HANDBOOK OF SOFTWARE QUALITY ASSURANCE

Second Edition

Edited by
G. Gordon Schulmeyer, CDP
and
James I. McManus

VNR VAN NOSTRAND REINHOLD
New York

Library of Congress Catalog Card Number 91-44322
ISBN 0-442-00796-5

I(T)P   Van Nostrand Reinhold is an International Thomson Publishing company.
ITP logo is a trademark under license.

Manufactured in the United States of America

Van Nostrand Reinhold   International Thomson Publishing GmbH
115 Fifth Avenue   Königswinterer Str. 418
New York, NY 10003   53227 Bonn
                                           Germany

International Thomson Publishing   International Thomson Publishing Asia
Berkshire House,168-173   221 Henderson Bldg. #05-10
High Holborn, London WC1V 7AA   Singapore 0315
England

Thomas Nelson Australia   International Thomson Publishing Japan
102 Dodds Street   Kyowa Building, 3F
South Melbourne 3205   2-2-1 Hirakawacho
Victoria, Australia   Chiyoda-Ku, Tokyo 102
                                           Japan

Nelson Canada
1120 Birchmount Road
Scarborough, Ontario
M1K 5G4, Canada

RRDHB   16   15   14   13   12   11   10   9   8   7   6   5   4   3

Library of Congress Cataloging-in-Publication Data

Handbook of software quality assurance / edited by G. Gordon
    Schulmeyer and James I. McManus.—2nd ed.
        p.   cm.
    Includes bibliographical references and indexes.
    ISBN 0-442-00796-5
    1. Computer software—Quality control. I. Schulmeyer, G. Gordon.
II. McManus, James I.
QA76.76.Q35H36   1992
005.1—dc20   91-44322
                                              CIP

for
Bonnie, Gordon, and Sean
and
for
Janice

Contributing Authors

Emanuel R. Baker (Ch. 4) is president of Software Engineering Consultants, Inc., a consulting firm in Los Angeles, California, specializing in software engineering services. He has been a consultant in this field since 1984. Prior to that, he was manager of the Product Assurance Department of Logicon's Strategic and Information Systems Division. In that capacity, along with his duties of managing the department, he also had responsibility for the contract to develop the new software quality standard for the Department of Defense, DOD-STD-2168.

From 1962 to 1980, he was employed at TRW. In 1972, he assumed the position of section head in the Software Systems Engineering Department on the Site Defense Program, a landmark program in the development of standards and procedures for software development, configuration management, and quality assurance practices. Later, he transferred into the Product Assurance area, playing an important role in the continuing development of software configuration management and quality assurance procedures used at TRW.

From 1959 to 1962, Dr. Baker was employed at Aeronutronic (now Ford Aerospace) as head of the Data Reduction Unit, where he was involved in the conversion of a manual data reduction system to a computerized one. Prior to that, he was an aerodynamics flight test project engineer at Hughes Aircraft. It was there that he had his first exposure to software, learning to program missile failure trajectories on a Burroughs E-102 computer.

Dr. Baker is an author and co-author (with Matthew J. Fisher) of numerous papers and articles on software quality and configuration management. In addition, he has appeared as a panelist at conferences and workshops, speaking on the topic of software quality.

He has a B.S.M.E. from New York University and the M.S.M.E. from the University of Southern California. In addition, he holds a M.S. and a Ph.D. in Education from the University of Southern California.

William E. Bryan (Ch. 13) has been in the computer software field since 1960, and has a broad range of experience in software engineering and software product assurance for command systems, management information systems, and process control systems.

Since joining Grumman-CTEC, Inc. (a wholly owned subsidiary of Grumman Data Systems Corporation) in 1979, Dr. Bryan has been performing software configuration management, independent verification and validation, acceptance testing and evaluation, and software quality assurance in a variety of applications.

He has lectured nationally and internationally on the subjects of software configuration management and software product assurance, is co-author of a number of articles on these subjects, and is co-author (with Stanley G. Siegel) of a textbook on software product assurance (to be published by Elsevier Science Publishing Co. in early 1987).

Dr. Bryan holds a Doctorate in Computer Science from George Washington University.

Chin Kuei Cho (Ch. 17), an internationally recognized expert in software engineering and quality assurance, is president of Computa, Inc. Dr. Cho has been Staff Scientist and Chairman of the Singer Artificial Intelligence Committee and of the Ada Steering Committee at the Singer Company, with responsibilities for development of technologies in software engineering and quality assurance, computer performance evaluation, Ada software engineering, very large data base management systems, and the Picture Archiving and Communication System (PACS) for military, industrial, and medical applications.

He has served as director of software technology at International Software Systems, Inc., and as systems engineer at the MITRE Corporation was responsible for software quality assurance during the development of the real-time Automated En Route Air Traffic Control Testbed System (AERA) for the Federal Aviation Administration. Dr. Cho's many successful software projects include worldwide satellite tracking and data networking tools, operations research and management science projects, and design and development of management systems. He is the author of *An Introduction to Software Quality Control,* published by John Wiley & Sons, 1980, and translated into Japanese by Kindai Kagaku Sha, Tokyo, 1982.

Dr. Cho is an Associate Professorial Lecturer in the Department of Electrical Engineering and Computer Science at George Washington University and also lectures in the Electrical Engineering Department and Department of Computer Science at the University of Maryland. He is a member of ACM and the IEEE Computer Society.

Dr. Cho holds a B.S. in Business Administration from National Cheng Kung University, an M.S. in Industrial Engineering from the University of Houston, and a Ph.D. in Computer Sciences from the University of Texas.

James H. Dobbins, CQA (Chs. 8, 9, 19) is an internationally recognized expert in software quality and reliability management, with over 28 years experience in these and related disciplines. Prior to joining the faculty at Defense Systems Management College (DSMC) in October 1990, he was a professor of systems management at the National Defense University. His current responsibilities include that of course director of the Management of Software Acquisition Course (MSAC) and software management instructor in the Program Management Course (PMC).

Following his tenure of service as a communications officer in the U.S. Air Force (SAC), he had 21 years of service with IBM Federal Systems Division, participating in the development of numerous DOD and NASA programs. These included the Gemini Program, Apollo Program, Air Force satellite programs, and Navy ASW systems. Following his service with IBM, he joined American Management Systems, Inc. as a principal of the company and Director of Software Quality Engineering.

He is active in numerous professional organizations and has presented many invited papers at conferences throughout the world. Most recently he participated as a featured debater at the International Software Debate in San Diego, and was a featured speaker at the Quality Assurance Institute national conference on quality measurement held in March 1992. As a senior member of the Institute of Electrical and Electronics Engineers (IEEE), he chaired the working group which developed the industry standard for software reliability management, IEEE Std. 982.1 and associated Guide 982.2.

In 1985, and again in 1986, he was chosen to participate in the French-American exchange of engineers and scientists program and visited France as a state guest to discuss his work in software reliability with several French companies, interfacing with the French Society for Industrial Quality Control and the French Standardization Society. He was a recipient of the NASA Apollo Achievement Award, and received a special Navy Letter of Commendation for his software test and evaluation effort on the LAMPS Program.

He has served as a consultant to NCR Corporation, UNISYS, RAND Corporation, and Time-Life Books. He authored *Software Quality Assurance and Evaluation,* published by ASQC Quality Press, three chapters of *Handbook of Software Quality Assurance,* Van Nostrand-Reinhold Publishing Company (1987 and 1992), and one chapter of *Software Validation,* North Holland Publishing Company

(1983). He is author of one chapter of *Total Quality Management for Software* to be published in 1992 by Van Nostrand-Reinhold, and three chapters of *Military Project Management Handbook,* to be published in 1992 by McGraw-Hill.

His biography has appeared in Marquis' Who's Who in America, Who's Who in American Education, Who's Who in the South and Southwest, Who's Who in the East, Who's Who in the Computer Graphics Industry, Who's Who in Science and Engineering, Who's Who in American Law, West's Who's Who in U.S. Executives, and Personalities of the South.

He holds a B.S. in Physics, an M.S. in Information Systems, and is an attorney-at-law. He received his certification as a Certified Quality Analyst from the Quality Assurance Institute, and has completed the training program conducted by the Software Engineering Institute required to conduct Software Capability Evaluations (SCE).

He is a member of the talent bank of the United States Congress on the subjects of software quality and reliability, a member of ASQC, a Senior Member of IEEE, a member of the IEEE Computer Society, The Boston Computer Society, American Defense Preparedness Association (ADPA), Mathematical Association of America (MAA), MENSA, the Virginia State Bar, the Virginia Trial Lawyers Association, and the Association of Trial Lawyers of America. He is licensed to practice law in Virginia and various Federal Courts.

He and his wife, Mary Beth, live in Stafford, Virginia, and have a four year old son, Nathan, and a three year old son, Daniel.

Robert H. Dunn (Ch. 18) an independent consultant, is the principal of Systems for Quality Software (107 Buck Hill Road, Easton, CT 06612). Until recently he was manager of Advanced Design and Test Technology of the Software Systems Technology Division of ITT's Advanced Technology Center in Connecticut.

Until early 1983, Mr. Dunn was with ITT Avionics Division, where he held various positions in software management and software quality assurance. He has held several offices within the National Industrial Security Association (NSIA), and has represented industry to the Defense Logistics Agency and the Quality Directorate of the DOD. He also chaired panels at the Joint Logistics Commanders' 1979 and 1981 software workshops in Monterey, California. His extensive publications on software engineering and software quality include two books: *Quality Assurance for Computer Software* (with Richard Ullman), McGraw-Hill, 1981; and *Software Defect Removal,* McGraw-Hill, 1984.

Mr. Dunn holds a B.S. in Engineering Physics from New York University, College of Engineering, and an M.S. in Mathematics from New Jersey Institute of Technology.

Matthew J. Fisher (Ch. 4) is currently Chief of Software Programs and Management Directorate for the Life Cycle Software Engineering Center (CECOM) at Fort Monmouth, New Jersey. This Directorate is responsible for advanced planning and systems engineering for the Life Cycle Software Engineering Center.

A civilian employee with the Federal government for 20 years, Dr. Fisher has worked as a research engineer in computer technology and software, navigation systems, and software product assurance. He has worked with the Avionics Research and Development Activity and with the Communication-Electronics Research and Development Command, also at Fort Monmouth.

Dr. Fisher was the Army's representative to the Joint Logistics Commanders subgroup for Computer Resource Management, which is responsible for efforts to standardize computer resource policies within DOD, and is co-editor, with John D. Cooper, of *Software Quality Management* (Petrocelli Books, 1979). The author of more than 25 published technical papers on software quality, Dr. Fisher has lectured at numerous seminars.

He has a M.A. from the University of Pennsylvania, and a Ph.D. from Drexel University; both degrees are in Electrical Engineering. Dr. Fisher is a member of the Tau Beta Pi, Eta Kappa Nu, and Phi Kappa Phi honor societies.

James H. Heil (Ch. 15) is the manager of Software and Firmware Quality Assurance Engineering at ITT Avionics in Clifton, New Jersey (a Division of the ITT Defense Corporation). In this role, he directs the Software Quality Program for all projects, as well as Firmware Quality for both hardware-intensive and software-intensive elements. He also manages the Statistical Product Assurance Group which handles all quality, yield, defect, and failure data collection and reporting. Prior to this, he was ITTAV Manager of Electronic Warfare Software Engineering, where he was responsible for the software requirements, design, coding, documentation,

software integration and acceptance testing, and field test support for several successful projects.

Prior to joining ITTAV, Mr. Heil was a Software Development Manager at IBM Federal Systems Division, where he developed real-time software for large sensor-based systems, and played a key role in the Systems Test Planning and scenario design for the SAFEGUARD Anti-Ballistic Missile System. Earlier at IBM, he was

Manager of Development for the CHQ Information Center at IBM Corporate Headquarters, and (before that) a Project Manager at the IBM Advanced Systems Development Division.

At Systems Development Corp., he helped develop the operational software for both the Command & Control Subsystem and the Planning Subsystem for the Air Force (SAC) 465L Command & Control System. Prior to that, Mr. Heil was a Project Engineer at the Aircraft Laboratory at Wright-Patterson AFB, Ohio.

Mr. Heil is past-Chairman of the NSIA Software Quality Assurance Group, and has been active in the organization of the NSIA Software Quality and Productivity Conferences since 1983. He served as Chairman of the CODSIA (Council of Defense and Space Industry Associations) Task Force to review both DOD-STD-2167 and 2167A, plus the related DIDs and Handbook. He also was the senior NSIA member of the CODSIA Task Force to review DOD-STD-2168 (Software Quality Program). He was Chairman of the ITT—North American Software Quality Council, and has participated in audits of other ITT Divisions' SQA Programs. Mr. Heil is a widely-known lecturer and frequent presenter at major conferences on Software Development, Software Quality, and Software Standards. Mr. Heil was an invited participant at both the Orlando II and San Antonio I Workshops on Software Standards sponsored by the Joint Logistics Commanders Computer Resources Management Group.

Mr. Heil holds a Bachelor's Degree in Mechanical Engineering and a Master's Degree in Electrical Engineering from NYU, a Master's Degree in Industrial Engineering and Operations Research from Ohio State University, and an MBA Degree from the New York Institute of Technology. He is a member of Tau Beta Pi, ORSA, ASQC, DPMA and AOC.

Thomas J. McCabe (Ch. 11) is president and CEO for McCabe & Associates, Inc. He is widely known as a consultant and authority in software development, testing, and quality control.

He has held a variety of high-level positions within the Department of Defense, accumulating extensive hands-on experience in the following areas: software specification, design, testing, and maintenance, software quality assurance, compiler construction, optimization, operating systems, software acquisition, and project management.

Mr. McCabe is best known for his research and publication on software complexity (*IEEE Software Engineering Transactions,* December 1976) and by the complexity measure which bears his name. (This measure allows the quantification of the paths within a module, leading to an understanding of its complexity). He has personally developed and published a structured testing methodology now being adopted extensively throughout the U.S. and internationally. He has developed advanced state-of-the-art courses in software quality assurance, structured testing, software specification and design, and software engineering, which he and his company present monthly throughout the U.S., Canada, and Europe.

Mr. McCabe holds both a B.S. (Providence College) and M.S. (University of Connecticut) in Mathematics.

James I. McManus (Chs. 2, 5, 12) is a software advisor at Westinghouse Electronic Systems Group. He supervised a Government funded research program to evaluate the feasibility of implementing zero defects on software development programs. The team successfully developed a prototype tool to support zero defects concepts during development.

He was formerly the director of consulting at McCabe & Associates; responsible for providing consultant services to businesses in need of state-of-the-art structured software techniques and software quality assurance.

His experience is with large-scale military and Department of Defense software/systems development. For 24 years, he has been actively involved in every phase of the software development cycle from proposal stage to sell-off. His background ranges from research analyst in underwater acoustics to aerospace engineer, from systems software support to software quality assurance.

He has previously worked for IBM, Singer, Martin Marietta, Vitro Laboratories, McCabe & Associates, and the RAIL Company.

Mr. McManus has a M.S. in Aerospace Engineering from the University of Maryland, a B.S. in Aerospace Engineering from the University of Maryland, and a B.S. in Engineering Physics from Loyola College.

Kenneth Mendis (Ch. 7) is manager of software quality assurance at Raytheon Company, Submarine Signal Division. He has over 10 years' experience in design-proving activity in system and hardware engineering, and more recently in software engineering.

Prior to joining Raytheon in 1978, Mr. Mendis worked for Control Data Corporation and NCR. At Raytheon, he has been responsible for developing and instituting the Submarine Signal Division's SQA program.

Mr. Mendis holds a B.S. in Electrical Engineering and an M.B.A. in management, and has done graduate work in computer science. He is a chairman of the National Security Industrial Association (NSIA) Software Quality Assurance Subcommittee, and chairman of Raytheon's Software Quality Assurance Committee of the Product Assurance Council (PAC).

Lawrence E. Niech (Ch. 16) is the Director of the Quality Assurance and Test Organization at Automatic Data Processing (ADP)—the largest dedicated software service company in the United States.

His previous positions have been at ITT Avionics, Singer-Kearfott (Guidance & Navigation Division) and Burroughs Corp. He has played major roles in implementing first time or enhanced Software Quality Assurance Programs as a Manager (ADP, Singer), Engineer (ITT) and consultant (various commercial and defense companies).

Mr. Niech has published papers, presented tutorials, taught at the College level and lectured extensively in the areas of software engineering management, software quality assurance, software/hardware test engineering and computer programming.

He is a member of the ASQC (Software Quality Division Conference Chairman), the NSIA SQA Subcommittee (Vice-Chairman) and the IEEE.

Mr. Niech holds a MBA from the Rutgers Graduate School of Management and a B.S. in Electrical Engineering from Rutgers, The College of Engineering.

William E. Perry (Ch. 20) is executive director of the Quality Assurance Institute (Suite 350, 7575 Dr. Phillips Blvd., Orlando Florida, 32819, (407) 363-1111). Under Mr. Perry's direction the QA Institute acts as a "catalyst" to promote quality within the data processing profession, and to assist vendors who produce data processing products. The QA Institute is also dedicated to assist and gain recognition for the individual specializing in quality assurance.

Mr. Perry is also president of William E. Perry Enterprises, Inc. He has been executive director of the Accounts Computer Users Technical Exchange (ACUTE), and prior to that was director of professional practice for the Institute of Internal Auditors. In this capacity, he worked closely with researchers in the field of internal auditing and data processing to bring to publication the latest developments in the many-faceted field. Prior to the Institute of Internal Auditors, he was supervisor of corporate computer auditing for Eastman Kodak Company.

He has had numerous articles published in the major accounting and financial journals and is a regular contributor for Auerbach Publishers and EDPACS. Mr. Perry is co-author of *EDP Control and Auditing* (Wadsworth), and a major contributor and editor for FAIM's *Auditing Computer Systems Manual.* His other books are *Effective Methods of EDP Quality Assurance* (Q.E.D. Information Sciences), How to Manage Management (Vanguard Press), and *Orchestrating Your Career* (CBI).

Mr. Perry is director of publications and publicity for the EDP Auditors Foundation and editor for Auerbach's *EDP Auditing Manual.* He also has written a control curriculum series of video courses for Advanced Systems, Inc. (ASI), and he has recently completed an encyclopedic manual, *Developing and Assessing Internal Controls* (FAIM Technical Products).

Mr. Perry is a graduate of Clarkson College and holds his M.B.A. from Rochester Institute of Technology, along with an M.Ed. from the University of Rochester. He is a New York CPA, and holds a certificate as a Certified Internal Auditor from the Institute of Internal Auditors, and a certified Quality Analyst from the Quality Assurance Institute.

G. Gordon Schulmeyer (Chs. 1, 3, 6, 10, 14) has 30 years' experience in management and information processing technology. He is presently a manager of software engineering at Westinghouse Electronic Systems Group, and was formerly manager of software quality assurance, also at Westinghouse.

Mr. Schulmeyer is the author of *Zero Defect Software* (McGraw-Hill Book Co., 1990), and *Computer Concepts for Managers* (Van Nostrand Reinhold, 1985). He has published numerous other papers and lectured on software and software-quality subjects. He was a panelist on DOD-STD-2168 *(Software Quality Evaluation)* at the October 1985 IEEE COMPSAC Conference. He has taken two long-term foreign assignments to provide information processing technology abroad.

Since 1968, Mr. Schulmeyer has been a holder of the CDP, issued by the Institute for the Certification of Computing Professionals (ICCP). He is a member of the Association for Computing Machinery and the American Management Association.

Mr. Schulmeyer is the 1992 recipient of the prestigious Shingo Prize, the First Prize for Professional Research, administered by the Utah State University College of Business. Mr. Schulmeyer received this award in May of 1992 for his work in Zero Defect Software. He is the first recipient from the business sector.

He holds the following degrees: B.S. Mathematics, Loyola College; J.D. Law, University of Baltimore; and M.B.A. Management, Loyola College.

Stanley G. Siegel (Ch. 13) has been active in the computer field since 1970. Since 1976, Dr. Siegel has been with Grumman-CTEC, Inc., a wholly owned subsidiary of Grumman Data Systems Corporation, specializing in software product assurance which encompasses quality assurance, testing, verification and validation, and configuration management. Most of his energies at Grumman-CTEC are devoted to the application of software product assurance principles to a broad range of software projects.

Dr. Siegel is co-author of the first textbook on software configuration management, which appeared in 1980. He lectures internationally on this subject and on the subject of software product assurance. He has published a number of articles in these areas and is co-author (with William L. Bryan) of a textbook on software product assurance (to be published by Elsevier Science Publishing Co. in early 1987).

Dr. Siegel received his Doctorate in Theoretical Nuclear Physics from Rutgers University.

Preface

Over the past two decades, the software industry has witnessed a dramatic rise in the impact and effectiveness of software quality assurance (SQA). From its day of infancy, when a handful of software pioneers tentatively first applied the basic principles of quality assurance to the development of software, software quality assurance has become integrated into all phases of software development.

This *Handbook of Software Quality Assurance* capitalizes on the talents and skills of the experts who deal with the implementation of software quality assurance on a daily basis. To have their accumulated knowledge at hand makes this *Handbook* a valuable resource. Each author, because of his or her special skills, talents, foresight, and interests, has contributed to the maturing process occurring in the field of software quality today.

What this *Handbook* brings to the reader, then, is a collection of experiences and expectations of some of the most notable experts in the field of software quality assurance. Because of their early involvement in software quality and continued pursuit to discover improved methods for achieving better on-the-job success, each author offers an insightful presentation of their personal involvement in software quality assurance.

The structure of this *Handbook* is relatively straightforward; twenty chapters covering many key areas of software quality assurance.

The first half of the *Handbook* sets the stage. Relevant terms are initially defined. Then the interaction of software quality assurance with several software speciality areas is covered. The knowledge gained in the quality field is directed toward improving the quality of software. Organizational considerations for a software quality program are presented. The importance of negotiation, compliance, and regression to software quality assurance management is captured. The history and future direction of the standardization of software quality assurance are discussed. The backbone of success in any enterprise—the people performing software quality assurance—is discussed in terms of how to identify, get, and keep those most suited for quality assurance. "Quality is free"; but whether this dictum applies to software quality is the subject of the "Cost of Software Quality," discussed in Chapter 8.

The second half of the *Handbook* focuses on applications and techniques. Attention is given to inspections, Pareto Analysis, software configuration management, software quality assurance and Computer Aided Software Engineering (CASE) tools, metrics, practical SQA applications for mission critical software and for commercial software, and statistical testing methods. Software reliability is covered next; specifically how to identify, remove and measure defects in software. Finally, the role of quality assurance for Electronic Data Processing (EDP) is discussed.

A brief summary of each chapter highlighting its main thrust is provided for the reader to decide which topic is of immediate interest. Revisions for each chapter are also highlighted here. If information is required from another chapter for additional insight, adequate cross-references have been provided within each chapter.

Chapter 1 defines each of the important terms relevant to this *Handbook*. Revision to this chapter includes a discussion of internal, independent, verification and validation. The Appendix to this chapter summarizes those definitions.

Chapter 2 discusses the relationship of software quality assurance to the various stages of software development. A discussion of the spiral model is also included. The chapter also addresses the relationship of software quality assurance to various techniques, such as Just In Time software, Zero Defect Software and Software Factory development.

Chapter 3 is an overview of the contributions and roles of the dominant figures in the quality field. The individual contributions of the dominant quality experts—Ishikawa, Juran, Sandholm, Deming and Crosby are assessed. Newly surveyed in this revision are Shingo and Taguchi.

Chapter 4 discusses the software quality organization. This chapter has been revised to include a discussion of what commercial organizations require to conduct software quality assurance. Other revisions include the role of assessing and measuring product quality during development and the controversy over the independence of SQA versus being part of the development organization.

Chapter 5 focuses on negotiation, compliance, and regression as the heart of software quality assurance management. How these three activities help management succeed and support Total Quality Management (TQM) through quality improvement is also discussed. A V-diagram helps illustrate the software development process and its interrelationships.

Chapter 6 traces the history of the standardization of software quality assurance. The Department of Defense (DOD), Federal Aviation Administration (FAA),

North Atlantic Treaty Organization (NATO), and the Institute of Electrical and Electronic Engineers (IEEE) standardization activities are discussed. New directions of DOD-STD-2167A (Defense Systems Software Development) and DOD-STD-2168 (Software Quality Evaluation) are given special emphasis. An important evaluation criteria table is provided from DOD-STD-2167A. Revision to this chapter incorporates discussion of the recent documents in SQA (formerly Appendix B in the first edition of this *Handbook*).

Chapter 7 discusses personnel requirements for a qualified software quality engineer and how a software quality organization should deal with personnel issues, such as training, roles for software quality engineers, paraprofessional activities and career paths. Successes recently achieved and up to date statistics on SQA personnel are also presented as revisions to this chapter.

Chapter 8 addresses the total cost of software quality and examines input required, value added, and expected output. Concerns such as major task elements, productivity, and potential misuse are evaluated. Also discussed are the "Price of Nonconformance" and the effect of budgetary constraints on the implementation of SQA.

Chapter 9 deals with the widely acclaimed use and application of inspections and the impact of inspections during the software development cycle. The inspection process is described and numerous results of inspections are provided to give the reader a first hand picture of what to look for when evaluating inspection data.

Chapter 10 focuses on the constraints of implementing the Zero Defect Software methodology. Emphasis is on investigating new improved methods for prevention and for early resolution of defects to prevent their delivery to the customer.

Chapter 11 applies the well known Pareto principle (80/20 rule) to the concerns and issues of software quality assurance. The impact and advantage of performing a Pareto analysis is supported by two real examples: one deals with WWMCCS (World Wide Military Command and Control System), the other with the Federal Reserve Bank.

Chapter 12 addresses Computer Aided Software Engineering (CASE) tools available for use by the SQA organization. This chapter provides insight into some of the software development tools which would be helpful in the production of a quality software product.

Chapter 13 looks at the role of software configuration management (SCM) and what that role implies for software quality and software development. Key issues discussed are staffing for SCM, the configuration control board, auditing the SCM process, and allocating resources to perform SCM.

Chapter 14 provides a survey of metrics proposed and currently used to determine the quality of the software development effort. The discussion is based on the experiences of the author who has been the chairperson of the Software Metrics Working Group at Westinghouse for the past three years.

Chapter 15 discusses how to successfully perform the job of software quality assurance in a real development environment for mission-critical software programs. Discussions are based on lessons learned and success stories from practical applications in mission critical software.

Chapter 16 discusses how to successfully perform the job of software quality assurance in a real development environment for commercial programs. Discussions are based on lessons learned and success stories from practical applications in commercial environments, and contrasted with mission-critical environments.

Chapter 17 treats statistics as a means of achieving software quality control. This chapter provides a quantitative method of assessing the effectiveness of testing. The cornerstone of this method is the development of the Symbolic Input Attribute Decomposition (SIAD) tree. Revisions include recent practical results using the statistical methods.

Chapter 18 is an overview of what is important to improve the reliability of the software product. Key concerns are software defects, their origin, detection and prevention, and how to improve software reliability by actively identifying and eliminating errors as early as possible.

Chapter 19 is updated, based on the latest events surrounding IEEE Project 982, which was established to enhance measurement of software reliability. The discussion is a follow up of the initial effort to bring together several key measures of software reliability.

Chapter 20 discusses the quality assurance of software in the Electronic Data Processing (EDP) environment. This chapter is updated with a summary of the 1989 Quality Assurance Institute EDP Quality Assurance Survey and explains software quality metrics and their implementation.

Appendix A is a glossary of acronyms used throughout the handbook.

The editors thank each and all of the contributors for their time, energy, and foresight in bringing to this handbook an excellent collection of original papers. This collection provides, in a single source, a wide spectrum of experiences and issues of concern not only to software quality assurance, but also to the future of software development.

The editors also appreciate the patience and help of Ms. Dianne Littwin, Senior Editor, and Pam Touboul, Manuscript Editor, Van Nostrand Reinhold, without whose assistance this *Handbook* would not have been accomplished.

G. Gordon Schulmeyer
James I. McManus

Contents

8. THE COST OF SOFTWARE QUALITY
James H. Dobbins

9. INSPECTIONS AS AN UP-FRONT QUALITY TECHNIQUE
James H. Dobbins

131

151

10. THE MOVE TOWARD ZERO DEFECT SOFTWARE   189
G. Gordon Schulmeyer, CDP

11. THE PARETO PRINCIPLE APPLIED TO SOFTWARE QUALITY ASSURANCE   225
Thomas J. McCabe   G. Gordon Schulmeyer, CDP

17. STATISTICAL METHODS APPLIED TO SOFTWARE QUALITY CONTROL   427
C. K. Cho, Ph.D.

18. THE QUEST FOR SOFTWARE RELIABILITY   465
Robert H. Dunn

TRADEMARKS

The following trademarks referenced within this book are noted as follows:

Bell and UNIX are registered trademarks of American Telephone and Telegraph Co.

Foundation is a registered trademark of Andersen Consulting.

Macintosh is a registered trademark of Apple Computer, Inc.

Software Backplane and Softboard Series are registered trademarks of Atherton Technologies.

Teamwork is a registered trademark of Cadre Technologies, Inc.,

IDEF/Leverage is a registered trademark of D. Appleton Co., Inc.

CDD/Plus, COHESION, DECdesign, DECwindows, NAS, ULTRIX, VAX BASIC, VAX C, VAX COBOL, VAX DIBOL, VAX DOCUMENT, VAX FORTRAN, VAX LISP, VAX OPS5, VAX Pascal, VAX RALLY, VAX Rdb/RMS, VAX RMS, VAX SCAN, VMS are registered trademarks of Digital Equipment Corp.

Adamat is a trademark of Dynamics Research Corp.

Hewlett-Packard is a registered trademark of Hewlett-Packard Co.

Statemate is a registered trademark of i-Logix.

Excelerator is a trademark of Index Technology Corp.

FOCUS is a trademark of Information Builders, Inc.

4GL is a trademark of Informix Software, Inc.

Software Through Pictures is a trademark of Interactive Development Environment.

Technical Publishing Software is a trademark of Interleaf, Inc.

DB2 and IBM are registered trademarks and CICS, OS/2, AIX, SAA, AD/Cycle are trademarks of International Business Machines Corp.

X-Window System is a trademark of Massachusetts Institute of Technology.

Mentor/Case is a trademark of Mentor Graphics Corp.

RTrace, and Protocol are trademarks of Zycad Corp.

SMARTsystem is a trademark of PROCASE Corp.

T is a trademark of Programming Environments, Inc.

Saber-C is a trademark of Sabre Software, Inc.

ARANDA is a trademark of Soft-Set Technologies, Inc.

Smartstar is a trademark of Smartstar, Inc.

SUN and NFS are trademarks of Sun Microsystems, Inc.

Ada is a registered trademark of the U.S. Government, Ada Joint Program Office.

DesignAid II is a registered trdemark of CGI Systems, Inc.

1

Software Quality Assurance— Coming to Terms

G. Gordon Schulmeyer, CDP

Westinghouse Electronic Systems Group

1.1 INTRODUCTION

What is software quality assurance (SQA)? This chapter addresses that question and related questions of:

- What is software quality control?
- What is software reliability?
- What is software maintainability?
- What is independent verification and validation (IV&V)?
- What is internal, independent verification and validation (I^2V&V)?
- What is software test and evaluation (T&E)?

The individual questions are first discussed and then the concepts are brought together to explain a coherent software quality program. How do all of these interrelated concepts work together? What is the goal to be achieved? How can it be achieved? All these questions are answered in relationship to the software quality program.

1.2 QUALITY—THE ELUSIVE ELEMENT

Perhaps the best expository material in popular literature about quality occurs in Robert M. Pirsig's *Zen and the Art of Motorcycle Maintenance.* The difficulty of explaining quality is addressed in the following passage:

Any philosophic explanation of Quality is going to be false and true precisely because it is a philosophic explanation. The process of philosophic explanation is an analytic process, a process of breaking something down into subjects and predicates. What I mean (and everybody else means) by the word *quality* cannot be broken down into subjects and predicates. This is not because Quality is so mysterious but because Quality is so simple, immediate and direct.[1, p. 224-225]

Further difficulties of coming to grips with quality are explained through the following dilemma exposed by Pirsig:

If Quality exists in the object, then you must explain just why scientific instruments are unable to detect it. . . .
   On the other hand, if Quality is subjective, existing only in the observer, then this Quality is just a fancy name for whatever you like. . . .
      Quality is not objective. It doesn't reside in the material world. . . .
      Quality is not subjective. It doesn't reside merely in the mind.[1, p. 205-213]

To define quality, Pirsig turns from philosophy to reality in the following brief passage:

When traditional rationality divides the world into subjects and objects it shuts out Quality, and when you're really stuck it's Quality, not any subjects or objects, that tells you where you ought to go.
   By returning our attention to Quality it is hoped that we can get technological work out of the noncaring subject-object dualism and back into craftsmanlike self-involved reality again, which will reveal to us the facts we need when we are stuck.[1, p. 253]

In approaching the definition of quality from the more traditional technological point of view, some of the thoughts of J. M. Juran are appropriate:

The basic building block on which fitness for use is built is the *quality characteristic.* Any feature (property, attribute, etc.) of the products, materials, or processes which is needed to achieve fitness for use is a quality characteristic.[2, p. 2-4]

Recognizing some of the same difficulties encountered by Pirsig, Juran goes on to say:

Because the unqualified word "quality" has multiple meanings, it is risky to use it in unqualified form.[2, p. 2-5]

Webster's Unabridged Dictionary, however, must qualify the meaning of quality:

1. that which belongs to something and makes or helps to make it what it is; characteristic element; attribute; as, purity of tone is an important *quality* of music.
2. any character or characteristic which may make an object good or bad commendable or reprehensible; the degree of excellence which a thing possesses; as, a fabric of poor *quality.*
3. superiority; excellence; as a person of *quality.*[3, p. 1474]

1.3 SOFTWARE—THE DEBATED ELEMENT

The IEEE Software Engineering Terminology Standard immediately focuses the debate in the definition of software:

Computer programs, procedures, rules, and possibly associated documentation and data pertaining to the operation of a computer system.[4, p. 31]

The use of the word "possibly," including associated documentation and data, says that differing factions believe documentation and data should be included and others not. For instance, the definition in the Department of Defense Standard on Defense System Software Development (DOD-STD-2167) for software takes in data, but excludes documentation:

A combination of associated computer instructions and computer data definitions required to enable the computer hardware to perform computational or control functions.[5, p. 5]

For the purpose of this *Handbook,* the term "software" derives from the definition of Matthew J. Fisher and William R. Light, Jr., in "Definition in Software Quality Management." Computer programs, procedures, rules, and associated data and documentation pertaining to the operation of a computer system; where the subordinate definitions are:

Computer program—a series of instructions or statements in a form acceptable to computer equipment and designed to cause the computer to execute an operation or operations.
    Computer data—a representation of facts, concepts, or instructions in a structured form suitable for acceptance, interpretation, or processing by computer equipment. Such data can be external to (in computer-readable form) or resident within the computer equipment.
    Computer program documentation—technical data, including program listings and printouts in human-readable form which document the requirements, design, implementation, and other details of the computer program. It also provides instructions for using and maintaining the computer program.[6, p. 5-6]

1.4 SOFTWARE QUALITY—
THE ATTRIBUTE

A number of good definitions have been proferred for software quality. An appreciation of what software quality is may be garnered from an examination of each of these definitions. Moving from the more general to the more specific definitions should aid comprehension.

First, in the *IEEE Standard Glossary of Software Engineering Terminology,* software quality is defined as:

The degree to which software possesses a desired combination of attributes.[4, p. 32]

What does this tell without knowledge of what the "desired combination of attributes" are? The usual attributes for software would be the "ilities" of reliability, maintainability, availability, and so on.

Next, we have from Fisher and Light in "Definitions in Software Quality Management";

> The composite of all attributes which describe the degree of excellence of the computer system.[6, p. 7]

Again, we have the "composite of all attributes" as discussed above; but here the concept of "excellence" enters into the software quality definition.

From Don Reifer in his *State of the Art in Software Quality Management* and also from Fisher and Baker in "A Software Quality Framework" comes the following definition:

> The degree to which a software product possesses a specified set of attributes necessary to fulfill a stated purpose.[7, p. 72; 8, p. 99]

This definition continues in the vein of a "set of attributes," but points out the added ingredient of fulfillment of "a stated purpose."

Going back to another IEEE definition:

> Totality of features and characteristics of a software product that bear on its ability to satisfy given needs; for example, conform to specifications.[4, p. 32]

This definition comes close to the definition of Philip B. Crosby in *Quality Is Free* of quality as "conformance to requirements"[9, p. 15], which when extended to software quality becomes "conformance to software requirements." The problem encountered in this definition is: what are the software requirements? Are they the technical requirements defining only what the software should do? Or, do they also include the requirements (imposed by the contract) for software quality?

Another sub-definition of IEEE for software quality is:

> The degree to which a customer or user perceives that software meets his or her composite expectations.[4, p. 32]

This definition brings in the customer/user expectations and the subjective nature of quality discussed above.

Turning more to the objective nature of software quality, the Department of Defense Standard on Software Quality Evaluation (DOD-STD-2168) provides this definition:

> The ability of a software product to satisfy its specified requirements.[10, p. 2]

By taking this definition and combining it with the J. M. Juran quality notions, we can derive the definition of software quality which will apply in this *Handbook: the fitness for use of the total software product.*

1.5 SOFTWARE QUALITY ASSURANCE— THE ACTIVITY

J. M. Juran in his *Quality Control Handbook* defines quality assurance as:

Quality Assurance is the activity of providing to all concerned the evidence needed to establish confidence that the quality function is being performed adequately.[2, p. 2-23]

Borrowing heavily on this base, both the IEEE software engineering terminology *Glossary* and George Tice, Jr., in his software quality control seminar use the following definition for quality assurance:

Quality Assurance is a planned and systematic pattern of all actions necessary to provide adequate confidence that the item or product conforms to established technical requirement.*[4, p. 28; 11, p. 1-A]

Because of the placement of this definition in software-related documents, both consider it the same as software quality assurance.

James Dobbins, a contributor to this *Handbook,* notes the difference between hardware and software in their definition of software quality assurance:

Unlike hardware systems, software is not subject to wear or breakage; consequently, its usefulness over time remains unchanged from its condition at delivery. Software quality assurance is a systematic effort to improve that delivery condition.[12, p. 108]

Fisher and Baker, who discuss the software quality organization in Chapter 4 of this *Handbook,* tie their definition to the organizational aspect of responsibility for performance:

Software quality assurance is the functional entity performing software quality assessment and measurement.[8, p. 105]

Donald Reifer provides a definition that brings in the concept of a system which captures the broader quality assurance idea:

Software quality assurance is the system of methods and procedures used to assure that the software product meets its requirements. The system involves planning, measuring and monitoring developmental activities performed by others.[7, p. 43]

---

*Adapted from DOD Directive 4155.1, Quality Assurance, 9 February 1972.

In this *Handbook,* the narrowing of the software quality definition provides the definition for software quality assurance: *the systematic activities providing evidence of the fitness for use of the total software product.*

1.6 SOFTWARE QUALITY CONTROL— THE ACTION

We turn again to J. M. Juran for a general definition of quality control:

> Quality Control is the regulatory process through which we measure actual quality performance, compare it with standards, and act on the difference.[2, p. 2-11]

This definition is very reminiscent of the "the control loop" provided in systems to ensure proper functioning of the system.

Applying this general definition to software very nicely, Fisher and Light in their "Definitions in Software Quality Management" derive this definition:

> Quality Control is the assessment of procedural and product compliance. Independently finding these deficiencies assures compliance of the product with stated requirements.[6, p. 13, 14]

According to Fisher and Light, quality control and quality design make up software quality management, where quality design involves participation in the insertion of quality attributes into the software development.[6, p. 13, 14]

Software quality control is equated with software verification by Donald Reifer:

> Software quality control is the set of verification activities which at any point in the software development sequence involves assessing whether the current products being produced are technically consistent and compliant with the specification of the previous phase.[7, p. 20]

Further narrowing of the software quality assurance definition leads to the definition of software quality control in this *Handbook: independent evaluation to assure fitness for use of the total software product.*

1.7 SOFTWARE RELIABILITY— KEEP CHUGGING ALONG

Turning to the expert J. M. Juran for a definition of reliability for hardware/systems is a good starting point.

> Reliability is the probability of a product performing without failure a specified function under given conditions for a specified period of time.[2, p. 2-7]

Now we move to software reliability, for a series of definitions which relate to software design quality:

Software reliability is really concerned with software design quality.[13, p. 182]
For software, reliability becomes a question of correctness, confidence, accuracy, and precision rather than the time to the next failure.[6, p. 9]
Extent to which a program can be expected to perform its intended function with required precision.[14, p. 129]

This next definition from George Tice, Jr., starts out sounding much like the definition of software quality, but then qualifies it for a time period of execution, and finally ties in the cost of failure to the user:

Software Reliability is the degree to which a software product satisfies its requirements and delivers usable services. The probability that the software will execute for a particular period of time without failure, weighted by the cost to the user of each failure encountered.[11, p. 3]

The *IEEE Draft Standard Measures for Reliable Software* provides a definition of software reliability that ties it to "deviation from required output":

The probability that a software failure which causes deviation from required output by more than specified tolerances, in a specified environment, does not occur during a specified exposure period.[15, p. 3]

whereas the *IEEE Standard Glossary of Software Engineering Terminology* ties the definition to "the inputs to the system," stressing software as a sub-part of the system:

The probability that software will not cause the failure of a system for a specified time under specified conditions. The probability is a function of the inputs to and use of the system as well as a function of the existence of faults in the software. The input to the system determines whether existing faults, if any, are encountered.[4, p. 32]

Norman Schneidewind stresses the difference between hardware reliability (error occurrence) and software reliability (error detection):

The passage of time is related to error detection and not to error occurrence; the errors which are detected were made at a previous time.[16, p. 175]

Harking back to the pure reliability definition of J. M. Juran, the IEEE *Standard Glossary* provides the definition of software reliability which most closely meets the requirement of this *Handbook* (italics ours):

The ability of a program to perform a required function under stated conditions for a stated period of time.[4, p. 32]

1.8 SOFTWARE MAINTAINABILITY—
ONLY ONE ERROR LEFT

This is the traditional definition for hardware that J. M. Juran provides:

> Maintainability is (1) the use of conducting scheduled inspections and servicing, called serviceability, and (2) the case of restoring service after failure, called repairability.[2, p. 2-8]

There is no clear relationship between serviceability and a counterpart in the area of software maintenance.

As one of the many "ilities" discussed by James McCall in the software measurement (metric) area, maintainability for software receives the following definition:

> Effort required to locate and fix an error in an operational program.[14, p. 129]

This definition is too narrow for what is being done with software under the name of software maintenance. Sixty to seventy percent of the expenditure for software is allocated to software maintenance rather than to new software development. In order to capture the activity that is being called software *maintenance*, the following definition from the *IEEE Standard Glossary of Software Engineering Terminology* is most appropriate (italics ours):

> *Software maintenance is the modification of a software product after delivery to correct faults, (to improve performance or other attributes, or to adapt the product to a changed environment).*[4, p. 32]

This is the definition favored by this *Handbook*.

1.9 INDEPENDENT VERIFICATION AND
VALIDATION (IV&V)—ON THE
RIGHT TRACK

There is crossover and confusion between independent verification and validation (IV&V) and test and evaluation (T&E). In this section the elements of V&V are defined and how they fit together is discussed. The next section discusses T&E and its interrelationship with V&V.

It is usually the developing contractor's job to deliver a complete system; so, depending on its facilities and capabilities it could provide testing at all levels. The Atlas Missile Program hired an "independent software tester" to provide additional unbiased software test support in the late 1950s. This outside source now called a validation and verification (V&V) contractor, performs the testing job which sometimes extends over the module, functional area, software system, and, sometimes even the target system.[17, p. 275]

In a V&V paper, Robert Lewis gives a broad definition:

> Verification and Validation is the systematic process of analyzing, evaluating, and testing system and software documentation and code to ensure the highest possible quality, reliability and satisfaction of system needs and objectives.[18, p. 238]

This definition incorporates all the testing within it.

The IEEE *Standard Glossary* gives two definitions that vary in their emphasis on the independence of the V&V activity:

> Verification and validation of a software product by individuals or groups other than those who performed the original design, but who may be from the same organization. The degree of independence must be a function of the importance of the software.[4, p. 21]
>
> Verification and validation of a software product by an organization that is both technically and managerially separate from the organization responsible for developing the product.[4, p. 21]

The Department of Defense clearly relates the requirement for independence in the definition provided in DOD-STD-2167A, *Defense System Software Department:*

> Independent Verification and Validation (IV&V)—Verification and validation performed by an organization that is both technically and managerially separate from the organization responsible for developing the product or performing the activity being evaluated.[5, p. 6]

A most succinct definition is provided by Barry Boehm. It, however, does not address the independence issue.

> Verification is doing the job right and validation is doing the right job.[19, p. 728]

The process discussed above needs further breakout in definitions to clarify what verification is and what validation is. For each of these, the IEEE Glossary definition is given first and followed by the DOD-STD-2167A definition. There is little difference between the definitions and all are acceptable within this Handbook (italics ours):

> *Verification is the process of determining whether or not the products of a given phase of the software development cycle fulfill the requirements established during the previous phase.*[4, p. 37]
>
> *Verification is the process of evaluating the products of a given software development activity to determine correctness and consistency with respect to the products and standards provided as input to that activity.*[5, p. 7/8]
>
> *Validation is the process of evaluating software at the end of the software development process to ensure compliance with software requirements.*[4, p. 37]
>
> *Validation is the process of evaluating software to determine compliance with specified requirements.*[5, p. 7/8]

1.10 INTERNAL INDEPENDENT VERIFICATION AND VALIDATION (I²V&V)—A DIFFERENT PERSPECTIVE

The use of the term internal independent verification and validation (I²V&V) may be considered an oxymoron. According to Robert O. Lewis software V&V Rule 1 is: V&V must be an independent, third-party activity.[18, p. 238] The independence of I²V&V is immediately brought into question. Perhaps it is best approached by that portion of the IEEE *Standard Glossary* which states, "The degree of independence must be a function of the importance of the software."

An examination of that definition would logically produce an independence of IV&V that means:

Importance	*Independence*
life critical	different company
organizational survival	different company (unless proprietary)*
very important	same company—separate organization*
important	same company—separate organization
trivial	same company—same organization

*same company may subcontract to different company.

It is expensive to have independent V&V—up to 30 percent of the cost of development.[20, p. 60] For a task of any significant size this becomes very costly, so there is a strong desire to do the independent V&V internally; thus less costly. The I²V&V personnel can use the development community which helps relieve costliness, but the independence is less independent.

Tom DeMarco in *Controlling Software Projects*[21, p. 220] recommends separate teams for software development—construction team, measurement team, and testing team. The test team with expanded tasks is closely approximated by a V&V team and could readily exist within one's own company.

1.11 TEST AND EVALUATION (T&E)— SEE HOW THEY RUN

A discussion of test and evaluation (T&E) is now appropriate. Then, this section concludes with a distinction between V&V and T&E.

The IEEE *Standard Glossary* defines testing in a rather broad manner:

Testing is the process of exercising or evaluating a system or system component by manual or automated means to verify that it satisfies specified requirements or to identify differences between expected and actual results.[4, p. 36]

Donald Reifer closes in more to software testing rather than the broad testing described above:

> Software quality testing is the systematic series of evaluation activities performed to validate that the software fulfills technical and performance requirements.[7, p. 60]

"Evaluation," following the standard dictionary definition, means "to appraise"[3, p. 632], and "to appraise" means "to judge the quality or worth of."[3, p. 91]

Therefore software T&E is defined as *the process of exercising complete programs to judge their quality through the fulfillment of specified requirements.*

The difference between V&V and T&E is that V&V can be accomplished without testing the software (but usually is not). The essence of V&V rests in the traceability of requirements. First, verification can be accomplished through the tracing of requirements embodied in the development specification to the design specification, and finally to the units of code. Second, validation can be accomplished by a test closure traceability for which the entire set of requirements is formally established in an approved test plan and test procedures, and finally proven as valid at the various levels of tests. The essence of T&E is in the actual exercising of the computer programs during test. As each test is made and evaluated, the validation assurance which traces requirements to software under test can be checked off for each test until all tests have been passed.

1.12 SOFTWARE PRODUCT ASSURANCE—BRINGING IT ALL TOGETHER

How do all these diverse areas fit together to achieve software quality? Once again, J. M. Juran helps to set the tone from his *Quality Control Handbook* for understanding software product assurance. He defines the quality function:

> Quality function is the entire collection of activities through which we achieve fitness of use, no matter where these activities are performed.[2, p. 2-11]

This "collection of activities" for software is performed in various functional organizations today. Thus software product assurance, if independent, is composed of software quality control (QC), *independent* verification and validation (IV&V), and *independent* test and evaluation (T&E). In most organizations, independent approach is not the usual way software product assurance is accomplished. When not specifically independent, software product assurance is composed of software quality assurance (SQA), V&V, and T&E. Outside consultants may be employed to provide independence in this case.

In the latter case, software reliability determinations are made by various personnel within the organization, sometimes within software product assurance, sometimes by the software developers, and sometimes by reliability engineering. It is not unreasonable that all three work together to make the software reliability determination.

Software maintainability is a factor that is to be considered when developing software in order to ease its modification after operation. Software maintenance is the modification of the software after delivery. Depending on the extent of the modification, it could be a process as complex as the initial development or it may be a simple fault correction. Achieving software maintenance usually involves V&V and T&E.

References

1. Pirsig, Robert M., *Zen and the Art of Motorcycle Maintenance* (New York: William Morrow & Co., 1974).
2. Juran, J. M. "Basic Concepts," in *Quality Control Handbook,* ed. by Juran, J. M., Gryna, Frank M., Jr., and Bingham, Frank M., Jr., (3rd ed. New York: McGraw-Hill Book Co., 1979).
3. McKechnie, Jean L., ed. *Webster's New Twentieth Century Dictionary of the English Language Unabridged,* 2nd ed. (Cleveland: The World Publishing Co., 1965).
4. Software Engineering Technical Committee of the IEEE computer Society, *IEEE Standard Glossary of Software Engineering Terminology,* IEEE-STD-729-1983 (New York: IEEE, 1983).
5. U.S. Depart. of Defense, DOD-STD-2167A *Defense System Software Development* (Washington, DC., NAVMAT 09Y, 1988).
6. Fisher, Matthew, J., and Light, William R., Jr., "Definitions in Software Quality Management" in *Software Quality Management,* ed. by Fisher, Matthew J. and Cooper, John D., (New York: Petrocelli Books, 1979).
7. Reifer, Donald J., *State of the Art in Software Quality Management* (Torrance: Reifer Consultants, 1985).
8. Baker, Emanuel R., and Fisher, Matthew J., "A Software Quality Framework," in *Concepts, The Journal of Defense Systems Acquisition Management,* ed. by Moore, Robert Wayne. Vol. 5, No. 4 (Fort Belvoir VA: Defense System Management College, Autumn 1982).
9. Crosby, Philip B., *Quality Is Free* (New York: New American Library 1979).
10. U.S. Dept. of Defense, DOD-STD-2168, *Defense System Software Quality Program* (Washington, DC: NAVMAT 09Y, 1988).
11. Tice, George D., Jr., *Developing Your Software Quality Control Program—A Seminar* (Pittsburgh: Westinghouse Corporate Quality College, 1983).
12. Dobbins, James A., and Buck, Robert D., "Software Quality Assurance," in *Concepts, The Journal of Defense Systems Acquisition Management,* op. cit.
13. Kline, Melvin B., "Software and Hardware Reliability and Maintainability: What are the Differences," in *1980 Proceedings, Annual Reliability and Maintainability Symposium.*
14. McCall, James A., "An Introduction to Software Quality Metrics," in *Software Quality Management,* op. cit.
15. Technical Committee on Software Engineering of the IEEE Computer Society, *IEEE Standard 982.1-1988, June 12, 1989 and IEEE-Guide 982.2-1988, June 12, 1989 (New York: IEEE, 1989).

16. Schneidewind, Norman F., "The Applicability of Hardware Reliability Principles to Computer Software," in *Software Quality Management,* op. cit.
17. Nelson, J. Gary, "Software Testing in Computer-Driven Systems," in *Software Quality Management,* op cit.
18. Lewis, Robert O., "Software Verification and Validation (V&V)," in *Software Quality Management,* op. cit.
19. Boehm, Barry, *Software Engineering Economics* (Englewood Cliffs, NJ: Prentice Hall, 1982).
20. Dunn, Robert, *Software Defect Removal* (New York: McGraw-Hill Book Company, 1984).
21. DeMarco, Tom, *Controlling Software Projects* (New York: Yourdon Press, 1982).

Appendix (Chapter 1)

Definitions

IV&V. organizationally independent V&V (verification and validation).

I²V&V. V&V (verification and validation) performed by a separate organization (independent) within one's own company (internal).

Quality. fitness for use; conformance to requirements.

Software. computer programs, procedures, rules, and associated data and documentation pertaining to the operation of a computer system.

Software maintainability. ability to modify a software product after delivery to correct faults (to improve performance or other attributes, or to adapt the product to a changed environment).

Software product assurance. composed of software quality control, IV&V, and independent T&E (if independent); composed of SQA, V&V, and T&E (if not specifically independent).

Software quality. the fitness for use of the total software product.

Software quality assurance. the systematic activities providing evidence of the fitness for use of the total software product.

Software quality control. independent evaluation to assure fitness for use of the total software product.

Software reliability. the ability of a program to perform a required function under stated conditions for a stated period of time.

Test and evaluation (T&E). the process of exercising computer programs to judge their quality through the fulfillment of specified requirements.

Validation. the process of evaluating software to determine compliance with specified requirements.

Verification. the process of determining whether or not the products of a given phase of the software development cycle fulfill the requirements established during the previous phase.

2

How Does Software Quality Assurance Fit In?

James I. McManus

Westinghouse Electronic Systems Group

2.1 INTRODUCTION

It is important to understand the interaction of software quality assurance (SQA) with different types of software and with specialized software-related activities. In this chapter, there is discussion of how SQA activities differ depending upon the software areas in which they are performed. Even though there are basic activities for SQA, there is a shift in emphasis according to the environment in which SQA personnel are acting. Although several elements remain essential to the success of the SQA function, emphasis within these elements must be shifted to focus attention where concern and risk are of the highest priority.

Within this chapter, five major software areas have been identified; each requiring a shift in emphasis in the role of SQA. These areas are operating systems software, mission critical software, real-time systems software, interactive software, and business software.

The role of SQA within each of these major software areas is discussed in terms of four elements of concern to SQA. These elements are software configuration management (SCM), software testing, software reviews and audits, and software documentation.

A separate discussion is also provided which highlights the relationship of SQA with several software specialty areas. These are software configuration management, software maintenance, and independent verification and validation (IV&V).

For other related discussions throughout this *Handbook* on SQA and SCM* or SQA and software maintenance.[+]

2.2 SQA IN OPERATING SYSTEMS SOFTWARE

Operating systems software is a collection of programs written to coordinate the operation of all computer circuitry allowing the computer to run efficiently.[1, p. 185] System software is the operating system which is composed of control programs and processing programs. *Control programs* control the efficiency and effectiveness of the computer on which they reside. *Processing programs* control the efficient processing of programmer preparation.

The actual development of system software is a common activity within the computer manufacturer, such as, IBM, Digital Equipment Corp., Burroughs, and so on. There is a basic similarity between this and the development of applications software by non-computer manufacturers. It is a question of emphasis: What is the main area to concentrate on for software quality?

With the knowledge that thousands of customers will be receiving delivery of the system software, the greatest emphasis must be on keeping everything under configuration control. It is not unusual to have to control multiple versions in the field and "at home" simultaneously. So, because of this aspect, the SQA personnel must ensure that software configuration management (SCM) is the top priority for system software.

Reviews and audits are necessary early on in the development cycle; first to assure that the intended operability of the operating system is designed—in as stated in the approved requirements documents, and second that test procedures provide adequate and thorough coverage prior to test.

Testing must be witnessed and certified by software quality assurance to assure that operability meets reliability requirements. This is necessary to prevent costly maintenance and loss of customer confidence after the system is released.

2.3 SQA IN MISSION-CRITICAL SOFTWARE

Mission-critical software is that software which executes on "mission-critical resources." "Mission-critical computer resources" include

computers and services for the conduct of the military missions of the Department of Defense related to:

—Intelligence activities;
—Cryptology activities related to national security;

---

*See Chapter 13 for further coverage of this area.
[+]See Chapter 18 for further coverage of this area.

—Command and control of military forces;
—Equipment integral to a weapon or weapons system;
—Equipment critical to direct fulfillment of military or intelligence missions, but
—Not routine administrative and business applications. [2, p. 38]

The Department of Defense describes "embedded computers" as

incorporated as an integral part of, dedicated to, or required for direct support of, or for the upgrading or modification of major or less-than major systems.

The most common definition of this term may include a broad spectrum of technologies from simple chips to computer systems with multiple processors. It is also associated with an array of complex military operations and equipment.[2, p. 38] Embedded software is that software which executes on "embedded computers".

The term "embedded computers" has persisted in relation to "mission-critical computer resources", but the "embedded computers" terminology is considered passé.

Mission-critical software must be reliable. So, reliability is the first issue and primary focus of SQA activities in this arena. Two issues for the reliable functioning of mission-critical software to be considered are that the software functions in a systems environment, and more often than not, winds up as nonvolatile firmware*.

Mission-critical software (see Chapter 15) requires detailed analysis and trade-off analysis of requirements at the systems level. The critical point of focus is performance reliability. Down time essentially is unacceptable during any of the defined critical missions. The complexity of the system's operations and interfaces and the specific allocations of performance requirements to major software components requires dedicated front end evaluation. Rapid prototyping is highly desirable.

The first role of SQA is to promote tighter controls on the front end of the life cycle to assure that performance reliability is extensively evaluated to reveal all facts about the system. Both internal systems requirements reviews and systems design reviews are required to expand the functional baseline to include derived requirements. Ambiguous, untestable, non-quantified, and assumed requirements are inadequate and are cause of real concern if development proceeds without these uncertainties resolved at the front end of the life cycle.

A well known example of reliability in mission critical software is the space shuttle. The initial flight was delayed because one of five on-board computers did not agree with information supplied by the other four.

This second issue of nonvolatile firmware makes the process of reviewing the "burning" of the firmware devise (e.g., PROM, UVPROM, etc.) a crucial SQA activity. It is really a two-step activity for SQA personnel. The first step is that the

---

*Firmware—an assembly composed of a hardware unit and a computer program integrated to form a functional entity whose configuration cannot be altered during normal operation. (IEEE Std. 729-1983)

software to be "burned in" is the appropriate software (a SCM activity), and the second step is to audit the "burn-in" process itself to see that it is successful.

The area of documentation for mission-critical software has in the past been weak, but is improving. The new standards discussed in Chapter 6 place a phase-by-phase of the development cycle emphasis on software-quality documents (products) evaluation. This will provide better documentation in the future for mission-critical software.

2.4 SQA IN REAL-TIME SYSTEMS SOFTWARE

> Real-time software is that software that controls a computer that controls a real-time system. A real-time system is one that provides services or control to an on-going physical process.[3, p. vii]

Software that executes in real-time is software that is subject to very strict performance requirements and constraints. Real-time software must interact with other external entities (other computer programs, terminals, subsystems, etc.) and execute all required processing in a real-time window. This software is therefore restricted by timing constraints, and in many instances also by sizing constraints. The software is usually complex and may exist in several forms such as firmware, assembly language, microcode, and a recompiled version of the developmental high-order language (HOL). With the advent of Ada and C++, many of the concurrent tasks associated with real-time can now be programmed in these HOLs.

Real-time tasks are performance driven using timing and sizing allocations for various parts of the system (hardware, software and user to machine interface). Timing and sizing estimates are required during each phase of software development. These estimates should be based on dependable models and simulations. Rapid prototyping is recommended for large, complex, state of the art, real-time programs.

System/software architectural trade-offs should be conducted early in the life cycle. Since hardware is difficult to undo later on, software can get stuck downstream with unplanned add ons to make up for hardware inadequacies. This results in last minute changes to software which increases complexity and hurts maintenance.

Whenever trade-offs are necessary, design should be simple not complex, flexible not rigid, modular and not all in one unit. This is necessary to accommodate changes, when needed, to adjust the design to keep up with the dynamics of real-time trade-offs. For example, a development program, requiring tightly controlled multi-processors in a real-time environment, needs not only to have trade-offs conducted in architectural design during the design phase, but must have the design tested early on to optimize performance. The method of testing may be innovative and may require several changes and iterations to verify the fitness of the system/software design.

System/software design trade-offs should also include concurrent engineering techniques. Reliability, Maintainability and Availability and Logistics considerations should be designed in up front, not added on later.

Such software is also subject to priority and interrupt processing for efficiency, recovery requirements, and a high reliability requirement for the system. In order to keep real-time programs intellectually manageable, Niklaus Wirth recommends

> that they first be designed as time-independent multiprograms and that only after analytic validation they be modified in isolated places, where the consequences of reliance on execution time constraints are simple to comprehend and document.[4, p. 141]

The SQA person has a responsibility to ensure overall efficiency of the real-time systems software. The best area in which to prove efficiency is testing. Here, the pieces of software are assembled and the interactions of real-time response may be measured. Checking on speed may be done by various timers and the computer(s), but the results are to be monitored by SQA personnel. After all, on real-time systems software the chief requirement is to complete execution of the software in a time certain.

Next, because many pieces make up the real-time systems software, special attention is required by SQA personnel on SCM. If the advice mentioned above by Wirth is followed by starting with "time-independent multiprograms" and then putting them together, then SCM is very important.

It has been a common experience in real-time systems software that when the computer programs come together, one of them causes the time constraint to be blown. By testing incrementally and controlling closely the new increments of software added, the SQA person can significantly enhance the probability of success for the system.

The reviews, audits, and documentation, as usual, are not to be underestimated as to their importance to the real-time system software. Without their proper build up within the development activity, the final product would just not be complete, or correct.

2.5 SQA IN INTERACTIVE SOFTWARE

Interactive software is software that drives interactive systems. Interactive systems are those systems which require an interface (interaction) with a human operator in real-time or non-real-time. All of the types of software discussed in this chapter are interactive to a greater or lesser degree.

Some examples are appropriate for a better description of the scope of this man-machine interface. In a fighter aircraft, the radar system will find the target only when turned on. The fire control system will fire only when ordered to do so. The command to the controlling software to lock onto a given target or to fire at the selected target must come from the fighter pilot.

When security is a factor, sometimes a two-person operation can be set up. One person must initiate a response or command, but the system will not accept it unless the second person provides a second response or command within a limited time frame. The interaction required is a two-part action within a given time frame, and unless this occurs the system will not execute as commanded and may even trigger an alarm.

Another type of interactive system is the word processor or the personal computer, where a high degree of interaction on the part of the user is required. Formatting and generating reports, filing and retrieving data within the system, and management of information using word processors and personal computers have quickly become a way of doing business at the office.

What is the role of SQA personnel in all of these? First, it is important to note that some common concerns exist for both the fighter aircraft system and the personal computer (PC). The fighter pilot interacts based on what he sees on a screen within the cockpit. The PC user may spend long hours at a terminal. Both systems require human factors engineering. What appears on the screen; how much information appears at any given time; how big are the words, figures, and symbols; how bright; what the background looks like; what is most important to be easy to find—any of these questions may be important to SQA personnel.

For example, the real-time aircraft system would require minimal interaction time if all information could be displayed all at once. However, the time to decipher, interpret, and find what is most important at any given time may take so long that the real-time requirement cannot be met. This suggests that SQA should assure that only menus of related information be shown on the screen at any one time to assure that the pilot can react quickly to a given situation.

The second example deals with the role of SQA personnel with PC software. Major issues facing most companies are: who controls (SCM) the software being written and purchased within the company, who assures that the software is performing as it should (testing), who has access to the corporate data base and who controls it (security). The SQA person must have an awareness of and play an active part in the assurance of controls for the PC software and its interaction with the corporate files.

In addition to the human-factors engineering aspects of interactive software, another aspect involving SQA personnel is that of training. Training programs are required to assure that fighter pilots and PC users know how to interact with the software. The role of SQA for the aircraft system example would be to assure that all software simulation programs are fully tested, verified, and calibrated prior to training a pilot how to use the operational system. The role of SQA for the PC would be to assure that the software to be used on the PC is PC-compatible, does what it says it does, and is fully documented to assure that a user can train and become self-sufficient on the PC. When software is developed by a PC manufacturer for a given PC, the manufacturer's internal SQA department should approve the software to be sold with the PC prior to the software's release. Future programs developed by the manufacturer should also be approved by its SQA prior to their release.

A severe problem facing SQA today is the increasing number of third-party software vendors who develop independent software packages to run on various manufacturers' PCs. These software packages do not come with any guarantees and are not necessarily approved by any manufacturer's internal quality assurance department prior to release.

The role of SQA here is to protect one's own corporation from any misuse or misrepresentation on the part of a vendor by requiring proof of performance. An adequate trial demonstration should be required of any vendor, plus a trial time period after initial purchase to determine fitness for a purpose.

Thus the aspect of control is of primary importance to SQA personnel in the business of vendor interactive software. The reviews and audits, and software documentation reviews mentioned in Section 2.4, though important, are secondary here.

2.6 SQA IN BUSINESS SOFTWARE

The primary application of software in the business environment is usually called the electronic-data processing (EDP) system. William Perry covers effective methods of EDP quality assurance in Chapter 20.

The role of the SQA person is to perform an audit of the EDP system to determine the adequacy of procedures, security of the system, adequate documentation, whether the ledger's are accurate and up-to-date, and that the system is functioning properly.

To prepare for an EDP audit, a checklist should be established prior to the audit (if none exists) to concentrate on the key issues relevant to each area audited. Besides focusing on the required issues and concerns during the audit, a checklist provides consistency from one audit to the next so that the person(s) audited knows what to expect time after time.

SQA personnel may also utilize one of the audit packages that are available to help assess and evaluate files within the EDP system. These audit packages, however, should only be one aspect in conducting the EDP audit.

The EDP auditor performs that myriad of activities mentioned above. There should be some EDP auditors who are software specialists. Within the context of EDP in this Handbook, the SQA person referred to is the EDP auditor specialized in software.

For business software, then, the SQA person must ensure accuracy of the software as the primary focus. That is accomplished mainly through comprehensive reviews and audits as the development of the software takes place. Because a high percentage of the business software on hand is in a maintenance phase, the importance of the software documentation is very high. The SQA person must constantly review software documentation to see that it correctly reflects the present EDP system. SQA personnel involvement is then rounded out for business software in the areas of testing and SCM.

2.7 SQA IN SOFTWARE CONFIGURATION MANAGEMENT

Software configuration management (SCM) is an internal function within an organization to properly identify, control, and assess the status of software and software documentation. For further coverage of these functions, see Chapter 13.

The role of SCM is of the highest priority when software has been approved and sold to a customer. It is a simple fact of life that software is subject to change.

Changes required after a product has been developed are of the highest concern. This concern is multifaceted. First, any rework is costly.[5, p. 40] Second, resources spent on rework are lost to new projects. Third, if changes are not identified and controlled accurately, the version or versions of software that exist become untraceable due to unknown, unaccounted fixes. Fourth, the ripple effect due to a change can be very time-consuming to trace and complete and if not completed will show up as future changes. Fifth, even if a good SCM function exists, a system can still diverge when subject to change after change.

The role of SQA therefore is critical when such an environment of changes is in effect. The divergent system is the worst case, in which each change begets two or more new changes. When such occurs, closure can never be obtained until changes start to disappear as the program progresses.

When such a system exists, SQA personnel must assure that each new correction actually resolves a known problem and that the impact of the change on other systems functions is traced, tested, and verified to eliminate or minimize any ripple effect.

The importance of doing the job right during development becomes extremely obvious when things go wrong in production or in the operations and maintenance phases. The role of SQA is to avoid downstream change by assuring that early development cycle changes are identified, controlled, and subject to status accounting by the SCM function and that all changes are individually approved by the configuration control board (CCB).

One step further back, if changes exist early in the life cycle of a software product's development, it is an SQA person's responsibility to assure that an adequate SCM function exists at that time to control changes from inception to closure.

Changes should be logged and maintained as part of the software library. The role of SQA is twofold here: first, are library control procedures in place to define how changes will be identified and controlled as part of the library, and who has access to library items; and second, are all versions, baselines, and revisions up-to-date and are library materials updated to reflect the latest status? SQA must therefore review library control procedures to determine their adequacy and audit the library to assure compliance with procedures.

2.8 SQA IN SOFTWARE MAINTENANCE

Software maintenance, defined fully in Chapter 1, includes fixing software, enhancing software, or adapting software after delivery. Studies conducted by Bennet Lientz uncovered three major software quality problems related to software maintenance:

1. Adequacy of application system design specification.
2. Quality of original programming of application system.
3. Quality of application system documentation.[6, p. 277]

These problems must be corrected prior to maintenance activity. Therefore the SQA person must investigate these areas to ensure their adequacy before maintenance activity proceeds.

Another aspect of system software (section 2.2) is that most businesses have resident system software specialists who "maintain" the system software for the local computer environment. Here, "maintain" means to investigate local system software problems and inform and work with the manufacturer's personnel to achieve resolution of problems. "Maintain" also means to know enough to answer local system software inquiries. Lastly, "maintain" means the traditional software maintenance of correcting or enhancing the local, unique version of the system software.

These activities of the system software specialists make it clear that the SQA person must be primarily concerned with control (SCM) and testing (reliability) of the system software under maintenance. As discussed in section 2.7 (SCM), all maintenance changes must be approved by formal configuration control board (CCB) action. If a CCB does not exist, it is in the interests of quality that one be formed to provide adequate review, approval, analysis, reworking, regression testing, and reverification of the change when implemented. Additionally, the impact of the change on the system must be revalidated through appropriate regression testing.

In the event that major requirements or design changes, or both, are required during the maintenance phase, the software modification to the system should be treated the same as during development with the exception that formal change control is required. As mentioned at the start of this section, software documentation is a major problem in maintenance, so SQA personnel must review original documents and updated-in-process documents. Lastly, reviews and audits are conducted by SQA personnel as in development for the proposed changes.

2.9 SQA IN IV&V

Independent verification and validation (IV&V) is defined in Chapter 1; its activities are to independently verify, validate and certify that the products produced comply with approved requirements and satisfy customer needs. The formation of an internal IV&V team (i.e., an I²V&V Team) is also discussed in Chapter 1. In I²V&V the contractor/developer takes on the role of IV&V agent.

SQA personnel must monitor the testing of the IV&V contractor. This is done by auditors watching the progress and success of the testing. SQA personnel ensure that each test is repeatable and that it follows the test procedure. A check is made of expected results versus actual results, with a note made of the actual results.

Since a major part of IV&V is the production of test documents, the SQA person stresses the *independent* review of the test documents. The flow of testable requirements to the actual tests must be ensured by the SQA person.

Finally, the reviews and audits and SCM typically performed in the development process take on a minor position for SQA review of IV&V activities.

TABLE 2-1   SQA Emphasis

TYPES OF SOFTWARE	SCM	TEST-ING	REVIEWS & AUDITS	SOFTWARE DOCUMENTA-TION	COMMENTS
System software	1	4	3	2	Customer emphasis (control)
Mission-critical software	3	1	2	4	Reliability
Real-time system software	2	1	3	4	Efficiency; control
Interactive software	1	2	3	4	Control
Business software	4	3	1	2	Accuracy

SOFTWARE-RELATED ACTIVITIES				SCALE 1 2 3 4	EMPHASIS Most ↑ Least
Software CM	Null	1	3	2	Auditor
Software maintenance	1	2	4	3	Control; test
IV&V	4	1	3	2	Auditor

2.10 SUMMARY

The question of how software quality assurance fits in has been asked in this chapter. It is a question related to SQA fitting in with different types of software and other software-related activities. Table 2-1 indicates the degrees of SQA emphasis required for the different types of software and software activities discussed above.

References

1. Mandell, Steven, L., *Computers and Data Processing* (St. Paul: West Publishing Co., 1979).
2. Becker, Louise G., "Military Computers in Transition: Standards and Strategy," in Moore, Robert W., ed., *Concepts, The Journal of Defense Systems Acquisition Management* Vol. 5, No. 4 (Autumn 1982) (Fort Belvoir, VA: Defense System Management College, 1982).
3. Glass, Robert L., *Real-time Software* (Englewood Cliffs, NJ: Prentice-Hall, 1983).
4. Wirth, Niklaus, "Toward a Discipline of Real-time Programming," in Glass, Robert L., op. cit.
5. Boehm, Barry, W., *Software Engineering Economics* (Englewood Cliffs, NJ: Prentice-Hall, 1981).
6. Lientz, Bennet P., "Issues in Software Maintenance," *Computing Surveys* Vol. 15, No. 3 (September 1983).

General References

Burrell, Claude W., and Ellsworth, Leon W., *Quality Data Processing* (Tenafly, NJ: Burrell-Ellsworth Associates, 1982).

Glass, Robert L., *Software Reliability Guidebook* (Englewood Cliffs, NJ: Prentice Hall, 1979).

Perry, William E., *Effective Methods of EDP Quality Assurance* (Wellesley, MA: Q.E.D. Information Sciences, Inc., 1981).

Wright, Bruce J., *How to Audit and Control Computer Systems* (Sandy, UT: Wright & Associates, 1981).

3

Software Quality Lessons From the Quality Experts

G. Gordon Schulmeyer, CDP

Westinghouse Electronic Systems Group

Quality is never an accident; it is always the result of intelligent effort.

John Ruskin

3.1 INTRODUCTION

The time has come for personnel performing software quality assurance to apply the teachings of the quality experts. What important lessons have been learned in the past that eminent quality experts have been telling us? The results achieved in Japan by following the lead of such significant thinkers have caused us in the Western World to turn to the Japanese to learn about quality.

In general, the quality concepts put to use in Japan have not been accepted in the Western World, though the trend is changing. Identifying those quality concepts that the Japanese have capitalized on so successfully and applying them to the area of computer software development is a significant step that needs to be taken.

The principles of these quality experts have not as a rule been applied to software development. The issue of duplicating the other person's answers for a different problem could be raised and should be addressed. The generic nature of "quality" production is applicable whether the product be automobiles, stereos, or computer software.

Although production lines—being machine intensive, repetitive, and resulting in many units—and computer software—being people intensive, intellectual, and resulting in one software system—do differ; the transition of quality principles is reasonable. A fundamental principle of transition training is learning from other people's experience; and so the software development and software quality assurance personnel may learn from the quality principles covered in this chapter.

This chapter looks to the works of Kaoru Ishikawa, Joseph M. Juran, Lennart Sandholm, W. Edwards Deming, and Philip Crosby. Some major points from each quality expert are noted and conclusions applicable to software development are drawn.

The works of each of these contributors contain important quality messages which are applied to software development. Typically, quality applications to software development have been supplied by software specialists. However, the concepts available that address quality production must now be used for the production of quality software. The definition of quality more narrow than "fitness for use" as discussed in Chapter 1, but in Chapter 1 is that by Philip Crosby: "conformance to requirements."[1] The logical extension of that definition to software quality is "to conform to requirements and to provide useful services,"[2] which parallels that provided in Chapter 1: "the fitness for use of the total software product."

First we look to Japan for the six major features of quality as seen by Kaoru Ishikawa. Second to be scanned is Joseph M. Juran's three ways for the Western World to meet the Japanese quality challenge, followed by a look at the four-point attack to achieve quality by Lennart Sandholm.

Then we review the statistical methods to achieve quality control provided by W. Edwards Deming, along with an application of his 14 points to software development. The goal of reduced variability in production of Genichi Taguchi through on line quality control and off line quality control are covered. The zero quality control methods of Shigeo Shingo with source inspections and the *poka-yoke* system are applied to software development. Finally, we survey the implementation concepts successfully incorporated at International Telephone & Telegraph (ITT) by Philip Crosby.

The key points in each section devoted to a quality expert are flagged with bullets at the beginnings of the relevant paragraphs. Occasionally the statements of one expert reinforce a point of another expert; for example, Lennart Sandholm is quoted in the section on Joseph M. Juran.

A simple diagram (Figure 3-1) borrowed from Joseph M. Juran graphically portrays what all the excitement is about concerning quality.

This chart, which compares results for Japan and the Western World since 1950, illustrates the impact of quality taught by the experts. Japan, originally behind the Western World in quality, took heed of the quality concepts and principles proposed by the quality experts. The Western World, formerly the quality leader, basically ignored the quality concepts and fell behind. The impact of this result is further amplified by the fact that from 1970 to 1980 the United States' share of world high-technology exports (excluding agricultural chemicals and plastics and synthetic materials) dropped an average of 3.5 percent.*

The chart shows us that Japan listened to these quality experts for management concepts, while the Western World did not. For software in the 1980s, the Western World (led by the United States) had a relative superior position in software quality

---

*Source: United States Department of Commerce

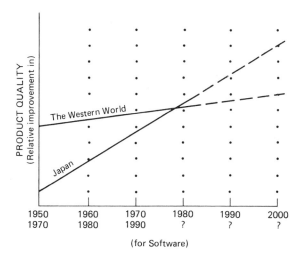

FIGURE 3-1. Quality growth in Japan and the West (adapted from reference 3).

similar to that which existed in the 1960s for overall product quality. The point of this paper is that as cost and importance of software development increases through the years, the Western World does not want a duplication of the relative product quality loss in software quality. Therefore, software development must learn from the quality experts.

3.2 KAORU ISHIKAWA

To explain the quality "miracle" in Japan, Kaoru Ishikawa gives six features of quality work there.

- Company-wide quality control.
- Top management quality control audit.
- Industrial education and training.
- Quality circles (QC) activities.
- Application of statistical methods.
- Nationwide quality control promotion activities.[4]

   • Company-wide quality control means that all departments and all levels of personnel are engaged in systematic work guided by written quality policies from upper management. The consequences of this point to software quality is that the software developers are committed to producing a quality product guided by software development management ("upper management") trying to achieve the same objective. This is how to build quality into the software product.

   • A quality control audit team of executives visits each department to uncover and eliminate any obstacles to the productivity and quality goals. Normally this auditing of software is placed in the hands of the software quality experts, but periodically an executive audit team is required to evaluate software quality. Directed conversations with the users of the software product, software quality management, software development management, and workers will uncover much that the executive audit team can act upon.

- Education and training in quality control must be given to everybody in all departments at each level because company-wide quality control requires participation by everyone involved. The initial training has to take place within the software quality assurance organization so that the software quality personnel "train ourselves before we are fit to train others." Then, to concentrate an intensive training program on software quality to be attended by software developers and their managers is the necessary, but not sufficient way to make quality software. Education about how to make "quality" software brings the awareness and discipline necessary for meeting that objective. The teachers in this arena should be the software quality personnel who also carry out the evaluation functions on a daily basis. Software quality personnel as the teachers bring uniformity to the effort by providing knowledge common to all quality software development.

- A *quality circle* (QC) is "A small group (which met) voluntarily to perform quality control within the workshop to which they belonged."[5] The QC has traditionally been applied to the manufacturing process, and has recently been used to enhance some management and professional (engineering) quality. The software developers could use the QC as another tool to guide the production of quality software. The QC provides a forum to discuss software production problems.

The QC frequently uses Ishikawa diagrams to highlight influential factors. Ishikawa diagrams are usually drawn to identify control points, the ingredients including people, materials, machines, organization, processes, and so on.[6] Using Ishikawa's "fishbone" cause and effect diagram provides a useful tool to find the cause(s) of each software production problem and the problem's resolution.

A sample Ishikawa diagram (Figure 3-2) explores the possible causes of a slipped software development schedule. Each probable cause is written onto the "fishbone" in relation to the major control points of manpower, machines, methods, and materials (the "4 M's"). The group then reviews all the possible causes in detail to determine the most likely ones. The most likely causes are circled and receive the appropriate attention. In the sample, "insufficient development computers" is the most likely cause of the software development being behind schedule.

- Statistical methods for quality control include Pareto analysis, cause and effect diagram, stratification, check sheet, histogram, scatter diagram, and Shewhart control chart. Thomas McCabe has advocated the use of Pareto analysis to software quality techniques, further explored in Chapter 11. Suffice it to say here that these various statistical concepts were so influential in Japan through the guidance of W. Edwards Deming that they brought about "the quality revolution." Each of these statistical methods may provide help to the software developer and a

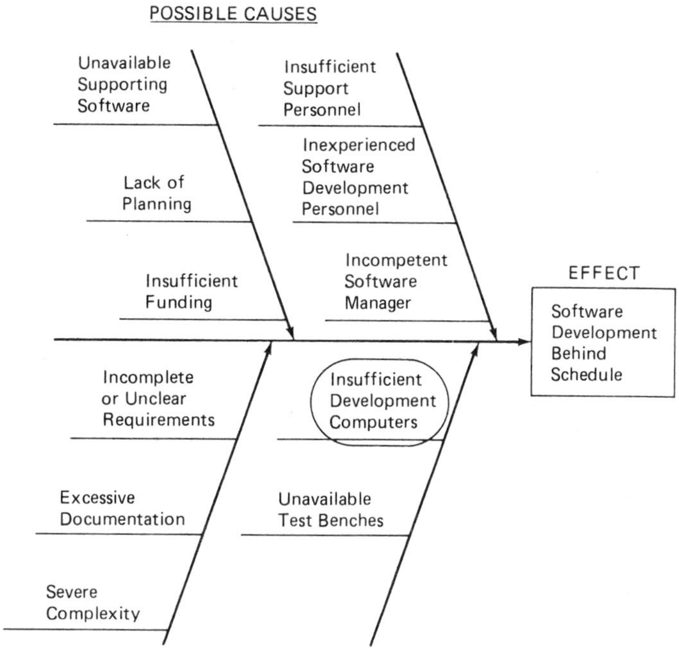

POSSIBLE CAUSES

FIGURE 3-2. Sample Ishikawa diagram.

few are explored in the Deming section in this paper. Since these methods are sufficiently covered in various textbooks of statistical analysis, they are not covered in detail here.

• Nationwide quality promotion activities peak in Japan in November—Quality Month—when the Deming Prize is awarded. The Deming Prize is used to advertise the company's products because it instills such a high degree of customer confidence that he or she can be sure of a quality product. Why not stimulate quality interest in software by awarding the yearly Lovelace Award (after Lady Ada Lovelace, the first programmer) for special quality achievement in software? Why not stimulate quality interest more locally by providing incentives in contracts for measurable software quality achievements? This type of awareness continually reinforces quality concepts for software developers.

3.3 JOSEPH M. JURAN

To meet the challenges of the solid Japanese campaign for quality achievement shown in Figure 3-1, Joseph M. Juran prescribes the following:

• Structured annual improvements in quality.
• A massive quality-oriented training program.
• Upper management leadership of each company's approach to product quality.[3]

• In the early 1950s, the Japanese faced a grim reality. No alarm signal is as insistent to industrial managers as inability to sell the product. Since their major limitation was quality, not price, they directed their revolution at improving quality. They learned how to improve quality, became proficient at it, and are now reaping the rewards of their efforts. Their managers are equally at home in meeting current goals and in making improvements for the future.[3]

This story of the Japanese electronics industry with transistor radios, for example, illustrates the dedication to annual improvements in quality that exists in Japan. The results of this commitment are shown in Figure 3-1.

There is a grim reality in software development that quality needs immediate attention and can stand improvement yearly. Too many software systems never meet their requirements, either because development has to be stopped short due to financial or time budgets, or because the user is unsatisfied. Software management must plan for and make a total commitment similar to Japan's, to quality software improvements from within. Software managers are aware of the structured analysis, structured design, structured programming, and structured testing; now is the time for software managers to be aware of structured annual improvements in quality.

To accomplish these annual quality improvements Joseph M. Juran advises that a team:

1. Study the symptoms of the defects and failures;
2. Develop a theory on the causes of these symptoms;
3. Test the theory until the cause(s) is known;
4. Stimulate remedial action by the appropriate department(s).[3]

Software quality assurance personnel are beginning to identify and categorize the defects in the software (see Chapters 9 and 18). As techniques for error identification mature, the steps required for annual quality improvements can be applied to computer software development.

Defects can be separated into those that are worker-controllable and management-controllable. The latter category includes defects that cannot possibly be avoided by workers. Whether a certain defect should be regarded as a worker-controllable defect or a management-controllable defect depends on the extent to which the following conditions are met:

1. The worker knows what to do.
2. The worker knows the result of his or her own work.
3. The worker has the means of controlling the result.

If all three conditions are met and the work is still defective, the worker is responsible. However, if one or more of the conditions have not been met, this is a management-controllable defect.[7]

Two relevant points made by W. Edwards Deming on the responsibility for defects which apply to software development (substitute "software developer" for "worker"):

> To call to the attention of a worker a careless act, in a climate of general carelessness, is a waste of time and can only generate hard feelings, because the condition of general carelessness belongs to everybody and is the fault of management, not of any one worker, nor of all workers.[8]

Many managers assume they have solved all the problems once they have brought worker-controllable defects under control. They, in fact, are just ready to tackle the most important problems of variation, namely, the *management-controllable* causes.[9]

During software development many worker-controllable defects can be controlled by software developers. However, there is a wide class of defects in software that arises because the developer does not know what to do. This condition occurs because of the inevitable intertwining of specification and implementation. In more direct wording, the basic problem is that during the software development (the implementation), the requirements (the specification) are continually being changed. That is, many times the software developer is continually "engineering" something new without the benefit of "frozen" requirements.

Contrary to claims that the specification should be completed before implementation begins ("worker knows what to do"), there are two observations concerning why the two processes must be intertwined. First, limitations of available implementation technology may force a specification change. That is, the hardware hosting the computer software may require software work-arounds because of hardware limitations. Second, implementation choices may suggest augmentations to the original specification. That is, as more is accomplished, more is learned, making it reasonable to augment with a better approach what was originally specified.

Only because these already-fixed and yet-to-be-done portions of this multi-step system development process have occurred unobserved and unrecorded, the multi-step nature of this process has not been more apparent.[10] This is especially true of the software development for large prototype systems where the entire system is pushing the technology of both the involved hardware and software. In most of these systems, the hardware does not even exist to test the software, but is under concurrent development with the software.

That "the worker (software developer) knows the result of his or her own work" in software is very immediate and sometimes humbling for the worker who made a "stupid mistake." For the developer receives the results immediately from the computer *exactly* as commanded, whether correctly or incorrectly. On the other hand are the subtle errors that are not found for years. This is a worker-controllable defect, but one where the worker does *not* know the result of his or her own work. Quality software development must continually resolve to remove this type of error.

In software development, "the worker has the means of influencing the result." Assuming a reasonable task assignment, the worker is directly involved in the production of the result (computer program) and is the first to see that result. Consider as one example a situation in which the worker loses that influence because the computer is unavailable. It is usually not worker-controllable that the computer is or is not available.

To summarize this discussion of the annual quality improvements suggested by J. Juran, it is clear that software developers must first know where they stand before setting up the program for improvement. In this specialty area, to know where one stands from a quality viewpoint is essential. The sole way to know such is to identify the defects (errors) and determine their causes. Only when this is accomplished is movement toward quality improvement possible.

• To date, selective training in quality sciences in the Western World has been largely confined to members of the specialized quality departments, which constitute only about 5 percent of the managerial and specialist forces in the companies. In contrast, the Japanese have trained close to 100 percent of their *managers* and specialists in the quality sciences.

This massive quality-oriented training program carries the education and training nostrum of Kaoru Ishikawa to its logical conclusion. J. Juran points out that common quality training needs to include:

1. The universal sequence of events for improving quality and reducing quality-related costs (creation of beneficial change).
2. The universal feedback loop for control (prevention of adverse change).
3. Fundamentals of data collection and analysis.[3]

Particular training for software developers in quality disciplines should include design reviews, reliability analysis, maintainability analysis, failure mode and effect analysis, life-cycle costing, quality cost analysis, concepts of inspection for design and code, and similar disciplines.

• An example of Japanese upper management commitment to quality is an observation made by Lennart Sandholm to the International Quality Control conference held in Tokyo in 1978. Almost half of the Japanese participants at the conference were from upper management—presidents, general managers, division heads, and directors. At conferences held in Europe or the United States, almost all participants are from the quality profession—quality assurance engineers, reliability engineers, quality managers, etc. There are few upper managers.[11]

W. Edwards Deming has also observed that in Japan top people in the companies take hold of the problems of production and quality. All the reports showing successful implementation of quality principles quoted in his paper were written by men with the rank of President of the company, Managing Director, or Chairman of the Board.[12]

As Deming stresses:

All of the top management came, not only to listen, but to work. They had already seen evidence from their own engineers that what you've got is this chain reaction. As you improve the quality, costs go down. You can lower the price. You capture the market with quality and price. Americans do not understand it. Americans think that as you improve quality, you increase your costs.[13]

The need for upper management leadership stems from the need to create major changes, two of which include annual improvements in quality and a massive quality-oriented training program, already discussed above. The recommended step for Western upper management is to perform a comprehensive company-wide quality audit to understand what needs to be done.

An organizational weakness in the West is the *large* central quality department with numerous functions of quality planning, engineering, coordination, auditing, inspection, and test. In Japan, most of these quality-oriented functions are carried out by line personnel (who have the necessary training to carry out such functions). The Japanese do have quality departments, but they are small in terms of personnel and they perform a limited array of functions: broad planning, audit, and consulting services. Upper management quality audits evaluate the effectiveness of the organization and only upper management has the authority to institute the necessary changes.

For the software development process, senior software management is the upper management. The commitment, then, of senior software management to producing quality software is necessary to institute the needed changes. Also, putting responsibility for software quality in the software development department is a correct posture for senior software management to enforce. The most obvious benefit of this posture is the close awareness of software quality brought to the software development organization.

3.4 LENNART SANDHOLM

To achieve quality, there is a four-point attack provided by Lennart Sandholm at Westinghouse Defense Center in May 1983:

- Quality policy.
- Quality objectives.
- Quality system.
- Quality organization.[14]

- The quality policy is a statement that expresses the need for corporate-wide quality. It is supported by a statement of commitment to quality by the corporation. It provides the direction for all employees to implement the quality policy. As with all policies, it emanates from the highest executive in the corporation.

Particularly, a quality policy for software should be promulgated by the senior software executive. It should explain the reasons for the production of quality software and indicate that only a strong commitment by the software developers to provide quality software will make it happen. A broader view of software quality policy, taken from George D. Tice, Jr., includes a policy statement, professional software quality management audit of performance against policy, recognition of achievement, and provision of the wherewithal for the program.[2]

- Quality objectives are statements of measurable improvements usually achievable on an annual basis. The implication is that there is a quality baseline established so that the quality improvements may be measured. The presumption is that each professional software developer knows the quality of the software produced. Actually, it depends on maturity, degree of professionalism, and many intangibles about people. With that awareness in mind, quality objectives are set with the software managers to improve in a quantitative way the quality of the software produced. For example, keep a record of the ratio of number of errors per thousand lines of source code (NOE/KLOSC) and measure its improvement for a software developer from project to project.

- The quality system is the means used to achieve the quality objectives. Traditionally, this is the book of procedures for quality personnel to follow step-by-step—not very effective, but necessary to meet documentation requirements. To have real quality awareness pervasive throughout the organization with every manager and worker striving to achieve the quality objectives would be more effective.

For software development, a quality system should include standards and procedures decided by and committed to by senior software management. Examples of these standards and procedures include, but are not limited to, software quality assurance (SQA) procedures, design guides, programming guides, coding standards, testing guides, and documentation guides. The SQA procedures and guidelines need to be particularized for each software development project; this is usually accomplished via a SQA project plan for each software development project.

- The quality assurance organization should be small and efficient in keeping with the previous statements. Such a quality assurance organization can then act as a monitoring mechanism to focus the total organizational effort toward quality improvement.

3.5 W. EDWARDS DEMING

W. Edwards Deming is the guiding consultant for the application of statistical methods to quality control as laid out by Walter A. Shewhart. The namesake of the coveted annual Deming Award in Japan has declared:

> (The) economic and social revolution, which took hold in Japan, upset in fifteen years the economy of the world, and shows what can be accomplished by serious study and adoption of statistical methods and statistical logic in industry, at all levels from the top downward.

The statistical control of quality is the application of statistical principles and techniques in all stages of production, maintenance, and service, directed toward the economic satisfaction of demand.[12]

Statistics have proven to have wide application in many different aspects of business, which would lead one to believe that there are many different statistical theories. However, Dr. Deming has cleared up this point:

> Rather than a separate and distinct theory for probability for process-control, another theory for acceptance sampling, another for reliability, another for problems of estimation, another for design of experiment, another for testing materials, another for design of studies for statistics, another for engineering, there is instead one statistical theory.[9]

This statistical theory may be applied in many ways to software development. Some proven statistical methods for software are covered next.

- This body of statistical knowledge has a variety of applications to the production of quality software. *An Introduction to Software Quality Control* by Chin-Kuei Cho compares a statistical sampling method for testing of software to the statistical sampling method used for manufactured products.[15] It is usually impossible to test every input to a computer program. With Dr. Cho's sampling method, a broad range of input values previously *never considered* can be evaluated. Chin-Kuei Cho further discusses these concepts in Chapter 17 in this Handbook.

- The analysis of errors for either type or cause will help control errors. An accepted method of error analysis in software quality assurance is the *inspection technique.* Both design and code error types are categorized in a post-inspection analysis which leads to a determination of the cause of the error. James Dobbins covers the direction and details of this method in Chapter 9, this Handbook.

- The statistical technique *seeding models,* covered in Chapter 18, estimates the total number of errors actually in the computer program. This technique baselines the defects in the software so that quality improvements can be made.

- In hardware quality determination, statistical measures of reliability include *mean time between failures* (MTBF). This statistic tells how long the unit is expected to operate. *Mean time to repair* (MTTR) tells how long it will take to repair the unit once it ceases to operate. In software quality, a more fitting statistical measure of reliability would be *number of errors left* (NOEL), which estimates the errors still in the computer program(s), and the *estimated time to fix* (ETTF), which estimates how long it will take to fix the computer program(s) once an error occurs. The tagging technique discussed above is an aid to determining NOEL. Determining ETTF would have to be based on prior experience and knowledge concerning types of error. It is not an easy measure because of the creativity and insight required to fix a computer program.

An extension of the NOEL measure could be to determine the probability that the error would cause a system malfunction. If it does not, may it not be acceptable to ignore it? A similar extension to the ETTF measure could be to determine the probability that the error would even be reached. Robert Dunn offers more about the reliability of software in Chapter 18.

- Important observations made by W. Edwards Deming:

Mr. Harold Dodge of Bell Telephone Labs said, "You can not inspect quality into a product." He meant that you must build quality: you must make the product so that it has quality in it, if you want quality. Quality is not built by making a great number of articles, hoping that some of them will be good, and then sorting out the bad ones.[12]

Even 100 percent inspection using automatic testing machines doesn't guarantee quality. It's too late — the quality is already there.[16]

These remarks apply directly to the production of quality software. The test and evaluation phase of software development is too late to retrofit quality into the software. The software has to be built with quality foremost from the beginning.

- In addition to statistical knowledge, Deming urges that everyone learn a common method of attacking and describing problems. This commonality of method is essential if people from different parts of the company are to work together on quality improvement. The method is referred to as the "P-D-C-A approach" (Plan-Do-Check-Analyze and Act), and is usually represented as the "Deming circle" (Figure 3-3).

When the president visits the various operations of the company to discuss their performance, he or she comes prepared to discuss intelligently how each operation is doing and what can be done to improve the system by reading the P-D-C-A information ahead of time. This approach should be contrasted with the usual "management by exception" approach under which, when things go wrong, the manager then tries to figure out what is wrong and what to do about it.[6]

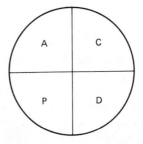

FIGURE 3-3. The Deming circle.

A significant step can be taken when senior software management uses the Deming circle in conjunction with the software development cycle so that each development phase is subject to the P-D-C-A approach. This method focuses attention as the development proceeds and so allows time to "Act" when required.

The quality approach of Deming is a management approach for continuous improvement of quality. Richard Zultner has adapted Deming's 14 points for management, seven deadly diseases, and obstacles to quality to software development. Table 3-1 contains the Fourteen Points for Software Development, Table 3-2 contains the Seven "Deadly Diseases" for Software Managers, and Table 3-3 contains the Obstacles to Software Quality.

TABLE 3-1   The Fourteen Points for Software Managers

1. Create constancy of purpose for the *improvement* of systems and service, with the aim to become excellent, satisfy users, and provide jobs.
2. Adopt the new philosophy. We are in a new age of software engineering and project management. Software managers must awaken to the challenge, learn their responsibilities, and take on leadership for change.
3. Cease dependence on mass inspection (especially testing) to achieve quality. Reduce the need for inspection on a mass basis by building quality into the system in the first place. Inspection is not the answer. It is too late and unreliable—it does not produce quality.
4. End the practice of awarding business on price alone. *Minimize total cost.* Move toward a single supplier for any one item or service, making them a partner in a long-term relationship of loyalty and trust.
5. Constantly and forever improve the system development process, to improve quality and productivity, and thus constantly decrease the time and cost of systems. Improving quality is not a one time effort.
6. Institute training on the job. Everyone must be well trained, as knowledge is essential for improvement.
7. Institute leadership. It is a manager's job to help their people and their systems do a better job. Supervision of software managers is in need of an overhaul, as is supervision of professional staff.
8. Drive out fear, so that everyone may work effectively. Management should be held responsible for faults of the organization and environment.
9. Break down barriers between areas. *People must work as a team.* They must foresee and prevent problems during systems development and use.
10. Eliminate slogans, exhortations, and targets that ask for zero defects, and new levels of productivity. Slogans do not build quality systems.
11. Eliminate numerical quotas and goals. *Substitute leadership.* Quotas and goals (such as schedules) address numbers—not quality and methods.
12. Remove barriers to pride of workmanship. The responsibility of project managers must be changed from schedules to quality.
13. Institute a vigorous program of education and self-improvement *for everyone.* There must be a continuing training and education commitment by software managers and professional staff.
14. Put *everyone* to work to accomplish the transformation. The transformation is everyone's job. Every activity, job, and task is part of a process. Everyone has a part to play in improvement.

TABLE 3-2   The Seven "Deadly Diseases" for Software Quality

1. Lack of constancy of purpose to plan systems that will satisfy users, keep software developers in demand, and provide jobs.
2. Emphasis on short-term schedules—short term thinking (just the opposite of constancy of purpose toward improvement), fed by fear of cancellations and layoffs, kills quality.
3. Evaluation of performance, merit rating, and annual reviews—the effects of which are devastating on individuals, and therefore, quality.
4. Mobility of software professionals and managers. Job hopping makes constancy of purpose, and building organizational knowledge, very difficult.
5. Managing by "visible figures" alone—with little consideration of the figures that are unknown and unknowable.
6. Excessive personnel costs. Due to inefficient development procedures, stressful environment, and high turnover, software development person-hours are too high.
7. Excessive maintenance costs. Due to bad design, error ridden development, and poor maintenance practices, the total lifetime cost of software is enormous.

TABLE 3-3   The Obstacles to Software Quality

1. Hope for instant solutions. The only solution that works is knowledge—solidly applied, with determination and hard work.
2. The belief that new hardware or packages will transform software development. Quality (and productivity) comes from people, *not* fancy equipment and programs.
3. "Our problems are different." Software *quality* problems simply aren't unique—or uncommon.
4. Obsolescence in schools. Most universities don't teach software quality—just appraisal techniques.
5. Poor teaching of statistical methods. Many software groups don't have good statistical-oriented training in quality or project management.
6. "That's good enough—we don't have time to do better"—but time *will* be spent later to fix the errors. Doing the right things right the first time (and every time) is fastest.
7. "Our quality control people take care of all our quality problems." Quality is management's responsibility, and cannot be delegated. Either management does it, or it doesn't happen.
8. "Our troubles lie entirely with the programmers." Who hired the programmers? Trained them (or not)? Manages them? Only management can do what must be done to improve.
9. False starts with quality (or productivity). Impatient managers who don't understand that quality is a long term proposition quickly lose interest.
10. "We installed quality control." Quality is a never-ending *daily* task of management. Achieve consistency (statistical control)—then continuously improve.
11. The unmanned computer—such as a CASE package used without solid knowledge of software engineering.
12. The belief it is only necessary to meet specifications. Just meeting specifications is not sufficient. Continue to improve consistency and reduce development time.
13. The fallacy of zero defects. Constant improvement doesn't end with zero defects (all specs met). The mere absence of defects is no guarantee of user satisfaction.
14. Inadequate testing of prototypes. The primary purpose of testing prototypes is to *learn*—and then apply that knowledge to a robust production system.
15. "Anyone that comes to help us must understand all about our systems." Software managers may know all there is to know about their systems and software engineering—except how to improve.

3.6 GENICHI TAGUCHI

Dr. Taguchi has been using and teaching methods to reduce variability at Bell Labs and throughout Japan, Taiwan, and India from 1955 through 1980. The Taguchi Method shows techniques for reducing variability in products and processes at the design stage, thus enhancing their ability to overcome the many uncontrollable changing conditions in production. In the United States of America these methods are taught by the American Supplier Institute, Inc.[22] which has given permission to use the material in this section.

Off line quality control (Figure 3-4) attempts to reduce product or process variability by controlling noise factors and control factors. Noise factors are items categorized as outer noise—environmental conditions such as thermal, mechanical, electrical, customer misuse; inner noise—deterioration such as wear and embrittlement; and piece to piece variation. Control factors are items categorized as (increase robustness—change location and robustness); (adjust location—change location); (increase robustness—change robustness); and (reduce cost—change neither).

The application of off line quality control to software development would place development variables under control factors. This makes the analogy that the software development process is the manufacturing process for the production of software units. The key control factors for software development are personnel, software tools, methodologies (i.e., object oriented design, structured analysis, structured programming, etc.), workstations, languages, data base management systems, work areas, and desk layout. The measurement of these factors would be elements in the matrices resulting in signal to noise (S/N) ratios that would provide indications of what controls need be applied.

Even after optimal production conditions have been determined, Dr. Taguchi says that the following remain:

- Variability in materials and purchased components
- Process drift, tool wear, machine failure, etc.
- Variability in execution
- Measurement error
- Human error

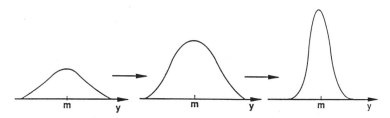

FIGURE 3-4. Off line quality control.[22] Copyright © 1988 American Supplier Institute, Inc. Reprinted by permission.

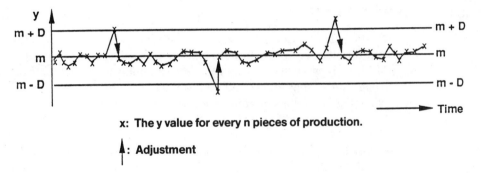

x: **The y value for every n pieces of production.**

↑: **Adjustment**

FIGURE 3-5. On line quality control.[22] Copyright © 1988 American Supplier Institute, Inc. Reprinted by permission.

These sources of variability are dealt with by quality control during normal production by on line (real time) quality control (Figure 3-5), which is truly feedback control. There are three on line quality control techniques: measurement and disposition, prediction and correction, and diagnosis and adjustment. *Measurement* is made on every product (100% is Taguchi's philosophy) and a *disposition* of deliver, scrap, or repair is made. To control variable quality characteristics in a production line, measurement is made every n^{th} unit. From the measurement, the average quality of the next n units is *predicted*. If the predicted value deviates from a target value by more than specified limits, *corrective action* is taken by adjusting a controllable variable. A manufacturing process is *diagnosed* at a constant interval. When normal, production continues; otherwise, the cause of the abnormality is investigated, and *adjustment* to the abnormality is made.

On line quality control applies to software development when a company has a defined, repeatable process. Such a process is subject to measurement, prediction and diagnosis. In fact, on line quality control methods are exactly right to provide insight into how to constantly improve the process. Process measurement is very difficult for the software development process.

3.7 SHIGEO SHINGO

Mr. Shigeo Shingo has written a book called *Zero Quality Control: Source Inspection and the Poka-yoke System.*[23] The English translation is copyrighted by Productivity, Inc., and much of the following information in this section is provided with their permission.

The book's title refers to three critical and interrelated aspects of quality control as taught by Shigeo Shingo. *Zero Quality Control* (Zero QC) is the ideal production system—one that does not manufacture any defects. To achieve this ideal, two things are necessary.

Poka-yoke (in English, "mistake-proofing"), looks at a defect, stops the production system, and gives immediate feedback so that we can get to the root cause of the problem and prevent it from happening again. *Source Inspection* looks at errors before they become defects and either stops the system for correction or automatically adjusts the error condition to prevent it from becoming a defect. Using poka-yoke devices and source inspection systems has enabled companies like Toyota Motors to virtually eliminate the need for statistical quality control (SQC), which has been the very heart of quality control in this country for years.[23, p. v, vi]

G. Gordon Schulmeyer, in his book *Zero Defect Software*[24, p. 33], has followed many of Shigeo Shingo's ideas as applied to software development. The primary elements of the zero defect software method are the software development process chart and its associated activities checklist, inspections and the zero defects software checklists, poka-yoke (software tools) methods, and the importance of the concept of an internal and external customer.

Error prevention and detection techniques at predefined checkpoints are basic to the zero defect software method. In defining a zero defect software program, a distinction must be made between an "error" and a "defect."

An "error" is an unwanted condition or occurrence which arises during a software process and deviates from its specified requirement.

A "defect" is that specific kind of unwanted condition or occurrence which has defied all attempts (inspections, reviews, walkthroughs, tests, and corrective action measures) to be eliminated during development and so is delivered to the customer.

Inspection methods are based on discovering errors in conditions that give rise to defects and performing feedback and action at the error stage so as to keep those errors from turning into defects, rather than stimulating feedback and action in response to defects. Every product, whether it be a document or work product of software development, has an informal review to check its integrity which is the self-checking by the worker who produced it. This also takes place whenever a work product is updated, which happens frequently during software development. This is called source inspection.

If this work product is to be handed off to another, this is the time to get that other person—the internal customer—into the process. The receiver has a vested interest in what he or she is going to have to work with and so will be critically sure that this is a good product. This is called a successive inspection.

How is poka-yoke (mistake-proofing) applied to the zero defects software program? Throughout the process, software tools need to be incorporated to automate the process and the inspection thereof. These software tools will make the process more "mistake proof."

Inherent in the zero defect software program is the need for consistency. Checklists, as applied to products and processes, will reveal where consistency can be or (more importantly) needs to be stressed. Where such consistency is desirable, new tools can be integrated into the process to reinforce the "expected" level of achievement.[24, p. 38]

3.8 PHILIP CROSBY

The five maturing stages of

- Uncertainty
- Awakening
- Enlightenment
- Wisdom
- Certainty

through which quality management evolves are shown in the Quality Management Maturity Grid (Table 3-4) developed by Philip Crosby in his book *Quality Is Free*. The measurement categories in the Grid include management understanding and attitude, quality organization status, problem handling, cost of quality as a percent

TABLE 3-4   Quality Management Maturity Grid[1]

MEASUREMENT CATEGORIES	STAGE 1: UNCERTAINTY	STAGE 2: AWAKENING
Management Understanding and Attitude	No comprehension of quality as a management tool. Tend to blame quality departments for "quality problems."	Recognizing that quality management may be of value but not willing to provide money or time to make it all happen.
Quality Organization Status	Quality is hidden in manufacturing or engineering departments. Inspection probably not part of organization. Emphasis on appraisal or sorting.	A stronger quality leader is appointed but main emphasis is still on appraisal and moving the product. Still part of manufacturing or other.
Problem Handling	Problems are fought as they occur; no resolution; inadequate definition; lots of yelling and accusations.	Teams are set up to attack major problems. Long-range solutions are not solicited.
Cost of Quality as % of Sales	Reported: unknown Actual: 20%	Reported: 3% Actual: 18%
Quality Improvement Actions	No organized activities. No understanding of such activities.	Trying obvious "motivational" short-range efforts.
Summation of Company Quality Posture	"We don't know why we have problems with quality."	"Is it absolutely necessary to always have problems with quality?"

of sales, quality improvement actions, and a summation of company quality posture. Drawing upon the Quality Management Maturity Grid as a guide, the Software Quality Assurance Measurement category is added to produce Table 3-5. The quality maturity stages established by Philip Crosby are examined below in relation to the production of quality software.

- In the stage of uncertainty, there are a number of deeply rooted "facts" that "everybody knows" about software quality:

1. Quality means goodness; it cannot be defined.
2. Because it cannot be defined, quality cannot be measured.
3. The trouble with quality is that American workers don't give a damn.

TABLE 3-4   (Continued)

STAGE 3: ENLIGHTENMENT	STAGE 4: WISDOM	STAGE 5: CERTAINTY
While going through quality improvement program learn more about quality management; becoming supportive and helpful.	Participating. Understand absolutes of quality management. Recognize their personal role in continuing emphasis.	Consider quality management an essential part of company system.
Quality department reports to top management, all appraisal is incorporated and manager has role in management of company.	Quality manager is an officer of company; effective status reporting and preventive action. Involved with consumer affairs and special assignments.	Quality manager on board of directors. Prevention is main concern. Quality is a thought leader.
Corrective action communication established. Problems are faced openly and resolved in an orderly way.	Problems are identified early in their development. All functions are open to suggestion and improvement.	Except in the most unusual cases, problems are prevented.
Reported: 8% Actual: 12%	Reported: 6.5% Actual: 8%	Reported: 2.5% Actual: 2.5%
Implementation of the 14-step program* with thorough understanding and establishment of each step.	Continuing the 14-step program* and starting Make Certain program*.	Quality improvement is a normal and continued activity.
"Through management commitment and quality improvement we are identifying and resolving our problems."	"Defect prevention is a routine part of our operation."	"We know why we do not have problems with quality."

* Names of specific programs used to make a quality improvement.

TABLE 3-5   Software Quality Management Maturity Grid*

MEASUREMENT CATEGORY	STAGE 1: UNCERTAINTY	STAGE 2: AWAKENING
Software Quality Assurance (SQA)	There are five quality "facts" that software development believes.	SQA is called upon in crisis situations.

STAGE 3: ENLIGHTENMENT	STAGE 4: WISDOM	STAGE 5: CERTAINTY
The SQA Plan is written first as the "driver" to the software development effort.	SQA management and software development management are working together to produce quality software.	Quality software is produced on time within cost every time.

* Adapted from reference 1.

4. Quality is fine, but we can't afford it.
5. Data Processing is different—error is inevitable.[17]

Among software developers there will usually be agreement about these quality "facts," especially the inevitability of errors in software. Education is required to dispel these erroneous "facts," better identified as mindsets.

When education is completed, there is usually a lip service to quality: people will say "yes" from their minds while they feel "no" in the pits of their stomachs; they will pay lip service to quality without really realizing it.[17] They will say they want quality but will continue to judge performance solely by schedule and budget.

There seems to be an implied assumption that the three goals of quality, cost, and schedule are conflicting, mutually exclusive. It is not true. Significant improvements in both cost and schedule can be achieved *as a result of focusing on quality.*[18] Fundamental to W. Edwards Deming's teachings is that the only way to increase productivity and lower cost is to increase quality.[6]

Company policy must be to supply exactly what a customer orders every time, seemingly too elementary to be important; but it *is* important. Remember that software quality is "to conform to requirements and to provide useful services" to the customer. Too often companies emphasize making the shipment, whether it's right or just close to right.[19]

Some cost will be incurred from the massive educational and procedural reworking effort that will be required. Each project will have to relearn what it really takes to achieve quality software production. To effectively increase quality, the SQA person will have to get involved with the management of software development to assure that relearning takes place on every project.

• In stage 2 of software quality, Awakening, the only times that SQA personnel are looked toward are times of crisis for the software development activity. One crisis during stage 2 is customer complaints about the integrity of the software development activities. SQA personnel can contribute by acting as a buffer to absorb these complaints. Usually this takes the form of special intensive quality investigations into the software development resulting in a report to the customer. There is value to be gained by highlighting the quality perspective of the software development.

Another crisis in software development is the software documentation trap. Software documentation is usually a deliverable item along with the computer programs, but due before the computer programs. Often the format and content requirements are so stringent that the computer programs are neglected to meet these documentation requirements. The SQA person is ultimately requested to perform a detailed software documentation audit which leads to the establishment of a checklist that may quickly be fulfilled. The checklist makes it much easier for the software development team to meet the format requirements.

• Philosophically, the Enlightenment stage occurs when it is understood that SQA contributes in a meaningful way to the role of software development management. Quality goals and objectives must be established first as a matter of corporate policy and then enforced through management involvement, procedural policy, and universal commitment. In essence, the quality role becomes a management role in which software quality principles and objectives are upheld at the start of the contract by software management, and development practices are driven by the quality objectives of those developing the software.

In the typical case of a software development project, requirements are imposed on the contractor to produce plans for software development, software configuration management, and SQA. The usual organizational alignments are such that each of these plans is developed independently by software development, configuration management, and SQA.

Because of this planning process, each organization has its "job" to do and goes on to do it. When organizational interactions are required to implement the plans, each of the organizational elements tolerates the activities of the others. Meanwhile, the quality of the software under development is being assured by SQA personnel through its use of planned tools, techniques, and methodologies.

Contrary to the usual practice of writing the software development plan before or concurrently with the SQA plan, there is a strong case for requiring the SQA plan to be written first. For software development to "build quality in," the software development plan written by and subscribed to by the software development team must follow the concepts included in the SQA plan.

The SQA plan, then, should be the first document written in a software development project. The SQA plan has to reveal more than the usual implementation auditing techniques. It must set the tone for those developing the software and espouse the quality principles inherent in producing quality software. These software quality principles may vary on different software development projects, so the particular software quality principles for this project are written into the SQA Plan.

With the "guidance system" in place for quality software, software development can then write the software development plan following the principles in the SQA plan. Only in this manner can software development write a software development plan that has quality inherent in the product.

- The Wisdom stage occurs when it is realized that software quality can only be built-in, with a conscious effort on the part of all involved. And must the management objective of the software development management and software quality assurance management teams! Since software development management is responsible for making the decisions for planning the project, software quality assurance management must contribute to this up-front decision-making process. Software quality assurance personnel must be active participants in the entire software development effort. (This concept is strongly reinforced by James I. McManus in Chapter 5.)

Throughout the software development cycle, software development management can produce quality software and software quality assurance management can ensure the quality of that product. As a result of putting increased emphasis on the *quality* of everything we do, we are beginning to realize some very significant gains—to repeat, *as a result of,* not in place of or instead of other performance measures.[18] In software, there is often a subcontractor producing software that must integrate with the overall software system. By emphasizing the quality of that subcontractor-provided software, the quality of the overall software system gains.

- In the Certainty stage, the objective of software development management and software quality management, producing quality software on time within a set cost everytime, is possible. The guidance given here by the quality experts as applied to the development of quality software should help lead to this objective.

3.9 CONCLUSION

This chapter applies the overall quality principles of leaders in the quality revolution to the specialty area of software quality. These principles lead to the application of what may appear to be remote principles to the reality of producing quality software.

Kaoru Ishikawa has laid a quality framework of six features, each of which has applicability to development of quality software. Joseph M. Juran's three methods for meeting the Japanese quality challenge all have applicability to the production of quality software. The quality policy, quality objectives, quality system, and quality organization of Lennart Sandholm also show applicability to software quality. Statistical methods and the Deming Circle taught by W. Edwards Deming have very specific application to software reliability and quality. Also, Dr. Demings 14 Points are applicable to software development. The Taguchi Method of reduction in variability of production is applied to the production of software. Shigeo Shingo's zero quality control with source inspections and poka-yoke provided the inspiration for the zero defect software methodology. Software quality can be shown as progressing through the five maturing stages of Philip Crosby's Quality Management Maturity Grid.

These experts have been responsible for a revolution in world economics brought about by attention to quality. The generally poor state of computer software will improve significantly by applying these revolutionary quality principles to the development of software. The groundwork has been surveyed by this paper, but there is so much to learn and apply from each expert that it is hoped others will expand the scope of the quality experts application to software development. The key message from Juran, Deming and others in the quality movement is that long-term improvement results only from systematic study and action, not from slogans or arbitrary objectives.[25, p. 95]

This paper started with a quotation: "Quality is never an accident; it is always the result of intelligent effort." It concludes with a statement from Robert Pirsig about understanding quality to use it:

> A real understanding of quality doesn't just serve the System, or even beat it or even escape it. A real understanding or quality *captures* the System, tames it and puts it to work for one's own personal use, while leaving one completely free to fulfill his inner destiny.[20]

References

1. Crosby, Philip, *Quality is Free* (New York: New American Library, 1979), pp. 32-33.
2. Tice, Jr., George D., "Management Policy & Practices for Quality Software." *ASQC Quality Congress Transactions—Boston,* 1983, Copyright American Society for Quality Control, Inc. Reprinted by permission.
3. Juran, Joseph M., "Product Quality—A Prescription for the West: [Part I] Training and Improvement Programs" *Management Review,* June 1981. © J. M. Juran 1981.
———— "Product Quality—A Prescription for the West: [Part II] Upper-Management Leadership and Employee Relations," *Management Review,* July 1981 © J. M. Juran 1981.
4. Ishikawa, Kaoru, "Quality Control in Japan," 13th IAQ Meeting, Kyoto, 1978.
5. *QC Circle Koryo,* "General Principles of the QC Circles," (Tokyo: JUSE, 1980).
6. Tribus, Myron "Prize-winning Japanese Firms' Quality Management Programs Pass Inspection," AMA Forum, *Management Review,* February 1984.
7. Juran, Joseph M., "Quality Problems, Remedies and Nostrums," *Industrial Quality Control,* Vol. 22, No. 12 (June 1966), pp. 647-653. Copyright American Society for Quality Control, Inc. Reprinted by permission.
8. Deming, W. Edwards., "On Some Statistical Aids Toward Economic Production," *Interfaces,* Vol. 5, No. 4 (August 1975), p. 8.
9. Deming, W. Edwards., "What Happened in Japan?" *Industrial Quality Control,* Vol. 24, No. 2 (August 1967), p. 91. Copyright American Society for Quality Control, Inc. Reprinted by permission.
10. Swartout, W. and Balzer, R., "On the Inevitable Intertwining of Specification and Implementation," *Communications of the ACM,* Vol. 25, No. 7 (July 1982), pp. 438-440. Copyright 1982. Association for Computing Machinery, Inc. Reprinted by permission.
11. Sandholm, Lennart, "Japanese Quality Circles—A Remedy for the West's Quality

Problems?" *Quality Progress,* February 1983, pp. 20-23. Copyright American Society for Quality Control, Inc. Reprinted by permission.

12. Deming, W. Edwards, "My View of Quality Control in Japan," *Reports of Statistical Application Research, JUSE,* Vol. 22, No. 2 (June 1975), p. 77.

13. Gottlieb, Daniel, "The Outlook Interview: W. Edwards Deming, U. S. Guru to Japanese Industry, talks to Daniel Gottlieb," *The Washington Post,* January 15, 1984, p. D3.

14. Sandholm, Lennart, "Quality Overview," Quality Department Lecture Series, Westinghouse Defense and Electronics Center, May 1983.

15. Cho, Chin-Kuei, *An Introduction to Software Quality Control* (New York: John Wiley & Sons, 1980).

16. Deming, W. Edwards, "It Does Work." Reprinted with permission from *Quality,* (August 1980), A Hitchcock Publication, p. Q31.

17. Burrill, Claude W. and Ellsworth, Leon W., *Quality Data Processing, The Profit Potential for the 80's* (Tenafly, NJ: Burrill-Ellsworth Associates, 1982), p. 176.

18. Walter, Craig, "Management Commitment to Quality: Hewlett-Packard Company," *Quality Progress,* August 1983, p. 22. Copyright American Society for Quality Control, Inc., Reprinted by permission.

19. Turnbull, Don. "The Manual—Why?," *Quality,* August 1980, p. Q5.

20. Pirsig, Robert M., *Zen and the Art of Motorcycle Maintenance* (New York: William Morrow & Co., 1974), p. 200.

21. Zultner, Richard, "The Deming Way—A Guide to Software Quality (Adapted by Richard Zultner)", brochure from Zultner & Co., 12 Willingford Drive, Princeton, NJ 08540, Copyright © 1988 Zultner & Co., Reprinted by permission.

22. Taguchi Method One Day Seminar, 10 August 1988, Copyright © 1988 American Supplier Institute, Inc., 15041 Commerce Drive South, Dearborn, MI 48126, (313) 336-8877, Reprinted by permission.

23. "*Zero Quality Control: Source Inspection and the Poka-yoke System,* by Shigeo Shingo, Copyright 1985 © by the Japan Management Association, Tokeyo; English Translation Copyright © 1986 by Productivity, Inc., P. O. Box 3007, Cambridge, MA. 02140. 1-(800) 274-9911 Reprinted by permission."

24. Schulmeyer, G. Gordon, *Zero Defect Software* (New York: McGraw-Hill Book Company, 1990).

25. Fowler, Priscilla and Rifkin, Stan. *Software Engineering Process Group Guide,* Software Engineering Institute Technical Report CMU/SEI-90-TR-24, September, 1990.

4

Software Quality Program Organization

Emanuel R. Baker, Ph.D.

Software Engineering Consultants, Inc.

Matthew J. Fisher, Ph.D.

Research, Development & Engineering Center (CECOM)

4.1 INTRODUCTION

The relationship between the quality of a software product and the organization responsible for that product is multi-dimensional. This relationship depends upon many factors including the business strategy and business structure of the organization, available talent, and resources to produce the product. It also depends upon the combination of activities selected by the organization to achieve the product quality desired. To reduce the dimension of this problem, let us consider the following precepts.

First, consider the definition of software quality. Software quality is defined as, "The degree to which a software product possesses a specified set of attributes necessary to fulfill a stated purpose."[1] As explained in the referenced work, this definition implies that "Quality is everybody's business." When we consider how software development projects are organized, this translates to: "Quality is affected by many, but effected by few." Virtually everyone working on the project, from the program/project manager (PM) on down to the most junior member of the staff, affects the quality of the software product; however, only those actually producing the product (the developers performing the requirements analysis, design, and coding) build the quality into it. Because of this, the person ultimately responsible for the quality of the software product is the PM — the "manager of quality" for the system produced. It is the PM's responsibility to integrate the efforts of "the many" and "the few" and bring them to bear on the development effort to accomplish the quality objectives. The PM may, of course, delegate the authority for this function, but, ultimately, he or she is responsible.

Second, there is a method for structuring the project to control the product quality, and that is to implement a software quality program (SQP). The SQP has three critical elements, each of which will be described below. Each of these elements spawn a series of tasks. The PM must determine the allocation of these tasks to the available personnel or organizations supporting the program, express them in an SQP plan, and obtain the commitment of the supporting organizations. The main topic of this chapter is how organizations could be structured to implement the SQP and better achieve the quality objectives.

Fundamental Software Quality Program Concepts

4.2 SOFTWARE QUALITY PROGRAM

The software quality program is the overall approach to influence and determine the level of quality achieved in a software product. It consists of the activities necessary to:

- Establish requirements for the quality of a software product.
- Establish, implement, and enforce methodologies, processes, and procedures to develop, operate, and maintain the software.
- Establish and implement methodologies, processes, practices, and procedures to evaluate the quality of a software product and to evaluate associated documentation, processes, and activities that impact the quality of the product.

Figure 4-1 illustrates the elements of the SQP.

The foundation of the software quality program is not how well one can measure product quality nor the degree to which one can assess product quality. While these are essential activities, they alone will not achieve the specified quality. Software quality cannot be tested, audited, evaluated, measured, or inspected into the product. Quality can only be built in during the development process. Once the quality has been built in, the operating and maintenance processes must not degrade it. It is that understanding that lays the basis for the software quality program.

The foundation of the SQP stems from the definition of software quality. It is the concept that product quality means, in effect, compliance with its intended end use, as defined by the user or customer. Does the software do what it is supposed to do? In other words, does it meet correctly specified requirements? The consequence of this concept is that product requirements are really quality requirements. These include the software functional and performance requirements, and also include requirements for maintainability, portability, interoperability, and so on. Software requirements are, in fact, the requirements for the quality of the software.

Figure 4-2 illustrates the elements of the software quality program and how it affects software quality. The interaction of the SQP with the other parts of the

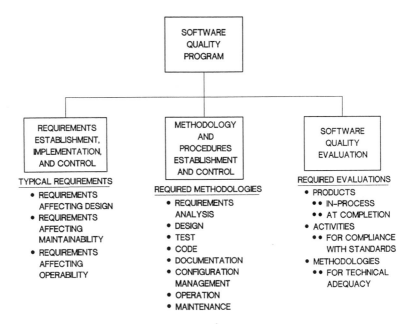

FIGURE 4-1. Software quality program elements.

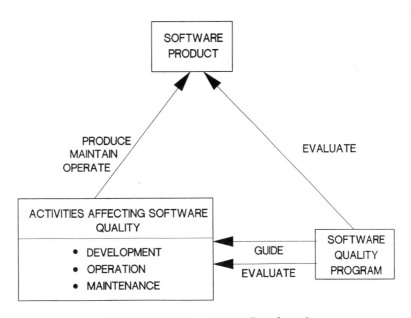

FIGURE 4-2. What creates quality software?

project elements as depicted in the figure is necessarily complex. The involvement is at all levels of the project organization and takes place throughout the project's life. In some cases, the SQP directs the other activities; in other circumstances, it can only influence those activities. In any case, all the project activities, in some way, affect software product quality.

The software quality program covers both technical and management activities. For instance, if we look at the element of the SQP concerned with methodologies for software development, enforcing these methodologies (in order to build quality into the software) is a management activity, while the specification of the methodologies is a technical activity.

Establishment of Requirements

The first element of the software quality program is the establishment of the requirements for the software to be produced on the project. As previously pointed out, the requirements for the software are, in fact, the requirements for the quality of the software. Consequently, the requirements must accurately reflect the functionality, performance, etc., that the customer or user expects to see in the software. This activity includes not only defining the requirements but also baselining (formalizing) them, as well.

However, merely defining and formalizing the requirements is insufficient. Changes to the product requirements, after they have been baselined, must also be controlled. Furthermore, the baselined software requirements must be enforced, i.e., implemented as stated, and in full. The developers must not be allowed to unilaterally deviate from implementing them. Failure to implement the requirements as stated can result in software products that do not meet user needs and requirements. The resultant impact on software product functionality and performance will range from negligible to severe (see Chapter 11). Deviation, intentional or otherwise, may not always cause significant problems, but the potential is clearly always there.

The process of defining and establishing the requirements and controlling changes to them involves interfaces with the other two elements of the SQP: establishment of methodologies and quality evaluation. Two kinds of interfaces with the establishment of methodologies exist. One has to do with the methodology for performing requirements analysis. To illustrate, the use of data flow analysis or object oriented analysis to define requirements is a result of establishing one or the other as the methodology for performing requirements analysis. The second has to do with baselining requirements and controlling changes to them. This process, or methodology, is known as a "configuration management process." This is a management methodology implemented to:

- Prevent uncontrolled changes to baselined items
- Improve the likelihood that the development effort will result in quality software, and that software maintenance will not degrade it.

The interface between this element of the SQP and the software quality evaluation element is concerned with the adequacy of the requirements. As pointed out in Chapter 11, total compliance with requirements does not guarantee quality software. If the requirements have not been properly defined, and errors exist in them, then compliance with requirements will produce software that does not satisfy the intended end use. Clearly, requirements must be evaluated for adequacy while they are being developed.

Establishment of Methodology

The second element of the SQP pertains to the establishment, implementation and enforcement of methodologies for the development, operation, and maintenance activities for the software product. These are the processes by which the software will be developed, operated, and maintained.

There is a very strong link between software quality and the processes used to develop it. If the processes in use by a software development organization are not well defined or organized, the quality of their software products will not be predictable or repeatable from project to project. The dependency of software quality on processes has been characterized by the Software Engineering Institute (SEI) at Carnegie Mellon University in a capability maturity model (CMM).[2] Five levels of maturity are described by the CMM. The levels, their names, and the characteristics that describe when the organization has reached that level are identified below:

- Level 1: *Initial:*   Chaotic, ad hoc; not even the most rudimentary procedures exist for project planning or management—neither do any exist for configuration management or quality assurance.
- Level 2: *Repeatable:*   Development process is intuitive, rather than codified; procedures for project planning and management, configuration management, and quality assurance exist and are implemented. Success of development projects, however, are very much dependent on key individuals, and not on process. In times of crisis, established procedures are abandoned.
- Level 3: *Defined:*   Procedures and tools for software development exist and are implemented. Processes are codified and followed for all projects. When faced with a crisis, the organization continues to use the defined process.
- Level 4: *Managed:*   Minimum basic process measurements have been established. A process data base and the resources to manage it have also been established. Resources to gather and maintain the data have been established.
- Level 5: *Optimizing:*   Process measurements are being taken and entered into the process data base. The process data base is being used to fine tune and optimize the development processes.

A methodology, called the software process assessment, has been developed by the SEI to determine the level at which software development organizations are functioning.[3,4] As of June 1989, 167 organizations have been surveyed. Of these organizations, 86% were found to be functioning at Level 1, and 13% at Level 2.[5] This means that 99% of the organizations surveyed do not have well-established, codified software development processes. Data gleaned from various sources indicate that the Japanese software industry is achieving defect rates two orders of magnitude better than those of the "best in class" U.S. companies.[6] A reason why the Japanese are achieving such low defect rates, based on reviews of the Japanese software industry conducted in 1984 and 1989, is because of their emphasis on understanding and improving the software development process. The same report also indicates that many of the Japanese companies are operating at Levels 3, 4 and 5, whereas barely 1% of U.S. companies are operating at Level 3 or above.

From the foregoing, it can be seen why establishment of methodologies is such an important element of the Software Quality Program.

Establishment of the methodologies refers to the definition of the methodologies to apply to the development, operation, and maintenance efforts. Implementation of the methodologies is accomplished by codifying them in the form of standard practices and procedures. Implementation of the methodologies may be facilitated by the acquisition of tools (see Chapter 12) compatible with the methodologies and the standard practices and procedures. Enforcement is accomplished through the commitment of corporate management. Management must consistently and unequivocally require the application of the selected methodologies from project to project, and under all conditions of schedule pressure. (This is not to preclude the acquisition, development or use of different methodologies; but, the appropriate scheduling of their introduction must be observed.) Some tools, such as automated process environments, can facilitate the enforcement of the methodologies and the associated standard practices and procedures.

"Development," as used here, refers to the requirements definition, design, and test phases of the project and the documentation produced during these phases. Development procedures refer to those needed to define how to establish requirements and to design, code, test, and document the software: for example, utilization of structured analysis, implementing top-down design, the use of software development folders[7], coding standards to be implemented, configuration management, and the like.

Operation refers to production or operational usage of the software. Quality can be affected by improper operation of the software system or by inadequacies in instructions contained in the user's manual. Chapter 11 illustrates this point quite well. It describes a situation where the software was apparently correctly designed and implemented, but the instructions in the user's and operator's manuals were not properly written. A large number of abnormal terminations occurred because the software was not correctly operated. Reference 1 points out that "quality is in the eye of the beholder." If the software does not operate the way that the user of the system *expects,* it will *not* be perceived as quality software. As the example in Chapter 11 shows, this can occur even when the software has been properly designed and coded, i.e., in compliance with the requirements.

The maintenance activities pertain to those activities that occur after development has been completed and a baseline has been established for the software (code, design, documentation). At this point, acceptance testing has been completed, and the software is ready for operational or production usage. If adequate procedures have not been established to handle software maintenance, the quality initially built into the software product may suffer degradation. For example, inadequate change control procedures or inadequate definition of procedures to "repair" the code in the event of a failure, would result in such degradation.

At present, the process for selecting the methodologies to apply is based on experience, intuition, literature search, and common knowledge. No formalized techniques exist for specifying methodologies; however, a formalized technique for specifying development methodologies to impose is being developed by Arthur and Nance at Virginia Polytechnic Institute.[8] This technique is oriented toward providing the capability to specify, prior to beginning development, the quality objectives such as adaptability or correctness for each software product or class of software product (e.g., geological models, Management Information System (MIS) applications, inertial navigation systems) to be developed. The degree to which each quality objective should be attained could be specified for each product or class of products. Theory says the quality objectives would be attainable by the degree to which a specific set of software engineering principles, such as information hiding or stepwise refinement were applied. The degree to which the principles are attained, in turn, are a function of the extent to which specific attributes of the software, such as readability, complexity, and cohesion, are achievable in the implementation of the methodology. Each candidate methodology, then, would be evaluated for its capability to provide the required levels of the attributes, principles, and objectives.

The paper by Nance and Arthur[8] reports on the work completed to date, and describes the work planned for the next phase of the activity. The results to date carry promise for eventual improvement in the capability to correctly select and apply development methodologies to the software development enterprise, thus enhancing the capability to achieve the specified quality requirements.

Evaluation of Process and Product Quality

The third element pertains to those activities necessary to evaluate the software development process and the resultant products. This element is referred to as the software quality evaluation (SQE) program. SQE is a set of assessment and measurement activities performed throughout the software development cycle to evaluate the quality of software products and to evaluate associated documentation, processes, and activities that impact the quality of the products. "Assessment" pertains to qualitative evaluation while "measurement" pertains to quantitative evaluation.

The "set of evaluation activities" refers to the actions, such as reviews, evaluation, test, analysis, inspections, and so on, which are performed to determine that technical requirements have been established, and that products and processes conform to these established technical requirements, and ultimately, to determine software quality. These activities vary as a function of the phase of the development cycle; and they can be performed by several organizations, some or all of which may be within a program manager's immediate organization. The "set of evaluation activities" are generally documented in project plans, software development plans, project-specific software quality procedures, and/or company quality plans and related software quality procedures.

In the case of the products, determination of the state of the software can be performed by comparing the products against pre-established criteria. However, evaluation of product quality is difficult, especially since the definition of software quality is hard to express quantitatively within the current state-of-the-art. A large volume of research has been directed toward the establishment of quantitative definitions of quality, e.g., software reliability (refer to Chapter 19). We see much of this effort expressed in terms of software metrics. Numerous definitions for software metrics have been proposed and applied to specific cases. However, the software development community has not come to a common agreement in the selection and use of these metrics for the measurement of software quality. Chapter 14 provides further illumination regarding the software quality metrics issue.

On the other hand, the technology is available to establish and enforce various forms of meaningful quality criteria. The approach is relatively straight forward: Establish criteria based upon measurable entities; entities that lend themselves to validation during software development. As long as the project believes that these criteria reflect the type of quality it desires ("quality is in the eye of the beholder"), it can use them to gauge the quality. For example, the metric of cyclomatic complexity is a measurable entity. If the project believes that software exhibiting some level of cyclomatic complexity is high quality software, then this metric is adequate for the project to use to determine the product quality.

The evaluation program also includes assessment and measurement of the software development process and the activities/procedures making up this process. It may be that the process is being properly implemented, but the products are not achieving the desired level of quality. Such evaluations are a check against the initial analysis done prior to the start of the development, that is, during the methodology selection process discussed above. This originates from the concept of Total Quality Management (TQM), i.e., the improvement of product quality through the continuous improvement of the processes used to produce the product. Continuous improvement is achieved by focusing on the processes, and using product evaluations as indicators of process adequacy (see, for example, Reference 9). This evaluation may be implemented by examining interim software products, such as initial specifications, or the products which result from the process itself, such as Software Development Folders.

Generally, the basis for determining which process to implement has been to look at a candidate process or set of processes and compare the proposed process against established development practices and methodologies. The assumption is that if the process has been shown to produce "high quality software" in the past, then proper implementation of the process will result in a high quality product. This argument is somewhat misleading. There has been no conclusive demonstration of a definite link between the process selected for the software development and the resultant quality of the software product itself. Establishment of such links has been more heuristic or intuitive rather than analytical. For example, Ada promotes information hiding which, in turn, should make the software more adaptable. But, the actual cause and effect link has not been clearly demonstrated.

Typical of the difficulty in such research is the work of the Department of Defense (specifically, the Air Force) in defining a software quality framework leading to software quality metrics. Upon close examination, it may be seen that this framework actually measures the adherence to good programming practices rather than the actual quality of the software. Other work attempting to link processes to product quality can be found in Reference 8, as previously discussed.

An often confused aspect of SQE is the role of Software Quality Assurance (SQA).

Historically, SQA has been incorrectly interpreted by some as the only means to achieve software quality. This originates from an inspection-oriented approach to software quality, rather than a total quality approach. SQA has also been identified as a specific functional entity within a development organization or within a government agency. Both considerations have resulted in quite a bit of difficulty. SQA in and of itself is not an organized discipline with a single, unambiguous meaning. Furthermore, SQA organizations are not the sole organizations performing all the evaluations defined by SQE as necessary to verify and validate that the software and the processes producing that software meet all requirements.

Compounding this problem is the difference in approaches to SQA from company to company. SQA to one organization may mean a checklist approach to assure the development process is proceeding as expected, while other organizations could conceivably assign all SQE activities to the SQA organization. Because of non-uniform assignment of responsibilities to SQA functional entities from organization to organization, conflict arises about the performance of SQA. As a result, very often the implementation of "quality assurance" falls by the wayside. Some evaluations may be overlooked and not performed. Many times software developers successfully promulgate an image of an SQA organization as ill-equipped (from the perspective of technical know-how) to perform any meaningful quality evaluations of the software. More often, organizational charters circumscribe what assessments and measurements are actually performed by the SQA entity, leaving other equally valid and significant evaluations to fall through the cracks.

Thus, if an SQA entity exists in a corporate structure and the capability of this group is limited, let us say, to a checklist approach, then a program manager may mistakenly conclude that the effort performed by this SQA group is sufficient to satisfy all the SQE needs of his or her program. This situation may preclude vital measurements (or tests) on critical software modules.

The point to be learned from this is that SQE and SQA are not necessarily synonymous. SQE is a set of activities and SQA is a functional entity within an organization. The degree of SQE performed by an SQA organization is related to an SQA organization's competence (and independence) to perform those activities and, to a large extent, the size of the company.

What is crucial to any software development project is the definition and implementation of the activities necessary to assess and measure the quality of the software products produced by that project, in accordance with the requirements established for the project. When the SQE activities have been defined, the assignment of these activities to specific organizations is a management prerogative. Where SQA organizations have the capability to perform many or most of the SQE activities, these can be assigned to the SQA organizations.

Organizational Aspects of the Software Quality Program

4.3 ORGANIZING TO IMPLEMENT A SOFTWARE QUALITY PROGRAM

Each of the elements of the SQP discussed above involve a number of organizations or functional entities within a company. The discussion that follows describes the functions or activities these organizations perform in the implementation of the SQP. It also explores how these organizations interact to implement the SQP.

Often the functions that will be described are not necessarily performed by separate organizations, but may sometimes be performed by different individuals within a single organization. For instance, within an MIS department, the responsibility for some of the SQP functions may be shared between the Data Administrator, Data Base Administrator, and Quality Administrator. In consideration of that, for convenience, the word "organization" will be used to refer to both actual organizations and to the situation where the functions are performed by separate individuals within an organizational entity, rather than separate organizations.

Organizational Relationships to Implement the Software Quality Program

Requirements Definition
A number of organizations participate in establishing, implementing, and controlling the software quality requirements (for example, the functional and performance requirements). The kinds of organizations that are involved will depend on the type of software under development. To illustrate, the kinds of organizations that will be involved in this effort for data-intensive systems, such as MIS applications, will be very different from the kinds of organizations that will be involved for engineering applications, such as an inertial navigation system. Nonetheless, the activities that occur in establishing, implementing, and controlling the requirements, and the sequence in which they occur, will be effectively the same for all types of applications (with minor variations).

The typical sequence of events is as follows:

a. Define the system requirements.
b. Review and approve the system requirements (using in-process reviews as well as a formal review).
c. Baseline the system requirements.
d. Allocate the system requirements to hardware and software elements (subsystems) of the system.
e. Define the hardware and software subsystems requirements.
f. Review and approve the subsystems requirements (using in-process reviews as well as a formal review).
g. Baseline the subsystem requirements.
h. Define the processing requirements for the individual software applications.
i. Review and approve the processing requirements (using in-process review as well as a formal review).
j. Baseline the processing requirements.

Where the system is reasonably uncomplicated, subsystems may not exist. Consequently, for that situation, the steps associated with subsystem requirements definition and baselining may be eliminated.

The foregoing is not intended to characterize the requirements development process as occurring in any kind of software development waterfall model. For example, as the system requirements are being developed, the allocation of the system requirements may sometimes have begun, even though the definition of all the system requirements has not been completed. Furthermore, there may be some iteration back and forth between the system requirements development and the subsystems requirements development to make sure that the requirements make sense. In any event, there always has to be some amount of "crawling before you learn to walk," i.e., some kinds of activities must precede other activities, even if the precedent activity has not been completed. The intent of the foregoing is only to show the general flow of events in defining software requirements.

In developing the system requirements, a number of organizations are involved. For engineering or scientific applications, although systems engineering takes the lead for developing the requirements, software engineering organizations should be involved in a cooperative effort to jointly develop the system requirements and define the allocation of them to software elements. The using organization must also be involved in order to assure that the system requirements reflect what is needed in the production system. Where the software is developed under contract, such customer (user) involvement may be difficult to achieve without affecting the contract costs and/or schedule.

For MIS or similar applications, the development of the system requirements should be performed by the using organization and specified in a user specification, which defines the functionality of the system (and does not specify how it is to be implemented in software). The participation of the user is essential in order to ensure that the requirements are responsive to the user's needs. In parallel to this, as the user specification is being developed, preliminary processing and data base design requirements are being developed by the MIS organization. Within the MIS organization, this process could involve system analysts, data analysts, and the Data Administrator.

A formal review occurs after the system requirements have been defined and documented, and the system requirements specification is then baselined in accordance with procedures established by the configuration management group. For engineering/scientific systems, this review may involve project management and personnel from the user or customer organization; system engineering; major subsystems engineering (including software engineering), configuration management and quality assurance groups; and various groups concerned with operating, fielding, and supporting the system. For MIS systems, the review would involve project management and personnel from the user organization, MIS development organization (system analysts, data analysts, and Data Administrator), and MIS configuration management and quality assurance administrators. After the formal review is successfully completed, the configuration management group is then charged with the responsibility for overseeing the control of the documented requirements to prevent unauthorized changes to them.

In developing the processing requirements for the software, there are also a number of organizations involved. For engineering or scientific applications, the software engineering organization should take the lead for developing the processing requirements. The systems engineering organization should be involved in the effort to ensure that the system requirements have been correctly allocated to the software and are being implemented, and to satisfy themselves that the software requirements are traceable to the system requirements. The using organization should also be involved in order to make sure that the software requirements reflect what is needed in the production system. Where the software is developed under contract, again, the using organization becomes the customer, and such involvement may be difficult to achieve without affecting the contract costs and/or schedule.

For MIS or similar applications, the development of the software processing and data base requirements should be performed by the MIS development organization. Within the MIS organization, this process typically involves system analysts, data analysts, and the Data Administrator. The user organization is also involved, insofar as they have a role to play in verifying that the processing requirements reflect the functionality they want in the system.

A formal review of the software requirements is quite similar to the formal review for the system requirements. It occurs after the software processing requirements have been defined and documented, and the software requirements specification is then baselined in accordance with procedures established by the configuration management group. For engineering/scientific systems, this review may involve project management and personnel from the software engineering, configuration management, software test, system engineering, and quality assurance groups, and various groups concerned with operating, fielding, and supporting the software. For MIS systems, the review would involve project management and personnel from the user organization, MIS development organization (system analysts, data analysts, and Data Administrator), and MIS configuration management and quality assurance administrators. After the formal review is successfully completed, the configuration management group is then charged with the responsibility for overseeing the control of the documented requirements to prevent unauthorized changes to them.

The manager (and subordinate managers) responsible for software engineering (or MIS development) is responsible for implementing the requirements as established and for assuring that they are not changed in an unauthorized manner. The quality assurance group may be responsible for monitoring the configuration management process to verify that no unauthorized changes have occurred.

For this element of the Software Quality Program, then, we see that at least the following organizations are active in establishing, implementing, and controlling the software quality requirements for engineering/scientific applications: user/customer organizations, system engineering, software engineering, software test, configuration management, quality assurance, project management, and various support groups, such as a logistics group, field maintenance group, and the like. For MIS systems, it involves the user organization, MIS development, quality assurance, and configuration management.

Methodology Definitions

Establishing and implementing methodologies to develop the software and maintain its quality include establishing the methodologies themselves and institutionalizing them in the form of standard practices and procedures. These methodologies, practices, and procedures cover a wide number of areas. They include requirements analysis, documentation, design, coding, test, configuration management, installing and operating the software, and software support (how to make changes to the code after it is delivered).

In implementing this element of the SQP, interactions occur with a number of organizations. Software Engineering must be involved in the definition process since they will be the ultimate users of the methodologies, standards, procedures, and associated tools (if applicable). An interface with the quality evaluators exists. From time to time, changes are made to the specified methodologies and implementing documentation and tools. This occurs under two conditions: (1) the specified methodologies, documentation, or tools are not producing the required levels of quality, or (2) new methodologies have become available which will materially improve the quality of the product. Once the changes have been made to the processes, they must be monitored to determine if, in fact, improvements have been made. The determinations of methodology adequacy result from product and process evaluations. The personnel performing software quality evaluations typically provide the raw data for evaluating existing, new, or modified methodologies and tools, while software engineering personnel generally do the analyses of the data or of the methodologies. The Project Manager must be consulted regarding the adoption of new methodologies and/or tools to determine if such changes will negatively impact productivity, schedule, and/or cost for that project. Operations personnel, such as Software Librarians and Data Base Administrators, must be consulted to determine the effect on operations. Personnel must be assigned the task of producing standards and procedures for implementing the methodologies and using the tools in a manner compatible with the established standards. Clearly, company management must be involved in this element of the SQP because of the investment in personnel to staff the function, as well as approval or disapproval for the acquisition of new methodologies and tools to implement the methodologies.

One can deduce from this that many organizations are involved in establishing and implementing the methodologies for development and maintenance and producing standard practices and procedures for these functions. Again, the multi-disciplinary nature of the Software Quality Program is evident.

Evaluation

Finally, we come to software quality evaluation or SQE. Activities involved here cover the establishment of standard practices and procedures and implementation of activities to evaluate the quality of software products and processes impacting the quality of the products. Any evaluative undertaking that requires reasoning or subjective judgment to reach a conclusion as to whether the software meets requirements is considered to be an assessment. It includes analyses, audits, surveys, and both document and project reviews.

On the other hand, measurement encompasses all quantitative evaluations, specifically, tests, demonstrations, metrics, and inspections. For these kinds of activities, direct measures can be recorded and compared against pre-established values to determine if the software meets the requirements. Accordingly, tests for unit level, integration, and software performance can be considered as measurement activities. Similarly, the output of a compare program or a path analyzer program can also be considered measurement.

The number of organizations involved in performing SQE can be large. Considering that SQE includes analytical as well as measurement activities, it is easy to see that SQE is a discipline that encompasses engineering as well as support groups. For example, analyses may be performed by systems engineering or a software engineering group. Tests may be performed by an integration test team or an independent software test group (or both), possibly with a quality assurance group monitoring. In some companies, the quality assurance group does testing as well.

Project reviews may include project management, and the system engineering, software engineering, configuration management (for a further discussion see Chapter 13), and quality assurance groups. Certainly a quality assurance entity would participate in and conduct audits. The configuration management and quality assurance groups would be involved in document reviews as would the system and software engineering groups.

In any event, it can be seen that the activities involved in SQE require the talents of almost all groups participating in the development process.

To complete this discussion of SQE, it is imperative to introduce the concept of independence. Relative to SQE, independence implies performance of software quality evaluation by an organization (or individuals) different from the organization (or individuals) that has produced the products or documentation, or that execute the processes and activities being evaluated.

To elaborate further on this concept of independence, the project's designated evaluators should be precluded from participating in establishing the software development practices and methodologies to be used on that project. The reason is that an unbiased review of the benefit of these practices is desired. If an evaluator helps establish these practices, the evaluator may be inclined toward one or more of them, and his or her review could be biased in that direction. As will be shown later in this chapter, this problem is averted by the introduction of the Software Engineering Process Group concept, and the interaction of the roles of that group, the project's software quality manager, and the project's quality evaluators.

In some cases, independence of quality evaluators is also extended to preclude them from establishing the criteria against which the project's outputs are being gauged. Here again, such preclusion helps reduce the perception of promoting self interest (or the potentiality for it), as might occur with the use of an outside V&V agent. Evaluators with a hidden agenda can hardly be considered independent. By removing them from the responsibility for establishing the evaluation criteria, such problems cannot arise. It should be the PM or the corporation who decides how the project should be gauged, not the software quality evaluator. The criteria for the evaluations should be based on the requirements for the product, hence the importance of establishing good requirements, and ensuring that the user's or customer's needs are accurately reflected in the requirements documents.

Independence, as a concept, has two aspects. One is independence exercised within an organization, such as the use of a test team comprised of individuals different from those who designed and developed the code. The second form of independence is perhaps, the most stringent. Here, independence is exercised by employing agencies totally outside the project organization, for example, an independent verification and validation agent from outside the organization producing the software product. Either way, the notion of independence is applied to reduce errors resulting from oversight due to extensive familiarity with the product being evaluated.

One effort within independent SQE is the collection of the objective evidence that technical requirements have been established, products and processes conform to technical requirements, and that software products meet the specified quality requirements. This may mean that one organization does a specific measurement or assessment, but another organization establishes the criteria for measurement and assessment, verifies that the measurement and assessment that has been performed, and impounds the data for eventual use in certifying the product or service. "Objective evidence" includes such items as audit reports, certified test data sheets, verification and validation (V&V) reports, resolved software trouble reports, and the like.

The point stressed here is that the activities described as software quality evaluation are very often performed as an independent activity which can take many forms: independent organizations within a structure, independent agency within the corporation, and/or independent contractor acting on behalf of the corporation. Decisions as to the application of independence, the degree of independence to apply, and the types of independent agencies to employ are a function of a number of variables. Examples of key variables entering into these decisions are the size and complexity of the software project, corporate policy, available funds, and criticality of software to its end use (e.g., human safety, destruction of equipment, severe financial loss, etc.).

Applying the Software Quality Program to Projects

Numerous organizational structures can be applied to implement a software quality program. The important point is the allocation of the associated tasks to corporate organizations available to the PM. This allocation depends upon several interrelated factors. Obviously, one factor is the business structure and guidance established by the corporation or by the PM to accomplish the project. The structure and guidance given to the PM eventually reduces to authorized funding and permissible execution control within the corporate structure, both of which limit the flexibility the PM has to conduct projects. Another factor is the extent of the tasks and the availability of personnel to perform these tasks.

In many cases, the corporation has predetermined responsibilities for its elements, thereby predetermining the allocation of tasks. This a priori assignment of tasks does restrict the PM in how he or she mobilizes a particular project. It is recommended that instead of imposing corporate assignment upon the project, that the PM be allowed to structure the project. This recommendation is especially applicable to the software quality program, which involves the coordination of so many disciplines. One way a PM can ensure this coordination is to appoint a software quality manager to his or her staff.

If we assume that most, if not all, necessary resources and talent are usually available for the program manager's execution of the SQP, the PM's task reduces to coordination of assigned activities. If the necessary resources and talent are not available, the PM must secure these through negotiation with company management.

The purpose of delegating a software quality manager is to support the PM in providing software quality on the project and, more importantly, making the quality program more visible to the rest of the PM's organization. The quality manager does this by ensuring that a software quality program is planned as part of the overall software development process, by insuring that the SQP is implemented, and by keeping the PM informed and on track with the overall software development.

Planning
The software quality manager must be an integral part of the program planning to ensure that the software quality program is addressed. He or she must play a very active role in this effort, setting up all the steps to follow in executing the software quality program, including those in the SQE effort.

Important in performing this role is the development of the software quality program plan. This can be either a major subset of the software development plan, or may be a separate document that is referenced within the software development plan. In any event, the vital task for the software quality manager during the planning phase is to produce this plan.

The software quality manager must work very closely with all participants in the project in order to generate the SQP plan, specifically, to ensure that:

1. The SQP plan is produced;
2. The SQP plan is complete and the elements of the SQP are integrated into the total management plan;
3. The plan contains realistic schedules;
4. The plan describes assignment of responsibilities and designates necessary authority to the appropriate performing organizations.
5. Expected program outputs are specified; and,
6. Criteria for successful completion of tasks are stipulated.

It is important that project personnel understand how the SQP will effect them and what they are expected to input to the program. This interface definition is particularly sensitive for the assessment and measurement portion of the SQP. No one, especially in engineering, appreciates others constantly reviewing, testing, and analyzing its work. So it is important to establish what the SQE effort consists of and how it may be structured to alleviate or reduce this sensitivity.

During software development, the software quality manager uses the result of the SQE effort to track the progress of the software quality program against the program plan. A primary concern is not simply to determine compliance with the plan, but, more importantly, to determine if application of the planned SQP will achieve the quality, or, if the plan must be changed, to affect the desired quality.

Requirements Definition

During the process of establishing the software requirements for the project, the software quality manager must have the authority to represent the program manager. Here, he or she actually manages the process. As indicated earlier, a number of organizations (or functions within an organization) may be involved in defining and establishing functional and performance requirements. These may include software engineering, user organizations, system engineering, etc. Other groups, such as those representing human factors or maintenance, must have a chance to influence the requirements. What kinds of groups are involved will depend on the type of application under development. As the number of these groups increases, the job of establishing the requirements becomes more and more difficult. Having the software quality manager coordinate or manage this process for the PM simplifies control to ensure that requirements are established and that they are quantitative, testable, complete, and so forth.

The software quality manager can use several methods of accomplishing this process, orchestrating the various groups involved. For example, he or she may depend totally upon the software engineering group or MIS development group to both specify the processing requirements and perform checks (assessments) as to their adequacy. On the other hand, the quality manager may use some groups to define the requirements, and other groups to perform the evaluations. In some cases, the evaluations may be split between the developers and the evaluators. For instance, the assessment for traceability might be performed by the software developers, instead of other designated evaluators, utilizing the traceability capabilities embedded within the computer aided software engineering (CASE) tool being used to develop the requirements, or utilizing a traceability tool external to the CASE tool, such as Program Statement Language/Program Statement Analyzer (commonly known as PSL/PSA). Whoever is assigned to making these evaluations is designated in the SQP Plan.

As pointed out previously, there is an interface between the requirements definition element and the SQE element of the SQP. Requirements development involves a strong interplay between requirements analysis and SQE. The requirements must be evaluated as they are being developed to make sure that the job is being performed completely and correctly. The software quality manager utilizes those personnel designated in the SQP Plan to make such assessments (perform SQE). The two functions are buffered from each other by the quality manager (see Figure 4-3). This technique is normally quite effective in reducing sensitivity on the part of those whose products (or efforts) are being assessed. The quality manager uses the outputs of the assessments to:

- Ensure that the evolving requirements are modified where necessary,
- Assist in revising the process of establishing requirements,

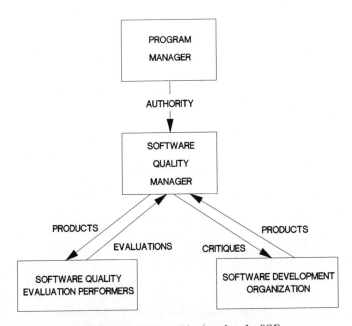

FIGURE 4-3. Non-sensitive interface for SQE.

- Assist in changing methodologies used in this process, and
- Enforce the procedures originally planned for this part of the SQP.

Communication between the two elements can be conducted totally through the software quality manager.

Methodology Definition

As with the requirements portion, the second element of the SQP is easy to accomplish within the project structure by assigning the job to the software quality manager. There are really three parts to this job: establishing the methodologies to be used for the project, enforcing the methodologies, and modifying the selected methodologies, when necessary.

One way in which the accomplishment of this element of the SQP can be facilitated is by establishing a Software Engineering Process Group* (SEPG).[2] It is the focal point for the methodology element of the SQP. Its main function is to serve as the initiator, sustainer, and evaluator of process change. Based on data collected through the SQE element of the SQP, the SEPG determines if the established processes for software development and maintenance are satisfying the quality requirements, especially in the form of product quality. If they are not, the SEPG researches other available methodologies to determine a suitable replacement. It also evaluates new methodologies as they become available to determine their applicability to the company's products, and their capability to meet quality criteria. If the introduction of a new methodology can effect a material improvement in product quality, the SEPG may recommend its introduction. In making this recommendation, it examines the impact of introducing the new methodology to determine if that will create excessive disruption, and significantly degrade the execution of the development or maintenance processes.

At the very outset, the applicability of the established methodologies, techniques, and tools for the software to be developed on the project is determined. If an SEPG exists within the company, the software quality manager must consult with that function in order to adequately carry out this assignment. The methodologies, which are established by the SEPG, are established for use throughout the entire organization according to the different types of software products produced by the organization. It may be necessary to modify these methodologies to suit the unique requirements for the software to be produced on this project. The software quality manager, in conjunction with the SEPG, makes this determination and oversees the modifications, if required. These modifications will be reflected in the form of project-specific modifications to the standards and procedures.

When an SEPG does not exist, the software quality manager then must assume much of the responsibility and coordination effort that the SEPG would have performed. In establishing methodologies to use in order to achieve the desired quality attributes for the software, the software quality manager must bring to bear

---

*In MIS organizations, it may be known as the MIS Standards Committee. It may be known by other names, as well, in other organizations, but its functions are essentially the same, no matter what it is called. For ease or reference, it will be referred to as the SEPG.

a wide range of disciplines, not just software engineering. The intent of this effort is to select those software engineering methodologies which offer the best promise of producing a software product meeting all the specified requirements—an extremely difficult process due to varying maturity in available software engineering techniques. The software quality manager must further assure that the interfacing disciplines (e.g., software engineering, testing, configuration management, etc.) are communicating with each other and coordinating on the methodologies to be employed on the project to assure that they are mutually compatible.

Once the project is started, the quality manager is responsible for enforcing the implementation of the methodologies. This is accomplished by setting policy and monitoring the development, operation, and maintenance activities to verify that the policy is being followed. Enforcement often depends upon an assessment or measurement of products and development, operation, maintenance activities, creating an interface between this element of the SQP and the SQE element of the SQP. Products include preliminary and final versions of documents and preliminary software releases. Since methodologies are procedural in nature, other kinds of products may be used to evaluate whether the methodologies are being properly implemented in the development activities. For example, software development folder audit reports and reports of walkthroughs may be used to determine if the developers have followed the prescribed methodologies.

The methodologies established for the project must also be evaluated during the life of the project to determine if they are, in fact, the correct ones to use. They must be modified if they are not achieving the desired results. As indicated earlier, this activity also creates an interface between this element of the SQP (methodology definition) and the SQE element of the SQP. The basic information on which a decision to alter the methodologies is based is an output of software quality evaluation. Process measures can be used to make this determination. Although no adequate means exists at the present time to perform this assessment during the life of the project, the means to perform this assessment quantitatively is under development, as reported elsewhere in this chapter. For the most part, the present capability is limited to an after-the-fact process evaluation, based on measures of product quality, and restricting the utility of the information to "lessons learned" to be used on the next similar project.

Because of the interfaces that exist between this element of the SQP and SQE element of the SQP, it becomes readily evident that the software quality manager is the most logical individual to assign as the one responsible for ensuring that this job is properly accomplished on the project.

Software Quality Evaluation

The software quality manager is also responsible for the implementation of the SQE program. The software quality program plan should have defined the totality of assessment and measurement activities and assigned these to the appropriate performing organizations. Clearly, the SQA organization can be a major performer, and as indicated previously, a number of other organizations are likewise involved. Accordingly, it is essential that the software quality manager completely and totally define the tasks and performers.

SQE is the major instrument defining the health of the product and hence the project. Through the evaluations performed, the PM can determine if his or her product will satisfy the customers' or user's needs within cost and within schedule. Because of the number of organizations involved in the SQE process, coordination of the results of this process is an essential role to be performed by the software quality manager.

Whatever decision management makes, it must be sure that all SQE activities have been assigned to an organization competent to perform that function and, where independence is specified, to an organization with the proper detachment as well.

Software Quality Program Example Implementations

4.4 IMPLEMENTATION

To varying degrees, the principles discussed in this chapter are slowly coming into practice. A number of organizations have begun to incorporate the elements of the SQP, including the SEPG, into the structure of their software development organizations.

Although many organizations have implemented SEPGs, and do many of the SQP activities described in this chapter, what is still lacking in most organizations is the coordination of the elements of the SQP, and the coordination of the SEPGs (when they do exist) with the elements of the SQP.

Clearly, a major determinant as to how the SQP is to be implemented is the size of the organization. A small organization, comprised of a number of small projects, cannot implement the SQP in the same way that a large organization would. This section discusses strategies for implementing the SQP, based on the experience of these organizations. It also discusses the implementation of the SEPG concept.

Software Engineering Process Group (SEPG)

Many companies have begun to adopt the SEPG concept. It is an important factor in successful implementation of the second element of the Software Quality Program, the establishment of methodologies. As pointed out earlier, the SEPG is the focal point for methodology selection and evaluation. Many of the companies that have been assessed by the SEI, or that have been trained by the SEI to perform self-assessments, now use SEPGs. This has come about as an outgrowth of the assessment results. Many MIS departments have established Standards Committees which perform many of the same functions that an SEPG does. Some of these organizations have established SEPG structures without having an assessment performed. They were established because these organizations recognized that the function performed by such a group is vital for the production of quality software and, consequently, to the success of the organization.

Reference 3 describes strategies for the implementation of SEPGs into the organizational structure. Organizational size is taken into account in the strategies discussed.

Large Organizations

Clearly, the easiest organization structure to describe is that which exists for large organizations producing engineering or scientific applications. Figure 4-4 illustrates one organization chart. In the figure, the acronym "APM" means Assistant Project Manager. In this structure, the software quality manager, or Project Software Quality Manager (PSQM) as this person is called, is responsible for planning the performance of the SQP and documenting the output of the planning effort in the appropriate plans, coordinating the activities of the performers of the SQP activities, and monitoring their performance to verify that it is being performed properly.

For the requirements element of the SQP, the organizations involved in the requirements definition effort include Systems Engineering, Software Development, and Logistics. The Logistics organization participates in the definition of the maintainability and software supportability requirements for the operational software. In this structure, the PSQM is responsible for coordinating and integrating the requirements definition activities of these areas of the project. The PSQM, as can be seen from the figure, also coordinates with the Configuration Manager with regard to establishing the baseline for the requirements.

To establish and maintain the methodologies to be utilized on the project, the PSQM coordinates with the SEPG. The SEPG is responsible for coordinating with the other organizations within the company with regard to establishing the methodologies in general usage and for determining their effectiveness.

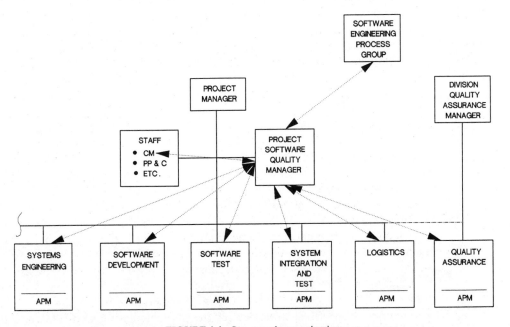

FIGURE 4-4. One sample organization.

Software quality evaluation is performed by Quality Assurance, Software Test, System Integration and Test, and Software Development. The PSQM coordinates and monitors the performance of the software quality evaluation elements of the SQP. The functions that each organization performs in support of the quality evaluation element of the SQP are documented in the Software Quality Evaluation Plan (SQEP). Feedback of the evaluation results into the development, operations, and maintenance activities and products is provided for in the SQEP. The coordination and monitoring of the feedback process is another function performed by the PSQM.

Because the PSQM is a staff function to the project manager, he or she has a direct line of communication to the PM to ensure that all project staff members comply with the requirements of the SQP. In the event of a non-compliance that cannot be resolved directly with the individual or organization involved, the PSQM can call on the project manager to enforce compliance. This type of a project structure can also deal effectively with recalcitrant project managers. Direct lines of communication also exist with the Quality Assurance organization, and these lines can be used to resolve any such conflicts.

Small Organizations

Small organizations face a totally different picture when it comes to implementing the elements of the SQP. In this situation, a number of conditions may exist. Two example situations are: (1) the company may be a one-project company, or (2) the company may be working entirely on a number of small projects. MIS organizations in many companies are an example of the latter. Figure 4-5 is an example of how one MIS department organized to implement the SQP.

Within the MIS Department, the MIS Standards Committee fulfills the function of the SEPG. It is comprised of key members of the Department including the MIS Quality Administrator, and representatives of the development, system resources, data administration, and configuration management areas of the department. Because of the size of the department, none of the members are assigned full time to the Standards Committee to do its work.

The MIS Quality Administrator reports administratively to the MIS Manager, and is an employee of that department. By company policy, the MIS Quality Administrator is deputized to act on behalf of Corporate Quality Assurance to ensure that the provisions of the corporate quality program are carried out. The MIS Quality Administrator has a responsibility to Corporate Quality Assurance to provide periodic reports on the activities of the MIS Quality Program. Note that in this case the Quality Administrator is not independent. The intent of independence is achieved, however, through a reporting channel to Corporate Quality Assurance and periodic audits by Corporate Quality Assurance to ensure that the provisions of the applicable policies and procedures are being correctly implemented.

In this structure, the MIS Quality Administrator acts more as a coordinator and monitor with respect to the SQP functions. The responsibility for defining requirements is shared between the user community and the project. Requirements

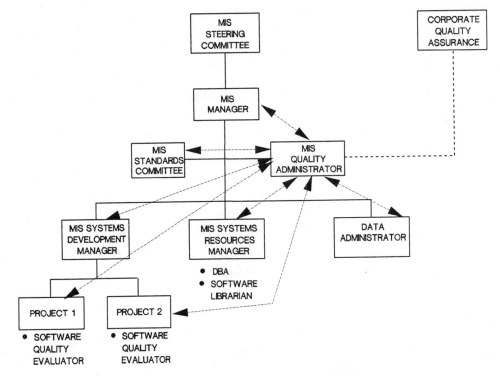

FIGURE 4-5. Another sample organization: an MIS department.

definition is performed in accordance with the procedures defined in the MIS Standards Manual, and the individuals responsible for performing this task, the outputs they produce, the informal and formal reviews to be held, and the schedule for the entire activity is documented in the Software Development Plan (SDP) for the project. The MIS Quality Administrator monitors the activity to ensure that it is being performed as prescribed by the MIS Standards Manual and the SDP. Any conflicts regarding implementation that cannot be resolved directly with the development or user project leaders are raised with the MIS Systems Development Manager for resolution.

The responsibility for the methodology element of the SQP is vested in the MIS Standards Committee. They perform the function of the SEPG. The MIS Quality Administrator is a member of the MIS Standards Committee and ensures that this function is being properly executed. The project-specific modifications, if applicable, to the standardized methodologies are documented in the SDP. Project-specific adaptations to the standards and procedures are also identified in the SDP. The MIS Quality Administrator is a signatory party to the SDP, and consequently can coordinate and monitor the application of this aspect of the SQP to the project.

The SQE element of the SQP is handled in a unique way by this company. A typical project size is approximately 3-4 developers. Because of the size of the entire organization, and the size of the projects, only two people, the MIS Quality Administrator and one assistant, are dedicated full-time to quality program tasks. Each project has its own part-time quality evaluator, and this person is also a part-time developer. He or she is responsible for performing the quality evaluations. Where necessary, the quality evaluators can call on other resources elsewhere within the MIS Department or within the affected user community to assist in the quality evaluations. For instance, in performing a quality evaluation of a requirements specification for a payroll program, the quality evaluator can call on personnel within Accounting to assist in the review of the document.

The results of each evaluation are documented on a quality evaluation record. These are entered into a log and into a data base. Both are available on-line. A major function performed by the MIS Quality Administrator is auditing each individual project for compliance with the SQEP and the standards and procedures specific to SQE contained in the MIS Standards Manual. Since the SQEP contains the definition of the SQE tasks to be performed, the person responsible for performing it, and the schedule for its performance, the MIS Quality Administrator uses it to determine when to perform the audits. The data base is queried to determine if a record exists of a given evaluation's performance. The MIS Quality Administrator has the authority to review the record and can spot check the product itself to ensure that the review was performed in accordance with the approved procedures. The MIS Quality Administrator can also participate in a review performed on an activity or product.

Another responsibility assigned to the MIS Quality Administrator is the audit of the configuration management functions. The configuration management functions are distributed to various projects. The development baseline is under the control of the development project leader, which results in another interface with the project leader, and the production baselined is under the control of the MIS Software Configuration Control Board, which is chaired by the MIS Manager. Changes to the applications software, corporate and project data dictionaries, and data bases are handled by the librarian, data administrator, and data base administrator, respectively, and their functions are audited by the MIS Quality Administrator.

Audits performed on the MIS area by Corporate Quality Assurance determine if these functions are being properly performed by the MIS Quality Administrator.

4.5 SUMMARY

In organizing to implement the Software Quality Program, several concepts must be kept in mind.

First, it must be emphasized that the foundation for the organization is tied to achieving the requisite quality in the software product. One must understand what software quality is and the technical aspects of specifying, designing, and testing for it. Software quality is achieved with proper software design and implementing appropriate processes. Quality cannot be achieved by "assuring" and testing the product.

Second, the ideas associated with software quality lead to the software quality program. General principles of such a program have been in some detail; these elements interact not only with each other but also with all other project activities. This interaction is extremely complex, occurring at many levels within the software project and throughout the project's life.

From the perspective of the software quality program, an organization can be derived based upon corporate structure (controlling policies) and available talent. It is recommended that the program manager be allowed to structure his or her own project organization without the restriction caused by a priori corporate organizations. The program manager needs to recognize and understand the SQP. Given this understanding, the PM allocates tasks of the SQP to those with appropriate talent. Because of its broad nature, the SQP requires a range of disciplines including software engineering as well as evaluation expertise. It is recommended that a software quality manager be appointed who is steeped in this expertise and in the methodologies needed to achieve software quality.

References

1. Baker, Emanuel R., and Fisher, Matthew J., "A Software Quality Framework," in *Concepts— The Journal of Defense Systems Acquisition Management,* ed. by Robert Wayne Moore; Vol. 5, No. 4 (Autumn 1982) (Fort Belvoir VA: Defense Systems Management College, 1982).
2. Humphrey, Watts S. "Managing the Software Process," New York; Addison-Wesley, 1989.
3. Humphrey, W. S., and W. L. Sweet. "A Method for Assessing the Software Engineering Capability of Contractors," Technical Report CMU/SEI-87-TR-23. Software Engineering Institute, Carnegie Mellon University, September 1987.
4. Humphrey W. S., and D. H. Kitson. "Preliminary Report on Conducting SEI-Assisted Assessments of Software Engineering Capability," Technical Report CMU-SEI-87-TR-16. Software Engineering Institute, Carnegie Mellon University, July 1987.
5. Tutorial, "Software Process Assessment", Software Engineering Institute, Carnegie Mellon University, September 1990.
6. Yacobellis, Robert E. "A White Paper on U.S. vs. Japan Software Engineering", January 1990.
7. Ingrassia, Frank S., *The Unit Development Folder (UDF); An Effective Management Tool for Software Development,* in "Tutorial; Software Management", Reifer, Donald J. ed., third edition, Washington, DC; IEEE Computer Society Press, 1986.
8. Arthur, James D. and Richard E. Nance. "Developing an Automated Procedure for Evaluating Software Development Methodologies and Associated Products", Technical Report SRC-87-007. System Research Center, Virginia Polytechnic Institute, Blacksburg, VA, 16 April 1987.
9. "Total Quality Management for Software", Schulmeyer, G. Gordon and McManus, James I., ed., New York: Van Nostrand Reinhold Company, Inc., 1992.

5

The Heart of SQA Management: Negotiation, Compliance, Regression

James I. McManus
Westinghouse Electronic Systems Group

5.1 INTRODUCTION

Effective management of software quality assurance (SQA) is a major challenge in today's software development environment. Books[1,2] have been written discussing the virtues of establishing an SQA organization within a corporation. Most corporations that develop software today practice some form of SQA. However, the effectiveness of SQA among corporations is not uniform and generally less than optimal.

A nationwide survey of how well corporations apply SQA is a recommended task. The focus of this chapter, however, is more basic: the effective application of the principles of SQA to achieve known quality objectives.

Several aspects of managing software quality assurance in order to be consistent and effective in achieving SQA objectives are explored. A greater awareness of where attention is needed by management should eventually lead to some form of standardization in planning for, establishing, and effectively practicing SQA.

Sections 5.2 and 5.3 discuss two interrelated quality concerns—process quality management and product quality management.

Under process quality management, SQA is discussed from four points of view. First is the delicate task of integrating SQA personnel into software development as active team players; second, the degree with which SQA personnel should become involved in software development; third, emphasis on the role of SQA personnel within each phase; and fourth, SQA management in terms of three inherent stages of SQA management.

Under product quality management, the impact of the software quality process on the software product is discussed. If a quality product is to be developed, quality must be managed.

A product-driven process is discussed to demonstrate that product quality can never be presumed and is a summation of every step that precedes the current state of the product. Just as a product cannot be separated from the development activities that bring it about, neither can the quality of the product be separated from the management goals, objectives, tools, techniques, and directives employed to achieve the quality goal.

Section 5.4 summarizes the importance of measurement to software quality assurance management.

5.2 PROCESS QUALITY MANAGEMENT

In a general sense, the two broad concerns of SQA management are the quality of the actual process and the final quality of the software product.[3] These concerns are characterized here as

- Process quality management.
- Product quality management.

This section focuses on the functional aspects of software quality management and discusses the following areas as they relate to software development processes:

- Integrating SQA into software development.
- Degree of SQA involvement.
- Phases of development.
- Management and assurance.

Integrating SQA into Software Development

Engineers and programmers are familiar with the process of integrating software through builds (successively more functionally complete bodies of computer programs) during unit test, integration test, and acceptance test. Several disciplines coordinate their activities to bring about a total testable software system.

In a management sense, and analogous to the integration effort noted above, the elements of SQA must also be coordinated with the elements of software development, i.e., systems engineering, software engineering, test engineering, and software configuration management. Management's first chance at planning an effective role for SQA is during the proposal phase: here the objectives of quality must first be defined. Defining quality objectives is particularly important to software quality and must be specifically and uniquely tailored to the project. How these objectives will be achieved is an important aspect that must be considered. In this sense, the what and how of SQA must be related to developmental processes and therefore described for each phase of the software life cycle.

The proposal phase, then, is management's (both development and quality) first look at the plans and objectives for development. This is not a phase whose only objective is winning contracts. How tasks will be performed (process quality) and what the end products must do (product quality) are being firmly established in a legal and contractual sense.

Realistic alternatives, risk areas, required resources, and so on also must all be evaluated up front to prevent major problem areas of cost and schedule after contract award.

This quality assessment must therefore be done during this phase to properly coordinate the planned activities of SQA with all of the concerned organizational areas.

SQA managers should also be active participants during the feasibility study to provide insight based on their previous experience into:

- Preventing problems.
- Performing trend analyses of key problem areas.
- Defining major risk areas.
- Defining the way review processes and inspections are to be conducted.
- Defining the need and use of procedures.
- Assessing how to modify existing procedures to fit a project.

This list is not intended to provide a complete set of SQA activities during the proposal phase but to emphasize the need for SQA personnel to be active participants in defining and proposing what must be accomplished and how these developmental activities will be processed. The proposal effort, then, is the product of an integrated activity conducted by peers. These peers are responsible to each other to review each other's contributions, provide constructive criticism, and proffer good advice to produce a set of well-coordinated plans and objectives for doing quality work and developing a quality product.

Degree of SQA Involvement

The degree to which an SQA team gets involved in a project is not fixed. An SQA team may remain completely independent from the development team in terms of tasks, or may take a more active role in performing some of the developmental activities. These decisions must be tempered in the best interests of software quality management and software development management as a function of the project. A guideline on the degree of involvement is found in Reference 4 at the end of this chapter, and further covered in Chapter 4 of this *Handbook*.

The important thing to remember is that SQA must never lose sight of its role as an independent management team when it comes to matters of quality. No matter how involved it is in the project itself, the sole justification for a quality team on a project is to "assure" that processes are in compliance with established quality procedures for doing work and that products are being developed in accordance with approved product specifications and requirements.

However, since quality team players should be experienced as to how developmental activities are performed, having been involved in non-SQA tasks should not be overlooked by quality management as a virtue for SQA personnel. How analysis or design or testing is performed must be well understood by SQA personnel, down to the nitty-gritty details. This "hands-on" experience is invaluable to the SQA person, since this very same work is that which must be evaluated by quality auditors an inspectors when adjudging the quality of the process.

Then exactly how does this kind of experience fit into SQA? First, SQA management requires adequate insight into development practices to sufficiently manage and assure software quality. Second, the specific methodologies used by SQA to get the required knowledge are to audit, inspect, review, monitor, witness, assess, evaluate, and analyze, and to attend meetings. Third, SQA needs to understand the software development activities of defining requirements, designing, coding, building, testing, and so on in order to accurately report and status what was audited, inspected, or reviewed. As a result, any direct experience SQA has or can obtain on the project via its personnel will go a long way in helping it assure the quality of the process and product.

Phases of Development

The basic phases of development are well documented in many studies.[1, 5, 6] In this subsection on process quality management, it is proposed that the management of each phase be weighted equally in terms of importance to the outcome of the final product. No phase must be considered lightly or be weighted more than any other relative to the final product. If management accepted each phase in terms of what each phase must *accomplish* and directed efforts within each phase to accomplish its specific objectives, then no one phase would be singled out, receive preferential treatment, receive inadequate attention, or cause undue concern or risk downstream in the development cycle.

This is where SQA can play a lead role. Before the next phase is entered, each phase must be required to pass some form of test or inspection. The risks of proceeding downstream when the project is not ready to enter the next phase are well-known. An example of such restraint at the end of a developmental phase is embodied in the peer inspection process discussed in Chapter 9. Cost-oriented studies in the same vein are found in the literature[1] and in Chapter 8.

The implication is that SQA management must concern itself with how well the specific objectives of each phase are being accomplished on a day-to-day basis. Concerns should be:

- What are the objectives of this phase?
- Are the objectives well-understood?
- If the objectives (or subset) are unclear, from whom do I seek resolution?

The objectives should be stated, approved by the entire management team, and coordinated among the project-specific plans:

- Software development plan.
- Test plan.
- Software configuration management plan.
- SQA plan.

The objectives should also be directed at requirements which are identified in the proposal, contract, statement of work, and other similar requirements documentation.

Figure 5-1 (the "V" diagram) illustrates a most important aspect of the software life cycle: *before you build something, you must first break it* [conceptualize it] *down into its most elementary parts.*

As simple as this concept appears, there are numerous projects for which software teams have started building software prior to tearing down the requirements and refining them to the point from which software can be built properly.

In the "V" diagram, the left side of the "V" is the Requirements side, to be associated with the TEAR-DOWN process. This side of the "V" diagram is concerned with a top-down evaluation, definition, refinement, and redefinition of requirements.

The right side of the "V" is the Validation side, to be associated with the BUILD-UP process. This side of the "V" diagram is concerned with a bottom-up evaluation of the product as it is being built and integrated into a total system — essentially a *validation* of the as-built product in terms of how well it meets the requirements of the TEAR-DOWN process. This process includes unit test, Computer Software Component (CSC) test, CSC integration test, Computer Software Configuration Item (CSCI) test, CSCI integration test, subsystem integration test, and systems acceptance and validation of the fully integrated system. Table 5-1 defines several key terms used in Figure 5-1.

A set of matched phases has been established to relate the Requirements side of the "V" diagram to the Validation side of the diagram:

Matched Phases

1. Systems requirements   vs.   Systems validation
2. Subsystems requirements   vs.   Subsystems integration testing
3. Software requirements   vs.   CSCI integration tests
4. CSCI requirements   vs.   CSCI testing
5. Build requirements   vs.   CSC integration tests
6. CSC requirements   vs.   CSC testing
7. Unit requirements   vs.   Unit testing

SQA is the independent team responsible for assessing the quality of each process and how that process does or does not lead toward a quality end product. The "V" diagram illustrates the need for SQA to:

• Concern itself with early requirements phases in the software development cycle, not just code and test.
• Be routinely involved in the early phases of development to understand and know the requirements on a per-phase basis.
• Concern itself with each phase of requirements refinement as the driving force for each corresponding test and validation phase, where operational and performance requirements must ultimately be verified.
• Work with software development management to maintain visibility, foster constructive communication, and provide positive feedback in order to

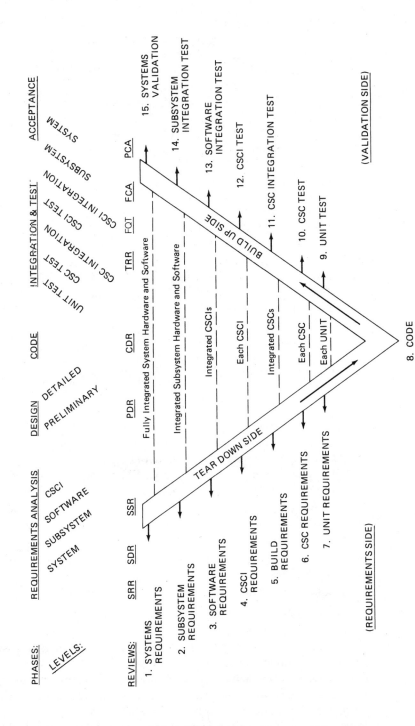

FIGURE 5-1. "V" diagram.

TABLE 5-1   Acronyms "V" Diagram

Within the "V" diagram, several acronyms require definition:

CDR — Critical design review (detailed design review)

CSC — Computer software component (major component of a CSCI)

CSCI — Computer software configuration item (a program under configuration control)

FCA — Functional configuration audit (audit of performance verification)

FQT — Formal qualification test (CSCI level)

PCA — Physical configuration audit (audit of the as-built configuration of the software)

PDR — Preliminary design review

SDR — Systems design review

SRR — Systems requirements review

SSR — Software specification review

TRR — Test readiness review

---

prevent future problems, detect current problems, control risks, discuss alternatives and solutions, and assure that quality is built-in phase-by-phase.

The life-cycle phases in the "V" diagram are closely related to the software development cycle phases noted in the Department of Defense standard DOD-STD-2167A.[6] However in the "V" diagram four system-level phases are shown; the systems requirements analysis phase, subsystem requirements analysis phase, subsystem integration test phase, and the systems validation phase. This provides a more complete picture because software must ultimately reside and be tested within a larger system.

DOD-STD-2167A defines six phases for the development of a single CSCI. The "V" diagram contains 15 phases. Four are system and subsystem phases. The remaining eleven are a refinement of the six DOD-STD-2167A phases, each emphasizing a different aspect of software development with which SQA should be concerned. For instance, the software requirements analysis phase is actually concerned with the operational and performance requirements of all CSCIs when integrated as well as the performance of each individual CSCI. Similarly, the performance of all CSCs (computer software components which must be integrated to make up a single CSCI) is as important an aspect of development, with its own set of integration requirements for each build, as is the performance of each individual CSC.

The "V" diagram attempts to point out that management of the up-front Requirements Definition phases cannot be considered complete unless the impact of each phase on its counterpart, validation phase has also been analyzed and defined. This dual analysis of both requirements phase and corresponding validation phase is of particular importance to the quality of the product.

At the beginning of this chapter, it was noted that a lack of standardization for effectively applying software quality assurance was missing from the industry. DOD-STD-2167A is the latest attempt by the Department of Defense (DOD) to establish a consistent way for all branches of the service and DOD contractors to develop software. Additionally, DOD-STD-2168 is also an attempt by the Department of Defense to bring some consistency and standardization to the use and application of software quality assurance. For more on standards, see Chapter 6 of this *Handbook*.

Management and Assurance

To gain a perspective of SQA as a management discipline, note first that quality software in and of itself can only be developed if the software development is receptive to and incorporates quality practices throughout. But this can only occur if management supports and condones effective quality practices, which results in quality being built-in.

Since management controls the up-front decision-making process, then quality must begin there—up-front; it can't be added later.

And since it is management who must enforce quality (if quality is to be achieved), then management must set quality objectives which foster visibility and control over software development practices to assure itself that the desired software quality is there.

SQA may not be where it should be. To effectively manage software quality over the software development cycle, SQA needs management authority and control in its own right. This management authority and control can only come about if it is essentially legislated and chartered by a corporate policy placing product quality on a par with profits.

Table 5-2 is the quality management, or QM, diagram. Three stages of SQA management are defined:

Stage   I—Negotiation
Stage II—Compliance
Stage III—Regression

All three are critical to effective management to achieve software quality. Similar to the way that analysis, design, coding and testing are generic to the development life cycle, so, too, the three stages of negotiation, compliance, and regression are generic to SQA management.

Stage I—Negotiation
The first stage is negotiation. What must SQA do to assure that software development is on target; that project quality objectives are well-defined, well-documented, and well-understood by all concerned; and that these same project quality objectives are supported by the proposed plans and procedures which govern how tasks will be performed? How will SQA effectively carry out its tasks as an integral part of the development team, not as some bench-warmer or high and mighty judge? How will SQA be involved in the day-to-day development of the project? These are the questions that SQA management must answer and coordinate in the best interest of the project.

TABLE 5-2   QM Diagram

NEGOTIATION	COMPLIANCE	REGRESSION
• Apply to life cycle.	• Apply to life cycle.	• Apply to life cycle.
• Apply to each phase of life cycle.	• Apply to each phase of life cycle.	• Apply to each phase of life cycle.
• Define objectives, goals.	• Monitor, audit, inspect practices, procedures, progress.	• Update records.
• Define how to achieve.	• Review, inspect software*	• Support regression techniques.
• Define role of SQA: • Where does SQA fit in? • How does SQA fit in?	• Review, inspect documentation	• Peer inspections of design.* • Peer inspections of requirements.*
	• Witness verification tests*	• Peer inspections of code.* • Perform trend analysis.
• Tailor plans to requirements. • Select tools, metrics, etc.	• Participate at software configuration review board*	• Certify verification processes, test results*
	• Monitor corrective action	• Assure follow-up activities
	• Write up reports on non-compliant items	• Validate software*
	• Prepare status report for upper management	• Validate documentation*
		• Enforce regression of non-compliant items before proceeding to next phase

* As applicable per phase.

These and similar questions must be answered and resolved during the proposal phase and at the beginning of each later phase. It is precisely this up-front aspect of quality management that negotiation beings to SQA; negotiation therefore is critical to the success of the QA organization.

Quality can only be built-in if it is an up-front concern with a well-planned, coordinated set of management activities. Only by negotiating up-front in the life cycle and within each phase can the management team (of development and quality) come to agreement on what must be done, how it shall be done, and to what degree any given task will be implemented to improve product quality.

Only by negotiation can differences be resolved, controlled and agreed upon internally. By placing negotiation first (hence stage I), tasks can be properly planned and budgeted and all disciplines accurately represented, each knowing ahead of time what to expect from the other. No group will stand alone as dominant or as subservient to another. Each will function as a team player with well-defined and well-understood rules. The risk of surprise downstream in the software development cycle will also be reduced.

From an SQA point of view, how each discipline executes its plan must be coordinated with how other disciplines execute their plans. The software development plan therefore must reflect and support the SQA plan, software configuration management plan, test plan(s), management plan, and so forth; and vice versa. An important aspect of the negotiation stage then is that the software development plan does not drive the other plans. It has often been stated that quality must come first, but this can only happen if all concerned disciplines strive as peer players to arrive at a set of well-thought-out, coordinated, integrated, negotiated positions.

When negotiating those tasks which must be performed in the systems requirements phase, consideration must also be given to the systems validation phase which exists solely for the purpose of validating systems level requirements. Similarly, the subsystems requirements phase must be negotiated not only to define what is essential to this phase itself but also how it impacts its counterpart phase of subsystems testing; and so on, until the unit code and unit testing level is negotiated.

Therefore, an important aspect of negotiation within any up-front life cycle phase is the impact any plan, procedure or process will have on the corresponding Validation phase as illustrated in the "V" diagram (Figure 5-1).

Here is a case study to illustrate negotiating. The subject is the use of software development files (SDFs) when they are not required by the contract.

From a *positive* viewpoint, SDFs can be an excellent way of organizing and saving important data on computer software components within the software development cycle. Program-related requirements, design charts, program design language (PDL), code, unit tests, and so on, can be saved component by component. A high degree of visibility can be provided on each program component. This affords easy access for review, audit, inspection, trend analysis, progress assessment, problem analysis status, and so forth, for SQA in its role.

From a configuration management viewpoint, SDFs are an excellent way for defining and identifying the software configuration items. A place is available for noting which software components are ready for baselining and for performing the role of status accounting. The SDFs also support physical configuration audits (PCA) as a means of preparing for and identifying the as-built software configuration.

From a development programmer's viewpoint, SDFs are an organized way of referencing a program's requirements, design, code and unit test results, for supporting walkthroughs, for reference when changes have to be made, and for reference when deliverable documents have to be written by software analysts.

From a *negative* viewpoint, major drawbacks to SDFs do exist:
- Continual maintenance of SDFs is time-consuming on the project.
- They are formalized in that everyone must follow the same procedure regardless of need.

- They reveal considerable information and may be a problem in terms of customers having access to proprietary information.
- Some data is classified and programs may have to be artificially separated, which creates inconvenience when showing something in the SDF file.
- They create more work.
- Analysts may be forced to place information in SDFs before they are ready to, resulting in poor reviews (not good for morale).

With SDFs there are advantages and disadvantages, as with any enforceable procedure. These advantages and disadvantages must be negotiable (not mandated as blanket requirements) in terms of what is possible and most effective for the project. Without negotiating, conflicts arise as to when SDFs should start (during preliminary design or detailed design or just during the code phase), what items should be contained (requirements, PDL, code and unit test, or just code and unit test results, etc.), who has access to these files, what happens if SDFs are not up to date, and so on. These and other concerns, if not resolved early-on, have an uncanny way of haunting a project and lingering on throughout the development cycle.

Stage II—Compliance

The compliance stage follows negotiation. Once the negotiated position has been fully integrated among all disciplines, the role of SQA is one of assuring compliance, as follows:

- That project team leaders know and understand contractual requirements.
- That project team leaders are in agreement as to the roles of all the players on the team.
- That approved plans and procedures exist for doing work.
- That SQA personnel are team players responsible for monitoring compliance in accordance with approved plans, procedures, and contractual requirements.
- That SQA personnel can assure compliance only if they have visibility to processes and products through monitoring, auditing, inspecting, reviewing, witnessing, meeting, etc.
- That SQA personnel will generate status reports of findings and will provide reports to appropriate team players of their action, concern, enlightenment, and disposition of risk-oriented problems.

This stage is a natural fallout of the negotiation stage. However, past experience has shown that what we are defining as the compliance stage is the only stage of SQA that has existed in many corporation. This limited scope of SQA has completely precluded the benefits of both the negotiation stage and regression stage (Stage III) on many projects. We have discussed an example of the lack of negotiation above; we will discuss the benefits of regression in Stage III. It is unfortunate that many organizations perceive the role of SQA solely as a function of monitoring for compliance only.

Stage III—Regression

The regression stage is as critical as the negotiation stage. If the agreed-upon requirements, objectives and milestones are not being successfully achieved and verified, then who will assure that they are? In the battle to meet cost and schedule, who will stand up for the quality of the product?

It is in this sense that we define the role of regression as an SQA management function. SQA must have the management authority and responsibility to assure that each phase has accomplished what is required of it.

The idea of regression is not new, but the application to software quality is. Regression is used during the test phase to retest modules which have changed. Regression is also applicable to other phases of the software development cycle.

Within every phase, specific objectives, goals, milestones, and requirements must be met. These requirements, milestones, and so forth, have already been defined, and how they are to be achieved has been negotiated in stage I. How well they have been met has been monitored in the compliance stage (II) and what remains to be accomplished has been documented in the compliance reports. At some point in the software development cycle, the schedule will call for completion of the current phase prior to moving into the next phase. The role of SQA in its management function here is to assure that all milestones, goals, objectives, and requirements have been met before the next phase is entered. If not, then the project should be held up, that is, not allowed to proceed to the next phase; this takes real management authority. This is the make-or-break point for SQA as a real contributor to the project.

Many readers will feel that this kind of authority and management responsibility is out of the question. But it is precisely the imposition of this kind of authority and management responsibility that has proved to be both the correct and effective way to accomplish goals. Should we ask anything less of SQA management?

Successful regression requires authority to enforce the required level of regression which is nothing more than redoing whatever is required to bring quality up to what it should be to meet the exit criteria of any given development phase.

Regression is a software quality process! It is a powerful quality management methodology to be applied at specific control points in the development process. As a Quality process, regression is to be applied in each and every phase, including analysis, preliminary design, detailed design, code, and unit test, and, finally, testing, where, unfortunately, regression has been enslaved for decades.

The basic question to ask is: is it correct to proceed to the next phase? If not, then regression is in order.

Regression as a quality process is different in that it invokes quality to act as a management discipline with specific authority and control to enforce what everyone agrees should be done but otherwise would not do.

Figures 5-2 and 5-3 illustrate regression as a series of in-phase processes. Figure 5-2 is a typical, modern-day, software life cycle characterized by the way engineers, analysts, and managers think and do business. This life cycle is schedule-driven.

A better way to conduct the business of software development is shown in Figure 5-3, which proposes a regression-driven cycle as opposed to the schedule-driven cycle of Figure 5-2. (Regression is indicated by the shaded boxes in each figure.) By regression-driven we mean a life cycle that actively promotes and supports those activities which assure that the software is correct, that software

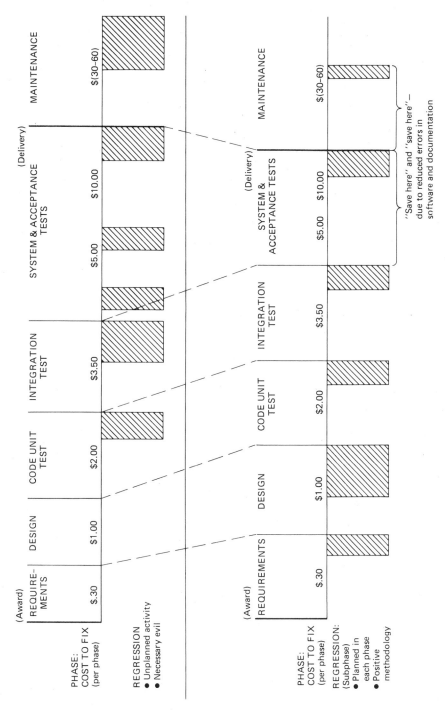

FIGURE 5-2. Schedule-driven cycle.   **FIGURE 5-3.** Regression-driven cycle.

satisfies requirements, and that errors are actively pursued and eliminated at their source. Specifically, the time required to find and eliminate errors when they are found should be not only a top management concern but everyone's concern.

In comparing Figures 5-2 and 5-3, note that the regression-driven cycle is heavily loaded on the front end whereas the schedule-driven cycle is not. The regression-driven cycle also has a regression stage for each and every phase, not just the test phase. The schedule-driven cycle has regression only during test.

The big difference in management's approach is that in the regression-driven cycle, regression is a *positive* influence on the program and is a planned activity required by management as the essential way to verify that software is where it should be and is what it should be at specific control points in the life cycle. The schedule-driven cycle, on the other hand, never plans on any regression whatsoever but is forced into it because perfect software is never built the first time around. Regression is even considered as a *negative* activity.

Many feel that the regression-driven cycle takes too long because of its heavy loading on the front end. However, studies[7] have shown that time spent during the front end in verifying correctness of software is cost-effective and saves time later during test and acceptance. Not only is time saved but the cost of fixing many serious errors during test is reduced simply because the errors have been eliminated early in the development cycle where rework is less costly.[1] This is what Figures 5-2 and 5-3 show.

Regression provides a way of verifying the correctness of software in every phase. Regression should no longer be looked upon as a last-minute, necessary evil of the test phase, but as a powerful and positive force within the life cycle with much to offer for each of the life cycle phases.

In Figure 5-1, the "V" diagram, it is clear that regression should be practiced in all of the tear-down phases on the left-hand (or Requirements) side.

5.3 PRODUCT QUALITY MANAGEMENT

Software is a major influence on our daily lives. At the office, word processors and graphics processors appear everywhere. We either work to develop software in-house or we use commercial applications (or adapt it) to make our work easier, or both. At home, software is also commonplace in the form of video games or consumer applications. Microprocessors are also widely used in automobiles and appliances. The quality of today's software product can mean the difference between a user-company's survival and nonexistence.

Whether the software product is commercially available, developed in-house, or occurs as a large Department of Defense (DOD) prototype system, an SQA group will be demanded by corporate management to support its quality goals and objectives.

The development of software as a product has not yet been reduced to a science. However, many structured and other methodologies exist today. Some conformity and consistency in approaching the development of quality software also exists. However, many products do not measure up to customer expectations;

products in development do not come in on time or within budget. Today there are as many varied and different ways to approach software development as there are software developers. Each company brings its own unique and proprietary techniques to the profession.

Measuring Quality—Metrics

The industry is, however, being drawn in the right direction. With the advent of *metrics,* first popularized by McCall and Richards[8] and later expounded by McCabe,[9] a concern and awareness of measuring product quality was presented. Instead of just building products through a series of development activities, a quality *measure* of the product was proposed for each early phase of the software development cycle. For the first time, the product could be defined in terms of measurable software quality factors and software quality attributes.[3, 8, 9, 10]

The introduction of metrics provided a way to define acceptable criteria within a given phase of development and a way to quantitatively answer the following broad questions:

- What do you want the product to do?
- How must it perform?
- What do we mean by "user-friendly" and are we achieving it?
- How well does the product perform at some downstream point in the life cycle?

The software quality factors and attributes measure a product's quality in terms of numbers. For instance, a product's requirements can be counted and traced to software units. The measure of traceability shows how many requirements are unaccounted for at any given point in the software development cycle. Details of metrics are provided in Chapter 14.

Product quality can be evaluated using metrics *during* development, not just after. Specific metrics are chosen[3] which best represent the required characteristics of the product and are then measured at specific points in the software development cycle to determine the degree of progress at those points (times). If any required action is necessary, the desired level of regression is enforced by management.

Process Control

The use of metrics and when they should be quantified fits very well into managing a product through *process control.* Process control is a management technique for enforcing a limited form of control at specific application points in the development cycle. In the case of software, the "V" diagram (Figure 5-1) defines all of the up-front phases which require process control. Each phase of the Requirements side of the V-diagram should undergo some form of process control. This process control can be applied through the use of metrics to measure a product's progress and determine the need for regression (i.e., re-code, re-design, re-analysis, and so forth, or any combination thereof). As opposed to schedule-driven or cost-driven, product quality becomes the driving force behind development.

The use of metrics does *not* do away with any stages of quality management. The measurement results are the data required to make proper management decisions. The selected metrics must be used to measure quality. The existence of any measurable quality deficiencies must then result in the corresponding regression to correct them.

But no matter which way one approaches the development of a software product, from a product standpoint or a process standpoint, one should still arrive at with the same real concerns during development and the same management objectives for building software. Whether one concentrates on using metrics to measure a product's quality or concentrates on compliance with quality processes, the action must be focused through all the software development cycle phases to effectively eliminate costly errors at their source.

5.4 SUMMARY

We have just discussed the role of metrics as a way of measuring product quality. Measures provide required insight into whether or not the efforts of software development are producing the desired product. However, there are few requests for proposal (RFP), statements of work (SOW), or contractual specifications that require the use of metrics in spite of the advantages of being able to measure progress in terms of quality. Management should take advantage of every option to objectively determine whether problem areas exist.

The role of software quality assurance is clear. It must assume its management role and provide the necessary set of data to assure the quality of both process and product.

In the eyes of software quality assurance, the quality of the product cannot be compromised. By placing SQA into its proper management position, the outlook for achieving quality objectives is tremendously enhanced; and, in the long run, so are cost and schedule.

References

1. Boehm, Barry W., *Software Engineering Economics* (Englewood Cliffs, NJ: Prentice Hall, 1981).
2. Crosby, Philip B., *Quality Is Free* (New York: McGraw-Hill, 1979).
3. Carpenter, C. L., Jr., and Murine, Gerald E., "Applying Software Quality Metrics," in *ASQC Quality Congress Transactions-Boston,* 1983.
4. Baker, Emanuel R., and Fisher, Matthew J., "A Software Quality Framework", *CONCEPTS: Journal of Defense Systems Acquisition Management,* Vol. 5, No. 4 (Ft. Belvoir, VA: Defense System Management College, Autumn 1982).
5. U.S. Navy, MIL-STD-1679, *Military Standard—Weapon System Software Development* (Washington, D.C.; NAVMAT 09Y, 1978).
6. U.S. Dept. of Defense, DOD-STD-2167A, *Defense System Software Development*

(Washington, D.C.; Commander, Space & Naval Warfare Systems Command; 29 Feb. 1988).

7. Fagan, Michael E., "Design and Code Inspections and Process Control in the Development of Programs", in IBM-TR-00.73, June 1976.

8. McCall, J. A., Richards, P. K., and Walters, G. F., *Factors in Software Quality*, RADC-TR-77-369, Vol. I–III (Rome, NY, Nov. 1977).

9. McCabe, Thomas J., *Software Quality Assurance—A Survey*, (Columbia, MD: By the author, 5501 Twin Knolls Rd., 1982).

10. Bowen, T. P., Wigle, G. B., and Jay, T. T., RADC-TR-85-37, Vol. 1-3, Feb. 1985, Rome Air Development Center, Air Force Systems Command, Griffiss Air Force Base, Rome, NY.

General References

ANSI/IEEE Std. 730-1981, *IEEE Standard for Software Quality Assurance Plans* (New York: 1981).

IEEE, U.S. Air Force, MIL-Q-9858A, *Military Specifications Quality Program Requirements*, Air Force—HQ USAF, 16 Dec. 1963.

U.S. Army, MIL-S-52779A, *Military Specification—Software Quality Assurance Program Requirements* (Washington, D.C.: NAVMAT 09Y, 1979).

U.S. Dept. of Defense, DOD-STD-2168, *Defense System Software Quality Program* (Washington, D.C.: 29 April 1988).

6

Standardization of Software Quality Assurance

G. Gordon Schulmeyer, CDP

Westinghouse Electronic Systems Group

6.1 INTRODUCTION

"Ruth made a big mistake when he gave up pitching," said the baseball expert Tris Speaker, in 1921.

Many software engineers have said, "You can't apply standards or controls to something as *creative* as developing software." There are some still saying this.

This chapter addresses not those standards specifically, but the standardization of software quality assurance (SQA), which ensures that there are discipline and controls in the software development process via independent evaluation.

An historical perspective is given showing which organizations have done what in SQA standardization. Then, the following 'organizations' standards are examined briefly: Department of Defense (DOD), Federal Aviation Administration (FAA), Institute of Electronic and Electrical Engineers (IEEE), and North Atlantic Treaty Organization (NATO). A brief look at the United States Air Force Pamphlet 800-14 on *Software Quality Indicators* is provided.

The Joint Logistics Command (JLC) of the DOD has been putting together proposed standards that are receiving wide acceptance; these JLC proposed standards are discussed in some detail.

A tabular comparison of the various requirements imposed in the standards is given with a brief discussion of ramifications of the differences.

6.2 HISTORICAL PERSPECTIVE

Table 6-1 provides a chronological list of software quality-related standards and plan guidelines. It lists 22 of the major ones, but does not claim to be all-inclusive. Throughout this chapter, the reference name will be used instead of the long title. Thus it may be necessary for the reader to refer back to Table 6-1.

TABLE 6-1   **Chronological List of Software Quality-Related Standards and Plan Guidelines**

Ref. No.*	Reference Name	Title	Date	Sponsor
1	MIL-S-52779	*Software Quality Program Requirements*	5 Apr. 1974	Army
2	FAA-STD-018	*Computer Software Quality Program Requirements*	26 May 1977	FAA
3	DI-R-2174	*Software Quality Assurance Plan*	29 Nov. 1978	Navy
4	MIL-STD-1679	*Software Development*	1 Dec. 1978	Navy
5	MIL-S-52779A	*Software Quality Program Requirements*	1 Aug. 1979	Army
6	ANSI-IEEE STD 730	*IEEE Trial-Use Standard for Software Quality Assurance Plans*	Jan. 1980	IEEE
7	(U)-E-759/ESD	*Software Quality Assurance Plan*	20 May 1980	Air Force
8	AQAP-13	*NATO Software Quality Control System Requirements*	Aug. 1981	NATO
9	ANSI/IEEE STD 730-1981	*IEEE Standard for Software Quality Assurance Plans*	13 Nov. 1981	IEEE
10	MIL-STD-SQAM	*Software Quality Assessment and Measurement*	1 Oct. 1982	DOD/JLC
11	R-DID-126	*Software Quality Assessment and Measurement Plans*	1 Oct. 1982	DOD/JLC
12	DI-R-X105	*Software Quality Assurance Plan*	Undated (1982)	DOD/JLC
13	DOD-STD-1679A	*Software Development*	22 Oct. 1983	Navy
14	DI-R-2174A	*Software Quality Assurance Plan*	22 Oct. 1983	Navy
15	IEEE STD 730-1984	*IEEE Standard for Software Quality Assurance Plans*	30 Jun. 1984	IEEE
16	DOD-STD-2168	*Software Quality Evaluation Program* (draft)	26 April 1985	DOD/JLC

TABLE 6-1   Continued

Ref. No.*	Reference Name	Title	Date	Sponsor
17	DI-MCCR-80010	*Software Quality Evaluation Plan* (draft)	4 June 1985	DOD/JLC
18	DOD-STD-2167	*Defense System Software Development*	4 June 1985	DOD/JLC
19	DOD-STD-2167A	*Defense System Software Development*	29 Feb 1988	DOD/JLC
20	DI-MCCR-80030A	*Software Development Plan*	29 Feb 1988	DOD/JLC
21	DOD-STD-2168	*Defense System Software Quality Program*	29 Apr 1988	DOD/JLC
22	DI-QCIC-80572	*Software Quality Program Plan*	29 Apr 1988	DOD/JLC
23	DOD-HDBK-287A	*A Tailoring Guide for DOD-STD-2167A*	11 August 1989	DOD/JLC
24	MIL-HDBK-286	*A Guide for DOD-STD-2168* (draft)	15 June 1990	DOD/JLC

*Reference numbers 10, 11, 12, 16, 17, and 24 had been proposed in draft form when this paper was written (some disappeared, but others became standards).
Reference numbers 3, 6, 7, 9, 11, 12, 14, 15, 17, 20, and 22 had been written as outlines for plans.

The preponderance (19 of 24) of those listed were established by the DOD driven by the high defense expenditure on weapons systems of which an ever-increasing percentage is allocated to software development. Eleven of these (3, 6, 7, 9, 11, 12, 14, 15, 17, 20, and 22) are plan guidelines or outlines usually employed in conjunction with a standard.

Three items of the list in Table 6-1 are IEEE outlines for SQA plans. Each is a direct update from the previous version; the dates are 1980, 1981, and 1984.

There was one standard provided rather early (1977) by the FAA that envelops a complete software quality program. Similarly, there was one standard for a complete program provided by NATO in 1981 with the issuance of the allied quality assurance publication (AQAP-13).

The first major standard was MIL-S-52779, which has had significant input on software quality standards. Every following standard and plan guideline was influenced strongly by this landmark standard. That influence is shown in Section 6.9 (this chapter), where the various standards are compared.

A major software quality standards effort has been pursued by the Joint Logistics Command (JLC) of the DOD. This effort has been gaining support outside the DOD from the FAA, National Aeronautics and Space Administration (NASA), and National Oceangraphic Atmospheric Administration (NOAA). More detail will be provided in Section 6.7 of this chapter about this effort.

6.3 DOD STANDARDS

The essence of software quality requirements, management and acceptance for the DOD is summarized by Dennis L. Wood in "Department of Defense Software Quality Requirements":

> (1) contractual specification of both computer program requirements and requirements for a quality program for managing software quality;
> (2) Government and contractor monitoring and assessment of implementation of the contractor's quality program, including its effectiveness; and
> (3) Government acceptance of the software upon demonstration of contractor compliance with contract quality requirements, particularly for computer program performance.[1, p. 101]

These three major points, contractual requirement, assessment, and acceptance, have been guideposts in the DOD software quality program.

The landmark MIL-S-52779, released in 1974, required the establishment of an SQA program. There are nine requirements the SQA program under MIL-S-52779 must reference:

- Work tasking and authorization procedures;
- Configuration management;
- Testing;
- Corrective action;
- Library controls;
- Computer program design;
- Software documentation;
- Reviews and audits;
- Tools, techniques, and methodologies.

Also, these requirements must be passed on to software subcontractors. Consideration of related military standards such as MIL-STD-483 (configuration management), MIL-STD-490 (specification practices), and MIL-STD-1521 (reviews and audits) is to be given in relationship to software quality. Finally, consideration is to be given an SQA plan.

The refinement of MIL-S-52779 to MIL-S-52779A was released by the Army in 1979. The key revisions are:

- "Software" takes in not just "computer programs and related documentation," but also "computer data".
- Both deliverable and non-deliverable software developed for the contract come under the requirements imposed by this specification.
- Firmware* is considered software for the purpose of this specification.

---

*Firmware is an assembly of a hardware unit and a computer program integrated to form a functional entity whose configuration cannot be altered during normal operation. (IEEE Std. 729-1983)

TABLE 6-2   Overview of Three DIDs

DI-R-2174 AND DI-R-2174A	(U)-E-759/ESD
Introduction	Introduction
Organization	Software Development Resources
Quality Assurance Procedures	Computer Program Design
Software Development Management	Work Certification
Configuration Management	Documentation
Software Specification, Design,	Computer Program Library Controls
and Production	Review and Audits
Software Testing	Configuration Management
Corrective Action	Testing
Subcontractor Control	Corrective Action
Plan Implementation	Subcontractor Control
Reporting and Control System	

- An SQA plan is required.
- The organization(s) responsible for carrying out the requirements must be defined.
- "Tools, techniques, and methodologies" is expanded to also include records.

MIL-STD-1679, released by the Navy in 1978, deals with software development, but has significant software quality requirements incorporated within it. The significantly distinct requirements in MIL-STD-1679 other than those covered above in the MIL-S-52779A requirements include: providing external responsibility from the developing organization, resolving conflicts at the next higher management level, ensuring program coding, monitoring correctness of deliverable items, and handling and reporting software problems.

The updated DOD-STD-1679A, released by the Navy in 1983, mainly uses more software-related terminology. For example, "software configuration management" rather than "configuration management," "software operation" rather than "program operation," and so on. (There is also a new appendix in DOD-STD-1679A on resource capacity measuring, but not applicable to this discussion).

The next three documents are DIDs for SQA plans. Data item descriptions (DIDs) are DOD documents that provide outlines of how required deliverable documents are to be formatted. Two DIDs, (DI-R-2174 and DI-R-2174A, are coordinated to be worked with MIL-STD-1679 and DOD-STD-1679A. The third is an Air Force DID referenced (U)-E-759/ESD, coordinated to be worked with MIL-S-52779A, and in fact is practically an outline of it. Table 6-2 provides an overview of the three DIDs.

The remaining DOD documents concerning actual and proposed standards and DIDs as of the time of the writing of this chapter will be discussed in Section 6.7.

6.4 FAA STANDARD

FAA-STD-018 was promulgated in 1977 and follows the basic concepts established in MIL-S-52779. It requires an SQA plan to be written in the format as shown in

TABLE 6-3   FAA-STD-018 Outline

Organization
Development process flow
Standards of software quality
Computer software work instructions
Indication of process status
Configuration management
Design review
Corrective actions
Test controls
Tools, techniques and methodologies
Subcontractor control
Records
Audits

Table 6-3. Four different items in FAA-STD-018—development process flow, standards of software quality, indications of process status, and records—are discussed for the first time in this section.

Development process flow requires the description of, and/or the charting of, the sequence of operation from concept through delivery of the software and the software quality activities. Typically, a chart interrelating the two is provided in the SQA plan to show pictorially what will happen on the project.

Standards for the "design, development and evaluation of computer software programs and related documentation" are required by the Standards of Software Quality section. The Indication of Process Status section requires a description of procedures and controls of the work-in-process. These indications may be accomplished by such actions as stamping, typing, and so forth. The Records section requires objective evidence of software quality activities throughout the software life cycle. It requires descriptions of the "initiation, verification, validation and retention of such records."

6.5 IEEE STANDARDS

The IEEE provided its first trial-use standard for SQA Plans in 1980, and then followed up with two revisions in 1981 and 1984. An outline of the 1984 version is provided in Table 6-4.

The purpose of the standard as written in the standard is "to provide uniform, minimum acceptable requirements for preparation and content of Software Quality Assurance Plans (SQAP)." The standard applies to "critical software; for example, where failure could impact safety or cause large financial or social losses." Tailoring is recommended where all the parts of the SQAP are not needed.

Minimum requirements for Documentation and for Reviews and Audits are nicely provided. The unique requirement not previously covered in the other standards or DIDs is Media Control (3.11). This section deals with the methods "used to protect computer program physical media from unauthorized access or inadvertent damage or degradation."

TABLE 6-4   IEEE STD 730-1984 Outline

3. Software Quality Assurance Plan
    3.1 Purpose (Section 1 of the Plan)
    3.2 Reference Documents (Section 2 of the Plan)
    3.3 Management (Section 3 of the Plan)
        3.3.1 Organization
        3.3.2 Tasks
        3.3.3 Responsibilities
    3.4 Documentation (Section 4 of the Plan)
        3.4.1 Purpose
        3.4.2 Minimum Documentation Requirements
            3.4.2.1 Software Requirements Specifications (SRS)
            3.4.2.2 Software Design Description (SDD)
            3.4.2.3 Software Verification and Validation Plan (SVVP)
            3.4.2.4 Software Verification and Validation Report (SVVR)
            3.4.2.5 User Documentation
        3.4.3 Other
    3.5 Standards, Practices, and Conventions (Section 5 of the Plan)
        3.5.1 Purpose
        3.5.2 Content
    3.6 Reviews and Audits (Section 6 of the Plan)
        3.6.1 Purpose
        3.6.2 Minimum Requirements
            3.6.2.1 Software Requirements Review (SRR)
            3.6.2.2 Preliminary Design Review (PDR)
            3.6.2.3 Critical Design Review (CDR)
            3.6.2.4 Software Verification and Validation Review
            3.6.2.5 Functional Audit
            3.6.2.6 Physical Audit
            3.6.2.7 In-Process Audits
            3.6.2.8 Managerial Reviews
    3.7 Software Configuration Management (Section 7 of the Plan)
    3.8 Problem Reporting and Corrective Action (Section 8 of the Plan)
    3.9 Tools, Techniques, and Methodologies (Section 9 of the Plan)
    3.10 Code Control (Section 10 of the Plan)
    3.11 Media Control (Section 11 of the Plan)
    3.12 Supplier Control (Section 12 of the Plan)
    3.13 Records Collection, Maintenance, and Retention (Section 13 of the Plan)

The difference between the 1984 and 1981 versions are first discussed. In the 1984 version (Sections 3.4.2.3, 3.4.2.4, and 3.6.2.4), the term "verification" is updated to "verification and validation"; a new minimum documentation requirement called "User Documentation" is added; and Section 3.7 is updated to "Software Configuration Management" from "Configuration Management."

The differences between the 1981 and 1980 versions follow. The additions in the 1981 version are: a new minimum documentation requirement called "Software Verification Report," two new minimum reviews and audits requirements called "Software Verification Review" and "Managerial Reviews," and a new section

TABLE 6-5   AQAP-13 Outline

General
Organization
System Review
Planning
Documentation
  Procedures
  Work Instructions
Corrective Action
Reviews
Configuration Management (CM)
Sub-Contractor Control
Software Support—Tools, Techniques and Methodologies
Purchaser Supplied Material
Testing
Preparation for Delivery of Software
Accommodation and Assistance

called "Records Collection, Maintenance, and Retention." Because of the new "Software Verification Review" section, the 1979 section called "Verification Control" was deleted.

6.6 NATO STANDARD

A working group for software quality assurance was established by NATO under the auspices of the NATO Advisory Committee (AC)/250 Group. The United States Government was designated to chair the working group, and the Army had the primary responsibility for developing the publication.[1, p. 110] The result in 1981 was AQAP-13. It, also, primarily follows MIL-S-52779. The outline of AQAP-13 is shown in Table 6-5.

The unique features of AQAP-13 are System Review, Purchaser Supplied Material, and Recommendations and Assistance. The System Review section requires a periodic review of the software quality control system by the contractor and customer. The Purchase Supplied Material section requires "procedures for the acceptance, storage, and maintenance of all supplied material." The Accommodation and Assistance section requires that the contractor supply assistance and accommodations as needed by the customer.

All of the sections following "Planning" in Table 6-5 are required to be addressed in what AQAP-13 calls the Software Quality Control Plan.

6.7 DOD STANDARDS—JLC-PROPOSED

In January 1979, the Joint Logistics Commanders (JLC) Joint Policy Coordinating Group on Computer Resources Management (JPCG-CRM), recognized an opportunity for service standardization and chartered a subgroup to review policies, procedures, regulations, and standards related to computer software acquisition and support. The subgroup, called the Computer Software Management (CSM) Subgroup, planned and conducted a software workshop in April 1979 to examine the services' software acquisition guidelines, management procedures, and standardization efforts to determine if there was a basis for coordination and adoption of joint-service policy and standards. The workshop panels concluded that the services should develop common policy, development standards, and documentation standards instead of continuing to approach software development in a service-unique manner. It was felt that economics were certainly one reason for developing a joint approach, but not the only one. By developing a joint approach the best methods of each service could be adopted for all to use.[2, p. 192]

The JLC activities have continued since 1979, resulting in a number of proposed documents applicable to software quality. The initial emphasis was placed on software development standardization. Various draft copies were submitted for government and industry reviews. The latest draft DOD-STD-2167, dated 30 January 1985, resulted in an official release on 4 June 1985.

Much of the content of DOD-STD-2167 derives from MIL-STD-1679, which was briefly discussed in Section 6.3 of this chapter. There are sections of DOD-STD-2167 specifically addressing software quality requirements and these again flow from the ideas initially in MIL-S-52779. Section 4.3 discusses general software quality requirements, Section 5.1.1.1e discusses preparation of the Software Quality Evaluation Plan (SQEP), and Section 5.8 contains the specific software quality evaluations.

The more detailed outline of the software quality requirements from DOD-STD-2167 is shown in Table 6-6. There was an evolutionary process to get to these requirements. The earlier software quality requirements in DOD-STD-SDS (Software Development Standard) were more related to Software Quality Assessment and Measurement (SQAM), which is discussed below with software quality standards. The requirements in Table 6-6 are more related to Software Quality Evaluation, which is more recent and also discussed below.

A draft DOD-STD-2167A *Defense System Software Development* dated 4 September 1987 streamlines the software quality requirements, and resulted in formal release on 28 February 1988. The outline of software quality requirements from DOD-STD-2167A is shown in Table 6-7.

Two items of special benefit to the software quality community from DOD-STD-2167A are included here. First, the software development cycle chart with products included in each phase, with reviews, or audits for each phase, and baselines and developmental configuration identified is reproduced in Figure 6-1.

The other special contribution is the explanation provided for the evaluation criteria in Table 6-8. For convenience, the explanations use the word "document" for the item being evaluated, even though in some instances the item being evaluated may be other than a document.

There have been major releases from the JLC for draft software quality standards. Initially, there was MIL-STD-SQAM, released in 1982. Then there was DOD-STD-2168 (formerly called MIL-STD-2168 [draft *Defense System Software Qual-*

TABLE 6-6   DOD-STD-2167 Software Quality Requirements Outline

4.3 General Software Quality Requirements
Contractor shall build in quality by:
a) Maintaining standards
b) Implementing a complete development process
c) Maintaining a software quality evaluation process
    5.1.1.1e Prepare Software Quality Evaluation Plan:
        1) Evaluate development plans, standards, and procedures
        2) Evaluate compliance with (1)
        3) Evaluate software development products
        4) Implement reporting system
        5) Implement corrective action system
5.8 Software Quality Evaluation
Contractor shall establish and implement procedures to:
1) Evaluate software requirements
2) Evaluate software development methodologies
3) Evaluate software development products
4) Provide feedback to effect software quality improvements
5) Perform corrective action with controlled software
5.8.1 Software Quality Evaluation—Activities:
    5.8.1.1 Contractor shall perform necessary planning.
    5.8.1.2 Contractor shall conduct *internal reviews* to evaluate compliance to
    standards. The internal reviews shall be:
    5.8.1.2.1 Evaluation criteria for reviews are:
        a) Adherence to required format
        b) Compliance with contractual requirements
        c) Internal consistency
        d) Understandability
        e) Technical adequacy
        f) Degree of completeness appropriate to the phase
    5.8.1.2.2 Internal reviews—all phases
        a) SDP, SSPM, SCMP, and SQEP*
        b) Evaluate:
            1) Software configuration management
            2) Software development library
            3) Documentation control
            4) Storage and handling of project media
            5) Control of non-deliverables
            6) Risk management
            7) Corrective action
            8) Conformance to all approval standards and procedures
    [5.8.1.2.3 through 5.8.1.2.8. Internal reviews during the
    phases: Software Requirements Analysis, Preliminary
    Design, Detailed Design, Coding and Unit Testing, CSC
    Integration and Testing, CSCI Testing.

    Review of the following documents and activities during
    these phases: OCD, Requirements, SRS, IRS(s), STLDD,
    STP, CSCM, SUM(s), CSDM, CRISD, SDDD, IDD(s),
    DEDD(s), STD, SDF, Unit tests, Integration tests, SPM,
    FSM, Source code, STPR, CSCI testing, STRs, SPS, VDD.

TABLE 6-6   Continued

Review the documents and activities for the following: (1) criteria in 5.8.1.2.1, (2) consistency, (3) understanding, (4) traceability, (5) testability, (6) appropriateness, (7) adequacy, (8) accuracy, (9) compliance, and (10) correctness. Also, monitor CSCI testing to ensure that (1) current controlled code is used, (2) testing is conducted in accordance with approved test plans, description and procedures, and (3) includes all necessary retesting.]

5.8.1.3 Ensure all products are available for formal reviews and audits.

5.8.1.4 Ensure all products are available and all procedures performed and documented to support acceptance inspection.

5.8.1.5 Evaluate installation and checkout.

5.8.1.6 Evaluate software or documentation for completeness, technical adequacy, and compliance.

5.8.1.7 Evaluate and certify commercially available, reusable, and Government furnished software.

5.8.1.8 Prepare and maintain written quality records.

5.8.1.9 Prepare quality reports showing results and recommendations.

5.8.1.10 Implement a corrective action system.

5.1.8.11 Collect quality cost data.

5.8.2 Software Quality Evaluation—Products

5.8.2.1 Prepare and maintain quality evaluation records

5.8.2.2 Prepare and maintain quality reports.

5.8.2.3 Certify compliance with the contract of each contract line item.

5.8.3 Independence sufficient to perform evaluation activities as required.

* All acronyms are defined in Appendix A, this *Handbook*.

ity Program]), dated 1 August 1986. Then, there was the DOD-STD-2168 draft dated 18 August 1987.

The major steps that MIL-STD-SQAM proposed were to divide detailed requirements to the phases of software development to agree with the proposed MIL-STD-SDS, and to subdivide the evaluation effort within each phase to an activities evaluation and a products evaluation.

A point of major concern to the community receiving the draft MIL-STD-SQAM for review was the immaturity of the software measurement process. The standard implied metric evaluation of the quality of the software. That concept was mostly rejected because of lack of experience in determining software quality metrics.

In the draft software quality standard DOD-STD-2168 released in 1985, are the welcome innovations of MIL-STD-SQAM, but the unwanted metric requirement is gone.

Draft DOD-STD-2168, *Defense System Software Quality Program,* dated 1 August 1986, was released in response to CODSIA Task Group 14-85, which raised twelve main issues with the 24 April 1985 draft:

1. DOD-STD-2168 should specifically state the requirements for a software quality program and it should state its relationships to MIL-Q-9858.

TABLE 6-7   DOD-STD-2167A Software Quality Requirements Outline

4.4   Software product evaluation
    4.4.1   Independence in product evaluation activities
    4.4.2   Final evaluations
    4.4.3   Software process records
    4.4.4   Evaluation criteria

5.x.4   Software product evaluations
    where x=1   System requirements analysis/design
        =2   Software requirements analysis
        =3   Preliminary design
        =4   Detailed design
        =5   Code and CSU testing
        =6   CSC integration and testing
        =7   CSCI qualification testing
        =8   System integration and testing

For each x there is a list of products being evaluated and an evaluation criteria table provided. Below is a sample evaluation criteria table for detailed design:

Item to be Evaluated	Internal Consistency	Understandability	Traceability to the indicated documents	Consistency with the indicated documents	Appropriate analysis, design or coding techniques used	Appropriate allocation of sizing and timing resources	Adequate test coverage of requirements	Notes: Clarification or Additional Criteria
Software Design Document(s) (SDDs) —Detailed Design	•	•	IRS SRSs	IDD	•	•		Consistency between data definition and data use. Accuracy and required precision of constants
Interface Design Document (IDD)	•	•	IRS SRSs	SDDs				
CSU test requirements and test cases	•	•		SDDs IDD			•	Adequate detail in specifying test inputs, expected results, and evaluation criteria
CSC test cases	•	•	IRS SRSs	SDDs IDD			•	Adequate detail in specifying test inputs, expected results, and evaluation criteria
Contents of CSU and CSC SDFs	•	•	See Notes	See Notes				Traceability of CSU SDFs to CSC SDFs
Software Test Descriptions (STDs) —Test cases	•	•	IRS SRSs				•	Adequate detail in specifying test inputs expected results, and evaluation criteria

Evaluation Criteria (See Table 6-8)

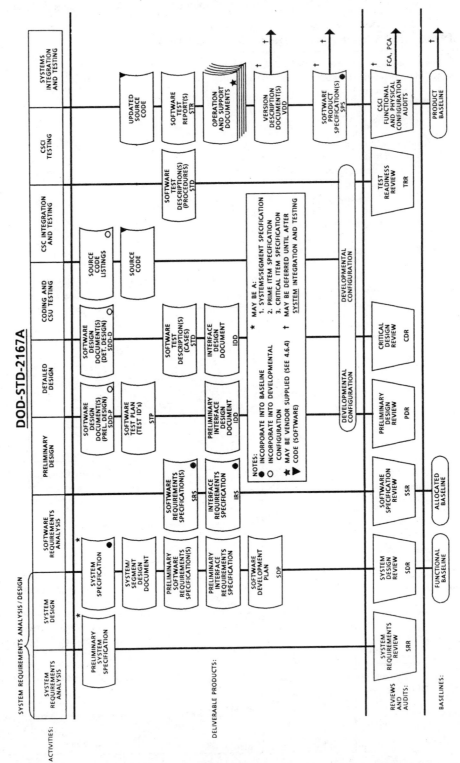

FIGURE 6-1. The software development cycle.

TABLE 6-8   Evaluation Criteria Explanation (from DOD-STD-2167A)

For convenience, the definitions use the word "document" for the item being evaluated, even though in some instances the item being evaluated may be other than a document.

Internal consistency. Internal consistency as used in this standard means that: (1) no two statements in a document contradict one another, (2) a given term, acronym, or abbreviation means the same thing throughout the document, and (3) a given item or concept is referred to by the same name or description throughout the document.

Understandability. Understandability, as used in this standard, means that: (1) the document uses rules of grammar, capitalization, punctuation, symbols, and notation consistent with those specified in the U.S. Government Printing Office Style Manual, (2) all terms not contained in the U.S. Government Printing Office Style Manual or Merriam-Webster's New International dictionary (latest revision) are defined, (3) standard abbreviations listed in MIL-STD-12 are used, (4) all acronyms and abbreviations not listed in MIL-STD-12 are defined, (5) all acronyms and abbreviations are preceded by the word or term spelled out in full the first time they are used in the document, unless the first use occurs in a table, figure, or equation, in which case they are explained in the text or in a footnote, and (6) all tables, figures, and illustrations are called out in the text before they appear, in the order in which they appear in the document.

Traceability to indicated documents. Traceability as used in this standard means that the document in question is in agreement with a predecessor document to which it has a hierarchical relationship. Traceability has five elements: (1) the document in question contains or implements all applicable stipulations of the predecessor document, (2) a given term, acronym, or abbreviation means the same thing in the documents, (3) a given item or concept is referred to by the same name or description in the documents, (4) all material in the successor document has its basis in the predecessor document, that is, no untraceable material has been introduced, and (5) the two documents do not contradict one another.

Consistency with indicated documents. Consistency between documents, as used in this standard, means that two or more documents that are not hierarchically related are free from contradictions with one another. Elements of consistency are: (1) no two statements contradict one another, (2) a given term, acronym, or abbreviation means the same thing in the documents, and (3) a given item or concept is referred to by the same name or description in the documents.

Appropriate analysis, design, and coding techniques used. The contract may include provisions regarding the requirements analysis, design, and coding techniques to be used. The contractor's SDP describes the contractor's proposed implementation of these techniques specified in the contract and SDP.

Appropriate allocation of sizing and timing resources. This criterion, as used in this standard, means that: (1) the amount of memory or time allocated to a given element does not exceed documented constraints applicable to that element, and (2) the sum of the allocated amounts for all subordinate elements is within the overall allocation for an item.

Adequate test coverage of requirements. This criterion, as used in this standard, means that: (1) every specified requirement is addressed by at least one test, (2) test cases have been selected for both "average" situation and "boundary" situations, such as minimum and maximum values, (3) "stress" cases have been selected, such as out-of-bounds values, and (4) test cases that exercise combinations of different functions are included.

Additional criteria. The following definitions apply to criteria that are not self-explanatory.

Adequacy of quality factors. This criterion applies to the quality factor requirements in the Software Requirements Specification (SRS). Aspects to be considered are: (1) trade-offs between quality factors have been considered and documented, and (2) each quality factor accompanied by a feasible method to be used to evaluate compliance with it is required by the SRS Data Item Description (DID).

TABLE 6-8   Continued

Testability of requirements. A requirement is considered to be testable if an objective and feasible test can be designed to determine whether the requirement is met by the software.

Consistency between data definition and data use. This criterion applies primarily to design documents. It means that each data element is defined in a way that is consistent with its usage in the software logic.

Adequacy of test cases, test procedures, (test inputs, expected results, evaluation criteria). Test cases and test procedures should specify exactly what inputs to provide, what steps to follow, what outputs to expect, and what criteria to use in evaluating the outputs. If any of these elements are not specified, the test case or test procedure is inadequate.

Completeness of testing. Testing is complete if all test cases and all test procedures have been performed, all results have been recorded, and all acceptance criteria have been met.

Completeness of retesting. Retesting consists of repeating a subset of the test cases and test procedures after software corrections have been made to correct problems found in previous testing. Retesting is considered complete if: (1) all test cases and test procedures that revealed problems in the previous testing have been repeated, their results have been recorded, and the results have met acceptance criteria, and (2) all test cases and test procedures that revealed no problems during previous testing, but these test functions are affected by the corrections, have been repeated, their results have been recorded, and the results have met acceptance criteria.

2. All requirements for independent verification and validation (IV&V) should be removed from this standard.
3. Redundancy and unnecessary detail should be removed.
4. Subjective quality factors and evaluation criteria should be clarified.
5. Independent organization evaluation should be clarified.
6. Excessive requirements for quality records and reports will increase acquisition costs.
7. Tailoring guidance should be removed.
8. Software quality program requirements for non-deliverable software should be clarified.
9. Software quality program requirements for firmware should be clarified.
10. "Cost of Quality" data requirements should be clarified or deleted.
11. Standard definitions and terms should be used throughout DOD-STD-2168.
12. Action on the Handbook should be deferred.

The draft DOD-STD-2168, *Defense System Software Quality Program,* dated 18 August 1987 was released because the 1 August 1986 over-corrected. It has too much of MIL-S-52779A mentality of check compliancy against the plan and not evaluating compliance with contractual requirements. The April 1985 draft of DOD-STD-2168 had a total quality approach for all products and evaluation to improve product quality. In this August 1987 draft, the evaluation has disappeared; it takes a check and stamp approach. The quality community is viewing DOD-STD-2168 as their document, whereas the product and process must be viewed as a whole so that there is a quality linkage throughout software to tie all aspects together.[3]

A formal release of DOD-STD-2168 was made 29 April 1988. A summary of DOD-STD-2168 is provided in Table 6-9. DOD-STD-2168 is using "software quality program", whereas previous standards called quality activities "software quality evaluation" (DOD-STD-2167) and "software quality assurance" (DOD-STD-1679A).[4, p. 4-160]

Various DIDs have also been proposed in draft form by the JLC for software quality plans. The one to go with the SQAM standard of 1982 was included as an Appendix to the SQAM and is called R-DID-126. R-DID-126 is an outline for a

TABLE 6-9   DOD-STD-2168 (29 April 1988) Summary

1.2.1 Application to non-deliverable software
1.2.2 Application to firmware
1.2.3 Application to software support
1.2.4 Application to government agencies
1.4 Tailoring of this standard
4. General requirements
  4.1 Objective of the software quality program
  4.2 Responsibility for the software quality program
  4.3 Documentation of the software quality program
  4.4 Software quality program planning
  4.5 Software quality program implementation
  4.6 Software quality evaluations
  4.7 Software quality records
    4.7.1 Software quality evaluation records
    4.7.2 Other software quality records
  4.8 Software corrective action
  4.9 Certification
  4.10 Management review of the software quality program
  4.11 Access for contracting agency review
5. Detailed requirements
  5.1 Evaluation of software
  5.2 Evaluation of software documentation
    5.2.1 Evaluation of software plans
    5.2.2 Evaluation of other software documentation
  5.3 Evaluation of the processes used in software development
    5.3.1 Evaluation of software management
    5.3.2 Evaluation of software engineering
    5.3.3 Evaluation of software qualification
    5.3.4 Evaluation of software configuration management
    5.3.5 Evaluation of software corrective actions
    5.3.6 Evaluation of documentation and media distribution
    5.3.7 Evaluation of storage, handling, and delivery
    5.3.8 Evaluation of other processes used in software development
  5.4 Evaluation of software development library
  5.5 Evaluation of non-developmental software
  5.6 Evaluation of non-deliverable software
  5.7 Evaluation of deliverable elements of the software engineering and test environments
  5.8 Evaluation of subcontractor management
  5.9 Evaluation associated with acceptance inspection and preparation for delivery
  5.10 Participation in formal reviews and audits

SQAM Plan and requires planning what the SQAM standard specifies to be accomplished.

The DID to go with the SDS standard of 1982 was called DI-R-X105 and is shown in Table 6-10. It is a SQA plan outline and follows closely those DIDs (DI-R-2174 and DI-R-2174A) devised to go with MIL-STD-1679, all discussed earlier. There is not much new here.

The 1985 draft document DI-MCCR-80010 (SQEP outline) when laid side-by-side with DOD-STD-2168 provides an outline for the requirements shown in that proposed 1985 Software Quality Evaluation Program standard. Thus the DID carries all the advantages discussed for the standard forward into the planning document.

As a part of 1986 draft DOD-STD-2168 release, a draft DID DI-MCCR-8XXXX, *Software Quality Program Plan* (SQPP) dated 1 August 1986 was released. This DID states the purpose of the SQPP: "The software quality program plan describes the organizations and procedures to be used by the contractor to determine the quality of the software and associated documentation and activities and to perform related tasks that are an outgrowth of the evaluation activities."

The 19 November 1987 draft DID DI-MCCR-8XXXX—a companion to DOD-STD-2168 dated 18 August 1987—changes the purpose of the SQPP by stating "... to be used by the contractor to evaluate the quality ..." instead of stating

TABLE 6-10   DI-R-X105 (SQA Plan) Outline

Scope
   Identification
   Introduction
Applicable Documents
   Government documents
   Non-Government documents
Organization
   Organizational structure
   Personnel
   Resources
Quality Assurance Procedures
   Critical performance factors monitoring
   Quality audits
   Reporting and control
   Reviews
     Specification reviews
     Design documentation review
     Code reviews
   Testing
     Software Test Plan
     Software Test Description
     Software Test Procedures
     Conducting the software test
     Software Test Reports
Notes
Appendix

". . . to be used by the contractor to determine the quality . . ." An outline of the SQPP as provided by DI-MCCR-8XXXX is given in Table 6-11.

The official released DID DI-QCIC-80572 dated 29 April 1988 states that "The SQPP identifies the organizations and procedures to be used by the contractor to perform activities related to the Software Quality Program specified by DOD-STD-2168." The outline of this SQPP is the same as DI-MCCR-8XXXX and so is also given in Table 6-11. Ada PROS, Inc. teaches the following main points concerning the SQPP:

- Typically, one per Software Development Plan (SDP)
- No required deadline for completion—should be during System Design, usually done during Software requirements analysis
- Identifies organizations and procedures to be used by the company performing activities related to DOD-STD-2168
- Used by the government to evaluate the company's plans for implementing the software quality program.[4, p. 4-174]

DOD-HDBK-287A, *A Tailoring Guide for DOD-STD-2167A,* provides guidance for using DOD-STD-2167A on software development contracts. The tailoring guidelines for selecting which deliverables are required for individual contracts given factors such as life cycle considerations, managerial considerations, and system considerations are useful, but overall this Guide is more relevant to development than to software quality.[5] However, it should be pointed out that the DOD-STD-2167A DID for the Software Development Plan (DI-MCCR-80030A) highlights software quality activities as shown in Table 6-12.

MIL-HDBK-286 (draft), *A Guide for DOD-STD-2168 Defense System Software*

TABLE 6-11   DI-MCCR-8XXXX and DI-QCIC-80572 SQPP Outline

1. Scope
    1.1 Identification
    1.2 System overview
    1.3 Document overview
    1.4 Relationship to other plans
2. Referenced documents
3. Organization and Resources
    3.1 Organization
    3.2 Resources
        3.2.1 Contractor facilities and equipment
        3.2.2 Government furnished facilities, equipment, software, and services
        3.2.3 Personnel
        3.2.4 Other resources
    3.3 Schedule
4. Software quality program procedures, tools, and records
    4.1 Procedures
    4.2 Tools
    4.3 Software quality records
5. Notes
    Appendices

TABLE 6-12   DI-MCCR-80030A SDP Outline Quality Highlights

Software product evaluations
   Organization and resources
      Organizational structure
      Personnel
   Software product evaluations procedures and tools
      Procedures
      Tools
   Subcontractor products
   Software product evaluation records
   Activity-dependent product evaluations
      Software products evaluation—(activity name)

Quality Program, dated 15 June 1990 provides useful guidance to DOD-STD-2168 implementation. Explanations are given as to applicability; tailoring; relationship to MIL-Q-9858A, *Quality Program Requirements;* organization; definition; requirements; evaluations; and evaluation criteria.

DOD-STD-2168 applies to software products, software development processes; software development contracts; any time during acquisition or support when software products are specified, developed, or changed. To tailor DOD-STD-2168 means to delete, partially delete or modify section 5. When there are both hardware and software on a contract, MIL-Q-9858A applies to the hardware elements and DOD-STD-2168 applies to the software elements.

DOD-STD-2168 does not impose an organizational structure, nor does it require a '2168 shop,' i.e., a company is not required to have procedures for every requirement in DOD-STD-2168, only those required by the contract. Software quality is defined in DOD-STD-2168 as: "The ability of a software product to satisfy its specified requirements." The standard does *not* specify requirements for software, documentation of that software, or software development processes and activities.

DOD-STD-2168 requires on-going evaluations of products and processes, as well as other evaluations, such as, software development library, subcontractor management, preparations for acceptance inspection, preparation for delivery, and participation in formal reviews and audits. The evaluation criteria of DOD-STD-2168 are compliance with the contract and adherence to software plans.

6.8 SOFTWARE QUALITY INDICATORS

To provide the appropriate perspective for AFSCP 800-14, *Software Quality Indicators* [25] pamphlet dated 20 January 1987, requires a brief initial look at the *Software Management Indicators* [26] pamphlet. This AFSCP 800-43 pamphlet, released in August 1990, has found wide acceptance within DOD and industry because of its common-sense approach to software management. The tri-services have adopted its use in their software projects.

In AFSCP 800-43, *Software Management Indicators,* eight indicators are described. These indicators are primarily aimed at gaining insight into the software development process. They also provide some secondary insight into the quality of the software products. The eight indicators which are presented in graphical form are the following: software development progress, computer resource utilization, software development personnel, requirements and design stability, software development tools, software size, requirements and design progress, and incremental release content.

AFSCP 800-14 builds upon the AFSCP 800-43 indicators to provide the same common sense approach to gaining insight into the quality, reliability, and maintainability of the software products being developed. These quality indicators are not to be interpreted as software quality metrics. The software quality metrics have not yet reached a state of maturity that allows consistent interpretation of each metric. The indicators, however, will support the software quality metrics when the metrics have reached a mature state that can be implemented.

Lt. Col. Anthony Shumskas, author of both pamphlets, states, "The software quality indicators are to provide trends rather than absolutes. The indicators are to get the total community to look at the quality of software. It is not currently known if the software products are doing what they are supposed to do. The indicators are consistent and provide information on the concerns for major milestones. The set of software quality indicators were chosen because they look throughout the full software development cycle, whereas in-depth expansion of the indicators will come later from the individual program offices and be tailored to meet their specific needs."[3]

The seven software quality indicators, also represented graphically are the following: completeness, design structure, defect density, fault density, test coverage, test sufficiency, and documentation.

The indicators are described from the AFSCP 800-14 pamphlet. Indicators are just that: indicators. They do not, nor are intended to, replace sound quality practices. These indicators, properly applied and meticulously followed up, will lead to those areas requiring additional management attention.

The completeness indicator provides insight into the adequacy of the software specifications, beginning during the requirements analysis phase of the software development process. The indicator can be used effectively throughout the software development life cycle. It lays the foundation for quality software and is crucial to obtaining a reliable and maintainable system. The values determined from the components of the completeness indicator can be used to identify specific problem areas within the software specifications and design.

The design structure indicator is used to determine the simplicity of a CSCI detailed design. Simplicity should not be confused with complexity. Several different ways of determining the complexity of the software design have been published. This indicator looks at "simplicity" or clarity of design, independent of the overall complexity of the implemented functions. The values associated with the inputs and components of the indicator can also be used to identify problem areas within the design that could affect the future maintainability of the software. This indicator can also be used to identify the potential for hidden or missing linkages in the CSCI.

The defect density indicator provides early insight into the quality of the

TABLE 6-13   Comparison of Requirements

Subject Matter	Software Quality Standards & DIDs							
	MIL-S-52779	FAA-STD-018	DI-R-2174	MIL-STD-1679	MIL-S-52779A	ANSI/IEEE STD 730	(U)-E-759/ESD	AQAP-13
1. Organizational Structure	X	X	X	X	X	X		X
2. Personnel Required				X				
3. Resources Required				X			X	
4. Schedules		X		X				
5. Evaluation Procedures, Methods, Tools, and Facilities (Tools, Techniques and Methodologies)	X	X	X	X	X	X		X
6. Evaluation of Development Processes	X	X	X	X	X	X	X	
7. Configuration Management	X	X	X	X	X	X	X	X
8. Software Development Library	X	X		X	X	X	X	X
9. Documentation Reviews	X	X	X	X	X	X	X	X
10. Evaluation of Media Distribution	X	X		X	X	X		
11. Storage and Handling	X	X	X		X	X		
12. Evaluation of Non-Deliverables					X			
13. Evaluation of Risk Management				X				
14. Subcontractor Controls	X	X	X	X	X	X	X	X
15. Reusable Software Controls (Supplied Material)								X
16. Records		X		X	X	X		
17. Corrective Action	X	X	X	X	X	X	X	X
18. Quality Evaluation Reports		X	X	X				
19. Certification				X	X		X	
20. Software IV & V Contractor Interface				X				
21. Government Facility Review	X	X		X	X			
22. Quality Cost Data								
23. Activities Evaluation (Reviews and Audits)	X	X	X	X	X	X	X	X
24. Products Evaluation	X	X	X	X	X	X		X
25. Software Test and Evaluation	X	X	X	X	X	X	X	X
26. Acceptance Inspection				X				X
27. Installation and Checkout								
28. Code Reviews				X	X	X	X	
29. Deviations and Waivers								
30. Work Tasking, Authorization, and Instructions	X	X		X	X	X		X
31. Accommodations and Assistance								X
32. Evaluation Criteria								
33. Transition to Software Support								
34. Safety Analysis								
35. Software Development File								
36. Non-developmental Software								

ANSI-IEEE STD 730-1981	MIL-STD-SQAM	R-DID-126	DI-R-X105	DOD-STD-1679A	DI-R-2174A	IEEE STD 730-1984	DOD-STD-2167	DOD-STD-2168	DI-MCCR-80010	DOD-STD-2167A(draft)	DOD-STD-2167A	DI-MCCR-80030A	DI-QCIC-80572	MIL-HDBK-286	DOD-HDBK-287A(draft)	MIL-HDBK-287A(draft)
X			X	X	X	X			X	X	X	X	X	X	X	X
			X	X					X	X	X	X	X	X	X	X
		X	X	X					X	X	X	X	X	X	X	X
	X	X		X					X	X	X	X		X		X
X	X		X	X	X	X	X		X	X	X	X		X		X
X	X	X	X	X	X	X	X	X	X	X	X		X		X	X
X	X	X		X	X	X	X	X	X	X	X		X		X	X
X				X			X	X	X	X	X		X		X	X
X	X	X	X	X	X	X	X	X	X	X	X		X		X	X
X	X	X		X		X	X	X	X				X		X	X
X	X	X			X	X	X	X	X		X		X		X	X
	X						X	X	X				X		X	
				X			X	X	X	X	X					X
X	X			X	X	X	X	X	X	X	X	X	X		X	X
							X	X	X	X	X			X		X
X	X			X		X	X	X	X	X		X	X	X	X	
X	X	X		X	X	X	X	X	X	X	X		X		X	X
	X	X	X	X	X		X	X	X	X	X		X		X	X
	X	X		X			X	X	X				X		X	
				X		X	X	X	X	X						X
				X			X	X					X		X	
							X	X								
X	X	X	X	X	X	X	X	X	X	X	X		X		X	X
X	X	X	X	X	X	X	X	X	X	X	X		X		X	X
X	X	X	X	X	X	X	X	X	X	X	X		X		X	X
	X	X		X			X	X	X	X	X		X		X	X
							X	X	X		X					X
X	X	X	X	X	X	X	X	X	X	X	X					X
	X							X								
X				X	X	X										
										X	X	X		X		X	X
											X	X					X
											X	X					X
											X	X	X	X		X	X
											X	X		X		X	X

software design and implementation into code. It is a transitory indicator that leads into the fault density indicator during integration and system test. It provides insight into the results of the design and code inspections. If, after these inspections, the defect density is outside of the norm for a particular software development effort, depending upon complexity, application, etc., it is an indication that the development and/or inspection process may require further scrutiny.

The fault density indicator is very similar to the defect density indicator. The primary differences are the application phases and an emphasis on test instead of inspection data. This indicator can be used in conjunction with the test coverage indicator to assess software reliability and maturity. It can also be used to determine if sufficient software testing has been accomplished.

The test coverage indicator presents a measure of the completeness of the testing progress from both a developer and a user perspective. It can also be used to quantify a test coverage index for software delivery. The indicator relates directly to the development, including unit, CSC, CSCI, system and acceptance test. It is also beneficial in assessing the readiness of the software under test to proceed to the next test level.

The test sufficiency indicator is a useful tool in assessing the sufficiency of software integration and system testing, based on prediction of the remaining software faults. This prediction is, in turn, based on the experienced fault density. Currently, there are insufficient data to make this an absolute indicator. However, many software developers do use this type of indicator as a rule of thumb for making a first approximation for test sufficiency, hence the need for a wide tolerance band at this time. If the indicator falls outside of a determined tolerance band, the software under test may need further testing prior to entering the next stage of test, or that the software design and test processes may require further scrutiny. The defect density and fault density indicators are directly related to this indicator and can be used, in conjunction with the test sufficiency indicator, to estimate the number of faults remaining in the CSCIs under development. If more faults are detected than expected (outside the maximum tolerance limit), error-ridden units may exist that require redesign and retest. If less faults are detected than expected (outside the minimum tolerance limit), an adequate number or variety of tests may not have been designed, or the tolerance coefficients may need to be redetermined due to a higher quality product entering test.

The primary objective of the documentation indicator is to gain insight into the sufficiency and adequacy of the software documentation products that are necessary in the operational and post deployment software support environments. The documentation indicator also provides a mechanism for the identification of potential problems in the deliverable software documentation and source listings that may affect the usability and maintainability of the operational and support software.

6.9 COMPARISON OF REQUIREMENTS[6,7]

The chart in Table 6-13 provides a matrix of the various subjects matters versus the standards and DIDs. It is a chart showing in which standards or DIDs the subjects are covered.

Most of the subjects have been taken from DOD-STD-2168 and DI-QCIC-80572 because they are the latest and most complete. Then the other standards and DIDs have been checked off where they conform. Finally, some few subjects were in early standards and DIDs, but not in DOD-STD-2168 or DI-QCIC-80572, so they have been included.

It is the author's belief that the use of DOD-STD-2167A, DOD-STD-2168, and DI-QCIC-80572 will provide a way to increase the quality of software developed. The use of the full requirements are for major software development efforts. Most efforts would be adequately covered by tailoring down the full-blown requirements.

6.10 CONCLUSION

It is hoped that this survey of standards and DIDs provides the reader with a better perspective of what is available and where to find it. Much work has been done since the early 1970s to standardize software quality requirements, and an introduction to these is provided herein.

The items of particular value in this chapter are the figure and the tables:

- The summaries of the standards.
- The outlines of the DIDs.
- The software development cycle (Figure 6-1).
- Evaluation criteria explanation (Table 6-8).
- Chronological list (Table 6-1).
- Comparison of requirements (Table 6-13).

References

1. Word, Dennis, L., "Department of Defense Software Quality Requirements," in *Software Quality Management* ed. by John D. Cooper and Matthew J. Fisher (New York: Petrocelli Book, 1979).
2. Klucas, Casper H., Lt. Col.; Fry, Leroy A., Major; Barnes, John W, Lt. Col. and Fisher, Matthew, "Joint Service Software Policy and Standards," *Concepts,* ed. by Robert Wayne Moore (Vol. 5, No. 4) (Ft. Belvoir, VA: Defense System Management College, Autumn 1982), p. 192.
3. Private conversation with Lt. Col. Anthony Shumskas in late 1986.
4. Ada PROS, Inc., "Joint Logistics Commanders (JLC), Joint Policy Coordinating Group on Computer Resources Management (JPCG-CRM), Subgroup on Computer Software Management (CSM), "Software Development Under DOD-STD-2167A: An Examination of Ten Key Issues," in Gray, Lewis (ed.) *Implementing the DOD-STD-2167 and DOD-STD-2167A Software Organizational Structure in Ada,* Association for Computing Machinery (ACM), Special Interest Group on Ada (SIGAda), Software Development Standards and Ada Working Group (SDSAWG), August 1990." Copyright © 1990 by Ada PROS, Inc. Reprinted with permission.
5. Roetzheim, William H., *Developing Software to Government Standards* (Englewood Cliffs: Prentice-Hall Inc, 1991) Copyright © 1991, Adapted by permission of Prentice-Hall, Inc., Englewood Cliffs, NJ 07632, p. 198.

6. Tice, George D., Jr., *Developing Your Software Quality Control Program—A Seminar* (Pittsburgh: Westinghouse Corporate Quality College, 1983), p. M-1.
7. McCabe, Thomas J., *Software Quality Assurance—Seminar Notes* (Columbia, Maryland: By The Author, 5501 Twin Knolls Rd., 1980), p. 56.

General References

IEEE, ANSI/IEEE STD 730-1981, *IEEE Standard for Software Quality Assurance Plans* (New York: IEEE, 1981).

IEEE, IEEE STD-730-1984, *IEEE Standard for Software Quality Assurance Plans* (New York: IEEE, 1984).

IEEE, *IEEE Trial-Use Standard for Software Quality Assurance Plans* (New York: IEEE, 1980).

McCabe, Thomas J. *Software Quality Assurance—A Survey* (Columbia, Maryland: By the Author, 5501 Twin Knolls Rd., 1980).

North Atlantic Treaty Organization AQAP-13, *Allied Quality Assurance Publication—NATO Software Quality Control System Requirements* (Washington, D.C.: NATO International Staff—Defense Support Division, 1981).

U.S. Air Force, (U)-E-759/ESD, *Data Item Description—Software Quality Assurance Plan* (Washington, D.C.: NAVMAT 09Y, 1980).

U.S. Air Force, AFSCP Pamphlet 800-14, *Software Quality Indicators* (Andrews Air Force Base, D.C., Headquarters AFSC, 1987).

U.S. Air Force, AFSC Pamphlet 800-43, *Software Management Indicators* (Andrews Air Force Base, D.C., Headquarters AFSC, 1990).

U.S. Army, MIL-S-52779, *Military Specification—Software Quality Assurance Program Requirements* (Washington, D.C.: NAVMAT 09Y, 1974).

U.S. Army, MIL-S-52779A, *Military Specification—Software Quality Assurance Program Requirements* (Washington, D.C.: NAVMAT 09Y, 1979).

U.S. Dept. of Defense, DOD-STD-2168 (draft), *Military Standard—Software Quality Evaluation Program* (Washington, D.C.: NAVMAT 09Y, 1985).

U.S. Dept. of Transportation, FAA-STD-018, *Federal Aviation Administration Standard—Computer Software Quality Program Requirements* (Washington, D.C.: Government Printing Office, 1977).

U.S. Joint Logistics Command, DI-R-X105 (draft), *Data Item Description—Software Quality Assurance Plan* (Washington, D.C.: NAVMAT 09Y, 1982).

U.S. Joint Logistics Command, DI-MCCR-80010 (draft), *Data Item Description—Software Quality Evaluation Plan* (Washington, D.C.: NAVMAT 09Y, 1985).

U.S. Joint Logistics Command, DOD-STD-2167 (draft), *Military Standard—Defense System Software Development* (Washington, D.C.: NAVMAT 09Y, 1985).

U.S. Joint Logistics Command, MIL-STD-SQAM (draft), *Proposed Military Standard—Software Quality Assessment and Measurement* (Washington, D.C.: NAVMAT 09Y, 1982).

U.S. Joint Logistics Command, DI-MCCR-80030A, *Data Item Description—Software Development Plan* (Washington, D.C.: NAVMAT 09Y, 1988).

U.S. Joint Logistics Command, DI-QCIC-80572, *Data Item Description—Software Quality Program Plan* (Washington, D.C.: NAVMAT 09Y, 1988).

U.S. Joint Logistics Command, DOD-STD-2168, *Military Standard—Defense System Software Quality Program* (Washington, D.C.: NAVMAT 09Y, 1988).

U.S. Joint Logistics Command, DOD-STD-2167A, *Military Standard—Defense System Software Development* (Washington, D.C.: NAVMAT 09Y, 1988).

U.S. Joint Logistics Command, MIL-HDBK-286 (draft), *Military Handbook—A Guide for DOD-STD-2168 Defense System Software Quality Program* (Washington, D.C.: NAVMAT 09Y, 1990).

U.S. Joint Logistics Command, DOD-HDBK-287A, *Military Handbook—A Tailoring Guide for DOD-STD-2167A* (Washington, D.C.: NAVMAT 09Y, 1989).

U.S. Navy, DI-R-2174, *Data Item Description—Software Quality Assurance Plan* (Washington, D.C.: NAVMAT 09Y, 1978).

U.S. Navy, DI-R-2174A, *Data Item Description—Software Quality Assurance Plan* (Washington, D.C.: NAVMAT 08Y, 1983).

U.S. Navy, DOD-STD-1679A, *Military Standard—Software Development* (Washington, D.C.: NAVMAT 09Y, 1983).

U.S. Navy, MIL-STD-1679, *Military Standard—Weapon System Software Development* (Washington, D.C.: NAVMAT 09Y, 1978).

7

Personnel Requirements to Make Software Quality Assurance Work

Kenneth S. Mendis

Raytheon Company

7.1 INTRODUCTION

Obtaining qualified engineers and keeping them motivated in what they are doing is a problem most of the engineering disciplines have been facing for some time. The problem is compounded when we focus on the software engineering discipline. At the level of software quality assurance (SQA), we find ourselves battling with the software developers for the few software engineers who are available.

To be effective and contribute to a project's success in a manner that is professionally acceptable, the SQA organization must be staffed with qualified software engineers. In addition, these individuals must also possess the credentials that make them good quality assurance representatives. Achieving any of the promised benefits of SQA is directly related to an organization's ability to staff the operation. Some of the issues the manager will be confronted with are engineer motivation, career training, and recruiting techniques.

The standard for Defense System Software Development DOD-STD-2167A, Defense System Software Quality Assurance DOD-STD-2168 and their companion handbooks MIL-HDBK-286 and DOD-HDBK-287 define a structured approach to developing quality software (see Chapter 6). With that approach comes the need to staff positions within the organization to enforce the plans that have been set in motion. Unfortunately, the glamor and challenges provided by a developing environment attracts the interest of the majority of software engineers. This leaves SQA with a limited number of qualified personnel from which to choose.

More recently the Defense Logistic Agency (DLA) has developed and introduced a new approach to software quality assurance. The new procedure known as IQUE for In-Plant Quality Assurance replaces the current Contractor Quality Assurance Program and makes use of continuous improvement tools and problem solving techniques to examine the adequacy of a contractor's process to continuously produce conforming products and to identify opportunities for process improvements.

The concept of IQUE includes management commitment, people development, quality excellence, and user satisfaction. Implementation of IQUE embraces techniques that use process and product quality to evaluate the quality of an organization's software products. IQUE focuses on working with the software developer, working with the software user, and working with contracting agencies to develop a product that meets the users needs. It means working as a team to measure and continuously improve the process. How does the SQA engineering staff face these Challenges?

7.2 FACING THE CHALLENGE

Our academic institutions today do not provide the required training for SQA engineers. By an SQA engineer is meant a software engineer trained in the disciplines of software quality assurance. Today, little or no training is provided in the techniques of software design review, good software documentation, software reliability and maintainability. Training is also inadequate for software attributes such as the use of program design languages, top-down development, and structured programming techniques, which are used to assess and measure the progress of software development. About the only way an individual becomes knowledgeable of SQA principles and disciplines is by hands-on work-related experience, which only makes the SQA staffing problem even more difficult.

As an individual involved with developing, staffing, and maintaining an SQA organization with a major company, I have battled almost daily with this problem of SQA staffing. I have searched through countless resumes and interviewed hundreds of applicants in an effort to find those individuals who would make good SQA engineers. In many instances, if an applicant is technically acceptable, then he or she still lacks those special attributes that make a software engineer a software quality assurance engineer.

Therefore, recruiting and hiring the personnel to staff SQA positions is expensive and time consuming. Thus, before the organization proceeds on a recruiting campaign, it is necessary to define and set priorities for those issues and positions that are critical to the success of the SQA function. The organization must consider these factors:

- Is it possible to promote from within and train individuals to fill the openings?
- Can contract employees help fill the organization's needs, and, if so, in what capacity should these employees be utilized?
- Should the recruiting effort be national, regional, or local?

The other problem one has to face is to hold these individuals' interest and motivation in the job assignments. Developing and outlining career paths is another important factor in the problems facing SQA staffing. Indeed, in my opinion, the most serious problem a manager faces is to prevent his or her department from becoming a stepping stone to other opportunities within the organization. The SQA department, if it is to develop into an effective organization dedicated to assuring a product's software quality, must consist of professionals both seasoned in software and dedicated to quality; and capable of providing guidance, training, and quality-consciousness within the organization.

Lastly, top management support is of serious concern. The lack of top management support or clear understanding of SQAs needs is perhaps the major issue confronting most SQA organizations today. To properly staff the organization, management must clearly understand the problems of personnel and assurance goals and be willing to address them. Support and understanding must go hand in hand; one without the other is ineffective. James McManus discusses this issue in depth in Chapter 5.

7.3 ORGANIZATION STRUCTURE

In April, 1979 the Software Management Subgroup of the Joint Coordinating Group on Computer Resource Management (JCG, CRM) sponsored a Joint Logistics Commanders software workshop. One of the key findings of the workshop stressed the difficulties facing the implementation of SQA, such as the lack of a well-defined and consistent set of requirements, differences in SQA approaches across the various branches of the services, and the unavailability of experienced personnel.

My experience has shown that independence is the key to success in implementing SQA programs. The SQA organization should be situated in the overall organization so that it always reports to the same level as the department which it must evaluate and audit. The Quality organization must have the organizational status and access to top management as do the other functions. Figure 7-1 shows how this concept may be instituted within an organization and how the assurance

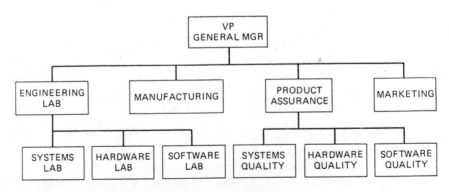

FIGURE 7-1. Organization structure.

function can use its position within an organization to achieve its goals and objectives.

An industry survey conducted by the National Security Industrial Association in 1983 reveals that the typical profile of most SQA organizations possess the following attributes:

- The SQA organization is located within the product assurance organization.
- SQA is staffed with people who possess approximately 1-5 years of software engineering experience.
- The person in charge of the SQA organization has over 5 years of software experience and is a middle manager within the organization.

The SQA function, established to support the software development effort, must provide the objective and authoritative controls required. An SQA function that reports to the development organization lacks the independence needed to get the job done properly. Moreover, the members of the development organization are by first love software designer/programmers, therefore making their quality tasks secondary in nature. An organizational structure of the type shown in Figure 7-1 allows itself to develop the SQA engineers into a position of responsibility, leadership, and independent management reporting. It is from here that the SQA engineer derives a perceived responsibility that allows him or her to translate that into getting the job done right.

A common problem of many organizations arises from appointing project-related software engineers as SQA personnel. These individuals function as senior staff members within the project organization, directing and managing the SQA effort of the project while reporting to project management. The shortcoming of this approach to SQA is that SQA is relatively new, not completely defined, and therefore varies sharply from individual to individual trying to enforce it—particularly those with a loyalty divided between the project and assurance.

Experience has shown that to establish any new discipline within an organization, a central motivating force is needed. Fragmented efforts are diluted and end up being ineffective. In my own experience, project-related SQA activity generally lacks depth and maturity. All too often, the SQA activity functions as a workhorse of the developer performing tasks for the developer.

SQA will work effectively only if all project SQA personnel report to a single SQA manager. This organizational posture allows for specialization; i.e., all personnel meeting the needs of the project as well as uniformity; all projects meeting the same minimum acceptance criteria. Members of the SQA staff should have relatively high technical expertise and a thorough knowledge of good software and quality assurance practices. The manner in which the staff is organized depends largely on staff size, estimated work load, and personnel skills.

7.4 CHARACTERISTICS OF A GOOD SQA ENGINEER

As mentioned earlier, the shortage of software professionals makes recruiting software engineers into the quality assurance profession a difficult task. Two factors appear to work against SQA: (1) developing software is far more attractive to the software engineer, and (2) the career path for someone in the development environment is clearly more attractive. Although, Dunn and Ullman[1] suggest that software engineers command salaries substantially greater than those of quality engineers. This is a differential that can and should be eliminated by all organizations developing software on any significant scale. Then the subtler prestige and glamor aspects can be addressed.[1]

If an organization is willing to take the time, it can probably find suitable candidates within its wage and salary guidelines. But time is money, and the longer it takes to hire the talent required, the longer it takes to bring the SQA function up to the engineering level now required to produce quality software products.

What makes a good software quality assurance engineer? I look for the following characteristics in an individual:

- The individual who seems to work the best appears to have spent approximately 3-5 years developing software. This individual recognizes the limited involvement he or she has had in the total developmental effort, and now wants a bigger piece of the pie. SQA clearly will provide this opportunity. This is an opportunity to get system and managerial exposure in a relatively short period of time. It is to the SQA manager's advantage to point this out to a prospective new hire. However, finding such an individual with the necessary qualities, as listed below, can be difficult and would require a national recruiting policy.
- The experienced software engineer who has seen it all and has survived the software battles. This individual can truly contribute to improving software development methodologies, being inherently familiar with the existing developing techniques and capable of assuming a position of leadership in a very short time. However, I must caution you that lack of motivation may sometimes be a problem for individuals in this group.
- The individual seeking to advance to management or a program manager's position clearly is a good candidate. It is within the SQA organization that one learns how to deal with people, learns about design and development approaches and techniques, and how to manage and report on software development projects—some of the attributes one would look for when recruiting for a management position.
- A good SQA engineer must possess good communication skills. This is especially true if he or she is to be effective in performing SQA duties. As we are well aware, software engineers by nature are an unfriendly breed of professionals, very possessive of their work, and always protecting what they have designed as confidential. An SQA engineer has to be able to deal with this and win the trust and respect of software design engineers. Communication skills play a vital role in this regard; the individual should be skillful in expressing ideas both orally and in writing.
- An academic background in computer science is essential. Over the years many individuals who possess a degree in education or the liberal arts have

made the switch to software. They were hired as programmers and function in this capacity. I have found that for the most part their ability in the software engineering field is limited to that of being programmers rather than being effective in design. These individuals work well under the supervision of a good software designer. They do, however, make poor SQA engineers.

- The individual who will succeed as an SQA engineer must be willing to meet and accept new challenges, and be able to carry out independent research and analysis assignments that deal with analysis of the techniques used to develop software. Such an individual must be capable of evaluating software development methodologies with an eye to improving software productivity and performance.

- The introduction of Total Quality Management tools such as continuous improvement, and problem solving techniques places additional demands upon the SQA engineer (see Reference 2, *Total Quality Management for Software*). For the first time SQA engineers are now being called upon to help establish and manage the cultural environment and monitor performance improvement goals set by the development organization, therefore requiring the SQA engineer to sharpen the needed people development skills.

7.5 TRAINING THE HARDWARE QA ENGINEER

Training the hardware QA engineer is one method of obtaining and retaining good SQA engineers. Some hardware QA engineers of yester-year now may be in a very unmotivated position because of obsolescence in hardware engineering. Selecting those individuals willing to be retrained in software engineering is the first step. Such individuals will tend to stay within the SQA field the longest. Furthermore, they bring to the function the needed expertise to deal with designers and managers, a quality that is learned over years of on-the-job training.

A hardware QA engineer requires a number of years of training to become an effective SQA engineer. However, the return on this type of investment is, in my opinion, the surest method of developing a staff of good qualified engineers in software quality. This approach to SQA staffing allows for a permanent core within the function, essential if the SQA activity is to survive as a long-range objective of the company.

Training of hardware QA engineers in software should follow one of two paths. The engineer should be encouraged to pursue a degree in computer science. Also, in-house training and learning by example should be pursued, with job assignments utilizing newly learned skills.

7.6 TRAINING THE SOFTWARE ENGINEER

The optimal approach—the one I have found to work the best with software engineers—is the *mentor approach* to training in the SQA discipline. A mentor in SQA is a teacher or an advisor, someone who has worked in SQA for a number of years. This individual is charged with teaching the software engineer the principles of SQA engineering. This technique to training works well with recent college graduates. Selective training is needed if this approach is to be applied to the more experienced software engineer.

The basic principle under this approach to staffing is to hire software engineers into the SQA organization and to assign them to an experienced SQA engineer. The mentor's responsibility will be to outline a program of task training and to closely monitor the new hire's work output. This mentor-new hire relationship gives the new hire access to someone who will provide guidance and leadership during the learning phase. For this approach to training to work, it is imperative that a training plan exist. An example of such a plan is outlined below.

The following steps will be taken to indoctrinate new personnel into the software quality assurance team:

- Describe the organization surrounding the project to which the new hire is to be assigned, and explain what each department does and how it interacts with the other departments. As a minimum, the departments to be discussed should include the following:

  System engineering
  Software engineering
  Software configuration management
  Data management
  Software integration
  Software quality assurance
  Software test

- Indoctrinate the new hire in the use and availability of existing tools and how to utilize tools to their full potential.
- Assign as reading assignments project-related software development plans, software quality assurance plans, and software configuration management plans. The objective in these assignments is to orient the new hire in the company's software development and quality assurance process.
- Define SQAs involvement in the development process. Include the following areas:

  Requirements review
  Design reviews (PDR, CDR, etc.)
  Documentation reviews
  Testing
  Software discrepancy reporting tracking and resolution
  Audits
  Software reliability

The benefits to be derived from such a program are twofold. The new hire has easy access to someone who is capable of guiding him or her in the performance of work assignments. Most important, the new hire is able to learn first-hand from someone who has been through the process and knows all of its ups and downs.

7.7 ROTATING SOFTWARE ENGINEERS

Rotating software engineers through the SQA function is an approach that brings to the software QA function bright and capable software professionals. They should be expected to serve a minimum of at least one year within the SQA function. But the following problems will have to be worked out before such an approach to SQA engineering will benefit the organization:

- There exists a shortage of qualified software professionals within the software development environment. A software manager would be hard pressed to release a good software engineer to SQA if he or she is facing a manpower problem that could impact schedule completion of a project. In many instances the tendency is to release those individuals who are poor performers.
- A rotating SQA policy requires support from upper management to become effective and not to end up as a dumping ground for the bad programmer or software engineer. The choice of who makes the rotation into the SQA section should be mutually agreed to by all concerned. Motivating the software engineer to participate willingly in such a program is necessary, and the only sure means of accomplishing this is to institute a promotional policy that gives special consideration to individuals who have already served as SQA engineers. The same policy should also hold true for one being considered for a manager's position in software engineering.

Today I know of three organizations that have tried such a program IBM, Raytheon, and ITT. The benefits these organizations have derived from such a program have been limited to how successful they have been in retaining the services of the individuals that participated in the rotation program. Because the majority of those participating in the program were recent college graduates all companies reported that many participants had left for assignments in other companies. For a rotation policy of this type to succeed as a means of increasing the awareness of SQA within an organization, what is needed is a core of resident SQA experts to learn from so as to continue the smooth operation of the SQA function. Furthermore individuals selected to participate in the program should have between 3-5 years of industry experience, therefore reducing the possibility of their departure after the rotation assignment.

7.8 NEW COLLEGE GRADUATES

The recent college graduate is ideal for certain specialized tasks within the SQA organization. Today's SQA organizations are evolving from a labor-intensive approach to a more computerized approach to quality software (see Chapter 12). Such a transition requires developing SQA tools to perform tasks that were once manually performed, hence the transition from a labor-intensive approach to QA to an automated approach. In my experience, the recent college graduate is an excellent source of expertise to perform some of the tasks needed to orchestrate such a transition.

It is a well-known fact that the interest and professional development of recent college graduates in computer science tends to follow the following broad guidelines. First, the graduate seeks out programming tasks and appears to find satisfaction in the activities associated with such a task. After a short period, from 3 to 6 months, his or her interest focuses on the challenges provided with being involved in software design. Some time later in terms of career growth, task assignments in software architecture become appealing. Employing a recent college graduate to perform SQA tasks at the onset has been proved to be a poor management decision, and the organization runs the risk of losing that employee because of a lack of interest in the work assigned.

The procedure that appears to work best is to combine programming tasks with SQA tasks. Obviously the mixture of programming and SQA tasks must be tailored to the needs of both the organization and the individual. During the first six months of a college graduates' employment, a 60/40 ratio of programming tasks to SQA tasks seems to work well. The benefits to be derived from such a mixture are many, but most of all the recent college hire's perception is that of performing a constructive task. He or she is also able to observe the benefits of these efforts while the benefits to be derived from purely SQA tasks are more subjective and therefore a demotivator.

Orienting the new hire to the SQA methodology employed by the organization is an important training procedure that must not be ignored. Typically the SQA training process takes somewhere between and 2 years before such an individual should be allowed to make independent SQA decisions without supervision. This orientation should involve exposure to overall company policies and procedures as well as the specific software tools and techniques employed by the organization to develop software.

7.9 SQA EMPLOYMENT REQUISITIONS

Recruiting, hiring, and training software engineers in quality assurance can be very expensive and time-consuming. It would be wise for the SQA organization to define and set priorities for key positions in the form of job descriptions and responsibilities. Before proceeding, the organization should consider these issues:

- Is the organization located in an area that can provide a local pool of software quality people? Should recruiting policy be national, regional, or local, considering that the degree of staff turn-around is directly related to where the new hire comes from? Can contract employees help and how best can they be utilized? Can the company promote from within and train individuals to fill SQA openings?
- What tasks should be assigned to a new SQA organization?

Whether SQA personnel are acquired from within or outside of the company, care must be given to distinguishing between software professionals and paraprofessionals. Job descriptions for these individuals should be documented to inform the placement office of the specific tasks they will be called on to perform and the backgrounds needed to sustain these tasks. Furthermore, the careful allocation of tasks between professionals and paraprofessionals will determine the attrition rate the organization will experience. Typical professional job titles within the SQA function are:

- Software quality assurance manager
- Engineer software quality assurance
- Software reliability engineer
- Software configuration management specialist

The SQA manager is typically responsible for supervising the operation of the SQA section through planning and directing the utilization of personnel. This position in the organization also requires that counseling and guidance be given to company management in matters pertaining to the quality and reliability of software products developed or purchased. From a global viewpoint, the SQA manager must set the framework that will dictate the use of a software development methodology that lends itself to quality software. The engineering reliability and configuration staff supporting this effort will provide the technical expertise necessary to assure that the objectives of the QA effort are achieved and maintained. Specific duties of the SQA function should include but not be limited to the following:

- Provide SQA support and improve upon the existing SQA system. Develop SQA tools that sense software problems during the design, development, and life-cycle phases.
- Keep management aware of the quality status of software development projects during the design, development and life-cycle phases.
- Monitor the continuing needs and requirements of the SQA program and implement them.
- Participate in software design reviews, testing, configuration control, problem reporting and resolution, and change control.
- Provide inputs to technical and cost proposals relative to the company's participation in computer software quality.
- Audit, monitor, evaluate, and report on subcontractor software development efforts.

Many of the tasks within the SQA function can be performed by individuals who are paraprofessionals. It would be to the benefit of the organization to use these individuals to perform those tasks. This category may include the following positions:

- Software librarian aide
- Senior software librarian
- Software quality assurance engineering assistant
- Software quality engineering assistant
- Software quality assurance aide

The role of these paraprofessionals can be viewed as assisting the professionals in achieving the SQA objectives defined by management. Work assignments are in many instances related to performing tasks that have been defined in detail by the professionals assigned to the SQA function. The manager employing the services of such paraprofessionals should realize that, properly trained and with formal education, these individuals could in the future make excellent SWA professionals.

7.10 WHAT TO EXPECT FROM YOUR SQA ENGINEERING STAFF

Members of the QA staff should have a relatively high level of technical expertise and a thorough knowledge of good software quality assurance policies. The manner in which the staff is organized depends largely on staff size, estimated work load, and personnel skills. Several alternatives are suggested:

- Each SQA staff member could be specialized to perform one task for all software products.
- Each SQA staff member could perform all software QA tasks associated with a particular product, or
- The SQA organization could act as a team in which all members would cooperate in performing the QA tasks.

If it is properly staffed and organized, you can expect the following from your SQA organization:

- The ability of the staff to work independently.

    If your staff and organization are to grow and meet the demands placed upon them, the individuals assigned to perform SQA tasks must possess an understanding and involvement in their assigned projects. This understanding and involvement is achieved if the system requires their independent involvement and participation. The part-time SQA engineer is ineffective and does little to improve the quality and reliability of the software product. Productivity with minimum supervision is achieved only if the policies and procedures in place lend themselves to a team approach to quality assurance. Productivity with supervision does not permit individuals the freedom to develop into professionals who function independently.

- Ability to devise new and improved methods to perform SQA tasks.

    The discipline of SQA is relatively new, and the whole process is being transformed from an approach that is labor-intensive to one that can be automated. The SQA engineer must be expected to develop the necessary tools, techniques, and methodologies to accomplish tasks that have been assigned.

- Good judgment and objectivity in approaching problems.

    It is imperative that the SQA engineer be able to apply good judgment and objectivity when dealing with other members of the software development team. These attributes are important, because the SQA engineer must have the support of the software development team to function effectively. If an

SQA engineer alienates himself or herself from the development team, the SQA function is no longer contributing to the team's effort.

- Communication skills for a better understanding.

   The SQA engineer must possess good communication skills. Skill in expressing ideas both orally and in writing are crucial; for example, when communicating SQA review and audit findings to the software development team, or making presentation to upper management. Since most findings are of a negative nature, challenge provided by the developing environment to these findings will require considerable skill to get the message across. Furthermore, SQA is frequently called upon to present its needs and requirements to the developers. Good communication can make this job easier.

- Technical competence and knowledge of the project are imperative.

   An SQA staff (or member or portion of the staff) not knowledgeable about software development cannot support the objectives of the SQA organization. Moreover, these individuals cannot provide the expertise needed to perform the software QA tasks that the position will demand. Such individuals will therefore not be able to complete assignments rapidly or at all without compromising standards of quality.

7.11 DEVELOPING CAREER PATHS

A software quality assurance organization without engineering-defined career paths will not survive the tests of time and effectiveness. It is essential that SQA engineers have the opportunity to ascend the corporate ladder. One of the disadvantages of some corporate organizational structures is that many of the SQA organizations exist within a hardware matrix organization, which limits the career paths for the software professionals within the product assurance organization. It is imperative that the organization recognize this critical shortfall and take steps to remedy it in order to permit the SQA function to develop into an essential and capable factor in software development.

What should be done? Obviously, if the organization is to survive, career paths from SQA to other disciplines within the organization must exist, such as SQA engineers becoming lead software engineers or SQA management moving into software development management. Specifically, a dual ladder system must exist; this allows highly competent technical employees to continue their career growth without assuming management responsibilities. It also allows management-oriented engineers to jump ladders and assume management responsibilities. (In fact, one of the Handbook's editors moved from Manager of Software Quality Engineering to Manager of Software Development Engineering. Another example, at the same firm, occurred when an experienced software quality engineer transferred into Software Systems Engineering.)

This parallel structure bridges the gap between engineering and management. The organization's main goal, however, for such an approach to staff development must be to allow engineers to progress up the ladder without becoming managers if they desire not to.

7.12 RECOMMENDATIONS

The organizational environment plays a decisive role in how successful the software QA function will be. Success can be measured only in terms of a team of dedicated individuals contributing in a supportive posture to a project. To give this success its best chance, the following recommendations are offered:

- The salaries of the SQA engineers should be generally competitive and specifically in line with those of software development engineers.
- Project-related SQA functions are disfunctional and present too many problems. A central, independent SQA function driving all projects is a more effective method to achieve SQA goals.
- A rotating SQA policy should be used as a long-range plan and only after a core of experienced SQA individuals already exists. The rotation program is not a recommended approach to starting up an SQA function.
- Responsibilities of SQA must be clearly defined and firmly supported by corporate management.
- The best approach to starting an SQA function is to first create a position within the corporate organization for an SQA manager, then promote or hire an individual to fill that position.
- The SQA organization should be situated in the corporate organization so that it always reports to the same level as the department which it must evaluate and audit.

References

1. Dunn, Robert, and Ullman, Richard, *Quality Assurance for Computer Software* (Englewood Cliffs, NJ: Prentice-Hall, 1983).
2. Schulmeyer, G. Gordon, and James I. McManus, *Total Quality Management for Software* (New York: Van Nostrand Reinhold Co., Inc., 1992).

General References

Arthur, L. J., *Measuring Programmer Productivity and Software Quality* (New York: John Wiley & Sons, 1984), pp. 12-35.

Mendis, Kenneth S., "A Software Quality Assurance Program for the 80s," *ASQC Technical Conference Transactions* (1980), pp. 379-388.

Mendis, Kenneth S., "Software Quality Assurance Staffing Problems," *ASQC Technical Conference Transactions* (1983), pp. 108-112.

Ryan, J. R., "Software Product Quality Assurance," *Proceedings of the National Computer Conference* (1982), pp. 393-398.

8

The Cost of Software Quality

James H. Dobbins, CQA

Defense Systems Management College

8.1 INTRODUCTION

The discipline of quality has been the focus of a paradox. The slogan *Quality is Free* is ever before us, in books,[1] posters, slogans and other media input. Yet the perpetual question asked by all program managers whenever a quality goal is required or suggested is, "What is it going to cost me?." It is as if everyone speaks of quality being free, but no one believes software quality is free. The real issue is one of investment, not cost.

It is time to examine the question of the cost of software quality and to draw some conclusions which, it is hoped, will enable the program managers to ask the correct questions about the cost of software quality, recognizing that the net value of a software quality investment is in terms of costs avoided. The investment in software quality, like any investment, has an immediate cost, with an expected net payback. The worth of the investment is determined by the value of the gain realized. If the gain realized from the quality investment is sufficient, then the net result is positive. To make this assessment, quantitative methods of evaluation are necessary.

8.2 CONCEPTS OF THE COST OF SOFTWARE QUALITY

The concepts of the cost of software quality have to be understood before the activities and measures related to the cost of software quality can be addressed in meaningful terms. Traditionally, the cost of quality, with its roots in hardware analysis, focused on failure related issues and activities. These included spoilage, defects, or the effort required to bring an item into, or back into, conformance with a set of requirements. The costs were usually tracked as the costs of scrap, rework, and repair. The costs were largely limited to labor and materials, and were often tracked in terms of their percent of total production cost, or percent of total sales volume.

Today, we recognize the cost of quality as being those segmented in terms of error *prevention, appraisal* (or product and process evaluation), and *failure* related activities. The drive is to minimize the failure related activities by making the proper level of investment in the prevention and evaluation activities. The categories of the cost of software quality and how they relate to each other must be understood in terms of the activities comprising each category and the measures describing and evaluating the cost of each of the software quality activities.

Visibility

A key consideration in any analysis of the cost of quality is visibility. The only reason for undertaking the analysis is to gain the visibility needed to make the enlightened decisions which result in highly effective software engineering processes producing high quality software products and their improvements. It is the visibility gained from cost of quality analysis which enables the project personnel to focus their attention on those activities which discover, and correct, the root causes of software defects. This root cause analysis allows the project personnel to determine how the development processes can be improved to prevent further defects. This visibility also provides the vehicle for excellent communication across all functions supporting the project, regardless of the organizational structure. The activities and resultant measures which provide the visibility are diverse, and are conducted across the life cycle phases. They can include inspections, audits, tests, vendor surveys, subcontractor audits, proposal evaluations, cost analysis, incorporation of CASE tools (Chapter 12), and any of several other such activities.

The Nature of Quality

A prerequisite to any meaningful discussion of the cost of software quality is an understanding of the nature of software quality. One of the impediments to a true understanding of cost of quality analysis, and identification of quality activities and measures, is the set of traditional "baggage" that comes with the term quality. This traditional view is founded in several myths, which are:

- Quality is defined by the producer, not the customer.
- Quality relates only to the final product.
- Software development is the biggest contributor to defects.
- Improving quality always costs more money.
- Quality is the responsibility of the Quality Assurance Department

The real story behind quality is that:

- The customer (user) defines quality.
- Quality is determined by every process, support function, and subproduct.
- Software defects are traceable to the requirements as a major contributor, and can occur during any life cycle phase.
- Improving quality will result in a lower life cycle cost.
- Quality is everyone's job, on every task they perform.

Why is There a Cost of Software Quality?

The cost, or more accurately the investment, of software quality for activities conducted is rooted in the requirement to assure that the developed product meets the approved requirements. The nature and size of the investment involved will be determined by several diverse elements. Some of these are:

- the requirements imposed by the buyer
- whether or not the contract is a government contract with specific activities mandated by standards and regulations
- the kinds of technologies used
- the kind of product being developed
- the internal development environment
- the project budget
- the degree to which repeatable processes and measures are incorporated into the everyday working practices of the developers
- the domain knowledge possessed by the development team

The objective of a cost of software quality analysis is not to reduce the cost, or investment, of software quality, but to make sure that the costs expended are the right kinds of costs and that the maximum benefit is derived from that investment. This requires a level of management understanding which recognizes the need for, and economic advantage of, error prevention in the early phases as opposed to error detection and correction during the later test phases. This cannot be accomplished without a management team sufficiently sophisticated and educated in the concepts, processes, and measures necessary for error prevention and process evaluation, and possessed of the wisdom to put into effect the activities needed to reap the maximum rewards for the investment.

As has been noted, the traditional view of the cost of quality, inherited from the hardware production disciplines, revolved around failure related activities. These costs were typically discussed in terms of scrap, rework and repair. Very little attention was given to defect prevention. More recently the hardware producers have adopted the concepts of total quality management, and the focus has shifted to the same kinds of concepts which are relevant to the cost of software quality. The major categories of activities are Prevention, Evaluation, and Failure. By shifting the emphasis from failure to prevention and evaluation, significant return on the quality investment, the Quality Return on Investment (QROI), can be realized.

Activity Assessment

In any assessment of quality, the question of cost can be quantified in terms of those activities which are done or not done. Things which are done can be costed in terms of the manhours and material expended in those tasks, and the cost benefit of doing those activities. Things which are not done can be costed, perhaps not as definitively, in terms of the impact of their not having been done, or not having been done at the right time. In either case, measurements have to be established by which management can evaluate both the activities and their effects.

In order to determine the activities to be performed, and therefore budgeted, an assessment must be made of the labor hours to be expended, any material resources costs, any costs related to the software equivalent of "scrap and rework," and the schedule impact on the life cycles during which the activities are performed. The value added benefit derived from these activities is evaluated in terms of process improvement, personnel skills improvement, product quality at delivery, overall project cost, impact on total project schedule, total manpower and material resources, warranty costs, competitive advantage in the marketplace and the post-delivery software maintenance costs.

In any analysis of activity, the effects of the activities must be measured for quality impact. If there is no impact on product quality, the value of the activity is zero. There must be a set of determinants which drive the questions asked and which focus the issue on the benefits derived. There must be a relationship between the objectives of the project and the activities performed.

8.3 INPUTS

Inputs to the cost of software quality analysis are the base elements necessary to conduct the analysis. This includes the requirements for data, material, customer needs, costs related to training, resources needed to support the process, and the procedures and standards required or followed.

Data

In order to perform a task which is to be measured as a cost of quality, the relevant data must be observable or measurable. This may be data directly observed, derived from analysis, provided by the customer, gathered as a result of the performance of some other task, provided as the output of another project, or data necessitated by the physical aspects of the project itself (such as the requirements of a nuclear energy project which are a function of the nuclear process itself). The data must be categorized as to whether it is related to error prevention activity, evaluation activity, or related to failures which occur at various life-cycle phases. Once the determination is made regarding the data required, the cost of obtaining that data can be determined by the process chosen to obtain the data.

Material

Any requisite material needed for the task must be determined. This may be the acquisition of a personal computer for analysis of the data to be obtained, or it may be something as simple as the forms necessary for recording data or activity results. In any case, the material involved has a cost of purchase or a cost of creation. The cost is determinable as long as the material is identifiable and available.

Customer Needs

The needs of the customer are among the lesser identifiable parameters of the set of input requirements for quality assessment. It is not uncommon for customers to have an overall idea of their needs, but a lack of specific requirements which they can communicate to the developer. It is very important to determine the project requirements, and the allocated software functional requirements. There is little doubt that software requirements which are not well defined or are constantly changing have a significant impact on the product quality and adversely affect the development processes. Each identified requirement must be measurable and testable. If it is not measurable and testable it is not a true requirement. If not, there can be no pass-fail criteria for determining whether the requirement has been met. Customers must also understand the difference between requirements and desirements. Customers often want everything, but they are only willing or able to pay for a portion of what they desire.

The way in which the requirements are specified can have a quality determinant and associated cost of its own. If written in prose, there will be a quality impact different from the impact of requirements written in a structured requirements definition language. The quality analysis activity will likewise be quite different. The quality cost is not the cost of writing the requirements, but is in terms of the cost of the error prevention processes employed in the requirements generation process, the requirements volatility, investments made in training or CASE tools to better produce requirements, and the difference in the product production cost when the requirements are produced in different ways.

Training

Quality activities often require training in certain process techniques. The type of training, the extent of the training, the travel, if any, required for obtaining or providing the training and the resources which must be expended to conduct or receive the training are all elements whose cost can be determined. The training must also be evaluated in terms of whether it is a one-time event or a continuous requirement.

The benefit derived from the software training in terms of process and product quality must be compared to the prior cost of not performing the activities, plus the cost of the training. In software development, how the beneficial cost of training is to be measured, and over what time period, has to be determined. This is not as easy as it might at first appear. Training is given to people, and when people are trained there is an initial skill increase which is beneficial, but there is often also a long range educational benefit derived from the application of that new skill in solving the problems of the tasks needed by the project.

Resources

The cost of resources required for providing or obtaining the necessary input data or material or training must be determined. The cost of facility resources for these elements must be determined in terms of space, utilities and other overhead impacts. Management involvement in all of these activities is a resource which must be accounted for but one which is often overlooked.

Procedures

Any activity will likely be done in accordance with some set of requirements, and will therefore be, or should be, in response to a set of procedures. If the procedures are not already available, they must be created and the cost of that creation recorded.

Standards

In many instances, the activities associated with the product production will have to conform to the requirements of certain standards. These standards may be government, industry, or internal. If an activity is performed only because a standard is invoked, and not because it would be done anyway, the cost of that activity must be considered a cost of quality. However, this must be assessed realistically. If the activity is treated as pure cost, and is not offset by benefits derived, the manager is saying that the activity has no cost benefit, but is done only because of the standard. If the standard imposes activity but adds no quality, the standard must be questioned. Alternatively, if the processes required by the standard add quality, but the activity associated with the standard would be done anyway as part of the normal development process even if the standard was not in place, then there is no added cost due to the standard.

8.4 VALUE ADDED ACTIONS

For each type of input, there must be a value added activity associated. Value added activities are those which add value to the product itself or to the process of producing that product. The value added can be in terms of increased quality of the product, positive impact on processes or procedures implemented in the production, and activities which lower the production cost without impacting product quality.

Overshadowing all of these activities are the customer needs. Clearly, there may be a compelling case for a defect free product. Associated with this, of course, are the costs related to attempt to achieve such a state of quality. Other customer needs may include systems which are "man-rated" (i.e., systems in which people are an active part of the system) or which will affect personal safety, such as the manned spaceflight projects or some nuclear applications or weapons systems. But there may be many instances where a defect free system is desirable but quite unnecessary. The degree of reliability of the system must be optimized on the basis of cost, schedule, resources, and available technological skills. It is important for the customer, as well as the contractor, to understand what the realistic needs really are for the system which is under contract.

8.5 OUTPUTS

The outputs of the cost of software quality analysis are the result of the application of the quality related processes and activities. These outputs are affected by the product, related services, and information.

Product

The product produced by the development activities will have a level of performance which is determined in part by the degree to which it is free of defects and is maintainable. The product will have performance requirements which will or will not be met depending in part on whether or not the inputs necessary are available and whether or not the value added actions have been performed. The product will have a reliability, however acceptable or unacceptable, which should be optimized based on all of the determining factors of cost, schedule, resources, and technology. The customer may desire a system with proven reliability of 100%, but can seldom afford the activity it would take to reach such a goal.

Services

The output of the value added actions may be in the form of a service performed for other departments or agencies. While not the product to be delivered, the service may be necessary for the product to be produced with the requisite level of quality. For example, performance of formal design and code inspections[2] may be a non-deliverable service, but the impact on the product quality can be significant. Document inspections are another form of quality service performed which tends to assure the customer that the product delivered—the document—is as defect free as the implemented procedure will allow.

It is worthy of note that the inspection process used in software is different from inspection of hardware. In hardware, the product is sample inspected to look for flaws in the production. Various things, such as loose or cold solder joints, missing fasteners, and the like are identified, the product is pulled from the line, and the defective product is returned for rework: it is a failure related activity.

In software, the inspection process is both a defect detection process and a defect prevention process. Software is an intellectual activity performed only once, and recorded. It is not mass produced, using new pieces each time, but merely copied as needed. The inspections are conducted at each step in the software life cycle to make the software product the best it can be at that time. It is an in-process activity which is largely analytical. Software is the recordation of the thought process of the designer and programmer, and inspections are essentially a group analysis and validation of the work of the author, performed while the product is in the various stages of being developed.

Information

Information is often the result of quality activities, even though the information itself is non-deliverable. This may take the form of quality analysis reports, such as the analysis of the design and code inspection data, or audit reports wherein the quality performance or activity or product of another group or department is assessed. Information may take any of several other forms, and any which are quality related activities are part of the cost of quality.

8.6 TOTAL COST OF QUALITY

In assessing the total cost of quality, all of the questions which many program managers fail to ask must be asked. When the program manager, who does not understand the real elements of quality, asks what the cost of an activity will be, he is asking what the specific cost of the performance of the activity will be, not the resultant impact of doing or not doing the task. If the task costs one amount, but the result of performing that task saves another amount, the real cost is the difference between the two, not the initial cost of the activity. However, it is never this difference about which the uneducated program manager is seeking information. If the real answer is a negative cost, and if the program manager does not really understand these relationships, he or she will be tempted to ask for a cut in budget for that activity since the total cost is perceived as a negative.

Because the program manager may not be conversant enough in quality processes to ask the real question or to assess the real impact of performing a quality activity, it is necessary to provide a means for assessing the real cost of quality on a project and offer the complete picture to the program manager to ensure that the proper questions are asked and the proper evaluations conducted.

To do this, each department should go through a quality assessment activity analysis, gather the proper data, and present the true picture to the program manager. Once the true picture is presented, and the program manager is educated thereby, the education process has the opportunity to work and the task of performing the quality activities is encouraged.

8.7 ACTIVITY ANALYSIS

In going through a process of quality cost analysis, there are four major steps. They are:

1. List all MAJOR Activities
2. For Each Activity:

   - List inputs: What? From Where?
   - Determine value added: Why do?
   - List outputs: What? Where?

3. For Each Activity:

   - Determine customer requirements
   - Determine supplier requirements
   - Determine measurements

4. For Each Activity:

   - Analyze measurement requirements
   - Determine level of effort: Estimate Cost of Effort.
   - Divide Cost into Categories

To accomplish this, a form should be used by each person in the department so that the activities associated with the product production may be assessed for quality cost/benefit/impact. This is not as intuitively simple as it may seem.

The activities must first be identified. A brief general description must be provided for each major activity in order to properly assess that activity. This may be done through the use of a form such as that shown in Figure 8-1. This is a very simple form, which can be used in multiple copies, if the list of activities will not fit on one page; it is easily scanned to determine the number of activities as well. This form prioritizes the activities, and can be used to group the activities by number, by type of activity, or other such pertinent classification.

The next step is to determine the requisite information for each of these tasks in terms of input required and value added by the performance of that activity. The output for the activity must also be determined. An example of a form for this purpose is shown in Figure 8-2. The advantage of the form is the removal of the guess-work involved and a clear indication of where vital information is missing. Each activity should have a separate form of its own for this purpose.

The work required to complete such an analysis may not be as simple as it seems, however. The Impact If Not Done part of the form is not always easy to specify, especially in terms of a cost element. The answer to this question may be an educated evaluation based on data from past projects.

The next step is to determine the answers to the requirements questions. Figure 8-3 shows a form for recording such information, but the information for large projects may reference another document. The output requirements must be

Department Activity Analysis

Department Name: _____

Department Number: _____

Function Name: _____

General Description of Work (Major Activities):

_____

_____

_____

_____

_____

_____

_____

_____

_____

_____

Manager's Signature   **date**   **phone**

_____

FIGURE 8-1. Department activity analysis.

determined and, finally, the measurements must be identified which will show whether the requirements are met.

To identify a set of measurements that are going to prove the requirements are met may necessitate considerable investigation. The arena of software measurements is just reaching a stage of development where companies are becoming comfortable with the idea of software quantification.

The assessment process recently developed by the Software Engineering Institute (SEI) at Carnegie-Mellon University,[3] and which is now being used by the Department of Defense as one of the contractor source selection criteria, has a five step scale for assessment. At Level 1, "the contractor has ill-defined software engineering procedures and controls. . . . the organization does not consistently

Department Value Added Analysis

Department Name: _____

Department Number: _____

Activity: _____

Prepared by: _____

INPUT:

WHAT: _____

_____

FROM: _____

VALUE-ADDED WORK ACCOMPLISHED

Why Do? _____

Value Added: _____

_____

Impact if Not Done: _____

_____

OUTPUT:

WHAT: _____

TO: _____

_____

FIGURE 8-2. Department value added analysis.

apply software engineering management to the process, nor does it use modern tools and technology".[4] It is not until an organization reaches Level 3 that meaningful metrics become part of the normal software engineering process, and are used by management in decision making. In the initial studies conducted, 86% of the companies assessed by SEI were at Level 1. Because of this, the measures, if any, which are selected by the contractor may not necessarily be understood or acceptable to the customer. Each measure selected must be identified, justified, and documented.

It is advisable for contractors to develop sets of measures for each development stage of the software rather than one measure at the very end of the development or test phase. This will afford the development management a means for continual assessment and correction throughout the software development process. In addition, if the company is a defense contractor, the revised DODI 5000.2, signed into law in February 1991, mandates the use of metrics in the software development process. The Department of Defense will no longer have the option of deciding whether or not to require contractors to incorporate metrics into their software engineering environment.

Department Requirements Activity Analysis

Department Name: _____

Department Number: _____

Activity: _____

Prepared by: _____

AGREED INPUT REQUIREMENTS:

_____

_____

_____

_____

AGREED OUTPUT REQUIREMENTS:

_____

_____

_____

_____

_____

_____

_____

_____

MEASUREMENTS:

_____

_____

_____

_____

FIGURE 8-3. Department requirements activity analysis.

The measurement selection process is one which should be governed by several factors, such as the input data requirements, the availability of support software to make the necessary computations or evaluations, the ease with which the results can be understood and evaluated by management, and the amount of information contained in the measurement result. It is clear that a measure which only indicates that a problem exists is far less valuable than one which indicates that a problem exists and also why it exists. All too often, measurement tools provide lengthy printouts of data, but the data are not converted to information, and especially not information that can be quickly and easily understood and utilized by management. In some instances, the measurement tool output is so involved, the company which developed the tool requires that one of their employees be always available, and paid, to interpret the results. Perhaps this approach is why so many managers have struggled with implementation of software metrics.

Once the activity analysis, i.e., the activities, input requirements, output requirements and measurement requirements have been determined, then the final set of questions must be asked. As is seen in Figure 8-4, for each activity, the manager (either the SQA and/or Program Manager) must determine whether the measurement is possible now, if it is possible at all, and whether the activity should be measured. It may cost more to perform the measurement than to accomplish the task.

Department Quality Activity Cost Analysis

Department: _____

Activity: _____

Prepared by: _____

MEASUREMENT ANALYSIS:

IS ACTIVITY MEASURED NOW: NO ○ YES ○

CAN THIS ACTIVITY BE MEASURED: NO ○ YES ○

SHOULD ACTIVITY BE MEASURED: NO ○ YES ○

LEVEL OF ACTIVITY

ESTIMATED HRS/WK SPENT ON THIS ACTIVITY:_____

IS ACTIVITY A "COST OF QUALITY"?

NO ○   YES   ○   PARTIALLY   ○

ESTIMATED "COST OF QUALITY" HRS/WK SPENT ON THIS ACTIVITY:

_____

COST OF QUALITY CATEGORIES:

PREVENTION: HRS/WK:_____   COST:_____

APPRAISAL: HRS/WK:_____   COST:_____

FAILURE: HRS/WK:_____   COST:_____

TOTAL: HRS/WK:_____   COST:_____

FIGURE 8-4. Department quality activity cost analysis.

The activity itself must be costed in terms of the man-hours required to perform the task. The activity may be purely a quality activity, it may be an activity which is only partially a quality activity, or it may be a totally non-quality activity.

The cost of quality should then be categorized in terms of Prevention activity, Appraisal activity, or Failure activity (see Figure 8-4).

8.8 FOCUS

Once these actions have been completed, the department manager has the information necessary to go to the program manager and present a true picture of the real cost of producing a quality product. The focus should be on two factors:

1. Cost to Analyze Problems
2. Cost to redo task

The analyses tasks provide the means for identifying errors in the system and for prioritizing the errors for corrective action. The attention is on the means to accurately identify non-conformances, and this requires that the employees get involved in the task. Involving the employees in a quality process to this degree builds up their quality awareness—the key to quality program success.

The result of the analysis process must be documented and presented to those who have to make decisions based on the information.

8.9 TASK ELEMENTS

Non-Cost of Quality

In making the assessments discussed, the non-quality portion of tasks has to be determined. To do this, the manager or employee must decide if the task is purely one of the following:

Design
Development
Fabrication
Documentation
Assembly
Process
Creation
Upgrade

Any of these, done the first time, is a non-quality task element. They are tasks which would be done just to get the product out the door, regardless of quality considerations. But note well the phrase, done the first time.

Cost of Quality

Task elements, which are part of the cost of quality, are generally grouped into three categories and two classifications. The classifications are Conformance and

TABLE 8-1   Categorizing Task Elements

Conformance		Non-Conformance
Prevention	Appraisal	Failure
Training	Inspection	Rework
Planning	Testing	Service
Simulation	Audits	Modification
Modeling	Monitoring	Expediting
Consulting	Measurement	Recall
Qualifying	Verification	Correction
Certifying	Analysis	Retest
		Error Analysis

Non-Conformance. The categories are Prevention, Appraisal, and Failure. They are cataloged according to the relationship which exists between the categories and the classifications. Prevention and Appraisal are under the Conformance category and Failure is under the Non-Conformance category. These relationships can be tabularized (also see Table 8-1) as follows:

In performing the conformance activities, care must be taken to distinguish between the work of others and of oneself. The review and checking methods may be the same if all is done in-house. However, if the work is done by a subcontractor, then the methods may be quite different and the cost elements different.

When this activity of categorization and classification is accomplished, an overall Quality Activity Analysis can be performed. This can be done using a simple form designed for that purpose, such as that shown in Figure 8-5. On this form the summary of the information gathered can be collected in one place, making it easier to present it to the Program Manager and providing the means for making the case for quality activity.

Department Quality Activity Analysis

Department: _____

Date: _____

ACTIVITY	NCOQ	CONFORMANCE PREV	EVAL	NON-CONFORMANCE FAILURE	TOTAL
PROGRAM DESIGN	616				616
DESIGN REVIEWS		63	42		105
CODE	432				432
CODE REVIEWS		57	36		93
UNIT TEST			329		329
INTEG TEST			458		458
SYSTEM TEST			379		379
CONFIG MGMT			273		273
PROBLEM SOLVING				184	184
REWORK				123	123
RETEST				167	167
TOTAL HRS	1048	120	1517	474	3159
% OF TOTAL	33.2%	3.8%	48%	15%	

FIGURE 8-5. Department quality activity analysis.

As an example, this form has been filled out for a software development department as shown in Figure 8-5. In this example, approximately two thirds of the total department cost is a cost of quality. If these data points are maintained regularly, and if they are summarized on an annual basis, the annual costs can be determined, as shown in Figure 8-6. Here the data shows that of the $288,000 dollars spent as a cost of quality, $186,000 was spent on fixing problems. Clearly, this can be attacked by the introduction of error prevention activities and by the introduction of methods and techniques for detecting and removing, early in the development cycle, errors that do slip by.

It has been estimated, for example, that removal of an error after delivery to the field may typically cost as much as 80 times the cost of removal during software design. If the time expended and the costs incurred by performing cost of quality activity are the result of poor production or design processes or procedures, then the failure related cost of quality can be reduced in proportion to the degree to which the design and production processes and procedures are improved. This reduction in the cost of quality can be measured and, if related to the production and design activity, can afford a means of assessing the effectiveness of the improvements made.

ESTIMATED ANNUAL COSTS

	HOURS	DOLLARS	%
NON-COST OF QUALITY	10,272	312,000	52
COST OF QUALITY	9,408	288,000	48
TOTAL ANNUAL COST	19,680	600,000	

CATEGORIES OF COQ

	HOURS	DOLLARS	%
PREVENTION	960	30,000	5
EVALUATION	2,304	72,000	12
FAILURE	6,144	186,000	31
TOTAL YEAR	9,408	288,000	48

FIGURE 8-6. COQ activity analysis.

8.10 POTENTIAL MISUSE

As is true of most good things, the Cost of Quality Analysis, once published, can be misused. The cost of quality is not a normal financial program activity. Few finance departments have anything resembling a cost of quality analysis as is described here. The typical finance or cost analysis department in all likelihood knows the total cost of a software quality assurance department, but that cost is not the actual cost of performing quality assurance. Conversely, the cost of quality analysis is not a financial program. It is not a substitute for an existing accounting system.

The misuse of the cost of quality analysis is typically related to the focal point of the analysis. There is a tendency to place too much emphasis on the "cost" and not enough on the failure elements of the analysis. The "cost" is just a means of bringing attention to bear on the failure elements and their effect on the program. There is no need for absolute and infallible accuracy to the last dollar as is required in accounting departments.

There is a requirement for understanding the impact of the failures and the cost picture is the most convincing means of conveying that impact. This is not to say that the figures are erroneous or unimportant. The failures do give life to the cost elements; it is a question of focus. The focus should be on the failures and what can be done to prevent them. Developing the cost should be a means of tracking the effectiveness of the failure reduction program.

The figures should also not be used to compare departments or functions for the purpose of punishment. Again, the emphasis should be on failure removal from software being developed, with emphasis on trends within a department or function. If the trend is in the correct direction, then the process is working. If it is working, don't break it; improve it. If the focus and trend analysis is on defect prevention, this in itself will have a significant leverage on quality costs. If the focus is on cost alone, it is likely that very little will be accomplished.

8.11 PRODUCTIVITY

Closely allied to the cost of quality, and intimately related to the failure elements, is the question of productivity. Here again, the questions asked are seldom the correct questions. The program manager or the customer is most likely to track productivity in terms of the number of lines of code generated per unit of time. This is usually expressed in terms of lines per manmonth. This measure, in itself, is counterproductive and encourages the development departments to overlook or eliminate quality tasks and procedures which they should be performing. If productivity is examined in conjunction with the cost of quality analysis, then the emphasis will be on lines produced correctly per manmonth. For example, if a programmer produces 1000 lines in one month, and 900 have to be corrected, then the programmers productivity should really be measured as 100 lines per month, or even less depending on how many lines have to be added per line corrected. If another programmer produces 500 lines in a month, but only 100 have to be corrected, then that programmers productivity is 400 lines per month, or four times the productivity of the other, supposedly the more prolific programmer.

This emphasis on productivity as a measure of correctly produced products requires considerable customer and manager education. It is often the combination of customer perception and manager ignorance of true programmer productivity which drives the definition, the measure, the reporting scheme, the schedule, and the overall program cost. Many contracts have built-in incentive fee awards, and if productivity is correctly assessed, this will afford a means of establishing an incentive fee award, which is truly meaningful. This concept can be applied to software production, and to those related elements upon which correct production depends, such as functional specifications. If the specification is produced quickly, but is full of defects, then the programmer productivity will be impaired. If the specification is produced with a minimal percent of defects, then that has a positive impact on the programmers' productivity and should be encouraged with incentives.

The foregoing aspects of productivity should be incorporated into a cost of quality analysis. It is these peripheral activities that can be major elements of the cost of quality and which can be most effective for improving cost and productivity.

8.12 MAJOR COMPONENTS

When the activities of software development are being assessed, along with the related cost components and the outputs, it is helpful to understand the differences between the software activities themselves and the software development attributes. The software activities are shown in Table 8-2, which gives the typical software development activities, the related cost components, and the outputs. These can be used as a basis for performing a cost of quality analysis for a software development department.

In Table 8-3, the relationships of software development are shown: the various elements (design features and practices) which impact attributes, such as reliability, accuracy, and others, are given (design objectives). This table, when used in

TABLE 8-2   Software Activities

Activity	Related Cost Component	Outputs
System Definition	• SW Requirements Definition • SW System Description • SW Development Planning • Engineering Change Analysis	• SW Sys Req Spec • SW Sys Descrip Doc • SW Dev Plan • Eng Chng Proposals
Software Design	• Functional Design • Program Design • Test Design • Software Tools • Design Evaluation	• Funct Des Spec • Prog Des Spec • Test Des Spec • Data; Analysis • Eval Report
Software Development	• Module Development • Development Testing • Problem Analysis and Correction	• Module Libraries • Test Documents • Program Modification

TABLE 8-2   Continued

Activity	Related Cost Component	Outputs
Software System Test	• Test Planning and Design • Integration and Test	• Test Procedures • Integration Library • Test Reports
System/Acceptance Test	• Test Support • Test Planning and Design • Test Media Control	• Test Library • Test Documents • Delivered System
Operational Support	• System Operation Support • Training • Site Deployment Support	• Assistance; Modification • Training Manuals, Courses • Logistics
General Support	• Project Management • Configuration Management • Software Cost Engineering • Software Quality Assurance • Administrative Support	• Development Decisions • Procedures; Config Control • Cost Analysis • Quality Evaluation Reports • Administrative Activities

TABLE 8-3   Software Attributes for Design

Design Objectives / Design Practices	Reliability	Accuracy	Testability	Maintainability	Change	Growth
Top-Down Architecture	X		X			
Module Size			X	X		
Low Complexity	X		X	X	X	
Structured Programming	X		X	X	X	X
Statement Grouping			X	X	X	
Symbolic Parameterization			X	X	X	X
Uniform Naming Convention			X	X	X	X
Module Listing Convention			X	X	X	X
Reserve			X			X
Timing and Sizing Analysis	X		X			X
Accuracy Loss Monitoring		X	X			
Low Number of S/W Paths	X		X	X	X	
Design Optimization		X				X
Minimize Dynamic Mods.	X		X	X	X	

conjunction with Table 8-1, can help formulate a program of reduction of quality costs by emphasizing activities that will have the most significant impact on the "ility" which requires the most attention.

8.13 CONCLUSION

The Cost of Quality itself may be zero, but only if the proper activity, based on clear analysis, is performed. Quality is *free* provided that the effort is made to perform failure reduction tasks and to seek ways and means to move the failure prevention, detection and removal activity closer to the front end of the development process. The closer to the front the failure removal activity is accomplished, the greater the impact and the more significant the cost reduction. It is only in this way that the cost of performing quality will become less than the cost of not performing quality tasks. Quality costs can be properly evaluated only in terms of the impact created when they are not incurred. It is that impact cost which will drive home the point that quality itself truly can be free.

References

1. Crosby, Philip, *Quality is Free,* (New York: McGraw-Hill Publ. Co., 1979).
2. Fagan, Michael E., "Design and Code Inspections to Reduce Errors in Program Development," *IBM Systems Journal,* Vol 15, Number 3, July 1976.
3. Humphrey, W. S., W. L. Sweet, *A Method for Assessing the Software Engineering Capability of Contractors,* Software Engineering Institute, Carnegie-Mellon University, Preliminary Version, Technical Report ESD-TR-87-186, September 1987.
4. *Ibid;* page 23.

9

Inspections as an Up-Front Quality Technique

James H. Dobbins, CQA

Defense Systems Management College

9.1 INTRODUCTION

Ever since the publication of Michael Fagan's paper[1] on the design and code inspection process, inspections have been used as a quality improvement and cost reduction technique. There has been considerable discussion as to whether or not inspections are necessary and whether or not they are any different or any better than walkthroughs. After considerable time expended in performing inspections and after collection of data from many inspections on a wide variety of projects, it has become apparent that the use of design and code inspections during development is one of the most productive activities which a software development team can employ. In spite of the initial reluctance most programmers exhibit when the inspection process is first imposed, programmers enthusiastically perform inspections as a routine part of their development once they become aware of the increase in their productivity and in the correctness of their product which they achieve through inspections.

Program managers initially question the cost-effectiveness of program inspections and the impact they will have on milestone schedule deliveries. However, once a program manager has had firsthand experience with properly conducted inspections, and understands the implications of early defect removal as opposed to costly error correction during tests, the value added by the application of inspections will become more than apparent to him or her.

Over the years, since inspections were first begun, the process has been examined and training methods have been streamlined, but the fundamental process and the requirements for the proper conduct of an inspection remain essentially the same as described in Fagan's paper. An overview of the inspection process is provided in this chapter, with cross-references to other chapters discussing inspections. The emphases of this chapter will be the lessons which have been learned through application of the process, how management can gain a measure of control over software projects, through proper analysis of the data collected, how to anticipate the results which should be obtained through application of inspections, with examples of application and analysis, and the impact the inspection process should have on any test program. Current practices will be surveyed, and speculation as to the impact software technology improvements might have will be pursued.

9.2 THE INSPECTION PROCESS

There are both primary and secondary purposes for conducting inspections. The primary vs. secondary categorization has more to do with the process of conducting the inspections than the net impact of having done inspections.

Primary Purpose

The Inspection, whether design or code, has only one primary purpose; that is, to remove defects as early as possible in the development process. The purpose of the inspection preparation and meeting is to:

1. Identify potential defects during preparation and validate them at the meeting;
2. Validate the fact that identified items are actual defects;
3. Record the existence of the defect; and
4. Provide the record to the developer to use in making fixes.

It is not the intent of the inspection process to find solutions to identified defects, although not finding solutions is extremely difficult for some people. The fact that a defect exists will be sufficient cause to search for a solution. However, the time of the inspection process preparation and meeting is to be used to identify and record the existence of defects. It is the sole responsibility of the author to define the solution. It is also in the province of the author to request, outside the inspection process, assistance in finding a solution.

Therefore, one of the most difficult tasks many moderators face is keeping the discussion centered on finding defects and away from discussing solutions. In some cases, the mere identification of the defect may be sufficient also to state the solution, but in most cases this is not true and the inspection process will be unreasonably lengthened if the solutions are pursued when the defects are identified. It is also a usurpation of the right of the author to fix his or her own defects.

Secondary Purposes

The secondary purposes resulting from the inspection process are:

1. Provide traceability of requirements to design.
2. Provide a technically correct base for the next phase of development.
3. Increase programming quality.
4. Increase product quality at delivery.
5. Achieve lower life-cycle cost.
6. Increase effectiveness of test activity.
7. Provide a first indication of program maintainability.
8. Encourage entry/exit-criteria software management.

These secondary purposes are all part of the net effect of performing inspections properly and professionally. The fact that they are secondary purposes does not in any way diminish their importance to the overall software development effort.

If the inspections are performed properly and according to the procedures described, and limited to that, then these secondary benefits will occur naturally. Some of the secondary purposes will be achieved directly as a result of the inspections, and others will be achieved by the inspections working in concert with other activities. In other words, inspections are not the sole cause, but they are a significant, and in some cases a primary, cause of the secondary purposes being achieved.

Inspection Phases

The *moderator* of an inspection is responsible for the entire inspection process for the software product. There are six distinct inspection phases: planning, overview, preparation, inspection meeting, rework, and follow-up.

Planning
The planning phase is that phase during which the moderator establishes the conduct and progress for the entire inspection. This requires that the moderator

1. Assure the identification of the inspection team:
2. Assure that the team members will be able to adequately prepare for the inspection;
3. Assure that the materials to be inspected are available and conform to standards;
4. Determine whether the entry criteria have been met;
5. Determine the need for an overview;
6. Assure that the place for the inspection meeting is available and reserved for the inspection;

7. Schedule the inspection meeting time and place; and
8. Give all inspection team members and other interested parties notice of the inspection meeting time and place.

Some of these tasks may be accomplished by someone other than the moderator, and often the author will actually schedule the meeting place, pass out the materials, and other such tasks. However, it is still the responsibility of the moderator to assure that these tasks are accomplished.

Overview

An overview meeting is an educational meeting usually conducted prior to a design inspection. It is a short meeting in which the author of the product to be inspected gives the inspection team members, and others who will be interfacing with the author's product, a brief description of the software, what task is being performed, how it will perform that task, what interfaces are to be active, and a description of the interface functions. Such a meeting provides insight to the inspection team members and makes their job easier. It also provides other programmers who will interface with this program the opportunity to learn how the interface will be handled and, if necessary, identify any problems with the described approach. If there are any significant problems, the inspection can be cancelled and the problems addressed.

The overview meeting is held at the beginning of the preparation phase and it is at this meeting, if held, that the moderator gives the inspection materials to the inspection team members and also gives them the inspection meeting notice. Otherwise, the moderator assures the materials are distributed to the team members at the beginning of the preparation phase. The moderator may not do the actual distribution, but the moderator does have the responsibility to assure the distribution is made.

Whether there is an overview meeting held or not is discretionary with the moderator. This is the only discretionary phase.

Preparation

The preparation phase begins when the inspection team members receive the inspection materials and the notice of the inspection meeting. Everything needed for the inspection should be provided to the inspectors at one time, at least five (5) working days in advance of the inspection meeting. This lead time is to give the inspectors the opportunity to properly examine the materials and record any discrepancies found. Since each inspector has other responsibilities, the lead time is to allow them to perform their assigned tasks and also prepare for the inspection meeting. It is expected that the inspection team members will spend at least as much time preparing for inspections as is required for the inspection meeting, which should not exceed two hours.

During this time, the *reader* prepares to present the material to the inspection team. The reader makes particular note of any difficulty in understanding the design, code, or commentary. Each inspector examines the material for all possible defects. The defects are recorded on the *inspection-defect log form,* which is included in the inspection materials provided to each inspector by the moderator. Each inspector also keeps track of his or her preparation time and records it on the inspection defect log.

Inspection Meeting

The inspection meeting is that phase of the inspection process at which the team members come together to discuss the discrepancies which have been detected. The moderator is responsible for the proper conduct of the meeting and for assuring that the team members approach this task in a professional manner. The reader is responsible for presenting the product to the team in a logical and orderly manner so that discussion of the material and any inherent defects is not hindered.

During this phase, the moderator calls the meeting to order, records the preparation time for each team member, and directs the reader to begin the discussion.

As defects are identified, they are discussed and recorded. Particular attention is paid to previously undetected defects which are discovered as a result of the discussion and interaction between the team members. Also important is verification that items identified for discussion are true defects. The defects are then recorded by each team member, the defect type is noted, and, at the end of the inspection meeting, the defects are counted.

During the inspection meeting, the moderator, to assure that the team members conduct themselves in a professional manner, at a minimum holds the participants to only one discussion at a time; and sees to it that they address problems in as objective, professional, and impersonal a manner as possible, and tries to convey the feeling that the person whose product is being inspected is being helped, not criticized.

As noted, the activity during the meeting is limited to finding defects, not solutions. It is the responsibility of the author to find the solutions. If a defect is a type which repeats itself, the team need discuss it only once. When the defect is encountered again, there need only be a reference back to the original defect detection point, and a note made that the same defect is repeated at this point. When summarizing defects, the moderator counts a defect once for each occurrence.

When defects are repeated in a product, the team should wait until the reader gets to the place each repeated defect is found before mentioning its repetition. The fact of repetition should *not* be mentioned when the first defect is found. To do so will distract from the flow of the material presented by the reader and tend to place unwarranted emphasis on this one defect or defect type.

When the inspection meeting is over, the moderator collects the individual defect logs from the team. If the moderator is able to ascertain from the meeting that a reinspection will or will not be required, it is announced then. If the defects will have to be examined first, then the moderator should do this in a timely manner.

When the inspection team has been dismissed, the moderator summarizes on the *defect summary log form* the defects found, records the preparation and inspection time, notes the author, department (or sub-contractor company name), notes the requirement for a reinspection, whether this inspection was a reinspection or not, notes the type of inspection, and sends a copy of the data to the author and to the software quality engineering (SWQE) department.

Rework

During the rework phase, the author examines the defects found and makes the necessary corrections. After the corrections are verified, the author discusses the corrections with the moderator. If the moderator determines that a reinspection is required, the author begins preparation for the reinspection.

Follow-Up

The follow-up phase is that activity engaged in by the moderator to assure that all of the defects detected during the inspection have been corrected. The moderator is responsible for the activity in this phase, and the inspection is not completed until the follow-up phase has been completed by the moderator.

The moderator has the responsibility to assure that each defect has been corrected. This verification is done in person, not by phone. If necessary, the moderator brings a member of the inspection team to assist in the verification process. The fix date (or the date when the fix is verified), is noted on the defect summary log. When verification is completed, the moderator sends a copy of the summary log to SWQE with the notation that this is a fix notification. When this last task is accomplished, the task of the moderator for the inspection is completed, and the inspection itself for the software product is also completed.

Inspection Types

There are three types of inspections typically performed. These are high-level design inspection (I_0), low-level design inspection (I_1), and code inspection (I_2). Requirements-document-inspections, designated as R_0 and R_1, are not addressed in this chapter, though mentioned in the last section.

High-Level Design Inspection (I_0)

During the high-level design phase, the overall design for a module or function is produced. This stage commences with the issuance of a preliminary program performance specification (PPS), the initiation of the interface design specification (IDS), and ends with the completion of the I_0 inspection. In this stage, the high-level architecture of the software is determined and recorded in the initial program design specification (PDS) material. This PDS information is examined during the I_0 inspection. For each function, the PDS will provide:

1. The source of the design (new, other contract, etc.).
2. A graphical presentation of the function allocation to hardware resources.
3. A graphical presentation of function flow.

4. A description of scheduling, timing, and synchronization.
5. A definition of interfaces.
6. The process of decomposition.
7. The design definition as follows:

- Retained modules: reference to an existing PDS, if applicable.
- Modified modules: reference to an existing PDS, where applicable, and a narrative description of the changes.
- New modules: high-level description of the interfaces and processing.

During the I_0, the PDS information is further expanded to include a description of each new task/module, including interfacing and processing. An I_0 is held for each new function. For the retained and modified modules, an inspection plan is written by the programmer to define the scope of requirements for any additional I_0 inspections. These requirements are based on the anticipated extent of modification.

Resource utilization estimates are generated during this design phase and are collected and maintained by the system engineering organization, with the software development organization periodically providing input. The system engineering organization reviews and approves the PDS and the I_0 material to assure compliance with the baseline documentation.

All six phases of the inspection process (with the possible exception of the overview phase) are conducted for each I_0.

PURPOSE

I_0 inspection conducts a formal examination of the software product to verify that the functional design at the task level is a correct expansion of the PPS at the mode level. A mode-level function may be class, tracking, and so forth. Verification is performed by identifying the allocation of PPS requirements to processes and tasks. A single I_0 is typically performed for each mode.

Low-Level Design (I_1)

The low-level design, or what is more commonly called *detailed design* or *module design,* reflects back on the overall design objectives. Key objectives considered in designing the software are:

1. Accuracy with high performance.
2. Reliability and fault-tolerance, enabling the system to continue to perform in the event of hardware intermittent failures or other unexpected occurrences.
3. Flexibility to accommodate change and growth.
4. Easy testability.
5. Readily maintainable.

Key features of the design process that facilitate the achievement of these objectives are described in Table 9-1.

TABLE 9-1 Relationship of Software Design Practices to Design Objectives

DESIGN OBJECTIVES DESIGN PRACTICES	RELIABILITY	ACCURACY	TESTABILITY	MAINTAINABILITY	CHANGE	GROWTH
Top-Down Architecture	X		X			
Module Size			X	X		
Low Complexity	X		X	X	X	
Structured Programming	X		X	X	X	X
Statement Grouping			X	X	X	
Symbolic Parameterization			X	X	X	X
Uniform Naming Convention			X	X	X	X
Module Listing Convention			X	X	X	X
Reserve			X			X
Timing and Sizing Analysis	X		X			X
Accuracy Loss Monitoring		X	X			
Low Number of Software Paths	X		X	X	X	
Design Optimization		X				X
Minimization of Dynamic Mods.	X		X	X	X	
Emphasis on Design Reviews	X	X	X			

Detail module design is developed and I_1 inspections are held for all modules which meet any of the following criteria:

1. New module development.
2. Any change to the external interface or function of an existing module.
3. A structural change in an existing module.
4. A 40% or greater change in the source lines of code (SLOC) in an existing module. This percentage presumes that the size requirements as specified in the military standards are adhered to. In the case of unrestricted module size, where the module is large, this percentage criteria may not be proper.

To improve maintainability, each new module, member, or subroutine process is self-documenting as follows:

- It contains a prologue, or preamble, which describes the routine function, inputs, outputs, revision levels, and process flow.
- Comments for each section are blocked and delineate the routine into logical segments and describe the function of each segment.
- Inline comments clarify specific statements.

PURPOSE

The objective of I_1 is to stepwise refine the I_0 design to an intermediate level before translation to the target language code is authorized. All interfaces between processes, tasks, and procedures are defined to the field or bit level. The level of decomposition must be sufficient to show the highest level of control structure for each procedure and the operations performed on the inputs and outputs. This does not, however, necessarily define completely all the control structures and internal data structures.

All six phases of the inspection process (with the possible exception of the overview phase) are conducted for each I_1.

Only after the successful completion of the I_1 inspection, and any required reinspections, can the module coding process begin. Managers have the responsibility to assure that no code begins on a module until the successful completion of the design inspection for that module. This is a technical and product quality decision and should not be controlled by schedule.

The portion of the PDS for that software which has completed the I_1 phase should be complete by the end of that inspection.

Code Inspections (I_2)

A code inspection (I_2) is held for all new code or code from another task which is being modified to meet the requirements of the new task or contract. The code inspection is not performed until after there has been an error-free compilation. All six phases of the inspection process (with the possible exception of the overview phase) are conducted for each I_2. In some cases where there is a very minor program trouble report (PTR) fix, the lead programmer may decide not to hold an I_2 inspection. There should be a person designated with the responsibility to make this judgment and this decision should be a purely technical decision, not one driven by schedule.

PURPOSE

The code inspection will serve the following purposes before the program test functions proceed:

1. Verification that the code conforms to the PPS, PDS, and IDS requirements for operational software.
2. Confirmation that the design has been correctly converted to the target language.
3. Verification that the code conforms to the requirements where there may be on-line interfaces.
4. Early audit of code quality by the programmer's peers.
5. Early detection of errors.
6. Verification that the code meets level-to-level module interface requirements.
7. Review of module test specification, which is provided with the inspection materials package.
8. Verification that the module test specifications (module test plan) are necessary and sufficient to test the requirements specified for that module and reviewed during the design inspection (I_0 and I_1).

9. Verification that the proper test tools and test environment have been identified and are available.
10. Verification that the test dependencies are correct and the module is testable based on the dependencies.
11. Decision whether to allow module test (unit test) to begin.
12. Verification that the software product conforms to the contract or internal standards and conventions.

Code inspections for each software module are typical of the pass/fail events which serve as milestones in software development schedules.

The result of a successful code inspection should be a complete code which conforms to the high-level design, low-level design, and PPS.

Only after successful completion of the code inspection can the module test begin.

Inspection Defect Types and Definitions

The inspection defect logs and design/code inspection summary logs used by the inspectors and the moderator require the categorization and typing of defects found. The types of defects and their definitions follow:

Design defect—function description does not meet the requirements specification.
Logic defect—data is missing; wrong or extra information.
Syntax defect—does not adhere to the grammar of the design/code language defined.
Standards defect—does not meet the software standards requirements. This includes in-house standards, project standards, and military standards invoked in the contract.
Data defect—missing, extra, or wrong data definition or usage.
Interface defect—incompatible definition/format of information exchanged between two modules.
Return code/message defect—incorrect or missing values/messages sent.
Prologue/comment defect—the explanation accompanying the design/code language is incorrect, inexplicit or missing.
Requirements change defect—change in the requirements specification which is the direct and proximate reason for the required change in the design or code.
Performance improvement defect—code will not perform in the amount of time/space/CPU allocated.

Inspection Initiation

Inspections are initiated upon the completion of software design, either high or low level, or upon the completion of the first clean compilation of code. Developers should not spend any time doing desk-checking of the product if these conditions have been met.

There is always the feeling that doing desk-checking saves time, and minimizes exposure of one's mistakes. In most instances, no time is really saved since the inspections must be held and the inspection team will still have to review the material. In addition, in desk-checking the only eyes, experience, and talent being applied to the product are those of the author. Often, this is insufficient. The whole idea is to make good use of the variety of backgrounds, experiences, and talents of the entire team to get a full, rigorous, and thorough examination of the product. Having it done twice, or more, by the author does not really accomplish much other than to alleviate some imaginary wounds to his or her pride.

The negative exposure the author receives from the inspection process is not nearly as great as it might seem to be at the time of the inspection. The inspectors do not really care how many defects are found. They are there to do a job, do it professionally, and then return to their assigned tasks. They are not going to spread out upon the office gossip line the number of defects everyone has in his or her product. Even if they did, the number of inspections held is so great that the numbers of defects would soon blend in everyone's mind to the point of becoming meaningless.

The real negative exposure occurs when the inspections are not held properly. If the defects are not found in inspections, they must be found in test. If found in test, they are recorded on a PTR or other equivalent form and entered into some data base. Usually, everyone on the project has access to the data base and all of the errors assigned to one individual are there for everyone to see.

Inspection Prerequisites

The requirements for the proper conduct of an inspection are:

1. A team of technically competent, trained inspectors.
2. A trained moderator.
3. Proper planning and distribution of materials.
4. A good professional attitude.
5. Full preparation *prior* to the inspection meeting.
6. Completed design or cleanly compiled code.
7. Updated resource requirements.

The training required is that which should be provided by the SWQE department for moderators and inspectors. SWQE also should have a course available for managers describing the inspection process and how it can be used to help achieve their project and department goals.

Inspection Teams

Establishing the Team

The moderator has the responsibility for identifying the inspection team. In the day-to-day activity, the moderator may not always personally select/identify the team members, but the moderator is responsible for assuring that the team is identified, that the team make-up is proper, and that the required materials are distributed.

In establishing the team, care should be taken to pick those who are willing and able to contribute in a positive and professional manner. Care should also be taken to avoid overloading good inspectors. Unless unusual conditions dictate otherwise, no one should be involved in inspecting the work of others more than 25% of his or her time. Otherwise, the inspector will either not have time to properly prepare for an inspection or, conversely, will have his or her own work suffer as a result.

The inspection team should be limited to no more than five (5) people unless special conditions warrant an increase.

Inspection Team Members and Duties

Inspection team members include the moderator, the author, and, depending on which type of inspection, individuals from the system engineering organization, the software integration and test (SWIT) organization, other developers, and SWQE.

RESPONSIBILITIES OF THE MODERATOR

The moderator has certain well defined responsibilities during an inspection.

Prior to the Inspection Meeting

1. Completion of the SWQE training course.
2. Determination whether the entry criteria for this level of inspection has been met.
3. Work with author to establish the team membership:

   - System Engineering Personnel for I_0.
   - Possibly System Engineering for I_1 or I_2.
   - Developers with related design or interface knowledge.
   - SWIT personnel.
   - SWQE personnel.

4. Preview the material for conformance to standards.
5. Insure the team size and mix is proper.
6. Insure there are at least 5 working days of preparation.
7. Insure proper materials are distributed.

During the Inspection Meeting

1. Insure adequate attendance.
2. Insure adequate preparation; if not, postpone to a later time.
3. Lead the inspection meeting.

4. Log defects (if not already on inspectors' defect logs) and all open items.
5. Require reinspection for major defects, specification changes, or greater than 50 defects per 1000 source lines or code (KSLOC).

After the Inspection Meeting

1. Review results with author.
2. Provide manager with estimate of rework completion data.
3. Eliminate duplicate defect log entries and send inspection summary to SWQE.
4. Add inspection summary and detail report to the software quality notebook kept by the departments or authors.
5. Verify correction of all defect log entries.
6. Add completion notice to quality notebook and send copy to SWQE.
7. Log open items in software quality notebook or open issues log.

RESPONSIBILITIES OF THE AUTHOR

The author also has well-defined responsibilities, both before and after the inspection meeting.

Prior to the Inspection Meeting

1. Prepare material to address all inspection level checklist items. Include as appropriate:

   - PPS or PPS section.
   - High-level design.
   - Low-level design.
   - Clean compilation of code.
   - Defect logs.
   - Result of prior inspections.
   - Updated resource utilization estimates.

2. Review material with moderator for completeness.
3. Provide cover page with all included material identified:

   - Major function or process.
   - All referenced packages.
   - Procedures or modules listing.
   - SLOC count estimate vs. allocated resources.
   - CPU estimates vs. allocated resources.
   - Memory and I/O estimates vs. allocated resources.
   - Any flows which might aid the inspectors.

4. Prepare for overview if one is to be held.

5. Work with moderator to schedule time and place for meeting.
6. Work with moderator to establish team membership.
7. Produce materials distribution package in timely manner.

After the Inspection Meeting

1. Complete all rework required.
2. Verify fixes will correct problem and not cause any additional problem.
3. Verify to moderator that changes have been made.

RESPONSIBILITIES OF THE READER

1. Guide the team through the material during the meeting; paraphrase or verbalize the review material.
2. Present material with clarity and understanding.
3. Note any items difficult or impossible to understand.
4. Be able to tie-back to specification or design.
5. Fulfill normal inspector responsibilities.

RESPONSIBILITIES OF ALL INSPECTORS

1. Attend the SWQE training class.
2. Thoroughly review all material against the checklist.
3. Assure understanding of function; consult with author if necessary.
4. Record detected defects on *inspection defect log form* prior to the inspection meeting.
5. Record the inspection-meeting preparation time.

RESPONSIBILITIES OF THE MANAGER

While not a part of the inspection team itself, the manager has an important role in assuring the success of the inspection process. The manager's responsibilities are:

1. Establish schedules which allow adequate review time and resulting follow-up. Preparation and rework time must be scheduled with the same attention as the inspection meetings themselves.
2. Insure all team members are aware of inspection procedures.
3. Meet with moderator and author to review open items and obtain rework estimate.
4. Monitor individual inspection time, to

   - Insure sufficient inspection preparation time
   - Insure sufficient inspection meeting time
   - Insure particular individuals are not overloaded

5. Review SWQE defect summary report for defect trends and perform defect-trends analysis.

The programmer schedules should indicate when the actual rework from an inspection is complete, not when the inspection meeting is held. In addition, any open items which remain unresolved should prohibit the inspection from being considered complete, or the item should be logged in a highly visible action-item data base.

9.3 LESSONS LEARNED

After several years of performing inspections on a variety of different programs ranging in size from 60,000 lines to in excess of 4,000,000 lines, it has become evident that the most effective way to perform inspections is to utilize *only* personnel trained in the proper conduct of inspections. It is likewise clear that the only way inspections can be effectively utilized as a management development technique is to perform inspections on 100 percent of all new code developed. Experiments have been tried in which inspections are performed on a selected basis according to program size, complexity, or function, and even programmer experience. In each case, the conclusion reached is that the process should be applied to *all* code.

The Psychological Factor

In order to properly conduct inspections, programmers must be trained in the *psychology* of inspections as well as the mechanics of the process. This is particularly important to the success of a project because inspections, by their very nature, cause people to become defensive.

If people have a particular physical makeup which prevents them from becoming star athletes, they can accept this physical limitation. But in programming, the situation is somewhat different. No one wants to admit that someone else thinks more efficiently than he or she does. Every program that has been written is nothing but an extension of some person's mental process displayed on a printout.

There is a creative pride in the results which are subjected to inspection. The primary purpose of an inspection is to find every possible defect in the program. The working peers of the programmer are the ones who are engaged in this detailed search for defects. The roles people must play in the inspection process are critical to its success, but can lead to many difficulties if not properly understood. On the one hand, you have a programmer who takes great pride in the creative endeavor which is placed before the inspectors, and on the other hand, you have a group of associates who are attempting to use every available technique at their disposal to find as many flaws as they can.

Without the proper psychology being employed, the inspection process could be a total disaster. The personnel involved must understand the sensitivity of the author and the natural tendency to be defensive about one's own work. Without proper training, the inspectors will not possess the proper techniques, or sensitivity, for error detection necessary to allow the author to leave the inspection feeling as if he or she has been helped rather than crucified.

One particularly sensitive aspect of inspections is the recording and dissemination of the data. The results of every inspection should be recorded. The data which results from each of these inspections must be summarized and analyzed so that the most effective use can be made of the process. This means that information will be provided to the management team so that proper decisions can be made, yet it must be done in such a way that any individual programmer will not feel intimidated or degraded. Inspections will work only if the programmers feel at ease with the way the data collected is being used. This means that the resultant information must *not* be used by management as a club to hold over the head of any programmer.

Making Inspections Impersonal

To accomplish this, the data must be provided to management in such a way that the result of any individual inspection is not discernable in the summary data. With a properly prepared summary, the visibility into the inspection process which management requires to make proper decisions can be made available without having to repeat the result of any individual inspection. Managers should, therefore, not participate personally in the inspection process and should not attempt to obtain results of individual inspections.

If the programmers feel comfortable with the inspections, the benefits are significant. If they feel threatened by the process, the results are virtually worthless. In an experiment to test the impact of management's presence, managers were told to attend the inspections. As soon as the managers began to participate, the number of errors detected by the inspection team per 1000 source lines of code (KSLOC) decreased significantly and the number of recommendations and suggestions by the inspection team went up correspondingly. When the managers stopped attending, the suggestions went away and the recorded defects returned to normal. Analysis of the results indicated that this was not any sort of conscious conspiracy on the part of the programmers, but rather a clear example of human nature at work. Most people are reluctant to expose their own failures or those of their fellow workers to those who are in a position of authority over them.

Inspectors Limited to Small Groups of Peers

Inspections were designed to be entirely a peer-group process and should remain that way. As mentioned above, the number of people involved in any one inspection should also be limited. Groups of various sizes have been tried as experiments, and the conclusions reached indicate that an inspection should never be conducted by more than five individuals. The author of the product always participates. There should also be an attempt to provide a proper mix of disciplines at inspections, with the mix driven by the type of inspection conducted. In addition to the designer and the implementer, during design inspections the engineers who wrote the software specification should participate; during code inspections, the test engineers should participate.

Consistency of Data Collections

Data collection during inspections is critical to both the programmers and to the management team. Consistency in the data collected is likewise important. If a standard set of data collection forms is used, and if the process is conducted by those who have been properly trained, then a historical data base can be generated which will provide the management team with the necessary insight into how well the inspections are being conducted and, more important, the impact of any change in software technology which has been introduced. If each project is allowed to collect whatever data there was in whatever form happens to be at hand or convenient, then the availability to the management team of any sort of comparison between contracts or between time periods is out of the question. For valid comparisons, the necessity is a standard set of data collection forms, a standard format for data presentation, and a standard method for training programmers in how to conduct inspections.

9.4 MANAGEMENT CONTROL

Inspections provide a degree of visibility into the early development process which is particularly useful in making early schedule and milestone decisions. By proper use and interpretation of inspection data, managers are able to gain useful insight into the level of correctness of the developing system and can make such critical decisions as whether they should halt development, better formulate specifications, or cancel the project altogether.

The Problem of Software Specifications

One of the areas in software development most in need of attention is the generation of clear, unambiguous software specifications. Most specifications are written in prose form, and indeed most or all of the military requirements which govern the production of specifications are written on the assumption that the documents will be produced in prose form. It is generally felt, however, that specifications written in this way are more error-prone than specifications written in almost any other format. A software development manager confronted with specifications which are incomplete, inconsistent, vague, or inaccurate has no way of determining the real extent of the problem without some measure of its impact on the programmers. Through proper application of inspections, the specification document is examined along with the software design which is the primary object of the inspection. By an examination of not only the software design but also that which was the determinant of the design (the specification document), that defects inherent in the specification document itself can be detected and recorded.

If the specification defects are tracked as a separate and distinct item on the inspection report, multiple benefits result. The programmers will not feel that they are being criticized for having to make a change in the design or code because the error is in the specification itself, not in the programmer's thought process. The managers have a means of assessing the impact of the specification defects and are able to make critical management decisions effecting the workload of the programmers. If a given functional area of the specification has significant problems, and these problems are evident from the number of changes required in the software because of requirements problems, the manager will have sufficient information at his or her disposal to address the issue with higher-level management, or perhaps even halt work on one or more functional tasks until the requirements have been more fully determined. These decisions must be backed by hard evidence and cannot be made purely on the basis of instinct or programmer complaints.

Recording Inspections

Because of the rigor which is required by the proper conduct of inspections, the software defects are recorded, analyzed, and reported. The specification defects are counted and the changes necessary to correct the defects within the software, per KSLOC, are computed, thereby providing management with a measure of the modification density required in the software because of specification errors. This independent assessment of requirements defects is a useful aid to programmers as well.

Software defects are tracked by density and by type. The most common defect types are tracked independently and the density of each is determined separately from the total defect density. Each program module is separately inspected three times and the data for all three inspections recorded. The data for a given function is reported as a summary of the data of the module(s) performing that function, and the totality of functions is reported as a summary of the entire project. Examples are discussed in Section 9.6.

The management team can then assess the software by major function and by project. Different levels of management will examine the reports for different reasons. Program managers are primarily concerned with project summary information and with information comparing one project with another. Line managers are primarily concerned with the functional data for which they are responsible. Managers who are conversant with the inspection process know that it should only be used as a positive management tool and never to intimidate programmers.

Line managers examining inspection data look for functional areas which are particularly error-prone, and they look for specific types of problems at different levels of inspection. During design inspections, the most predominant areas of interest will necessarily be design errors and functional specification defects; therefore design defects should be uncovered at this inspection with a greater frequency per KSLOC than other defect types such as language errors or standards errors. During code inspections, it is expected that design errors will be minimal and that commentary or interface errors will predominate.

Benefit of Structured Languages

If a design language is not used on the project, and the design is done using flowcharts or other such devices, then inspections at the design stage will be virtually impossible and problems which should be detected at this stage will have to be uncovered during code inspections. Inspections, therefore, encourage the use of structured design languages such as PDL for business or scientific programs or Ada. Program managers from projects which have used inspections during several development efforts universally conclude that the use of structured design languages in combination with inspections is the most powerful set of development tools which can be employed to assure a high-quality product.

9.5 NATURAL NUMBERS OF PROGRAMMING

After several applications of inspections to a variety of projects and types of code, certain key parameters begin to project a stability in value which allows them to be key elements in the assessment of software quality during early development. These parameters may be considered part of *a set of the natural numbers of programming.* They are the key parameters which show not only the quality of the software under development but also the impact on the programming process of new software technologies.

The concept of natural numbers of programming is relatively new and undiscussed in the literature. Natural numbers of programming can be defined *as measures of software processes or products which are almost constants and are virtually independent of programming personnel, environments, or type of code.*

As an example, consider the measure of defects per KSLOC. This measure, when applied to new code development as opposed to modification of old code, will invariably reach a stable value after approximately 10,000 lines of code have been inspected and will remain almost unchanged no matter how large the code volume is thereafter.

When this phenomenon was first noticed, it was thought to be a peculiarity of the particular facility involved. After all, the same programmers and managers were doing the work on a group of somewhat similar projects. Therefore, some consistency was to be expected. The values for this measure were extremely consistent and remained so regardless of the type of code. It seemed to make no difference whether the programmers were writing algorithmic software, purely process software, or hardware diagnostic software. In each case, the defect density for new code fell within a very narrow range of values. This phenomenon was discussed with software quality assurance personnel at other facilities within the division and with those at a commercial division in another state. The results were the same: when the inspection process was applied rigorously to new code development, after approximately 10,000 lines of code were inspected the measure of defects per KSLOC settled out to within a very predictable tight range of values.

Other natural numbers appear to be evident in the products currently being developed. One such number has to do with the efficiency of the inspection process. If detected errors are separated into major and minor categories, "major" being a defect which affects the functional performance of the software and "minor" the remainder of the defects, and if the man-hours expended in the inspection process are recorded, the man-hours per major defect detected appear to be another natural number of programming. This measure also falls within very narrow limits, exhibiting the same sort of independence as seen in the previous measure discussed.

Although some of the natural numbers which are discovered may be proprietary, it is hoped that a sufficient number will be discovered so that investigation into this phenomenon will be worthwhile.

9.6 EXAMPLES

In the following examples, various results of the inspection process are shown and interpreted. In some cases, emphasis will be on the product itself, and in other cases on management use of the data results. Since subcontractors are given orientation in the inspection process, results are shown where subcontractors have applied the process themselves.

In Figure 9-1, the defects per thousand lines (K-lines) are shown for high-level inspections (I_0), for low level inspections (I_1), and for code inspections (I_2). The total values 23.52, 12,67, and 3.04 show a significant drop in defect density as the product proceeds through the different levels of inspection.

In this particular program, new technologies have been introduced for the development of software specifications. As a result, the defect density at the I_2 level is significantly lower than would have been expected without the introduction of this new specification technique. The design defects at the I_2 level are reduced to zero and the interface defects are likewise reduced to zero. The number of lines inspected is almost 18,000, and so these values have considerable credibility. The interface defects and the design and logic defects appear to have been largely removed during the design inspections. There is little indication from this data that managers should be concerned.

In Figure 9-2, which shows a different function from the same project, the same general trend is seen. However, the number of lines inspected is too low during the I_0 stage to allow any real conclusions, and it is borderline at the I_1 stage. Nonetheless, the same general trend appears to be present and one should anticipate a low level of defect density upon completion of the code inspection phase.

In Figure 9-3, again from the same project, the same trend is seen as far as defect density values are concerned. Closer examination of the I_2 data indicates that some attention should be given to this functional area in spite of its low defect density. The number of design defects, logic defects, data defects, language defects, and interface defects together with a significant number of changes due to changes in requirements (i.e. 37) indicate that this module is addressing an area for which the requirements are still in a state of considerable flux. The impact of this module, because of its expected number of interfaces with other modules, will have to be watched very closely.

In Figure 9-4, the function has just completed design inspection: the results show that the defect density is what would certainly be desired, and design defects are well below those seen in the previous figure. There is nothing exhibited which would be a cause for concern to the management or customers. The prologue and commentary defects have remained constant, but these defects have little or no

Total I0 Inspection Data Information:

Lines Inspected	=	4421	# Modules =	16		
Hours Preparation	=	74.50	Average Lines Per Preparation		Hour =	59.34
Hours Inspection	=	60.50	Average Lines Per Inspection		Hour =	73.07
Hours Total	=	135.00	Average Lines Per Total		Hour =	32.75
			Average Defects Identified Per Total		Hour =	0.77
Lines Rework Estimate	=	265	Which is 5.99% of the Lines Inspected			
Design	Defects =	33	Average Defects Per K-lines =	7.46		
Logic	Defects =	13	Average Defects Per K-lines =	2.94		
Language	Defects =	5	Average Defects Per K-lines =	1.13		
Standards	Defects =	2	Average Defects Per K-lines =	0.45		
Data	Defects =	12	Average Defects Per K-lines =	2.71		
Interface	Defects =	14	Average Defects Per K-lines =	3.17		
Ret.Code/Msg	Defects =	1	Average Defects Per K-lines =	0.23		
Prologue/Com	Defects =	18	Average Defects Per K-lines =	4.07		
Req. Change	Defects =	6	Average Defects Per K-lines =	1.36		
Other	Defects =	0	Average Defects Per K-lines =	0.0		
Total I0	Defects =	104	Average Defects Per K-lines =	23.52		

Total I1 Inspection Data Information:

Lines Inspected	=	11601	# Modules =	50		
Hours Preparation	=	72.00	Average Lines Per Preparation		Hour =	161.12
Hours Inspection	=	67.80	Average Lines Per Inspection		Hour =	171.11
Hours Total	=	139.80	Average Lines Per Total		Hour =	82.98
			Average Defects Identified Per Total		Hour =	1.05
Lines Rework Estimate	=	397	Which is 3.42% of the Lines Inspected			
Design	Defects =	36	Average Defects Per K-lines =	3.10		
Logic	Defects =	26	Average Defects Per K-lines =	2.24		
Language	Defects =	4	Average Defects Per K-lines =	0.34		
Standards	Defects =	3	Average Defects Per K-lines =	0.26		
Data	Defects =	28	Average Defects Per K-lines =	2.41		
Interface	Defects =	27	Average Defects Per K-lines =	2.33		
Ret.Code/Msg	Defects =	1	Average Defects Per K-lines =	0.09		
Prologue/Com	Defects =	18	Average Defects Per K-lines =	1.55		
Req. Change	Defects =	4	Average Defects Per K-lines =	0.34		
Other	Defects =	0	Average Defects Per K-lines =	0.0		
Total I1	Defects =	147	Average Defects Per K-lines =	12.67		

Total I2 Inspection Data Information:

Lines Inspected	=	17784	# Modules =	42		
Hours Preparation	=	33.50	Average Lines Per Preparation		Hour =	530.87
Hours Inspection	=	19.75	Average Lines Per Inspection		Hour =	900.46
Hours Total	=	53.25	Average Lines Per Total		Hour =	333.97
			Average Defects Identified Per Total		Hour =	1.01
Lines Rework Estimate	=	95	Which is 0.53% of the Lines Inspected			
Design	Defects =	0	Average Defects Per K-lines =	0.0		
Logic	Defects =	15	Average Defects Per K-lines =	0.84		
Language	Defects =	28	Average Defects Per K-lines =	1.57		
Standards	Defects =	0	Average Defects Per K-lines =	0.0		
Data	Defects =	7	Average Defects Per K-lines =	0.39		
Interface	Defects =	0	Average Defects Per K-lines =	0.0		
Ret.Code/Msg	Defects =	0	Average Defects Per K-lines =	0.0		
Prologue/Com	Defects =	3	Average Defects Per K-lines =	0.17		
Req. Change	Defects =	1	Average Defects Per K-lines =	0.06		
Other	Defects =	0	Average Defects Per K-lines =	0.0		
Total I2	Defects =	54	Average Defects Per K-lines =	3.04		

FIGURE 9-1. Inspection results—function *x*.

```
_____ Total I0 Inspection Data Information:

Lines Inspected          =     2005  # Modules =        6
Hours Preparation        =    10.00  Average Lines Per Preparation    Hour =   200.50
Hours Inspection         =     7.50  Average Lines Per Inspection     Hour =   267.33
Hours Total              =    17.50  Average Lines Per Total          Hour =   114.57
                                      Average Defects Identified Per Total  Hour =     1.43
Lines Rework Estimate    =       75  Which is 3.74% of the Lines Inspected
Design        Defects =           5  Average Defects Per K-lines =    2.49
Logic         Defects =           7  Average Defects Per K-lines =    3.49
Language      Defects =           2  Average Defects Per K-lines =    1.00
Standards     Defects =           0  Average Defects Per K-lines =     0.0
Data          Defects =           8  Average Defects Per K-lines =    3.99
Interface     Defects =           2  Average Defects Per K-lines =    1.00
Ret.Code/Msg  Defects =           0  Average Defects Per K-lines =     0.0
Prologue/Com  Defects =           1  Average Defects Per K-lines =    0.50
Req. Change   Defects =           0  Average Defects Per K-lines =     0.0
Other         Defects =           0  Average Defects Per K-lines =     0.0
Total I0      Defects =          25  Average Defects Per K-lines =   12.47

_____ Total I1 Inspection Data Information:

Lines Inspected          =     9202  # Modules =       60
Hours Preparation        =    64.00  Average Lines Per Preparation    Hour =   143.78
Hours Inspection         =    26.50  Average Lines Per Inspection     Hour =   347.25
Hours Total              =    90.50  Average Lines Per Total          Hour =   101.68
                                      Average Defects Identified Per Total  Hour =     0.48
Lines Rework Estimate    =      165  Which is 1.79% of the Lines Inspected
Design        Defects =           9  Average Defects Per K-lines =    0.98
Logic         Defects =           7  Average Defects Per K-lines =    0.76
Language      Defects =           0  Average Defects Per K-lines =     0.0
Standards     Defects =           0  Average Defects Per K-lines =     0.0
Data          Defects =           4  Average Defects Per K-lines =    0.43
Interface     Defects =           3  Average Defects Per K-lines =    0.33
Ret.Code/Msg  Defects =           0  Average Defects Per K-lines =     0.0
Prologue/Com  Defects =           8  Average Defects Per K-lines =    0.87
Req. Change   Defects =          12  Average Defects Per K-lines =    1.30
Other         Defects =           0  Average Defects Per K-lines =     0.0
Total I1      Defects =          43  Average Defects Per K-lines =    4.67

_____ Total I2 Inspection Data Information:

Lines Inspected          =        0  # Modules =        0
Hours Preparation        =      0.0  Average Lines Per Preparation    Hour =     0.0
Hours Inspection         =      0.0  Average Lines Per Inspection     Hour =     0.0
Hours Total              =      0.0  Average Lines Per Total          Hour =     0.0
                                      Average Defects Identified Per Total  Hour =     0.0
Lines Rework Estimate    =        0  Which is 0.0% of the Lines Inspected
Design        Defects =           0  Average Defects Per K-lines =     0.0
Logic         Defects =           0  Average Defects Per K-lines =     0.0
Language      Defects =           0  Average Defects Per K-lines =     0.0
Standards     Defects =           0  Average Defects Per K-lines =     0.0
Data          Defects =           0  Average Defects Per K-lines =     0.0
Interface     Defects =           0  Average Defects Per K-lines =     0.0
Ret.Code/Msg  Defects =           0  Average Defects Per K-lines =     0.0
Prologue/Com  Defects =           0  Average Defects Per K-lines =     0.0
Req. Change   Defects =           0  Average Defects Per K-lines =     0.0
Other         Defects =           0  Average Defects Per K-lines =     0.0
Total I2      Defects =           0  Average Defects Per K-lines =     0.0
```

FIGURE 9-2. Inspection results—function y.

_____ Total I0 Inspection Data Information:

Lines Inspected	=	46775	# Modules =	85		
Hours Preparation	=	340.50	Average Lines Per Preparation		Hour =	137.41
Hours Inspection	=	321.80	Average Lines Per Inspection		Hour =	145.35
Hours Total	=	662.20	Average Lines Per Total		Hour =	70.64
			Average Defects Identified Per Total		Hour =	1.26
Lines Rework Estimate	=	3377				
Lines Rework Estimate	=	7.22%				
Design	Defects =	170	Average Defects Per K-lines =	3.36		
Logic	Defects =	41	Average Defects Per K-lines =	0.88		
Language	Defects =	43	Average Defects Per K-lines =	0.92		
Standards	Defects =	23	Average Defects Per K-lines =	0.49		
Data	Defects =	43	Average Defects Per K-lines =	0.92		
Interface	Defects =	108	Average Defects Per K-lines =	2.31		
Ret.Code/Msg	Defects =	0	Average Defects Per K-lines =	0.0		
Prologue/Com	Defects =	32	Average Defects Per K-lines =	0.68		
Req. Change	Defects =	17	Average Defects Per K-lines =	0.36		
Other	Defects =	360	Average Defects Per K-lines =	7.70		

_____ Total I1 Inspection Data Information:

Lines Inspected	=	5632	# Modules =	12		
Hours Preparation	=	52.30	Average Lines Per Preparation		Hour =	107.69
Hours Inspection	=	113.75	Average Lines Per Inspection		Hour =	49.51
Hours Total	=	166.05	Average Lines Per Total		Hour =	33.92
			Average Defects Identified Per Total		Hour =	1.06
Lines Rework Estimate	=	545				
Lines Rework Estimate	=	9.68%				
Design	Defects =	45	Average Defects Per K-lines =	7.99		
Logic	Defects =	14	Average Defects Per K-lines =	2.49		
Language	Defects =	5	Average Defects Per K-lines =	0.89		
Standards	Defects =	12	Average Defects Per K-lines =	2.13		
Data	Defects =	5	Average Defects Per K-lines =	0.89		
Interface	Defects =	32	Average Defects Per K-lines =	5.68		
Ret.Code/Msg	Defects =	9	Average Defects Per K-lines =	1.60		
Prologue/Com	Defects =	35	Average Defects Per K-lines =	6.21		
Req. Change	Defects =	3	Average Defects Per K-lines =	0.53		
Other	Defects =	16	Average Defects Per K-lines =	2.84		

_____ Total I2 Inspection Data Information:

Lines Inspected	=	29831	# Modules =	90		
Hours Preparation	=	216.10	Average Lines Per Preparation		Hour =	138.04
Hours Inspection	=	149.25	Average Lines Per Inspection		Hour =	199.87
Hours Total	=	365.35	Average Lines Per Total		Hour =	81.65
			Average Defects Identified Per Total		Hour =	1.11
Lines Rework Estimate	=	2557				
Lines Rework Estimate	=	8.57%				
Design	Defects =	31	Average Defects Per K-lines =	1.04		
Logic	Defects =	60	Average Defects Per K-lines =	2.01		
Language	Defects =	29	Average Defects Per K-lines =	0.97		
Standards	Defects =	9	Average Defects Per K-lines =	0.30		
Data	Defects =	13	Average Defects Per K-lines =	0.44		
Interface	Defects =	9	Average Defects Per K-lines =	0.30		
Ret.Code/Msg	Defects =	0	Average Defects Per K-lines =	0.0		
Prologue/Com	Defects =	82	Average Defects Per K-lines =	2.75		
Req. Change	Defects =	37	Average Defects Per K-lines =	1.24		
Other	Defects =	137	Average Defects Per K-lines =	4.59		

FIGURE 9-3. Inspection results—possible requirements problem.

_____ Total I0 Inspection Data Information:

Lines Inspected	=	8443	# Modules =	47		
Hours Preparation	=	24.00	Average Lines Per Preparation		Hour =	351.79
Hours Inspection	=	30.00	Average Lines Per Inspection		Hour =	281.43
Hours Total	=	54.00	Average Lines Per Total		Hour =	156.35
			Average Defects Identified Per Total		Hour =	1.31
Lines Rework Estimate	=	210	Which is 2.49% of the Lines Inspected			
Design	Defects =	13	Average Defects Per K-lines =	1.54		
Logic	Defects =	20	Average Defects Per K-lines =	2.37		
Language	Defects =	0	Average Defects Per K-lines =	0.0		
Standards	Defects =	1	Average Defects Per K-lines =	0.12		
Data	Defects =	7	Average Defects Per K-lines =	0.83		
Interface	Defects =	15	Average Defects Per K-lines =	1.78		
Ret.Code/Msg	Defects =	0	Average Defects Per K-lines =	0.0		
Prologue/Com	Defects =	13	Average Defects Per K-lines =	1.54		
Req. Change	Defects =	2	Average Defects Per K-lines =	0.24		
Other	Defects =	0	Average Defects Per K-lines =	0.0		
Total I0	Defects =	71	Average Defects Per K-lines =	8.41		

_____ Total I1 Inspection Data Information:

Lines Inspected	=	9929	# Modules =	139		
Hours Preparation	=	13.00	Average Lines Per Preparation		Hour =	763.77
Hours Inspection	=	12.60	Average Lines Per Inspection		Hour =	788.02
Hours Total	=	25.60	Average Lines Per Total		Hour =	387.85
			Average Defects Identified Per Total		Hour =	2.03
Lines Rework Estimate	=	144	Which is 1.45% of the Lines Inspected			
Design	Defects =	9	Average Defects Per K-lines =	0.91		
Logic	Defects =	13	Average Defects Per K-lines =	1.31		
Language	Defects =	4	Average Defects Per K-lines =	0.40		
Standards	Defects =	0	Average Defects Per K-lines =	0.0		
Data	Defects =	5	Average Defects Per K-lines =	0.50		
Interface	Defects =	2	Average Defects Per K-lines =	0.20		
Ret.Code/Msg	Defects =	1	Average Defects Per K-lines =	0.10		
Prologue/Com	Defects =	13	Average Defects Per K-lines =	1.31		
Req. Change	Defects =	5	Average Defects Per K-lines =	0.50		
Other	Defects =	0	Average Defects Per K-lines =	0.0		
Total I1	Defects =	52	Average Defects Per K-lines =	5.24		

_____ Total I2 Inspection Data Information:

Lines Inspected	=	0	# Modules =	0		
Hours Preparation	=	0.0	Average Lines Per Preparation		Hour =	0.0
Hours Inspection	=	0.0	Average Lines Per Inspection		Hour =	0.0
Hours Total	=	0.0	Average Lines Per Total		Hour =	0.0
			Average Defects Identified Per Total		Hour =	0.0
Lines Rework Estimate	=	0	Which is 0.0% of the Lines Inspected			
Design	Defects =	0	Average Defects Per K-lines =	0 0		
Logic	Defects =	0	Average Defects Per K-lines =	0.0		
Language	Defects =	0	Average Defects Per K-lines =	0.0		
Standards	Defects =	0	Average Defects Per K-lines =	0.0		
Data	Defects =	0	Average Defects Per K-lines =	0.0		
Interface	Defects =	0	Average Defects Per K-lines =	0.0		
Ret.Code/Msg	Defects =	0	Average Defects Per K-lines =	0.0		
Prologue/Com	Defects =	0	Average Defects Per K-lines =	0.0		
Req. Change	Defects =	0	Average Defects Per K-lines =	0.0		
Other	Defects =	0	Average Defects Per K-lines =	0.0		
Total I2	Defects =	0	Average Defects Per K-lines =	0.0		

FIGURE 9-4. Inspection results—no real concern.

impact on functional performance even though they may have an impact on the eventual maintainability of the product.

In Figure 9-5, we see another example of a function which is in relatively good condition, the only real area drawing attention being that of the interface defects. They have gone up from 10 to 13 in going from the I_1 to the I_2 stage. Although there have been few requirements changes (3), the increase in interface errors would indicate the possibility, though clearly not the certainty, of changes in other areas causing interface errors in this particular function. It is something which bears watching, but is not cause for real concern at this time. The function should be watched carefully to see how the numbers settle out as the number of lines of code inspected reaches the 10,000 cut-off point. At that time, the manager will have a much better idea of what action, if any, is necessary. Any action taken should be done before the code goes under configuration management and into the test program.

In Figure 9-6, the function has no data for the I_0 design inspection, but the function has gone through the I_1 and I_2 inspections. The volume of code is such that the numbers are credible and the results are quite encouraging. Design defects have dropped from 1.7 per K-lines to 0.38 per K-lines. Interface defects are minimal and requirements changes have dropped from 21 to 0. It is significant that this function has been done by a subcontractor who has just recently received orientation in the inspection process but whose programmers have accepted the process at face value instead of exhibiting resistance to a new technique, as is often the case. There is no I_0 data shown because it was done by the prime contractor prior to passing the task to the subcontractor.

Figure 9-7 is another example of a function which appears to be in rather good shape, with low error density, and with a significant drop in design errors. It has been also done by a subcontractor. Again, a slight rise in requirements change errors is noted, but the increase is quite small and no cause for real concern at this time.

All of the foregoing are examples of modules which are in relatively good shape, and all are on a project which has initiated the use of a structured language to generate a significant portion of the requirements. It is the first time that has been tried and the impact on the project as a whole can be seen in the summary chart for the entire project, Figure 9-8. In this figure, the defect density is approximately one-third, at the I_2 stage, of what would be considered a natural number utilizing the technologies previously employed. This project is approximately 4-percent complete, but the final number should not be more than twice the current figure, even when all of the code is incorporated, including the code written to specifications which are not generated using the new technology. If so, this will mean a 30-percent decrease in defect density at the I_2 stage by application of this new documentation technique, even though the system itself is using an architecture new to this facility.

The next two figures will illustrate the necessity of looking at *all* of the data presented, not just one number or line of data.

Figure 9-9 shows a very high-defect density at the I_0 stage and at the I_1 stage. This

```
_____  Total I0 Inspection Data Information:

Lines Inspected          =    1500   # Modules =          8
Hours Preparation        =   41.00   Average Lines Per Preparation    Hour =    36.59
Hours Inspection         =   13.50   Average Lines Per Inspection     Hour =   111.11
Hours Total              =   54.50   Average Lines Per Total          Hour =    27.52
                                      Average Defects Identified Per Total  Hour =    0.37
Lines Rework Estimate    =     150   Which is 10.00% of the Lines Inspected
Design         Defects =        13   Average Defects Per K-lines =     8.67
Logic          Defects =         0   Average Defects Per K-lines =     0.0
Language       Defects =         0   Average Defects Per K-lines =     0.0
Standards      Defects =         6   Average Defects Per K-lines =     4.00
Data           Defects =         0   Average Defects Per K-lines =     0.0
Interface      Defects =         0   Average Defects Per K-lines =     0.0
Ret.Code/Msg   Defects =         0   Average Defects Per K-lines =     0.0
Prologue/Com   Defects =         1   Average Defects Per K-lines =     0.67
Req. Change    Defects =         0   Average Defects Per K-lines =     0.0
Other          Defects =         0   Average Defects Per K-lines =     0.0
Total I0       Defects =        20   Average Defects Per K-lines =    13.33
                                   ___  Total I1 Inspection Data Information:

Lines Inspected          =   12078   # Modules =         46
Hours Preparation        =  119.00   Average Lines Per Preparation    Hour =   101.50
Hours Inspection         =   81.30   Average Lines Per Inspection     Hour =   148.56
Hours Total              =  200.30   Average Lines Per Total          Hour =   .60.30
                                      Average Defects Identified Per Total  Hour =    0.39
Lines Rework Estimate    =     224   Which is 1.85% of the Lines Inspected
Design         Defects =        11   Average Defects Per K-lines =     0.91
Logic          Defects =         5   Average Defects Per K-lines =     0.41
Language       Defects =         3   Average Defects Per K-lines =     0.25
Standards      Defects =         8   Average Defects Per K-lines =     0.66
Data           Defects =         5   Average Defects Per K-lines =     0.41
Interface      Defects =        10   Average Defects Per K-lines =     0.83
Ret.Code/Msg   Defects =         0   Average Defects Per K-lines =     0.0
Prologue/Com   Defects =        24   Average Defects Per K-lines =     1.99
Req. Change    Defects =         7   Average Defects Per K-lines =     0.58
Other          Defects =         5   Average Defects Per K-lines =     0.41
Total I1       Defects =        78   Average Defects Per K-lines =     6.46
_____  Total I2 Inspection Data Information:

Lines Inspected          =    5427   # Modules =         44
Hours Preparation        =   39.50   Average Lines Per Preparation    Hour =   137.39
Hours Inspection         =   36.00   Average Lines Per Inspection     Hour =   150.75
Hours Total              =   75.50   Average Lines Per Total          Hour =    71.88
                                      Average Defects Identified Per Total  Hour =    0.29
Lines Rework Estimate    =     110   Which is 2.03% of the Lines Inspected
Design         Defects =         1   Average Defects Per K-lines =     0.18
Logic          Defects =         2   Average Defects Per K-lines =     0.37
Language       Defects =         0   Average Defects Per K-lines =     0.0
Standards      Defects =         0   Average Defects Per K-lines =     0.0
Data           Defects =         0   Average Defects Per K-lines =     0.0
Interface      Defects =        13   Average Defects Per K-lines =     2.40
Ret.Code/Msg   Defects =         0   Average Defects Per K-lines =     0.0
Prologue/Com   Defects =         3   Average Defects Per K-lines =     0.55
Req. Change    Defects =         3   Average Defects Per K-lines =     0.55
Other          Defects =         0   Average Defects Per K-lines =     0.0
Total I2       Defects =        22   Average Defects Per K-lines =     4.05
```

FIGURE 9-5. Inspection results—possible interface problem.

_____ Total I0 Inspection Data Information:

Lines Inspected	=	0	# Modules =	0		
Hours Preparation	=	0.0	Average Lines Per Preparation	Hour =		0.0
Hours Inspection	=	0.0	Average Lines Per Inspection	Hour =		0.0
Hours Total	=	0.0	Average Lines Per Total	Hour =		0.0
			Average Defects Identified Per Total	Hour =		0.0
Lines Rework Estimate	=	0	Which is 0.0% of the Lines Inspected			
Design	Defects =	0	Average Defects Per K-lines =	0.0		
Logic	Defects =	0	Average Defects Per K-lines =	0.0		
Language	Defects =	0	Average Defects Per K-lines =	0.0		
Standards	Defects =	0	Average Defects Per K-lines =	0.0		
Data	Defects =	0	Average Defects Per K-lines =	0.0		
Interface	Defects =	0	Average Defects Per K-lines =	0.0		
Ret.Code/Msg	Defects =	0	Average Defects Per K-lines =	0.0		
Prologue/Com	Defects =	0	Average Defects Per K-lines =	0.0		
Req. Change	Defects =	0	Average Defects Per K-lines =	0.0		
Other	Defects =	0	Average Defects Per K-lines =	0.0		
Total I0	Defects =	0	Average Defects Per K-lines =	0.0		

_____ Total I1 Inspection Data Information:

Lines Inspected	=	54161	# Modules =	397		
Hours Preparation	=	283.75	Average Lines Per Preparation	Hour =		190.88
Hours Inspection	=	210.50	Average Lines Per Inspection	Hour =		257.30
Hours Total	=	494.25	Average Lines Per Total	Hour =		109.58
			Average Defects Identified Per Total	Hour =		2.12
Lines Rework Estimate	=	1445	Which is 2.67% of the Lines Inspected			
Design	Defects =	92	Average Defects Per K-lines =	1.70		
Logic	Defects =	163	Average Defects Per K-lines =	3.01		
Language	Defects =	56	Average Defects Per K-lines =	1.03		
Standards	Defects =	11	Average Defects Per K-lines =	0.20		
Data	Defects =	342·	Average Defects Per K-lines =	6.31		
Interface	Defects =	1	Average Defects Per K-lines =	0.02		
Ret.Code/Msg	Defects =	0	Average Defects Per K-lines =	0.0		
Prologue/Com	Defects =	362	Average Defects Per K-lines =	6.63		
Req. Change	Defects =	21	Average Defects Per K-lines =	0.39		
Other	Defects =	0	Average Defects Per K-lines =	0.0		
Total I1	Defects =	1043	Average Defects Per K-lines =	19.35		

_____ Total I2 Inspection Data Information:

Lines Inspected	=	20780	# Modules =	402		
Hours Preparation	=	38.75	Average Lines Per Preparation	Hour =		536.26
Hours Inspection	=	41.75	Average Lines Per Inspection	Hour =		497.72
Hours Total	=	80.50	Average Lines Per Total	Hour =		258.14
			Average Defects Identified Per Total	Hour =		0.40
Lines Rework Estimate	=	170	Which is 0.82% of the Lines Inspected			
Design	Defects =	8	Average Defects Per K-lines =	0.38		
Logic	Defects =	8	Average Defects Per K-lines =	0.38		
Language	Defects =	4	Average Defects Per K-lines =	0.19		
Standards	Defects =	0	Average Defects Per K-lines =	0.0		
Data	Defects =	3	Average Defects Per K-lines =	0.14		
Interface	Defects =	0	Average Defects Per K-lines =	0.0		
Ret.Code/Msg	Defects =	1	Average Defects Per K-lines =	0.05		
Prologue/Com	Defects =	8	Average Defects Per K-lines =	0.38		
Req. Change	Defects =	0	Average Defects Per K-lines =	0.0		
Other	Defects =	0	Average Defects Per K-lines =	0.0		
Total I2	Defects =	32	Average Defects Per K-lines =	1.54		

FIGURE 9-6. Inspection results—subcontractor team.

_____ Total I0 Inspection Data Information:

Lines Inspected	=	0	# Modules =	0		
Hours Preparation	=	0.0	Average Lines Per Preparation	Hour =	0.0	
Hours Inspection	=	0.0	Average Lines Per Inspection	Hour =	0.0	
Hours Total	=	0.0	Average Lines Per Total	Hour =	0.0	
			Average Defects Identified Per Total	Hour =	0.0	
Lines Rework Estimate	=	0	Which is 0.0% of the Lines Inspected			
Design	Defects =	0	Average Defects Per K-lines =	0.0		
Logic	Defects =	0	Average Defects Per K-lines =	0.0		
Language	Defects =	0	Average Defects Per K-lines =	0.0		
Standards	Defects =	0	Average Defects Per K-lines =	0.0		
Data	Defects =	0	Average Defects Per K-lines =	0.0		
Interface	Defects =	0	Average Defects Per K-lines =	0.0		
Ret.Code/Msg	Defects =	0	Average Defects Per K-lines =	0.0		
Prologue/Com	Defects =	0	Average Defects Per K-lines =	0.0		
Req. Change	Defects =	0	Average Defects Per K-lines =	0.0		
Other	Defects =	0	Average Defects Per K-lines =	0.0		
Total I0	Defects =	0	Average Defects Per K-lines =	0.0		

_____ Total I1 Inspection Data Information:

Lines Inspected	=	69013	# Modules =	424		
Hours Preparation	=	126.25	Average Lines Per Preparation	Hour =	546.64	
Hours Inspection	=	131.95	Average Lines Per Inspection	Hour =	523.02	
Hours Total	=	258.20	Average Lines Per Total	Hour =	267.28	
			Average Defects Identified Per Total	Hour =	1.19	
Lines Rework Estimate	=	2321	Which is 3.36% of the Lines Inspected			
Design	Defects =	20	Average Defects Per K-lines =	0.29		
Logic	Defects =	58	Average Defects Per K-lines =	0.84		
Language	Defects =	15	Average Defects Per K-lines =	0.22		
Standards	Defects =	4	Average Defects Per K-lines =	0.06		
Data	Defects =	50	Average Defects Per K-lines =	0.72		
Interface	Defects =	0	Average Defects Per K-lines =	0.0		
Ret.Code/Msg	Defects =	2	Average Defects Per K-lines =	0.03		
Prologue/Com	Defects =	156	Average Defects Per K-lines =	2.26		
Req. Change	Defects =	2	Average Defects Per K-lines =	0.03		
Other	Defects =	0	Average Defects Per K-lines =	0.0		
Total I1	Defects =	307	Average Defects Per K-lines =	4.45		

_____ Total I2 Inspection Data Information:

Lines Inspected	=	28833	# Modules =	338		
Hours Preparation	=	29.50	Average Lines Per Preparation	Hour =	977.39	
Hours Inspection	=	27.50	Average Lines Per Inspection	Hour =	1048.47	
Hours Total	=	57.00	Average Lines Per Total	Hour =	505.84	
			Average Defects Identified Per Total	Hour =	0.88	
Lines Rework Estimate	=	127	Which is 0.44% of the Lines Inspected			
Design	Defects =	0	Average Defects Per K-lines =	0.0		
Logic	Defects =	0	Average Defects Per K-lines =	0.0		
Language	Defects =	41	Average Defects Per K-lines =	1.42		
Standards	Defects =	1	Average Defects Per K-lines =	0.03		
Data	Defects =	0	Average Defects Per K-lines =	0.0		
Interface	Defects =	0	Average Defects Per K-lines =	0.0		
Ret.Code/Msg	Defects =	0	Average Defects Per K-lines =	0.0		
Prologue/Com	Defects =	4	Average Defects Per K-lines =	0.14		
Req. Change	Defects =	4	Average Defects Per K-lines =	0.14		
Other	Defects =	0	Average Defects Per K-lines =	0.0		
Total I2	Defects =	50	Average Defects Per K-lines =	1.73		

FIGURE 9-7. Inspection results—subcontractor team 2.

Total I0 Inspection Data Information:

Lines Inspected	=	193352	# Modules =	694		
Hours Preparation	=	1417.60	Average Lines Per Preparation		Hour =	136.39
Hours Inspection	=	1348.70	Average Lines Per Inspection		Hour =	143.36
Hours Total	=	2766.30	Average Lines Per Total		Hour =	69.90
			Average Defects Identified Per Total		Hour =	0.69
Lines Rework Estimate	=	7810	Which is 4.04% of the Lines Inspected			
Design	Defects =	479	Average Defects Per K-lines =	2.48		
Logic	Defects =	145	Average Defects Per K-lines =	0.75		
Language	Defects =	101	Average Defects Per K-lines =	0.52		
Standards	Defects =	47	Average Defects Per K-lines =	0.24		
Data	Defects =	110	Average Defects Per K-lines =	0.57		
Interface	Defects =	242	Average Defects Per K-lines =	1.25		
Ret.Code/Msg	Defects =	7	Average Defects Per K-lines =	0.04		
Prologue/Com	Defects =	580	Average Defects Per K-lines =	3.00		
Req. Change	Defects =	162	Average Defects Per K-lines =	0.84		
Other	Defects =	32	Average Defects Per K-lines =	0.17		
Total I0	Defects =	1905	Average Defects Per K-lines =	9.85		

Total I1 Inspection Data Information:

Lines Inspected	=	321197	# Modules =	2087		
Hours Preparation	=	1807.50	Average Lines Per Preparation		Hour =	177.70
Hours Inspection	=	1311.00	Average Lines Per Inspection		Hour =	245.00
Hours Total	=	3118.50	Average Lines Per Total		Hour =	103.00
			Average Defects Identified Per Total		Hour =	1.36
Lines Rework Estimate	=	12440	Which is 3.87% of the Lines Inspected			
Design	Defects =	723	Average Defects Per K-lines =	2.25		
Logic	Defects =	723	Average Defects Per K-lines =	2.25		
Language	Defects =	290	Average Defects Per K-lines =	0.90		
Standards	Defects =	146	Average Defects Per K-lines =	0.45		
Data	Defects =	734	Average Defects Per K-lines =	2.29		
Interface	Defects =	172	Average Defects Per K-lines =	0.54		
Ret.Code/Msg	Defects =	8	Average Defects Per K-lines =	0.02		
Prologue/Com	Defects =	1291	Average Defects Per K-lines =	4.02		
Req. Change	Defects =	135	Average Defects Per K-lines =	0.42		
Other	Defects =	5	Average Defects Per K-lines =	0.02		
Total I1	Defects =	4227	Average Defects Per K-lines =	13.16		

Total I2 Inspection Data Information:

Lines Inspected	=	101427	# Modules =	948		
Hours Preparation	=	288.75	Average Lines Per Preparation		Hour =	351.26
Hours Inspection	=	220.25	Average Lines Per Inspection		Hour =	460.51
Hours Total	=	509.00	Average Lines Per Total		Hour =	199.27
			Average Defects Identified Per Total		Hour =	0.90
Lines Rework Estimate	=	1301	Which is 1.28% of the Lines Inspected			
Design	Defects =	39	Average Defects Per K-lines =	0.38		
Logic	Defects =	109	Average Defects Per K-lines =	1.07		
Language	Defects =	107	Average Defects Per K-lines =	1.05		
Standards	Defects =	20	Average Defects Per K-lines =	0.20		
Data	Defects =	51	Average Defects Per K-lines =	0.50		
Interface	Defects =	23	Average Defects Per K-lines =	0.23		
Ret.Code/Msg	Defects =	1	Average Defects Per K-lines =	0.01		
Prologue/Com	Defects =	89	Average Defects Per K-lines =	0.88		
Req. Change	Defects =	13	Average Defects Per K-lines =	0.13		
Other	Defects =	5	Average Defects Per K-lines =	0.05		
Total I2	Defects =	457	Average Defects Per K-lines =	4.51		

FIGURE 9-8. Inspection results—entire project summary.

```
————————————————————————————  Total I0 Inspection Data Information:

Lines Inspected         =     814  # Modules =        17
Hours Preparation       =   12.25  Average Lines Per Preparation    Hour =   66.45
Hours Inspection        =    9.00  Average Lines Per Inspection     Hour =   90.44
Hours Total             =   21.25  Average Lines Per Total          Hour =   38.31
                                   Average Defects Identified Per Total  Hour =    2.12
Lines Rework Estimate   =     110  Which is 13.51% of the Lines Inspected
Design        Defects =     7  Average Defects Per K-lines =    8.60
Logic         Defects =     4  Average Defects Per K-lines =    4.91
Language      Defects =    27  Average Defects Per K-lines =   33.17
Standards     Defects =     0  Average Defects Per K-lines =    0.0
Data          Defects =     0  Average Defects Per K-lines =    0.0
Interface     Defects =     7  Average Defects Per K-lines =    8.60
Ret.Code/Msg  Defects =     0  Average Defects Per K-lines =    0.0
Prologue/Com  Defects =     0  Average Defects Per K-lines =    0.0
Req. Change   Defects =     0  Average Defects Per K-lines =    0.0
Other         Defects =     0  Average Defects Per K-lines =    0.0
Total I0      Defects =    45  Average Defects Per K-lines =   55.28
————————————————————————————  Total I1 Inspection Data Information:

Lines Inspected         =    4535  # Modules =        13
Hours Preparation       =   73.00  Average Lines Per Preparation    Hour =   62.12
Hours Inspection        =   19.75  Average Lines Per Inspection     Hour =  229.62
Hours Total             =   92.75  Average Lines Per Total          Hour =   48.89
                                   Average Defects Identified Per Total  Hour =    1.98
Lines Rework Estimate   =     458  Which is 10.10% of the Lines Inspected
Design        Defects =    36  Average Defects Per K-lines =    7.94
Logic         Defects =    25  Average Defects Per K-lines =    5.51
Language      Defects =    51  Average Defects Per K-lines =   11.25
Standards     Defects =     9  Average Defects Per K-lines =    1.98
Data          Defects =     2  Average Defects Per K-lines =    0.44
Interface     Defects =     2  Average Defects Per K-lines =    0.44
Ret.Code/Msg  Defects =     1  Average Defects Per K-lines =    0.22
Prologue/Com  Defects =    56  Average Defects Per K-lines =   12.35
Req. Change   Defects =     2  Average Defects Per K-lines =    0.44
Other         Defects =     0  Average Defects Per K-lines =    0.0
Total I1      Defects =   184  Average Defects Per K-lines =   40.57
————————————————————————————  Total I2 Inspection Data Information:

Lines Inspected         =       0  # Modules =         0
Hours Preparation       =     0.0  Average Lines Per Preparation    Hour =    0.0
Hours Inspection        =     0.0  Average Lines Per Inspection     Hour =    0.0
Hours Total             =     0.0  Average Lines Per Total          Hour =    0.0
                                   Average Defects Identified Per Total  Hour =    0.0
Lines Rework Estimate   =       0  Which is 0.0% of the Lines Inspected
Design        Defects =     0  Average Defects Per K-lines =    0.0
Logic         Defects =     0  Average Defects Per K-lines =    0.0
Language      Defects =     0  Average Defects Per K-lines =    0.0
Standards     Defects =     0  Average Defects Per K-lines =    0.0
Data          Defects =     0  Average Defects Per K-lines =    0.0
Interface     Defects =     0  Average Defects Per K-lines =    0.0
Ret.Code/Msg  Defects =     0  Average Defects Per K-lines =    0.0
Prologue/Com  Defects =     0  Average Defects Per K-lines =    0.0
Req. Change   Defects =     0  Average Defects Per K-lines =    0.0
Other         Defects =     0  Average Defects Per K-lines =    0.0
Total I2      Defects =     0  Average Defects Per K-lines =    0.0
```

FIGURE 9-9. Inspection results—reinspection recommended.

information certainly does make a manager take notice, but there is no real cause for panic, at least not yet. The I_0 data is based on only 814 lines inspected. This is certainly not enough to merit any conclusions. It is too early to take any decisive action. At the I_1 stage, the volume of data inspected, 4535 lines, is more significant, but still about half of the volume required before any drastic action based on the results should be taken. If the volume doubles, and no new errors are detected, the defect density will be near normal values for a standard project. Since the likelihood that no new errors will be detected during inspection of the next 4535 lines is slim, the probability is that the function is going to need some attention, especially since the problems do not seem to be of the interface or requirements category. The manager, as a minimum, should insist on reinspections after the required corrections are made.

In Figure 9-10, we again have an example of a very high-defect density, but the volume inspected is so low at this time that no conclusions can be reached. The data has no real significance.

In Figure 9-11, an example is shown of a function which has a defect density significantly higher than is acceptable. The defects are spread throughout the range of defect types; at the I_2 stage there is still a high density of design defects being discovered. Clearly, this is a function which is having some real problems and needs a lot of help and attention. If this function is going to survive even a rudimentary test, a lot of rework is required and reinspections should be mandated. This function, even though it has theoretically gone through inspection, is not ready to proceed to the next phase. Any program manager who would push this function into test just because of schedule or other pressures is making a very serious mistake. The passage to the next phase is only compounding the problem due to the effort, manpower, cost, and schedule impact of correcting the defects *after* the system is under configuration management instead of *before*—while still in the inspection stage.

At the inspection stage, the program manager has visibility, a workable level of control, and the opportunity and time to take necessary action. He or she also has a means of measuring the impact of corrective action. When used alone, or in conjunction with other quality and reliability measurements, the inspection process is an extremely valuable tool for early defect detection and removal and for gaining valuable visibility into a system in real time.

9.7 IMPACT ON TEST RESULTS

The test program on a real-time system is usually conducted in multiple stages, moving from integration to final system test. The impact on the test results, and the level of control achieved during test due to inspections can be seen in a very simple way. If the record of all test problem reports is tracked over time, and if a cumulative graph beginning at the start of integration testing and ending with acceptance test is maintained for the errors, the result is an error detection rate chart showing the rate at which errors are being detected at any one point in time and for the time since the test's beginning. This rate chart, such as the one shown

```
_____ Total I0 Inspection Data Information:

Lines Inspected        =      179  # Modules =           6
Hours Preparation      =    12.00  Average Lines Per Preparation      Hour =   14.92
Hours Inspection       =    17.50  Average Lines Per Inspection       Hour =   10.23
Hours Total            =    29.50  Average Lines Per Total            Hour =    6.07
                                   Average Defects Identified Per Total  Hour =  0.51
Lines Rework Estimate  =       45  Which is 25.14% of the Lines Inspected
Design       Defects = 7  Average Defects Per K-lines =   39.11
Logic        Defects = 2  Average Defects Per K-lines =   11.17
Language     Defects = 0  Average Defects Per K-lines =    0.0
Standards    Defects = 0  Average Defects Per K-lines =    0.0
Data         Defects = 2  Average Defects Per K-lines =   11.17
Interface    Defects = 1  Average Defects Per K-lines =    5.59
Ret.Code/Msg Defects = 0  Average Defects Per K-lines =    0.0
Prologue/Com Defects = 0  Average Defects Per K-lines =    0.0
Req. Change  Defects = 3  Average Defects Per K-lines =   16.76
Other        Defects = 0  Average Defects Per K-lines =    0.0
Total I0     Defects = 15 Average Defects Per K-lines =   83.80
_____ Total I1 Inspection Data Information:

Lines Inspected        =        0  # Modules =           0
Hours Preparation      =      0.0  Average Lines Per Preparation      Hour =    0.0
Hours Inspection       =      0.0  Average Lines Per Inspection       Hour =    0.0
Hours Total            =      0.0  Average Lines Per Total            Hour =    0.0
                                   Average Defects Identified Per Total  Hour =  0.0
Lines Rework Estimate  =        0  Which is 0.0% of the Lines Inspected
Design       Defects = 0  Average Defects Per K-lines =    0.0
Logic        Defects = 0  Average Defects Per K-lines =    0.0
Language     Defects = 0  Average Defects Per K-lines =    0.0
Standards    Defects = 0  Average Defects Per K-lines =    0.0
Data         Defects = 0  Average Defects Per K-lines =    0.0
Interface    Defects = 0  Average Defects Per K-lines =    0.0
Ret.Code/Msg Defects = 0  Average Defects Per K-lines =    0.0
Prologue/Com Defects = 0  Average Defects Per K-lines =    0.0
Req. Change  Defects = 0  Average Defects Per K-lines =    0.0
Other        Defects = 0  Average Defects Per K-lines =    0.0
Total I1     Defects = 0  Average Defects Per K-lines =    0.0
_____ Total I2 Inspection Data Information:

Lines Inspected        =        0  # Modules =           0
Hours Preparation      =      0.0  Average Lines Per Preparation      Hour =    0.0
Hours Inspection       =      0.0  Average Lines Per Inspection       Hour =    0.0
Hours Total            =      0.0  Average Lines Per Total            Hour =    0.0
                                   Average Defects Identified Per Total  Hour =  0.0
Lines Rework Estimate  =        0  Which is 0.0% of the Lines Inspected
Design       Defects = 0  Average Defects Per K-lines =    0.0
Logic        Defects = 0  Average Defects Per K-lines =    0.0
Language     Defects = 0  Average Defects Per K-lines =    0.0
Standards    Defects = 0  Average Defects Per K-lines =    0.0
Data         Defects = 0  Average Defects Per K-lines =    0.0
Interface    Defects = 0  Average Defects Per K-lines =    0.0
Ret.Code/Msg Defects = 0  Average Defects Per K-lines =    0.0
Prologue/Com Defects = 0  Average Defects Per K-lines =    0.0
Req. Change  Defects = 0  Average Defects Per K-lines =    0.0
Other        Defects = 0  Average Defects Per K-lines =    0.0
Total I2     Defects = 0  Average Defects Per K-lines =    0.0
```

FIGURE 9-10. Inspection results—insufficient data.

Total I0 Inspection Data Information:

Lines Inspected	=	54220	# Modules =		187		
Hours Preparation	=	302.23	Average Lines Per Preparaticn			Hour =	179.40
Hours Inspection	=	351.11	Average Lines Per Inspection			Hour =	154.42
Hours Total	=	653.35	Average Lines Per Total			Hour =	82.99
			Average Defects Identified Per Total			Hour =	1.83
Lines Rework Estimate	=	5120	Which is 9.44% of the Lines Inspected				
Design	Defects =	315	Average Defects Per K-lines =		5.81		
Logic	Defects =	31	Average Defects Per K-lines =		0.57		
Language	Defects =	84	Average Defects Per K-lines =		1.55		
Standards	Defects =	41	Average Defects Per K-lines =		0.76		
Data	Defects =	86	Average Defects Per K-lines =		1.59		
Interface	Defects =	151	Average Defects Per K-lines =		2.78		
Ret.Code/Msg	Defects =	0	Average Defects Per K-lines =		0.0		
Prologue/Com	Defects =	157	Average Defects Per K-lines =		2.90		
Req. Change	Defects =	14	Average Defects Per K-lines =		0.26		
Other	Defects =	318	Average Defects Per K-lines =		5.86		
Total I0	Defects =	1197	Average Defects Per K-lines =		22.08		

Total I1 Inspection Data Information:

Lines Inspected	=	64311	# Modules =		1354		
Hours Preparation	=	651.00	Average Lines Per Preparation			Hour =	99.56
Hours Inspection	=	581.80	Average Lines Per Inspection			Hour =	111.40
Hours Total	=	1232.80	Average Lines Per Total			Hour =	52.57
			Average Defects Identified Per Total			Hour =	3.08
Lines Rework Estimate	=	400	Which is 0.62% of the Lines Inspected				
Design	Defects =	1163	Average Defects Per K-lines =		17.94		
Logic	Defects =	291	Average Defects Per K-lines =		4.49		
Language	Defects =	247	Average Defects Per K-lines =		3.81		
Standards	Defects =	311	Average Defects Per K-lines =		4.80		
Data	Defects =	501	Average Defects Per K-lines =		7.73		
Interface	Defects =	173	Average Defects Per K-lines =		2.67		
Ret.Code/Msg	Defects =	15	Average Defects Per K-lines =		0.23		
Prologue/Com	Defects =	991	Average Defects Per K-lines =		15.29		
Req. Change	Defects =	58	Average Defects Per K-lines =		0.89		
Other	Defects =	44	Average Defects Per K-lines =		0.68		
Total I1	Defects =	3794	Average Defects Per K-lines =		58.54		

Total I2 Inspection Data Information:

Lines Inspected	=	44807	# Modules =		826		
Hours Preparation	=	575.30	Average Lines Per Preparation			Hour =	77.88
Hours Inspection	=	333.40	Average Lines Per Inspection			Hour =	134.39
Hours Total	=	908.70	Average Lines Per Total			Hour =	49.31
			Average Defects Identified Per Total			Hour =	2.23
Lines Rework Estimate	=	34	Which is 0.08% of the Lines Inspected				
Design	Defects =	370	Average Defects Per K-lines =		8.26		
Logic	Defects =	642	Average Defects Per K-lines =		14.33		
Language	Defects =	198	Average Defects Per K-lines =		4.42		
Standards	Defects =	96	Average Defects Per K-lines =		2.14		
Data	Defects =	216	Average Defects Per K-lines =		4.82		
Interface	Defects =	58	Average Defects Per K-lines =		1.29		
Ret.Code/Msg	Defects =	12	Average Defects Per K-lines =		0.27		
Prologue/Com	Defects =	403	Average Defects Per K-lines =		8.99		
Req. Change	Defects =	10	Average Defects Per K-lines =		0.51		
Other	Defects =	23	Average Defects Per K-lines =		0.51		
Total I2	Defects =	2028	Average Defects Per K-lines =		45.26		

FIGURE 9-11. Inspection results—defect density unacceptable.

in Figure 9-12, will provide continuous visibility into the rate of error detection, and can be drawn for the entire system, for each major function, or, within any of those categories, for each defect priority. If a priority scheme such as that found in DOD-STD-1679A (see Chapter 6) is chosen, with the five levels of severity described, then five separate graphs may be drawn for each major function or for the entire system. The production and update of these charts and graphs is a positive influence that can be provided by software quality assurance personnel.

The utility of this chart is that the actual number of errors is less important than the *slope* of the line. This may seem to be contrary to instinct, but it is true. If the plot of actual locks like the curve shown in Figure 9-12 for cumulative defects, then the project is under control. The cumulative curve should begin to show a marked transition at about the mid-point of test (MPT), and the slope should begin to approach zero as an asymptote.

The proper implementation of the inspection process can provide this control. If the cumulative slope is as shown, the program manager can be reasonably sure that the project will complete on time and with minimal defect density at delivery. Without the inspection process, the likeliest shape of the cumulative curve will be a continual positive slope of a level which would indicate the system is just not ready for delivery. In many such cases, the program manager who, for whatever reason, had thought the system was under control, realizes that disaster is imminent. He or she decides to take immediate steps to resolve the problem and issues the order to fix all known problems so that the system can proceed to acceptance test with few, hopefully zero, open errors.

In such a case, the cumulative curve will go dead flat a few weeks before system test and the curve displaying the number of open errors will drop rapidly toward zero. These wholesale error correction activities will usually introduce new errors due to the panic atmosphere surrounding the project. The program manager will

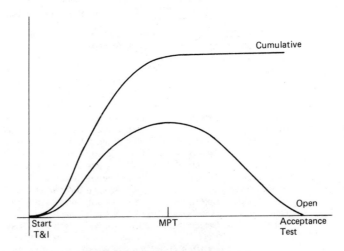

FIGURE 9-12. Error-detection rate chart.

be trying to figure out where things went wrong, not realizing that they were wrong from the beginning, and that disaster was inevitable.

Naturally, the reason for cumulative curve goes flat is that everyone on the project is so busy correcting known problems, or verifying the fixes to known problems, that no one has the time to find the rest of the errors still in the system. The delivery defect density will be a total unknown and unpredictable, and the program enters acceptance test with everyone, especially the program manager, crossing fingers in the hope the system will squeak through the test.

The solution is to maintain control throughout the entire development process. Without control, it is impossible to tell the state of health of the system, and without measurement, there is only minimum control. It is the measurement programs which provide the visibility essential to any real system control. The measurements must be effective, but they need not be complex or elaborate. It is also not necessary to automate the measurements in all cases, although that is the most efficient means for most systems. The cumulative rate charts, for example, can be prepared by hand from the error reports. They can also be automated by accessing the error report data base. In either case, the data can be obtained and used.

In Figure 9-13, the cumulative and closed curves are shown by accessing the data base. Different projects can be compared as is done here. The actual raw data will never show the sort of smoothness as is shown in Figure 9-12, but the *trend* in the curve, the change in slope, will be quite evident.

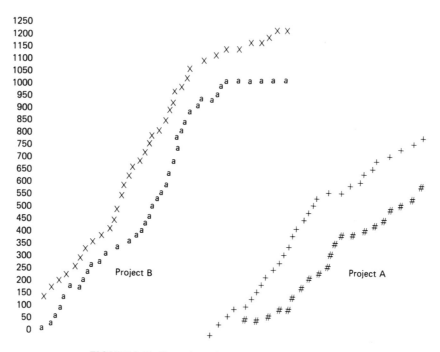

FIGURE 9-13. Error-detection rate charts for two projects.

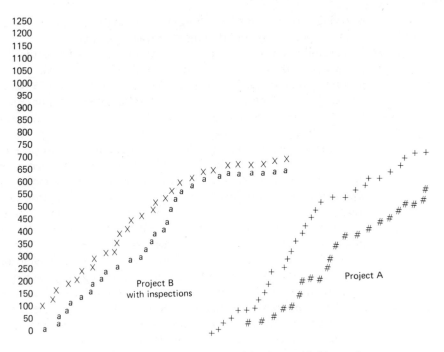

FIGURE 9-14. Error-detection charts with volume-added inspections.

In Figure 9-14, the same type of plot is shown and the inflection point is quite evident. The change in slope is clear and the program manager has a means of assessing the validity of what has preceeded the test program. The value added by the inspections becomes self-evident. The control achieved, the relaxed and panic-free environment, assures that the system will proceed to acceptance test with no surprises and the customer will be able to utilize effectively the system delivered. Each major step in the development process, from initial design to acceptance test, provides a level of visibility, measurement, and control which assures the program manager of a successful delivery.

It also affords the manager the opportunity to seek customer counsel if a problem is visible early which requires the customer to make a choice. The visibility is available early enough to make the change without disrupting the entire program.

9.8 CURRENT PRACTICES

The practice of design and code inspections is no more static than is the discipline of software quality assurance itself. These practices are constantly under review and their effectiveness is continually examined. The process as a whole, and each of its parts, is also under consideration for automation. Which parts of the inspection process, if any, will be automated have not yet been determined. With continuing advances in technology and with the widespread use of personal computers, both individually and tied to a central system, it is natural to expect that any process as critical to the success of software development as properly conducted inspections will be a subject of major interest. The more we can automate, the more we can free the participants in software to concentrate on matters not inherently amenable to automation.

R_0 Inspection

The success of the design and code inspection process has prompted hardware design engineers to adapt it for hardware design, especially in disciplines such as VLSI and VHSIC. The system engineers who produce software requirement specifications are also adapting the technique. It has been identified as the R_0 inspection, which is analogous to the high-level design inspection being taken one step backward in time. It is important to understand that this step can only be effectively taken if implemented in conjunction with other improvements in software technology, such as the use of a structured language for the requirements document. It would be difficult or impossible to move the inspection practice back to the requirements stage if the requirements were still written in prose. The foregoing is just one example of the interrelationship of many of the subdisciplines, techniques, and measurements (see Chapter 19) being developed to address the overall discipline of software quality assurance.

As technology progresses, the improvements being currently made will impact on all which has gone before, including the inspection process. For example, the development of Ada, a language which is projected to be a compilable design language, will eliminate the need for I_2 inspections. With the increasing use of distributed systems in real-time applications, the inspection process may correspondingly change to implement techniques for detection of an entirely different group of defects (see Chapter 18) from those now commonly found.

It is virtually certain that as each new software technology is introduced, the natural numbers of programming associated with inspections will also change. These changes will be reflected in the defect densities and in the measures of the efficiencies of developmental techniques and processes. They will also be reflected in the densities of the various types of defects detected.

The requirements documents inspections, R_0 (and R_1, which is analogous to the low-level design inspection), will probably exhibit their own set of natural numbers which will aid in shifting the error detection and removal process just that much farther toward the front end of the project's life cycle. The more this is done, the less testing will be required as a primary error detection and removal process.

The knowledge gained from these processes will enable the practitioners of software quality assurance to determine the types of errors which are made, where they are introduced, and why they are introduced. Inevitably leading to effective error prevention techniques and tools.

All of this can be accomplished, but only if there are sufficient data on which to make judgments, and a consistent set of data obtained from well-recognized processes affording a common means of communication between disciplines and between persons actively involved in the field. We are not far from the time we will have to answer, not whether we will be able to deliver defect-free software, but when.

References

1. Fagan, Michael E., "Design and Code Inspections and Process Control in the Development of Programs," IBM-TR-00.73, June 1976.
2. Myers, Glenford J., *The Art of Software Testing* (New York: John Wiley & Sons, 1979).

The Move Toward Zero Defect Software

G. Gordon Schulmeyer, CDP

Westinghouse Electronic Systems Group

10.1 INTRODUCTION

Is it meaningful to talk of zero software defects? Is it achievable? This chapter traces through a number of steps and concepts which the author believes will lead to zero defect software as is detailed in his book, *Zero Defect Software.*[1]

First, the zero defects programs that have been used in industry are discussed as precursors to their application to software development.

A number of models and issues concerning the software process are next investigated highlighting inspection points.

The synergism of the important concepts in Shigeo Shingo's book, *Zero Quality Control: Source Inspections and the Poka-yoke System* (pronounced POH-kah YOH-kay) and the procedure charting of value analysis leads to a guide toward the achievement of zero defect software.

With the outline provided by the Software Development Process Chart (Appendix herein), the key issues of importance to its successful implementation are discussed. The customer is discussed in terms of the next person in line in the development process.

Errors are human and will always be made. The secret to successful zero defect software is to isolate the errors humans make along the way and remove them. Here, a software defect is any software failure delivered to the ultimate customer. Source inspections and successive inspections isolate errors manually, and poka-yoke techniques help prevent errors with an automated device, so no software defects get delivered.

The responsibilities of both the individuals (workers) and the managers in the software development process are next examined. This emphasizes that it is only through people that the achievement of the zero defect software goal may be obtained.

10.2 ZERO DEFECTS PROGRAMS

In his book, *Quality is Free,* Philip B. Crosby discussed quality through defect prevention, which led him to the idea of a zero defects program. He states the underlying reasons for the zero defects program, as follows.

People are conditioned to believe that error is inevitable. We not only accept error, we anticipate it. We figure on making errors in typing a letter, programming a computer, etc, and management plans for errors to occur. We feel that human beings have a "built-in" error factor. However, as individuals, we do not have the same standard of error acceptance. We do not go home to the wrong house periodically or drink salt water for lemon juice. We have a double standard—one for ourselves, one for the company.

The family creates a higher performance standard for us than the company. The company allows 20 percent of sales for scrap, rework, warranty, service, test, and inspection. Errors by people cause this waste. We must concentrate on preventing the defects and errors that plague us to eliminate this waste. The defect that is prevented does not need repair, examination, or explanation. All personnel must adopt an attitude of zero defects in the company.[2]

In some things, people are willing to accept imperfection; in others, the amount of defects must be zero. Mistakes are caused by lack of knowledge and lack of attention. Knowledge can be measured and deficiencies corrected. Lack of attention must be corrected by the person himself or herself. Lack of attention is an attitude problem that may be corrected if there is a personal commitment to watch each detail and carefully avoid error. This leads to zero defects in all things.

When management and employees committed to zero defects, people communicated an error-cause removal system. Errors dropped 40 percent almost immediately.

Zero defects is a management performance standard, not a "motivation" program. In 1980 Tokyo, there was a party for Philip Crosby to celebrate 16 years of the zero defects programs in Japan. The United States, particularly the defense industry, went zero defects-happy for two years. Then the "motivation" wore off because American quality professionals never took time to understand zero defects.[3]

There are conflicting schools of thought about quality. One says only zero defects is acceptable. The other says set an acceptable quality level (AQL) because the cost and effort to achieve zero defects is not worthwhile. Figure 10-1 gives an AQL chart where producing above AQL quality is out of control, but producing below AQL is too expensive to be practical.

Burrill and Ellsworth in *Quality Data Processing* point out that Figure 10-1 does not adequately represent the cost of software systems (critical products) failure.

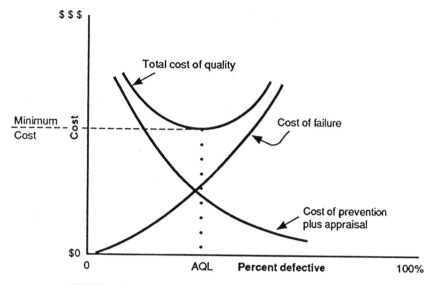

FIGURE 10-1. Traditional view of costs versus percent defective.[4]

Their malfunction can generate costs that are extremely large compared with the cost of system development. This means that the cost of failure rises steeply as the percent of defectives increase.

Second, consider the cost of prevention plus appraisal. The traditional view is that this cost must become almost infinite to achieve zero defects. But this is not true for software systems. Examples of no defect software in the first year of operation show that zero defects can be achieved at a cost of prevention plus appraisal that is finite and reasonable. Also, the increase in this cost is not excessive as the percent of defects trends to zero.

For failure costs and prevention plus appraisal costs as shown in Figure 10-2, the total cost of failure decreases steadily as the percent defective trends to zero. So the minimum total cost of failure is at the point of zero defects. For these curves, the AQL is zero defects.[5]

10.3 THE PROCESS

"A process may be described as a set of operations occurring in a definite sequence that operates on a given input and converts it to some desired output."[7] For software development, explicit requirement statements are required as input. The series of processing operations that act on this input must be placed in the correct sequence with one another, the output of each operation satisfying the input needs of the next operation. The output of the final operation is the explicitly required output in the form of a verified program. Thus, the objective of

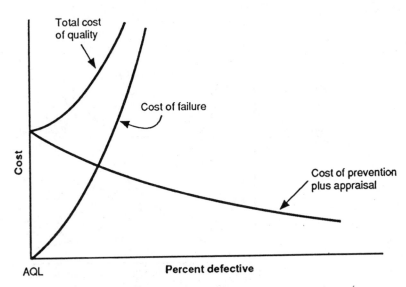

FIGURE 10-2. Cost versus percent defective for software systems.[6]

each processing operation is to receive a defined input and to produce a definite output that satisfies a specific set of exit criteria. A well-formed process can be thought of as a continuum of processing during which sequential sets of exit criteria are satisfied, the last set in the entire series requiring a well-defined end product.[7]

Would you calculate every week the results that go on your listing: i.e., correct the listing every week (Figure 10-3).[8] No one is so ignorant that they would not correct the program once, instead of continually correcting the results.

Figure 10-4 shows the same situation with some labels changed. It shows a staff repeatedly correcting defective products of a system rather than correcting the system that produced those defective products. There are billions of dollars spent correcting system defects without realizing the wrong system is being corrected. The system for building systems should be corrected.

When a software developer says, "This is the problem" while pointing to listings, he or she is really only pointing out the symptom, not the problem. The real problem is a defective development procedure that allows defective code to be put there. We do not remove defects from the system for building systems, because we never go looking for them. It is better to correct the system for building systems so that it does not insert defects in the first place.[10]

Michael Fagan's landmark work on the software development process using inspections to improve quality provided several charts showing that fewer errors resulted the closer to the work the inspection was held. Figure 10-5 shows an example of how design inspections, I_1, code inspections, I_2, and test inspections, I_3, resulted in 38 percent fewer errors per thousand lines of code (KLOC). Figure 10-6 compared the old approach with the one Michael Fagan proposed showing a

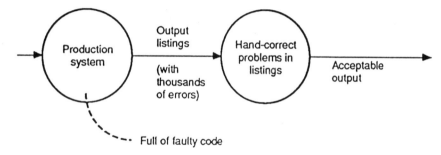

FIGURE 10-3. Correct the program.[8]

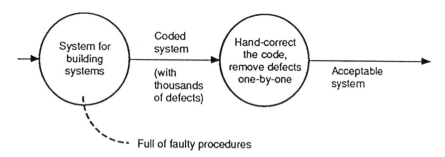

FIGURE 10-4. Correct the system.[9]

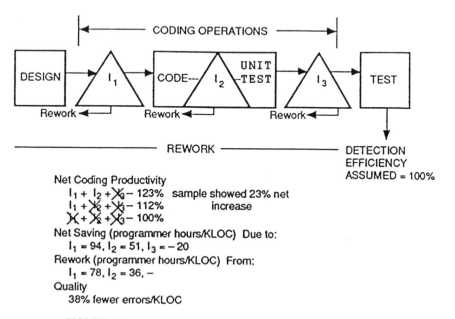

FIGURE 10-5. Inspection model with statistics from sample problems.[11]

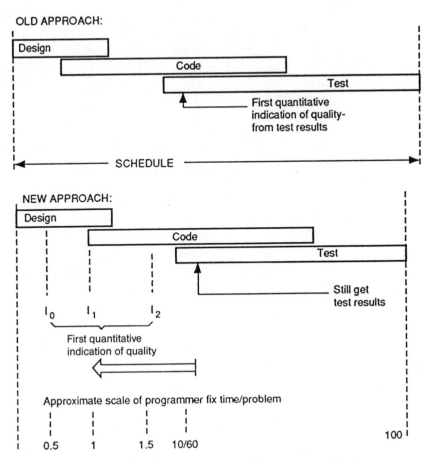

OLD APPROACH:

Design

Code

Test

First quantitative
indication of quality-
from test results

← SCHEDULE →

NEW APPROACH:

Design

Code

Test

Still get
test results

I_0 I_1 I_2

First quantitative
indication of quality

Approximate scale of programmer fix time/problem

0.5   1   1.5   10/60   100

FIGURE 10-6. Effect of inspection on process management.[12]

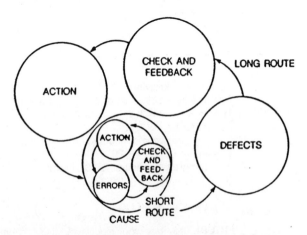

CHECK AND
FEEDBACK   LONG ROUTE

ACTION

DEFECTS

ACTION

CHECK
AND
FEED-
BACK

ERRORS

SHORT
ROUTE

CAUSE

FIGURE 10-7. Cycle for managing errors and defects.[14]

reduction in overall schedule using requirements inspections, I_0, and I_1, and I_2 inspections embedded in the process.

Shigeo Shingo[13] has devised a process cycle for the managing of errors and defects (Figure 10-7). The check and feedback portion is analogous to inspections I_0, I_1, I_2, and I_3 shown in Figures 10-5 and 10-6. Note that the short route similar to Fagan's approach gets closer to the worker. Getting the worker involved in the process of quality improvement of their own process is one of the driving forces behind the software development process chart discussed next.

10.4 SOFTWARE DEVELOPMENT PROCESS CHART

Shigeo Shingo's book, *Zero Quality Control: Source Inspections and the Poka-yoke System* convinced the author that Shingo's fundamental manufacturing ideas to achieve zero defects could be applied to software development. Shingo's approach, combined with concepts of Value Analysis, facilitated generating the Software Development process chart. (See the Appendix to this chapter.)

The Software Development Process Chart starts with a modified collection of symbols usually used in value analysis to show paper flow in a company.

The appendix continues with the entire software development chart based upon the value analysis symbols[15] produced by the author to highlight how to improve the process. It is derived primarily from software development methods as outlined in DOD-STD-2167A, *Defense System Software Development.*

Every product, whether it be a document or work product of software development, has an informal review which is the self-checking by the worker who produced it to check its integrity. This also takes place whenever a work product is updated, which happens frequently during software development. This is called a self-check inspection, to be discussed in more detail later.

If this work product is to be handed off to another, this is the place to get that other person—the internal customer—into the process. The receiver has a vested interest in what he or she is going to have to work with and so will be critically sure that the product is good. This is called a successive check inspection, also discussed later.

After the generation or update of each work product, a quality review of the work product takes place. Of course, this is after the worker has reviewed his or her own work. The quality review requires independence of judgment to best achieve its results.

Every formal customer review, such as a critical design review (CDR), has an internal practice run to ensure readiness for the real thing. This dry run ensures that the customer sees only the correct results, not intermediate errors that previously occurred. This is work that already has been through multiple reviews. Poka-yoke techniques do not show up in this portion of the chart. This does not imply that they should not be used here. A discussion of their usage and how they could be used in the process is in Section 10.6 entitled Isolating the Errors.

The software development process chart deals with the computer program production and associated documentation. It has been noted by C.K. Cho. Ph.D.

(Chapter 17) in his various publications that the "software" itself should be treated as a factory having inputs and producing a population of output data. By thinking this way, statistical methods may be applied to the "software" to produce a confidence level in the goodness of its output. This statistical quality control is another recommended (poka-yoke) method to help achieve zero defect software. In this sense, the software development process chart is directed also to "software" (in the Cho sense) that produces a population of output data that is error-free, culminating in zero defects software that is usable.

10.5 THE CUSTOMER

Make the customer come alive for all employees. It is one thing to produce a quality product for an abstraction called the customer and a very different thing to do the job for the customers who are people, too.

The customer should be made to come alive for all employees, especially those who do not normally come into contact with the customers. Some methods are: distribute stories how customers use the products, allow customers to address employees telling what it is like to do business with them, and have employees visit customer sites on field trips to see the product being used.

Where direct contact does not exist with the customer, explicitly identify and strengthen all customer connections for the employee. Specifically show how the employee's job has an effect on the customer or if no effect where the job might be eliminated.

The quality professionals in an organization have the know-how to preach the quality gospel. The employees must truly get into the church to hear it and respond to it. The focus of the sermon is one simple question: "What can I do to deliver more value to our customer?"[16] (Reprinted by Permission from Trainer's Workshop June/1987 Copyright © 1987. American Management Association, New York. All rights reserved.)

Customer satisfaction must be considered from two viewpoints: (1) it is the ultimate customer who is paying for the product or service; (2) customer consideration relates to the next person in the chain of operations within an organization. Both must be satisfied for successful quality improvement.

Three major points to improve employee involvement with the ultimate customer are that every contact should be a quality interface, responsiveness to the customer is important, and involving customers in activities (for example, design reviews) related to their work helps to build a team approach that results in openness and trust.

The concepts applied to the ultimate customer are applicable to the internal customer. Meeting the internal customer's requirements completely and in a timely manner usually contributes to the ultimate customer's satisfaction. Infrequently, there is a conflict and, when that occurs, the ultimate customer must come first.

Everyone has customers and success comes from satisfying those customers. This is achieved by meeting customer expectations, which, of course, is meeting requirements. Customer satisfaction is an integral part of any quality improvement process. Goals, objectives, and action plans for internal and ultimate customer satisfaction must be established, measured, and managed.[17]

Successful companies are customer oriented. They work to please customers because *only customers can define quality.* Most companies in the United States are share-price oriented, they work to please the equity market—not the customers.

In order to be truly customer-oriented, every worker must find out what the next person in line needs in order to do a good job and must provide it. In a well-managed business, each employee considers the next person in line as the customer and works to help him to do a better job.[18] This is a vital concept in the software development process chart that can lead to zero defect software.

Customer satisfaction is the core of the revolution in quality. Every person on a production line is the customer of the preceding operation. Therefore each worker's goal is to make sure that the quality of his or her work meets the requirements of the next person (called the internal customer). When that happens throughout the organization, the satisfaction of the ultimate customer should be assured. This concept was revolutionary to some workers who realized that they have a customer.[19]

10.6 ISOLATING THE ERRORS

Since defects are generated during the process, you only discover those defects by inspecting goods at the end of the process. Adding inspection workers is pointless because you will not reduce defects without using processing methods that prevent defects from occurring in the first place.

It is an unalterable fact that processing produces defects and all that inspections can do is find those defects. So approaching the problem only at the final inspection stage is meaningless. Defects will not be reduced merely by making improvements at the final inspection stage, although such improvements may eliminate defects in delivered goods.

The most fundamental concept is to recognize that defects are generated by work and all final inspections—judgmental inspections—do is to discover those defects. Zero defects can never be achieved if this concept is forgotten.[20]

In terms of its effect on defect density, software testing borders on the irrelevant. In the United States, the range of defects per thousand lines of executable code is from 0.016 to 60, a factor of nearly 4000. The way to make a drastic improvement in the quality of code that comes out of the testing process is to make a drastic improvement in the quality of code that goes into the testing process.[21] One way is to use computer-based systems to analyze product quality while the design details are merely images and symbols on a computer screen. Do this because 80 percent of all product defects get "designed in."[22]

There are three major inspection methods: (1) judgment inspections that discover defects; (2) informative inspections that reduce defects; and (3) source inspections that eliminate defects. Judgment inspections were just discussed in paragraph three above.

In an informative inspection, information of a defect occurring is fed back to the specific work process, which then corrects the process. Consequently, adopting informative inspections regularly should gradually reduce production defect rates. There are three categories of informative inspections:

- Statistical Quality Control Systems (SQCS)
- Successive Check Systems (SuCS)
- Self-Check Systems (SeCS)

Statistical Quality Control Systems (SQCS) include the notion of informative inspections and use statistically based control charts. SQC systems use statistics to set control limits that distinguish between normal and abnormal situations. The essential condition identifying a method of inspection as an SQC method is the use of statistical principles.[23]

SQC systems suffer from two shortcomings:

1. Sampling is used. Would it not be better to use 100-percent inspections to find all abnormalities. One-hundred percent inspections, however, are expensive and time consuming. If low-cost, 100-percent inspections could be devised, would not they be preferable? This leads to poka-yoke devices.
2. SQC methods are too slow to be fully effective concerning feedback and corrective action.

The best way to speed up feedback and corrective action would be to have the worker who finds any abnormality carry out 100-percent inspections and immediately take corrective action. But objectivity is essential to the performance of inspections, and that is why inspections have been carried out by independent inspectors. An inspection can be carried out by any worker other than the one who did the processing. If this task is given to the nearest person, then one could have a successive check system of the following sort:

1. When A completes processing, he passes it on to B for the next process.
2. B first inspects the item processed by A and then carries out the processing assigned to him. Then B passes the item to C.
3. C first inspects the item processed by B and then carries out the processing assigned to him. Then C passes the item to D.
4. Similarly, each successive worker inspects items from the previous process.
5. If a defect is discovered in an item from the previous process, the defective item is immediately passed back to the earlier process. There, the item is verified and the error corrected. Action is taken to prevent the occurrence of subsequent errors.

Successive check systems represent an advance over control chart systems because it makes it possible to conduct 100-percent inspections, performed by people other than the workers involved in the processing.[24] This does not imply a look at the entire output data population for software, but a look at the computer programs and associated documentation.

The nature of informative inspections remains such that rapid feedback and swift action are desirable, and it would be ideal to have the actual worker involved conduct 100-percent inspections to check for defects. However, there are two flaws to be reckoned with: workers are liable to make compromises when inspecting items that they themselves have worked on and they occasionally forget to perform checks on their own.

If these flaws could be overcome, then a self-check system would be superior to a successive check system. In cases where physical, rather than sensory, inspections are possible, poka-yoke devices can be installed within the process boundaries, so that when abnormalities occur, the information is immediately fed back to the worker involved. Because abnormalities are discovered within the processes where they occur rather than at subsequent processes, instant corrective action is possible. So, a self-check system is a higher order approach than the successive check system to cut defects even further.[25]

Source inspections are inspection methods that are based on discovering errors in conditions that *give rise to defects* and performing feedback and action at the error stage so as to keep those errors from turning into defects, rather than stimulating feedback and action in response to defects.

Many people maintain that it is impossible to eliminate defects from tasks performed by humans. This stems from the failure to make a clear separation between errors and defects. Defects (delivered to the customer) arise because errors are made; the two have a cause-and-effect relationship.

It is impossible to prevent all errors from occurring in any task performed by humans. Inadvertent errors are possible and inevitable. However, if feedback and corrective action are optimized, errors will not turn into defects. The principle feature of source inspections eliminates defects by distinguishing between errors and defects; i.e., between causes and effects.[26]

Bakayoke is Japanese for "foolproofing." A foolproofing device to prevent seat parts from being spot-welded backwards was installed in an Arakawa Auto Body plant around 1963. A worker asked hysterically if she was a "fool" who could mix up left- and right-hand parts. She was told she was not a "fool," but the device was inserted because anyone could make an inadvertent mistake.

When Shigeo Shingo was told that story, he sought a suitable term. He used poka-yoke (mistake-proofing) for the devices because they serve to prevent (or "proof" in Japanese, yoke) the sort of inadvertent mistake (poke in Japanese) that anyone could make. Since the word poka-yoke has been used untranslated into English, French, Swedish, and Italian books, it is now current throughout the world.[27]

For software an example is the Software Life-Cycle Support Environment (SLCSE). Rather than supporting a single development methodology, SLCSE uses a modifiable tool-based approach where an almost unlimited number of tools can be integrated to support various methodologies. Off-the-shelf or custom tools may be used so that changes in the modes or the development paradigm may be supported. Table 10-1 shows initial tool categories and representative generic tool types for each category that will be supported by SLCSE. The tool categories reflect life-cycle phases or activities that span the entire cycle.[28] More details on software quality tools in a CASE (computer aided software engineering) environ-

TABLE 10-1   Example Software Tool Types and Categories. Copyright © 1987 IEEE[28]

General Support
- Text Editor
- Document Formatter
- Command-Language Editor
- Electronic Mail

Requirements Analysis
- Requirements Generator
- Requirements Documentor
- Consistency Analyzer

Design
- Design Generator
- Design Documenter
- Consistency Checker

Coding
- Language-Sensitive Editor
- Assembler
- Compiler
- Linker
- Debugger
- Assertion Translator

Testing
- Instrumeter
- Postexecution Analyzer
- Test-Summary Reporter
- Test Manager
- Simulator

Prototyping
- Window Prototyper

Verification
- Data Tracer
- Code Auditor
- Static Analyzer
- Dataflow Analyzer
- Interface Checker
- Quality Analyzer

Configuration Management
- Software Manager
- Documentation Manager
- Test-Data/Results Manager
- Change-Effect Manager

Project Management
- Project Planner
- Project Tracker/Reporter
- Problem-Report Processor
- Change-Request

Environment Management
- Method Script Editor
- Menu Editor
- Keypad Editor
- Command-Procedure Editor
- Global-Command Setup
- Tool Installer/Deleter

ment are given by James McManus in Chapter 12. These tools are the equivalent of poka-yoke techniques for the software development process.

A poka-yoke system is a means and not an end. Poka-yoke systems can be combined with successive checks or self-checks and can fulfill the needs of those techniques by providing 100-percent inspections and prompt feedback and action. Successive checks and self-checks function only as informative inspections in which feedback and action take place after a defect has occurred. In cases where repairs can be made, it looks as though no defects occurred, but these methods are inherently unable to attain zero defects.

Source inspections and poka-yoke measures must be combined to eliminate defects. The combination of source inspections and poka-yoke devices make zero quality control systems possible. This same combination applies to the software development process as outlined in the chart in the Appendix. One must never forget, finally, that the poka-yoke system refers to a means, not an end.[29]

10.7 RESPONSIBILITY FOR ZERO DEFECT SOFTWARE

Success in quality—conformance to requirements—is a management issue. Management must recognize the weaknesses of the organization and see that quality applied correctly will eliminate them. Management establishes the organizational purpose, makes measurable objectives, and takes action required to meet the objectives. Management sets the tone for the people in the organization to look to. If people perceive management indifference to quality, indifference will permeate the organization. On the other hand, when management is perceived to have a quality commitment, quality will permeate the organization.[30]

Management must organize for quality. Simplicity with clear reporting enhances the ability to achieve quality. A clean, well-defined organizational structure and operation philosophy go together with process simplification. Process simplification such as proposed in the software development process chart leads to quality performance.

Many managers think they are committed to quality, while their subordinates perceive that they are not committed. This is cause for failure of many quality improvement programs. If it is perceived that quality is not a high management priority, then it will not be a high priority with the people. People must see management leading the quality improvement process and making it work on a continuing basis.

To achieve this commitment, management must understand quality and be involved in the process with active participation (Figure 10-8). Each person in the organization must see participation by the level above him.

Management shows its commitment to quality by establishing a quality policy. The policy should set the expectations for quality and should apply to all departments and individuals in the organization. The policy needs to be simple, direct, and concise. With proper management attention to establish the policy as the basis for quality performance, it becomes a rallying point for people to determine actions and priority.

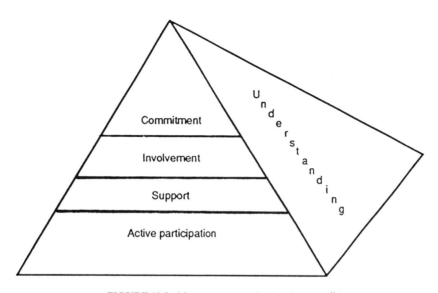

FIGURE 10-8. Management quality involvement.[31]

Management must show patience in its commitment to quality, because the quality improvement culture change is a long-term process. There is usually short-term improvement, but the big payoffs occur in future years. Management must show the tenacity necessary to leave no doubt as to their long-term quality commitment.

Management must eliminate all temptations to compromise conformance to requirements. It only takes one compromise to create doubt—forget that software unit test, ship that software design specification without software quality review. Once there is doubt, long-term consistent behavior on the part of (software) management is the only way to diffuse the doubt.

Management has the responsibility to educate, coach, and sell quality to the organization continually. Education provides the understanding, coaching defines the application, and selling establishes the desire.

The greater challenge usually comes from those few people who do not believe in or resist getting involved in the quality process. They can be educated and they can be coached. The problem is usually getting them to participate in the quality process. Management may make them responsible for some important action or expose them to a "nonquality" situation (such as irate customers). Doing this is a way to sell them on the movement.[32]

Attention has been focused on management's responsibilities, it is also appropriate to focus some attention on worker's responsibilities. The differences among software workers as shown in Figure 10-9 is enormous. Expect variations on the order of 10 to 1 in performance in all but the smallest project team. These variations are not caused solely by the extreme cases; they apply across the entire

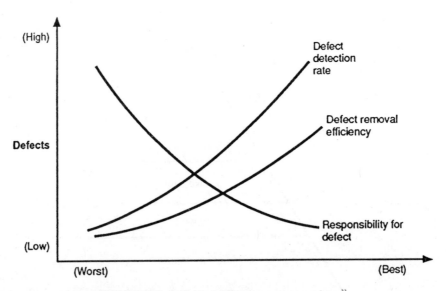

FIGURE 10-9. Individual differences among workers.[33]

spectrum of workers. Even if your workers are not at the extremes, you will see differences of three of four to one in your software project teams.

Poor performances are responsible for an order of magnitude more defects than the best performer; lower-average performers are responsible for twice as many as upper-average. There are people on almost all projects who insert spoilage that exceeds the value of their production. Taking a poor performer off your team can often be more productive than adding a good one. In a software project team of 10, there are probably 3 people who produce enough defects to make them net negative producers. The probability that there is not even 1 negative producer out of 10 is negligible. A high defect producing team (above 30 defects/thousand lines of executable code) may have fully half in the negative production category.

There are two reasons why not much is done about negative producers: defect-prone people *do not appear* to be bad developers and the idea of measuring the individual is slightly repugnant to most people.

When we measure and allocate defects fairly and when we make the idea palatable to the people affected, we will find the worker who is defect prone. When we find defect-prone workers, it does not mean they should be fired, but only that they should not be allowed to write code. If A writes nearly defect-free products and B excels at defect detection and diagnosis, they assign them accordingly; let A write all the code and B do all the testing. It is unconscionable to ignore the differences between A and B, assign them correctly and the differences in project results are quite significant.

Switching roles has been shown to improve quality by more than 75 percent. Making these changes illustrates the difference in cost between removing defects ($18,000) and abstaining from defects ($0). There were 36 more defects inserted when A and B were assigned without regard to B's defect production.

If you collect accurate defect rates and efficiencies without upsetting the people involved, note the results achieved. Not only has quality improved, but *each person's value to the project has been increased.* No one need be embarrassed to have been assigned tasks that make optimal use of individual strengths. Even worker B, temporarily chastened to learn that all his testing and diagnostic skill barely made up for a high defect insertion rate, will know (once you have assigned him properly) that his prior low value to the project was due to management failure, rather than worker B failure.

A most important function of management is defaulted if the difference between people are ignored and they are assigned homogeneously. Measuring defect rates will prove that 25 percent or more of the staff should not be coding at all, and that some of the best coders should not be allowed to test.[34]

10.8 CONCLUSION

As a software development manager and former software quality manager, I believe it is my duty to not only "preach" zero defects in software, but also to provide direction toward achieving it. I must also act on element 3 of the TQM movement of education and training to utilize TQM methods in software development. Using the software development process chart as a guide with source inspections and automated tools (poka-yoke), the direction is set. It has been successfully demonstrated in manufacturing by Shigeo Shingo. Now is the time for similar success in software development.

The payoff in software development is very high indeed. William Mandeville of the Carman Group, Inc. relates that 30% to 50% of product life-cycle costs are wasted as the costs of poor quality. However, quality improvements of up to 75% of that loss are attainable.[35]

References

1. Schulmeyer, G. Gordon, *Zero Defect Software* (New York: McGraw-Hill Book Co., 1990).
2. Crosby, Philip B., *Quality Is Free* (New York: New American Library, Inc. 1979), pp. 145, 146.
3. *Ibid,* pp. 83, 84.
4. Burrill, Claude W. and Ellsworth, Leon W., *Quality Data Processing* (Tenafly: Burrill-Ellsworth Associates, Inc., 1982), p. 50.
5. *Ibid,* pp. 49-51.
6. *Ibid,* p. 52.
7. Fagan, Michael E., "Design and Code Inspections and Process Control in the Development of Programs," *IBM-TR-00.73,* June 1976, p. 125.
8. DeMarco, Tom, *Controlling Software Projects: Management, Measurement & Estimation;* Copyright © 1982, Adapted by Permission of Prentice-Hall, (Englewood Cliffs: Prentice-Hall, Inc., 1982), p. 206.
9. *Ibid,* p. 206.
10. *Ibid,* pp. 205-207.
11. Fagan, Michael E., *op. cit.,* p. 127.
12. *Ibid,* p. 144.
13. *Zero Quality Control: Source Inspection and the Poka-Yoke System,* by Shigeo Shingo, Copyright © 1985 by the Japan Management Association, Tokyo; English translation copyright © 1986 by Productivity, Inc., P.O. Box 3007, Cambridge, MA. 02140. 1-(800) 274-9911. Reprinted by permission.
14. *Ibid,* p. 53.
15. Graham, Jr., Ben S., "Procedure Charting," prepared for Ben S. Graham Conference, copyright 1977.
16. Guaspari, John, 'The Role of Human Resources in "Selling" Quality Improvements to Employees,' *Management Review,* March 1987, pp. 20-24, Copyright 1987 American Management Association, pp. 23, 24.
17. Cooper, Alan D., *The Journey Toward Managing Quality Improvement* (Orlando: Westinghouse Electric Corp., 1987), pp. 13-16.
18. Tribus, Myron, "The Quality Imperative," *The Bent of Tau Beta Pi,* (Spring 1987), pp. 24-27.
19. "The Push for Quality," *Business Week,* June 8, 1987, pp. 130-143.
20. Shigeo Shingo, *op. cit.,* pp 35-39.
21. DeMarco, Tom, *op. cit.,* pp 216-218.
22. Kotelly, George V., "Competitiveness = Quality," *Mini-Micro Systems,* Vol. xx, No. 12, December 1985, Cahners Publishing Co., Div. of Reed Publishing, Denver, CO., p. 9.

23. Shigeo Shingo, *op. cit.,* pp. 58-59.
24. *Ibid,* pp. 67-69.
25. *Ibid,* pp. 77.
26. *Ibid,* pp. 83-85.
27. *Ibid,* pp. 45, 46
28. Cavano, Joseph P. and LaMonica, Frank S., "Quality Assurance in Future Development Environments," *IEEE Software,* September 1987, p. 29, Copyright © 1987 IEEE.
29. Shigeo Shingo, *op. cit.,* pp. 92, 93.
30. Cooper, Alan D., *op. cit.,* p. 6.
31. *Ibid,* p. 18.
32. *Ibid,* pp. 17-20.
33. DeMarco, Tom, *op. cit.,* p. 208.
34. *Ibid,* pp. 207-210.
35. Mandeville, William A., "Defects, and Software Quality Costs Measurements" *NSIA Fifth Annual National Joint Conference Proceedings* February 1989, p. 6.

Appendix (Chapter 10)

Symbol Definitions

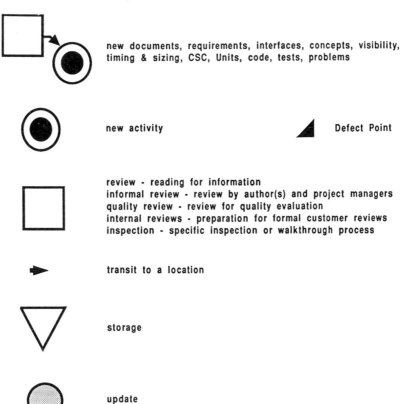

new documents, requirements, interfaces, concepts, visibility, timing & sizing, CSC, Units, code, tests, problems

new activity

Defect Point

review - reading for information
informal review - review by author(s) and project managers
quality review - review for quality evaluation
internal reviews - preparation for formal customer reviews
inspection - specific inspection or walkthrough process

transit to a location

storage

update

⌠ collection of items

① numbered return point

OK acceptable to proceed

$\overline{OK}$ must be updated

D long term delay (days to months)

△ researching or retrieving - time spent reading, obtaining information

Acronym List

CDR - Critical Design Review
CIDS - Critical Item Development Specification
CRISD - Computer Resources Integrated Support Document*
CSC - Computer Software Component
CSCI - Computer Software Configuration Item
CSOM - Computer System Operator's Manual*
CSU - Computer Software Unit
D.C. - Developmental Configuration
Doc. - Documentation
FCA - Functional Configuration Audit
FSM - Firmware Support Manual*
FQT - Formal Qualification Testing
Funct. - Functional
IDD - Interface Design Document
IRS - Interface Requirements Specification
Mgmt. - Management
PCA - Physical Configuration Audit
PDR - Preliminary Design Review
PIDS - Prime Item Development Specification
Prelim. - Preliminary
Qual. - Qualification
RFP - Request For Proposal
Rqmts. - Requirements
SCCB - Software Configuration Control Board
SDD - Software Design Document
SDF - Software Development File
SDP - Software Development Plan
SDR - System Design Review
SOW - Statement of Work
Spec. - Specification
SPM - Software Programmer's Manual*
SPR - Software Problem Report
SPS - Software Product Specification
SQPP - Software Quality Program Plan
SRR - System Requirements Review
SRS - Software Requirements Specification
SSDD - System/Segment Design Document
SSR - Software Specification Review
SSS - System/Segment Specification
STD - Software Test Description
STP - Software Test Plan
STR - Software Test Report
SUM - Software User's Manual*
TRR - Test Readiness Review
VDD - Version Description Document

*May be vendor supplied

Software Development
Process Chart

**System
Requirements
Analysis/Design**

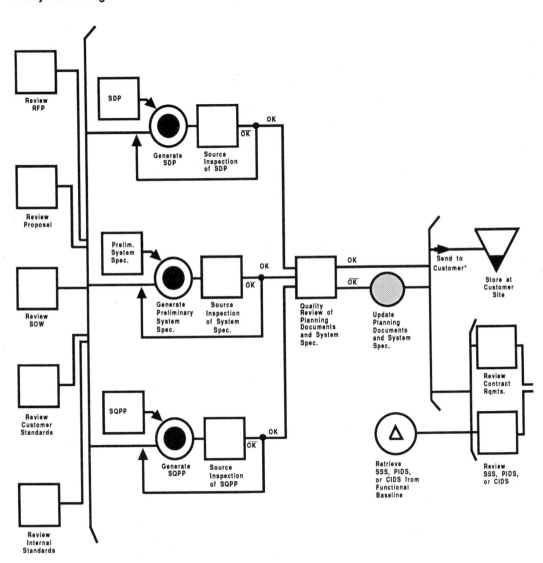

* Formal Delivery of SDP, SQPP

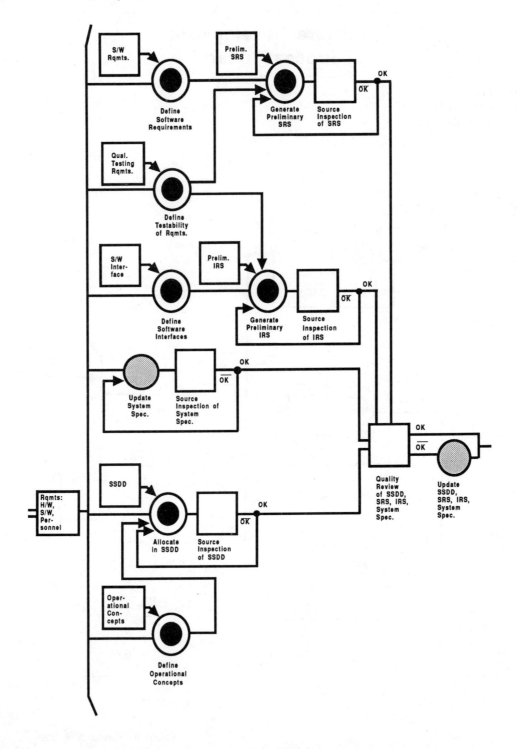

Software Requirements Analysis

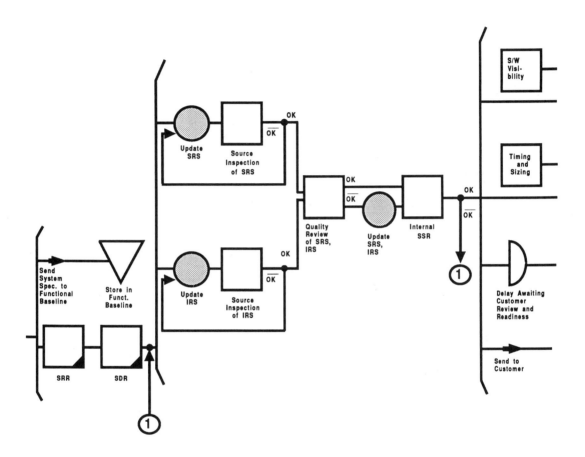

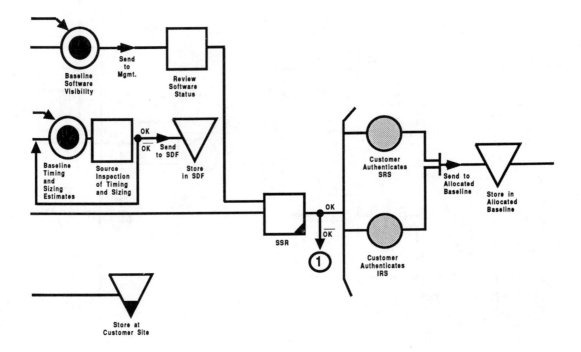

Preliminary
Design

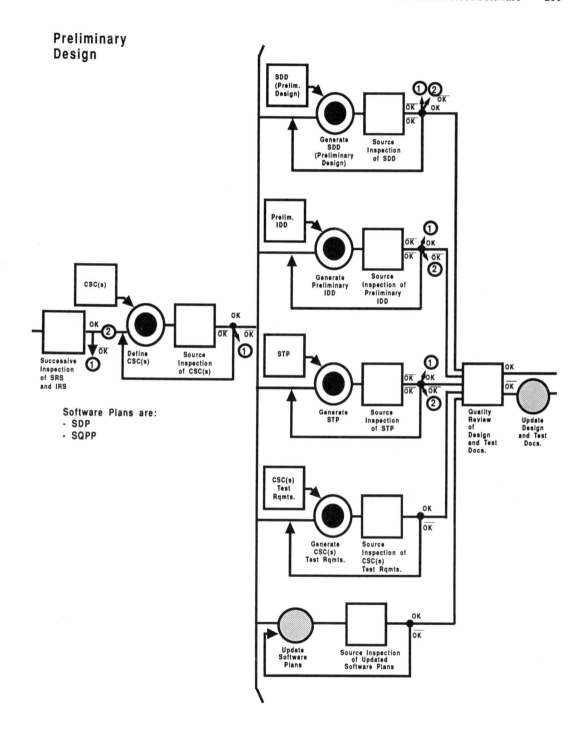

Software Plans are:
- SDP
- SQPP

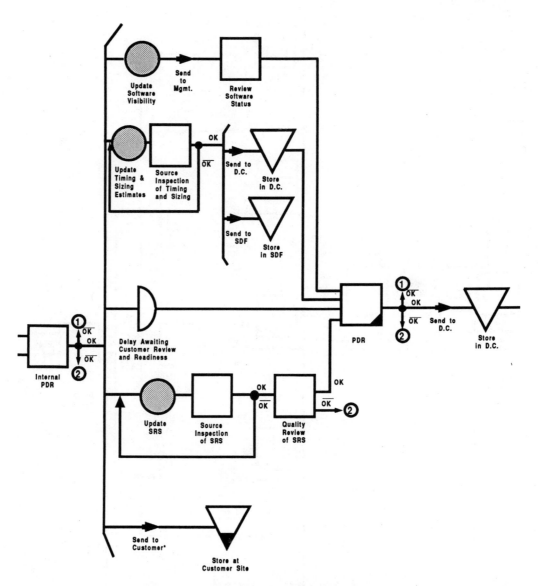

* **Formal Delivery of STP and Preliminary SDD and IDD**

Detailed Design

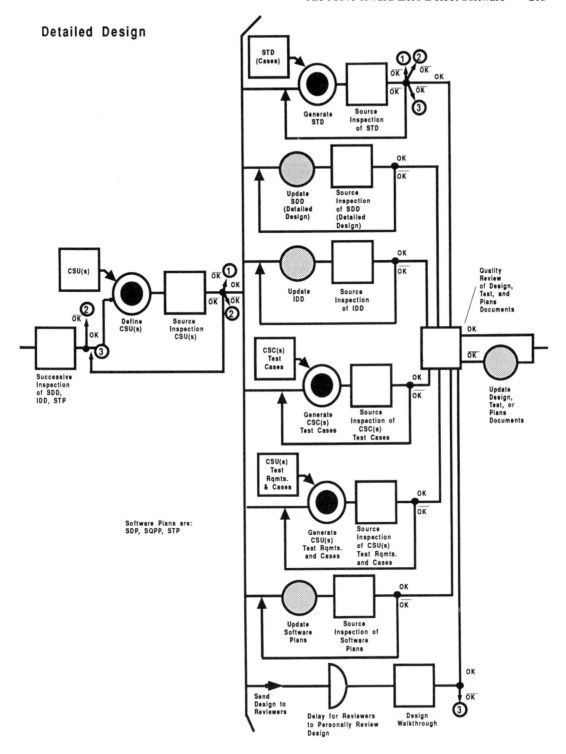

Software Plans are:
SDP, SQPP, STP

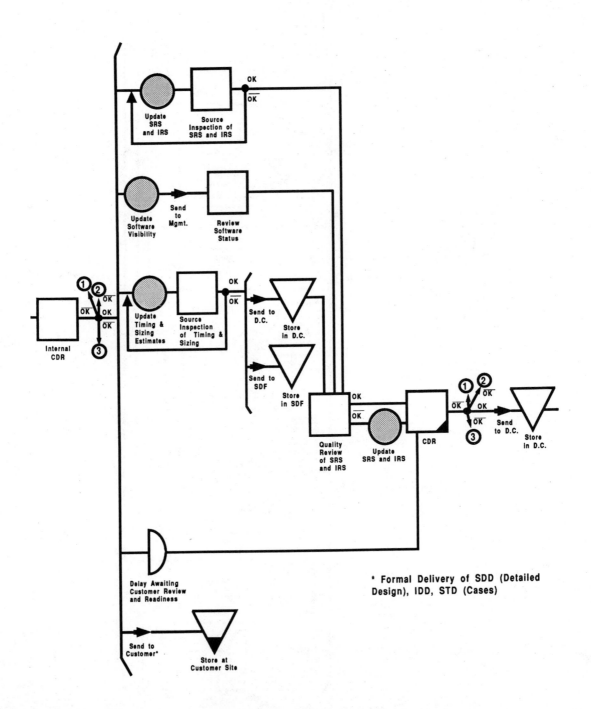

Coding and CSU Testing

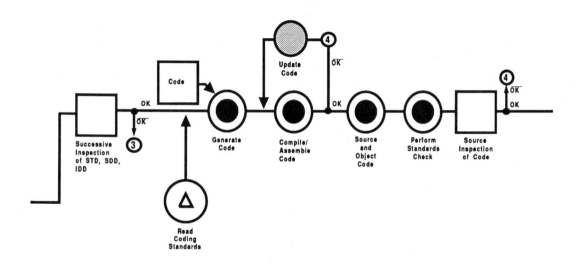

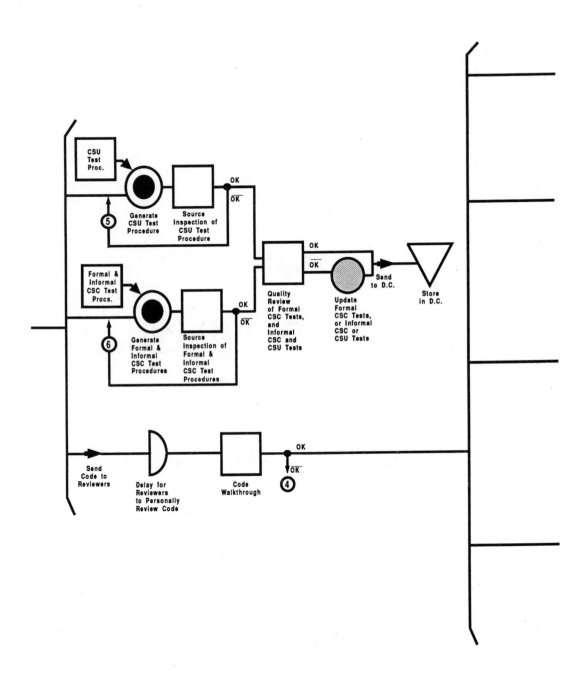

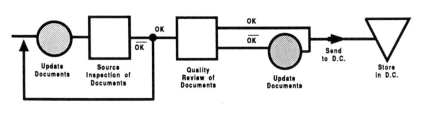

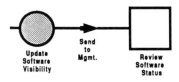

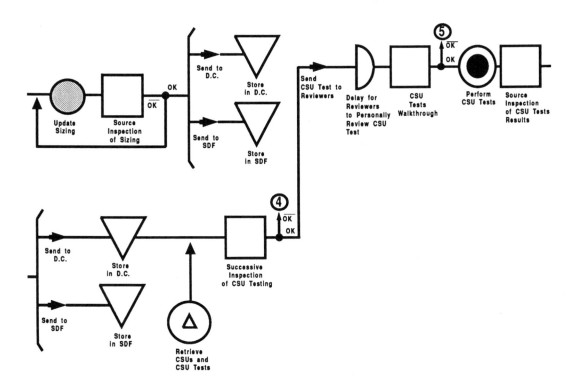

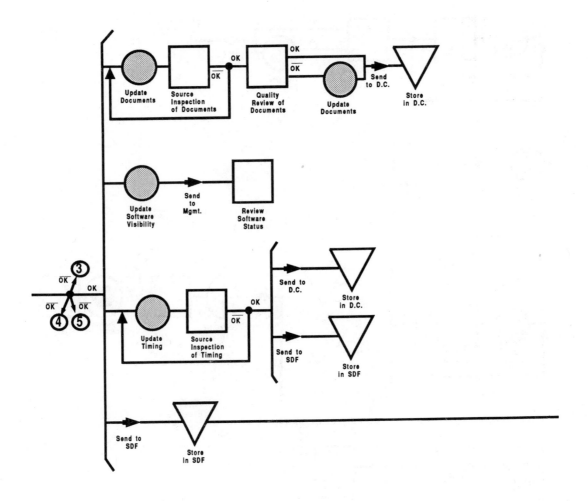

**CSC Integration
and Testing**

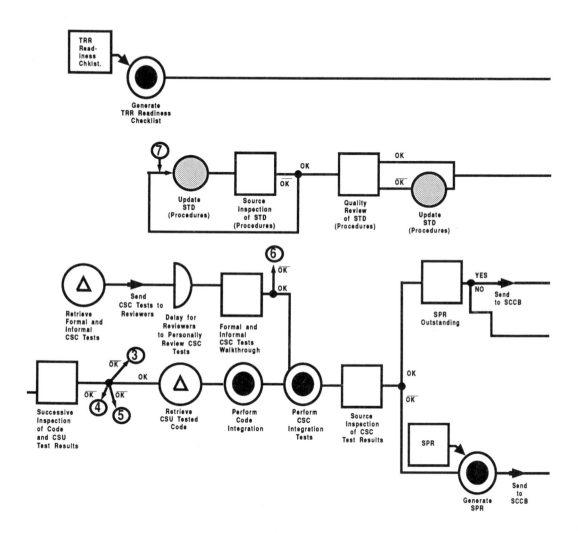

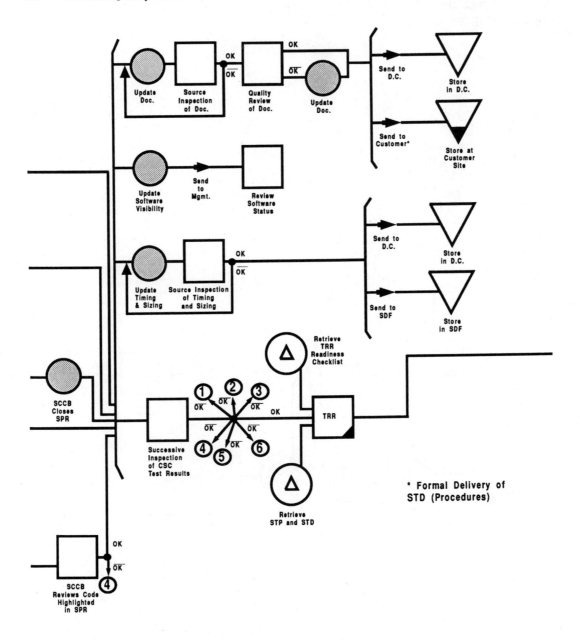

* Formal Delivery of
STD (Procedures)

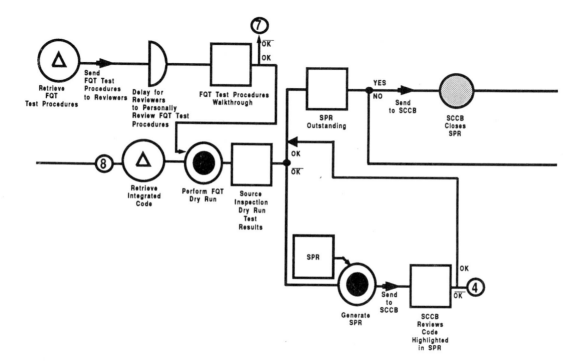

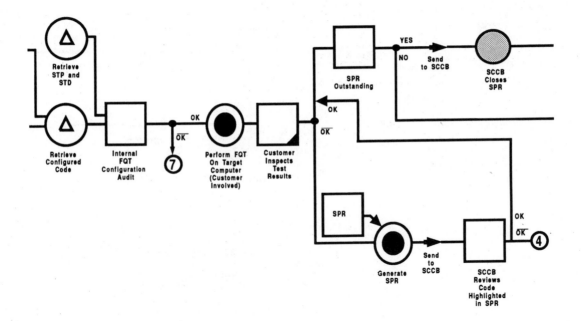

Retrieve
STP and
STD

Retrieve
Configured
Code

Internal
FQT
Configuration
Audit

OK

OK

⑦

Perform FQT
On Target
Computer
(Customer
Involved)

Customer
Inspects
Test
Results

OK

OK

SPR
Outstanding

YES

NO

Send
to SCCB

SCCB
Closes
SPR

SPR

Generate
SPR

Send
to
SCCB

SCCB
Reviews
Code
Highlighted
In SPR

OK

OK

④

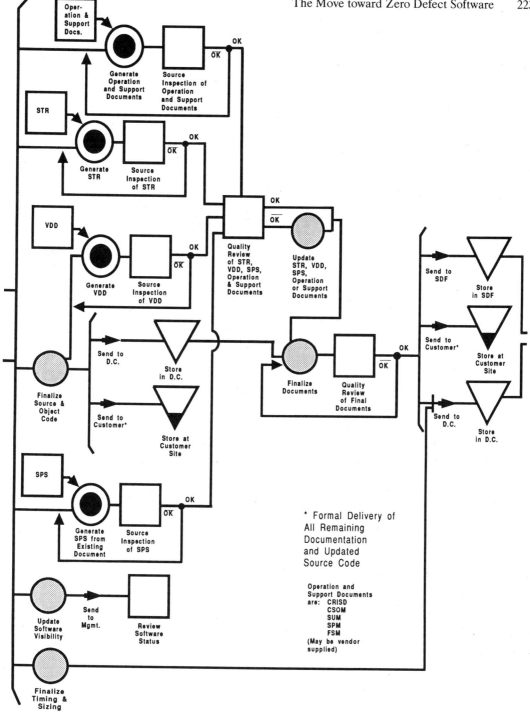

* Formal Delivery of
All Remaining
Documentation
and Updated
Source Code

Operation and
Support Documents
are: CRISD
        CSOM
        SUM
        SPM
        FSM
(May be vendor
supplied)

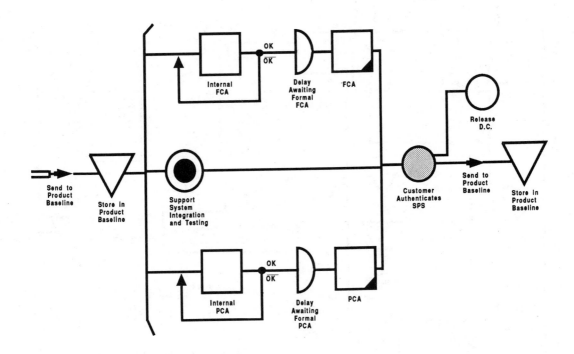

11

The Pareto Principle Applied to Software Quality Assurance

Thomas J. McCabe

McCabe & Associates, Inc.

G. Gordon Schulmeyer, CDP

Westinghouse Electronic Systems Group

11.1 INTRODUCTION

Concentrate on the vital few, not the trivial many. This admonition borrowed from J. M. Juran, the quality consultant, epitomizes the Pareto principle as he applied it to quality management. Thomas J. McCabe has extended the Pareto principle to software quality activities.

This chapter explores many aspects of the Pareto principle and each aspect is then related to software. It is during the software development cycle that the application of the Pareto principle pays off. SQA personnel should be aware of how to apply the Pareto principle during the software development cycle, this application is what this chapter covers. So, while reading this chapter, SQA personnel should remember that the processes are for their use and benefit even though the following discussion focuses primarily on the software development process.

First, a brief historical background is provided to set the stage. Then two specific examples undertaken by McCabe & Associates, Inc., for the World Wide Military Command and Control System (WWMCCS) and the Federal Reserve Bank are covered in some detail. The various ways that the Pareto principle is applied to software and the results of the applications are discussed.

Some extensions of the Pareto principle to other fertile areas previously exposed by J. M. Juran are defect identification, inspections, and statistical techniques. Each of these areas is discussed in relation to software and its probable payoff in better quality.

For defect identification in software, some of the common symptoms of defects in software are exposed, and suggestions as to the basic causes of defects are made.

Inspections have been a mainstay in the factory to ensure the quality of the product. That inspections have been applied to software is well-known, but tying the Pareto principle to inspections is not usually done. Thus the explanation of that application is covered in this chapter.

The use of statistical techniques based upon error types is explored in relation to software. The frequency of error types in software and the use of statistics for assuring software quality are covered.

11.2 HISTORICAL BACKGROUND

J. M. Juran is the "father" of the Pareto principle in quality management. He coined the terms *vital few* and *trivial many* as applied to the Pareto principle. Fundamentally, the Pareto principle is to concentrate on the vital few, not the trivial many.

The historical development of the Pareto principle illuminates its application to software quality. The oldest application of the idea of the vital few (the "exception principle" for management decision-making) is provided by Juran in his book *Managerial Breakthrough*[1, p. 49]:

> The principle is very old. An early example is charmingly related in the Old Testament. Following the exodus of the Israelites from Egypt, their leader Moses found himself the sole judge of the disputes which arose amoung the people. The number of such disputes was enough to make this solitary judge a bottleneck in decision making. In consequence, the people "stood by Moses from the morning into the evening," waiting for Moses to make decisions. Moses' father-in-law, Jethro, saw this spectacle and ventured advice. (For which Jethro has become regarded by some as the first consultant on record).
>
> *Jethro's advice:* "And thou shalt teach them ordinances and laws, and show them the way wherein they must walk, and the work they must do." (Exodus 18:20)
>
> *Translated into modern management dialect:* "Establish policies and standard practices, conduct job training, and prepare job descriptions."
>
> *Jethro's advice:* "Moreover thou shalt provide out of all the people able men, such as fear God, men of truth, hating covetousness, and place such over them, to be rulers of thousands, and rulers of hundreds, rulers of fifties and rulers of tens." (Exodus 18:21)
>
> *Translated into modern management dialect:* "Set up an organization; firstline supervisors to have 10 subordinates; second-line supervisors to have 5 subordinates, etc.; appoint men who have supervisory ability."
>
> *Jethro's advice:* "And let them judge the people at all seasons; and it shall be that every great matter they shall bring unto thee, but every small matter they shall judge; so it shall be easier for thyself, and they shall bear the burden with thee." (Exodus 18:22)
>
> *Translated into modern management dialect:* "Institute delegation of authority; routine problems to be decided down the line, but exceptional problems to be brought to higher authority."

Next, a quantum time jump to the 1940's, when Joseph Juran noticed that the concept that a vital few members of the assortment account for most of the total effect, and contrariwise, the bulk of the members (the trivial many) account for very little of the total effect was a universal. He named the phenomenon "the Pareto principle" (after the Italian economist, Vilfredo Pareto [1848-1923]), which has endured.

Juran later footnoted in his *Quality Control Handbook* that is was a mistake to name it the Pareto principle, [2, pp. 2-17, -18], Pareto quantified the extent of inequality or nonuniformity of the distribution of wealth, but had *not* generalized this concept of unequal distribution to other fields. In fact, the first edition of Juran's *Quality Control Handbook* illustrates cumulative "Pareto" curves which rightfully should have been identified with M. O. Lorenz, who had used curves to depict concentration of wealth in graphic forms.

McCabe & Associates have been giving a seminar on software quality assurance since 1978. It is during sessions of this seminar that Thomas McCabe has introduced the application of the Pareto principle to software quality. The Pareto principle is presented in light of Juran's contribution to overall quality and then made specific for software quality in the *SQA Survey Book*[3, pp. 153-154] and the *SQA Seminar Notes*[4, p. 11] prepared for the seminar. The actual application of the concept to software quality in two real examples (WWMCCS and Federal Reserve Bank) by McCabe and Associates are explored below in some detail.

11.3 WWMCCS EXAMPLE

The example cited is from an actual study of quality assurance conducted by Thomas McCabe in 1977 for WWMCCS (World Wide Military Command and Control System).[3, pp. 154-156] At that time, WWMCCS was a large network of 35 Honeywell H6000s with a specialized operating system and hundreds of user application programs. WWMCCS ADP Directorate is the organization responsible for WWMCCS software acquisition, integration, and testing. The quality assurance program studied by McCabe was for the WWMCCS ADP Directorate organization; the following are ways in which the Pareto principle was applied to the WWMCCS ADP Directorate.

Manpower

This heading represents internal WWMCCS ADP Directorate personnel expenditures. Identify the different functions performed in WWMCCS ADP Directorate (e.g. planning, scheduling, task preparation, demonstration test, integration, stability testing, regression testing, and so on) and then analyze the WWMCCS ADP Directorate personnel expenditure on each task. The few functions that the Pareto analysis determines consume 80 percent of the manpower would then be strong candidates to be placed "under the microscope" to determine the reasons for this consumption. The goal is to reduce personnel expenditures by reducing the number of people required to complete the task, that is, without diminishing

TABLE 11-1   Hours Expended on Personnel Tasks

PERSONNEL TASKS	HOURS EXPENDED	% OF HOURS EXPENDED	CUMULATIVE HOURS EXPENDED	CUMULATIVE % OF HOURS EXPENDED
*Managerial Personnel**				
Scheduling	600	43	600	43
"Crisis Reaction"	300	21	900	64
Planning	200	14	1100	78
Decision-Making	150	11	1250	89
Contract Administration	100	7	1350	96
Controlling	30	3	1380	99
"Task Preparation"	20	1	1400	100
*Technical Personnel**				
Software Purchase analysis	2500	25	2500	25
Planning	2000	20	4500	45
Contract Administration	1500	15	6000	60
Integration	1200	12	7200	72
Stability Testing	1000	10	8200	82
Regression Testing	1000	10	9200	92
Demonstration Tests	500	5	9700	97
"Crisis Reaction"	300	3	10000	100

*Assumes 3 management and 22 technical.

the quality of the complete job. In doing this, one should distinguish between technical and managerial manpower. Two initial distributions to qualify assurance will result in identifying two distinct classes of internal WWMCCS ADP Directorate functions.

A chart similar to the one in Table 11-1 aids in the analysis. The statistics assume a 3-month time frame.

For managerial personnel note that scheduling and "crisis reaction" require over half of the expended time, and for technical personnel note that software purchase analysis and planning utilize just under half of the expended time. A particular interesting WWMCCS ADP Directorate function in the table is "crisis reaction." It is informative to determine how much of personnel resources this

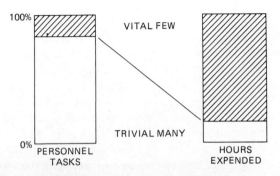

FIGURE 11-1. Pareto principle simplified (adapted from reference 1, p. 47).

category actually consumes and then see which types of "crisis" are most frequently repeated and most costly. The "crisis reaction" function for managerial personnel has turned out indeed to be significantly expensive. So, a key point is that a program should be directed at more careful planning and coordination.

For a simpler representation, in graph form, for the data shown in Table 11-1, see Figure 11-1.

Cost of Contracts

This is the amount and distribution of money spent on contracts to support the WWMCCS ADP Directorate activities. A distribution of the funds spent by contractor—HIS, PRC, MITRE, and so on—can be constructed and then analyzed with the Pareto principle. The results will indicate to which contractors the program should first be applied. An illuminating facet of this analysis is the internal WWMCCS ADP Directorate personnel expenditure on contract administration, which is really part of *Manpower,* discussed above.

Quality of the Product

This category of examination is concerned with the internal software quality of a WWMCCS release. There are two steps in applying the Pareto principle to the quality of the product. First, the WWMCCS ADP Directorate decides how to define quality—this could be done by prioritizing the software quality factors (metrics) listed in Table 11-2, and selecting a subset of the factors as an operational definition of quality as shown in Table 11-3. The hurdle rates shown in Table 11-3 are the values set up-front that must be achieved during the measurement of these factors in the development phases when the evaluation (count) is made.

TABLE 11-2   Software Quality Factors*

Correctness	Reliability	Efficiency
Integrity	Usability	Maintainability
Testability	Flexability	Portability
Reusability	Interoperability	

*See page 417 for definitions of Factors.

TABLE 11-3   Example Hurdle Rates for Selected Software Quality Factors

SOFTWARE QUALITY FACTOR	HURDLE RATE*
Correctness	97%
Reliability	95%
Maintainability	95%
Useability	90%
Testability	85%

Hurdle rate—the values set up-front which must be achieved during the measurement of these factors in the development cycle when the evaluation (count) is made.

Once the definition of quality is agreed upon, the second step is to apply it to the different modules, software documentation, and Software Development Notebooks (SDNs), which are components or packages in a WWMCCS release. That is, the quality of each of the components of the WWMCCS release is analyzed. This results in a "quality distribution" through which Pareto analysis can identify the critical components.

By Release

Analyze historically the various releases processed by WWMCCS ADP Directorate and rank their quality. By identifying and analyzing the releases with the poorest quality, some pitfalls can be avoided, and the beginning of a corrective

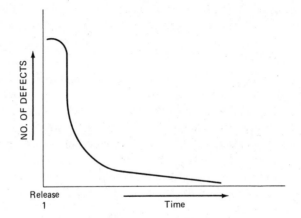

FIGURE 11-2. Software release defects.

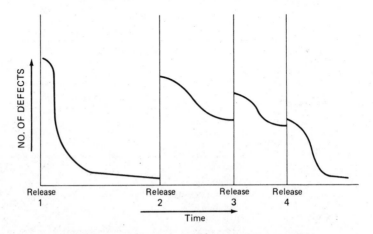

FIGURE 11-3. "Moving mountain" software releases defects.

program formed. Analyzing the best-quality releases will likely result in positive principles to follow that would become part of a standards program.

The "moving mountain" phenomenon occurs with the issuance of new releases. This phenomenon refers to the graphical representation of the number of defects in a software system plus the new defects which are uncovered in a new release. The basic graph, Figure 11-2, shows defects being removed over time with a software system.

The "moving mountain" occurs when the basic graph is drawn for each *new release* of the software system on the same graph, as shown in Figure 11-3.

With a graph such as Figure 11-3 it becomes easy to recognize that release 4 is rather good in comparison to releases 1, 2, and 3. It even seems likely that one is better off by remaining with release 1, but of course release 1 lacks the enhancements incorporated in releases 2, 3, and 4.

By Function

Analyze the "quality" of the various WWMCCS ADP Directorate functions. The first step is to list the various WWMCCS ADP Directorate functions as under *Manpower* discussed above. Second, determine which of the functions lead to the most problems and direct the corrective program at these troublesome functions.

A chart similar to Table 11-4 aids in the "by function" analysis of problems. The statistics assume 3 months time. Implicit in this approach is that a Pareto analysis

TABLE 11-4   Problems Encountered by Personnel Functions

PERSONNEL TASKS	PROBLEMS ENCTRED	% OF PROBLEMS ENCTRED	CUMULATIVE PROBLEMS ENCTRED	CUMULATIVE % OF PROBLEMS ENCTRED
Managerial Personnel				
Contract Administration	10	48	10	48
"Crisis Reaction"	8	38	18	86
Scheduling	2	9	20	95
Decision-Making	1	5	21	100
Planning	0	0	21	100
Controlling	0	0	21	100
"Task Preparation"	0	0	21	100
Technical Personnel				
Software Purchase Analysis	110	42	110	42
Contract Administration	58	22	168	64
Integration	40	15	208	79
"Crisis Reaction"	25	9	233	88
Planning	15	6	248	94
Stability Testing	7	3	255	97
Regression Testing	5	2	260	99
Demonstration Tests	4	1	264	100

TABLE 11-5   Problems Encountered by Personnel Sub-Functions

PERSONNEL TASKS	PROBLEMS ENCTRED	% OF PROBLEMS ENCTRED	CUMULATIVE PROBLEMS ENCTRED	CUMULATIVE % OF PROBLEMS ENCTRED
Managerial Personnel				
Contract Administration:				
Monitor Contract Fulfillment	5	50	5	50
Receive Contract	2	20	7	70
Resolve Contractual Conflict	2	20	9	90
Discover Contractual Conflict	1	10	10	100
Close Out Contract	0	0	10	100
Send Out Contract	0	0	10	100
"Crisis Reaction":				
System Crashes	5	56	5	56
Loss of Best Analyst	2	22	7	78
Previously Unplanned Customer Presentation Tomorrow	1	11	8	89
System Late for Delivery	1	11	9	100
Boss Needs Report by Tomorrow	0	0	9	100
Technical Personnel				
Software Purchase Analysis:				
Program to Aid in Vendor Analysis	50	45	50	45
Package History Check	45	41	95	86
Vendor History Check	10	9	105	95
Benchmark Conduct	4	4	109	99
"Perfect" Package Costs Too Much	1	1	110	110
Contract Administration:				
Contractor Disputes	30	52	30	52
Contractor Inadequate	20	34	50	86
Contractor Delivers Late	7	12	57	98
Monitor Contract Fulfillment	1	2	58	100
Letter Recommending Cancellation	0	0	58	100

is applied recursively within individual functions to determine which of the sub-steps have the most problems. A chart such as Table 11-5 aids in the "by sub-steps" analysis of problems.

Also resulting from this approach is the formulation of internal "quality criterion" to be applied to each of the internal WWMCCS ADP Directorate functions.

It should be noted that the function of the various vendors can be analyzed in a similar manner. In this case, the program would monitor the quality of the functions performed by the various vendors.

11.4 FEDERAL RESERVE EXAMPLE

The example cited is from another actual study of quality assurance conducted by McCabe & Associates, in 1982 for the Federal Reserve Bank.[12] As a part of a functional management program to improve the operations of the General Purpose Computer Department of the Federal Reserve Bank of New York, and to establish a departmental quality assurance program, McCabe & Associates was asked to conduct a software quality assurance study. The scope of the study is defined, the analysis process is described and the conclusions are stated below.

The scope of this effort was restricted to the ongoing operations and related interfaces of the General Purpose Computer Department of the Federal Reserve Bank of New York and how the quality of those operations might be improved. Specifically related to the project development cycle, the nature and extent of General Purpose Computer Department involvement in the following phases was investigated:

```
Project Proposal (Stage I)
    Development Schedule
    Resourse Requirements for:
        Acceptance Testing
        Production Operations
Design Phase (Stage II)
    Data Conversion Plan
    Acceptance Test Planning
    User's Guide Review
Implementation Phase (Stage III)
    Completion Criteria for "Run Books"
    Completion Criteria for Operator/User Training
Post Implementation (Stage IV)
    Post Implementation Review
    Post Implementation Evaluation
```

Further, the effort was limited to those software quality factors directly affecting the General Purpose Computer Department as currently chartered. The primary factor for this project was *usability*.

Attributes, or criteria, as developed by McCabe & Associates and others* associated with the usability factor are as follows:

Operability   Those attributes of the software that determine operation and procedures concerned with the operation of the software.

---

*William E. Perry, *Effective Methods of EDP Quality Assurance* (Wellesly, MA: Q.E.D. Information Sciences, Inc., 1981).

| Training | Those attributes of the software that provide transition from the current operation or initial familiarization. |
| Communicativeness | Those attributes of the software that provide useful input and output which can be assimilated. |

Of these criteria, operability and training were considered to have impact on the General Purpose Computer Department, with communicativeness impacting mainly the user.

The metric for stating requirements and measuring the accomplishments of the above criteria is the number of occurrences of program failures (ABENDS in the General Purpose Computer Department environment) attributable to operator error.

Other, or secondary software quality factors which have a high positive relationship with usability are *correctness* and *reliability*. These features were not analyzed in as much depth as the primary factor, usability.

The process used to conduct the analysis consisted of three major components:

- An analysis of the process used by the General Purpose Computer Department in accepting new or modified applications and placing them in production.
- An investigation of the classes or errors occurring.
- An investigation of the causes of the errors.

The analysis of the General Purpose Computer Department acceptance and production process was divided into two parts: (1) the introduction and acceptance of new or modified applications, including documentation, training, testing activities, as well as General Purpose Computer Department participation in the development process; and (2) running the applications in production including acceptance of user inputs, job setup and scheduling, and delivery of output. In both cases, the analysis included studying input, procedures, output, supporting documentation, and error reporting and correction procedures.

The investigation of the classes of error occurrence dealt with objective errors, i.e. those causing reruns of a portion or all of the application, and also subjective errors, i.e. those which, while not causing reruns, contributed to inefficiency and lack of management control. In this investigation, formal error (ABEND) reports were analyzed using the Pareto technique to determine which classes of errors occurred most frequently and had the most severe impact on operations and/or the user.

The final, and most detailed, analysis was aimed at determining potential causes for the various types of errors. Specifically, an attempt was made to attribute the cause of failure to one of the following areas:

System design
Operating procedure

Training
Documentation

Part of the document review consisted of a review of a typical set of application operations documents called "runbooks." The payroll system was chosen as an example of a large system which was frequently run, and which was considered to be of below-average quality. The payroll system is normally run 90 times a year, sometimes as often as three times in a single week. The system consists of 23 jobs (and hence 23 runbooks) in three major categories: pre-payroll processing, payroll processing, and post-payroll processing. Each runbook contains about 20 pages of information (460 pages total), and an average of eight control cards in a plastic pouch (177 cards total). These 23 jobs are set up, including reading in the control cards and mounting at least one tape for each job, each time payroll is run. The setup is done manually and the payroll system ABENDs approximately every other time it is run. In addition, sometimes the attempted rerun also ABENDs. The ABENDs are almost always caused by human error in setup or processing. The conclusion reached was that the runbook procedure is largely a manual process. Thus, it is excessively error-prone.

The most detailed step in the analysis process was to review the file of General Purpose Computer Incident (ABEND) Reports of the past year. This file consisted of a stack of completed "ABEND" forms. The origin of the form is as follows:

When a job or job step is unable to complete normally, for whatever reason, the job is suspended by the system and the operator is notified with a diagnostic code. This event is called an "ABEND" and the codes provided are "ABEND CODES." Upon the occurrence of such an event, the operator fills out the top portion of a General Purpose Computer Incident Report and notifies the shift production support analyst. The analyst is provided the report and any supporting documentation, such as printouts. The analyst then takes action to diagnose and correct the error and initiate a rerun of the job, if appropriate. The analyst then completes the ABEND form as to corrective action and disposition.

The review of the ABEND file was performed using Pareto-type analysis to identify which of the potentially many error types were most frequent and thus impacted most severely on productivity and quality. The analysis yielded a relatively small number of error types, and an even smaller number of classes of errors which occurred with dominating frequency. A disturbing aspect of the analysis was that, of the 1536 forms reviewed, 21 percent of the forms had no information entered as to cause of error and another 21 percent were unclear as to cause although job disposition was given; there remained only 58 percent of the file for meaningful analysis. The results of the analysis are shown in Table 11-6.

What can be inferred from this analysis is that a relatively small number of error types (9) have occurred during the past year. Six of these types comprising 78% of the total can be classified as human errors on the part of either the operator or the user as shown in Table 11-7.

TABLE 11-6   ABEND Analysis

CORRECTIVE ACTION	NUMBER	% OF TOTAL	% OF SAMPLE
Change JCL Card	195	12.6	22
System Error (Hardware/Tape/System)	154	10	17
Return to User	127	8.3	14
Change Procedure	115	7.4	13
Override File Catalogue	115	7.4	13
Incorrect Job Setup	97	6.3	11
File Not Found (Late Mount)	41	2.6	5
Contact Programmer	23	1.5	3
Restored and Rerun (Error not Found)	14	0.9	2
Sample Total	882	58.0	100
No Information	324	21	
Insufficient Information	330	21	
Total	1536	100	

TABLE 11-7   Rate of Human Errors Inferred from Analysis

JCL Card in Error	22%
User Input in Error	14
Procedure (JCL) in Error	13
File Catalogue/Designation in Error	13
Job Improperly Set Up	11
Tape Not Mounted on Time	5
Total	78%

The other significant error class is hardware or system errors. These are primarily tape read errors which are corrected by varying the drive off-line or by switching drives. The large proportion of human error can be attributable to one or more of the following:

- Poor human factors design of the application.
- Inadequate training of operators and users.
- Inadequate performance aids for the operators and users, i.e., runbooks, checklists and automated tools.

These human errors relate directly to the usability factor discussed earlier. In fact, these errors are the metric measurement for the operability and training criteria.

With regard to the software quality factors and their criteria, as discussed above, the following conclusions may be drawn:

- The usability of the software application being run in production by the General Purpose Computer Department must be considered low. The per-shift

rate of 1.6 ABEND represents a high resource cost and an unpredictable and disruptive environment.
- The operability criteria in particular is not being adequately met by systems development, as evidenced by the high error rate, i.e. every other run for payroll. Nor are operability requirements being fed to system development during the project development cycle.
- The involvement of the General Purpose Computer Department in the Project Development Cycle is minimal. No requirements for the usability of systems are fed in on a formal basis and review of development documentation is informal and inadequate.
- There exists an opportunity to reduce the number of error-prone human procedures through the use of installed packages such as APOLLO and ABENDAID and SCHEDULER. Other, related quality factors such as correctness and reliability appear to be satisfactory. This judgment is based on the lack of user complaints and the relatively infrequent need to call for programmer assistance. However, it should be noted that no evidence could be found that these factors were formally and rigorously tested prior to production.

The impact of the above findings and conclusions upon the operation of General Purpose Computer Department can be characterized as follows:

The 1536 ABEND, plus an estimated additional 384 (25%) errors not causing ABEND, create an extremely disruptive environment. As has been stated, this is approximately two (2) ABEND per shift, with at least one application ABENDing every other time it is run. Some recoveries and reruns require more than a day to accomplish.

In financial terms, the recovery and rerun procedures require an estimated 65 percent of the production support personnel resources of the Central Support Division. The dollar value of these services is approximately $150,000 annually, or 20 percent of the Division's budget. This cost can also be stated as 6 percent of the General Purpose Computer Department salary budget. If this 6 percent were extended to the entire General Purpose Computer Department budget, the dollar value would be $390,000 annually. If the useful life of an average application is 5 years, this would amount to almost $2 million merely to deal with operational errors over a 5-year period. Probably most important is the consideration that as applications become more complex and data-base-oriented, the ability of the production support team to maintain processing may be exceeded.

11.5 DEFECT IDENTIFICATION

Defect identification is a fertile area for Pareto analysis in the software field. Some examples from other fields are first identified; how this information points to other useful tools in software is explained with these examples, then demonstrated for the software field. The extensions discussed in this section are the concepts of common symptoms, basic causes of defects, and cost of defects.

TABLE 11-8   Defect Costs in a Foundry[2, p. 16-5]

DEFECT NAME	% OF ALL DEFECT COSTS		ANNUAL COST $000
	THIS DEFECT	CUMULATIVE	
Pits	36	36	315
Light	9	45	78
Physical Excess	8	53	73
Hard	5	58	41
Wide Gaps	4	62	39
Thin Face	4	66	32
Rough Sides	3	69	30
Broken (Foundry)	3	72	30
Casting	3	75	24
Broken (Machining)	3	78	23
All Others	22	100	186
Total	100	—	871

Table 11-8 shows the estimated cost of various defect types in a foundry. The most costly defects are the pits. Pareto analysis highlights this highest cost item.

The list of defects in Table 11-8 defines how the symptoms manifest themselves as defects, and so are called the *principal symptoms* or *common symptoms.* Whenever the causes for the principal symptom categories are "obvious" (i.e., all knowledgeable hands agree) from the nature of the symptoms, then an analysis can be made by *basic cause* categories. In still other cases where defects might be the result of any of several possible causes, it is nevertheless instructive to attempt to classify by basic cause categories.

An example is given in Figure 11-4: the depicted symptoms appeared during the operations of a sheet metal fabrications shop. Figure 11-4 is a true Pareto diagram because it is a bar graph showing the frequency of occurrence of various concerns, ordered with the most frequent ones first.[9, p. D-13]

The symptoms in Figure 11-4 were not sufficiently distributed to allow concen-

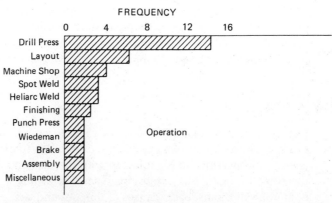

FIGURE 11-4. Symptoms Pareto diagram.[2, p. 45-19]

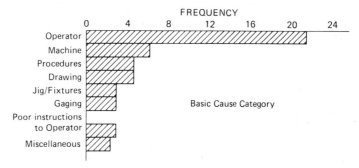

FIGURE 11-5. Basic causes Pareto diagram.[2, p. 45-19]

tration on the vital few. So a special study was set up for a limited period, during which each rejection or error was carefully traced to its origin by a task force representing Engineering, Production, and Inspection. Based on the facts uncovered, the task force's members tried to agree on the cause classification. Figure 11-5 represents Pareto analysis basic cause category for the sheet metal fabrication shop. The most promising direction for study appears to be the basic cause category "operator error," since operator errors (acknowledged as such by the operator in each case) are by a wide margin the biggest single class.[2, p. 45-19]

For computer software, some data for frequency of occurrence of errors is available. First, Rubey's "Quantitative Aspects of Software Validation"[6] data is presented. Table 11-9 shows the basic cause error categories. Then, for the major causes the common symptoms are shown in Tables 11-10, 11-11, 11-12, and 11-13.

TABLE 11-9   Basic Cause Error Categories for Software

ERROR CATEGORY	TOTAL		SERIOUS		MODERATE		MINOR	
	NO.	%	NO.	%	NO.	%	NO.	%
Incomplete or Erroneous Specification	340	28	19	11	82	17	239	43
Intentional Deviation from Specification	145	12	9	5	61	13	75	14
Violation of Programming Standards	118	10	2	1	22	5	94	17
Erroneous Data Accessing	120	10	36	21	72	15	12	2
Erroneous Decision Logic or Sequencing	139	12	41	24	83	17	15	3
Erroneous Arithmetic Computations	113	9	22	13	73	15	18	3
Invalid Testing	44	4	14	8	25	5	5	1
Improper Handling of Interrupts	46	4	14	8	31	6	1	0
Wrong Constants and Data Values	41	3	14	8	19	4	8	1
Inaccurate Documentation	96	8	0	0	10	2	86	16
Totals	1202	100	171	14	478	40	553	46

TABLE 11-10   Common Symptoms for Software Defects: Incomplete or Erroneous Specifications

ERROR CATEGORY	TOTAL		SERIOUS		MODERATE		MINOR	
	NO.	%	NO.	%	NO.	%	NO.	%
Dimensional Error	41	12	7	37	17	21	17	7
Insufficient Precision Specified	15	4	0	0	11	13	4	2
Missing Symbols or Labels	4	1	0	0	0	0	4	2
Typographical Error	51	15	0	0	0	0	51	21
Incorrect Hardware Description	7	2	3	16	3	4	1	0
Design Consideration Incomplete or Incorrect	177	52	8	42	47	57	122	51
Ambiguity in Specification or Design	45	13	1	5	4	5	40	17
Totals	340	100	19	6	82	24	239	70

TABLE 11-11   Common Symptoms for Software Defects: Erroneous Data Accessing

ERROR CATEGORY	TOTAL		SERIOUS		MODERATE		MINOR	
	NO.	%	NO.	%	NO.	%	NO.	%
Fetch or Store Wrong Data Word	79	66	17	47	52	72	10	83
Fetch or Store Wrong Portion of Data Word	10	8	10	28	0	0	0	0
Variable Equated to Wrong Location	10	8	4	11	6	0	0	0
Overwrite of Data Word	10	8	4	11	4	2	2	17
Register Loaded with Wrong Data	11	9	1	3	10	0	0	0
Totals	120	100	36	30	72	60	12	10

TABLE 11-12   Common Symptoms for Software Defects: Erroneous Decision Logic or Sequencing

ERROR CATEGORY	TOTAL		SERIOUS		MODERATE		MINOR	
	NO.	%	NO.	%	NO.	%	NO.	%
Label Placed on Wrong Instruction/Statement	2	1	2	5	0	0	0	0
Branch Test Incorrect	28	20	10	24	15	18	3	20
Branch Test Set Up Incorrect	2	2	1	2	1	1	0	0
Computations Performed in Wrong Sequence	9	6	1	2	2	2	6	40
Logic Sequence Incorrect	98	71	27	66	65	78	6	40
Totals	139	100	41	29	83	60	15	11

TABLE 11-13   Common Symptoms for Software Defects: Erroneous Arithmetic Computations

ERROR CATEGORY	TOTAL		SERIOUS		MODERATE		MINOR	
	NO.	%	NO.	%	NO.	%	NO.	%
Wrong Arithmetic Operations Performed	69	61	12	55	47	64	10	56
Loss of Precision	9	8	1	5	6	8	2	11
Overflow	8	7	3	14	3	4	2	11
Poor Scaling of Intermediate Results	22	20	4	18	15	21	3	17
Incompatible Scaling	5	4	2	9	2	3	1	5
Totals	113	100	22	19	73	65	18	16

Several inferences can be drawn from the data in Table 11-9 by SQA personnel. First, there is no single reason for unreliable software, and no single validation tool or technique is likely to detect all types of errors. Many possibilities are discussed in Chapter 18 to improve software reliability. Second, the ability to demonstrate a program's correspondence to its specification does not justify complete confidence in the program's correctness, since a significant number of errors are due to an incomplete or erroneous specification, and the documentation of the program cannot always be trusted. Third, intentional deviation from specification and the violation of established programming standards more often leads to minor errors than to serious errors. On the other hand, invalid timing or improper handling of interrupts almost always results in a significant error.

The data presented in Table 11-9 summarize the errors found in independent validations. In practice, however, the organization responsible for independent validation does not wait until the developer has completed program debugging. Instead, the independent validation organization often becomes involved at each program development phase to check that intermediate products (such as the program specification and program design) are correct.

The errors occurring in the categorization of Table 11-10, incomplete or erroneous specifications, indicate either deficiencies in, or the absence of, the verification of the program specification or program design, since there should be no errors in the final programs attributable to the program specification if the preceding verification efforts were perfect. As shown in Table 11-10, 19 serious and 82 moderate errors have escaped the verification efforts and have been found only during the checking of the actual coding. In 239 additional cases, an error due to incomplete or erroneous specification are considered of minor consequence; this is largely because the coding had been implemented correctly even though the program specification is itself in error.

If all of the 239 minor erroneous or incomplete specification errors were faithfully translated into coding, the total number of serious errors in the resultant coding would be 84 and the total number of moderate errors would be 162. Only 94 of the 239 minor errors would remain minor errors, even if the coding implemented the erroneous specification. This would make the incomplete or erroneous specification error category in Table 11-9 the largest error source by a factor of 2, and would increase the total number of serious errors by 38 percent and the total number of moderate errors by 12 percent. Obviously verification of the program specification and design in advance of coding and debugging is a very beneficial activity, and indeed is probably essential if reliable software is desired.[7, p. 7, 8]

Another source of data for a cost by type analysis is provided in *Software Reliability.*[8] This book presents an extensive collection of analysis of error data performed at TRW. The data has resulted from the analysis of seven projects; characteristics of the projects are shown in Table 11-14. Note that project 5 is broken down into 4 sub-projects. Each is a project unto itself because of the differing management, languages, development personnel, requirements, and so on.

Table 11-15 presents an analysis that is similar to the breakdown of the Rubey data. Although the definition of error types does not completely agree for the two studies there is a striking similarity in the two sets of data: logic errors and data-handling errors rank first and second in the serious error category in the Rubey data, and they likewise rank first and second in the TRW data (in fact, their respective percentages are similar).[7, p. 8]

The TRW study further analyzes various sub-types of errors. For example, logic errors are divided into the following types:

- Incorrect operand in logical expression.
- Logic activities out of sequence.

TABLE 11-14   Characteristics Breakdown of Projects Analyzed

PROJECT	SOFTWARE TYPE	OPERATING MODE	LANGUAGE	DEVELOPMENT APPROACH
2	Command and Control	Batch	JOVIAL J4	Single Increment*
3	Command and Control	Batch	JOVIAL J4	Single Increment*
4	Data Management	Time Critical Batch	PWS MACRO	Operational
5	Applications Software	Real-Time	FORTRAN	Top-Down Multiple Increment
	Simulator Software	Real-Time	FORTRAN	Top-Down Multiple Increment
	Operating System	Real-Time	Assembly	Top-Down Multiple Increment
	PA Tools	Batch	FORTRAN	Single Increment*

* "Single increment" refers to a typical development cycle in which each development phase is performed only once. This is in contrast to the top-down, multiple-increment approach, in which the cycle is repeated several times, first for a system of stubs and subsequently for replacement of stubs with deliverable software.

- Wrong variable being checked.
- Missing logic on condition test.

It is very important as well as interesting to examine this more detailed analysis of the two most costly errors—logic and data handling. The results are shown for Project 5. Table 11-16 shows the results for logic errors and Table 11-17 the detailed data handling errors. This data indicates that the most frequent error sub-type (according to TRW's data) and the most serious sub-type (according to Rubey's data) is *missing logic or condition tests.* The second most frequent and serious error sub-type is *data initialization done improperly.*

Another interesting study performed by TRW was to analyze error types according to major error categories. A particular error will have its source in one of the following stages of development: requirements, specifications, design, or coding. TRW performed this detailed analysis for 23 major error categories during

TABLE 11-15   Percentage Breakdowns of Code Change Errors into Major Error Categories

			PROJECT 5			
PROJECT 5 MAJOR ERROR CATEGORIES		PROJ. 3 (%)	PROJ. 4 (%)	APPLICATIONS SOFTWARE (%)	SIMULATOR SOFTWARE (%)	OPERATING SYSTEM (%)	PA TOOLS (%)
Computational	(A)	9.0	1.7	13.5	19.6	2.5	0
Logic	(B)	26.0	34.5	17.1	20.9	34.6	43.5
Data Input	(C)						
		16.4	8.9	7.3	9.3	8.6	5.5
Data Output	(E)						
Data Handling	(D)	18.2	27.2	10.9	8.4	21.0	9.3
Interface	(F)	17.0	22.5	9.8	6.7	7.4	0
Data Definition	(G)	0.8	3.0	7.3	13.8	7.4	3.7
Data Base	(H)	4.1	2.2	24.7	16.4	4.9	2.8
Other	(J)	8.5	0	9.4	4.9	13.6	35.2

TABLE 11-16   Project 5 Detailed Error Category Breakdown

		PERCENT OF MAJOR CATEGORY			
DETAILED ERROR CATEGORIES		APPLICATIONS SOFTWARE	SIMULATOR SOFTWARE	OPERATING SYSTEM S/W	PA TOOLS
B000	LOGIC ERRORS	2.1	8.3	0	4.3
B100	Incorrect Operand in Logical Expression	21.3	6.2	7.1	4.3
B200	Logic Activities Out of Sequence	17.0	29.2	10.7	10.6
B300	Wrong Variable Being Checked	4.3	8.3	14.3	2.1
B400	Missing Logic or Condition Test	46.8	39.6	60.7	76.6

TABLE 11-17   Project 5 Detailed Error Category Breakdown (cont.)

	PERCENT OF MAJOR CATEGORY			
DETAILED ERROR CATEGORIES	APPLICATIONS SOFTWARE	SIMULATOR SOFTWARE	OPERATING SYSTEM S/W	PA TOOLS
D000 DATA HANDLING ER-RORS	10.0	21.1	11.8	70.0
D100 Data Initialization not Done	6.7	10.5	17.6	0
D200 Data Initialization done Im-properly	20.0	10.5	41.2	10.0
D300 Variable Used as a Flag or Index Not Set Properly	20.0	5.3	23.5	10.0
D400 Variable Referred to by Wrong Name	6.7	21.1	0	0
D500 Bit Manipulation Done In-correctly	10.0	0	0	0
D600 Incorrect Variable Type	3.3	10.5	0	0
D700 Data Packing/Unpacking Error	10.0	5.3	0	10.0
D900 Subscripting Error	13.3	15.7	5.9	0

the design and coding stages of development for Project 3. The results are shown in Table 11-18.

The following observations are offered about the data in Table 10-18. The overall result shown—62 percent of all errors being design errors and 38 percent coding errors—is very representative of what other studies of similar data have shown. A rule-of-thumb used in the industry is that about 65 percent of all the errors will be design errors and 35 percent coding errors. The fact that 65 percent of all the errors are design errors suggests why the average cost of an error is so high.

Another strong point illustrated by Table 11-18 is the high cost of logic errors. Indeed logic errors are the most frequent, and, considering that 88 percent of logic errors are design errors, they contribute enormously to the cost of a given development. This data and observation reinforce the point made by Rubey's data; logic errors are the most serious error type. One of the implications of this result is that work done by SQA personnel with specifications should be heavily concentrated in the areas of logic and data handling.

A further interesting area to investigate is the identification of internal modules within a system that can result in high cost. That is, is there a way to identify the modules whose errors will have a large impact on the rest of the system? Specifically, a module's error becomes costly if that module has many affects on the rest of the modules in a system. A given module could be highly "coupled" with the rest of a system as a result of the parameters it passes, the global data it affects, the interrupts it can cause, or the modules it involves. If such a highly coupled module

TABLE 11-18   Project 3 Error Sources

MAJOR ERROR CATEGORIES		% OF TOTAL CODE CHANGE ERRORS	PROBABLE SOURCES	
			% DESIGN	% CODE
Computational	(AA)	9.0	90	10
Logic	(BB)	26.0	88	12
I/O	(CC)	16.4	24	76
Data Handling	(DD)	18.2	25	75
Operating System/ System Support Software	(EE)	0.1	(1)	
Configuration	(FF)	3.1	24	76
Routine/Routine Interface	(GG)	8.2	93	7
Routine/System Software Interface	(HH)	1.1	73	27
Tape Processing Interface	(II)	0.3	90	10
User Requested Change	(JJ)	6.6	83	17
Data Base Interface	(KK)	0.8	10	90
User Requested Change	(LL)	0	(2)	
Preset Data Base	(MM)	4.1	79	21
Global Variable/ Compool Definition	(NN)	0.8	62	38
Recurrent	(PP)	1.3	(1)	
Documentation	(QQ)	0.8	(1)	
Requirements Compliance	(RR)	0.4	89	11
Unidentified	(SS)	1.0	(1)	
Operator	(TT)	0.7	(1)	
Questions	(UU)	1.1	(1)	
		Averages	62%	38%

(1) Although errors in these major categories were changed, their source breakdown into design versus code is not attempted here since all other categories shown encompass 95 percent of the change errors noted.

(2) Enhancements or changes to the product's design baseline are considered "out of scope" for this study and therefore not accounted for.

has errors, it can be very costly since the erroneous assumptions made in the module can be spread throughout the rest of the system. The SQA personnel should look at module coupling to assure that it is minimized. It should be noted that the term *module* can be applied to any internal unit of a system.

The main references for this section are "Module Connection Analysis"[9] and *Applied Software Engineering Techniques.*[10]

Assume that a system is broken down into N modules. These are N^2 pairwise relationships of the form

P_{ij} = probability that a change in module i necessitates a change in module j

Let P be the N by N matrix with elements P_{ij}.

Let A be a vector with N elements that corresponds to a set of "zero-order" changes to a system. That is, A is the set of immediate changes contemplated for a system without considering intramodule side-effects. The total number of changes T will be much greater than A because of the coupling and dependency of the modules. An approximation of the total amount of changes T is given by:

$$T = A(I - P)^{-1}$$

where I is the identity matrix.

An example from the Xerox Timesharing System will be used to illustrate. The Probability connection matrix P for the Xerox Timesharing System is shown in Figure 11-6.

Let us look at P_{48}; $P_{48} = 0.1$, indicating a 10 percent probability that if module 4 is changed then module 8 will also have to be modified.

Let us assume that a global change to the system is to be made that will result in

	1	2	3	4	5	6	7	8	9	10	11	12	13	14	15	16	17	18
1	.2	.1	0	0	0	.1	0	.1	0	.1	.1	.1	0	0	0	.1	0	0
2	0	.2	0	0	.1	.1	.1	0	0	0	0	0	.1	.1	.1	0	.1	0
3	0	0	.1	0	0	0	0	0	0	0	0	0	0	0	0	0	0	0
4	0	.1	0	.2	0	.1	.1	.1	0	0	0	0	0	0	.1	0	.1	0
5	.1	0	0	0	.4	.1	.1	.1	0	0	0	0	0	0	0	0	.1	0
6	.1	0	0	0	0	.3	.1	0	0	.1	0	0	0	.1	0	0	.1	0
7	.1	0	0	.1	.2	.1	.3	.1	0	.1	0	0	0	.1	0	.1	.1	0
8	.1	.1	0	.1	.2	0	.1	.4	0	.1	0	0	0	.1	0	0	0	.1
9	0	0	0	0	0	0	0	0	0	.1	0	0	0	0	0	0	0	0
10	.1	0	0	0	0	.1	.1	.1	0	.4	.2	.1	.2	.1	.1	.1	.1	.1
11	.1	0	0	.1	0	0	0	0	0	.2	.3	.1	0	0	0	0	0	0
12	.2	0	0	0	0	.1	0	0	0	0	.2	.3	0	0	.1	.1	0	0
13	.1	.1	0	0	0	.1	.1	.1	0	.2	.1	0	.3	0	0	0	0	0
14	0	0	0	0	0	0	0	0	0	0	0	0	0	.2	0	0	0	0
15	0	0	0	0	0	0	0	0	0	0	0	0	0	0	.2	0	0	0
16	0	0	0	0	0	0	0	0	0	0	0	0	0	0	0	.2	0	0
17	0	0	0	0	0	0	0	0	0	0	0	0	0	0	0	0	.2	0
18	0	0	0	0	.1	0	.1	0	0	.1	0	0	0	0	0	0	0	.3

FIGURE 11-6. Probability connection matrix P.

modification to many of the modules. This global set of zero-order changes can be represented as a vector A (Table 11-19). (These are actual changes per module that were applied to the Xerox Training System during a specific period.)

Given A, one can now compute the approximation T of the total number of changes that will be required. This is done by computing

$$T = A(I - P){-1}, \text{ where } I \text{ is the } 18 \times 18 \text{ identity matrix}$$

The results are shown in Table 11-20.

TABLE 11-19   Changes Per Module

$A(1)$	2	$A(2)$	8
$A(3)$	4	$A(4)$	6
$A(5)$	28	$A(6)$	12
$A(7)$	8	$A(8)$	28
$A(9)$	4	$A(10)$	8
$A(11)$	40	$A(12)$	12
$A(13)$	16	$A(14)$	12
$A(15)$	12	$A(16)$	28
$A(17)$	28	$A(18)$	40

TABLE 11-20   Module Changes Required

XEROX TIMESHARING SYSTEM: INITIAL & FINAL CHANGES		
MODULE	INITIAL CHANGES (A)	TOTAL CHANGES $T = A(I - P)^{-1}$
1	2	241.817
2	8	100.716
3	4	4.4444
4	6	98.1284
5	28	248.835
6	12	230.376
7	8	228.951
8	28	257.467
9	4	4.4444
10	8	318.754
11	40	238.609
12	12	131.311
13	16	128.318
14	12	157.108
15	12	96.1138
16	28	150.104
17	28	188.295
18	40	139.460
Totals	296	2963.85

Notice the factor of 10 increase of total work over the initial set of changes; this is caused by the ripple effect of a change through highly coupled modules. The approximation of 2963.85 is within 4 percent of what Xerox actually experienced.[13]

The results in Table 11-20 clearly indicate that modules 10, 1, and 7 are highly coupled with the rest of the system. Module 10, for example, initially has 8 changes and ends up with 318 spill-over cumulative changes in all modules. On the other hand, module 3 initially has four changes and ends up with only four changes.

The point is that, by identifying the modules with the highest coupling (modules with maximum rows of probabilities in P), one can anticipate which modules are most dangerous to modify. Similarly, errors in these same modules will have an enormous impact on the rest of the system since the errors have to be removed not only from these modules but also from all the coupled modules. The errors made in these highly coupled modules will be the most costly.[7, pp. 17-21]

11.6 INSPECTION

The Pareto principle has been applied to assembly-line inspection by Juran. He suggests setting up a special study to secure the data for the needed distribution. Trained inspection personnel of proved accuracy are assigned to audit each work station for a period of time sufficient (about a month) to establish station-to-station variability. (The alternative of placing all inspectors at the end of the line is a waste of inspection effort. It also increases the lag between operation and detection. When prior operations are buried by later operations, no ready check is possible at the end of the line.) The operators are then classed A, B, C, etc., respectively. These classifications are then used, in accordance with the Pareto principle, as an aid in planning the distribution of inspection effort among the assembly line stations.[2, p. 41-12]

Like the assembly line, programming has a series of operations, each operation having its own exit criteria (see Chapters 5 and 9 for further details). There must be some means of measuring completeness of the product at any point of its development by inspection or testing. Then the measured data may be used by SQA personnel for controlling the process more effectively. This SQA activity has not been found to "get in the way" of programming, but has instead enabled higher predictability than by other means.

This section uses guidelines in Michael E. Fagan's "Design and code inspections to reduce errors in program development"[11] to govern the use of the Pareto principle in the programming process (detailed analysis of inspections is also made by James Dobbins in Chapter 9). For design inspection, participants, using the design documentation, literally do homework to try to understand the design—its intent and logic. To increase their error detection in the inspection, the inspection team first studies the ranked distributions of error types found by recent design and code inspections such as those shown in Tables 11-21 and 11-22. This study will prompt them to concentrate on the most fruitful areas (what we are calling the vital few).

TABLE 11-21   Summary of Design Inspections by Error Type (Order by Error Frequency)[11, p. 192]

VP INDIVIDUAL NAME	INSPECTION FILE				
	MISSING	WRONG	EXTRA	ERRORS	ERROR %
LO Logic	126	57	24	207	39.8
PR Prologue/Prose	44	38	7	89	17.1
CD ⌈CB Definition	16	2		18	3.5 ⌉
CU ⌊CB Usage	18	17	1	36	6.9 ⌋ 10.4
OT Other	15	10	10	35	6.7
MD More Detail	24	6	2	32	6.2
IC Interconnect Calls	18	9		27	5.2
TB Test & Branch	12	7	2	21	4.0
MN Maintainability	8	5	3	16	3.1
RM Return Code/Msg.	5	7	2	14	2.7
IR Interconnect Reqts.	4	5	2	11	2.1
PE Performance	1	2	3	6	1.2
RU Register Usage	1	2		3	.6
L3 Higher Lvl. Docu.	1			2	.4
PD Pass Data Areas		1		1	.2
FS FPFS	1			1	.2
MA Mod Attributes	1			1	.2
ST Standards					
	295	168	57	520	100.0
	57%	32%	11%		

TABLE 11-22   Summary of Code Inspections by Error Type (Order by Error Frequency)[11, p. 192]

VP INDIVIDUAL NAME	INSPECTION FILE				
	MISSING	WRONG	EXTRA	ERRORS	ERROR %
LO Logic	33	49	10	92	26.4
DE Design Error	31	32	14	77	22.1
PR Prologue/Prose	25	24	3	52	14.9
CU CB Usage	3	21	1	25	7.2
CC Code Comments	5	17	1	23	6.6
IC Interconnect Calls	7	9	3	19	5.5
MN Maintainability	5	7	2	14	4.0
PU PL/S or BAL Use	4	9	1	14	4.0
PE Performance	3	2	5	10	2.9
FI		8		8	2.3
TB Test & Branch	2	5		7	2.0
RU Register Usage	4	2		6	1.7
SU Storage Usage	1			1	.3
OT Other					
	123	185	40	348	100.0

TABLE 11-23   Basic Causes for Design Defects

	ERRORS	%	CUMULATIVE %
Unclear Requirements	17	3	100
Missing Requirements	34	7	97
Design	307	59	59
Poor Standards	125	24	83
Miscellaneous	37	7	90

TABLE 11-24   Basic Causes for Code Defects

	ERRORS	%	CUMULATIVE %
Unclear Design	84	24	91
Missing Design	117	34	34
Coder	115	33	67
Poor Standards	24	7	98
Miscellaneous	8	2	100

Tables 11-21 and 11-22 show the common symptoms for defects in the design and code respectively. From defect identification, it is a logical extension to probe the basic causes for these defects. The basic causes are shown in Tables 11-23 and 11-24.

One of the most significant benefits of inspections is the detailed feedback of results on a relatively real-time basis. When there is such early indication from the first few units of work inspected, the affected individual is able to show improvement, and usually does, on later work even during the same project.[11, p. 197]

11.7 STATISTICAL TECHNIQUE

The use of statistical analysis as an extension to Pareto analysis is discussed first in light of existing techniques, then extended to software techniques.

Figure 11-7 shows the frequency of errors of various types in a sampling of high-volume claim documents. Figure 11-8 shows the same data arranged according to the Pareto analysis.

The design and code inspections defect distributions shown in Tables 11-21 and 11-22 are adapted from Fagan (reference 11). Tables 11-25 and 11-26 show how they appear in the article. So, Table 11-21 and 11-22 are the result of arranging the data according to the Pareto analysis.

In preparing bids, experienced managers know that a few major components are decisive; the rest can be thrown in as a percentage. In valuing a plant, the experienced engineer singles out the major pieces of equipment and values them individually. The rest he or she figures as a percentage, or studies a sample and applies the findings to all.[1, p. 50] In the preparation of software bids, the details required are excruciatingly painful to supply. The rule of the trivial many espe-

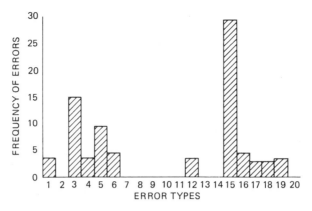

FIGURE 11-7. Frequency of error types in claim documents.[2, p. 46-11]

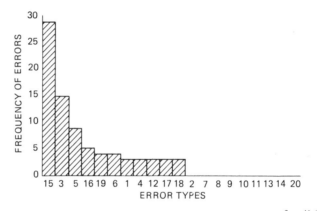

FIGURE 11-8. Pareto analysis of error types in claim documents.[2, p. 46-11]

cially applies here. The experienced manager should supply a software bid solidly based upon the vital few components, with percentages taken for the trivial many components.

Once a project is being executed, the job of controlling it in order to meet delivery schedules involves the Pareto principle. For instance to production control personnel, the "vital few" are the "bottlenecks". Formalized approaches—CPM (Critical Path Method) or PERT (Program Evaluation and Review Technique)—for predicting bottlenecks in complex system planning have coined the term "critical path" as a label for the vital few.[1, p. 47] Many software projects have been controlled by CPM or PERT, so there is nothing new here except the realization of either approach being another aspect of the Pareto principle.

For software testing, a unique statistical methodology has been devised by Dr. C. K. Cho and is covered in Chapter 17. The input domain of a piece of software can be represented by the Symbolic Input Attribute Decomposition (SIAD) tree.

TABLE 11-25   Summary of Design Inspections by Error Type[11, p. 192]

VP INDIVIDUAL NAME	INSPECTION FILE				
	MISSING	WRONG	EXTRA	ERRORS	ERROR %
CD DB Definition	16	2		18	3.5
CU CB Usage	18	17	1	36	6.9
FS FPFS	1			1	.2
IC Interconnect Calls	18	9		27	5.2
IR Interconnect Reqts	4	5	2	11	2.1
LO Logic	126	57	24	207	39.8
L3 Higher Lvl Docu	1			2	.4
MA Mod Attributes	1			1	.2
MD More Detail	24	6	2	32	6.2
MN Maintainability	8	5	3	16	3.1
OT Other	15	10	10	35	6.7
PD Pass Data Areas		1		1	.2
PE Performance	1	2	3	6	1.2
PR Prologue/Prose	44	38	7	89	17.1
RM Return Code/Msg	5	7	2	14	2.7
RU Register Usage	1	2		3	.6
ST Standards					
TB Test & Branch	12	7	2	21	4.0
	295	168	57	520	100.0
	57%	32%	11%		

(CD and CU bracketed together: 10.4)

TABLE 11-26   Summary of Code Inspections by Error Type[11, p. 192]

VP INDIVIDUAL NAME	INSPECTION FILE				
	MISSING	WRONG	EXTRA	ERRORS	ERROR %
CC Code Comments	5	17	1	23	6.6
CU CB Usage	3	21	1	25	7.2
DE Design Error	31	32	14	77	22.1
FI		8		8	2.3
IC Interconnect Calls	7	9	3	19	5.5
LO Logic	33	49	10	92	26.4
MN Maintainability	5	7	2	14	4.0
OT Other					
PE Performance	3	2	5	10	2.9
PR Prologue/Prose	25	24	3	52	14.9
PU PL/S or BAL Use	4	9	1	14	4.0
RU Register Usage	4	2		6	1.7
SU Storage Usage	1			1	.3
TB Test & Branch	2	5		7	2.0
	123	185	40	348	100.0

The choice of input units using the SIAD tree is a statistical application of Pareto Analysis since it is almost always impossible to use every available input in testing.

11.8 CONCLUSION

A broad survey of the Pareto principle has been presented, including an historical perspective leading to the use of the Pareto principle as an effective quality tool for detecting major error trends during the development of software projects. Extensions of the Pareto principle to software have been drawn from the areas of defect identification, inspections, and statistical techniques.

In summary, the steps for the application of the Pareto principle are succintly given by Juran[1, p. 44] as follows:

1. Make a *written* list of all that stands "between us and making this change."
2. Arrange the items of this list *in order of importance.*
3. Identify the *vital few* as projects to be dealt with individually.
4. Identify the *trivial many* as things to be dealt with as classes.

In software, as well as in general, the list of the vital few (through use of the Pareto principle) does *not* come as a complete surprise to all concerned: some of the problems on the list have long been notorious. But, to be sure, some of the problems will come as a genuine surprise. Indeed, the big accomplishment of the Pareto analysis is rather that! In summary,

1. Some notorious projects are confirmed as belonging among the vital few.
2. Some projects, previously not notorious, are identified as belonging among the vital few.
3. The trivial many are identified. This is not new, but the extent is usually shocking.
4. The magnitudes of both the vital few and the trivial many are, to the extent practicable, quantified. Ordinarily, this has not been done before.
5. There is established a *meeting of the minds as to priority* of needs for breakthrough. This is the biggest contribution of all since the Pareto analysis sets the stage for action.

The Pareto analysis also provides an early check on the attitude toward breakthrough. If either the vital few or the trivial many look like good candidates for change, then the original hunch is confirmed, so far. If, on the other hand, the Pareto analysis shows that none of these is economically worth tackling, that is likely the end of the matter.[1, p. 51-52]

Much has already been done in the application of the Pareto principle to software, but there is much more to work on. Emphasis on the vital few has produced a payoff, but there are always ways to improve the take. The guidelines presented in this chapter suggest how to identify these ways.

References

1. Juran, J. M., *Managerial Breakthrough* (New York: McGraw-Hill Book Co. 1964).
2. Juran, J. M., Gryna, Frank M., Jr., and Bingham, R. S. Jr., (editors), *Quality Control Handbook,* 3rd Ed. (New York: McGraw-Hill Book, 1979).
3. McCabe, Thomas J., *SQA—A Survey* (Columbia, MD: By the author, 5501 Twin Knolls Rd., 1980).
4. McCabe, Thomas J., *SQA—Seminar Notes* (Columbia, MD: By the author, 5501 Twin Knolls Rd., 1980).
5. Data Myte Corporation, *Data Myte Handbook—A Practical Guide to Computerized Data Acquisition for Statistical Quality Control* (Minnetonka, MN: Data Myte Corporation, 1984).
6. Rubey, R. J.; Dana, J. A.; and Biche, P. W., "Quantitative Aspects of Software Validation" *IEEE Transactions on Software Engineering,* SE-1(2), June 1975, pp. 150-155.
7. McCabe, Thomas J. "Cost of Error Analysis and Software Contract Investigation" *PRC Technical Note,* PRC 819-5, 20 February 1979, Contract No. DCA 100-77-C-0067.
8. Thayer, Thomas A.; Lipow, Myron; and Nelson, Eldred C., *Software Reliability* (New York: North-Holland Publishing Co., 1978).
9. Haney, F. A., "Module Connection Analysis", *AFIPS Conference Proceedings,* Vol. 4, 1972 Fall Joint Computer Conference, AFIPS Press.
10. McCabe, Thomas J., *Applied Software Engineering Technique,* Control Data Corp., 1975.
11. Fagan, Michael E., "Design and code inspections to reduce errors in program development," *IBM System Journal,* Vol. 15, No. 3 (1976), p. 182-211.
12. McCabe & Associates, Inc., Phase I Report of Software Quality Assurance Project for the Federal Reserve Bank of New York, General Purpose Computer Dept., July 29, 1982.

General References

Loucks, William N., and Whitney, William G., *Comparative Economic Systems,* 9th Ed. (New York: Harper & Row, 1957).

Miller, David W., and Starr, Martin K., *Executive Decisions and Operations Research,* 2nd Ed. (Englewood Cliffs, NJ: Prentice-Hall, 1969).

Samuelson, Paul A., *Economics, An Introductory Analysis* (New York: McGraw-Hill Book Co., 1951).

Thurow, Lester C., *The Zero-Sum Society* (New York: Penguin Books, 1981).

12

Software Quality Assurance Case Tools

James I. McManus
Westinghouse Electronic Systems Group

12.1 INTRODUCTION

What is CASE?

Over the past several years, roughly since 1985, there has been an explosion in what is known as CASE technology. By definition CASE stands for Computer Aided Software Engineering.

CASE refers to an integrated collection of tools designed to aid the life cycle process of developing compliant software products.

One of the first uses of the acronym CASE occurred in 1979. The application was specifically intended for distributed systems and stood for Computer Assisted Software Engineering.[1] Today CASE takes on a broader meaning for software. Its applications range from centralized systems to distributed, from the stand alone personal computer to large, complex, real time, embedded software systems.[2]

CASE can also take on the broader scope of software systems and in this sense is defined as Computer Aided Software/Systems Engineering.

Software Engineering Environments (SEE)

A Software Engineering Environment (SEE) also refers to an integrated collection of tools. However a SEE is characterized by the following additional attributes:[2] The environment enforces processes and methodologies such as configuration management and supports project management; processing is distributed but linked across different sites and across phases of the life cycle; the environment supports automated documentation and organizes information into documentation templates; the environment provides checks across development and project management activities; the environment is expandable and supports software reusability: the environment is user friendly and may use an expert system; and the environment contains powerful, automated, integrated tools to support software development. Currently, no one environment contains all of these characteristics.

Both industry and government have promoted SEEs. Examples include: Digital Equipment Corporation's (DEC) COHESION[3] which supports multiple platforms and integrated tools sponsored by DEC and third party vendors; the National Aeronautics and Space Administration's (NASA) software support environment Space Station Freedom (NASA-SSF);[4] and the Department of Defense's (DOD) SLCSE (pronounced slice), which stands for Software Life Cycle Support Environment. SLCSE was originally defined by the U.S. Air Force at the Rome Air Development Center (RADC) to support DOD-STD-2167A programs under development.[4]

CASE then is a subset of an SEE. As part of the support environment, CASE is the set of integrated tools within the environment. This implies restricting use of CASE tools to function within the set of enforceable processes defined by the SEE.

This chapter focuses on the emerging awareness of CASE tools as a means of improving the quality of the process of software development. Section 12.2 discusses the importance of CASE technology to the software development process. Section 12.3 discusses the state of the art in CASE tool integration. Section 12.4 presents a survey of the usage of tools by Software Quality Assurance (SQA) and discusses the role of SQA and CASE. Section 12.5 presents a CASE tool survey and discusses the application of several CASE tools as they support one or more phases of the software development life cycle. Section 12.6 presents a look ahead.

12.2 THE CASE FOR CASE

With the power of CASE, significant improvements to both process and product can be realized.

Benefits of CASE

Several benefits anticipated from application of CASE tool technology include cost benefits, reduced rework, automated support for the user, better managed processes, improved product performance, increased confidence going into development, and eventually the promise of industry wide standardization in CASE tool integration technology and in the software development processes that use them.

CASE Related Concerns

In addition to any benefits, the need for a fully integrated CASE environment is also highlighted by several other factors:

- the cost of software
- the quality of software
- consistency and confidence

The Cost of Software

The cost of software continues to rise in today's software environment. Witness the rise in fixed price contracts let by the Department of Defense (DOD). The days of cost plus contracts have, for all practical purposes, disappeared. Even the daily news carries events of major cost impact such as the January 7, 1991 television announcement that DOD would terminate one of its state of the art programs. According to the news it was reported, by congressional auditors, that delays and projected changes would probably push costs to at least five billion dollars over budget if bailed out by the government. Concerns such as these have also been noted in the past, such as the termination of one sizeable DOD contract in 1985, and the recent stop work order for an Air Force program in 1991. Notably, software costs have reached crisis proportions.

The Quality of Software

The quality of software has also suffered in the way that software is developed. The complexity of large software programs is on the rise making it more difficult than ever to know what is actually going on during development. Development today makes use of many concurrent processes, which must all come together for the first time during the software integration phase and later during the systems integration phase of the life cycle. Visibility needs to be exploited on the front end of software development, specifically where errors are introduced into the process.

Consistency and Confidence

How do we know what we are building when we are in the middle of the building process? What is there to tell us if we are, or even if we can, build software right the first time, as originally proposed by Philip Crosby[5] and now by the more recent Total Quality Management (TQM) approach to software?[6] Is most of software development subject to trial and error? What is there that provides a method of standardization and consistency that managers and engineers can rely on time and time again? How can we know and assess the real risks during the software development process? What is a true measure of progress? What is the true measure of performance?

These and other concerns are of increasing importance to the software community at large and to the customer. We can no longer afford to be at risk; vulnerable to the point where vital programs can be swept away by the tide of noncompliance and delays. Again witness the ripple effect through the economy of so many jobs lost in key industries across the country following the announcement of a recent DOD program termination. Not only are primes hurt but also the subcontractors, the vendors, and the individual.

It is specifically in the area of high risk where CASE technology can play a major role. The use of better control, widespread automated integration throughout a program, and high visibility are what is needed to reinforce up-front project management and technical decision making. These are but a few of the potential rewards awaiting evolution of CASE technology.

12.3 STATE OF THE ART IN CASE

The state of the art in CASE technology requires that two areas be examined; the state of the industry that produces software as a product, and the state of the art in CASE technology itself. It must be realized that considerable disparity can exist between the producer of software and the capability of tool technology.

On the one hand, the producer's company may be mature enough to use technology to improve its software production process, but the technology is not there. On the other hand, the technology may exist, but the producer's company may not be mature enough to use it. It is not uncommon for users to give up on adequate tools because their practices and procedures do not reinforce the need for such tools. Even worse, the producer may have inadequate procedures making the use of any tool arbitrary at best.

Self Assessment and Process Maturity Levels

It is recommended that serious companies evaluate their process for developing software to determine where they stand relative to the industry (i.e., benchmarking) and where they need to be. Companies behind the curve have the opportunity to take advantage of what others have accomplished in similar industries and markets. Companies on the leading edge of the curve have the satisfaction of knowing they are state of the art and are in a position to advance it to their benefit.

One way to rate your company is to compare the attributes which characterize your company's software development process with the criteria established for the Process Maturity Levels proposed by the Software Engineering Institute (SEI).[7] In this analysis a company is rated as to where it places on a five step ladder, as defined in Table 12-1 below. Level-1 is least desirable, Level-5 most desirable.

Findings show that most software companies are at a process maturity of Level -1 or -2. In a recent survey[8] conducted by SEI, of 250 companies including 50 of the top DOD contractors, 86% were at Level-1; none were at Level-4 or Level-5.

TABLE 12-1   Process Maturity Levels*[7]

"1. Initial: Until the process is under statistical control, orderly progress in process improvement is not possible. While there are many degrees of statistical control, the first step is to achieve rudimentary predictability of schedules and costs."

"2. Repeatable: The organization has achieved a stable process with a repeatable level of statistical control by initiating rigorous project management of commitments, costs, schedules, and changes."

"3. Defined: The organization has defined the process as a basis for consistent implementation and better understanding. At this point advanced technology can usually be introduced."

"4. Managed: The organization has initiated comprehensive process measurements and analysis. This is when the most significant quality improvements begin."

"5. Optimizing: The organization now has a foundation for continuing improvement and optimization of the process."

*Watts S. Humphrey, *Managing the Software Process,* © 1989, by Addison-Wesley Publishing Company, Inc. Reprinted with permission of the publisher.

At best, this implies the existence of procedures for conducting software development processes, but not the anticipated widespread adherence to them. In other words the methods for practicing software development are ad hoc.

Processes cannot be rigorously followed in such a culture. If software life cycle processes are not adequately defined, they can neither be measured nor improved, for there is no baseline to compare against. Without positive change and improvement, it is virtually impossible for a company to mature to the next level.

By conducting an internal self assessment of your company's process maturity level, two areas of significance will be revealed. First will be the adequacy of the processes used everyday to develop software, and second will be the readiness of your company to select tools to benefit those processes.

Tools should not be selected because they generically map to life cycle phases. This does not guarantee success. The processes must be defined first. Only then will the tools have a well defined role in supporting the process and also the outlook for success.

CASE Assessment

The second and more involved assessment is relative to the state of the art in CASE technology. This is an area that holds much promise for the concerns noted in Section 12.2. Much has been accomplished already. Prominent leaders in CASE tools today, such as Cadre Technologies, Mentor-Graphics, and Protocol to name a few,[4] offer products with integrated tools that support more than one phase of software development (for more on this refer to Section 12.5). However, future technological breakthroughs are still needed to achieve the much needed mechanism for integration. Within the industry, the two most likely candidates to advance the state of the art in future CASE integration technology are IBM and Digital Equipment Corporation (DEC).[4]

Dilemma for CASE

The problem for CASE is the lack of a standardized scheme[4] to integrate tools. There is not a clear, all encompassing, workable set of requirements from which a universally compatible, integration mechanism can be developed. Without a consistent means for integrating tools (even for a single vendor) achieving the flexibility to connect additional tools to the would-be integrated toolset becomes extremely difficult, if not impossible. To make matters worse, the cost of integrating tools into an existing tool set is also very expensive.

Although any one vendor can create a limited integrated toolset, using any one of the nonstandard integration schemes available today, each vendor is at high risk; first because of the considerable investment it takes to create CASE tools, and second because of the near term expectation that a major breakthrough may make their CASE tools obsolete.

Integration is an expensive proposition. Consequently, it behooves many small vendors to take a wait and see attitude[4] letting the giants battle over who will win out in standardizing a universally, acceptable, tool integration mechanism.

Technology can only move ahead so fast. Perceived needs are inconsistent. Consequently, direction is mixed at best. CASE tools will continue to be developed but will be targeted to well defined markets where identifiable needs can at least be partially met by existing levels of tool integration. Given this environment, vision for small companies may well remain near term to take advantage of existing markets and to minimize risk. Applications will be selectively focused and vendor tools will for the most part remain standalone to protect proprietary rights and market share.

CASE Integration

It is in the very definition of CASE tool integration where the point of focus breaks down. Witness the numerous versions and variations of CASE tools and environments produced in the 1980s. Over 250 SEEs with various tool applications have been or are under development according to one source.[2]

Integration applications can range from transfer of data between stand alone tools to a fully integrated support environment with strongly connected tools, including tools developed by different vendors, providing users both control over the tools and the data. In its implementation, integration is subject to various interpretations depending upon the objective of the user and/or the capability of the innovator.

Figure 12-1 illustrates several levels of integration with varying degrees of tool interfaces.[9] Although there is what can be termed an exchange of data, this condition offers minimal interface capability. In this case, data is exchanged between tools through a transformation, usually manually, or transfer of data, in whole or in part. For example, two stand alone word processor tools can access the same document by converting to a common format such as ASCII for input. Several characteristics of the data may be lost during the conversion process, but the text is transferred.

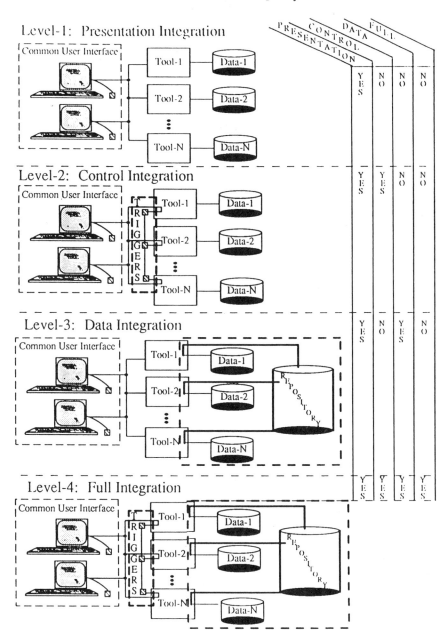

FIGURE 12-1. Levels of CASE Tool Integration.[9] Reprinted with permission of CASE Consulting Group, Lake Oswego, Ore. 97035, Copyright © 1989; Ref: *CASE Outlook.* Vol. 89. No. 2, Mar/Apr.

Integration for CASE technology is essentially defined as one or a combination of the following levels of integration:

Level-1. "Presentation Integration," is a mechanism for invoking CASE tools and tool functions through a Common User Interface.[3] An example would be a personal computer (PC) or workstation which has access to several software packages. The available packages could be presented to the user in a list, shell, or high level menu. The most widely accepted form of a common user interface today is the X-Window System,[3] a technology developed at the Massachusetts Institute of Technology. Note that presentation integration does not enhance the way data is exchanged between tools and still requires manual conversion and transfer of the data.

Level-2. "Control Integration,"[4] uses "triggers" to control the sequential execution of tasks through the use of integrated CASE tools based on information reporting among the tools. A trigger is a way for a tool to notify other tools of an event or occurrence within the system of tools. This might occur when a requirements tool executes an analysis task and triggers (i.e., sends) a signal to notify the design tool that it has completed its task.

Level-3. "Data Integration,"[4] is a mechanism which permits global sharing of data among integrated CASE tools either through direct or indirect means and includes access to both local and public data storage areas. The data may be accessible/stored in a shared data area or transferred through a utility.

A fourth level, considered the ultimate in CASE integration, is a combination of the above noted three levels. This is called fully integrated.

Level-4. "Full Integration." An environment (SEE) which ties all three levels of integration together into a fully integrated environment is generally referred to as an Integrated Project Support Environment (IPSE).[4] The IPSE is a tool coordination facility which provides the framework for full integration and utilization of CASE tool applications throughout the software development process.

A Framework[4] permits users to select the tools most appropriate for their applications and to integrate these tools into the system. The Framework ideally supports full integration and includes presentation integration, data integration, and control integration. Full integration is considered to be several years away. Figure 12-2 represents a model of a Framework for total integration.

CASE tools generally support at least one of the three levels of CASE integration: presentation integration, data integration, or control integration.

Within the Framework of Figure 12-2, the common user interface represents the front end of integration, what the user sees, and is referred to as presentation integration. Tools applicable here are X-Window System and DECwindows. These tools present the user with a multiple screen environment and user friendly features such as a mouse, pull down menus, icons and scroll bars.[3] Development tools may integrate with common user interface tools to take advantage of the pull down menus, mouse, etc.

The common repository interface shown in Figure 12-2 represents the second level of integration, control integration, which supports project management and configuration management services such as data integrity and security, versions of

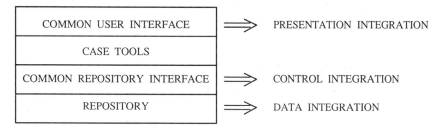

FIGURE 12-2. A framework for CASE Integration.[3] Based on *The Digital COHESION Environment for CASE.* Copyright © 1990 by Digital Equipment Corporation. Reprinted with permission of Digital Equipment Corp.

software programs and data files, object oriented management, control information using triggers, and procedural information. DEC has proposed "A Tools Integration Standard" (ATIS)[3] as an industry standard for the common repository interface. ATIS is an object oriented interface with rule processing capabilities.

Note, the Software Backplane, such as that produced by Atherton Technology, provides the mechanism for controlling the interfaces among the integrated CASE tools.

The Repository in Figure 12-2 represents the third level of integration, data integration. Data integration permits tools to share information throughout software development.[3] Information can be shared among tools from several vendors once integrated into the system.

Both Control Integration and Data Integration are dependent upon the Repository. The repository, unlike data dictionaries, offers the advantage of storing information about objects, including the methods of operating on those objects.

A repository[4] is an object oriented database that stores CASE tool data using object relationships and rule processing. The front runners in repository design are IBM with its Application Development/Cycle (AD/Cycle) and DEC's Common Data Dictionary/Plus (CDD/Plus).

AD/Cycle is IBM's CASE methodology which uses a common data repository based on IBM's Systems Application Architecture (SAA) development environment. CDD/Plus is DEC's CASE tool data repository which uses distributed access capabilities to support DEC's VAX environment.

The Framework of Figure 12-2 shows full integration of all levels and is representative of an IPSE. An IPSE presents a logical view of the system to the user. Several makes of an IPSE exist. One of the first (if not the first) and most comprehensive IPSEs was developed by Atherton Technology.[4] This environment was based on Atherton's internally developed Software Backplane and Softboard Series™ of integrated applications.

The Software Backplane is the environment that connects the CASE tools, the data and the project procedures together. The Software Backplane also allows the user freedom of choice in the selection and use of tools and methodologies.

Atherton's Softboard Series™ consists of Atherton's Integration Softboard— which integrates the development tools together, Atherton's Configuration Management Softboard—which automates tracking and statusing of project defined objects for baselines, and Atherton's Project Softboard—which tracks formal changes for the software project. The IPSE uses a data repository which stores and links data objects across different databases.

A more recent IPSE is DEC's COHESION, an evolving software development environment. The current COHESION environment supports the entire development and deployment cycle as well as the management of software. COHESION supports all phases of the software life cycle, accommodates multiple platforms, and interfaces with other computing environments which support transaction processing, information systems, and embedded systems.[3]

Major elements of COHESION are DEC's Network Application Support (NAS), CASE integration Framework, and CASE tools.

NAS is a distributed, networked environment which facilitates interoperability and portability. The CASE Integration Framework links the three levels of presentation, control and data integration shown in Figure 12-2. CASE tools integrated into the COHESION environment support both DEC tools and third party tools.

The Framework of Figure 12-2 shows a repository which acts as a central data storage and retrieval facility for CASE tool data and provides data integration. A repository makes data available to the accessing tool regardless of whether the actual data resides in the repository or elsewhere within the distributed system.

The current problem in data integration is that of data incompatibility[4] when moving data between tools. The rules and relationships surrounding databases are controlled by the tools creating the data. This results in data mismatches or lost meanings when data is transferred to secondary tools.

IBM and DEC are the apparent leaders in evolving state of the art repository design. IBM's repository, part of the AD/Cycle environment, is a DB2 based repository. Several vendors have been subcontracted to integrate their tools into the IBM environment. DEC's repository, CDD/Plus, currently runs under VMS, which is a strict platform for vendors to deal with when integrating under COHESION.

12.4 SQA AND CASE

The role of Software Quality Assurance (SQA) in relation to tools is primarily twofold. First, SQA in its role to assure compliance with enforceable processes has responsibility to negotiate the selection and use of specific tools by software development in its execution of these processes during development. The negotiation is a shared process conducted jointly with software development to select tools most appropriate for the success of the program and also as a means of posturing the company to become a Level 3 company (refer to Table 12-1). This is necessary particularly for companies at process maturity Levels 1 and 2. Appropriate tools not only promote the consistency, structure and discipline required in today's sophisticated programs, but assure that the ad hoc, chaotic activities characteristic of Level 1 and Level 2 companies are controlled and, over time, are replaced by well defined enforceable processes. This benefit serves not only the program but the entire company.

Second, in its role as assurer of quality for the program, SQA must make use of existing CASE tool technology to keep pace with development and to measure progress and performance. CASE tools should be selected by SQA to support such functions as trend analysis, metrics determination, increased visibility, and accurate current status reporting.

In this section a survey[10] of how well tools are used by SQA is presented. This is followed by a discussion of how SQA could more appropriately use tools as "Poka-Yoke"[11] devices to mistake-proof the software development process.

SQA Tool Survey

The information presented here is taken from the Software Quality Survey sponsored by the American Society for Quality Control (ASQC).[10]

According to the survey, many of the tools used by SQA to implement their programs are manual. These include brainstorming, use of checklists and standards. Very few of the numerous tools available in today's market are being used to automate SQA tasks. The one exception is the extensive use of an automated requirements tracer within the Aerospace industry. The reason given for this exception was the extreme difficulty of having to track requirements without an automated tool.

The list below identifies several of the tools available for use by SQA teams on programs. The figures status the percent of use each specific tool received within industry SQA departments. The percent of use is divided among three categories of industry users as follows: Aerospace Firms, Non-Aerospace Firms, and the average between them.

Figures 12-3, 12-4, and 12-5 show the percent of use by all three industry categories for the following tools:

Complexity Analyzer: An automated tool used to determine the complexity of software design or code using some metric like fan-in/fan-out, degree of nesting or other characteristic.

Database Analyzer: An automated tool used to investigate the structure of and flow within a database to determine whether performance goals can be realized.

Error Lists: A list of common errors typically distributed at a walkthrough or an inspection to help reviewers understand what to look for as they go through a design or code.

Histograms: Frequency distributions in which heights of rectangles placed upon the horizontal axis are used to indicate frequency information.

Logic Analyzer: An automated tool used to inspect the use of control logic within a program, determines if it is proper and mechanizes the specified design.

Reliability Models: Automated packages used to assess the probability with which the software will perform its required functions during a stated period of time.

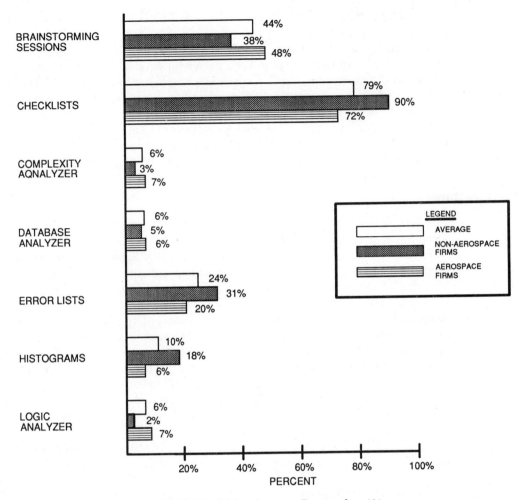

FIGURE 12-3. SQA tool survey—Percent of use (A).

Simulators: Automated tools (both hardware and software) used to represent certain features or functions of the behavior of a physical or abstract system.

Standards Analyzer: An automated tool used to determine whether prescribed development standards have been followed.

Test Drivers: An automated tool that invokes an item under test, often provides test input and reports test results.

Cause and Effect Graphs: A diagrammatic tool used to show cause and effect relationships for analysis purposes.

Comparator: An automated tool used to compare two software programs, files, or data sets to identify commonalities and/or differences.

Consistency Analyzers: An automated tool employed to identify inconsistencies in conventions used in requirements, designs or programs.

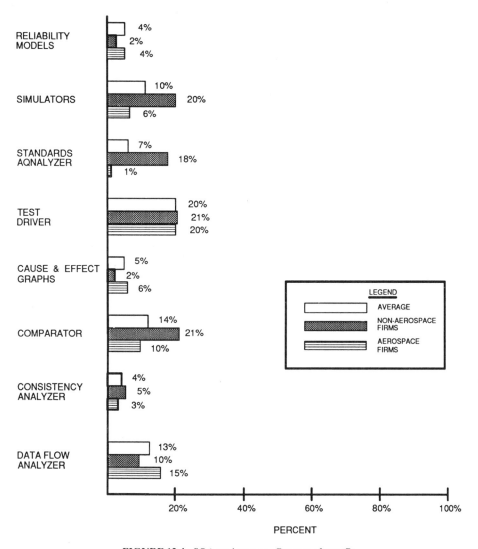

FIGURE 12-4. SQA tool survey—Percent of use (B).

Data Flow Analyzer: An automated tool used to determine if a data flow diagram is complete, consistent, and adheres to the established set of rules that govern its construction.

Fishbone Diagrams: A diagrammatic tool used to illustrate multiple relationships all at the same time.

Interface Analyzer: An automated tool used to determine if a range of variables is correct as they cross interface boundaries.

Metrics Analyzers: An automated tool used to collect, analyze, and report the results of metrics quantification and analysis activities.

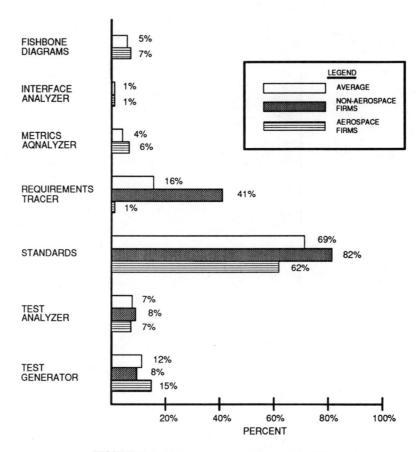

FIGURE 12-5. SQA tool survey—Percent of use (C).

Requirements Tracer: An automated tool used to trace how the requirements were realized in the design and code.

Test Analyzer: An automated tool used to determine test case coverage (i.e., whether a segment of code had been tested by any of the defined tests).

Test Generator: An automated tool used to generate test cases directly from some specification.

Standards: Standards are established rules to be followed during development and present a formalized basis for comparative evaluation.

Checklists: Checklists establish rules for development which are used as structuring guides.

SQA Model Survey

Also noted in the ASQC Survey[10] are the use of models by the SQA groups. Figure 12-6 statuses the percent of the SQA population who use models as an SQA resource and what the breakdown is within that percent.

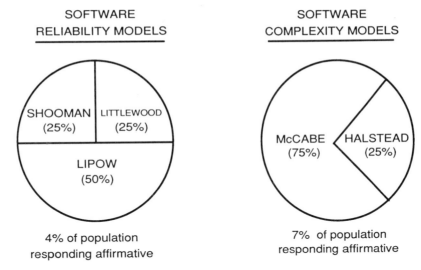

FIGURE 12-6. SQA model survey—Percent of use.

As shown, only a small percentage of the SQA population uses models; 7% use complexity models; 4% use reliability models. Of the 7% that use complexity models, Figure 12-6 shows a breakdown of 75% for the McCabe Cyclomatic Complexity Metric and 25% for the Halstead Metric. Of the 4% that use reliability models, Figure 12-6 shows a breakdown of 50% for the Lipow model, 25% for the Shooman model, and 25% for the Littlewood model.

"Poka-Yoke" and Zero Defect Software

In contrast to the findings of the ASQC Survey,[10] there is considerable need to exploit automation in software development processes. This need is best illustrated by the success attained by Shigeo Shingo[11] in his use of "Poka-Yoke" (i.e., mistake proofing) devices to prevent errors from occurring in the process.

Paraphrasing the description of Shigeo Shingo, a Poka-Yoke device is any device integrated into a process, at the point where a defect originates, to prevent the defect from occurring, thus mistake proofing the process. This approach is not limited to hardware and has ample ground for its application in software.

The use of CASE tools, as Poka-Yoke devices in software, is an extremely challenging and promising area for SQA. The need to eliminate errors at their source to produce defect free products is a goal too significant to ignore. And who is better to pursue it than SQA?

The philosophy is simple. First examine the suspect process, any process, to determine the reason for (root cause of) the mistake. Then determine the simplest means to prevent that mistake from recurring again and implement it.

One example,[11] (presented here with permission from *Zero Quality Control: Source Inspection & the Poka-Yoke System*, Shigeo Shingo, English Translation copyright © 1988 by Productivity Press, Inc., P.O. Box 3007, Cambridge, MA 02140. Phone (617) 497-5146), was that of an employee who worked on an assembly line inserting springs in ON/OFF switches. Note: this example is The number of defective switches being returned by the customer was cause for alarm and unacceptable to management. The reason for the returns was because either the "ON" spring or the "OFF" spring was missing. In examining the suspect process, Shigeo Shingo noticed that random numbers (a handful) of springs were taken from a box to be inserted individually. It was easy to lose track of how many springs were inserted in a switch after "N" number of switches. Mr. Shingo's solution was simple. He grabbed an available cup and said to take only two springs from the box and put them in the cup. When the cup was empty, the switch had to have the correct number of springs inserted; two. Only then could the switch be sent down the assembly line to the next station. Only then would the employee be permitted to take two new springs from the box and put them in the cup for the next switch. This simple procedure was adopted by all employees who inserted springs. After that, management far exceeded their expectations in reducing the number of returned switches.

The secret for the new success was in the process. By improving the process, the number of defects quickly approached zero.

In this example several chronological points are obvious.

First: Management's Awareness of the Problem. (Metrics). Management's immediate reaction was concern for the quality of its products. This concern was raised by the greatest metric of all; profit. The number of returned products was a true measure, reflecting customer dissatisfaction, fewer sales and less profit.

Second: Management's Commitment to Prevention. (Prevention, not Corrective Action). Corrective action (fixing defective switches) only corrects the product, does nothing to prevent new products from becoming defective and is a form of corrective maintenance. Preventive action corrects the process so that the worker can more readily to the job right the first time. To correct the process the root cause of the problem must be found and eliminated.

Third: Root Cause Determination Within the Process. (Maximum Process Visibility). Determination of the root cause requires an in-process evaluation and inspection of the process; not off-line analysis but live, in-person, face to face observation. The highest level of visibility is required. In the example above management was willing to reveal the process to an outsider to determine the root cause of the problem. By opening up the process to observation the root cause can be determined. (Essentially there was no visible way for the worker to verify that two springs were installed.)

Fourth: Eliminating the Root Cause from the Process. (Process Improvement(s) Defined). The preventive action must be incorporated into the suspect process. This requires a change to the process to bring about the desired prevention improvement(s). In the example, the cup was the "Poka-Yoke" device which provided the visibility required by the worker to verify that two springs had in fact been installed. Note however that the cup was not sufficient in and of itself. The actual process change was the requirement to place two and only two springs in the cup for each switch prior to installation.

Fifth: Adopting the New Process. (Acceptance in the Work Place). When the new/modified process is approved for use, the procedure for executing the new process is approved for use, the procedure for executing the new process must also be changed; reflecting management's commitment to prevention of defects and to acceptance of the new process in the work environment.

The above chronological steps are representative of a quality improvement process. They apply to software as well as manufacturing and hardware. Successes have been numerous in the manufacturing environment environment. Very little has been documented for software. As a step in the right direction, Table 12-2[12] lists several key elements within the software development process and the set of tools recommended for use as Poka-Yoke devices for each element.

There are two reasons for introducing this example in a discussion of SQA and CASE. The first is that Poka-Yoke devices are devices integrated into processes to prevent defective products from being produced. No greater benefit can accrue than to prevent defects which cause serious and costly problems later. Since the advent of CASE, there are many tools, some integrated, some standalone, that offer consistency and increased visibility; exactly what is needed to observe processes and determine the root cause of problems. Additionally with recent advances in repository design, the ability to store large quantities of data using compact disks, and the possibility of a major breakthrough in CASE tool integration technology, many new capabilities are on the horizon. CASE tools offer the software engineer a way to integrate Poka-Yoke software devices into the process. CASE tools (the device), if used properly (the process) can bring about the changes needed to effect prevention in the work place.

The second reason is that SQA in its role to effect quality assurance measures has the opportunity to recommend and negotiate (refer to Chapter 5) with management the use of specific CASE tools to support both quality and software development in the work place. These tools can be applied by SQA engineers on programs (such as ADAMAT which supports 150 metrics) or by software engineers (such as Teamwork or DesignAid to support front end structured analysis and design methods).

The role of SQA in software is not unlike that of Mr. Shigeo Shingo's concepts, to evaluate processes for quality improvement and prevention. SQA can recommend use of CASE tools as effective Poka-Yoke devices in software development processes. The use of such tools in this way to prevent defects is a step in the direction of zero defect software.

12.5 CASE TOOL SURVEY

CASE tools exist for all phases of the software life cycle. This section discusses several of the currently available tools being offered today. However it must be

TABLE 12-2   Zero Defect Software and Poka-Yoke.[12]

Element	Tools (poka-yoke)	Element	Tools (poka-yoke)
Requirements	a. Requirements tracking b. Templates for documents c. Structure analysis d. Data Flow Diagram (DFD) e. Data Dictionary (DD) f. Input, Processing, Output (IPO)	Documentation *(Continued)*	e. Word Processing f. Grammar checker g. Automated generation of: PDL-Program Design Language DFD—Data Flow Diagram DD—Data Dictionary DBDD—Data Base Design Document SDD (sections)—Software Design Document IDD—Interface Design Document Flow Diagram
Design	a. Requirements tracking b. Templates for documents c. PDL (Program Design Language) checker d. Hierarchy (CALL/CALLED) tree automation e. Automatic sizing from PDL f. Global software SYSGEN g. Flow diagram	Management visibility	a. Automate chart generation for a and b b. PERT or CPM charts c. Page & line progress counts
Code	a. Requirements tracking b. Templates for code c. Compiler, assembler, linker d. Pretty printer e. Standards checker f. Automated sizing g. Automated line of code (LOC) counter h. Language sensitive editor	Timing & sizing	a. Trend analysis/extrapolation b. Automated page & line updates c. Automated execution time recording d. Automated sizing recording e. Logic analyzer/Timing analyzer f. Line of code (LOC) counter g. SLAM or similar timing & sizing models
Test	a. Requirements testability b. Templates for documents c. Cyclomatic complexity measurement d. Path analysis identification e. Unit test tool f. Automated systems test tool g. Automated test setup h. Simulators/emulators i. Test drivers j. Subsystem emulators	Configuration management	a. Automated configuration control
Documentation	a. Requirements traceability through documents b. Templates for documents c. Available "boilerplate" d. Spell checker and dictionary	Software Development File (SDF)	a. Requirements flowdown b. Automate the file entry and retrieval
		Reviews	a. Automated presentation material

Table reproduced with permission of McGraw-Hill, Inc. and is taken from *Zero Defect Software*. G. Gordon Schulmeyer. Copyright © 1990, McGraw-Hill, Inc.

kept in mind that these tools are all subject to enhancement or replacement over time, particularly in light of the recent explosion in CASE tool technology.

The discussion herein is based on marketing information available in the open literature[3, 14, 17, 18, 19] and presents a brief summary of the tools. Each brief identifies the tool, its manufacturer, specific application(s) of the tool, and whether the tool is part of an integrated tool set. Table 12-3 also identifies the tools and groups the tools according to the phase of the life cycle they support.

Note: the software tools described herein not meant to be an exhaustive set of tools across the life cycle. Nor are they meant to be the most desirable for any given phase. The list of tools, as well as the descriptions provided within this text, are merely representative of some of the tools that exist in today's market. The selection process is user dependent (i.e., any candidate tool must meet specific requirements as defined by the individual user and as constrained by the environment within which the prospective tool must operate).

TABLE 12-3   CASE Tool Life Cycle Survey[3]

System/Software Requirements, Analysis, Design	Implementation	Integration and Test	Documentation
DECdesign	FOCUS	Source Code Analyzers	Aranda
DesignAid II	Foundation	Test Tools: • diff	Interleaf 5
Excelerator	Netron CAP Development Center	• shell	VAX Document
IDEF/Leverage and Personal IDEF Leverage	Saber C	Performance Analysis: • prof	
Mentor/CASE	SmartStar	• pixie • getusage	
Rtrace	RTrace	RTrace	
Software Through Pictures	SMART system	T	
Statemate	VAX Rally		
Teamwork 4	ADAMAT		
Editing Tools			
	Code Debuggers		

SOFTWARE EXECUTIVE BACKPLANE
(TOOL INTEGRATOR)

System/Software Requirements Analysis and Design

DECdesign: Digital Equipment Corporation.[3]

- Structured Analysis & Design Tool.
- Runs under the VMS Operating System. Requires a workstation with 12 mega-bytes and must integrate with DEC's Repository CDD/Plus.

DECdesign provides a graphics environment using DEC-windows (an X-window derivative for DEC) to model the behavior of processes and data within the software analysis and design phases of development. Graphics is based on Yourdon[13] and Ward-Mellor[20] methods.

DesignAid II: CGI Systems, Inc.
- PC Based CASE tool supporting Structured Analysis, Design & Documentation.
- Runs on IBM's PS/2, PC/XT, PC/AT, Compaq: uses PC/MS-DOS V3.1 or above; supports DOS V3.1 compatible LANs (Novell Advanced NetWare, IBM's Token-Ring, PC-Network, 3COM 3+Open & Banyan Vines). When bridged with CGI's PACBASE, provides a software engineering environment under IBM's Ad/Cycle.

DesignAid II is CGI's I (integrated—CASE tool providing analysts, designers and tech writers with integrated support over the software life cycle. As front end analysis and design tool, DesignAid II directly supports: Yourdon/DeMarco Process Modeling with automated balancing and validation; Data Modeling using Chen notation (tool option); Ward/Mellor and Hatley real time modeling (tool option); Information Engineering linking matrices with their diagrams in the Repository; and automated transformation of DFD processes and data stores into structure chart modules using the Design Module. Key features of DesignAid II are: an interactive multi-user Repository with data objects and file sharing; multi-file/multi-window environment with capability to nest and group files using menu files; automatic data normalization of data structures; Automated balancing & validation of parent-child diagrams using rule-based analysis; integrated text and graphics (the AutoDraw™ feature supports creation of diagrams from text and creation of text from diagrams); and an optional interface for some standard desktop publishing systems & word processing software.

Excelerator: Index Technology, Inc.[3]
- Structured Analysis and Design tool.
- Runs standalone on a PC and under VMS. Under VMS, Excelerator uses a bridge to interface with DEC's Repository CDD/Plus and also integrates with the VAX Language Sensitive Editor/Source Code Analyzer.

Excelerator provides real-time specification, data modelling and structured analysis and design.

IDEF/Leverage and Personal IDEF/Leverage: D. Appleton Company, Inc.[3]
- Analysis and Design Tools.
- Runs under VMS.

IDEF/Leverage products are automated database design tools. These tools provide computer aided integrated manufacturing and information system integration. The tools also support DOD's Computer-Aided Acquisition and Logistics Support (CALS) Initiative. As part of DEC's COHESION environment for CASE, IDEF Leverage tools run under DEC's VMS and use the VAX relational database management system, Rdb/VMS.

Mentor/CASE: Mentor Graphics Corporation.[3]
- Analysis and Design Tool.
- Runs under VMS and UNIX.

Mentor/CASE supports structured analysis and design techniques. Release 8.0 supports a graphical user interface, hypertext, object oriented database design and optical storage capabilities as part of Mentor's concurrent design environment.

RTrace™:   Protocol, a Division of Zycad Corporation.[14]
NOTE [14]: The following is reprinted with permission of Protocol, a Division of Zycad Corporation.

- Requirements Management/Traceability Tool.
- Runs under VMS. Using Protocol's Design Tool Interface Utility, RTrace™ can also be used with Cadre's Teamwork, version 3.0.3.2 or greater, running under SunOS 4.1 (or greater) with SUNVIEW or running under VMS 5.1 (or greater) with DECWindows.

In today's industry, the ability to demonstrate requirements compliance is key to having a product accepted and marketed. RTrace™ provides both developer and project manager the visibility to track all system and derived requirements from cradle to grave. RTrace™ Version 1.2 is a fifth generation software product, which helps users automate management of requirements during development and test. RTrace™ helps users to analyze and organize requirements through user defined attributes, maintain several architectures simultaneously, allocate and demonstrate traceability of requirements to components/objects, associate test cases with requirements, and generate reports (i.e., requirements reports, allocation object reports, orphan allocation object reports and unallocated requirements reports). RTrace™ Version 1.2 also supports maintenance and modification of documents using the Document Change Loader utility. RTrace™ is adaptable to any life cycle environment (DOD-STD-2167A, NASA, FAA, FCC, and private industry). RTrace™ will be released early 1993 with increased and fully integrated functionality such as X-Windows compatible user interface, multiple views of project data, improved access control, and improved report writing capability.

Software Through Pictures: Interactive Development Environments, Inc.[3]
- Structured Analysis, Design & Documentation Tool.
- Runs under VMS and UNIX. Runs on workstations such as Apollo, SUN and Aegis (UNIX), DECstation 3100 (VMS) and on mainframes (IBM). Also runs under DEC's ULTRIX. Interfaces with Interleaf's Technical Publishing System.

Software Through Pictures (STP) is an integrated set of CASE tools which provide real-time specification, requirements traceability, data modeling, rapid prototyping, and structured analysis and design techniques including both Yourdon & DeMarco[15] and Gane & Sarson.[16]

Under DEC's VMS, STP integrates with the Code Management System, Language Sensitive Editor/Source Code Analyzer and interfaces with Interleaf's Technical Publishing System (TPS).

Statemate: i-Logix, Inc.[3]
- Requirements Analysis and Design Tool.
- Runs on VAX, SUN and Apollo workstations. Runs under VMS and UNIX including DEC's ULTRIX.

Statemate is a powerful analysis and design tool for modeling and simulating real-time systems. Statemate has four integrated capabilities: Kernel generates graphic specifications based on analysis. Analyzer tests the specifications, Prototyper converts the specifications to Ada code, and Documentor uses the Kernel derived specifications to generate DOD-STD-2167A documents. As part of DEC's COHESION environment for CASE; Statemate, under VMS, interfaces with DEC's Code Management System and DEC's relational database management system Rdb/VMS; Statemate, under ULTRIX, interfaces with DEC's Source Code Control System (SCCS).

Teamwork 4:   Cadre Technologies, Inc.[17]
- Structured Analysis and Design Tool.
- Runs on HP's Apollo workstations under SR 10.2 OS. Teamwork 4 is planned ('92 time frame) for Sun Microsystems' UNIX workstations, IBM's RS/6000 under AIX, DEC's ULTRIX and VAX VMS, and HP's HP/UX workstations.

Note:[17] The following article is reprinted by permission of Ziff Communications Co. as taken from *PC WEEK*, Nov. 26, 1990, by John Pallatto, Copyright © 1990, Ziff-Davis Publishing Co., One Park Avenue, New York, N.Y., 10016, Phone: (212) 503-5448.

Cadre to Expand Suite of CASE Workstation Tools by John Pallatto

"Cadre Technologies, Inc. is expanding its palette of CASE tools for workstations with new reverse-engineering and program-simulation models.

The new Teamwork/4.0, scheduled for release in the first quarter of 1991, also will deliver enhancements designed to bolster the development of C, C++ and Ada applications, said Lou Mazzucchelli, chief technical officer for Cadre in Beaverton, Ore.

The reverse-engineering tool, called Teamwork/C Rev, scans existing C source code files, automatically composing flow charts that depict the structure and relationships of a program's functions, Mazzucchelli said. Armed with the charts, developers can easily redesign existing programs or create new ones from scratch, he said.

'I found that it was really easy to use,' said Dave Zegas, a beta tester of Teamwork/C Rev and a software engineer with Computer Consoles Inc., a Rochester, NY, software developer. 'I spent two or three hours with the sales representative getting familiar with Teamwork/C Rev, and that was all the training I needed to generate charts on my own.'

Computer Consoles will use the software to redesign directory assistance databases that it builds for North American telephone companies, he said.

'One thing that impressed everyone here was that it was quick. You put in the source code, and a few minutes later you have a chart that you work with,' he added. The other Teamwork/4.0 addition, Teamwork/SIM, is a simulation tool that analyzes specifications created by Teamwork/SA (Structured Analysis) and Teamwork/RT (Real-Time)—both system-modelling tools, Mazzucchelli said.

The resulting analysis, which is used to predict how a given software and hardware architecture will perform before a program is coded, can reveal design errors and processing bottlenecks that often aren't discovered until the test cycle, he explained.

Initially, Teamwork/4.0 will run on Hewlett-Packard Co.'s Apollo workstations running the proprietary SR 10.2 operating system. Later next year, Cadre will release Teamwork/4.0 versions for Sun Microsystems Inc. Unix workstations, IBM RS/6000s running AIX, Digital Equipment Corp.'s Ultrix and VAX/VMS systems, and Hewlett-packard's HP/UX workstations.

Cadre's Teamwork family is available directly from the company. Pricing for Teamwork/4.0 starts at $8500.00, depending upon the hardware and operating system configuration."

Implementation

FOCUS: Information Builders.[3]

- Fourth Generation Language.
- Runs under VMS. Integrates with DEC's CDD/Plus and DEC's Rdb/VMS.

FOCUS provides users a methodology for developing information systems applications and for generating reports, finance methods, graphics and spread sheets.

Foundation: Andersen Consulting.[3]
- Database Management and Development Facilities.
- Runs under VMS. Integrates with DEC's CDD/Plus.

Foundation is an integrated set of facilities that enable the user to develop distributed systems which utilize the capabilities provided by DEC's CASE environment.

NETRON/CAP Development Center: Netron, Inc.[3]
- Design, Code Generation and Test Tool.
- Runs under VMS and MVS/VM. Runs on IBM Mainframes.

The NETRON/CAP Development Center supports user applications throughout design, code and test activities. Applications can run under VAX VMS or IBM mainframes running MVS, CICS and DB2. As part of DEC's COHESION environment for CASE, this tool integrates with CDD/Plus and Rdb/VMS under DEC's VMS Operating System.

Saber C: Saber Software, Inc.[3]
- Integrated Programming Environment.
- Runs under UNIX.

Saber C provides source code editing, debugging, management, source code analysis, advanced static analysis, and test of software modules. Saber C also contains a DECwindows interface which supports it as a CASE tool within DEC's COHESION environment.

SmartStar: SmartStar Corporation, Inc.[3]
- SQL based Fourth Generation Language.
- Runs under VMS. Integrates with DEC's CDD/Plus and Rdb/VMS. SmartStar is a 4GL information and application development system.

SMARTsystem: PROCASE Corporation.[3]
- Integrated Programming Environment.
- Runs under VMS.

SMARTsystem provides source code editing, debugging, management, source code analysis, advanced static analysis, and test of software modules.

VAX RALLY: Digital Equipment Corporation.[3]
- Fourth Generation Language (4GL).
- Runs under VMS.

A 4GL tool for use by Management Information Systems professionals in application development and information centered environments. VAX RALLY can be used with DEC's relational database management system (Rdb/VMS) to support applications running under VMS and can be used to integrate applications into an ALL-IN-1 office automation system. As part of DEC's COHESION environment for CASE, VAX RALLY integrates with DEC's Repository (CDD/Plus).

Implementation Languages:
Supported by many vendors.

High Order Programming languages run under MVS, OS/2, VMS, MS DOS and UNIX among others.

Prominent Languages include Ada, APL, BASIC, C, C++, COBOL, DIBOL, DSM, FORTRAN, LISP, OPS5, Pascal, PL/1, RPG II, SCAN.

Language Evaluation Tools

ADAMAT: Dynamics Research Corporation.

- Evaluates Ada Source code.
- Runs under VAX with Ada Compiler.

ADAMAT analyzes the quality of Ada source code providing over 200 metrics and corresponding reports to reflect the users priorities and concerns. The metrics are related to one another in a top down hierarchical structure. Each high level metric is supported by two or more metrics at Level 2, with each Level 2 metric supported in turn by several metrics at Level 3 and so on through Level 8. Metrics evaluate Ada code by generating a score (i.e., a ratio between 0.00 and 1.00) or a total count of occurrences measured by a metric. A score measures the number of instances a condition occurred versus the total possible. These scores and counts may measure instances of good or bad programming practice depending upon the metric. In practice ADAMAT has three control files which the user (Software Quality Engineer or Programmer) has control over.

ADDSETFILE lists predefined names from which ADAMAT can distinguish pragmas, input/output names, and special words. This file contains default names for the standard Ada environment and normally requires no change.

METRICS contains over 200 metrics which the user may include or exclude. Scores are ignored for excluded metrics. For included metrics the user may selectively control whether they are reportable or nonreportable by specifying threshold values (two scores and a count). Only metrics within the thresholds are reported.

REPORT_FORMAT allows the user to control the output format and to select which metrics are to be reported. Since the reports contain a lot of information, processing is slow. Therefore it is recommended that ADAMAT be processed as a batch job with low priority.

Implementation Tools and Utilities under UNIX

Editing Tools: Supported by many vendors.[3]

- Generate and Modify Source files.
- Runs under UNIX.
  - set   (global batch editor)
  - vi   (standard 8 bit clean, full screen editor)
  - ex, ed   (alternate line editors)
  - EMACS   (public domain editor)
  - xedit   (DECwindows enhanced EMACS)
  - dxnotepad   (notepad editor for daily office use)

Code Debuggers: Supported by several vendors.[3]

- Code Debugging Tools.
- runs under UNIX.
  - dbx   (source level debugger for FORTRAN, C, Pascal and assembly code; performs high level and assembly language debugging, expression evaluation, stack tracking, breakpoints, single stepping, program state examination, and line by line variable tracing)
  - adb   (line oriented debugger version of "dbx")
  - dxdb   (DECwindows enhanced "dbx" with a front end menu interface, source code window, and mouse selection of operation; also displays C programs and permits users to set, change, and examine values line by line)

Code Management: Supported by several vendors.[3]

- Runs under UNIX.
  - crbSCCS   (source code control system; maintains source code files and their modification histories, permits recovery of prior versions, and flags current files to prevent inconsistent updates.)

- SCCS   (DEC's version of crbSCCS similar to above but allows third party users such as Cadre and Software Through Pictures to interface with SCCS to track application designs as well as code)

System Builders: Supported by several vendors.[3]

- Automated System Builders.
- Runs under UNIX.
  - make   (determines which recompiles are required to generate a program by comparing dates of source files, object files, libraries, and executable code; also performs macro and text substitution)
  - s5make   (System 5 version of "make")

Specialized Tools: Supported by several vendors.[3]

- Parsers & Filters.
- Runs under UNIX.
  - lex   (lexical analysis program generator; supports building structures for parsing grammar; a processor/pattern matcher for input streams)
  - yacc   (defines acceptable grammar; converts context free grammar into tables used by compilers and parsers)
  - awk   (used to scan and match patterns; can be customized to a C-like language)

Integration and Test

Static Source Code Analysis Tools: Supported by several vendors.[3]

- Source Code Analyzers.
- Runs under UNIX
  - cxref>grep   (pipeline transfer of "cxref" results through "grep" to build cross-reference tables and listings of static, dynamic and global symbols)
  - ctags   (creates a tag file for editors (ex, vi & EMACS) based on C, Pascal or FORTRAN Source code to identify the location of objects in groups of files)
  - lint   (detects program elements containing bugs, lacking portability, and redundant code; lint checks for dead code, loops entered incorrectly, constant logical expressions, functions containing variable numbers of arguments, unused values and inconsistently returned values.)
  - cflow   (execution flow analyzer for C, yacc, lex, assembler, object files, and external references)

Testing Tools: Supported by several vendors.[3]

- Runs under UNIX.
  - diff   (file comparator utility that handles graphics files)
  - dxdiff   (DECwindows enhanced version of "diff")
  - shell   (test tool scripts written in the "shell" interpretive language)

T: Programming Environments Incorporated (PEI)

T is a test tool for software. T verifies that individual descriptions of software (produced by other tools prior to test) use data in a consistent manner. T also generates test cases based on several specification based methods such as cause and effect graphs, functional specification, heuristic and boundary value analysis. Each test case generated by T is also supported by pass/fail criteria which is used to evaluate the amount of coverage provided by the test.

Performance Analysis Tools: Supported by several vendors.[3]

- Runs under UNIX.
    - prof   (locates/profiles execution intensive code, hot spots, and produces a feedback file for an optimizer)
    - pixie   (locates execution intensive code by partitioning programs into elemental blocks, writes instrumentation code, and counts the execution of each block)
    - vtimes, time, size
    - getusage   (obtains input/output (I/O) information)
    - gprof   (call profile/count)
    - ctrace   (system service calls)
    - perfmon   (shows I/O and paging)
    - perfmeter
    - vmstat   (virtual memory statistics)
    - iostat   (I/O statistics)
    - netstat   (shows network status)
    - nfsstat   (shows network file system (NFS) statistics)
    - ps   (print-process statistics)

Documentation

UNIX documentation Utilities: Supported by several vendors.[3]

- Documentation Utilities.
- Run under UNIX. Also accessible under DEC's ULTRIX.
    - troff   (text editor)
    - spell   (spell checker)
    - diction (dictionary)
    - style   (predefined document styles)

Aranda: Soft-Set Technologies Inc.*[18]

---

*Note: the following is based on information taken from Brad Andrews, "Aranda (Computer-aided software engineering software) (Software Reviews column)," Computer Language, Nov. 1990, Vol. 7, No. 11, pp. 101-103, Copyright © 1990 Miller-Freeman Publications. Reprinted with permission of the publisher.

- CASE Documentation Tool for Apple Macintosh.
- Runs on a 68000 or 68030 Macintosh with 2MBytes RAM. Needs hard disk space of four times the size of the source code files.

Aranda parses user selected source files from an existing database. These files are then displayed in desktop fashion. A top down structure of each module is presented, displaying the relationship among module elements. The top down structure allows the user to hide (or retrieve) information below any user specified level. The system creates flow charts as well as views of the source code. The use of Hypertext allows variable linking to other code modules permitting dynamic views of the software.

Internal graphics features can be appended to any display. External graphics and text can also be pasted to the display using the clipboard feature. The current version (version 1) only permits one view at a time, making it difficult to compare views. Printing is also limited to one page per printout.

The system is designed to support documentation maintenance activities which are notorious for frequent changes to documentation. Future capabilities are planned for Aranda to include on-line editing of source code modules, parsing in languages other than Think Pascal and MPW, such as C and C++. Systems compatibility is also planned for the IBM PC.

Interleaf 5, Technical Publishing System: Interleaf, Inc.†[19]

- Desktop Publishing System, Version 5.
- Interleaf 5 documents can be shared among workstations including DEC VMS, HP and Apollo, IBM mainframes, SUN Microsystems, UNIX, and 80386 based PCs and Apple Macintosh.

Interleaf interfaces with other tools such as Software Through Pictures to provide a flexible system within which engineering data, diagrams (control flows and data flows), and text can be cleanly and easily merged into a final, presentable document. As part of DEC's COHESION environment for CASE, Interleaf is accessible by the user.

Interleaf 5 employs the new "active document" technology to utilize information. "Active documents" run any Software Query Language (SQL) DBMS, access user specified data, and build text and graphics catalogs showing different sets of data to different users. Products of Interleaf 5 include "Professional Writer," "Interleaf Engineer," "Illustrator," "Production," "Academic and Passport," and "Point and Type" templates for easy learning.

VAX Document: Digital Equipment Corporation.[3]

- Electronic Publishing System.
- Runs under VMS.

VAX Document is a comprehensive publishing system for the entire publishing process; providing tools for text creation, a standard markup language, text and

---

†*Note:* the following is based on information taken from "Interleaf launches its first active document," *Computergram International,* Oct. 5, 1990, No. 1526, Copyright © 1990 APT Data Services Ltd, 12 Sutton Row, London W1V5FH England. Reprinted with permission of the publisher.

graphics integration, revision control, document formatting, and output to laser and line printers.

12.6 A LOOK AHEAD

The advent of CASE tools has brought much enthusiasm to the software development community. The promise of a fully integrated software development environment (or a SEE) looks feasible. The commercial sector seems further advanced in the pursuit of the Integrated Project Support Environment (IPSE) than the government. The leaders in the field are apparently IBM and DEC, who both have teaming agreements with Atherton Technology to develop the mechanism for full integration at all levels; presentation, control and data integration. The next generation in CASE technology foresees enhancement of the data Repository to utilize Object Oriented Design (OOD) features for storing and retrieving processing and behavior rules as well as data and other objects. SQA can play a major role in the use of currently available tools and in promoting awareness of up and coming advances in CASE tool technology to maintain a competitive edge in the marketplace.

References

1. Amey, W., *The Computer Assisted Software Engineering (CASE) System,* Proceedings Fourth ICSE, September, 1979.
2. Fedchak, Elaine, "An Introduction to Software Engineering Environments", *Proceedings of COMPSAT 1986, the IEEE Computer Societies' 10th Annual International Computer Software and Applications Conference, Chicago, IL., October 8..10, 1986,* pp. 456-463, IIT Research Institute, Copyright © 1986 IEEE. (Note: Material is reprinted with permission of IEEE).
3. *The Digital COHESION Environment for CASE,* Digital Equipment Corporation, 1990. (Note: Copyright © 1990, Digital Equipment Corporation. All rights reserved. Reprinted by permission.)
4. McKeehan, David, "Avionics Software Development for PAVE PILLAR & PAVE PACE Architectures," SEI-90-SR-15, July 1990. (Note: Material reprinted with permission of the Software Engineering Institute, Carnegie Mellon University, Copyright © 1990, SEI).
5. Crosby, Philip B., *Quality Without Tears,* (New York: McGraw-Hill Book Co., 1984).
6. Schulmeyer, G. Gordon, and McManus, James I., *Total Quality Management for Software,* (New York: Van Nostrand Reinhold, 1992).
7. Humphrey, Watts S., *Managing the Software Process,* SEI Series in Software Engineering, p. 5, (Addison-Wesley Publishing Co., October, 1989). (Note: Material from "Watts S. Humphrey, *Managing the Software Process,* © 1989, by Addison-Wesley Publishing Co., Inc., Reprinted with permission of the publisher".)
8. Wehner, Ross, "SEI Examines DOD's Software Maladies," *Washington Technology.* Vol. 4, No. 23, (p. 30), March 8, 1990.
9. Forte, Gene, "In Search of the Integrated CASE Environment", *CASE OUTLOOK.* Vol. 89, No. 2, Mar/Apr Issue, Copyright © 1989.
10. Reifer, Donald J., Knudson, Richard W., and Smith, Jerry. *Final Report: Software Quality Survey,* Software Quality Technical Committee, American Society for Quality Control, 20, November 1987.

11. Shingo, Shigeo, *Zero Quality Control: Source Inspection and the Poka-Yoke System,* Andrew P. Dillon, translator, pp. 42–46, (Cambridge, MA: Productivity Press, 1986). (Note: Material reprinted with permission of Productivity Press, Inc.: From *Zero Quality Control: Source Inspection & the Poka-Yoke System,* by Shigeo Shingo, English Translation Copyright © 1988 by Productivity Press, Inc., P.O. Box 3007, Cambridge, MA 02140. Phone (617) 497-5146.)

12. Schulmeyer, G. Gordon, *Zero Defect Software,* (New York: McGraw-Hill Inc., 1990), pp. 258, 259. (Note: Material reproduced with permission of McGraw-Hill, Inc.: from *Zero Defect Software,* G. Gordon Schulmeyer, Copyright © 1990 by McGraw-Hill, Inc.)

13. Yourdon, E., and Constantine, L. L., *Structured Design: Fundamentals of a Discipline of Computer Program and Structured Design,* Englewood Cliffs, NJ: Prentice-Hall, 1979.

14. *RTrace, Requirements Managements Concepts Document,* Copyright © 1991 by Protocol, A Division of Zycad Corporation, 17177 N. Laurel Park Drive, Ste. 161, Livonia, MI 48152.

15. DeMarco, Tom, *Structured Analysis and System Specification,* (Englewood Cliffs: Prentice-Hall, 1979).

16. Gane, C., and Sarson, T., *Structured Systems Analysis: Tools and Techniques,* (Englewood Cliffs: Prentice-Hall, 1979).

17. Pallatto, John, "Cadre To Expand Suite of CASE Workstation Tools", *PC WEEK,* Nov. 26, 1990, Vol. 7, No. 4, p. 4, Copyright © 1990, Ziff-Davis Publishing Co. (Note: Material "Reprinted from *PC WEEK,* November 26, 1990, Copyright © 1990, Ziff Communications Company", One Park Ave., New York, NY, 10016.)

18. Andrews, Brad, "Aranda. (Computer-aided software engineering software) (Software Reviews column)," *Computer Language,* November 1990, Vol. 7, No. 11, pp. 101–103, 1990. (Note: Material reprinted with permission of Miller-Freeman Publications: from *Computer Language,* Nov. 1990 Issue, Vol. 7, No. 11, Copyright © 1990 by Miller Freeman Publications, 600 Harrison St., San Francisco, CA, 94107.)

19. Interleaf Inc., "Interleaf launches its first active document product", *Computergram International,* Oct. 5, 1990, No. 1526. (Note: Material reprinted with permission of APT Data Services Ltd: from *Computergram International,* Copyright © 1990, "APT Data Services Ltd, 12 Sutton Row, London W1V5FH England".)

20. Ward, P., and Mellor, S., *Structured Development for Real Time Systems,* (New York: Yourdon Press, 1983).

21. *DesignAid II, The PC-based CASE Product with a True Multi-User Repository,* CGI SYSTEMS, Inc., One Blue Hill Plaza, P.O. Box 1645, Pearl River, New York 10965, (914) 735-5030.

13

Software Configuration Management—A Practical Look

William E. Bryan, D.Sc.

Grumman—CTEC, Inc.

Stanley G. Siegel, Ph.D.

Grumman—CTEC, Inc.

13.1 IT IS RAINING— WHERE IS AN UMBRELLA?

In providing motivation for their book *Principles of Software Engineering and Design,* the authors tell the following short story:[1]

> When the Verrazano Narrows Bridge in New York City was started in 1959, it was estimated to cost $325 million and was to be completed by 1965. It was the largest suspension bridge ever built, yet it was completed in November 1964, on target and within budget. . . . Would anyone care to base his or her reputation on such predictions for a large-scale software development?
>
> Software is often delivered late. It is unreliable. It is expensive to maintain. . . . Why can engineering be so exact while software development flounders?

Our response to the last question is illustrated in Figure 13-1. The raindrops in the figure pour down on many software projects and their archetypical participants—the user, buyer, and seller. These problem raindrops are the following:

- *Lack of Visibility.* Unlike the engineering of bridges (suspension or otherwise), the development of software involves the "crafting" of something that is inherently difficult to see (we formally define software below). This lack of visibility tends to confound management (how can you manage what you cannot see?) and confuse project participants (especially on large projects where different organizations develop different pieces of software).

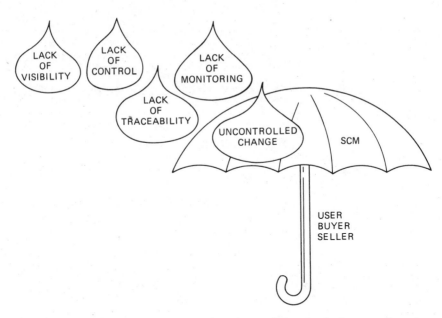

FIGURE 13-1. Why software development flounders—and the role of software configuration management.

- *Lack of Control.* Because software development is often characterized by a lack of visibility, this development often spins out of control—how can you control what you cannot see? Schedules slip and budgets overrun because management simply lacks the means to assess what has been accomplished (and at what cost) and what remains to be done.
- *Lack of Traceability.* Contributing to software project misfortunes is a lack of linkage between project events. This linkage—or traceability thread—provides management the means for reexamining events when projects encounter unexpected happenings (such as sudden budget changes or key personnel losses) and for rationally determining how to best proceed. Lacking this thread, projects already going out of control spin yet further out of control.
- *Lack of Monitoring.* Because of lack of visibility and traceability, management lacks the means to monitor project events. Management is thereby hampered in its ability to make informed decisions—and again schedules slip and budgets overrun.
- *Uncontrolled Change.* Software as its name implies, is highly malleable. This malleability, when coupled with a lack of visibility and control, leads to uncontrolled change—changes made without the knowledge of management and other key project participants. The effects of these changes frequently compound, consuming project resources while the participants who have been kept in the dark try to sort out these effects with (or without) the help of those who made the changes.

Then raindrops in Figure 13-1 are turning into a cloudburst that threatens to wreak havoc with both military and commercial applications. Our military systems are becoming increasingly dependent on software, and concern is increasing that systems simply will not perform when they are needed.[2-4] And the number of lawsuits involving computers and software in commerce is rising.[5-6, 19]

Why can't we in the software industry turn out products that work right, are delivered on time, and are within budget? Is it because we don't understand what it takes to achieve these objectives? Or is it because we don't know how to manage costs? Our contention is that some of us probably don't understand what it takes to achieve these objectives, but most of us simply aren't willing to commit to meeting them. In this chapter we offer some insight into what it takes and what it costs to provide software configuration management on a project as an important part in achieving overall software quality. Our orientation is toward the practical with specific suggestions, based on our experience, for raising the visibility of the software development process and infusing it with traceability, thereby bringing it under control.* We take a candid look at some things that our experience indicates are necessary (but not sufficient) to incorporate into the software development process to ward off the rain shown in Figure 13-1, and at some reasons which make good business sense to pay the price in time, effort, and budget to incorporate into the software development process. Our approach is the following:

- We define the configuration management discipline and explain its crucial role in the production of working software.
- We then describe some real-world considerations needed to convince management of the value of software configuration management (particularly to top management) and subsequently implement it on a software project.

13.2 SOFTWARE CONFIGURATION MANAGEMENT OVERVIEW

In this section, we present an overview of our concept of software configuration management. Our purpose is to establish the context for the discussion given in the next section, which presents real-world considerations for applying configuration management. Details of our configuration management concept are given elsewhere.[7-8]

Software configuration management is a template for visibly, traceably, and formally controlling software evolution. What is being controlled? Software configurations. What is a software configuration? To answer this question, we first need to define the notions of *configuration* and *software.*

The first notion is defined in Figure 13-2 (and taken from the dictionary) together with a simple hardware example. When it comes to bicycles, lawnmowers, and other hardware items, the utility of this notion is widely accepted. A parts list

---

*Our notions of visibility and traceability are formally defined in reference 11.

A <u>CONFIGURATION</u> is a RELATIVE ARRANGEMENT OF PARTS

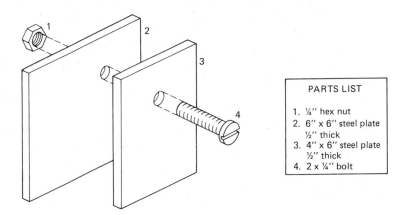

FIGURE 13-2. The concept of configuration.

and exploded parts diagram like those shown in Figure 13-2 serve as a set of instructions for assembling the hardware and for acquiring replacement parts when the hardware malfunctions and breaks down. It is interesting to note that, while we expect to receive "documentation" such as that shown in Figure 13-2 when we pay tens or hundreds of dollars for hardware "systems" such as bicycles or lawnmowers, many of us are typically willing to pay hundreds of thousands or even millions of dollars for software systems without such documentation.

Figure 13-3 defines our concept of software.[9] Note that this concept encompasses not only computer code but also predecessor documentation such as design specifications, software system concept papers, and requirements specifications.

The software concept used in this chapter is more panoramic than the software concept used elsewhere in this handbook. As becomes evident in this chapter, this panoramic concept provides a unified view of certain software management support processes that generally appear in different, sometimes disparate, contexts in the software management world. Consider, for example, the result of defining as software a design document that specifies the logic to be incorporated into computer code. The processes of determining whether the design in such a document conforms to a user requirements document and whether computer code (operating in an environment approximating the user's operational environment) conforms to a user requirements document are fundamentally the same. Both processes are software comparison exercises. The former is generally referred to as a "design review" in the literature, while the latter is generally referred to as "acceptance testing." By defining software in such a way, we can formulate a relatively small set of principles that applies to *any* stage of the software life cycle. We feel this formulation simplifies the task of controlling software development and maintenance.

SOFTWARE is INFORMATION

- Structured with logical and functional properties
- Created and maintained in various forms and representations during its life cycle
- Tailored for machine processing in its fully developed state

FIGURE 13-3. A concept of software. (Adapted from Bersoff, E.; Henderson, N.; and Siegel, S., *Software Configuration Management,* Englewood Cliffs, NJ: Prentice-Hall, 1980, p. 10)

A SOFTWARE CONFIGURATION is a RELATIVE ARRANGEMENT OF SOFTWARE PARTS

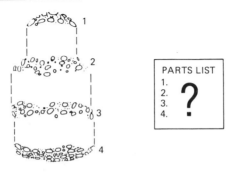

FIGURE 13-4. The concept of software configuration.

It follows from Figures 13-2 and 13-3 that a *software configuration* is a relative arrangement of software parts. (The term *baseline* is often used synonymously for *configurations.*) This concept is depicted in Figure 13-4, where we show an "exploded-parts" diagram of a four-piece software system. This figure also prompts the following question: What are the software analogues to the nut, bolt, and steel plates shown in Figure 13-2? The answer to this question follows from our definition of software. Examples of software parts are the following:

- 300-page specification document.
- Three-sentence paragraph in a design document.
- A single FORTRAN, COBOL, Ada®, PL/1, or assembly language statement.
- Recording of a computer program on a magnetic medium.
- Sequence of instructions executing in computer hardware.
- Keystroke recorded in the memory of a programmable calculator.

Basically, a software part can be any piece of information with the three characteristics listed in Figure 13-3. The key consideration regarding this concept is that

---

®Ada is the registered trademark of the Department of Defense (Ada Joint Program Office).

software project participants should formally agree to a parts list (by a mechanism we subsequently describe) and maintain this agreement until the project participants formally agree to alter this parts list (also by a mechanism we subsequently describe).

Figure 13-5 depicts our concept of software configuration management. Elaborating on our earlier statement, we can define software configuration management as a template molded from the integrated application of the four functions shown in Figure 13-5 for visibly, traceably, and formally controlling software evolution. More specifically, these four functions and the purpose of each are the following:

1. *Identification,* whereby each software part is physically labeled. In the figure we show a four-part software system, each part tagged with a numeric label. (the identification function is described at length in reference 8, Chapter 4.)

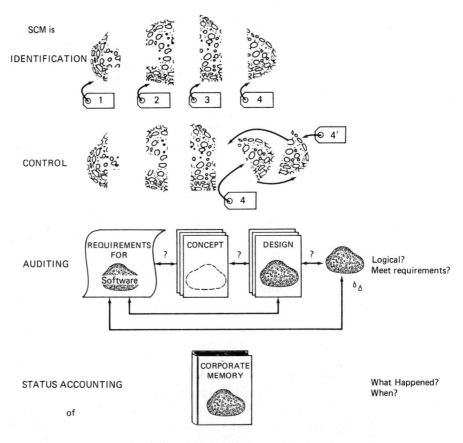

a relative arrangement of software parts

FIGURE 13-5. The four functions of software configuration management. (Adapted from Bryan, W., and Siegel, S., "Product Assurance: Insurance Against a Software Disaster," *Computer,* Vol. 17, No. 4 (April 1984, p. 79. |© 1984 IEEE])

2. *Control,* whereby proposed changes to software parts are reviewed, then subjected to the agreement of project participants, and finally incorporated into the currently approved software configuration. In Figure 13-5, part 4′ is shown replacing part 4. This transition is a two-step process. The first step is a review by an organizational body called a configuration control board (CCB) (whose composition and operation are discussed in section 13.3) of (1) the cost and schedule needed to effect the transition from part 4 to part 4′ and (2) the impact of this transition on the other parts in the configuration: the second step is CCB approval (or rejection or postponement) of the transition from part 4 to part 4′. (The control function is described at length in reference 8, Chapter 5.)

3. *Auditing,* which seeks answers to the following two questions:
   a. Is software evolution proceeding logically? The process of answering this question is termed verification. In terms of Figure 13-5, this question is asked three times as follows: Does the concept logically follow from the requirements specification? Does the design logically follow from the concept? Does the working code logically follow from the design?
   b. Is software evolution proceeding in conformance with requirements for the software? The process of answering this question is termed validation. In terms of Figure 13-5, this question is asked three times as follows: Is the concept shown in Figure 13-5 congruent with the requirements specification or, if not, what are the incongruencies? Is the design congruent with the requirements specification or, if not, what are the incongruencies? Is the computer code operating on the intended host hardware congruent with the requirements specification or, if not, what are the incongruencies?

   (The auditing function is described at length in reference 10 and reference 8, Chapter 6.)

4. *Status accounting,* which seeks answers to the following two questions:
   a. What happened on a software project? (E.g., what happened to the discrepancies between software code and software requirements, where these discrepancies are included in a test [i.e., audit] report?)
   b. When did an event happen on a software project? (E.g., when was a software design update approved by the CCB?)

   The status accounting function provides a corporate memory of project events that supports accomplishment of the other three configuration management functions. This corporate memory also serves as an experience bank whose contents can be exploited on other projects, to avoid repeating past mistakes and to capitalize on the successful approaches. (The status accounting function is described at length in reference 8, Chapter 7.)

In the previous section, we indicate that many software projects suffer from a lack of visibility and traceability. Now that we have described the four component functions of configuration management, we can indicate in specific terms how configuration management helps to raise the visibility of software projects and infuse them with traceability. Table 13-1 lists some of the ways each of the four

TABLE 13-1   How the Four Configuration Management Functions Infuse Visibility and Traceability into a Software Project

FUNCTION	VISIBILITY	TRACEABILITY
Identification	• User/buyer/seller can see what is being/has been built/is to be modified. • Management can see what is embodied in a product. • All project participants can communicate with a common frame of reference.	• Provides pointers to software parts in software products for use in referencing. • Makes software parts and their relationships more visible, thus facilitating the linking of parts in different software products and in different representations of the same product.
Control	• Current and planned configuration generally known. • Management can see impact of change. • Management has option of getting involved with technical detail of project.	• Makes baselines and changes to them manifest, thus providing the links in a traceability chain. • Provides the forum for avoiding unwanted excursions and maintaining convergence with requirements.
Auditing	• Inconsistencies and discrepancies manifest. • State of product known to management and product developers. • Potential problems identified early.	• Checks that parts in one software product are carried through to the subsequent software product. • Checks that parts in a software product have antecedents in requirements documentation.
Status Accounting	• Reports inform as to status. • Actions/decisions made explicit (e.g. through CCB meeting minutes). • Data base of events is project history.	• Provides history of what happened and when. • Provides explicit linkages between change control forms.

configuration management functions helps to achieve visibility and establish traceability on a software project. This table thus provides insight into the protective nature of the software configuration management umbrella shown in Figure 13-1.

Having overviewed software configuration management, we can now examine some considerations governing the practice of this discipline in the real world.

13.3   REAL-WORLD CONSIDERATIONS

This section presents some practical considerations involved in the establishment and practice of software configuration management (SCM). We discuss several

TABLE 13-2   Real-World Considerations in Software Configuration Management

SUBJECT	ESSENTIAL CONSIDERATION
Management Commitment	Management commitment to the establishment of checks and balances is essential to achieving benefits from SCM.
SCM Staffing	Initial staffing by a few experienced people quickly gains the confidence and respect of the other project team members.
Establishment of a CCB	As a starting point in instituting SCM, periodic CCB meetings provide change control, visibility, and traceability.
CM During the Acceptance Testing Cycle	CM integrated within the acceptance testing cycle maintains a visible and traceable product ready for delivery to the customer.
Justification and Practicality of Auditing	Although auditing consumes the greater part of the SCM budget, it has the potential of preventing the waste of much greater resources.
Avoiding the Paperwork Nightmare	The buyer/user and seller should agree on the paperwork needed to achieve a mutually desirable level of visibility and traceability.
Allocating Resources among CM Activities	Cost versus benefits must be evaluated for each individual project in determining the allocation of limited SCM resources.

aspects of configuration management as shown in Table 13-2. Our discussion is not simply theoretical; it is based on actual experience and observation in the practice of SCM. We begin with a discussion of the importance of management commitment of SCM. Next we present some ideas on the staffing of the SCM organization. We describe the mechanics of what we feel is the most important element of SCM—the configuration control board—in terms of its membership, organization, and procedures. This description is followed by a discussion of the integration of CM into an area of much importance in the development and maintenance cycle—acceptance testing. Next we present our views on the problems of coping with the high resource consumption of auditing and of avoiding the paperwork nightmare of SCM. Finally we provide some insights into how to allocate SCM resources among the SCM functions.

Management Commitment to Checks and Balances

How does one go about establishing a software configuration management program in his or her organization? One way might be by leading a software development coup—dazzle upper management one day with guarantees of software success and send in the storm troopers the next day, ready to control and discipline software development. Management by fiat and manifesto are necessary—after all, the poor developers don't yet realize how much they need SCM.

Monitor every action by the developers and have them prepare a report on every effort—plenty of traceability here and tremendous visibility. If upper management becomes uneasy with the approach, guarantee them long-range success and share some of your visibility with them.

Is this approach practical? Hardly. Its only guarantee is a high turnover rate on the software engineering staff. A much better approach is to proceed gradually and convincingly. Let's consider some practical steps to take in instituting SCM in an organization.

First of all, start at the top. If SCM is to become successful, the software project manager and his or her boss need to commit to some form of checks and balances with respect to the activities of the software product developers (see Figure 13-6). In the absence of this commitment, software configuration management has little likelihood of being effective. Without management commitment to back up the CM organization, CM efforts will be eroded and eventually ignored altogether. Checks and balances are needed to give management a perspective of the software development process other than that of the developers. Developers quite naturally have one viewpoint of the products they develop, the software configuration management personnel another. After all, these two groups have different goals and objectives. Provision of these checks and balances immediately increases the visibility to management of the software development process. One raindrop deflected already! We repeat, upper management commitment to the establishment of checks and balances is essential to achieving benefits from SCM.

How do you convince management to make such a commitment? There are several ways to achieve this goal. One way is to hire, or be fortunate enough to already have aboard, managers who have experienced firsthand what can go wrong on software projects. Such managers are generally receptive to alternative approaches to software development and should be sensitive to the intrinsic value of checks and balances. They can readily perceive the benefit to them of a different perspective and of increased visibility into the project. Obtaining a commitment for the establishment of checks and balances on the developers from such managers as these should be relatively easy.

If your organization is not fortunate enough to have such experienced managers,

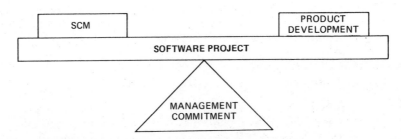

FIGURE 13-6. Keeping a software project on an even keel requires management commitment to checks and balances on product development—such as those provided through SCM.

obtaining an upper management commitment is a more difficult task. They must be sold at project outset on the benefits of the SCM checks and balances, and also honestly informed of their liabilities. The latter are readily perceived as the expenditure of additional resources—time and money. The benefits of SCM are the warding off of the raindrops shown in Figure 13-1. All four SCM functions provide increased visibility and traceability as shown in Table 13-1. With this increased visibility and traceability, management can establish control and provide adequate monitoring of a software development or maintenance project. And, as a final benefit, SCM can control change—after all, control is the underlying purpose of SCM.

Unfortunately, upper management often cannot objectively weigh the intangible benefits versus the tangible liabilities of providing SCM on software development projects. Knowing that they must spend time and money to perform SCM, they want to know the potential savings to be achieved through performance of SCM. We contend that, although SCM costs time and money, it increases the likelihood that even greater amounts of time and money will not be required to recover from a software disaster. It is difficult, however, to prove this contention. Empirical data could be provided for a project with SCM and for a different project without SCM. Such disparate data offers no sound basis for comparison. Experiments to prove this contention have not been conducted; they would be expensive, and in any case it would be difficult, if not impossible, to avoid biasing the experiments either toward or against SCM. (Reference 11 discusses the difficulty of conducting meaningful experiments to prove this contention.)

Perhaps the best rationale that can be offered to support the contention in the preceding paragraph is an analogy to replacement of oil filters in automobiles. Most automobile owners pay a modest sum to replace the oil filter in their car on a regular basis. Why? Because they believe that such an action will avert costly engine repairs in the future. How much money do they save? There is, of course, no way of knowing how much they might have to spend on engine repairs if they never change their oil filter. And some people who never change their oil filter drive many thousands of miles without engine trouble. Despite all these considerations, most people do believe the contention that spending money to change an oil filter saves money through avoidance of costly engine repairs. The problem is to convince upper management that resources expended on SCM may save expending considerably more resources; this contention, although unprovable, is indeed valid. The literature contains many accounts of software disasters.[5-6, 12-14, 19-20] In fact, we have stressed elsewhere that the scope of these disasters is so great as to constitute a crisis in the software industry.[11] DeMarco, for instance, concludes from a multi-year survey he conducted of over 200 projects that 15 percent of all software projects never deliver anything, and overruns of 100 to 200 percent are common.[12] We do not contend that all these disasters result from a lack of SCM. However, it is clear that too little visibility and/or traceability (both of which can be attributed at least in part to a lack of SCM) account for some of these disasters. On the other side of the coin, the literature does contain some accounts showing a correlation between the application of SCM and software project success.[11, 16] Our experience in the software industry has convinced us that the application of SCM is a necessary (though not sufficient) condition for software project success.

SCM Staffing

Staffing of the software configuration management organization with properly qualified people is extremely important to getting started in SCM (see Figure 13-7). Without qualified people to perform the SCM functions, the most comprehensive approach to SCM backed by fully committed top-level management will most likely fall short of helping to achieve the desired software products. If the people are available, the SCM team should be staffed initially with a few highly experienced (and thus probably highly paid) individuals rather than a larger number of less experienced people.

Generally, the SCM team is viewed as a group of antagonists by the other project team members. To reduce antagonism and to enhance the likelihood that checks and balances will not be circumvented, a few experienced people will get the CM task quickly off on the right foot and gain the confidence and respect of the other project team members. It is important to build the image that the SCM team has the objective of helping the other project team members achieve the overall team goals, that they are not a group of obstructionists and criticizers constantly harping on shortcomings, aberrations, and trivia. These experienced people generally will need to have the technical and diplomatic skills to analyze the developers' output from a broad perspective and to tactfully present the

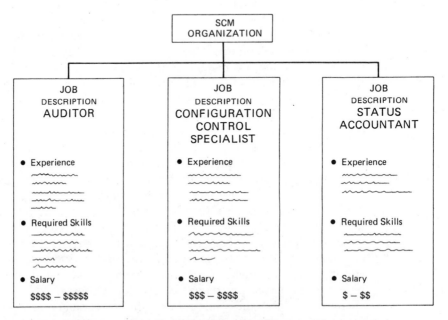

FIGURE 13-7. What kinds of people staff a proficient SCM organization?

TABLE 13-3   **Configuration Management Functions and Personnel Qualifications**

FUNCTION	PERSONNEL QUALIFICATIONS

Identification	• Ability to see partitions.
	• Ability to see relationships.
	• Some technical ability desirable:
	  –System engineering orientation
	  –Programming

Control	• Ability to evaluate benefits versus costs. • System viewpoint (balance of technical/managerial, user/buyer/seller). • An appreciation of what is involved in engineering a software change.
Auditing	• Extreme attention to detail. • Ability to see congruence. • Ability to perceive what is missing. • Extensive experience with technical aspects of system engineering and/or software engineering.

Status Accounting	• Ability to take notes and record data.
	• Ability to organize data.
	• Some technical familiarity desirable but not required:
	  –System engineering
	  –Programming

observed discrepancies and potential dangers perceived as development progresses. Important qualifications of these people are the ability to see congruence between software products and the ability to perceive what is missing from a software product. With these abilities, the SCM team member, freed as he or she is from the responsibilities of detailed design and development, can observe how change to the software system is visibly and traceably being controlled.

Need all SCM personnel be skilled programmers and analysts? No, these particular skills are not a necessity by any means, although personnel performing software configuration auditing should be technically skilled. Table 13-3 presents some recommended qualifications that members of the SCM team should possess to perform the four SCM functions. One can conclude from Table 13-3 that the job requirements for an SCM specialist are demanding. The SCM specialist is challenged to take a broad, comprehensive viewpoint in his or her tasks, while paradoxically being meticulous as to details in all work.

Establishment of a CCB

With management support and a cadre of CM personnel, how should you begin exercising SCM? We advise starting simply (particularly if your management remains somewhat skeptical of the benefits of SCM). Then, as confidence in the value of SCM grows, gradually expand the scope of SCM activities.

As a starting point, if you do nothing else, establish periodic meetings of a configuration control board (CCB). Why start with CCB meetings? We feel that the control function is central to the performance of SCM, and the CCB is the heart of the control function (see Figure 13-8). (A CCB meeting is *not* an alternative for the project status meeting, however; it may have many of the same participants as the project status meeting, but its purpose and focus are quite different.) The CCB meeting is a mechanism for controlling change during the development and maintenance of software (another raindrop deflected!).

Remember that change is indigenous to and continual on a software project and includes both *revolutionary change* (caused by discrepancies, requests for enhancements, and changes in environment) and *evolutionary change* (the planned succession of software products providing an increasing level of detail in the development of a software system). The CCB infuses sustained visibility into this process of change throughout the system life cycle. The likelihood that problems will go unnoticed or unresolved is thereby reduced. The CCB also infuses traceability into the process of change, thereby increasing maintainability of the software.

Membership

CCB members should be drawn from all organizations on the project team. After all, a prime purpose of the CCB is to increase visibility on the project. The CCB should include policy makers, as it is a decision-making body, whose decisions might impact project budget or schedule. But the CCB must also include technical specialists, whose opinions are needed to reach decisions on technical issues. Certainly, the project manager should be a member of the CCB. However, the leaders of software and hardware engineering groups for the project should also be active members, with the type and number of additional engineers participating dependent upon the issues on the CCB agenda. And also, the leaders of both the CM and the quality assurance (QA) teams for the project (if your company has separate CM and QA organizations) should be members of the CCB.

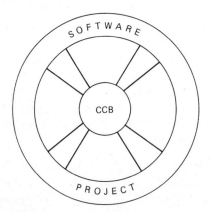

FIGURE 13-8. The hub of the project wheel—the CCB.

Note in the foregoing the underlying assumption is that all CCB members are from the *seller's* company. However, equivalent personnel from the buyer's organization should also be members of the CCB. These personnel include the buyer's project manager, technical people (both hardware and software), and CM and QA representatives. Further, user personnel should also attend CCB meetings.

The inclusion of buyer/user personnel on the CCB may seem ill-advised to many readers. After all, who wishes to air one's dirty linen before a customer? Our response is that everyone on the project team will benefit from the visibility that derives from having user, buyer, and seller representation on the CCB. The goal of the entire project team should be the satisfaction of *user* needs. Airing problems an successes at CCB meetings keeps the entire project staff informed as to the status of the project, facilitates reallocation of resources to problems, and helps keep the project on track, on schedule, and within budget.

Decisions Mechanism

With the recommended variety of representatives on the CCB, the question arises as to how decisions are made. A natural suggestion is to give each CCB representative one vote with the majority vote effecting a decision. This exercise in democracy allows all views equal consideration and makes all CCB members a part of the decision-making process. CCB members are motivated to participate in and contribute to the board meetings.

This mechanism does have its drawbacks, however. One consideration is that a specific definition of majority vote must be made. Should it be a strict majority? (What constitutes a quorum?) A plurality? Two-thirds of those present and voting? A much more important consideration, though, is that this decision-making mechanism tend to introduce politics into the CCB. Members may tend to vote in blocks, e.g., buyer versus seller or developers versus CM personnel. When this tendency develops, the number of representatives that an organization has on the CCB becomes more important than what the CCB is trying to do.

At the other extreme, all decision-making authority could be put in the hands of a single person, for example, the buyer's project manager. This arrangement, of course, fosters decision-making and allows flexible consideration of priority in making decisions. It appears, in the case of naming the buyer's project manager as the single voter, to be a reasonable choice, since he or she is the person who has ultimate responsibility for the project. On the other hand, this arrangement could stifle the interest of the other CCB members in the meetings. Why should they take an interest when they can't vote and feel their opinions don't count?

Another decision-making mechanism is to seek a consensus of the representatives on the CCB, that is, informal (non-voting) agreement by most of those present. This method is relatively expeditious and certainly allows all viewpoints to be expressed and considered. A fault of the method, though, is that, if a consensus of the board cannot be reached, the board does not make a decision. To prevent the board from bogging down in such cases, an escape mechanism should be provided. For example, if the board cannot reach a consensus in a reasonable period of time, then the buyer's project manager unilaterally should make the decision on the matter at hand (because the buyer put up the funds to develop the software).

Chairing the Board

Another issue related to the formation of a CCB is who should serve as chairperson of the board. A number of individuals could be designated in the precept for the CCB or selected by the CCB Table 13-4 lists some candidates and the rationale as to why they might be so designated. Note that some of these candidates may not participate in the decision-making process but rather simply preside over the meetings. For example, a CCB organization that we have observed in successful operation over a long period of time involves the following:

> The CCB secretary serves as the CCB chairman, keeping the meeting on track and recording its decisions. Decisions are generally made on a consensus basis. However, where consensus cannot be reached, the buyer's project manager makes the decisions in matters regarding cost and priority of effort, and the seller's project manager makes the decisions on technical matters within the cost and priority constraints.

TABLE 13-4   Candidate CCB Chairpersons

TITLE	RATIONALE FOR CHOICE
Seller's Project Manager	• Responsible for project development and maintenance. • Most technically competent of managerial personnel.
Buyer's Project Manager	• Ultimately responsible to the user for the end product. • Puts up the money for the project.
A Subordinate to the Buyer's Project Manager (e.g. a Deputy)	• On a large project, the project manager is generally a planner (as opposed to a day-to-day supervisor). He or she is therefore generally far separated from the project details, thus may delegate this responsibility to a deputy or other subordinate.
Seller's CM Representative	• CM is his or her prime responsibility and the CCB is the focal point of configuration management.
Buyer's CM Representative	• CM is his or her prime responsibility and the CCB is the focal point of configuration management.
CCB Secretary	• Serves as an orchestrator but not as a decision-maker. • Functions similarly to presiding officer of U.S. Senate.
Consultant from Outside the Project	• Unbiased orchestrator with no responsibility for implementation of any decision.
Jointly, Seller's and Buyer's Project Managers	• Two most responsible persons on CCB. • Buyer and seller both represented as orchestrators. (In case of disagreement, buyer's project manager should have ultimate authority, because buyer is putting up the money for the project.)

Minutes

An important aspect of CCB meetings is the configuration status accounting function of recording and publishing minutes of each meeting. These minutes give visibility to the decisions of the CCB and, through approval or modification at the next meeting, ensure that the decisions of the CCB are correctly recorded. The minutes provide traceability through stating what happened and when. Every entry in the minutes should be specific and precise so that there is no margin for misinterpretation. When action is to be taken, the minutes should specify who is to take the action and when the action should be completed. The names of all attendees at the meeting should be recorded and, also, the names of all board members absent. The minutes should be distributed not only to all attendees but also to upper-level management of the buyer and the seller, to permit management to track what is happening on the project. (The format and content of CCB minutes are subsequently discussed in this section under "Avoiding the Paperwork Nightmare.")

Preparation of minutes of CCB meetings is not for the purpose of formality, but rather for clarity and completeness. Format and style are less important than content and precision. Further, CCB minutes are necessary for small projects just as they are for large projects. They eliminate such later comments as, "I thought someone else was going to take action on that issue," or, "I don't remember that being decided on." People often leave meetings with conflicting ideas as to what has been agreed on, and the results of this natural confusion can be disastrous. The preparation of minutes helps to avoid such problems.

CM during the Acceptance Testing Cycle

Configuration management is most important, and often neglected, during the phase immediately preceding handover of the system to the user. The developers have completed coding and unit testing the software modules and have integrated those modules into a software system. Delivery and installation dates are fast approaching. During the time remaining, a test team is formed to check out the system as thoroughly as time allows. Typically, the testers exercise the system a few (four to eight) hours each day by executing a previously prepared set of test procedures. Of course, they will find at least a few troubles and duly report them to the developers. The developers, in turn, will scurry to locate the bugs in their programs causing the problems. Once the bugs have been located, the code is corrected, the system is rebuilt, and the software system is returned to the testers.

This cycle is repeated until delivery day arrives. At this point, an acceptance test is usually conducted to demonstrate to the buyer and users that the system delivered fulfills the contractual requirements. This acceptance test can be conducted at the seller's plant prior to shipping, at the user's site after installation, or at both places. (The reader who desires a fuller description of this testing cycle than what follows should see references 15 and 16.)

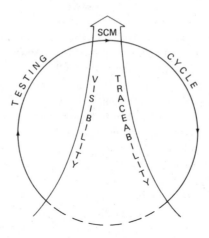

FIGURE 13-9. SCM—a means for elevating the visibility of and threading traceability into the testing cycle.

Why CM Is Necessary

SCM is essential to elevate the visibility of, and to thread traceability into, the testing cycle (see Figure 13-9). This cycle is characterized as a time of frequent and rapid change to the software code. Problems are reported, solutions are found, code is modified, documentation is (or should be) updated, and the system is rebuilt.

It is not difficult to lose control during such a period. Problems may be overlooked and go unreported. Reported problems may be lost in the shuffle and never corrected. Solutions may be incorrect or unworkable or may give rise to other problems. Solutions might not be adequately tested to verify that they have resolved problems without harmful side effects. Corrected code can be lost or may not be included in new system builds. Documentation may not be updated. The fact that documentation needs correcting may even be overlooked.

Control of the change process throughout the testing cycle is essential as the system evolves to its operational state. Visibility must be provided as to the status of the software throughout this period. Traceability has to be established so that the operational system can be maintained. In view of the definition of configuration management given earlier, it is easy to see why SCM is essential during the testing cycle.

CCB Role during the Testing Cycle

How is configuration management integrated into this testing cycle? Actually, as shown in Table 13-5, all four functions of CM come into play throughout the cycle. Let's take a closer look at the testing cycle (shown in detail in Figure 13-10), concentrating on how configuration management is injected into the process.

As in other phases of the development cycle, the CCB plays a central role in the

TABLE 13-5   Configuration Management Activities during the Testing Cycle

FUNCTION	ACTIVITIES
Configuration Identification	• Preparation of release notes (lists of changed software modules). • Identification of development baseline.* • Identification of incident reports. • Identification of operational baseline.*

Configuration Control	• CCB meetings:
	  –Establishment of development baseline.*
	  –Assignment of testing and incident report resolution priorities.
	  –Establishment of turnover dates.
	  –Approval of audit and test reports.
	  –Approval of incident report resolutions.
	  –Establishment of operational baseline.*

Configuration Auditing	• Comparison of new baseline to previous baseline. • Assurance that standards have been met. • Testing (verification and validation) of software system.
Configuration Status Accounting	• Logging and tracking of incident reports. • Publication of CCB minutes.

*See Figure 13-10.

testing cycle. The CCB should meet at two points during the cycle. The first kind of CCB meeting should occur whenever the developers turn software over to the testers, while the second should occur immediately following each test period. (For the moment, let us assume that the testing cycle consists of alternating periods of development/problem resolution and of testing. Subsequently, we discuss another practical approach involving overlapping periods of development and testing.) These CCB meetings establish configuration control over the testing cycle, as we will explain.

The Software Turnover CCB Meeting.   A CCB meeting is held at the beginning of the testing cycle, at which time the developers present a set of source code modules and a release note to the CCB. The release note lists all the modules turned over—a "parts list" that identifies the configuration of the software. The developers also present a list of all known discrepancies (with respect to requirements and/or design) in the modules turned over. These discrepancies are accepted by the CCB and logged (a function of configuration status accounting). The CCB places the code modules under control and establishes them as a baseline (another identification function). Recall from our discussion of Figures 13-2 and 13-3 that a *baseline* is a relative arrangement of software parts as embodied in a software product. We label this baseline as the *development baseline* (the name is clearly arbitrary). Based on the known discrepancies of the development baseline and the CCB's perception of the relative importance of the functions within the release, the CCB establishes priorities and areas of particular concern for testing, and selects a date for termination of the test period. The minutes of the CCB meeting are published and disseminated.

Building the software system from the development baseline should be a configuration management function. Prior to building the system, CM personnel perform a comparison (i.e., audit) of the source code in the new development baseline with the source code in the immediately preceding development baseline (if any; clearly there will be no preceding development baseline on the first iteration of the testing cycle for a new product). The results of this comparison make visible all changes that have been made to source code from one baseline to the next. The next step in this audit is to verify that the changes detected in the comparison process are all approved by the CCB. Another part of this audit is to compare the source code modules that have changed since the last development baseline was established to the standards adopted for the project. These standards might require, for example, certain commentary in the code and proper identification of the changes to the code modules. The findings of the audit are documented in an audit report, which is presented to the next meeting of the CCB.

The testers perform their tests using a documented set of test procedures. These test procedures specify a step-by-step set of operator actions. For each operator action, the reason for the action and the results expected from the action are documented. The test procedures are derived from two basic sources—the set of requirements for the project (*requirements baseline*) and the detailed design specifications for the software (*design baseline*). In performing the tests, the testers are assessing whether the development baseline logically follows from the design baseline and whether the development baseline is congruent with the requirements baseline. In the description of auditing in our SCM overview, we described the former process as *verification* and the latter process as *validation.* Thus the testers are performing verification and validation, which are the fundamental processes of configuration auditing. (For a discussion of how test and evaluation [T&E] and auditing can be viewed as equivalent processes, see References 11 and 16.)

The results of this audit/testing are documented in a test report, which is akin to an audit report. This test report is presented to the next meeting of the CCB for approval (see Figure 13-10). Individual discrepancies uncovered by this form of audit are documented in test incident reports. These incident reports (IRs) are logged by the configuration status accounting function and tracked until they have been resolved and all approved actions arising from them have been completed.

The Test Incident CCB Meeting.   The second kind of CCB meeting during the testing cycle occurs, as indicated in Figure 13-10, when the testers have executed the test procedures and written test incident reports. At this meeting, the CCB considers the audit report on the development baseline, the test report on the just-completed testing period, the discrepancies uncovered by the audit, and the incident reports resulting from the testing. On the first iteration of the testing cycle, the number of problems made visible is likely to be substantial, and the CCB

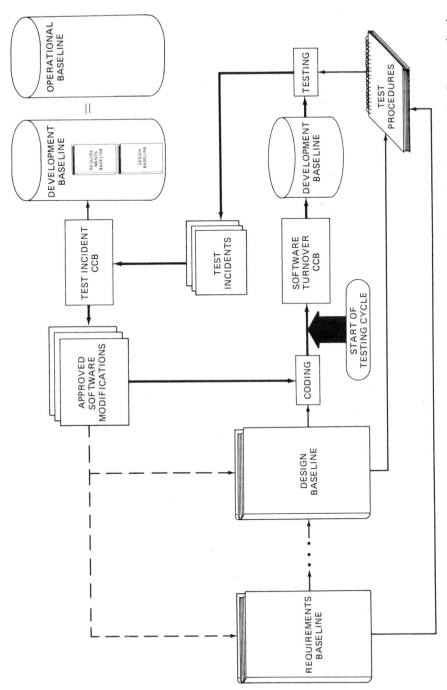

FIGURE 13-10. SCM and the testing cycle—iterating from the design baseline to the operational baseline with a development baseline created and controlled through CCB action. The cycle continues until the CCB determines that the development baseline incorporates the specifications of the requirements and design baselines (or approximations to these specifications). The resultant development baseline becomes the operational baseline.

probably will decide to continue the testing cycle. The problems are presented to the developers for investigation and recommendation of changes to be made to the software (both code and documentation). The CCB also sets a date for beginning the next iteration of the testing cycle.

As a result of this meeting, the CCB approves modifications to the computer source code and possibly to baselined documents (such as the requirements baseline or the design baseline—see Figure 13-10). The developers make the required software (source code and documentation) changes.

On the established date, the next iteration of the cycle begins with the repetition of the initial CCB meeting described above. At this meeting, the responses of the developers to the IRs and the discrepancies in the audit report are presented to the CCB. The release note for this meeting lists the software that has been changed since the last testing cycle began. If the CCB approves the recommended resolutions presented by the developers, the development baseline is updated with the changed software. The testers next audit the changed modules in the updated development baseline as they did on the preceding iteration. On this and subsequent iterations, the testers confirm that the problems whose resolutions have been approved by the CCB have actually been solved. In addition, the testers repeat the test procedures to ensure that the approved changes have not introduced new problems.

Terminating the Testing Cycle

At the CCB meeting following testing, the CCB will formally close out any problems whose satisfactory resolution has been demonstrated by testing. At each iteration of the testing cycle, the number of outstanding problems within the system should be reduced. When the number of remaining problems converges to only a few or possibly no problems remaining, the CCB will establish the software as an *operational baseline,* and delivery can be effected. Any remaining problems, still tracked and controlled, can be corrected through field changes or in the next release. The operational baseline is equivalent to the development baseline with the specifications of the requirements baseline and design baseline incorporated (see Figure 13-10).

If a firm delivery date is reached before this convergence point, the software can still be delivered together with a list of known discrepancies. This delivery of a still-defective product can be done because of the visibility as to the state of the software system that the process provides. Usually the seller has the contractual responsibility to correct these outstanding defects.

Notice how, throughout the testing cycle, SCM has continuously maintained control, has elevated the visibility of the testing cycle, enabling the project team to be aware of the status of the configuration at all times, and has threaded traceability of how the end product has been achieved into the testing cycle. Visibility, traceability, and control have been achieved through the pervasive application of configuration management.

Concurrent Development and Testing: An Alternative Cycle

As previously stated, the foregoing description is based on an alternating sequence of development/resolution periods and testing periods. It is also possible to successfully use another scheme, in which the development/resolution periods and test periods are concurrent. In this scheme, the development group uses the computer system on one shift, and the test group uses the computer system on a second shift. A brief CCB meeting generally is held each day between the two shifts. At these meetings, the CCB performs the same functions as at both CCB meetings in the sequential scheme described above. Incident reports arising from testing are introduced at the daily CCB meeting. Changed software code is released only periodically, however, perhaps weekly or biweekly. Otherwise, the testing cycle remains the same.

This concurrent scheme allows increased utilization of resources at the expense of some inconvenience to the project staff due to the two-shift workload. It doubles the utilization of the project computer system (assuming that the luxury of two available computer systems is lacking). It also allows both the development group and the test group to be working continuously, and it puts the observed problems into the hands of the developers for resolution at an earlier point—daily, rather than at the end of a test period. Configuration management is even more important to maintaining control under this scheme because of the high, concurrent activity level. Since SCM is integrated into the testing cycle, the benefits of control, visibility, and traceability are obtained, and a product that can be maintained is achieved.

Justification and Practicality of Auditing

The conduct of auditing can be a heavy consumer of configuration management resources. Auditing is the most technical and also the most labor-intensive of the CM functions. It requires an ability to understand and relate details, and to perceive not only what is present in a software product but also what is missing from it. As a result, the most experienced (and thus the most expensive) CM personnel generally are assigned to the auditing task. It is not difficult to see why auditing consumes such a large part of the CM budget. (This specific CM auditing activity is not to be confused with the auditing of the entire CM process by software quality assurance personnel as discussed in Chapter 2.)

In light of the high cost of auditing, management may well question the expenditure of valuable resources on this function (see Figure 13-11). This questioning is particularly likely to happen at project initiation, when an eager but ill-advised project manager is liable to say the following, as hypothesized by Boehm:[17]

> Don't worry about that specification paperwork. We'd better hurry up and start coding, because we're going to have a whole lot of debugging to do.

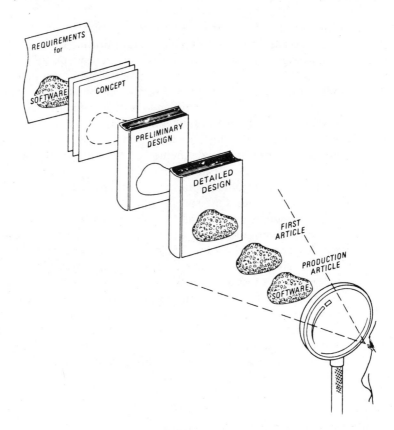

FIGURE 13-11. Paying an auditor to see what is (and is not) there—is the expenditure worth it?

This questioning may also occur in the latter stages of a development, when the harried project manager is likely to reason as follows:

> Look, I don't need anyone to tell me that I have problems. I know what my problems are—we are falling behind in our design and coding. I can hire two or three programmers for the cost of one auditor. That's where I need to spend my limited resources.

Often, the result of such reasoning is a sudden termination of auditing activities and a swarm of programmers coding as rapidly as possible. Such an approach can be extremely shortsighted. While the creation of gobs of code may seem productive on the surface, it can be very unproductive if the wrong code is produced and some customer requirements are left unaddressed. Elimination of auditing is false economy.

Likely Payoff
Auditing pays for itself through the avoidance of larger, unnecessary expenses. Boehm has indicated that savings of up to 100:1 for large projects and 4-6:1 for

small projects can be achieved by finding (through verification and validation) and fixing problems early in the life cycle.[17] Through verification, we avoid wasting resources on the development of inconsistent products (such as a detailed design that is inconsistent with a preliminary design); through validation, we avoid wasting resources on the development of something that hasn't been asked for (for example, including in a design document a capability that has no antecedent in a user's requirements specification).

Can we ever really be sure that the audit approach will save time and money? No, we cannot be certain. After all, auditing may not uncover latent problems, or there may not be any problems to uncover. Further, there is no guarantee that discrepancies or flaws detected through auditing will be accepted and corrected. The best that we can say is that money spent on auditing *may* result in saving more money over the life of a project.

Of course, there are circumstances in which auditing is necessary, even though it is accepted a priori that time and money may not be saved. We may have a sufficiently complex system under development whose failure would result in calamitous consequences (e.g., a missile system). Or we may be developing a system whose failure would result in serious political consequences (e.g., an election outcome prediction system or a national space project). In these circumstances, the value of auditing is that it provides assurance that a software product works, as opposed to its value in reducing overall project costs.

Audit Compromises to Reduce Costs

There are times project management appreciates the value of auditing but, owing to budget constraints, must limit the amount of auditing that can be performed. There are two basic compromises that can be made to reduce expenditures for auditing. One of these compromises is to reduce the depth of each audit but still to audit each baseline*. This approach maintains a degree of traceability with some loss of visibility. The second compromise is to eliminate one or more audits. Here, visibility is maintained, but traceability is impaired. If this latter approach is taken, the prime candidate for omission is the baseline established on completion of installation. This baseline is generally little changed from the baseline established at the end of the testing cycle. The most important baselines to be audited, which should *never* be omitted from audit, are the first baseline established (errors ferreted out here are much cheaper to repair than those discovered in later phases) and the first baseline containing code (this baseline is the first that has multiple representations, all of which must be congruent).

Both of the compromises indicated above increase project risk. They raise the likelihood that potentially serious discrepancies may not be detected. Further, extraneous and possibly costly items in the software may not be detected. Certainly, visibility or traceability is diminished. Management must decide whether these risks are acceptable, taking budget factors into account.

---

*See Chapter 11 for the possible use in this case of Pareto Analysis to determine key errors.—Editors.

Coping with Numerous Software Products

Another resource problem connected with auditing often occurs at the end of a phase of the software development cycle. Here, usually a number of software products are delivered by the developers at approximately the same time. For example, at the end of the design phase, the developers may produce detailed design specifications, a user's manual, a data specification document, and possibly other documents. Not only must all these documents be audited at about the same time, but often several of these documents are voluminous in size. To exacerbate the problem, a limited amount of time is frequently provided to the auditors to review these documents. To maintain progress on the project, generally the time between the publication of the documents and the establishment of the baseline is kept relatively brief. How to audit all these documents in these circumstances with limited resources is indeed a problem.

There are a number of ways to cope with this problem. One is to bring extra auditors onto the project for a brief period to alleviate this peak demand. Unfortunately, the extra resources are rarely available when most needed. Another solution to this problem is to stretch out the period during which auditing is performed, for example, by performing preliminary audits on draft documents. This tactic allows the auditors not only a longer period over which to audit but also allows them to become familiar with the documents, thus facilitating their audit of the final documents. This tactic also provides preliminary input to the document developers, which allows them to improve documents before producing the final versions.

It is possible and often practical to conduct only a partial audit prior to establishing a set of products as a baseline, and then to continue the audit to a greater depth after the baseline is established. The partial audit concentrates on establishing the basic validity of the baseline (e.g., by determining whether all paragraph headings in, for instance, a design document have antecedents in a requirements specification). Using the results of this partial audit, the CCB can establish the baseline subject to the satisfactory completion of the audit. The developers can then proceed from this provisional baseline into the next phase of the project, knowing that, in all likelihood, only minor adjustments need be made when the full audit is completed. When establishing the baseline, the CCB also can direct the auditors to concentrate on particular issues of concern to the board.

Auditing indeed consumes resources, often in great amounts. However, the payoff in these resource expenditures is the avoidance, through early discovery of incongruities among software products, of consuming even greater amounts of resources.

Avoiding the Paperwork Nightmare

A criticism often leveled against SCM is that the primary product of its application is paperwork and more paperwork (see Figure 13-12). It is true that the output of SCM functions is paper. Identification produces parts lists; control produces CCB minutes and a multitude of forms pertaining to software changes—incident reports,

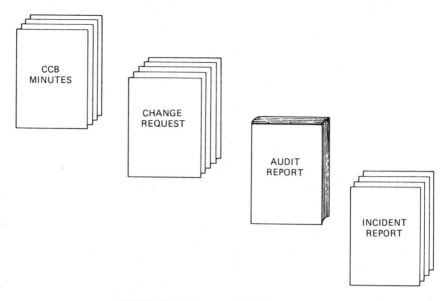

FIGURE 13-12. Some typical SCM paperwork.

prepared documentation modifications, patches to fielded code, and so forth; auditing produces discrepancy reports and test incident reports; and, of course, status accounting archives and disseminates the paper produced by the other three SCM functions. Thus unbridled application of SCM can precipitate literally mountains of paper which, in turn, can impede (or, in the extreme, stop) project progress.

A guiding principle whose application can serve to keep paperwork in check is the following:

> The buyer/user and seller should iteratively agree on how much and how frequently paper is needed to achieve a mutually desirable level of visibility and traceability.

To see how this principle works, we consider some of the paperwork associated with CCB meetings—CCB minutes. Of all the SCM paper produced on a project, these minutes are probably the most fundamental elements in establishing and maintaining a visible trace of project activities. For CCB minutes, the above principle translates into the following particulars:

1. Begin with an outline and format such as that shown in Table 13-6.
2. Use this format at the first few CCB meetings to generate minutes.
3. Because the minutes from one meeting should serve as the basis for conducting the next meeting, it should become clear to the meeting participants which topics are useful to the participants and how much detail should be recorded for each topic.

TABLE 13-6   Sample Format for CCB Minutes

CCB MINUTES

Date
Ident. No.

List of Attendees and Organizational Affiliation

1. Purpose of Meeting.

   – Agenda
   – Adoption of minutes from preceding CCB

2. CCB Actions

   – Software parts labeled/relabeled
   – Baselines reviewed/changed/established
   – Disposition of change control forms
   – New/unresolved/unscheduled issues

3. Discussion of CM Audits

   – Discrepancies reviewed
   – Plan for resolution of discrepancies

4. Items for Subsequent CCB Meetings

   – Action items
   – Agenda for next meeting
   – Time and place of next meeting

Distribution List

---

4. In this manner, the format and content of the CCB minutes should evolve to accommodate the needs of the CCB participants, thus, by definition, avoiding unnecessary paperwork.

A by-product of the above process is the paring down of other paperwork associated with the conduct of CCB business. Specifically, the primary business of the CCB is the review and approval of software changes. This review and approval process, to be performed in a visible and traceable manner, needs to be supported by paperwork to accomplish the following tasks:

1. To document incidents which may indicate problems with software code that is being tested prior to operational use or is in operational use.

2. To document CCB-approved changes to software code.
3. To document CCB-approved changes to software other than code (e.g., design specifications) and software-related documentation (e.g., user's manuals—documentation that describes in user language how to use software systems).
4. To document requests for enhancements or new capabilities that the CCB must act upon.

The number and format of the forms needed to perform the above tasks can be agreed upon and defined during CCB meetings in a manner similar to that used to refine the format and content of CCB minutes. A starting point for defining these forms can be found in Reference 8, Chapter 5.

In addition to the paperwork reduction process just described, electronic tools can also serve to reduce or eliminate paper. For example, word processors can be used to reduce paper by storing masters of forms, their contents, and CCB minutes. This information archive can then be tapped in response to specific requests from project participants, thus keeping paper flow regulated by project need. Electronic mail systems offer a potential for eliminating paperwork; the application of such a system to the SCM paperwork problem is described in Reference 18.

Avoiding the paperwork nightmare can thus be achieved through negotiation on the part of project participants on the form and content of project correspondence. The focus of this negotiation should be the CCB, through which the bulk of this paperwork flows. Judicious use of electronic tools is a further means to alleviate this flow, by regulating paper in response to specific needs.

Allocating Resources among CM Activities

Most software projects, particularly in the commercial world, where profit is an important—if not the single most important—success criterion, provide only relatively small dollar allocations to "overhead activities" such as SCM. Consequently, it is frequently necessary to make hard decisions regarding the percentage of already highly limited resources that should be parceled out to each of the SCM functions. Unfortunately, we are not aware of any general principles governing how these difficult decisions should be made (see Figure 13-13). The particulars of individual projects often establish the deciding factors. (Politics may dictate what SCM can and cannot do; for example, some software project managers simply do not want detailed audits of software products developed prior to code—they would rather wait until code testing to find out what the developers have been doing.) We will therefore illustrate some of the trade-offs involved with making such decisions by working through the following example based on a typical business-world situation:

Example

Suppose that you have just been put in charge of a software development effort that is just getting started. Suppose further that your past experience with software

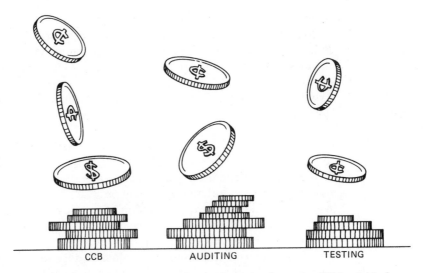

FIGURE 13-13. Where should limited resources be allocated to SCM activities?

projects has convinced you of the need for and importance of SCM. Finally, suppose that your management is (1) primarily interested in keeping project costs to an absolute minimum and (2) is unfavorably disposed toward "overhead functions" such as SCM. You are therefore placed in a position of reducing SCM to a bare minimum. After presenting various SCM proposals to your management, the guidance you receive is that you are permitted to fund *only one* of the following activities:

1. Weekly configuration control board meetings attended by yourself and the buyer/user to review project progress and to consider proposed software changes.
2. Development and execution of written test procedures to determine buyer/user acceptance of the coded software that you are responsible for developing. The coded software is assumed to be exercised in an environment that either is identical to or approximates the actual user environment.
3. Audits of selected software products (such as the functional specification, design documents, and code).

Given the above scenario, how would you make your selection? Table 13-7 lists the advantage and disadvantages associated with the above three SCM activities. Which activity you select depends upon how much weight you (or your boss) give to these advantages and disadvantages. This table thus illustrates typical trade-offs associated with allocating resources to various CM activities and (qualitatively) the types of paybacks offered in return for resources invested. The table also indicates the manner in which SCM activities complement one another, thus suggesting that their integrated application is really necessary if working software products are to be achieved on time and within budget.

TABLE 13-7   Trade-Offs in Deciding Which SCM Activities to Fund

ACTIVITY	ADVANTAGE	DISADVANTAGE
1. Weekly CCB Meetings	Sustained visibility forced on buyer/user/seller, which reduces the likelihood that problems will go unnoticed too long.	Does not provide definitive determination that delivered software code is doing what it is supposed to do.
2. Development and Execution of Test Procedures	Provides the most definitive indication (of all three activities) of the degree to which the final software product (i.e., the operating code) is doing what it is supposed to do.	A one-shot exercise late in product development cycle, whose application may be insufficient (or too late) to adequately deal with problems.
3. Audits of Selected Software Products	Provides an indication (long before testing) of potentially costly deviations from requirements (and design), thereby allowing corrective action to be taken at reduced schedule and cost risk to the project.	Probably conducted less frequently than the first activity, thus providing less visibility and thereby increasing the likelihood that problems will go unnoticed (or will be noticed later and thereby be more costly to rectify).

TABLE 13-8   Funding SCM Activities—Reallocation and Rescoping Considerations

ACTIVITY	ORIGINAL ALLOCATION	REALLOCATION	RESCOPING
1. Weekly CCB Meetings	$25,000	$18,000	Reduce frequency of meetings slightly (maybe to three per month).
2. Development and Execution of Test Procedures	25,000	12,000	Reduce depth and breadth of testing.
3. Audits of Selected Software Products	25,000	10,000	Audit to a lesser depth or do fewer audits (concentrating on initial software products).

To see in more quantitative terms some of the cost-versus-benefit trade-offs involving SCM activities, consider the following extension to the previous example:

Suppose that you estimate that it would cost $25,000 for *each* of the three activities. Suppose further that your management gives you $40,000 and allows you to fund *any* combination of the three activities. With this budget constraint, indicate how you would reallocate funds to these activities, and indicate how you would change their scope to reflect this reallocation.

Table 13-8 indicates one way to respond to the resource allocation and scope issues raised above. This table and the preceding one offer a specific example of the cost versus benefits associated with specific SCM activities.

13.4 SUMMARY

Software configuration management offers the buyer, user, and seller protection against the myriad problems that often beset software development and maintenance projects—problems that, if left unaddressed, can easily spell project disaster. To address these problems, the four SCM functions—identification, control, auditing, and status accounting—must be practiced in, and indeed integrated into, the software development process throughout the project life cycle.

Establishment of an SCM program on a software project of *any* size is practicable and economically justifiable. Management commitment to installing the checks and balances provided by SCM is of paramount importance. An SCM program should be established gradually, molded to the organization and functions of the company and its projects and to available personnel. An early endeavor should be the establishment of a configuration control board periodically meeting to maintain change control for the project. Other areas of importance for SCM are the conduct of audits of the software products, particularly early in the life cycle, and of acceptance testing of the completed software code prior to its delivery to its users.

In this chapter, we have made a number of practical suggestions for implementing an SCM program. With the installation of such a program, a large measure of protection will be provided to a project through an increase in visibility and traceability, through the establishment of project control and change control, and through provision of a capability to monitor project events. The end result is an increased likelihood of developing software systems that satisfy user needs and that are delivered on time and within budget.

References

1. Zelkowitz, M. W., Shaw, A. C., and Gannon, J. D., *Principles of Software Engineering and Design,* pp. 1-2. Reprinted by permission of Prentice-Hall, Inc., Englewood Cliffs, NJ. Copyright © 1979 by Prentice-Hall, Inc.
2. "Report of the DOD Joint Service Task Force on Software Problems," Department of Defense Report (Deputy Under Secretary of Defense, Research & Advanced Technology), July 30, 1982.
3. Bunyard, J. M., and Coward, J. M., "Today's Risks in Software Development—Can They Be Significantly Reduced?," *Signal,* Vol. 37, No. 7 (October 1982), pp. 18-29.
4. O'Toole, T., "Computer Failures Helped Put $100 Million Satellite Off Course," *The Washington Post,* January 29, 1984, p. A2.
5. Omang, J., "Firms Unhappy with Computers Are Taking to the Courtrooms," *The Washington Post,* February 22, 1983, p. A10.
6. "Getting Rid of the Bugs, Angry Systems Users Are Taking Their Complaints to Court," *Time,* Vol. 122, No. 14 (October 3, 1983), p. 68.
7. Bersoff, E. H., Henderson, V. D., and Siegel, S. G., "Software Configuration Management: A Tutorial," *Computer,* Vol. 12, No. 1 (January 1979), p. 6-14.
8. Bersoff, E. H., Henderson, V. D., and Siegel, S. G., *Software Configuration Management: An Investment in Product Integrity,* (Englewood Cliffs, NJ: Prentice-Hall, Inc., 1980).

9. *Ibid.,* p. 10. Reprinted by permission of Prentice-Hall, Inc., Englewood Cliffs, NJ. Copyright © 1980 by Prentice-Hall, Inc.

10. Bryan, W. L., Siegel, S. G., and Whiteleather, G. L., "Auditing Throughout the Software Life Cycle: A Primer," *Computer,* Vol. 15, No. 3 (March 1982), pp. 57-67.

11. Bryan, W. L., and Siegel, S. G., "Product Assurance: Insurance Against a Software Disaster," *Computer,* Vol. 17, No. 4 (April 1984), pp. 75-83.

12. Demarco, T., *Controlling Software Projects,* (New York: Yourdon Press, 1982).

13. General Accounting Office Report to the Congress by the Comptroller General of the United States, FGMSO-80-4, "Contracting for Computer Software Development—Serious Problems Require Management Attention to Avoid Wasting Additional Millions," November 9, 1979.

14. Weiss, D. M., "The MUDD Report: A Case Study of Navy Software Development Practices," Naval Research Laboratory Report 7909, May 21, 1975.

15. Bryan, W. L., and Siegel, S. G., "Configuration Management of Software Testing," *Proceedings of Software Maintenance Workshop,* Monterey, CA, December 6-8, 1983, pp. 15-16.

16. Bryan, W. L., and Siegel, S. G., "Making Software Visible, Operational, and Maintainable in a Small Project Environment," *IEEE Transactions on Software Engineering,* Vol. SE-10, No. 1 (January 1984), pp. 59-67.

17. Boehm, B. W., "Verifying and Validating Software Requirements and Design Specifications," *Software,* Vol. 1, No. 1 (January 1984), pp. 75-88.

18. Zucker, S., "Automating the Configuration Management Process," *Proceedings of SOFTFAIR,* July 25-28, 1983, pp. 164-172.

19. Kirchner, J., "Candy Maker, Software Firm in Legal Battle," *ACM SIGSOFT* No. 5 (January 30, 1984), pp. 1, 8.

20. "Gentlemen Prefer Platinum to Bonds—$32 Billion Overdraft," *ACM SIGSOFT Software Engineering Notes,* Vol. II, No. 1 (January 1986), pp. 3-7. (This account of a software disaster that befell a bank appears in the "Letter from the Editor" section of the journal. This letter, which is titled "Risks to the Public in Computer Systems," and appears on pp. 2-14, contains a collection of software failure stories of various magnitudes, the most dramatic being the one cited above.)

14

Software Quality Assurance Metrics

G. Gordon Schulmeyer, CDP

Westinghouse Electronic Systems Group

14.1 INTRODUCTION

The purpose of software quality metrics according to the IEEE Draft *Standard for a Software Quality Metrics Methodology,*[7, p. 4] is to make assessments throughout the software life cycle as to whether the software quality requirements are being met. The use of metrics reduces subjectivity in the assessment of software quality by providing a quantitative basis for making decisions about software quality. However, the use of metrics does not eliminate the need for human judgement in software evaluations. The use of software quality metrics within an organization or project is expected to have a beneficial effect by making software quality more visible.

Software quality assurance metrics have taken on various guises over the years, and this chapter gives an introduction to those used most. To introduce some relevant concepts in this section there are discussions of data collection methods and the idea of validation of metrics.

A software quality survey discussed in this chapter gives some information as to the state of the practice with software quality assurance metrics. The following section gives some help to the often inaccurate area of software estimating. Although, not specifically an SQA measure, it is of such significance to overall software success that it deserves some special notice.

Next, there are a number of examples given of various practical implementations of SQA metrics. That section covers Hewlett-Packard's experiences, Basili and Rombach's quantitative SQA, Walker Royce's TRW pragmatic quality metrics, The Carman Group's MIL/SOFTQUAL, and Hitachi's software quality measurements.

The IEEE Draft *Standard for a Software Quality Metrics Methodology* has a section devoted to its explanation of a coherent methodology for the capture of software quality metrics. That is followed by a section on what is being called the "omnibus" software quality metrics that derived from the work of McCall and Boehm.

Software quality indicators have been published and a brief survey of their intention and use is covered. Finally, the chapter has a few concluding remarks.

Data Collection

The three-stage procedure for implementing a data collection scheme is:

1. Set the goals (why are you collecting the data, what reports do you want to see and when?)
2. Model the production process and the data (what data do you need to collect and when?)
3. Devise a collection scheme and put it in place (how do you make it happen?)

As a result of significant data collection the following important lessons were learned:

- Recording large volumes of data on paper is useless
- A scheme starts by transcribing data, not collecting it
- Define the process model, then the metrics
- Technology changes during a long term collection project
- Target and prediction data is not the same as *actual* data

As a part of this data collection exercise, it was found that subjective metrics (subjective complexity, quality, and the like) are unreliable for preliminary identification of anomalies but very useful when diagnosing their causes.[18, pp. 80, 81, 85]

Experience has shown that software developers do not mind quality criteria targets and the collection of data to achieve their goal as long as they participate in setting those goals and agree with them. But when data collection and interpretation are hidden from them, they will wonder whether the ground rules have been changed without their being informed.[8, p. 32]

Validation of Metrics

The validation of software quality measures are of interest here. There are two levels of validation necessary, which are referred to as *internal* and *external*. A software quality measure is internally valid if, in the sense of measurement theory, it provides a numerical characterization of some intuitively understood attributes. In all cases one must know on which aspect of the product (or process) a given measure is defined and whether there is a formal model for such definition (ensuring no ambiguity). Thus, for example, a valid measure of the attribute of modularity of designs requires a formal model for designs and a numerical mapping which preserves any relations over the set of designs intuitively imposed by the attribute of modularity. Thus, the proposed measure of modularity should indeed measure precisely, that if it is generally agreed that D_1 has a greater level of modularity than design D_2, then any measure m of modularity must satisfy

$$m(D_1) > m(D_2)$$

A software quality measure is externally valid if it can be shown to be an important component or predictor of some behavioral software quality attribute of interest. For example, if it could be demonstrated that modularity of designs was an important factor in subsequent ease of maintenance of the implemented code, then it could be said that modularity was a validated indicator of maintainability.

Proponents of software quality measurement have said that we cannot control what we cannot measure. It is equally true that we cannot *predict* what we cannot measure, but this viewpoint has rarely been articulated or understood. It seems strange that so much effort has been placed on externally validating metrics, which predict attributes like cost, errors, changes, and certain external 'quality' attributes, when there are not yet agreed standards for their definition nor the ability to identify (let alone measure) these attributes properly after they have occurred! Unless this is done there is no hope for true validation of predictive metrics.

Thus, in the absence of any standards for their definition and means of measurement, the use of historical data for defects, changes, costs, etc. as a means of external validation should be treated with extreme caution.

There is another reason why one should be far more careful in the approach to predictive metrics, which can never be effectively validated without an explicit life-cycle model. In the absence of a generally agreed upon model, the use of even a validated predictive metric may be limited, except possibly in 'conservative' areas like predicting specific code or maintenance attributes from code measures, or code attributes from measures of the detailed design. This would be particularly true in the case of current trends such as *evolutionary* design by rapid prototyping, where 'traditional' life-cycle views are irrelevant.[4, pp. 75, 76]

At a software engineering lab described in reference 17, each project spends on average, 3 percent of its budget on data collection and validation. The organization spends an additional 4 to 6 percent on off-line data processing and analysis. However, you should expect a higher investment up front to build a new program.[17]

14.2 SOFTWARE QUALITY SURVEY

Some interesting metric information relating to software quality is contained in a recent software quality survey[18] conducted by the Software Quality Technical Committee of the American Society for Quality Control (ASQC). The survey is based upon 108 responses from industries that had 50 percent representation from aerospace/electronics and banking/financial, and the remaining 50 percent from other diverse industries.

Quality metrics, defined in the survey as a technique used to quantify the attributes of software quality through hard numbers, on average is used by 13 percent of those responding.

While a lot has been written in the area of quality metrics, few of the firms surveyed used these hard indicators to quantify characteristics of software quality. The metrics captured by firms responding as part of the survey were used to quantify quality goals in the areas of software size, complexity, maintainability, reliability and testability.

A little over 12 percent of the survey population employed metrics as an indicator of software reliability. The following three indicators were cited for this quality attribute: error rate, error density, and error severity. The metrics used for these are: error rate—errors/month and errors/release, error density—errors/ KSLOC(thousands of source lines of code) and number of problem reports, error severity—errors/category and number of rejections.

About 6 percent of the survey population employed some measure of software size as an indicator of quality. Both function points and lines of code were cited as metrics for this quality attribute. Lines of code were defined in over five different ways by those responding.

Less than 4 percent of the survey population employed metrics to bound the complexity, maintainability, and/or testability of their software. The most cited metric for these quality goals are for complexity (4%)—cyclomatic number, maintainability (2%)—number of maintenance requests, and testability (1%)—coverage.

An average of 4 percent of those surveyed used a metrics analyzer, which is defined as an automated tool used to collect, analyze and report the results of metrics quantification and analysis activities.

The survey respondents overwhelmingly responded as follows with their "wish list"; they want practical metrics available to measure both the characteristics and the cost/benefits of the quality of the firm's software life cycle processes and products.[16]

14.3 SOFTWARE ESTIMATING

Software developers are so poor at estimating because often, competent estimators, based on their superior performance, get promoted to positions where their skill is no longer required. Newly elected estimators rarely find adequate procedures or sufficiently available skilled consultants from whom they can learn. There is rarely a project history file available for reference. In organizations where there is generally an inadequate understanding of the planning process and its value, lack of commitment for time and resources also effects estimating results.[24, p. 58]

Several experienced managers estimated the size of 16 software projects on the basis of the complete specification for each project. The average expert predic-

TABLE 14-1.   Actual and Predicted Size of 16 Software Projects[9, p. 40]
© 1990 IEEE

Product	Actual Size	Predicted Size
1	70,919	34,705
2	128,837	32,100
3	23,015	22,000
4	34,560	9,100
5	23,000	12,000
6	25,000	7,300
7	52,080	28,500
8	7,650	8,000
9	25,860	30,600
10	16,300	2,720
11	17,410	15,300
12	33,900	105,300
13	57,194	18,500
14	21,020	35,400
15	8,642	3,650
16	17,480	2,950

tions are presented in Table 14-1 together with the actual size of each software project, after completed. The table shows that based upon expert judgment that the discrepancy between estimated and real size values is large enough to raise questions about the "expert judgment."

The assumption that estimates are unbiased toward underestimation or overestimation is not confirmed by current experience. In Table 14-1 it can be seen that 12 of 16 projects were underestimated by experts. The reasons for underestimating include the desire to please management, incomplete recall of previous experiences, lack of familiarity with the entire software job, and lack of enough knowledge of the particular project being estimated.[9, pp. 39, 40]

Estimating Recommendations

The following steps aid in estimating a project:

1. Select the estimating technique(s).
    If the participants are not experienced in the technique(s), allow extra time for the learning period.
2. Determine the data requirements
3. Define the planning process
4. Automate as much as possible
5. Produce the estimates

6. Save the results in an accumulated history file, recalibrate as necessary, and make the data available to everyone in the company.[24, p. 59]

14.4 PRACTICAL IMPLEMENTATIONS

Hewlett Packard

At Hewlett Packard (H-P) there has been a recent history of software quality improvement efforts that have been reported at various conferences. The following is a timeline of H-P company-wide efforts:

1980 Management awareness training for every General Manager and above.

1980 Developed FURPS (Functionality, Usability, Reliability, Performance, and Supportability) to describe software quality attributes, which was later revised to FURPS+ to include localization, predictability, and portability.

1981 Created the function of Productivity Manager in each Research & Development division.

1982 Formed a metrics council of interested engineers and managers, explored/ collected many metrics from divisions, highlighted in the 1986 book, *Software Metrics: Establishing a Company-wide Program.*[6] H-P has kept very detailed records of software defect data after product release for years, but only recently have they had some divisions analyze the causes of defects found prior to release.[6, p. 22]

1983 Set up the Software Engineering Laboratory in corporate engineering for tools and methods.

1984 Started the Software Engineering Productivity Conference, an internal forum with over 800 attendees, where practical implementations of productivity and quality improvements are discussed.

1985 Established a corporate software quality manager.

1986 Established the Software 10X improvement goal: John Young, H-P CEO, stated, "I want us to achieve a tenfold improvement in two key software quality measures in the next five years."

1987 A high management level software 10X task force reaffirmed the magnitude of the issues, and the need for focus on software.

1987 The BET (Break Even Time) metric was introduced. This focuses on getting the right product to market in a timely manner. The goal is to cut the Break Even Time in half in five years. Figure 14-1 provides a demonstration BET metric example.

Company-wide measures at H-P are very few and very focused. They serve as drivers for division efforts and programs which are resulting in a set of best practices at the divisions.[23 pp. 8B-41, 8B-42]

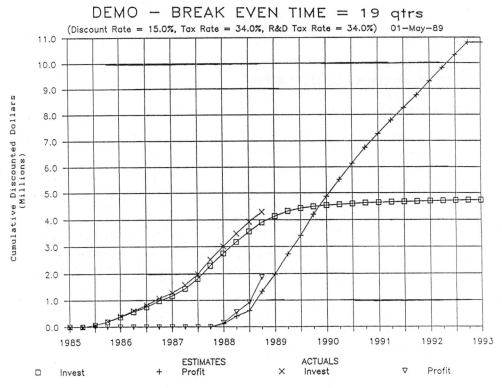

FIGURE 14-1. BET demonstration metric.[23]

Quantitative SQA

Basili and Rombach[1] suggest a model for quantitative SQA that consists of three phases:

1. Define quality requirements in quantitative terms. Select the quality characteristics of interest, define priorities among and relations between those quality characteristics, define each characteristic by one or more direct measures, and define the quality requirements quantitatively by assigning an expected value.
2. Plan quality control through adequate actions to assure fulfillment of the defined quality requirements, control the proper execution of these actions, and evaluate the results.
3. Perform quality control which consists of: (1) measurement, in which the methods and techniques specified during the planning phase are applied to gather actual values for all defined measures, and (2) evaluation, in which the direct measurements are compared to the quality requirements and indirect

measurements are interpreted to explain or predict the values of direct measures. Evaluation also involves deciding if the requirements were met for each quality characteristic and for the entire set of project requirements.

The quantitative SQA model considers the importance of the process, not just the product. One reason quality and productivity are perceived conflicting is that process quality is often neglected. It is believed that productivity increases if a high quality development process is employed.

Quantitative SQA model also accounts for the equal importance of analytic and constructive SQA activities. The term "assurance" (as opposed to analysis) indicates that the objective is both to determine if quality requirements are met (the analytic aspect) and, when they are not met to suggest corrective action (the constructive aspect).

The model covers all phases of software development so that effective software quality corrective action may be suggested.

Finally, the model stresses the importance of separating responsibilities for development and SQA. It is not important *who* performs the measurement part of quality control as long as it is planned for and evaluated by development-independent personnel.[1, p. 8]

Pragmatic Quality Metrics

Walker Royce at TRW Space and Defense has been calculating metrics of real time Ada projects. Simplicity is achieved by keeping the number of statistics to be maintained in an SCO database to five (type, estimate of damage in hours and SLOC, actual hours and actual SLOC to resolve) along with the other required parameters of an SCO. Furthermore, metrics for $SLOC_C$ (configured source lines of code) and $SLOC_T$, (total source lines of code) need to be accurately maintained.

- A Software Change Order (SCO) constitutes a direction to proceed with changing a configured software component.

The metrics described here were easy to use by personnel familiar with the project context. Furthermore, they provide an objective basis for discussing current trends and future plans with outside authorities. Table 14-2 provides raw data definitions for source lines, errors, improvements, and rework. Table 14-3 shows the in progress indicator definitions of rework ratio, backlog, and stability. Table 14-4 defines the end-product quality metrics of rework proportions, modularity, changeability, and maintainability; as well as some values determined from real projects.

There are enough perspectives that provide somewhat redundant views so that misuse should be minimized. The possibility of misinterpretation exists, and so it would be beneficial to obtain more experience to evaluate where misinterpretation is most likely.[19, pp. 5, 17, 18]

TABLE 14-2 Raw Data Definitions[19, p. 8]

Statistic	Definition	Insight
Total Source Lines	$SLOC_T$ = Total Product SLOC	Total effort
Configured Source Lines	$SLOC_C$ = Standalone Tested SLOC	Demonstrable Progress
Errors	SCO_1 = No. of Open Type 1 SCOs SCO_1 = No. of Closed Type 1 SCOs SCO_1 = No. of Type 1 SCOs	Test Effectiveness Test Progress Reliability
Improvements	SCO_2 = No. of Open Type 2 SCOs SCO_2 = No. of Closed Type 2 SCOs SCO_2 = No. of Type 2 SCOs	Value Engrg. Design Progress
Open Rework	B_1 = Damaged SLOC Due to SCO_1 B_2 = Damaged SLOC Due to SCO_2	Fragility Schedule Risk
Closed Rework	F_1 = SLOC Repaired after SCO_1 F_2 = SLOC Repaired after SCO_2	Maturity Changeability
Total Rework	$R_1 = F_1 + B_1$ $R_2 = F_2 + B_2$	Design Quality Maintainability

TABLE 14-3 In Progress Indicator Definitions[19, p. 9]

Indicator	Definition	Insight
Rework Ratio	$RR = \dfrac{R_1 + R_2}{SLOC_C} -$	Future Rework
Rework Backlog	$BB = \dfrac{B_1 + B_2}{SLOC_C} -$	Open Rework
Rework Stability	$SS = (R_1 + R_2) - (F_1 + F_2)$	Rework Trends

TABLE 14-4 End-Product Quality Metrics Definitions[19, pp. 11, 14]

Metric	Definition	Insight	Value
Rework Proportions	$R_E = \dfrac{Effort_{SCO_1} + Effort_{SCO_2}}{Effort_{Total}}$	Productivity Rework	10.7%
	$R_S = \dfrac{(R1 + R2)_{Total}}{SLOC_{Total}}$	Project Efficiency	23.4%
Modularity	$Q_{mod} = \dfrac{(R_1 + R_2)}{SCO_1 + SCO_2}$	Rework Localization	54 SLOC/SCO
Changeability	$Q_C = \dfrac{Effort_{SCO} + Effort_{SCO}}{SCO_1 + SCO_2}$	Risk of Modification	17 Hrs/SCO
Maintainability	$Q_M = \dfrac{R_E}{R_S}$	Change Productivity	0.46

MIL/SOFTQUAL

A software quality tool for assisting in metric evaluation is MIL/SOFTQUAL produced by The Carman Group, Inc. MIL/SOFTQUAL takes inputs based on development phases and subphases, it calculates Costs of Quality by project, phase, and subphases (Departments), and provides 145 different output charts. The MIL/SOFTQUAL outputs include:

- Cost of Quality
  - > Project
  - > Phase
  - > Department
- Defects
  - > Pareto
    Project
    Phase
    Department
  - > Defect Costing
  - > Liability
- Relational—Cost of Quality
  - > Budget
  - > Operating Expenses
  - > Headcount
  - > Lines of Code[11, pp. 15, 16]

Hitachi

In manufacturing, the Japanese have demonstrated that *productivity gains follow naturally from quality improvements in the process.* It is important to consider quality measurements during the development process as a link to improved productivity.

Japanese companies are measuring software quality with the same interest that they showed in manufacturing quality. At Hitachi they have plotted what they call "spoilage" since 1976, which represents the cost to fix postrelease defects. Figure 14-2 shows their success at improving software quality as a ratio of spoilage to total project cost. When a company can reduce rework by such a large amount, it frees up substantial resources to produce additional revenue-producing products.[6, p. 22]

14.5 SOFTWARE QUALITY METRICS METHODOLOGY

This section is abstracted from the IEEE DRAFT *Standard for a Software Quality Metrics Methodology.*[7] The software quality metrics methodology is a systematic approach to establishing quality requirements and identifying, implementing,

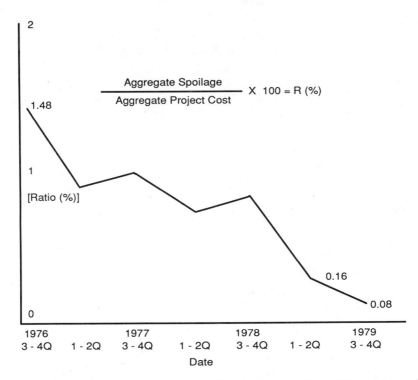

FIGURE 14-2. Quality improvement results from Hitachi. Copyright © May 1981, IEEE (6, p. 23).

analyzing and validating software quality metrics for a software system. It spans the entire software life cycle and is comprised of five steps, which are:

Establish software quality requirements
Identify software quality metrics
Implement the software quality metrics
Analyze the software quality metrics results
Validate the software quality metrics.

Establish Software Quality Requirements

The methodology starts by identifying quality requirements that may be applicable to the software system. Use organizational experience, and required standards, or regulations to create this list. Also, list other system requirements that may effect the feasibility of the quality requirements. Consider acquisition concerns, such as cost or schedule constraints, warranties, and organizational self-interest. Focus on direct metrics instead of predictive metrics. A direct metric value is a numerical target for a factor to be met in the final product. Whereas a predictive metric value is a numerical target related to a factor to be met during system development. It is an intermediate requirement that is an early indicator of final system performance.

Rate each of the listed quality requirements by importance. Importance is a function of the system characteristics and the viewpoints of the people involved. To determine the importance of possible quality requirements survey all the involved parties, and create an agreed upon final ordered list of quality requirements.

For each factor, assign a direct metric to represent the factor, and a direct metric value to serve as a quantitative requirement for that factor. For example, if "high efficiency" was one of the quality requirements, the direct metric "actual resource utilization/allocated resource utilization" with a value of 90% could represent that factor. This direct metric value is used to verify the achievement of the quality requirement. Without it, there is no standard to tell whether or not the delivered system meets its quality requirements.

Identify Software Quality Metrics

Create a chart of the quality requirements based on the hierarchical tree structure found in Figure 14-3. Only the factor level should be complete at this point. Now, decompose each factor into sub-factors for as many levels as are needed until the sub-factor level is complete. Then, decompose the sub-factors into metrics using the software quality metrics framework.

The software quality metrics framework (Figure 14-3) begins with quality factors which represent management-oriented views of system quality. Associated with each factor is a direct metric, which serves as a quantitative representation of the quality factor. For example, a direct metric for the factor reliability could be faults/KLOC. Each factor must have an associated direct metric and a target

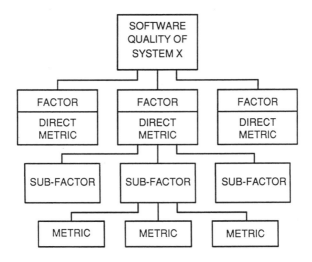

SOURCE: IEEE Standard for a Software
Quality Metrics Methodology (Draft) April 1990

FIGURE 14-3. Software quality metrics framework. Copyright © 1990 IEEE, (7, p. 6).

value, such as 1 fault/KLOC, that is set by project management. Otherwise, there is no way to determine whether the factor has been achieved.

At the second level of the hierarchy are quality sub-factors, which represent technically-oriented concepts. These are obtained by decomposing each factor into measurable software attributes. Sub-factors are independent attributes of software, and therefore may correspond to more than one factor.

At the third level of the hierarchy the sub-factors are decomposed into metrics used to measure system products and processes during the development life cycle. Direct metric values (factor values) are typically unavailable or expensive to collect early in the software life cycle. For this reason, metrics on this level are used, either collectively or independently, to estimate factor values.

For each validated metric on the metric level, assign a target value that should be achieved during development. To help ensure that metrics are used appropriately, only validated metrics (i.e., either direct metrics or metrics validated with respect to direct metrics) shall be used to access current and future product/process quality. Non-validated metrics may be included for future analysis, but shall not be included as a part of the system requirements. Each metric chosen must be documented on the form shown in Table 14-5.

After the software quality metrics framework is applied a cost—benefit analysis is to be performed. Identify all the costs associated with the metrics in the metrics

TABLE 14-5   Metrics Set © Copyright 1990 IEEE[7, p. 10]

Term	Description
Name	Name of the metric
Metric	The mathematical function which is used to compute the metric
Costs	The costs of using the metric
Benefits	The benefits of using the metric
Impact	An indication of whether a metric may be used to alter or halt the project
Target Value	Numerical value of the metric that is to be achieved to meet quality requirements
Factors	Factors that are related to this metric
Tools	Software of hardware tools that are used to gather and store data, compute the metric and analyze the results
Application	A description of how the metric is used and what is its area of application
Data Items	The data items (i.e., input values) that are necessary for computing the metric values
Computation	An explanation of the composition of the metric (i.e., steps involved in the composition)
Interpretation	An interpretation of the results of the metrics computation
Considerations	Metric assumptions, appropriateness (e.g., Can data be collected for this metric? Is the metric appropriate for this application?)
Training Required	Training required to implement or use the metric
Example Validation	An example of applying the metric
History	The names of projects that have used the metric and the validity criteria the metric has satisfied
References	References for further details on understanding or implementing the metric. List of projects, project details, etc.

set. For each metric, estimate and document the following impacts and costs: metrics utilization costs, software development process change costs, organizational structure change costs, special equipment, and training. Then, identify and document the benefits that are associated with each metric in the metrics set. Finally, view the costs versus benefits and adjust the metrics set accordingly.

Implement the Software Quality Metrics

For each metric in the metric set, determine the data that must be collected and assumptions made about the data (e.g., random sample, subjective or objective measure). The flow of data should be shown from point of collection to evaluation of metrics. Describe when and how tools are to be used. Identify the organizational entities that will directly participate in data collection. Describe the training required for this metric.

Test the data collection and metric computation procedures on selected software. Determine the cost of this prototype effort to further refine the cost estimates. Select the appropriate set of tools (manual or automated) to satisfy the requirements for data collection and metrics computation. Collect and store the data at the appropriate time in the life cycle. Compute the metric values from the collected data.

Analyze the Software Metrics Results

The results should be interpreted and recorded against the broad context of the project as well as for a particular product or process of the project. Software components which appear to have unacceptable quality shall be identified. During development validated metrics shall be used to make predictions of direct metric values. Predicted values of direct metrics shall be compared with target values to determine whether to flag software components for detailed analysis. Direct metrics shall be used to ensure compliance of software products with quality requirements during system and acceptance testing. Software components and process steps whose measurement deviates from the target values are noncompliant.

Validate the Software Quality Metrics

The purpose of metrics validation is to identify both product and process metrics that can predict specified quality factor values, which are quantitative representations of quality requirements. Remember, metrics validation is addressed in the introduction to this chapter. If metrics are to be useful, they must indicate accurately whether quality requirements have been achieved or are likely to be achieved in the future. To be considered valid, a metric must demonstrate a high degree of association with the quality factors it represents. This is equivalent to accurately portraying the quality condition(s) of a product or process. A metric may be valid with respect to certain criteria and invalid with respect to other criteria.

Metrics validation shall include the following steps: (1) Identify the quality factors sample, (2) Identify the metrics sample, (3) Perform a statistical analysis, and (4) Document the results. Additionally, it is necessary to re-validate a predictive metric each time it is used. Metrics validation is a continuous process. Confidence in metrics is increased over time and with a variety of projects as metrics are validated, the metrics data base increases and sample size increases. Confidence is not a static, one-time property.

To the extent practicable, metrics validation shall be undertaken in a stable development environment, and there shall be at least one project in which metrics data have been collected and validated prior to application of the predictive metrics.

Major Metrics Summaries

To aid understanding, the IEEE Draft *Standard for a Software Quality Metrics Methodology* contains summaries of some major metrics with advantages and limitations highlighted which conclude this section. Also, the Draft *Standard* contains a Mission Critical and a Commercial example to carry the reader through the methodology. The Appendix E of the Draft *Standard* has a comprehensive annotated bibliography of software quality metrics references.

The major metrics summarized include:

1. Halstead—Software Science
   advantages: Fairly easy to compute. Can automate. Tools exist.
   limitations: Cannot be computed until software is designed. Controversy about validity. Does not represent all aspects of complexity.
2. Boehm—Constructive Cost Model (COCOMO)
3. Albrecht—Function Points
4. McCabe—Cyclomatic Complexity
   advantages: Easy to compute. Tools exist. Can apply to both code and preliminary design.
   limitations: Must have some idea of design structure before it can be applied. Controversy about validity. Does not represent all aspects of complexity.
5. Source of Software Error
   advantages: Relates problem to source of error so problem can be fixed.
   limitations: Not easy to automate. Not easy to identify source of error.
6. Number of Changes Which Affect Module
   advantages: Easy to compute. Can automate. Tools exist.
   limitations: Cannot use until software exists.
7. Defect Metrics
   advantages: Evaluate reliability and design approach.
   limitations: Data may be difficult to collect.
8. Traceability
   advantages: Excellent for assessing whether software and documentation is fully integrated.

limitations: Subject to various interpretations. Difficult to define quantitatively. Difficult to automate.

9. Number of Program Paths (Np)

advantages: Representative of execution sequences in a program.

limitations: Can be difficult to compute because number of paths may be large. Computer time may be excessive.[7]

14.6 OMNIBUS SOFTWARE QUALITY METRICS

There have been several attempts to quantify the elusive concept of software quality by developing an arsenal of metrics which quantify numerous factors underlying the concept. The most well known of these metric systems are those developed by Boehm, Brown, Kaspar, Lipow, MacLeod, and Merrit,[2] Gilb,[5] and McCall, Richards and Walters.[13] The Boehm et al. and McCall et al. approaches are similar, although differing in some of the constructs and metrics they propose. Both of these systems have been developed from an intuitive clustering of software characteristics which are illustrated in Figure 14-4.

The higher level constructs in each system represent 1) the current behavior of the software, 2) the ease of changing the software, and 3) the ease of converting or interfacing the system. Here, we will stay with the McCall et al. set of metrics. McCall et al. identified 11 quality factors, and beneath this second level there are 23 criteria. For example, *self-descriptiveness* underlies a number of factors included under the domains of product revision and transition.

Primitive constructs and criteria are operationally defined by sets of metrics which provide the guidelines for collecting empirical data. There are 41 software metrics consisting of 175 specific elements.

No project can stay within a reasonable budget and maximize all of the quality factors. The nature of the system under development will determine the proper weighting of quality factors to be achieved in the delivered software.[3, p. 204, 205]

Factors (see Table 14-6) in software quality provide a framework for the acquisition manager to quantify concerns for the longer life cycle implications of a software product. For example, if the system is in an environment in which there is a high rate of technical breakthroughs in hardware design, the portability of the software should take on an added significance. If the expected life cycle of the system is long, finding and fixing errors as effectively as possible (maintainability) becomes a cost-critical consideration. If the system is an experimental system where the software specifications will have a high rate of change, flexibility in the software product is highly desirable. If the functions of the system are expected to be required for a long time, reusability is of prime importance in those units that implement the major functions of the system. Because of many networks available today, more systems are being required to interface with other systems, so interoperability is very important.[12, p. 130]

Each software system is unique in its software quality requirements relative to specific levels of quality. There are basic system characteristics which affect the

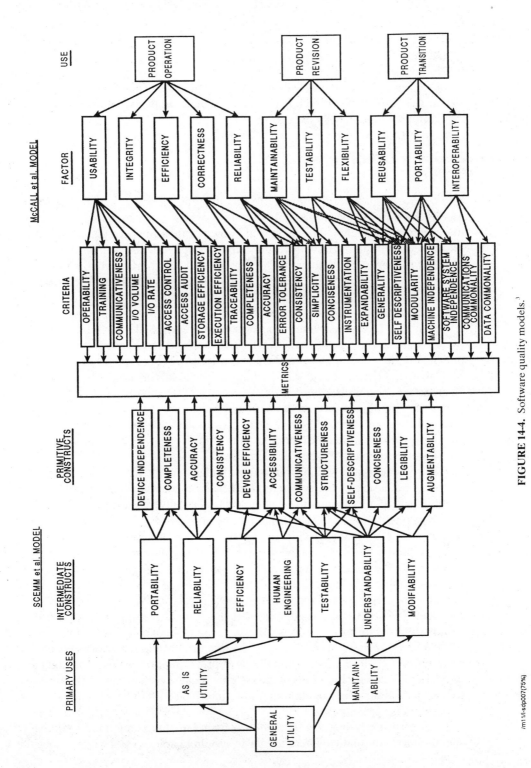

FIGURE 14-4. Software quality models.[3]

/m1/vl-sdp007(75%)

TABLE 14-6   Software Quality Factors[12, p. 129]

Correctness	Extent to which a program satisfies its specifications and fulfills the user's mission objectives.
Reliability	Extent to which a program can be expected to perform its intended function with required precision.
Efficiency	The amount of computing resources and code required by a program to perform a function.
Integrity	Extent to which access to software or data by unauthorized persons can be controlled.
Usability	Effort required to learn, operate, prepare input, and interpret output of a program.
Maintainability	Effort required to locate and fix an error in an operational program.
Testability	Effort required to test a program to insure it performs its intended function.
Flexibility	Effort required to modify an operational program.
Portability	Effort required to transfer a program from one hardware configuration and/or software system environment to another.
Reusability	Extent to which a program can be used in other applications—related to the packaging and scope of the functions that program performs.
Interoperability	Effort required to couple one system with another.

quality requirements and each system must be analyzed for its fundamental characteristics. Examples of these fundamental characteristics and the associated quality factors are:

Characteristic	*Quality Factor*
Human lives affected	Reliability
	Correctness
	Testability
Long life cycle	Maintainability
	Flexibility
	Portability
Real-time application	Efficiency
	Reliability
	Correctness
Classified information processed	Integrity
Interrelated with other systems[22, p. 144]	Interoperability

The above quality factors take a management perspective to software quality. To introduce a dimension of quantification, this management orientation must be translated into a software-related viewpoint. This translation is accomplished by defining a set of criteria for each factor (see Table 14-7). These criteria further define the quality factor and help describe the relationships between factors since one criterion can be related to more than one factor. The criteria are *independent attributes* of the software, or the software production process, by which the quality can be judged, defined, and measured.

TABLE 14-7   Criteria Definitions for Software Quality Factors[12, p. 133, 134]

Criterion	Definition	Related Factors
Traceability	Those attributes of the software that provide a thread from the requirements to the implementation with respect to the specific development and operational environment.	Correctness
Completeness	Those attributes of the software that provide full implementation of the functions required.	Correctness
Consistency	Those attributes of the software that provide uniform design and implementation techniques and notation.	Correctness Reliability Maintainability
Accuracy	Those attributes of the software that provide the required precision in calculations and outputs.	Reliability
Error Tolerance	Those attributes of the software that provide continuity of operation under non-nominal conditions.	Reliability
Simplicity	Those attributes of the software that provide implementation of functions in the most understandable manner. (Usually avoidance of practices which increase complexity.)	Reliability Maintainability Testability
Modularity	Those attributes of the software that provide a structure of highly independent modules.	Maintainability Flexibility Testability Portability Reusability Interoperability
Generality	Those attributes of the software that provide breadth to the functions performed.	Flexibility Reusability
Expandability	Those attributes of the software that provide for expansion of data storage requirements or computational functions.	Flexibility
Instrumentation	Those attributes of the software that provide for the measurements of usage or identification of errors.	Testability
Self-Descriptiveness	Those attributes of the software that provide explanation of the implementation of a function.	Flexibility Maintainability Testability Portability Reusability
Execution Efficiency	Those attributes of the software that provide for minimum processing time.	Efficiency
Storage Efficiency	Those attributes of the software that provide for minimum storage requirements during operation.	Efficiency
Access Control	Those attributes of the software that provide for control of the access of software and data.	Integrity
Access Audit	Those attributes of the software that provide for an audit of the access of software and data.	Integrity
Operability	Those attributes of the software that determine operation and procedures concerned with the operation of the software.	Usability
Training	Those attributes of the software that provide transition from current operation or initial familiarization.	Usability

TABLE 14-7   Continued

Criterion	Definition	Related Factors
Communicativeness	Those attributes of the software that provide useful inputs and outputs which can be assimilated.	Usability
Software System Independence	Those attributes of the software that determine its dependency on the software environment (operating systems, utilities, input/output routines, etc.)	Portability Reusability
Machine Independence	Those attributes of the software that determine its dependency on the hardware system.	Portability Reusability
Communications Commonality	Those attributes of the software that provide the use of standard protocols and interface routines.	Interoperability
Data Commonality	Those attributes of the software that provide the use of standard data representations.	Interoperability
Conciseness	Those attributes of the software that provide for implementation of a function with a minimum amount of code.	Maintainability

Quality metrics can be established to provide a quantitative measure of the attributes represented by the criteria. The measurements, represented by the quality metrics, can be applied during all phases of development to provide an indication of the progression toward the desired product quality. The measures themselves are predictive, and are of two types. The first, like a ruler, is a relative quantity measure; and the second is a binary measure (present or absent). Figure 14-5 provides example metric collection sheets.[12, p. 130-136]

Gerald Murine reports on some results from Japan using the omnibus software quality metrics with a customized program called SQMAT (software quality measurement and assurance technology). Motoei Azuma and others at Nippon Electric Company reported the following in 1985. Four pilot projects were undertaken that spanned a range of application, size, programmer experience level, and other parameters. Each produced interesting results (see Table 14-8) and the following conclusions:

- "The quality target can be concretely established because of the qualifying quality."
- "Quality can be assessed objectively because of small differences between reviewers' scores."
- "Visual management can be put into practice through displaying quality graphically."
- "Software Quality Measurement and SQMAT are necessary technologies to measure quality quantitatively for managing software quality . . ."
- "This methodology contributes to management engineering from a standpoint of not only controlling quality but also managing software development by means of quality."[15, p. 40, 41]

Factor(s): Reliability, maintainability, testability

CRITERION/ SUBCRITERION	METRIC	REQMTS		DESIGN		IMPLEMENTATION	
		Yes/No 1 or Ø	Value	Yes/No 1 or Ø	Value	Yes/No 1 or Ø	Value
Data and control flow complexity	SI. 3 Complexity measure (by module, see para. 6.2.2.6)				☐		☐
	System metric value: $\dfrac{\text{Sum of complexity measures for each module}}{\text{\# modules}}$				☐		☐

Factor(s): Correctness

CRITERION/ SUBCRITERION	METRIC	REQMTS		DESIGN		IMPLEMENTATION	
		Yes/No 1 or Ø	Value	Yes/No 1 or Ø	Value	Yes/No 1 or Ø	Value
Completeness	CP. 1 Completeness checklist:						
	(1) Unambiguous references (input, function, output).	☐		☐		☐	
	(2) All data references defined, computed, or obtained from an external source.	☐		☐		☐	
	(3) All defined functions used.	☐		☐		☐	
	(4) All referenced functions defined.	☐		☐		☐	
	(5) All conditions and processing defined for each decision point.	☐		☐			
	(6) All defined and referenced calling sequence parameters agree.			☐		☐	

FIGURE 14-5. Example metrics. (12, p. 137)

14.7 SOFTWARE QUALITY INDICATORS

Seven Software Quality Indicators

Remember from Chapter 6, the seven software quality indicators are completeness, design structure, defect density, fault density, test coverage, test sufficiency, and documentation.

The application and interpretation of the software quality indicators is not a "by rote" process. The indicators are not intended as a method of comparing the software development and quality status of Program A versus Program B. However, if the two programs are of similar size, complexity, and application the lessons learned on one program can be beneficial in improving the quality, reliability, and supportability of the second.

Although there are no widespread tools available to support application of software quality metrics, an evaluation should be made of the application of the 11 software quality factors identified in DOD-STD-2168.[21] These factors form a basis for evaluating the software products.

Table 14-9 from AFSCP 800-14 depicts the relationships between the 11 software quality factors and the software quality indicators.

TABLE 14-8   Nippon Electric Co. SQMAT Results[15, p. 41]

Project	A	B	C	D
Software Type	Operating System (Assembly)	Cost Control (COBOL)	Application (COBOL)	Telephone Exc (PL1)
Phases	All	Design, Code	Design, Code	Test
Factor(s)	Usability	Correctness Reliability	Correctness Reliability	Correctness Reliability
# Elements	28	15(D), 22(C)	9(D), 8(C)	3
SQM Staff	4	3	1	Not Complete
Cost	25%	20.8%	12.7%	Not Complete
Results	Reduce Spec 25% Reduce Cost 33%	Reduce Test 50.8%	Reduce Code 46.2%	Not Complete

TABLE 14-9   Software quality indicator and quality factor relationships

Software Quality Indicators \ Software Quality Factors	CORRECTNESS	EFFICIENCY	FLEXIBILITY	INTEGRITY	INTEROPERABILITY	MAINTAINABILITY	PORTABILITY	RELIABILITY	REUSABILITY	TESTABILITY	USABILITY
Completeness	X					X		X		X	
Design Structure		X				X		X		X	
Defect Density	X					X		X		X	X
Fault Density	X					X		X		X	X
Test Coverage	X					X		X		X	
Test Sufficiency	X					X		X		X	
Documentation	X					X		X		X	X

Eleven Software Quality Indicators

Scientific Systems Inc., under a contract to the Air Force Business Research Management Center, developed a set of software quality indicators (see Table 14-10) to improve the management capabilities of personnel responsible for monitoring software development projects. The quality indicators address management concerns, take advantage of data that is already being collected, are independent of

TABLE 14-10   Quality indicators by development phase [10, p.25]

	Software Requirements Analysis	Preliminary Design	Detailed Design	Code and Unit Testing	CSC Integration and Testing	CSCI Testing
PROCESS INDICATORS						
MANAGEMENT CONCERN:						
PROGRESS	Requirements Volume	Top Level Design Complete	Detailed Designs Complete	Units Completed	Tests Accomplished	Tests Accomplished
STABILITY	System Requirements Stability	Software Requirements Stability	Top-Level Design Stability	Detailed Design Stability	Software Stability	Software Stability
COMPLIANCE	Process Compliance	←				→
QUALITY EFFORT	Quality Evaluation Effort	←				→
DEFECT DETECTION						
1. TEST COVERAGE				Percentage of Paths Executed	Percentage of Paths Executed	Percentage of Functions Executed
2. DEFECT DETECTION EFFICIENCY		Defect Detection Efficiency	←			→
PRODUCT INDICATORS						
COMPLETENESS	System Requirements Traceability	Software Requirements Traceability				
1. DEFECT REMOVAL RATE	Open and Closed Problem Reports	←				→
2. ACI PROFILE	Problem Report Age Profile	←				→
3. DEFECT DENSITY	Defect Density	←				→
COMPLEXITY	Requirements Complexity	Design Complexity	Design Complexity	Code Complexity		

the software development methodology being used, are specific to phases in the development methodology being used, are specific to phases in the development cycle, and provide information on the status of a project.

Eleven quality indicators are recommended:

1. *Progress;* measures the amount of work accomplished by the developer in each phase.
2. *Stability;* assesses whether the products of each phase are sufficiently stable to allow the next phase to proceed.
3. *Process Compliance;* measures the developer's compliance with the development procedures approved at the beginning of the project.
4. *Quality Evaluation Effort;* measures the percentage of the developer's effort that is being spent on internal quality evaluation activities.
5. *Test Coverage;* measures the amount of the software system covered by the developer's testing process.
6. *Defect Detection Efficiency;* measures how many of the defects detectable in a phase were actually discovered during that phase.

7. *Requirements Traceability;* measures the percentage of the requirements that have been addressed by the system.
8. *Defect Removal Rate;* measures the number of defects detected and resolved over time.
9. *Defect Age Profile;* measures the number of defects that have remained unresolved for a long period of time.
10. *Defect Density;* detects defect-prone components of the system.
11. *Complexity;* measures the complexity of the design and code.

These quality indicators have certain characteristics. Quality measures must be oriented toward management goals. One need not have extensive familiarity with technical details of the project. Quality measures should reveal problems as they develop and suggest corrective actions which could be taken. Quality measures must be easy to use. They must not be excessively time consuming, nor depend heavily on extensive software training or experience. Measures that are clearly specified, easy to calculate and straightforward to interpret are needed. Quality measures must be flexible.[10, pp. 1, 2, 7]

14.8 CONCLUSION

There are many software quality assurance metrics to choose from and many are being used rather successfully by various companies. Personal experience has shown that any metrics program is very time consuming to implement and difficult to define. I have chaired a software metrics working group for the past two years. The progress shown by the working group has been slow, and seemingly every software metric needs to be redone for a myriad of reasons.

It is certainly interesting to note that DOD-STD-2168, *Defense Systems Software Quality Program,*[21] standard says nothing about the use of or not the use of software quality metrics.

While metrics remain controversial, that controversy is diminishing as research results show their usefulness, as issues of software reliability and safety become part of the public consciousness, and as government and industry realize the growing dependence on software and the concomitant need to measure software's functionality, reliability, cost, and schedule. Remember: You can't control what you can't measure.[14, p. 16]

References

1. Basili, Victor R. and H. Dieter Rombach, "Implementing Quantitative SQA: A Practical Model," *IEEE Software* March 1990, © 1990 IEEE.
2. Boehm, B. W. et al., *Characteristics of Software Quality* (Amsterdam: North Holland, 1978).
3. Curtis, Bill, "The Measurement of Software Quality and Complexity," collected in *Software Metrics* ed. Alan J. Perlis, Frederick G. Sayward, and Mary Shaw, (Cambridge: The MIT Press, 1981).

4. Fenton, Norman E., "Software Metrics: Theory, Tools and Validation," *IEEE Software Engineering Journal* January 1990, © 1990 IEEE.

5. Gilb, T., *Software Metrics* (Cambridge: Winthrop, 1977).

6. Grady, Robert B. and Deborah L. Caswell, *Software Metrics: Establishing a Company-Wide Program* (Englewood Cliffs: Prentice-Hall, Inc., 1987), Copyright © 1987, Adapted by permission of Prentice-Hall, Inc., Englewood Cliffs, NJ 07632, p. 22.

7. Reproduced from IEEE Standards Project P1061/D21, IEEE Standard for a Software Quality Metric Methodology, Copyright © 1990 by the Institute of Electrical and Electronic Engineers, Inc., with the permission of the IEEE. This is an unapproved draft and subject to revision.

8. Grady, Robert B., "Work-Product Analysis: The Philosopher's Stone of Software?," *IEEE Software* March 1990.

9. Laranjeira, Luiz A., "Software Size Estimation of Object-Oriented Systems," *IEEE Transactions on Software Engineering,* Vol. 16, No. 5, 5 May 1990, © 1990 IEEE.

10. MacMillan, Jean and John R. Vosburgh, *Software Quality Indicators* (Cambridge: Scientific Systems, Inc., 1986).

11. Mandeville, William A., "Defects and Software Quality Costs Measurements," *NSIA Fifth Annual National Joint Conference Tutorial Notes* 28 Feb. 1989.

12. McCall, James A., "An Introduction to Software Quality Metrics," collected in *Software Quality Management* ed. John D. Cooper and Matthew J. Fisher, (New York: A Petrocelli Book, 1979).

13. McCall, J. A., P. K. Richards, and G. F. Walters, *Factors in Software Quality* General Electric, Command & Information Systems Technical Report 77CIS02, Sunnyvale, CA, 1977.

14. Mills, Harlan D. and Peter B. Dyson, "Using Metrics to Quantify Development," *IEEE Software* March 1990, © 1990 IEEE.

15. Murine, Gerald E., "Integrating Software Quality Metrics with Software QA," *Quality Progress* November 1988, Copyright © 1988 American Society for Quality Control, Reprinted by permission.

16. Reifer, Donald J., Richard W. Knudson, and Jerry Smith, *Final Report: Software Quality Survey* prepared for American Society for Quality Control, 20 Nov. 1987.

17. Rombach, H. Dieter, "Design Measurement; Some Lessons Learned," *IEEE Software* March 1990, p. 20, © 1990 IEEE.

18. Ross, Niall, "Using Metrics in Quality Management," *IEEE Software* July 1990, © 1990 IEEE.

19. Royce, Walker, "Pragmatic Quality Metrics for Evolutionary Software Development Models," *Proceedings of Tri-Ada '90,* December 3-7, 1990, Reprinted by permission of the Association for Computing Machinery, Copyright © 1990 ACM.

20. U.S. Air Force, AFSCP Pamphlet 800-14, *Software Quality Indicators* (Andrews Air Force Base, D.C., Headquarters AFSC, 1987).

21. U.S. Joint Logistics Command, DOD-STD-2168, *Military Standard—Defense System Software Quality Program* (Washington, D.C.: NAVMAT 09Y, 1988).

22. Walters, Gene F., "Application of Metrics to a Software Quality Management (QM) Program," collected in *Software Quality Management* ed. John D. Cooper and Matthew J. Fisher, (New York: A Petrocelli Book, 1979).

23. Ward, T. Michael, "Software Measures and Goals at Hewlett Packard," *Juran Institute Conference Proceedings* Atlanta, 1989.

24. Zells, Lois, *Managing Software Projects: Selecting and Using PC-Based Project Management Systems* (Wellesley: QED Information Sciences, Inc., 1990).

15

Practical Applications of Software Quality Assurance to Mission-Critical Embedded Software

ITT Avionics

15.1 SPECIAL CONCERNS WITH MISSION-CRITICAL SOFTWARE

Mission-Critical Software has been defined by the U.S. Department of Defense (DOD) to be software that is used in Weapon Systems or Real-time Sensor Systems, and also in Command and Control and Intelligence Systems. The formal definition is in DOD Directive 5000.29. Mission-Critical software is characterized by having a direct effect on the operational success or failure of a military mission, usually involving significant risk to human life. Examples of software of this type include ground-based systems to detect and track ICBMs (Inter-Continental Ballistic Missles) and SLBMs (Submarine-Launched Ballistic Missiles), and satellite-based systems to detect military activity of various kinds (and transmit specific messages back to command and control nodes). Other examples include airborne avionics systems for communications/navigations, defense electronics counter-measures, and flight control.

Some Mission-Critical software systems are large, over a million executable Source Lines of Code (SLOC), and reside on large mainframe computers. Other systems are relatively small, and may be only 20,000 to 100,000 SLOC. These smaller systems usually reside on embedded microcomputer systems, which may have limited memory and addressing capability. Until recently, most of the real-time embedded applications were written in Assembly-language because of the very limited memory available (frequently 64K words or less).

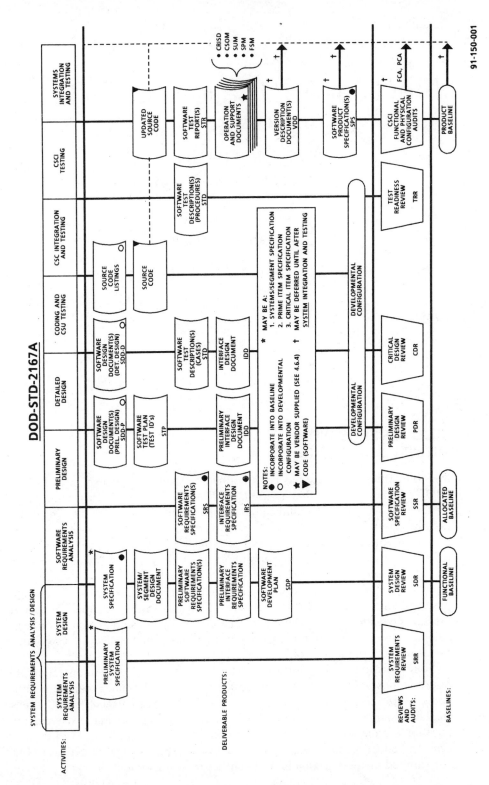

FIGURE 15-1. Deliverable products, reviews, audits, and baselines. (Based on Figure 2 in DOD-STD-2167A.)

344

In addition, there is usually a critical need to execute certain 'program paths' in a few milliseconds to meet system performance requirements. In the last ten years, the author has been involved primarily with small, embedded, real-time systems of this general type. However, it is important to note that software and microcomputer technology are improving rapidly, and software for such embedded systems can now be written for the most part in Ada, but with selective use of Assembly language for critical time-sensitive kernels.

Most Mission-critical software for DOD is now being developed per DOD-STD-2167A, Defense System Software Development, dated 29 February 1988. Figure 2 from DOD-STD-2167A provides a comprehensive overview of the activities, products, and reviews, etc., and how they interrelate. This figure is repeated here in Figure 15-1 with some additional annotations. This figure shows the nominal software development activities across the top of the diagram. The deliverable products, which normally are produced by each activity unless tailored out of the contract, are shown in the middle of the diagram. Six different formal reviews with the customer, plus the final Functional and Physical Configuration Audits are shown near the bottom of the diagram. Finally, the three baselines used for Configuration Management are shown at the bottom.

15.2 EMBEDDED MISSION-CRITICAL SOFTWARE

The Mission-critical software used in most embedded systems is characterized by very tight constraints on memory, processing power (MIPS*), input-output capability, and in some cases by the instruction set of the microprocessor. Of course, the capabilities of the assembler or compiler used for the source language can influence the performance of the delivered code, which can make a significant difference for some embedded systems.

Embedded computer systems are frequently composed of several microprocessors, rather than just one. Different functions are allocated to each microprocessor and its software. This functional allocation serves several purposes, including getting several aspects of the total processing job done in parallel to meet time deadlines. Usually software residing within a single microprocessor is controlled as a separate Computer Software Configuration Item (CSCI) for project management, configuration management, documentation, and cost purposes. Some CSCIs may have multiple instances (copies) to handle the load requirements for a System. Instances of 2-4 are reasonably common, and one system had over 40 instances of the same software. There may be cases where each instance of Software is slightly different because of the need to identify itself in its outputs.

The microprocessors in a system of multiple microprocessors are arranged in different patterns, and communicate in different ways. The architectures of federated, multiple microprocessor systems can be quite diverse. The following

---

*MIPS = Millions of Instructions Per Second

discussion considers three main types. The simplest form is a multiple, independent channel system (Figure 15-2a). Each microprocessor is separate and independent, and interfaces only with its own channel; it is not a "federated" system in the normal sense.

A second architecture is where several microcomputers are attached to a single bus, and each microcomputer has its own address or ID. The microcomputer only processes those messages that have its address, or an acceptable address or code. A message goes down the entire bus, and is usually processed only by the intended microcomputer(s) (Figure 15-2b). A broadcast message with a particular broadcast code may be processed by all of the microcomputers, for various systems functions, etc. In some cases, the bus may be in a ring structure, hence the term ring architecture.

Another form of architecture is the star pattern of microprocessors. In this system, a single microprocessor acts as the central supervisor or controller at the hub of the star. A bus then goes from each satellite processor to the Supervisor (Figure 15-2c). In a classic star architecture, there is no communication directly between the satellite processors (T, U, V, . . .). The Supervisor handles all commu-

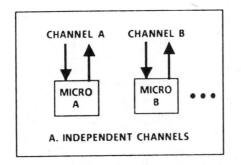
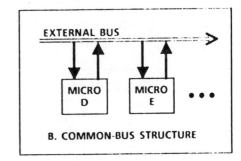

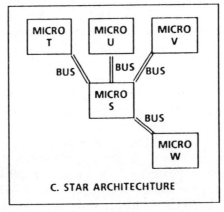

91-150-002

FIGURE 15-2. Some simple federated system architectures.

nications with the other processors, and may task the processors to do certain work or may interrupt the processors. The Supervisor will also initialize the system, and oversee the BIT (Built-In-Testing) at initialization and other times. In larger systems, there may be secondary supervisors, each with their own cluster of satellite processors; the secondary supervisor would communicate directly with the main supervisor.

15.3 THE SPECIAL DEVELOPMENT LIFE CYCLE FOR EMBEDDED MISSION-CRITICAL SOFTWARE

Embedded mission-critical software usually goes through several cycles of software development. The final stage of development is called the Full-Scale Development (FSD) phase, and the intent of this phase is to develop the final software that will be deployed for operational use. However, prior to the FSD phase, there is frequently a Demonstration and Validation (Dem-Val) Phase, where an initial version of the software and system is developed, as a prototype, to reduce risk in an effort considerably smaller than a FSD. A Dem-Val effort may be 10% to 50% of the FSD, assuming the go-ahead is given to proceed into FSD. In some cases, a Concept Exploration phase may even preceed the Dem-Val phase. Software may go through three or more macro cycles, and the "Spiral Model" for software development is one way to characterize these multiple macro cycles.[1]

The planning for the Software Quality Assurance (SQA) program (described in DOD-STD-2168) usually considered a full-blown effort for the FSD phase. Typical SQA efforts for FSD phases run about 9% to 12% of the Software Engineering effort, exclusive of software documentation. For the Dem-Val effort, if there is one, the SQA percentage of the smaller effort is normally in the 6% to 9% range, exclusive of software documentation. If there is a Concept Exploration phase at the front end, the SQA requirements imposed by Contract are usually tailored out, and only the Contractor's procedures guide the level of SQA effort, which could range from 0% to 5% of the Software engineering effort. A typical progression for a hypothetical project might be similar to the values shown in Table 15-1.

TABLE 15-1   Typical Relationships Between Software Engineering and SQA Efforts

	Concept Exploration Phase	Demonstration-Validation Phase	Full-Scale Development Phase
Software Engineering Effort (Person-years)	30	60	200
SQA Effort (Person-years)	0.9 (3%)	4.5 (7.5%)	20 (10%)

If we examine the software development activities within a macrophase, the nominal activities shown in DOD-STD-2167A may not be fully adequate, particularly for embedded mission-critical software. As noted in paragraph 4.1.1 of 2167A, the software development process actually used shall include certain major activities, but may include additional ones. The nominal software development activities from 2167A are shown here in Figure 15-3 which is the 'folded waterfall chart' used extensively by Dunn,[2] Niech, Heil, and others. Software Quality is concerned with the internal reviews, and the subsequent formal customer reviews.

For embedded systems, the process starts with the System Requirements Analysis and Design. The output of this process is the top-level system spec, usually an 'A-Spec' or a 'B1' Prime Item Development Spec. This output normally takes the system design down one level, usually to system elements that end up as a Critical Items. These Critical Items are typically major elements of the system that will have to be defined further, usually in a subsequent Critical Item Design Spec (a 'B2' Spec). The Critical Items, when defined, usually contain both hardware and software elements, each of which will require still further 'system design'. It is usually at these levels that software is synthesized, and becomes one or more CSCIs. Some of the Critical Item's functions are allocated to the software, and

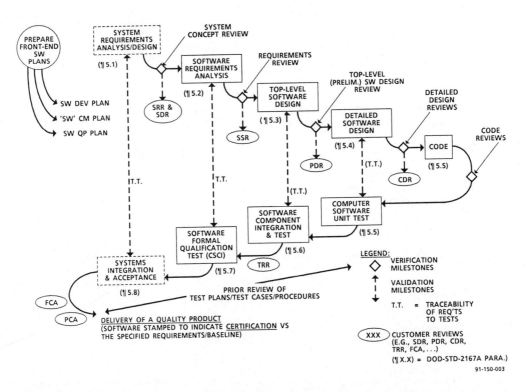

FIGURE 15-3. Nominal software development activities. (Showing internal reviews and customer reviews.)

interfaces between each CSCI and other system elements are defined or postulated. The external definition of the CSCI is iterated, and finally is hardened into a version that is presented in an internal design review for the Critical Item. Typically, Systems Engineering, Software Engineering, Quality Engineering, and SQA participate in this review. SQA and Software Engineering are concerned primarily with external definition of the CSCI(s) and the reasonableness of this definition.

Note that at this point the detailed definition asked for in the Software Requirement Specification (SRS) does not exist, just external, black-box definition exists. After the completion of the Critical Item's design reviews, and the resolution of any Action Items, the revised external definition of the CSCI serves as the basis for the Software Requirements Analysis phase, which is the second activity described in DOD-STD-2167A. Some large systems may even have additional intervening levels, e.g., distinct sub-systems, each made up of several Critical or Prime Items.

The subsequent phases of Software Preliminary Design and Detailed Design are similar to what is described in DOD-STD-2167A. However, sometimes an incremental build approach is applied to the design, code and test phases, such that each build is treated as a separate entity until the later stages of integration and test. Coding and CSU (Computer Software Unit) Testing for embedded systems are also similar to DOD-STD-2167A.

Computer Software Component (CSC) Integration and Testing may be different in two ways. First, the CSC Integration may be broken into two activities, the first of which is on a host development machine. The second activity is the integration of some of the CSCs in a hardware environment that includes the new target computer, actual hardware interfaces, and other real hardware from the newly designed system. This second phase is different because the new software is tested with the new hardware to see if it works together and to find as many errors as possible. This activity is called Hardware-Software Integration, and may start with only one or two CSCs, particularly, with a top-down, partial-build implementation strategy. The second way that CSC Testing & Integration can be different than what is outlined in DOD-STD-2167A is that multiple builds may be used, and extensive testing may be done with only part of the Software before other Software is incrementally added for additional testing.

CSCI Testing may involve a considerable amount of integration and testing for embedded systems. Where multiple, partial builds are utilized, the integration aspects can be somewhat complex and extensive. In some cases, all the integration and testing may be done on the host development machine. In any case, the final CSCI Testing is usually done on the target microcomputer with the other real hardware.

The final steps are the Acceptance Testing of the CSCI on the target hardware, etc. Partial software builds may have several informal sell-offs, one for each build. At some point, the complete CSCI is built and the entire CSCI is tested, culminating in a final sell-off of the entire CSCI which is witnessed by SQA and customer representatives.

Finally, once the software CSCIs have been tested and accepted, the several levels of system testing begin. This usually includes LRU* or WRA* level testing, followed by Subsystems and Systems Testing.

After sell-off and acceptance of the entire system (Hardware and Software), there are usually two additional phases. The first phase is the Development Testing (DT), where the software and testing are controlled by the contractor. The second is Operational Test (OT), where the government controls the tests and any changes to the software. Each of these phases could take from 3 to 9 months. After all approved changes have been made, based on DT and OT, then the system may be approved to go into production and to be deployed for operational use.

15.4 THE ROLE OF SQA FOR MISSION-CRITICAL SOFTWARE

Software Quality Assurance has been mandated by various government standards and specifications. MIL-S-52779A has provided the primary Software Quality Program requirements since August 1979 (see Chapter 6). In April 1988, DOD-STD-2168 was issued and replaced MIL-S-52779A. It is important to understand that 2168 sets the Software Quality Program for all DOD software, not only for software developed under DOD-STD-2167A. As noted in the foreword of 2168.

> "This standard implements the policies of DOD 4155.1, Quality Program, and provides all the necessary elements of a comprehensive quality program applicable to software development and support. This standard interprets the applicable requirements of MIL-Q-9858A, Quality Program Requirements, for software."

The provisions of DOD-STD-2168, plus the Software Product Evaluation and Formal Qualification Testing subsections of DOD-STD-2167A, provide a framework for an organization's Software Quality Program. Basically, there was no choice about establishing a SQA program if you developed software for DOD. In this sense, SQA in the DOD Software community is more mature and extensive than in the commerical area, although there are some notable exceptions. IEEE Standards in the software quality area have existed for several years, but their implementation in the commercial area has been largely voluntary. Standardization efforts in the international area have recently intensified, and many United States companies are interested in qualifying to the new international standards so that they can compete in various overseas markets in the coming years.

For mission-critical software, contractors must have a comprehensive SQA Program in place if they want to successfully compete for new business. The software quality program must cover deliverable and certain classes of non-deliverable software. The software quality program also must address the software-

---

*LRU is Line Replaceable Unit, an Air Force Term for a major black-box that can be replaced on the Flight-Line. WRA is Weapon Replaceable Assembly, and is an equivalent NAVY term.

intensive firmware, related to both the deliverable and non-deliverable software noted above. The contents of the firmware device is the computer software or data that must be carefully controlled. For production, exact copies of the correct versions must be 'burned' into the firmware devices and then verified. For embedded systems, all the software eventually gets burned into firmware devices of one kind or another during production. Even an error as small as one bit can cause a system to fail in a life-critical situation. Suffice it to say that if 200 or 300 systems are built, the firmware copies in each system must be verified as a natural part of the production quality process.

The SQA program must also ensure the quality of non-developmental software-software not developed under the particular contract. This software may be Commercial Off-the-Shelf (COTS) software, or it may be furnished by the government or another third party. Or the software may have been developed by the contractor's organization for an earlier contract or project. The software that is re-used without modification may have been developed under different standards or documented in a different manner or to different Data Item Descriptions (DIDs). For mission-critical software, there can be no 'trust me, it works'; the quality of all non-developmental software must be verified.

Most contractors find it advantageous to have a full set of SQA procedures written and approved. The procedures must cover all the requirements in the various government standards, such as DOD-STD-2168 and DOD-STD-2167A. A single set of these procedures defines how a company or division runs its Software Quality Program. It is too expensive and confusing to have several different sets of procedures. These procedures should be reviewed and updated on an annual cycle. The intent of DOD-STD-2168 is not to tell a contractor how he will meet the quality program requirements, just *what* he has to meet. The company or division SQA procedures tell how the requirements will be met. Each company's procedures will, of course, be different. Some will be fairly general, and others will be quite specific. At ITT Avionics, for example, there is a Policy and Standard Practice for SQA which provides a ten page division's overall product assurance policy. At a more detailed level, there is a family of Operating Instructions which describe, in greater depth, each of the SQA tasks, responsibilities, and procedures. They are grouped into areas such as:

- Internal Reviews
- SQA Planning
- Testing and Certification, etc.

Blocks of numbers were assigned to each area, and some blank numbers exist for possible future growth. The current SQA Operating instructions as of August 1991 are shown in Table 15-2.

With a generic software quality program documented and in place, and people trained in implementing the program, the next step is to document how this company software quality program will be applied to meet a specific contract's requirements. The Software Quality Program Plan (SQPP) is used to document how these procedures will be applied to a particular contract. The SQPP can be a

TABLE 15-2   Sample SQA Operating Procedures

	Internal Reviews
2.10.001	System-Level Concept Review (Internal)
2.10.002	Software Requirements Review (Internal)
2.10.003	Top-Level Software Design Review (Internal)
2.10.004	Detailed Software Design Review (Internal)
2.10.005	Software Code Inspections and Audits
2.10.007	Documentation Reviews (Internal)

	SQA Planning
2.10.021	Software Quality Plan and SQA Program Management

	Testing and Certification
2.10.032	Unit Testing
2.10.034	Software Integration and Testing
2.10.036	Software Formal/Qualification/Acceptance Testing
2.10.037	Software Certification and Product Delivery

	Software Configuration Management
2.10.051	Software Change Control Board
2.10.052	Software Configuration Control and Software Library Audits
2.10.054	Firmware Configuration Control

	SQA Reporting and Record Retention
2.10.062	SQA Record Retention
2.10.063	Software Quality Reporting
2.10.067	Software Quality Assurance Inspection Reports
2.10.069	Software Quality Assurance Checklists

	SQA Analysis
2.10.061	Software Defect Collection, Analysis and Reporting
2.10.065	Software 'Cost-of-Quality' System

	SQA Corrective Action and Control
2.10.071	Software Quality Assurance Corrective Action and Control

	Software Installation, Field Test and Production
2.10.081	Software Installation and Checkout
2.10.082	Software Field Testing (SQA Activities)
2.10.083	Control of Software in Production (SQA Activities)

	Support Software
2.10.091	Software Tools (SQA Activities)
2.10.092	Non-Deliverable Software (SQA Activities)

TABLE 15-2   Continued

External Interfaces

2.10.101	Subcontractor Surveys, Surveillance and Control (SQA Activities)
2.10.102	Commercially Available/Reusable/Government Furnished Software (SQA Activities)
2.10.111	IV&V Interface
2.10.112	DPRO Coordination
2.10.113	Customer Technical Meetings (SQA Activities)

Formal Reviews and Audits

| 2.10.121 | Customer Formal Reviews |
| 2.10.122 | Customer Formal Audits—FAC/PCA |

Note: There are some gaps in the Procedure Numbers to allow for possible future growth.

stand-alone document, per Data Item Description DI-QCIC-80572, or it can be incorporated into the Software Development Plan (such as the SDP for DOD-STD-2167A per DID DI-MCCR-80030A).

The author's experience is that it is very helpful to have a model SQPP ready to use, which represents the SQA state of the art at your organization. Conceptually, a copy of this model SQPP can be 'red-lined' for a particular project, thus saving a lot of time under a tight deadline. If it is good enough, the new SQPP may then become one of a family of model SQPPs kept in the SQA department's Library. An outline (sample) for a SQPP in accordance with DOD-STD-2168, and DI-QCIC-80572, is shown in Table 15-3. The sections that will vary significantly from one project to another are marked with an asterisk. Section 4 of the SQPP may present some problems, because it is organized into three broad headings—Procedures, Tools, and Quality Records—rather than by the specific Requirements in DOD-STD-2168.

One way to solve this problem in the SQPP and still be fully compliant with the DID is to add a Section 4.4 which is a cross-reference matrix to the specific 2168 requirements. Each 2168 requirement, in order, can be listed as a line item in the matrix or data base. In concept, there are three columns, one for procedures, one for tools, and one for the software quality records for each quality activity or requirement. The SQPP paragraph number or item number can be entered into the matrix. Any omission becomes very obvious. If a requirement is tailored out of the contract, it should be flagged, even if one is voluntarily complying with the requirement. Obviously, the first time you prepare the matrix, it will take some time, but it is a worthwhile investment.

An interesting question arises when a contract does not require you to do something that you normally do. The contract *requirements* may be tailored, but should your software quality program be tailored? Should one yield to the temptation to try to save time and money, possibly at the risk of quality? Is your normal way of doing business somewhat flexible? As discussed earlier, do you handle a Dem-Val project the same as an FSD project? To reduce the variability due to

TABLE 15-3   Sample Outline of a Software Quality Program Plan (for DOD-STD-2168)

1.0 Scope
    1.1 Identification (of system)*
    1.2 System Overview (purpose of system, and software function)*
    1.3 Document Overview (summarize purpose and contents on SQPP)
    1.4 Relationship to other Plans (e.g., to SDP, QPP . . .)
2.0 Referenced Documents
    (List all documents referenced or cited in the SQPP—include document number, title, revision, date).
    Note: Government Specs, Standards, Handbooks are listed first, then other Government documents, drawings, publications then ITT publications/standards then ITT forms.
3.0 Organization and Resources
    3.1 Organization (include authority and responsibilities of each organization; include an organization chart showing proper relationships)
    3.2 Resources (used for Software Quality)*
        3.2.1 Facilities and Equipment (desired for equipment software, tool and services to be used for SQ Prog.
        3.2.2 Government Furnished Facilities, Equipment, Software and Service
        3.2.3 Personnel (Describe number and 'skill levels' of personnel who will do SQ Pgm activities)
        3.2.4 Other Resources
    3.3 Schedule* (for SQ Program activities, plus key milestones—e.g., formal Reviews & Audits, Key Meetings, document reviews, Qualifications or Acceptance Tests, etc.)
4.0 Software Quality Program Procedures, Tools and Records
    4.1 Procedures (to be used in the SQ Program)
    (Identify, and map to requirements to which they apply.)
    (Do *NOT* include the procedure details on Revision & Date) should be in Section 2.
    4.2 Tools (to be used in the SQ Program)
    Identify, Description of tool, how used, in the SQ Pgm, and status (of development).
    4.3 Software Quality Records
    Plans for preparing, verifying, maintaining, and accessing for reviews the records. Indicate forms (and data content) 'such as' to allow for improvements. Indicate Software Quality Reports to be extracted from the records.
    4.4 Cross-Reference Matrix:
    for DOD-STD-2168 Requirements ** (vs. Procedures, Tools and Records in SQ Pgm Plan)
5.0 Notes
    General info, background info or details, glossary for terms, acronyms, abbreviations, . . .)
    Appendices (if needed)
    A.   (Sections 10.1, 10.2, . . .)
    B.   (Sections 20.1, 20.2, . . .)
    C.   (Sections 30.1, 30.2, . . .)

---

*These sections vary considerably from one Project to another.
**Requirements of DOD-STD-2168 are contained only in Sections 4 and 5 of the Standard. If the requirement is tailored, indicate it.

different development phases, first consider whether you should do the standard software quality tasks for all FSD projects even if the contract doesn't require them. To a great extent, it depends on how you did the proposal (which is an implied promise), and also on what you promised to do in the SQPP delivered after contract start.

The cost or budget of the software quality program could be a function of the perceived risk. A high risk project may be funded for higher levels of SQA effort to reduce the risk. Also, it may be desirable to focus more effort on some crucial elements of software.

Utilization of the SDP to document the SQPP, rather than a stand-alone SQPP document, is not very direct. There are some existing sections in the SDP DID that can be used (to varying degrees):

3.10 Corrective Action Process
3.11 Problem/Change Reports
4.1   Organizational Structure—Software Engineering
4.2   (and relationship to the organizations . . .)
5.1   Organization and Resources—formal qualification testing
5.1   Test Approach/philosophy
6.1   Organizational Structure—software product evaluations
6.2   Software Product Evaluations Procedures and Tools
6.4(and 6.5) Software Product Evaluation Records

However many topics covered in DOD-STD-2168 (such as "Evaluations of the processes . . .," "Evaluation of the Software Development Library," etc.) are not really addressed in DOD-STD-2167A and the SDP. Some of these topics can be addressed in a new Section 6.6 of the SDP. A hybrid approach can be useful, with a page or so of text on the Software Quality Program in a new Section 6.6, with a reference to the stand-alone SQPP. In any event, most contracts will call for a deliverable SDP document, but some will not call for a deliverable SQPP.

The author's experience suggests that an 'informal' SQPP must be prepared so that Project Management and the SQA department knows what its plan is, even if it is only a red-lined version of a model SQPP with a new cover attached. Even in this case, the preparer should sign and date the SQPP, and the SQA Manager should review it and sign it when it is approved.

The software product evaluations are a key part of the software quality program, but are not the exclusive province of the SQA department. Modern practice is that both the software development and the software quality groups are involved directly in product evaluations. To ensure that product evaluations are considered an in-line part of the software development process, these product evaluations were inserted in each of the activity phases in DOD-STD-2167A. Using the nominal paradigm shown in Figure 2 of DOD-STD-2167A, all of the software (or documentation) items to be evaluated from each activity phase are shown in a consistent series of matrix-like tables. The criteria to be used in the evaluations for each item or product are included in the Matrices. Although one may debate a few points here and there, the guidance provided by these sections of DOD-STD-2167A and the corresponding matrix tables is reasonably complete, and serves as a good basis for developing systems for Product Evaluations for your own special needs and software development processes. Table 15-4 summarizes the Product Evaluation requirements distributed throughout the various activity phase subsections in Section 5 of the Standard. Note that the results of the Product Evaluations are to

TABLE 15-4   Product Evaluations in DOD-STD-2167A

Activity Phase	Software Product Evaluations	Results of Product Evaluations
5.1 System Requirements Analysis	5.1.4 (Figure 4)	(SRR, SDR)
5.2 Software Requirements Analysis	5.2.4 (Figure 5)	Summarize at SSR(s)
5.3 Preliminary Design	5.3.4 (Figure 6)	Summarize at PDR(s)
5.4 Detailed Design	5.4.4. (Figure 7)	Summarize at CDR(s)
5.5 Coding & CSU Testing	5.5.4 (Figure 8)	—
5.6 CSC Integration & Testing	5.6.4 (Figure 9)	Summarize at TRR
5.7 CSCI Testing	5.7.4 (Figure 10)	(FCA, PCA)
5.8 System Integration & Testing	5.8.4 (Figure 10)	(FCA, PCA)

be presented at the formal reviews. Some general requirements are presented in Section 4.4 of 2167A, and the paragraphs on Independence, Final Evaluations, and Evaluation Records are particularly important to the Software Quality Program evaluations.

It is interesting to note that some Software Documents are not specifically covered in DOD-STD-2167A for Product Evaluations, such as the five operation and support documents listed in paragraph 4.6.4, Version Description Document, Software Product Specifications, and Computer Program Identification Number (CPIN) Requests. Obviously, these documents should be included in a comprehensive SQA program.

The tasks covered in DOD-STD-2168 and DOD-STD-2167A provide a good basis for preparing a set of SQA procedures. Analysis of these standards to identify each requirement and task is necessary; then use cross-reference or traceability techniques to ensure that all requirements are covered somewhere in your SQA procedures.

15.5 THE ROLE OF SQA DURING THE SYSTEM REQUIREMENTS AND SYSTEM DESIGN 'PHASE'

At the start of a contract, a preliminary system-level specification is normally part of, or appended to, the contract's Statement of Work (SOW). One of the first tasks is the analysis of the specification, and the development of a revised specification for the customer. This revised Specification is sent back to the customer after several months, and one or two months before the System Requirements Review. The System-level Spec usually does not have a lot of detail on software, which actually is fine. There may, however, be some constraints in place, such as the target processors to be used, the source language to be used, and sometimes the software support environment that must be used to support the software after the System is deployed. If any constraints exist, their impact on the project must be assessed; if the impact is major, it should become the subject of some tradeoffs and discussions with the customer.

The feasibility of handling the input-to-output transformation with the available information, within the allowable time, and with the required accuracy and precision represents the single thread performance of the system. These requirements have to be addressed for feasibility, and will become the basis for some of the system-level acceptance tests. The rates that the system has to handle under high-traffic conditions is another level of complexity that must be addressed, and will ultimately affect the size of the embedded computer resource segment. Most of these issues are the province of the system engineers, and there are usually a few senior software engineers on the team to provide the software expertise.

When the system design task starts, postulations of the various major components of the system are made. Usually, these system designs are based on extensive experience with prior systems in the same domain. At some level in the design hierarchy, CSCIs are postulated, and tasks assigned to them as "black boxes." At this level, it is possible to assess the loading under different scenarios to establish the worst case loading(s). The feasibility of the processor loadings during peak periods can be assessed at least on a preliminary basis. Particularly for "unprecedented" systems, the margin for processing power, to allow for uncertainties, should be significant, based on an agreed-upon margin. The memory utilization for embedded systems, in terms of the ROM (read-only memory) for the program and the dynamic RAM (random access memory), should also be sized to ensure that the estimated memory is below the target. The suitability of the microprocessors selected, if there is a potential speed or memory problem, has to be addressed. It may also be necessary to have multiple processors (and therefore multiple instances of a CSCI) to do a particular function.

The external requirements for the CSCI(s) are then analyzed and reviewed. SQA ensures that all the appropriate factors are considered and that any problems are identified and resolved as quickly as possible. SQA participates in the internal design reviews for the software elements and records the results of any action items on the SQA Inspection Report (SQAIR). Other elements such as safety, reliability, BIT (built-in-test), initialization/re-initialization, ease of modifying software, etc. also have to be considered. Areas of high-technical risk or schedule risk related to the embedded computers and software must be identified. The results of the internal reviews are then reflected in the System Design Document or its equivalent. Preliminary versions of the Software Requirement Specification (SRS) and Interface Requirements Specification (IRS) may not be required at this time.

At system design time, the SDP is also prepared and reviewed internally by engineering and SQA. When the SDP is acceptable, and all the problems are resolved, then the SDP is transmitted to the customer for review. As discussed in the prior section of this Chapter, a stand-alone SQPP may also be a required deliverable document at this time for the System Design Review, but under DOD-STD-2168 requirements.

15.6 SQA DURING THE CRUCIAL
SOFTWARE REQUIREMENTS 'PHASE'

The Software Requirements Analysis phase is geared to producing just two kinds of outputs:

- A Software Requirements Specification (SRS)—one for each unique CSCI.
- An Interface Requirements Specification (IRS)—for the system or segment.

However, these documents are very important because they are the foundation on which the whole software development effort is built.

The SRS contents and format are defined by Data Item Description DI-MCCR-80025A. Any deviations or additions to the SRS must be discussed and agreed to by Software Engineering, Systems Engineering, and SQA near the beginning of this phase. When the internal technical review for each CSCI's SRS is held, SQA should first verify that all the contents, as agreed, are included in the Draft SRS. About five working days must be allowed for each technical reviewer to read and analyze the Draft SRS, before the scheduled review meeting.

A second task is for SQA to review the requirements traceability. The system design material is reviewed to develop a list or database of all requirements allocated to the particular CSCI. Then, the SRS is reviewed to see if all of these requirements have been picked up in the SRS. There should be no gaps in the downward traceability of higher-level requirements down to the SRS.

A second aspect of the traceability analysis is to identify each software requirement in the SRS. To do this, assign a number to each SRS requirement, if not already assigned, and then determine the basis for each of these requirements. Normally, most of the SRS requirements will be traceable to a requirement in the higher-level requirement spec immediately above the SRS in the spec hierarchy. It is a concern to SQA if an SRS requirement has no predecessor or basis. In this case, this requirement must be flagged, and a determination must be made if the SRS requirement is a valid 'implicit' requirement or a derived requirement. If the SRS requirement is neither of these, it is an invalid requirement with no basis, and no justifiable reason for being there. Do not do it, if nobody wants it—the principle of parsimony in software development. Such an invalid requirement is sometimes referred to as an alien requirement (from outer space?).

Note that some requirements unique to data processing are introduced for the first time at the SRS level in the spec tree, e.g., initialization, re-initialization. These requirements are not always covered in the higher-level specs, although one could argue that they should be. These may constitute valid requirements which must be introduced in the SRS, to provide a comprehensive requirements base for software design. Any such valid implicit requirements should be flagged in the SRS, consistent with SRS paragraph 3.12. This would be the mapping of the SRS requirements back up to the higher-level requirements in the System/Segment Specification (SSS) (or PIDS or CIDS), or a flag indicating a valid implicit requirement with no predecessor or basis. This traceability analysis lends itself to a database, which can be printed out as an Appendix to the SRS.

If multiple (incremental) builds are to be used, the mapping of requirements to each build should be documented in some form in the SRS, or a companion document.

As noted earlier in this chapter, evaluation criteria for each product is shown in the matrix tables. The SRS evaluation criteria in Figure 5 of DOD-STD-2167A include:

- Internal consistency
- Understandability

In addition, the SRS should be consistent with the other SRSs and the IRS, which are at the same level in the Spec hierarchy tree. SQA must also check the appropriateness (not always yes or no) of the allocation of sizing and timing requirements to the CSCI (Section 3.6 in the SRS). Special areas related to safety (Section 3.7), security (Section 3.8), and design constraints (Section 3.9) must also be reviewed explicitly by SQA.

The adequacy of quality factor requirements (Section 3.10) must also be evaluated, but this is an emerging area that is not widely understood; note that only three system quality factors* are discussed in the Data Item for the SSS, and include reliability, maintainability, and availability (no quality factors are discussed elsewhere in 2167A or the DIDs, nor in 2168). However, the contractor may define other quality factors to apply to either the system of CSCI level. Human performance and human engineering requirements (Section 3.11) must also be reviewed for correctness, traceability, and feasibility. For some embedded systems, the user merely pushes an 'ON' button, and sees if the ON INDICATOR stays on, and all the other functions far transcend human capabilities and speeds.

The adaptation requirements must also be reviewed (Section 3.5) for completeness and correctness. The most technical reviews deal with the completeness and correctness of the capability or functional performance requirements in Section 3.2, the interfaces outside of the CSCI in Section 3.1, and for data elements internal to the CSCI in Section 3.4.

The test coverage of the requirements can be determined by reviewing Sections 4.1 and 4.2 of the SRS. However, analysis of database that shows each requirement, by requirement number and SRS paragraph, makes it easy to see how many of the requirements will be demonstrated or tested, or be qualified by analysis or inspection. The SDP should give a value of functional test coverage that must be met, e.g., 90% of all requirements not qualified by Analysis or Inspection must be qualified by demonstration. SQA can analyze the SRS qualification section to determine if the agreed-upon target has been met.

SQA must also review the SRS for the following are: the requirements explicit and unambiguous; and are they testable against a specific, feasible criteria with a well-defined pass-fail value or threshold?

---

*Other software quality factors exist,[3] and eleven of them were included in the August 1986 draft of DOD-STD-2168, e.g., correctness, efficiency, flexibility.

SQA prepares its list of discussion items for the internal software requirements review, and raises each point at the appropriate time. Any items that are not resolved on the spot are recorded as action items with a target date and a responsible person. SQA will write up a SQAIR, showing the results of the review, including all the Action Items. When all items are resolved, and validated by SQA, the SRS can be updated and issued to the customer for review usually at least 30 days before the SRR. Based on the SRR, the customer will agree on certain changes to the SRS, and the SRS will be updated and reissued. This reissued SRS becomes part of the Allocated Baseline for the System once it is approved and signed by the customer's representative. A practical problem is getting an agreement and signature from the customer for the SRS within a reasonable number of days, e.g., 30 days, to preclude delays.

15.7 SQA DURING THE TOP-LEVEL DESIGN 'PHASE'

Top-Level design is unique in that it is the bridge between software requirements and the actual design of the software. The software requirements usually are the responsibility of the systems engineering group, although the importance of some software engineering participation is well known. If this bridge is correctly handled, the software will be off to a good start. Otherwise, the problems that can be created during this phase will be very pervasive, and can be very expensive and time-consuming to fix. Few people would argue that a good software engineering development process would not be valuable at this phase, and would tend to consistently produce good software designs. In the broad sense, a mature software quality "process" is part of the larger software development process, and can contribute to producing a high-quality software design that will not be beset by many problems later on.

The software quality process must be concerned with the underlying *process* of software design, as well as looking at the products of software design. Errors of omission are usually more difficult to detect, unless there is a comprehensive framework available. To a great extent, good SQA procedures and supporting checklists can be helpful. It is even more helpful if the software developers have copies of the SQA procedures and checklists so there are no surprises. The developers want to do a good job, and if they understand the expectations, they will usually try to deliver a product that meets these expectations, rather than knowingly produce a product that will not pass.

The SQA Procedure for Top-Level design reviews is not the only "command media" that deals with Software Design Reviews. A Policy and Standard Practice that deals with the engineering aspects has been very helpful. The Standard Practice deals with all kinds of reviews, not just software reviews; however, it includes the various internal software design reviews, including Top-Level and detailed software design reviews. The inclusion of software design reviews, which is in essence, a product evaluation during the development process, in the Engineering Standard Practice makes quality an integral part of engineering's responsibilities, versus just something Quality Assurance has to worry about. The description in the Engineering Standard Practice is very brief, but is of the form shown in Table 15-5. Attendance at this design review shall be established in the procedures, and should include:

- Principal Software Designer (Originator)
- Software Engineering Section Head
- Electronics Engineering Representative
- Digital Engineering Representative
- Software Quality Assurance
- Systems Engineering

SQA should spot-check the top-level design process to see if software engineering is proceeding in accordance with the SDP, the detailed software engineering

TABLE 15-5   A Sample Engineering Standard Practice for the Top-Level Software Design Review

Top-Level Software Design Review

A. *Objective*
1) Assure that all requirements allocated to each CSCI are adequately covered by the Top-Level Design.
B. *Topics To Be Covered*
1) CSCI Top-Level Design
   - Functional Performance requirement
   - Memory, input/output, and real-time estimate
   - Design and Programming conventions
   - Data base design
   - CSC performance
   - Executive control methodology
   - Family tree (Software)
   - Configuration management
2) Preliminary Software Integration Plan
3) Preliminary Hardware/Software Integration Plan
4) CSCI Qualification Test Plan
5) Final Software Development Plan
6) Final Support Software and Hardware Requirements
7) CSC Test Requirements/Plans
C. *Documentation*
1) CSCI Top-Level Design Specification (SDD-Part I)
2) Preliminary Interface Design Document (IDD)
3) Preliminary Software Integration Plan
4) Preliminary Hardware/Software Integration Plan
5) Software Test Plan
6) Final Software Development Plan
7) Support Software and Hardware Requirements
8) SDF Information on CSC Test Requirements/Plans
D. *Responsibility.* This review shall apply to each CSCI, and shall occur when the CSCI software architecture has been designed to the point where it can serve as a baseline for detailed design. This review shall be scheduled by the responsible Software Engineer with the Design Review Chairman.

procedures, and any special contractual requirements. Depending on the risks and what was promised in the SQPP, one check or audit for each CSCI is usually sufficient. If problems are uncovered, follow-up process audits should be scheduled in that area. Each audit must be documented in a SQAIR.

Other reviews or audits are usually not done until the top-level design is considered ready by the responsible Lead Software Engineer. Then, that Lead Software Engineer schedules a design review with the Engineering Design Review Coordinator, usually for five working days in the future. Sufficient lead time must be allowed for the reviewers to study the design package, and identify any problems or questions. Some of the logistics of getting a large design package to each of the various five or six reviewers can be non-trivial, particularly if the design package is classified. Access to electronic media can help speed-up the process, but there are still some elements that are in paper form, and must be physically distributed. The announcement for the meeting must also be very clear on the scope, agenda, ground rules, classification levels, and the time and location of the meeting. Through trial and error, we have found that if a person cannot attend, they must notify the Design Review Coordinator of who will substitute for them. This allows a new schedule to be established, but only if most of the 'principals' cannot attend that day.

SQA looks at the design review in a slightly different way than the other attendees. SQA is concerned primarily with the quality of the design, but not directly with the cost or schedule. Therefore, the question becomes simply: Is the quality level fully acceptable? Not the question of a cost or schedule tradeoff with quality. SQA must insist that the quality be fully acceptable!

For the Top-Level software design, the SQA analysis of the design package usually starts with a quick pass reading of the SDD material for familiarity, e.g., what's there, and what's missing. Then, a detailed review of all the requirements allocated to the CSCI is done, based on the contents in the previously reviewed SRS, per the SRS requirements traceability section, 3.12. This SRS section will either contain a list of all the allocated requirements, or will refer to an SRS Appendix which has a printout from the requirements traceability database. SQA shall determine how and where each requirement is handled in the Top-Level design, one requirement at a time. The analysis must systematically address every requirement in the SRS, which can easily be in the hundreds. Because SQA is asking the question, 'are all the requirements covered?', all the requirements must be listed. Without a computer database system, this gets very tedious if the CSCI has over 100 requirements. A listing could be developed, by computer or manually, that looks like the one in Figure 15-4. As required by DOD-STD-2167A, every requirement has a unique Requirements ID. The following format could be used for CSCI-level requirements IDs:

AA	R	NNNN

The AA field would be a two alpha field to identify the CSCI. The 'R' simply identifies this as a requirement entity. The NNNN field would be the number of the

REQ'T ID*	SRS PARAGRAPH*	TLCSSC(S)	OK
AA—R NNNN	3.2.X	————	——
.			
.			
.			
AA—R 0072	3.2.14	3	Y
AA—R 0073	3.2.4	4,5	Y,Y
AA—R 0074	3.2.21	2	N
AA—R 0075	3.2.23	99**	——

*Based on SRS data
**99 = TL CSC cannot be found (in Top-Level Design)

FIGURE 15-4. Representative List for CSCI Requirement Analysis

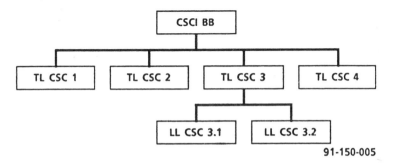

91-150-005

FIGURE 15-5. Sample CSCI top-level architecture chart (a partial family tree).

requirement within that CSCI, normally starting with '0001'. This CSCI Requirement ID and the SRS paragraph would be based on the information in the SRS document. The SQA reviewer would identify which Top-Level CSC in the design handles this requirement, and enter the TL CSC number or ID into the database or form. When the TL CSC seems to adequately handle the requirement, a yes "Y" code could be entered into the database. If it is handled, but *not* adequately, a no "N" code could be entered. In the Top-Level design package, if the organization is similar to the format of the SDD, each CSC will be described in a unique subsection within Section 3.2 (CSCI Design Description). There is something to be said for numbering the CSCs and the subsections such that CSC Number 1 is in subsection 3.2.1, etc. A rational numbering system for any lower-level CSCs (LLSCSs) would also help, as suggested in Figure 15-5.

When the requirements traceability analysis is done, any gap or uncovered requirements will be obvious. It may save time to call the Lead Software Engineer before the review meeting about any potential gaps. Remember, SQA may have missed them in the design package. The questions about not adequately handling the requirement is not quite as severe, and perhaps could wait until the design review meeting.

The review of the relevant portions of the Interface Design Document (IDD) must be done in concert with the SDD for the particular CSCI. The interfaces for that CSCI must be reviewed, even if the IDD was covered before as an entire document. Remember, the IDD is normally a single document for all CSCIs in the system or for a major segment. In some cases, there may be no Preliminary IDD required by the contract because it was tailored out. In any event, some level of detail of information on CSCI interfaces is still required for the SDD (Section 3.1). This information must be reviewed for consistency with the interface information in the SRS (Section 3.1) and the IRS (Section 3.1, and the appropriate interface discussions in sections 3.2, 3.3, etc. for each interface). If there are any inconsistencies or omissions, they must be identified for resolution at the internal Top-Level design review.

After the analysis of the CSCI-level design, SQA should then address the internal design of CSCI, down to the Top-Level CSCs. Note that the requirements traceability analysis already determined the requirements mapping to the TLCSCs. The actual mapping of requirements should then be compared with the information in the design package related to Section 3.2.X of the SDD for that CSC, because sometimes the two are not identical. The data flow into and out of each CSC should match the processing needed to meet the functional requirements. Check off the data elements for each requirement or function. Are there any extra or missing data inputs or outputs? Is the execution control adequate, reasonable, and fast enough to meet requirements. Use of non-developmental software should also be reviewed for risk and adequacy.

The memory, processing time, and input/output allocations for Section 3.1.3 in the SDD should be reviewed for reasonableness and consistency with hardware and software capacities. The total used should still provide an adequate reserve of design margin, consistent with the contract and Statement of Work. If the contract doesn't mandate a required margin, design standards should be used. If no standards are available, the project should document them. A 35% to 40% margin is suggested, and this margin is normally eroded by the time of Acceptance Tests. At this time, the budgets are just budgets or allocations (that hopefully can and will be met). It is not clear yet that the budgets will actually be met, but hopefully the totals for the CSCI provide reasonable margins within the available capacities.

At the Top-Level design review, other items are normally covered, although sometimes a separate meeting may be scheduled to avoid an overly-lengthy single meeting. DOD-STD-2167A requires that the Software Test Plan (STP) for the CSCI be prepared at this time, and presented at the Preliminary Design Review (PDR). SQA then will have to review the draft of the STP at about the same time as the SDD-Preliminary Design. The STP is only for the qualification tests for the CSCI, and most of the qualification tests are done at the CSCI level.[4] For some embedded systems, this means the qualification tests are at the end of the Hardware/Software Integration phase with the actual digital hardware and microcomputer. In a few cases, the qualification tests are conducted in the target system with a complete system. In any event, the tests are not necessarily for every requirement in the SRS, but should address the most important and most critical functions. The functional test coverage of the SRS requirements should normally be at the 70% to 80% level, as defined in the SDP.

In reviewing the Test Plan, SQA should compare the STP against the SRS qualification sections (4.1 and 4.2), particularly for those requirements which were to be tested, versus requirements to be validated by Analysis or Inspection. Any discrepancies have to be identified and resolved.

Special classes of tests such as stress tests, overload tests, erroneous input tests, etc. may also test some of the same requirements again, but from a different perspective. The types of data to be recorded, and the related reduction and analysis write-ups must be reasonable for each test. The test schedule should be feasible for the number of test teams to be used; if they are artificially tight, quality may suffer. It is important to note that the Test Plan is not very detailed. It is the Software Test Description (STD) which details out each test into test case descriptions; the STD is an output of the later detailed design phase.

The Preliminary Software Integration plan for the CSCI, and the Preliminary Hardware/Software Integration plan describe the test and integration for both activities, and must be reviewed for reasonable tests at each level of software build. The sequence and schedule must also be reviewed for reasonableness and completeness. Both plans are not specifically discussed in DOD-STD-2167A.

One item that is required by DOD-STD-2167A during the Top-Level design phase is the CSC test requirements, which are the tests for each CSC, based on the requirements mapped to the CSC, and the interfaces with that CSC, as defined in the SDD. The CSC test requirements are analogous to the CSCI Software Test Plan. Note that CSC test cases, with the details for testing each CSC, is an output of the later detailed design phase. There is no DID* for the CSC test requirements information, so this must be defined in the Software Procedures Manual. SQA should review the CSC test information, CSC test requirements at this time) for completeness against the CSC requirements, design and interfaces, plus testing standards and the definitions for the CSC test requirements.

At this point, the updated support software and hardware requirements must be reviewed to ensure that all elements required for development are identified and will be available, and an SQA checklist is helpful here. If a Computer Resources Integrated Support Document (CRISD) is under contract, a similar update and review cycle for this document that plans for the support environment for post-deployment support will also be needed, and should be reviewed together with the development environment information.

The SDP may require some additional updates at this time. Therefore, a review of the revised SDP is necessary. The SDP should be compatible with the other informal plans and the development environment. Hopefully, the SDP changes will not be extensive, but this plan is a living document which is likely to change over the development period.

To make the reviews of these various outputs more modular, it is suggested that separate SQAIRs be used for each one. This is especially important if the reviews extend over a period of time, or are performed by several SQA engineers.

At the internal review meeting(s), each item is briefly discussed but not resolved. Each action item is given a number, a due date, and assigned to a particular person. When all the action items are closed, the SQAIR can be closed out and considered

---

*DID = Data Item Description.

complete. Then, that item can be prepared as a final deliverable document if required by the contract. The internal review of the draft documents should be allowed for in the schedule. A scheduling parameter of reviewing five pages per hour seems acceptable. The completed document should be reviewed in its entirety, rather than in fragments. Document review forms should be used to document the comments. It saves time if the SQA person discusses any areas of disagreement with the document author face-to-face, and a resolution is sought. When all issues are resolved, SQA can approve the publication of the document.

The customer will then review the document and present formal comments, either by letter or at a Review Meeting. SQA will normally review the comments, and then the revised document to ensure it meets the customer's valid comments. A SQAIR and document review form are usually used for the revised document, too. When all items have been resolved, SQA can approve the revised document for shipment. It is usually a good practice for SQA to keep a copy of the document in its files, along with the customer's comments and the SQAIRs. If there are any agreements or clarifications from the customer, copies of these letters must also be retained in the SQA files.

15.8 SQA DURING THE DETAILED DESIGN 'PHASE'

The Detailed Design Phase not only expands the Software Design to greater levels of detail down to the CSU or data element, but it also refines the Top-Level design because of new insights. The Top-Level design is very rarely finished or constant at the end of the Top-Level design phase, and is modified to some degree, as a result of additional design effort during the detailed design phase. Barring any significant changes in requirements, the top-level design should be final by the end of the detailed design phase. However, in the real world, sometimes external factors may necessitate requirements changes even if there is a significant cost and/or schedule impact. The result in this case, is a new functional baseline and a new allocated baseline, which then can ripple down into the software design.

The products of the Detailed Design Phase are:

a. Revised SDD for each CSCI, with added detailed design sections 4, 5, 6.
b. Interface Design Document (IDD).
c. The Software Test Description (STD)—Part I, for the Test Cases.

In addition, it may be necessary to update the Software Test Plan (STP) in order to keep it current and valid.

Other information that is produced at this phase is:

d. The test cases for CSCs.
e. The test requirements for the CSUs.
f. The test cases for the CSUs.

This information (d-f) should reside in the appropriate Software Development Files (SDFs), which usually are not treated as deliverable data. However, DOD-

STD-2167A does require that a specified percentage of the SDFs be evaluated during this phase; the required precent is normally specified in the SDP, and may also be specified in a stand-alone SQPP if one exists. As discussed for prior phases, SQA shall review or evaluate these various products during the Detailed Design Phase.

A separate SQA operating procedure has been found useful to provide guidance for the software detail design reviews. The design parts of the reviews deal with the design of one or a few CSCs. In some cases, the internal, detailed design of an entire Top-Level CSC can be handled in one review meeting, which has several advantages over fragmenting the review into several smaller design reviews. The SQA procedure, out of self-defense, also stresses that the design package must be distributed and received at least five working days before the scheduled review, to allow enough time to prepare. If the design package deals with a software TLCSC that is likely to exceed 10,000 SLOC, more than five days is recommended.

With the design review for a CSC or TLCSC, the comparable parts of the IDD must be reviewed. Each CSCI external interface that relates directly or indirectly to the CSC shall be considered, but remember that external interfaces do not necessarily interface directly with the CSC under review. The interfaces between the CSCs in a CSCI are described in the SDD. The interfaces between CSUs are also covered in the SDD, under section 4.X for each CSC.

A separate review meeting dealing with the IDD is recommended, because this document details the interfaces between the CSCI and other configuration items, and is not directly related to the design of a particular TLCSC.

The SQA procedure for detailed design reviews should also be supported by a detailed SQA checklist. For the detailed design reviews, several checklists are helpful:

- CSC Design Checklist
- CSCI Interface Design Checklist
- Software Test Description—Test Cases Checklist
- CSC and CSU Test Cases Checklist
- CSC and CSU Test Requirements Checklist

In addition, SQA checklists for the audits of the CSC and CSU SDFs are useful at this phase of the development cycle.

The detailed design review is scheduled by the software engineer responsible for the CSC design. The lead software engineer also must distribute the CSC detailed design package in time to allow five days for analysis.

Attendees at the detailed design review should include:

- The Lead Software Engineer for the CSC
- Software Engineering Section Head
- Electronics Engineering representative (for certain CSCs)
- Digital Engineering representative

- Software Quality Assurance
- Systems Engineering

Representation at the design review is mandatory, and a delegate must be sent if the primary person cannot attend.

The description of the review in the Engineering Standard Practices is of the form shown in Table 15-6. As noted before, there are some advantages in breaking out the review of the Software Test Description of the CSCI because it is really a CSCI-level global matter, not directly related to any one CSC. The timing is the only common theme, they are both produced in the detailed design phase.

The Software Test Descriptions—Part I describes the test cases to test the CSCI requirements, consistent with SRS Sections 4.1 and 4.2. In fact, almost all the requirements in the SRS that are to be qualified by a test or demonstration should be covered in the STD by at least one test case. The STD is also built on, and is traceable back to the STP, and the various levels and classes of tests defined there. The test cases should provide the functional test coverage for the desired percent of requirements that are not otherwise qualified by analysis or inspection.

TABLE 15-6   A Sample Engineering Standard Practice for the Detailed Software Design Review

Detailed Software Design Review

A. *Objectives*
   1) Assure that the design of the individual software modules (in one or more CSCs) is compatible with the Top-Level design and CSCI requirements.
   2) Audit the algorithms, and the real-time processing and memory estimates.
B. *Topics To Be Covered*
   1) Review of detailed design of each module within the CSC Interface designs
   2) Detailed memory and real-time processing estimates
   3) Software Test Description—of Test Cases (CSCI)
   4) Software Integration Plan (for CSCI)
   5) Hardware/Software Integration Plan (for CSCI)
   6) Test Cases for the CSC
   7) Test Requirements & Test Cases for the CSUs
C. *Documentation*
   1) CSCI Software Design Document—Parts I and II
   2) Interface Design document (IDD)
   3) Software Test Description—Test Cases
   4) Revised Software Integration Plan (CSCI)
   5) Revised Hardware/Software Integration Plan (CSCI)
   6) Test Cases for the CSC
   7) Test Requirements for the CSUs
   8) Test Cases for the CSUs
D. *Responsibility.* This review shall be held when the CSC software design stage is completed. The responsible Software Design Engineer schedules this review with Design Review Chairman after completion of the detailed software design.

SQA must review the STD to see which requirements are, in fact, tested. A simple list or data base can be built from the STD test descriptions, as follows:

Requirement ID	Test Case ID
AA-R-NNNN	AA-T-NNNN
.	.
.	.
.	.
AA-R-0074	AA-T-0308
.	.
.	.
.	.

(The T indicates a test entity in the Test Case ID column.)

The requirements actually tested in accordance with the STD shall be checked against the STP and SRS. Any anomolies must be documented, and addressed at the review meeting for the STD. Also, the total number of requirements tested versus the total requirement not otherwise qualified are calculated as a percentage. *For example:*

310	Total requirements for the CSCI
−48	Requirements to be qualified by either inspection or analysis
262	Requirements addressable by testing
203	Actually tested, per the Software Test Description

Percent of functional test coverage (Net):
$203/262 = 78\%$

Percent of functional test coverage (Gross):
$203/310 = 66.5\%$

The net test coverage percentage is more useful since it eliminates the intervening variables of the numbers of requirements best handled by analysis or inspection. If the target value required for net coverage was 80%, then the number of requirements to be tested should be: $0.80 \times 262 = 209.6$, or 210 requirements should be tested. For this example, seven more "testable" requirements that are important in some sense should be tested. Some scale for identifying the important and critical requirements is needed, so that these requirements are tested. If you can only test 80%, test the most important 80%, not the easiest 80%.

For each test case, the information required is shown in the STD DID—see Section 4.X.Y. Preparations for the test are to include information per Section 3.X.2. SQA must ensure that the information is complete and reasonable for each test case. SQA must also review the definition of the CSCI-level regression test set, but this is normally defined outside the STD.

The CSC test cases for the complete CSC is similar to the problem of reviewing the CSCI test cases. A requirements first approach can be taken down to the CSC, if the SRS requirements are mapped to the CSC, and there is high functional cohesion within the CSCs.

Net functional test coverage for the CSC can similarly be determined, and compared with the target percent. White-box test planning techniques should be utilized to make sure all of the execution controls and subroutine calls are exercised, which are other kinds of test coverage that transcend intra-unit structural coverage.

The CSU test requirements, followed by the CSU test cases, are called for by DOD-STD-2167A as outputs during the detailed design phase. However, in most cases, these cannot be done meaningfully until the CSU is designed. The detailed, internal design of the CSU can be considered the most detailed level of design, and is done prior to the actual coding. However, the use of prototyping makes this distinction quite fuzzy. The general sequence of these steps is shown in Figure 15-6. The timing of the review(s) can be flexible. One variation used several years ago by the author was that a separate review was held for the unit level design, followed immediately by a second review (part 2) on the test requirements to test the unit. Because 100% structural testing was strongly encouraged, units tended to be non-complex, so they usually could be completely path tested with less than ten test cases. Boundary cases and error cases were additional. There were no subsequent reviews of the detailed test cases, but the coding seemed to go very well, and the unit testing progressed well, even with virtually complete path testing. The number of coding errors discovered in later test stages was strikingly low.

The person who designed the CSU and defined the CSU test requirements also did the coding and unit testing in about 80% of the cases, so there was a high knowledge carryover from the CSU design and test requirements steps.

A good point to stress is that the SDP defines how you will do the software development, and if you make a good case for a variation from the nominal process in DOD-STD-2167A, you will probably get approval to try it.

SQA, in any event, will analyze the various products, and prepare for the design reviews. All action items assigned at the review meeting are documented in a SQAIR, along with the due date and the responsible person. When all the action items have been resolved and verified by SQA, then the design review(s) can be considered complete. SQA must track the status and closure of all the action

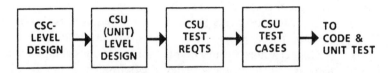

FIGURE 15-6. Detailed design phase steps for CSU-level activities.

items, and report when they are all closed. When all the CSCs for that CSCI have been completed, then the SDD detailed portion, plus the updates to the Top-Level design, can be documented or completed and published. The SDD is normally sent to the customer 30 to 60 days before the Critical Design Review (CDR). Normally the customer reviews the SDD prior to the CDR, and should be prepared to discuss it at the CDR. When all points raised at the CDR are finished and coordinated, a revised SDD can be published for final customer approval and authentication. It is in everyone's interest to try to resolve these issues quickly, because usually the developer has to start the coding and unit test, at the developer's risk, to meet the schedules and also to not have a big gap where everyone is just waiting for customer approval of the SDD.

SQA should also do a process audit in a few selected areas for the detailed design phase. Basically, the audit is to ensure that the activities are being done properly, in accordance with the SDP and the referenced Software Engineering Procedures, plus any special contractual requirements. If people are doing the right things in the right way, the consensus is that the software design will tend to be good. This is the underlying concept for the SEI software process maturity model developed by Watts Humphrey and others. Further, the process audits tend to keep everyone on their toes, so that no one is tempted to cut corners or get sloppy. Results of the audit are documented in a SQAIR. Any adverse trends must be identified, and correction action initiated, usually to the process.

Returning to the product reviews, SQA tracks the action items uncovered at the various reviews, and determines if there are an unusually large number of any particular kind of errors, e.g., requirements errors, top-level design errors, detailed design errors. Boris Beitzer[1] has developed a very detailed and comprehensive structure for error types and related statistics. Whatever system of error types are used, the point is to see if a larger than expected number of errors were introduced during a certain phase, or perhaps that the defect removal process at a particular point was not effective, and the errors were not found until a later phase when their removal could be much more costly. Getting statistics for a particular project can be very useful.

A simple illustration just for requirements errors might be helpful. The requirements errors found at each stage are shown in Table 15-7. In this illustration, 126 requirements errors were found during development. It is not known how many more exist, and of those, how many would be found in development testing or operational testing. Experience suggests a few more would be found during these kinds of tests. Without estimating the not-yet-found errors, we can say there were 126 requirements errors found so far, of which 61 were found in requirements reviews. In other words, about 48% of the requirements errors were found in the internal software requirements review. Does this mean that this review was effective? What about the detailed design reviews? Should detailed design reviews find many requirements errors, or are they geared more for finding design errors? The author thinks the latter is true. Other important questions are: Is the Software Requirements process itself within acceptable limits or norms since it produced at

TABLE 15-7   Requirements Errors Found at Different Points in the Development Process

	Number of Errors Found
Software Requirements Reviews	61
Top-Level Design Reviews	34
Detailed Design Reviews	4
Code Inspections	0
Static Analysis	0
Unit Test	1
CSC Integration & Test	4
CSCI Integration & Test	16
System Integration Test	6
Total Errors Found:	126
Total Errors Not Found:	?

TABLE 15-8   Defect Removal Effectiveness

	From	To
Requirements Reviews	20%	50%
Top-Level Design Review	30%	60%
Detailed Design Reviews	30%	70%
Code Inspections	20%	75%
Static Analysis	20%	75%
Unit Test	10%	50%
SW Integration Test	25%	60%
SW Qualification Test	25%	65%
(From T. C. Jones and Others)[6]		

*KLOC = Thousands of (Source) Lines of Code

least 126 requirements errors? What is an acceptable error density? For a system with 2000 software requirements, would 126 requirements errors be acceptable? For a small system with only 100 unique software requirements, 126 requirements errors would seem excessive, and something is probably wrong with the requirements process. In the illustration, the effectiveness of the requirements review process (48%) seemed to be within normal limits based on widely published values, based largely on the work of T. Capers Jones.[6] Table 15-8 shows these acceptable values for all kinds of defects, not just requirements errors, and implies that some defects will remain in the software at delivery time. Normal values of 2 to 3 defects per KLOC* of delivered source executable code are typical of current practice, but some cases exist with less than 1 defect per KLOC. Quality targets of less than 1 defect per delivered KLOC may be necessary if the United States is to maintain its competitive edge. For a system with one million lines of source code, i.e., 1000 KLOC, even one defect per KLOC doesn't seem that great!

15.9 SQA DURING THE CODING AND UNIT TEST 'PHASE'

The Coding and Unit Test 'Phase' is the point in the software development cycle where the design is finally implemented. The time and effort spent in this phase is a small part of the total effort for mission-critical software. This effort is about 20% to 30% of the effort from software design through hardware/software integration and CSCI sell-off qualification testing.

The products from the coding and unit test phase, as delineated by DOD-STD-2167A, are:

a. The Source Code—for each CSU
b. CSC Level test procedures (for the next phase)
c. CSU test procedures
d. CSU test results

Source listings are not separate products, but may be viewed on a computer display CRT screen or printed out whenever desired, based on the source code files (a, above) resident in the computer.

The SDFs, as described in Section 4.2.9 in DOD-STD-2167A, shall be evaluated on a sample basis, in addition to the four products listed above. The SDFs are not usually considered products although some of the information and artifacts in them is important. The sample percentage of SDFs evaluated in this phase need not be the same as that used in other phases.

For CSU-level SDFs, the contents of the SDF should include:

a. The source code for each CSU.
b. The relocatable object code for each CSU, and information of which version of the compiler or assembler was used to produce it. If there are special compiler instructions used, these instructions should be captured in the SDF.
c. The CSU test procedures—these are generally not needed* because of the skill levels of the personnel in this domain, and because of the test tools used.
d. The CSU test results for the last few sets of test runs. If any Software Problem Reports (SPRs) were generated, they should be cited in the test results. The version and date of the CSU that was tested are also important.
e. The CSU test requirements, test cases, and the test data (inputs).
f. Design information, data, constraints, and other design considerations.
g. Schedule and status information.

---

*If not needed, make sure this is documented in the SDP. Note that SPRs are not normally generated during unit test or code inspections, mainly due to the number of problems uncovered and fixed. However, it may be desired to collect the data for process improvement purposes.

Information on several related CSUs can be put into one SDF, but this can also cause some complications. A system of SDFs that match the unit reference numbers from the software architecture chart (software family tree) can simplify the use of one SDF for one CSU. The CSCI architecture chart shown earlier in the Top-Level design sub-section should be expanded down to the CSU level, although for a large CSCI this chart may be too complex for a single diagram. Take just one TLCSC, and expand it down for each level until all the units are enumerated, and the structure and numbering could look like that shown in Figure 15-7. The CSU SDFs for this TLCSC in CSCI BB would, conceptually, be organized in the equivalent numerical sequence, as follows:

USDF 3.1.1.1
USDF 3.1.1.2
USDF 3.1.1.3
USDF 3.1.2.1
USDF 3.1.2.2
USDF 3.2.1
USDF 3.2.2
(where USDF = Unit SDF)

The Unit SDFs for TLCSC 4 would follow those for TLCSC 3 in the data base, etc. Other CSCIs would be treated similarly, and Unit SDFs can be added or declared replaced, as needed. It is not a good idea to actually delete an SDF if a unit is dropped from the design.

The product evaluation of the source code usually takes the form of either a code review or a code inspection. The code inspection is a very rigorous, structured procedure, originally developed and codified by Michael E. Fagan.[7] In addition to the quality benefits, Fagan claimed a net improvement in productivity of 94 hours per KLOC.

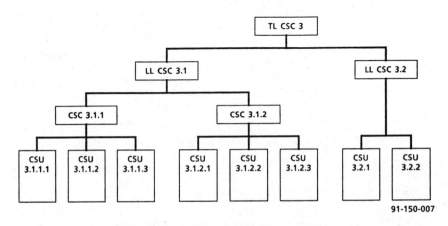

91-150-007

FIGURE 15-7. Software family tree for TLCSC 3

The code review or code inspection, in either case, is done before the unit is tested by execution on a computer in various test cases (dynamic testing). One reason for this sequence is that code inspections can more economically and more quickly find errors than path testing for all seven categories of defects (computational, logic, input-output, data handling, interface, data definition, and data base). Therefore, the code inspection is a good way to remove many defects before actual testing begins. However, subsequent testing will usually find a few errors that were not found by the code inspection, mainly because of a different perspective or approach.

The code inspection, or the less rigorous code review, is a product evaluation of one kind. The participants in this review meeting are the "coder," one or two technical experts in the application software domain, an SQA engineer, an inspection leader, and a recorder. Others may be added if necessary. Visitors and non-contributors should be discouraged. Managers may inhibit the free discussion and candor needed to flush out all the problems.

A code inspection may be scheduled to handle several closely related CSUs, particularly if they are all coded by the same programmer.

What is evaluated at a code inspection? (See Chapter 9.) There are six main areas, as follows:

1. Code functionality.
   Does the CSU code meet the specific requirements allocated to it? (Refer to the SDD). Does it do things it should not do, or that are not required? Also, is the code reasonable in terms of code efficiency, run time, memory utilization; and error control/error handling?
2. CSU interfaces.
   Do the CSU interfaces match the expectations of the other CSUs, etc.? Are the conventions and data definitions the same? (e.g., 1 = YES or 0 = NO, Least Significant Bit = 15, High Altitude = 1 or Low Altitude = 0.) Are error condition exits handled correctly? Are all interfaces handled on the other side of the interface?
3. Data.
   Is all data set or used by the CSC the same. Are there any data conflicts? Is the data initialized or reinitialized properly? Is the data redundant? Is the precision of the data sufficient? Are the data descriptions clear and unambiguous? Is there any data validation required? How often is the data used or set?
4. Specification conflicts.
   Does the CSU have any conflicts with the SRS requirements or the SDD design?
5. Prologues and comments.
   Is the prologue adequate to describe the processing, inputs and outputs, any subroutine calls, and configuration and data information? Are the comments in the code adequate to describe how the program works, and any anomolies or special considerations.

6. Programming conventions.
    Does the CSU adhere to the programming standards and conventions referenced in the SDP, and any special contractual requirements? Example:

    1. Structured coding constructs
    2. CSU size limits (executable source statements, memory requirements)
    3. CSU entry/exit limitations
    4. Nesting conventions and limits
    5. Prologue and comment requirements
    6. Labeling and naming conventions
    7. Prohibition of execution-time self-modification of the code.
    8. Limits on McCabe cyclomatic complexity[8] or equivalent.

At the risk of saying the obvious, the source language should be acceptable for this contract.

It is also useful to re-visit the CSU test cases, and analyze the paths tested by each test case. If the McCabe cyclomatic complexity is relatively low (10 or less), then it is feasible to path test every path through the code. Code that is not complex is not expensive to completely test, and is generally easier to maintain or modify over its operational life (and during testing). Once the code has been reviewed and any problems resolved, it is useful to see if all the code paths are tested by the set of test cases developed earlier. The actual code may be somewhat different than the detailed design logic was at design time. The set of test cases may not test all the paths of the actual code, so a glass-box view of these test cases and their path coverage is useful. Whenever possible, the test cases should exercise all the paths.

If there are redundant test cases, eliminate the redundant test cases so each path is tested exactly once. Also, look at the boundary case test cases from an input space viewpoint. Are all boundary cases covered? Finally, look at the error cases; are all the errors tested (or at least the critical ones?). In some of these cases, the analysis of the code is sufficient, based on each test case. Dr. Harlan Mills[9] makes an interesting point in his 'Clean Room' approach that unit testing may not be necessary at all if the code is thoroughly inspected by the programmer, or by a reviewer, for each test case. To implement the test case inspections (even with some unit testing retained), SQA and software engineering procedures would need to be modified from today's versions.

Static analysis of the source code can be utilized to find additional problems prior to test execution (dynamic analysis?) As Robert Dunn[10] points out, compilers (and some link editors) have been doing some degree of static analysis for many years, e.g., starting with Autocoder and FORTRAN, for example, way back in the early 1960s. Dunn lists typical outputs of static analysis, e.g., unused variables, uninitialized variables, cross-reference lists for operands, etc. The software engineering process and SQA process should capitalize on these capabilities which vary with the compiler (or other tools) actually used. Using these "static analyzers" should be encouraged, preferably before unit test.

If there is no shortage of computer power, particularly during off-hours, it is not wise to insist that the code inspections be done before compilation, because the compiler or other static analysis tools may quickly detect problems which can be fixed by the programmer before the code inspection, thus saving time for everyone in the code inspection activity. As a practical matter, it may be hard to prevent programmers from using these tools before the inspection, even if you wanted to; most programmers want to 'look good' at the inspection. In fact, some organizations require an 'error-free' compilation before the code inspection. SQA doesn't have to concern itself with this static analysis process, but may want to spot-check some units and run them through the static analysis toolset to see if there are still problems after the inspection or after code changes; this spot-check may encourage the programmers to use the available tools which should help improve Quality.

The next main activity in the Coding and Unit Testing phase is the unit testing activity, unless no unit testing is used, and the code is released directly to the CSC Integration Library and process. The product of the unit testing activity is revised source code, and a lot of unit test results. The goal is to end up with a version of the unit (by version and date) that has passed all the test cases, and the test results (data, and PASS/FAIL indications) in the unit SDF. SQA can audit the process by witnessing the unit tests and auditing the unit SDF, and documenting the results in a SQAIR. A final audit should be done on a sample of completed, released units to ensure that all the tests have been run on the final version of software, and that all the test data actually mean a 'PASS' for all the test cases. Release of a unit without successful testing all the test cases would be a serious matter, and not only would a SQAIR be written, but a more fundamental "Corrective Action Request" would be sent to software engineering regarding the apparent breakdown in the process. "We ran out of time and couldn't test everything" is not considered acceptable!

After a unit is released to the CSC test and integration library, it may still be maintained in the development library so that future problems can be addressed and fixed by the developer, without "playing around with" the version in the CSC Test & Integration (T&I) Library.

Tracking the status of the units completed provides good overall information on the Coding and Unit Testing phase. Tracking the individual problems, and CSU test case completions is usually left to the developer and the lead software engineer, to prevent 'micro management'. In this phase, SQA would track only serious breaches in the Unit Code/Test process, such as not completing the agreed-upon test cases or not properly recording the test results in the SDF.

15.10 SQA DURING THE SOFTWARE INTEGRATION AND TESTING 'PHASE'

Software Integration and Testing usually have several sub-phases for embedded mission-critical software. Software integration within a CSC would normally occur first. This integration can be done in two main ways, bottom-up or top-down. Then, several CSCs, after they have completed CSC integration, can be integrated and tested as part of the CSCI. Most or all of the CSCI integration and test is done in a simulated environment on a host development computer. At the planned point, the CSCI testing moves to a Hardware-Software Integration phase where the software runs on the actual target microcomputer, and interfaces with real, usually new hardware. The action here is to test the new software and the new hardware, and resolve any problems and incompatibilities.

At the end of the Hardware-Software Integration activity, the CSCI is completely built and tested, and Acceptance Testing of the CSCI begins in the 'real hardware' environment. When the software seems to work 100% correctly per the Acceptance Test Specification, SQA is called to witness a final "dry run" test. When the dry-runs are successfully completed, which may take several attempts before everyone including SQA is satisfied, customer and the government representatives (e.g., DPRO Quality in-plant personnel) are notified and the Formal Acceptance Test is scheduled. The point is that you do not want any surprises or embarrassments in front of the Customer, nor do you want to waste their time.

The products of the CSC-level integration and testing phase are the updated code built into various CSCs, and the updated Software Test Description updated to include any detailed test procedures, and any refinements to the Test Case Descriptions developed earlier during the Detailed Design Phase. For some embedded systems, the test procedures part of the STD is not needed, and is tailored out because the people running the CSCI tests are experts who really don't need the procedures.

For some embedded systems, the human interactions at this level of testing are virtually zero, and one particular signal is injected on top of background noise. This is far different from a large command and control system, where there are normally extensive human interactions and many carefully scripted 'threat' and 'environmental' (simulated or real) inputs.

Another output of this phase is the CSC integration test results for each CSC test case. At some point in time, these test results for the current CSC software version for all the test cases are contained in the CSC-level SDF.

The above three products are subject to product evaluations by engineering, SQA, and others. As with some of the prior phases, the updated SDFs for the CSC are subject to evaluation on a sample basis.

The activity of CSC Integration and Test is subject to process evaluations by SQA to ensure that the methods and procedures promised in the SDP and its references are being properly followed, and that all other contractual requirements for these activities are being met. For example, are the tests being conducted properly and completely, are all the test case results being recorded properly and accurately, are Software Problem Reports (SPRs) being written promptly for any observed anomalies, are changes to the software being controlled properly in the Developmental Configuration, are any unauthorized software changes being made, is the software design documentation being kept current (at least weekly) with the software changes?

A fundamental question is the CSC integration approach. Should the CSC be integrated 'all at once' or in an incremental approach. The incremental approach seems to work well for most situations in the embedded system arena. This incremental approach is planned around the major software functions and is briefly described as follows:

1. Design, code, and test one unit
2. Add another unit to the CSC
3. Test the collection of the two units (a 'partial build' of the CSC).
4. Repeat steps 2 and 3 for additional units, until all the units have been incorporated and tested.

One advantage of this incremental approach from a software quality viewpoint is that only a few 'new' units are added to the CSC build at one time, thus tending to isolate potential problems to either the few new units, or to interfaces with these units. This self-focusing approach can be helpful in isolating and finding the causes of problems. Further, it is easy to back-up to the prior build and do special testing whenever necessary. This incremental approach is also compatible with a top-down implementation approach, which is very useful in many kinds of systems, particularly embedded Mission-critical systems. The CSC builds should be functionally coherent to allow several units to work together to produce an overall result or output. Stubs may be necessary to substitute for real units until they are available. Whichever approach is used, SQA will periodically spot-check the CSC integration and test, and document the audit findings in a SQAIR.

When the CSC testing is reported to be complete, all the units for that CSC should be included in the build, and this complete aggregate of software should have successfully passed all the CSC-level test cases. SQA shall be notified of the completion; SQA should then validate completions of the CSC testing, using the results in the CSC-level SDF. On some projects, the Software Development Plan may also call for a small CSC Test Review Meeting, involving the Tester, the Lead Software Engineer, and SQA.

The other product of the CSC Integration and Test Phase is the updated STD—to be used in the next phase for CSCI-level qualification testing. (Note: In some cases, the qualification testing may be done at other levels than the CSCI-level, but this is not too common.) DOD-STD-2167A shows the test procedures being added to the STD at this time in the development process. If test procedures are required for the qualification tests i.e., have not been tailored out of the contract, then this information is added as Sections 4.X.Y.6 to the STD, where X is for the various "Tests," and Y is for the test cases within each "Test."

The required contents of each STD Test Procedure subsection are shown in Table 15-9, and these contents must be reviewed and evaluated by engineering and SQA before the document is published.

In addition, the Formal Qualification Test (FQT) preparations (Section 3 of the STD) are to be added for each of the "Tests" at this time (Section 3.1 for the first "Test", etc.) The specific contents for these STD sections are shown in Table 15-10.

SQA must also review the document to ensure the customer comments on the

TABLE 15-9   Software Test Description Test Procedure Information

4.X.Y.6   (Test Case Name) Test Procedure—for Test Case Y of Test X

Arranged as a series of sequentially numbered steps. For each step:
- Step Number
- Test Operator actions, and equipment operation required
- Expected Result
- Evaluation criteria (as applicable)
- Actions, in case of a program stop or indicated error
- Data Reduction and analysis procedures

In addition, the scripted time of the desired test operator action, either in absolute test time from T = O, or from some prior event. Also, special data recording instructions may be needed.

TABLE 15-10   Software Test Description Test Preparation Information

3.X.2   (Test Name) Pre-test Procedures—for Test Case X

3.X.2.1   Hardware Preparation
- Specific hardware to be used (by name and number)
- Diagrams to show hardware, interconnecting control, and data paths
- Switch settings and cabling (identify by name and location)
- Precise step-by-step instructions for placing hardware in a 'ready state'

3.X.2.2   Software Preparation (for the CSCI, and any support software)
- Storage medium of CSCI, and step-by-step instructions for loading the CSCI
- Storage medium of any support software, and step-by-step instructions for loading the support software
- When the support software is to be loaded
- Instructions for CSCI and support software initialization (common to more than one test case)

3.X.2.3   Other Pre-test Preparations

earlier STD are adequately resolved. SQA will review the completed draft of the updated STD, and write up any comments via a SQAIR before the document is published. If there are any disagreements or questions on the SQA comments, it is essential to meet promptly, discuss only these SQA comments in question, and resolve these open comments. The normal evaluation criteria of internal consistency and understandability apply. DOD-STD-2167A also requires adequate detail in specifying the test procedures, but the SDP and internal procedures should clarify adequately for whom and for what purposes. Also, the test procedures have to be traceable back to the test cases in the STD. When the last comment is resolved, SQA can sign off for the publication of the document. The document is then printed and distributed, with copies to the customer and others, including SQA. It is important that the customer respond promptly on the STD because it must be used in the next phase, CSCI Testing. There is little alternative but to allow 30 days for customer comments, and then proceed 'as is' if no comments are received by then; however, it is necessary to tell the customer that you must proceed at the end of 30 days to preclude a schedule impact. Also recognize the customer comments may take up to two weeks to analyze and address, so that an STD with problems can delay the CSCI Testing phase. On the other hand, a good STD will tend to prevent schedule impacts and reduce the rework effort.

A significant formal review called the Test Readiness Review (TRR) is held at the end of this phase. The requirements of this review are spelled out in MIL-STD-1521B. Sometimes this review is tailored out of the contract if the development effort is considered 'low risk.' One practical reason for this review was the very large time gap between CDR and the software qualification tests. Apparently, the government was getting too many surprises when they came in to witness the CSCI Acceptance Tests; the TRR was added to 2167 and 2167A as an intermediate checkpoint, i.e., an opportunity for midpoint corrections.

15.11 SQA DURING THE CSCI TEST 'PHASE'

The CSCI Testing phase is the culmination of the main part of the software development effort. The various CSCs that comprise the CSCI are integrated and tested, preferably one or two at a time. When the CSCI is complete, the entire CSCI can be tested as an entity, leading up to the CSCI acceptance testing, or Formal Qualification Testing (FQT). As shown in the folded waterfall diagram in Figure 15-3, each software FQT is based on the CSCI requirements documented in the SRS, and the test cases described in the STD. The tests in the STD are traceable back to the SRS, and are specifically covered in the SRS qualification requirement Sections 4.1 and 4.2. All the requirements to be addressed directly by testing are covered as demonstration items in the SRS. The mapping of the requirements (by ID number) to the test cases (by test case ID) was discussed earlier in subsection 15.8 as an SQA work-product. The advantages of including a verified printout from the test traceability data base in the STD are significant. Every requirement is listed, even ones that were deleted in subsequent changes approved for the SRS (Allocated Baseline). This listing is very useful to SQA, Project Management, and to the customer. It could take the form shown in Table 15-11.

The direct products of the CSCI testing phase are:

* The updated source code for all the CSUs in the CSCI
* The Software Test Reports for the qualification testing, primarily at the CSCI Level

Some of the other products of the CSCI Testing phase shown in DOD-STD-2167A are usually deferred for embedded mission-critical software. The reason for deferring these documents, such as the operation and support documents, and the Software Product Specifications is that the software usually undergoes additional changes as a result of Systems-level Integration and Testing. To reduce expense and the drawdown of project talent, these documents are normally done just once, after the "dust has settled." Usually, these documents are still subject to a few comments from the customer or from an Independent Verification and Validation (IV&V) contractor supporting the customer, but the time and energy

TABLE 15-11   Complete Requirements List For CSCI AA

Requirement ID	Requirement Name	SRS Paragraph	SRS Qualification Method (A, D, I)	STD Test Case ID
AA-R-0001	Change modes, per User Input	3.2.1	D	AA-T-0006
AA-R-0002	Automatic Mode Change	(deleted: ECN 0212)		—
•				
•				
•				
AA-R-0074	Determine Pulse Repetition Interval . . .	3.2.38	D	AA-T-0308

Qualification Methods:
A = Analysis
D = Demonstration (Test)
I = Inspection
Note: All requirements are shown for completeness, arranged by Requirement ID.

to resolve these comments is normally modest with computerized documentation/publishing systems.

The Version Description Document (VDD) is generated according to DI-MCCR-80013 when a new version of the software is established, based on a revised Allocated Baseline in the SRSs. The VDD describes the changes incorporated since the last version, and lists the media and related documentation for this software release. The VDD is delivered to the customer along with the software media. Because the software itself is not considered final until at least the completion of Systems-level test, the VDD is normally not sent at the completion of CSCI Testing, but is deferred.

Incremental CSCI testing, using incremental builds of the CSCI, have been found to be very effective for embedded software. The early builds allow debugging of the test facilities and test procedures. If a separate test team is used for CSCI testing, the early builds allow the team to get started and learn on a smaller problem, and facilitates the initial phases of CSCI testing. The CSCI integration plans included in Table 15-5 are in addition to the items required by DOD-STD-2167A. The Software integration plan covers the integration and testing done in a software environment on a host development machine. Although there may be advantages in going directly to the real hardware and target computer, the new hardware may not be available in time. Therefore, some meaningful testing can be done, and usually must be done to meet schedules, in a software environment with simulations of the real hardware.

The Hardware/Software Integration plan covers the CSCI test and integration done on the real hardware and target microcomputer. The circuit board with the computer and memory and other hardware elements is set-up in a test cage with other interfacing equipment, signal generators to provide certain inputs, and waveform analyzers to look at the outputs.

It is time-consuming to reburn PROMs each time a software change is made, so Test Console Systems to replace the PROMs and read the software from floppies or hard disks are used. Any software changes can be made and saved, at least temporarily during this process. At least weekly, these changes would be submitted to the software change control system, and would be formally released to the software library once approved. SQA is a member of the Software Change Control Board for each project, along with software engineering, software configuration management, and the systems engineering group.

SQA will do 'in-process' audits of the CSCI testing to ensure that engineering test logs are properly kept, test data are correctly recorded, and that the CSCI level SDFs and related data are maintained in correct and current form. SQA will prepare a SQAIR for each spot-check audit, even if there are no problems found.

When the CSCI integration testing is completed, and the CSCI is considered ready for the CSCI acceptance tests, a dry run is scheduled. The SQA operating procedure dealing with Software Test and Validation says simply: "SQA shall witness 'dry runs' of all Qualification and Acceptance Tests involving software."

The entire Software Test Description is followed in the dry run, and any anomalies in the STD are identified. If any anomalies require changes to the STD, some telephone calls with the customer to discuss the STD necessary changes are recommended. The STD changes can be 'red-lined' onto a Master Copy. SQA and engineering must both be assured that the CSCI satisfactorily and fully passes all the test cases in the STD. The dry run test results are stored in the CSCI SDF. SQA keeps a summary of the test results, by test case, and documents the results of the dry run in a SQAIR. If there are any problems, they must be fixed and a new revision of software processed through the Software Change Control Board, etc., and the full qualification test dry run must be re-run with the new software version.

Finally, when the software is 100% ready, the customer can be notified and the acceptance test scheduled. Even if customer representatives are on-site, it may take a few days before everyone can be available for the actual FQT.

Although some tests may take only a day or two, larger tests can take several weeks. For the illustrative CSCI case discussed in sub-section 15.8, 203 requirements of a potential 262 addressable by testing will be tested in the FQT. The mapping of requirements to test cases varies, but if the average is two requirements per test case, about 100 test cases will be run. If each test case requires a different input signal, data recording and reduction, plus an average of one hour of analysis and discussion, then two hours per test case is not unreasonable. For 100 test cases, this means about 200 hours of actual testing work. With at least four hours of introductory briefings, etc. on the front-end, and possibly four to six hours of summary briefings on the last day, the elapsed time totals about 26 normal work days. The customer should be a party to planning so the time commitment is known well in advance. If the test might take more than two weeks, two test teams could be considered. Along with two shift test operations.

In one recent case, two test teams were used, but they alternated the use of the facilities and equipment with only light contention. Work ran from about 7:30 AM to about 7:00 PM, with only 45 minutes for lunch. Each team had two software engineers, one system engineer, one SQA engineer, and one or two customer representatives.

It must be pointed out that not every customer sends a team to witness the FQT of each CSCI. In some cases, the customer will delegate the local government people to witness the testing for them. In other cases, they rely on the SQA group to witness and certify the testing, and validate the test results.

During the acceptance test, SQA keeps a separate test log, and records each event, the time, and anomalies, pass/fail information, and any other key data. This is in addition to the Engineering Test Log. At the end of each day, the test log is carefully reviewed for any gaps, problems, etc. by the test team. However, if a major phase completes, the review will be held at that time. Any additions or clarifications are discussed and entered in the log, along with initials and the time of the changes. When everyone agrees that this log represents a complete and accurate picture of the day's testing, all the parties sign and date each of the pages for that day. Copies of these signed pages are then given to the government representatives and to SQA. The customer seems to appreciate the procedures, and has a feeling of confidence that things are being done professionally. The customer also appreciates that no changes can be made to the test results or any other info in the test logs. SQA then locks up the master log books and other test materials for the night. SQA unlocks the test materials and log the next morning in the government's presence, and everyone takes a few minutes to review yesterday's results before the plan for the current day is established. If any changes have to be made to the STD, a master copy is red-lined and each change is initialed and dated, and changes noted in the test log. The red-lined copy of the STD becomes a new revision, and copies are made after the Test, with copies going to the customer, to SQA, and to software configuration management for release to the software library.

Because of the dry-runs, it is unlikely that there will be any surprises or problems during the FQT. Therefore, there should be no reason to stop and modify the software under test during the formal test. If a 'glitch' is observed, it is usually better to just record the anomaly and continue the testing. This approach gives some time to address any problems off-line, while testing continues. The anomaly is usually isolated in a day or two. In this case, the test will usually be considered by the Customer as a conditional acceptance, conditional on the software being fixed and retested in the next week or two.

At the end of the testing, a final out briefing is held to summarize the customer's view of the testing, and whether or not there were any problems or action items.

The Systems Test Report (STR) is a formal, deliverable document that uses the information from the Software Test Description, the test logs, the recorded test data, and the results summarized in the test "out-briefing." It normally takes several weeks after the completion of the testing to complete the document, and for SQA to review it. The heart of the STR is the Test Results section, section 4.

In the STR, each 'test' has a separate major section (e.g., 4.1, 4.2, etc.). Within each test, the results for each test case within that group is given, Section 4.X.Y. For each Test Case, two subsections are provided:

4.X.Y.1 (Test Case Name) Test Results

- Results for each step
- Description of any anomalies or discrepancies
- References to additional information

4.X.Y.2 (Test Case Name) Deviations from Test Procedure

- Discussion of any deviation from the STD Test Procedure (submitted prior to the Test).
- Rationale for allowing each deviation, and its impact on the validity of the test.

STR Section 5 is interesting in that it asks for an overall CSCI evaluation of the software's capabilities and any deficiencies or limitations, plus recommended improvements (section 5.2) to the software, its operation, or the testing.

An executive summary of the Test is to be provided in section 3.X.1 for each test group. Although not required, the use of a test results summary table is suggested in the STR DID. A sample of such a test results summary table for all the test cases in a test is shown in Table 15-12, based largely on the table in the STR DID.

TABLE 15-12   Sample Test Results Summary Table (for all test cases in a given test)

Test Case ID	Success (P = Pass)	Failure and Step No. (S)	Software Problem Reports	Remarks
•				
•				
•				
BB-T-0032	P			
BB-T-0033		F	SPR-018	Minor Problem
		Step 8		
BB-T-0034		F		
		Step 10	SPR-032	Response Time Problem*
		Step 22	SPR-033	Minor Problem
•				
•				
•				

Note:
CSCI: Time-Domain Pulse Sorter
Test: Single Threats, Light Noise Background
Test Class: Basic Performance
Level: CSCI
*Needs correction for full approval.

The STR DID is not very detailed, and each development organization should prepare a more detailed template for their standard model of an STR. Based on this model, SQA should prepare a detailed checklist to serve as a tool to guide the SQA review of the draft STR before it is published.

SQA should also review the updated code to make sure it meets all the coding standards, including current configuration information. SQA should particularly review the units affected by SPRs.

Similarly, the design documentation, primarily the SDD, should be reviewed by SQA to ensure that it is current for all approved Software Problem Reports that change the design, and therefore change the design documentation. If the contract does not call for a formal delivery of the updated SDD, at least a master copy of the SDD should be red-lined and kept current by the Lead Software Engineer. SQA should review this copy to ensure that all design-related changes have been incorporated.

As each CSCI completes testing, it can be promoted to the System-Level testing library.

15.12 THE ROLE OF SQA DURING SUBSYSTEM AND SYSTEM INTEGRATION AND TEST 'PHASE'

For embedded Mission-critical software, the testing does not end with the CSCI-level testing, even though this testing is a FQT of each CSCI. The software is embedded in a hardware system, and the total entity is a new design, and must work together to meet higher-level system specifications. Normally, there are between one to three levels of system integration and test, depending on the size and complexity of the system. For example, there could be testing at the Line Replaceable Unit (LRU) Level, then several LRUs could be integrated into a subsystem, and finally, several subsystems would be integrated to make up the entire "flyable" System.

In each level of testing, problems will be noticed, some of them traceable to the software. In other cases, the cause of the problem may not be in the software, but the solution will be to change the software to resolve the problem. SQA will be concerned with the software aspects of the System Testing. Anomalies or problems tracked to the software must be assigned an SPR number. Software changes approved by the Software Change Control Board will be cut into the software CSCI run-load files, as soon as possible. Each new software version/revision must identify the SPRs that are being incorporated in the new software release. At the various system levels of testing, the released software is normally burned into some type of PROM, so there are some additional steps that SQA must verify, basically, that the firmware is correct.

Hopefully, the number of software changes per week will not be too great. Where possible, new compilations will be made and a new build made with the revised software, using the project's link editor tools. It is a good idea to try to make a new build each week or two, so that the changes do not accumulate. This way, if there are any problems encountered during regression testing, the number of changes are somewhat limited, and the source of the problem is bounded to just the few modified units and their interfaces.

During system testing it may be necessary to temporarily patch the run-load with a temporary fix, and retest to see if the patch really solves the problem. If it does, at least system testing can proceed in the meantime. Software engineering can be working in parallel on the corresponding change to the source code. The Software engineering practices usually have guidelines on the maximum number and size of patches. SQA should track the maximum amount of memory used for patches and the number of patches, and help ensure that a new source code build will be used before the limits are exceeded. The original Navy Software Standard, MIL-STD-1679, limited the number of patches to one half a percent of the total Software Memory, but this was relaxed in MIL-STD-1679A, and also is not explicitly covered in DOD-STD-2167A. Therefore, the organization's internal standard practices will have to set the groundrules for patches. Some standard practices also limit the maximum size of a single patch to some reasonable value, e.g., 50 words.

The software products of the System Integration and Test Phase are:

- The updated source code
- The updated design documentation, as discussed in the prior subsection.

In addition, any changes to the software after the CSCI FQTs must be carefully documented, and the tests for those changes shall be documented as addenda to the STD. The tests must be witnessed and certified by SQA, and documented in a SQAIR, and addenda to the appropriate STRs prepared. The test results shall be available within the CSCI SDFs. These changes will have to be addressed later in the Software Functional Configuration Audit (FCA) and Physical Configuration Audit (PCA).

The system level acceptance test is supported by SQA for the software-related items. SQA must certify the correct version and revision of each CSCI under test, and the related firmware contents and labeling. SQA will ensure that any software anomalies are documented and addressed, and that no unauthorized changes are made to the software.

After the system test is completed, the various operation and support documents, the Version Description Document, and the Software Product Spec can be finalized, reviewed by SQA, and then shipped to the customer for review and approval.

The FCA and PCA are normally held after the system-level tests are completed. However, these audits are sometimes delayed until completion of DT/OT, Development Test/Operational Test. The FCA and PCA are discussed in a later subsection.

15.13 FUNCTIONAL AND PHYSICAL CONFIGURATION AUDITS FOR SOFTWARE

The Functional Configuration Audit (FCA) and Physical Configuration Audit (PCA) are the two final audits held for each Configuration Item, before going into Production. These audits are described in MIL-STD-1521B, Appendices G and H.

Functional Configuration Audit

For software, the FCA is used to determine and verify that the CSCI actually meets the requirements in the SRS and IRS. This is done primarily by reviewing the test results in the STR(s) for all the CSCI's requirements. In addition, the completed operation and support documents are reviewed to ensure that they are adequate to support the system once it is deployed. These user documents are:

- Computer System Operator's Manual (CSOM)
- Software User's Manual (SUM)
- Software Programmer's Manual (SPM)
- Firmware Support Manual (FSM)

To be able to conduct the FCA, the software requirements (SRS and IRS) must have been previously approved and authenticated for the correct version. These requirements form the Allocated Baseline for each CSCI. The STR for each CSCI's qualification testing should also have been made available for customer review prior to the FCA. The Software Product Specification (SPS), which describes the as-built CSCI that completed the FQT, is also needed by the customer prior to the FCA. In the 'real world,' the SPS may not be available much ahead of the FCA.

All of the CSCIs for the embedded software should be scheduled for one FCA. The contractor must notify the customer of the FCA agenda, including which items are to be covered, and the following specifics for each CSCI:

- Nomenclature of the CSCI
- Specification Number(s) of SRS and IRS
- Configuration Item Number and ID for the exact Version/Revision of software to be audited
- A complete list of deviations and waivers and their status
- Status of any Software Test Tools used in the CSCI qualification testing.

It is a good idea to also indicate the document numbers and status of the STRs and SPSs for each CSCI.

Because of the importance of the FCA—basic acceptance of the software for production and deployment, or not—internal planning meetings and an abbreviated dry run by the contractor is recommended. SQA must ensure that all items needed for the formal audit are identified and made ready for the FCA. These items include:

- The SRS for each CSCI
- The IRS
- The SPS* (Software Product Specification) for each CSCI
- The Software Test Plan for each CSCI
- The Software Test Description for each CSCI
- The Software Test Report for each CSCI

---

*The SPS includes the updated Software Design Document and the associated code listings.

- A list of all approved ECPs
- Approved minutes of the Software Preliminary Design Review
- Approved minutes of the Software Critical Design Review
- Briefing materials on the CSCI requirements and design
- Briefing materials on the CSCI testing, and the test results.

SQA, software engineering, software configuration management, and the Project Management Office are the principal parties in the FCA planning and preparation. SQA must verify that all the necessary information is, indeed, available and it is the correct version.

The FCA dry run is an internal walk-through of all the activities that must be done well before the formal FCA. These activities include:

- Briefings on each CSCI, and the testing
- If any requirements were not met, they must be discussed, along with proposed solutions
- Discussion of ECPs (Engineering Change Proposals) incorporated and test results
- Highlights of the test results, both problem areas and successful accomplishments
- Audits of the Software Test Plans, down to the Test Descriptions/Procedures, and the Software Test Reports, for consistency and traceability, and versus the actual recorded test data and test log data. Also, the completeness and accuracy of the actual test data and test logs must be checked.
- Audits of all approved ECPs, to ensure they are incorporated correctly and completely.
- Consistency of all the technical documents in the document set
- Audit of the PDR and CDR minutes, to ensure that all findings and action items have been fully incorporated.
- Audit of the interface testing against the IRS
- Audit of the final memory and storage allocation versus the requirements and margins for delivery time; also, the actual processing timing (including processor loading, path lengths, . . .) and input/output port loadings versus requirements and margins.
- Audit of the as-built data base characteristics versus requirements and design
- Adequacy of human interfaces, workloads, and human factors
- Adequacy of the operation and support documents
- Audits of the quality program records for those requirements qualified by analysis or inspection.
- Other tasks, as determined by the FCA planning group.

The results of the dry run should be documented, and any deficiencies noted and action items assigned to specific individuals with a due date. SQA should document the dry run results in an SQAIR, and track all the action items, and highlight the items due each week and any overdue items.

When all action items are resolved, then the real FCA can be held. For the real FCA with the customer, the activities are the same as noted above. Someone on the contractor's FCA team must be the recorder, and take careful minutes each day. A useful idea is to publish a draft of the FCA minutes each day for everyone to review and to ensure good sharing of information. If there are any problems, they can be addressed promptly that day, or early the next morning, to keep things moving ahead smoothly.

The final result of the FCA is that each CSCI is either accepted 'as is,' or some items must be fixed before the CSCI can be accepted. In some cases, non-critical deficiencies can be mapped into a future update, because the initial capability is considered adequate for now. These points all have to be discussed at the end of the FCA, and the customer has the final decision. There should be a good understanding of the final results, and of the customer's feelings about acceptance (or not) for each CSCI.

The contractor's FCA team puts together the formal minutes of the FCA, and submits them to the customer for approval. A draft should be put together and coordinated for all the days, with the possible exception of the last day, for informal review on the last day. The customer's contracting agency reviews the formal minutes, may ask for additional data, and ultimately determines one of three possible outcomes for each CSCI:

- Approval
- Contingent Approval—not approved until satisfactory completion of the indicated action items.
- Disapproval—the FCA was not adequate.

With the timely formation of an internal FCA team and some reasonable planning and preparation, the outcome should be either a or b, above. The dry run will tend to ensure that the results are full approval, if the dry run discrepancies are addressed seriously. SQA should act as a surrogate customer, and play the customer's role during the FCA dry run. These efforts are not free, but they do help make for a successful FCA and will enhance the reputation and success of your company with the customer, which will be considered for future business.

If sufficient test data is not available at the FCA, it is necessary to hold a separate review later, called a Formal Qualification Review (FQR), usually after both the FCA and PCA. However, the practice seems to be to have a single combined FCA, which obviates a separate FQR just to review the test results against the requirements.

Physical Configuration Audit (PCA)

The PCA for software is the audit and formal examination of the actual as-built software product versus the design documentation and user/support manuals. The PCA is done after the FCA.

The key items for a Software PCA include the following:

- The Software Product Specification (SPS) for each CSCI. The SPS includes the updated Software Design Document and the comparable final source code listings.

- The Version Description Document.
- The software operation and support manuals (Computer System Operator's Manual, Software User's Manual, Software Programmer's Manual, and the Firmware Support Manual).
- The SRS for each CSCI.
- The IRS.
- FCA minutes for each CSCI.
- Findings/status of the quality assurance program for the software.
- The coding standards used for the project.

The planning and preparation for the PCA should be done by a designated PCA team, including representatives from software engineering, SQA, and software CM. The agenda has to be prepared and coordinated with the customer. SQA must verify that all the necessary materials have been collected and organized in advance.

A dry-run PCA should be held with SQA acting as the surrogate customer. All action items from the dry-run must be documented, resolved and verified before the formal PCA with the customer.

The PCA itself consists of a series of steps:

1. Review the Software Products Specification (SPS) components for format, correctness, completeness, and compatibility.
2. Review the FCA minutes for any discrepancies, and the corresponding actions that must be taken.
3. Review the design descriptions in the SPS for proper entries, symbols, labels, tags, references, and data descriptions.
4. Compare the Top-Level software component design descriptions with its Lower-Level software components for consistency.
5. Compare the Lower-Level component design description with the actual software code listings for consistency, accuracy, and completeness.
6. Check the various user manuals for completeness, consistency, and correctness with the final version of code.
7. Examine the CSCI delivery media for conformance with SRS Section 5-Preparation for Delivery, e.g., media characteristics and format, labeling, packaging, classification marking, etc.
8. Review the annotated listings for compliance with the approved coding standards for the contract.

In preparing for the PCA, SQA should take pains to ensure that all recently approved STRs have been fully and consistently included in both the code and the documentation set. Further, SQA should verify that these code changes meet all the coding standards.

After completion of the PCA, the contractor must submit copies of the formal minutes, and the attachments, to the customer for review and the ultimate decision. The customer then either accepts, or rejects the PCA for each CSCI.

When both the FCA and PCA are approved for a given CSCI, that CSCI is then accepted for production and deployment. This approval defines the Product Baseline for production. SQA can play a significant role in the planning, preparation and actual conduct of the Software PCA, and contribute to the success of the PCA. A rejection of one or more CSCIs is costly to resolve, and impacts the deployment schedule.

Subsequent changes to the Product Baseline are possible, through Engineering Change Proposals (ECPs). Any such changes will ultimately create a new set of Baselines (Functional, Allocated, and Product) for that ECP, starting with a given effectivity point (e.g., effective Serial Number 122 and subsequent). Units already in the field may have to be retrofitted with the software change. New Baselines (with new requirements) will normally have mini-FCAs and mini-PCAs to ensure they are correct and complete before deployment.

15.14 DEVELOPMENT AND OPERATIONAL TESTING (THE 'REAL WORLD')

For most embedded, real-time systems, extensive testing is done outside the development laboratory after the System Acceptance Test. The purpose is to test the systems extensively in realistic environments, which usually are not practical in the contractor's development laboratory. These test sites are usually at government installations, such as test ranges or extensive simulation facilities.

The field test team that supports the testing normally consists of several systems engineers and a few software engineers. Usually there is not an on-site SQA or any software configuration management (SCM) person. The testing may be at one site for a few weeks, and then may move to another test site for additional testing, sometimes with a week or two gap in between.

The test schedule for each test flight must be met, if at all possible. For testing systems for aircraft, the flight schedule may, for example, call for flights every Monday, Wednesday, and Friday, starting about 7:00 AM or so. The software must be ready to go, which can mean fixing a problem that was observed on the last test, testing it on a test bench system of some sort, and then re-burning PROMs with the change and installing them on the Board, and re-installing the 'black box' back into the aircraft and re-testing the system. The total time to do this, from touchdown of one test to takeoff for the next test, is usually a little under 48 hours.

The activity starts, as you might expect, with a debriefing on the completed test based on observations, test logs, and 'QUICK-LOOK' data reduction. Problems, if any, are highlighted. A more detailed analysis, supported by more thorough data reduction, then occurs to examine all relevant parts of the test. A master list of any problems and anomolies from the test is assembled for control and tracking purposes. This process may only take a few hours, or could run 6 to 8 hours, depending on the complexity of the test, and the amount of analysis required to determine what really happened and where are the problems.

Problems that potentially are due to software are assigned to one of the software engineers as the principal investigator. A Software Problem Report number is assigned at this point, and an SPR is created. The SW engineer must try to repeat the error, based on similar inputs and other conditions. Analysis of the recorded data played over the logic of the software may also reveal what the software really does, given this set of inputs. If the error can be duplicated and confirmed, then it must be addressed further.* There is no way to estimate how long it will take to find the problems; some problems take only an hour or two; but some take days.

The problem, once found, must still be fixed. Usually this takes some careful design and desk-checking, because there isn't time to do it twice. It is usually a good idea to bounce the proposed solution off a second person as a double-check.

After the proposed change has been checked, then the change to the code is usually done as a binary patch to the run-load file for the CSCI. A patch is used because there isn't time to compile and re-link. Very careful records of the patches must be kept in a Field Test Patch Log. Each patch is assigned a number in the Patch Log, consistent with the Software Engineering Standard Practices, and the SPR number is referenced. The exact changes (both the 'FROM' and the 'TO') and the address for each WORD changed is noted. The patch could be a simple change in-place to a few consecutive instructions or to a single data value, or it may involve putting in a JUMP to a previously unused address where a significant number of new instructions can be added, followed by a JUMP, usually back to next instruction in the original program. These patch logs must be verified, and signed by both the originator and the on-site reviewer. Copies of the patch log pages must be mailed or faxed back to software engineering and to SQA and software CM at least once a week for review. Each set of new patches creates a new run load file, which receives a new file number. Software CM back at the lab keeps track of all the patches assigned to each run-load file, and of the various revisions and dates to the run-load files for each CSCI. For a sizeable field test, a hundred or so patches may be made, a few of which may later get removed or replaced by other patches. If there are three flights a week for 8 weeks, approximately 24 versions of the set of run-load files will probably be needed. However, not every CSCI will change for each flight, and some CSCIs will not change very often over the test period. Normally, one or two CSCIs will receive more changes than the others. Also, CSCIs that contain data elements that are 'tuneable' like a software trimpot will receive tuning changes to try to optimize thresholds, limits, timing values, weighting factors, etc.

Back at the lab, SQA should review the batch of new patch log pages, first to ensure no pages are missing (numbered and dated pages are highly recommended), and secondly, to ensure that the patch log contents are complete and consistent. If there is a problem, SQA should get on the phone immediately and try to correct the matter. Software engineering in the lab can validate that the change will do what it is supposed to do, but it's not always possible to predict if the patch will solve the problem, and also not create new problems. After the next flight test where that test case is re-run with the new patch, it is possible to tell if the patch worked. Patches that seem to fully solve a problem get a big checkmark, and may

---

*If the error cannot be duplicated, the SPR is closed out as a "CND" ('Can Not' Duplicate).

be re-sourced. Each verified patch is assigned to a programmer back at the lab to re-source, referencing the original SPR number. To provide support from the Lab, each CSCI is assigned to a software engineer such that the person has responsibility for about 10,000 to 15,000 executable source lines. Some CSCIs are less than 10,000 source lines, while others are greater than 50,000 source lines and will need to be split among several support people.

If the number of patches in the field grows so large that patches are on top of patches, etc., the patched software can be difficult to maintain, and at some point will be virtually impossible to maintain. At this point, it is necessary to ship a new, clean re-sourced load file to the site.

The new source run-load file will first have to be tested at the lab, and the testing shall be witnessed and certified by SQA. Modifying the source code does introduce some risks; therefore, regression testing should be done using a significant subset of the test cases for each CSCI, plus any test cases that are specific to the changes. A practical problem is obtaining time on the system to do regression testing at the system level; the modified CSCIs must work with the other hardware and software elements in the system. Usually, the system assets are very scarce, and test time is very hard to get. The problem is one of allocating time to a less-than-optimal number of test cases to get the most value of the limited test time available. This is a classic tradeoff of time versus risk; the more test time available, the lower will be the risk. When the testing is completed, and the revised source code is formally released, the Software Design Document also has to be updated, and sometimes the STD.

It is necessary for SQA to track the verified patches and their related SPRs. Each time a new software release of source code is prepared using a Software Engineering Release Notice (SERN), or equivalent, the release must be checked to make sure all the necessary patches have been included. Further, no unapproved patches should be included in the software release. The release is normally handled at the CSCI level at this stage. Each SERN lists the patch numbers and related SPR numbers that have been incorporated to advance the CSCI to the next configuration level. In a few cases, an SPR may be included but there was no field patch related to it. SQA will ensure that all the differences between the prior revision's source files and the new revision's source files are for approved SPRs, and that all approved SPRs are fully implemented.

A coding convention that highlights the changed code for an SPR with an initial comment line and a final comment line can be very helpful when reviewing the source code file or the corresponding source listing. These comment lines could look like the following:

"****** SPR #288 START ******

at the front of the change, and a trailing comment line at the end of the change, such as:

"****** SPR #288 END ******

and would be useful for highlighting the modified source code for each SPR. Some software engineering standards also require the SPR numbers for the current

TABLE 15-13   System-Wide Configuration of Software CSCIs to be Released to Production

Subsystem	CSCI	Version/Revision	SERN* and Release Date
Alpha	AA	03.07	288 - 8/14/91
	BB	03.03	279 - 8/09/91
	CC	02.04	201 - 6/05/91
	DD	02.05	218 - 7/01/91
Gamma	SA	03.24	289 - 8/14/91
	SB	03.06	246 - 7/17/91
	SC	03.04	247 - 7/17/91
Omega	WB	04.08	271 - 8/02/91
	WK	03.34	290 - 8/14/91
	WW	03.03	231 - 7/08/91
	WZ	03.08	248 - 7/17/91

*SERN = Software Engineering Release number for the Project

changes to be included as part of the configuration information in the prologue for the affected CSUs.

After all the field testing is finished, there will still need to be a final clean-up of the last patches. These patches must be cut into source code, re-compiled and re-linked, and a final set of software and system tests run to make sure the clean source code works properly. If the software is mature, the last group of patches shouldn't be too large (perhaps under ten or so), due to a low defect discovery rate with the mature code. In this sense, 'mature' means that virtually all of the latent defects have been found and fixed, and discovery of any of the few remaining defects will be relatively rare events. This is analogous to saying that the 'mean time between failures' is quite large, and the Software Reliability has grown to a respectable value which can be independently estimated using various reliability models.[11] The result is software that is sufficiently mature and reliable to deploy, and meets the performance requirements under a wide variety of realistic conditions (including stress and error tests). In some ways, Operational Testing is equivalent to Beta testing at a customer site in the commercial world.

If a significant number of DT or OT changes have occurred since the FCA/PCA 'audits', a 'mini' FCA and a 'mini' PCA should be held to cover these additional changes that are now in the Product Baseline. These versions of the CSCIs would be the configuration of the software released to production; an illustrative sample of the CSCIs for a system is shown in Table 15-13. This release would be for Production Lot I, and SQA should review the release to ensure the correct software versions. A new release would be used for LOT II, and the software VERSIONS/REVISIONS might be different for Lot II, at least for some of the CSCIs.

References

1. Boehm, B., "A Spiral Model of Software Development and Enhancement," *ACM SIGSOFT,* Vol. 11, August 1986, pp. 14-24.
2. Dunn, R. H., and Ullman, R. S., *Quality Assurance for Computer Software,* McGraw-Hill Book Co., New York, 1982, p. 159.

3. Bowen, T. P., Wigle, G. B., Tsai, J. T., Specification of Software Quality Attributes, Boeing Aerospace Company, RADC-TR-85-37 (Volume I), February 1985.

4. Heil, J. H., "Ensuring Good Test Plans and Test Descriptions," Automating Software Test & Evaluation Conference, Educational Foundation—Data Processing Management Association, Washington, D.C., May 1991.

5. Beitzer, B., "Bug Taxonomy and Statistics," Appendix, *Software Testing Techniques,* second edition, 1990, Van Nostrand Reinhold, New York.

6. Jones, T. C., Technical Report: Program Quality and Programmer Productivity, TR 02.764, IBM General Products Division, January 1977.

7. Fagan, M. E., "Design and Code Inspections to Reduce Errors in Program Development," *IBM Systems Journal,* Vol. 15, No. 3, 1976, pp. 182-211.

8. McCabe, T., "A Complexity Measure," *IEEE Transactions on Software Engineering,* Vol. SE-2, No. 4, December 1976, pp. 308-320.

9. Mills, H., "Engineering Discipline for Software Procurement," *Proceedings of NSIA QRAC Fall Joint Conference on Software Quality,* 30 Sept.-2 Oct. 1987, p. 88, NSIA, Washington, D.C., 1987.

10. Dunn, R. H., Ullman, R. S., *Quality Assurance for Computer Software,* pp. 166-168, McGraw-Hill, New York, 1982.

11. Heil, J. H., Gorenflo, F. M., Cannon, J., and Polizzano, J., "The Use of Software Reliability to Measure Software Quality Improvement," *Proceedings of NSIA QRAC Sixth Annual Software Quality and Productivity Conferences,* April 17-19, 1990, NSIA, Washington, D.C., 1990.

General References

DOD Documents

MIL-STD-1521B, Technical Reviews and Audits for Systems, Equipments and Computer Software, Dept. of Defense, Washington, D.C., June 4, 1985.

DOD-STD-2167A, Defense System Software Development, Dept. of Defense, Washington, D.C., February 29, 1988.

DOD-STD-2168, Defense System Software Quality Program, Dept. of Defense, Washington, D.C., April 29, 1988.

DIDS: DI-MCCR-80030A, Software Development Plan, DOD, Washington, D.C., February 29, 1988.

DI-QCIC-80572, Software Quality Program Plan, DOD, Washington, D.C., April 29, 1988.

Mission-Critical Computer Resources Software Support—Military Handbook MIL-HDBK-347, Dept. of Defense, May 1990.

IEEE Documents

IEEE Standard for Software Quality Plans, ANSI/IEEE Standard 730.1-1989, October 1989.

IEEE Standard Glossary of Software Engineering Terminology, IEEE Standard 729-1983, February 1983.

Other General References

Bersoff, E., "Elements of Software Configuration Management," *IEEE Trans, Software Engineering,* Vol. SE-10, January 1984.

Bersoff, E., Henderson, V., Siegal, S., "Software Configuration Management: A Tutorial," *IEEE Computer Society Magazine,* Vol. 12, No. 1, January 1979.

Boehm, B., *Software Engineering Economics,* Prentice-Hall, Englewood Cliffs, NJ, 1981.

Boehm, B. et al, "A Software Development Environment for Improving Productivity," *Computer,* June 1984, pp. 30-44.

Cooling, J. E., *Software Design for Real-Time Systems,* Chapman and Hall, London and New York, 1991.

Deutsch, M., *Software Verification and Validation: Realistic Project Approaches,* Prentice-Hall, Englewood Cliffs, N.J., 1982.

Dunn, R. H., *Software Defect Removal,* McGraw-Hill Book Co., New York, 1984.

Dunn, R. H., *Software Quality — Concepts and Plans,* Prentice-Hall, Englewood Cliffs, N.J., 1990.

Endres, A., "An Analysis of Errors and their Causes in System Programs," 1975 International Conference on Reliable Software, IEEE Cat. No. 75CH 0840-7CSR, pp. 327-336.

Gannon, C., "Error Detection Using Path Testing and Static Analysis," *Computer,* IEEE Computer Society Magazine, Vol. 12, No. 8, August 1979, pp 26-31.

Halstead, M., *Elements of Software Science,* Elsevier-North Holland, Inc., New York, 1977.

Humphrey, W. S., *Managing the Software Process,* Addison-Wesley Publishing Co., New York, 1989.

Kafura, D., and Reddy, G., "The Use of Software Complexity Metrics in Software Engineering," *IEEE Trans. Software Engineering,* Vol. SE-13, March 1987, pp. 335-343.

Lipow, M., and Thayer, T. A., "Prediction of Software Failures," *Proceedings 1977 Annual Reliability and Maintainability Symposium,* IEEE Cat. No. 77CH 1161-9RQC, pp. 489-494.

Meyers, W., "An Assessment of the Competitiveness of the United States Software Industry," *Computer,* March 1985, pp. 81-92.

Musa, J., "SOFTWARE ENGINEERING: The Future of a Profession," *IEEE Software,* January 1985, pp. 55-62.

Petschenik, "Practical Priorities in System Testing," *IEEE Software,* Vol. 2, September 1985, pp. 18-23.

Walston, C. E., and Felix, C. P., "A Method of Programming Measurement and Estimation," *IBM Systems Journal,* Vol. 16, 1977, pp. 54-73.

Wegner, P., "Varieties of Reusability," *Proceedings — Workshop on Reusability in Programming,* Newport, R.I., September 1983, pp. 30-45.

16

Practical Applications of Software Quality Assurance for Commercial Software

Lawrence E. Niech

Automatic Data Processing (ADP)

16.1 INTRODUCTION—SQA PRINCIPLES APPLIED

Previous chapters of this book discussed specific techniques, methodologies and philosophies which contribute to a successful Software Quality Assurance (SQA) program. The next step is to address the practical application of these topics.

The following chapter provides insight through experiences and lessons learned regarding how to successfully perform the SQA function in a commercial development environment. Specific issues which are addressed include: quality's role in the commercial software sector, SQA program philosophies, software testing within the quality framework and the similarities and differences between mission-critical and commercial software.

16.2 COMMERCIAL SOFTWARE DEFINED

The category of commercial software immediately excludes software which is produced for a government agency (e.g., NASA, DOD, FAA) where the software development process is subject to strictly enforced standards and contractual requirements. Typically, this class of software is known as mission-critical software (although an argument can be made that some commercial software should also be considered mission-critical).

Commercial software includes software produced in the non-government sector, i.e., not subject to government standards, targeted for a competitive consumer market and intended for multiple distribution as opposed to "one of a kind" solutions. Examples of commercial software or products containing commercial software include:

- Payroll/Personnel Systems (paychecks, taxes)
- Telecommunications Systems (voice mail, switches)
- Consumer Applications (games, tax filing, organizers)
- Business/Management Software (finances, spread sheets)
- Industrial Systems (robots, queuing devices)
- Software Development Aids (testers, code generators, compilers)

16.3 SOFTWARE QUALITY'S ROLE IN THE COMMERCIAL SECTOR

One philosophy is to view any Quality Assurance Program, whether software or hardware, as the last line of "quality defense" between a company and its customers. That is, the Quality Assurance Program should encompass the necessary methodologies and processes to ensure product quality prior to shipment. Essentially, the quality program is viewed as providing the last opportunity to decide a product's market worthiness in terms of a company's reputation and future.

Businesses and corporations are created to produce a product which fills a consumer's need while generating a profit. The overall business objective is to identify the areas of greatest need in order to maximize a profit. Since the upper bound of a commercial company's profits are not regulated (unlike military contractors) the potential for success, measured in dollars, is unlimited.

Although it is in the best interest of a business to produce quality software, quality programs in the commercial sector are strictly voluntary; again, unlike the military contracting segment. Consequently, companies which are considering a quality process must believe two things:

1. the approach to quality will not erode expected profits
2. the approach to quality will in fact provide a substantial return on investment (ROI)

Short of running two prototype projects in parallel, one with a quality program, the other without, it is usually quite difficult to provide quantitative evidence to justify a quality process prior to its implementation in terms of the two above criteria. Accordingly, organizations typically initiate a formal quality process only after they have felt the aftershocks of a poor or absent quality program. Thus, many companies tend to see quality as a defensive mechanism rather than an offensive weapon.

If viewed from the defensive prospective, there are several measurable advantages to implementing an effective formal quality program which addresses software.

Similar to a quality program for hardware, if the SQA program is ineffective, the results could be disastrous:

- slippage in project schedules/deliveries
- loss of revenue
- damage to company image
- loss of future business
- loss of market leadership

The philosophy outlined above has been a prime reason for many commercial organizations initiating or enhancing SQA Programs.

Once the commitment has been made to implement an SQA Program, the scope and ground-rules of the process must be established. An effective approach to planning, implementing and enhancing any SQA program involves providing services which are:

- incorporated into each phase of the software product life cycle
- consistent with software industry standard techniques
- planned, structured and documented
- automated and repeatable
- measurable

16.4 COMMERCIAL vs. MISSION-CRITICAL SQA PROGRAMS—AN OVERVIEW

Why is it important to address Mission-critical SQA in a chapter on commercial SQA? Well, for one thing, the discipline of SQA has its beginnings deeply rooted in the Mission-critical, i.e., military/government, software development segment. The SQA philosophy encompasses everything from management style and standards to development/quality techniques and processes. Because government contractors' early attempts at software development and management were lacking, the military decided to define and mandate an approach which they believed would lead to a quality software product. As software became more prevalent in military applications, the typical characteristics of a software intensive contract were: the product was delivered well beyond the scheduled completion date, total actual costs exceeded estimated costs and maintenance was a nightmare. Some of the factors contributing to these problems included poor project control methodologies and undefined software development processes. Thus, government standards and specifications covering everything from the software development process and configuration management to specification practices and quality assurance programs were born.[1]

Some software professionals contend that the commercial sector is lucky that it does not have to contend with the document-driven approach and regulations imposed by the government on software developers. Some insist that government standards negatively impact quality. The argument is that the government's mandated methodologies and overwhelming documentation requirements are cost drivers and thus other product development areas are affected by the need to scrimp and save on overall product cost. However, if the intent of the various government standards and methodologies are understood, they can be invaluable in any SQA Program.

Which brings us to the second reason for considering military SQA programs. Commercial SQA programs can benefit from reviewing, tailoring and implementing many of the processes defined in the government software standards and specifications. Later in the chapter a summary of which SQA techniques can be successfully transferred from the military to the commercial environment will be outlined. Also, the fundamental differences that exist between SQA programs in commercial companies and SQA programs in military contractors are examined.

16.5 SQA PROGRAM IMPLEMENTATION PHILOSOPHY

The term software quality assurance (SQA) often conjures up a vision of a department of people. The military sector traditionally (i.e., pre DOD-STD-2167/DOD-STD-2168) has forced the responsibility for quality upon a single organization. The commercial sector, unlike the military software environment, has always been free to define the organizations, roles, responsibilities, techniques, etc. necessary to achieve a quality software product.

However, in order to successfully produce quality software, the SQA task must be considered in broader terms.

> *Example 1:* The software standard for quality prior to DOD-STD-2168 (Software Quality Evaluations) was MIL-S-52779A (SQA Program Requirements). As a result of the independence requirement stated in MIL-S-52779A, most software quality organizations sprang up within the Quality/Product Assurance Department. Consequently, the quality responsibility was perceived to rest within the Quality Department and the Software Engineering Department only had to convince the software quality auditor that all was well.
>
> *Example 2:* An actual incident at a major defense contractor's manufacturing facility further illustrates how quality is sometimes perceived to be owned by one organization. The contractor, shut down due to poor quality, formed an investigative team to determine the causes of their problems. The team's finding was "that 'quality' was centered in a large quality assurance organization that inspected parts after they were built. Accordingly, no one on the production line felt responsible for quality; everyone felt it was quality assurance's job."[2]

Remember, commercial companies want to maximize product sales and hopefully the resulting profit. Inevitably, commercial organizations are going to exercise their freedom to define the proper mix of project roles and responsibilities in order to reduce cost, improve quality and ultimately maximize profit. More often than not, companies discover that the best quality role/responsibility mixture can be derived from the often repeated statement: "quality is everyone's business."

The sharing of the responsibility for quality is also the cornerstone of the Total Quality Management (TQM) philosophy. The TQM approach towards software quality is a common key attribute in the commercial market. Particularly since the average commercial software shop cannot afford to fund a full time quality organization to police quality, therefore employees find themselves wearing many "hats" and tasked with many diverse responsibilities. Sharing responsibility also suggests that commercial organizations are more apt to practice "true" SQA. This concept is further illustrated in the three SQA characteristic statements outlined below.

Software Quality Assurance is:[3]

- the approach which assures the effectiveness of a software quality program; it does not assure the quality of software
- an integral part of all software development, test and maintenance activities
- the set of activities that make up the software quality program

These characteristics imply that SQA is not meant to be a department; instead it must be a program/team approach involving various software professionals, each with his or her own area of expertise. In short, SQA is a managed set of activities utilized to achieve a quality software product. Thus, companies who have developed processes to improve software quality within the commercial market have probably developed "true" SQA *programs* without even realizing it. That is, the SQA concept was developed from a project team approach and not via defined organizational responsibilities.

16.6 TESTING WITHIN THE SOFTWARE QUALITY FRAMEWORK

A common trait among commercial software organizations is that software testing is assigned to organizations outside and independent of the software development group. It is quite common in the commercial environment that software testing is assigned to the Quality department. Regardless of the name of the organization which performs software testing, assigning responsibility for product validation to a group other than the developers themselves is a sound philosophy. "The use of organizationally independent testers is often thought, correctly to be a technique for reducing the risk of delivering software of poor quality."[4] Additionally, " . . . test groups represent the attitude of the potential users of the software. Handing the system—or in the case of integration testing, its parts—to another organization is tantamount to bridging the gap from chiefly technical concerns to those of the marketplace or the user community."[5]

As noted, the objectives of software testing can vary greatly. Usually the objectives vary with the level of testing that is being performed or the maturity of the software, i.e., how much of the software or system is available. For example, the typical levels or types of tests performed on commercial software include:

- unit
- software integration
- hardware/software integration
- functional
- system
- acceptance
- performance
- stress
- regression
- usability

Commercial tests must also consider various user environmental concerns. Consequently, the role of *diverse* testing to measure and improve product quality plays a vital role in an effective commercial SQA program. Examples of situations which involve environmental or installation diversity concerns include:

- multiple available versions of software operating systems
- multiple available versions of network operating systems
- multiple types of available network topologies
- multiple hardware product types of personal computers, modems, printers, etc.

16.7 IMPLEMENTING THE COMMERCIAL SQA PROGRAM: THE KEYS TO SUCCESS

A General Framework

Product Life Cycles
If the implementation of any software quality process is to have a chance of succeeding it must be preceded by changes in organizational cultures, management styles and most especially, product development philosophies.

A significant change in development philosophy would include adopting a well-defined software product life cycle (PLC) approach to producing a software product. The implementation of a software PLC aids the software quality effort because it allows the SQA program to utilize "review hooks" or "assessment windows" during the software production process in order to assess the progress and quality of the product under development. These "hooks" are most effective when mapped upon the software life cycle model. While there are many definitions of software PLCs and its overlapping "partner"—the waterfall model, a typical software PLC may include the phases and activities as depicted in Figure 16-1.[6] The review milestones denoted by the "diamonds" in Figure 16-1 are typical examples of "review hooks" or "assessment windows."

The orderly development process which is promoted by the PLC approach also complements the SQA Program's prime activity—verification and validation (V&V). Verification is the process of determining whether or not the product at a given phase of the PLC fulfills the requirements established during the previous phase. Examples of verification activities in Figure 16-1 include ensuring that:

- the top-level software design is traceable back to the software requirements
- the detailed software design is traceable back to the top-level software design

Validation is the process of evaluating software at the end of the software development cycle to ensure compliance with the software requirements. Examples of validation activities denoted by the dotted vertical lines in Figure 16-1 include performing:

- unit testing to ensure that all detailed design requirements are met
- software qualification testing to ensure that all software product requirements are met

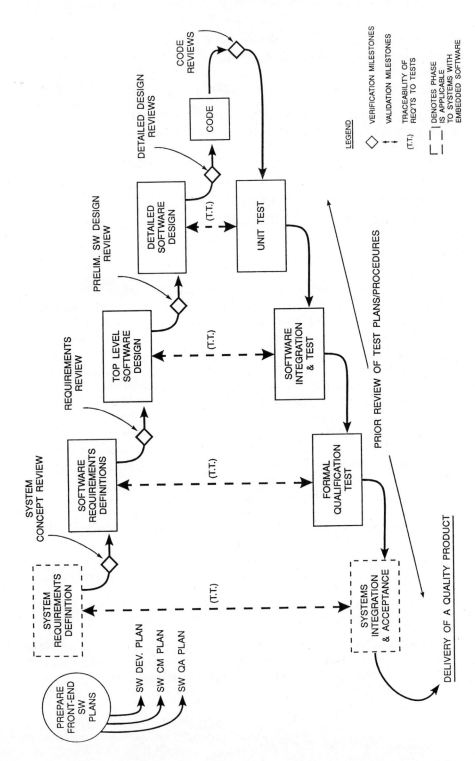

FIGURE 16-1. Typical software product life cycle (and major milestones).

SQA Program Roles

As previously noted, SQA is a management approach, not a department of personnel. As such, the implementation of the managed process can involve personnel from various organizations and disciplines. For example, a typical SQA project program for a PC-based payroll system which is commercial software, may involve the following organizations and roles:

Organization	Role(s)
Marketing	Research market activity and needs; define market/customer requirements; assess success/failure of delivered product.
Payroll Analysis Group	Translate marketing requirements into software requirements and the top-level design based upon knowledge of existing systems.
Software Product Development Group	Formulate detailed software design based upon Analysis information; generate code; perform unit and integration testing.
Quality Assurance and Test Group	Assess the activities during the PLC process; perform Functional, System Acceptance and other benchmark Testing.
Software Support	Assist customers after product roll-out; provide input to the development process based upon customer experience.
Implementation Group	Plan and coordinate pilot of developed software product; plan an orderly roll-out of the product.
Documentation Group	Create user documentation and on-line help text based upon software requirements and design specifications.

Quality Personnel within the SQA Program

The role of the software quality personnel depends upon several factors: industry requirements, organizational structures, the product being developed. Generally, software quality personnel are members of independent quality groups who monitor technical activities and provide product assessments. As Dunn points out, quality personnel can assume numerous roles in order to reach similar objectives:[7]

1. The Peacekeeper—ensure process standards and project plans are met, including audits of reviews/walkthroughs, documents, libraries and tests
2. The Surrogate—perform defect removal via independent testing
3. The Data Collector—perform measurements, collect project data
4. The Analyst—assess project status and progress via collected data
5. Planner—develop and document the project quality plan

Generally, the Surrogate role is quite common in commercial SQA Programs because of the test role played by quality personnel. Since quality auditing/reviewing are very weak methodologies in commercial software programs, quality personnel in commercial SQA programs do not often have the chance to fulfill the Peace-keeper role. The remaining roles, Data Collector, Analyst and Planner are at best addressed by most commercial quality personnel.

The role of software quality personnel also depends upon the responsibilities and capabilities of the other personnel participating in the SQA Program. Examples of the roles which software quality personnel can fulfill within an SQA Program are discussed in a case study later in this chapter.

Now that we have established the framework for an SQA program, the next section will discuss techniques for ensuring that the program is successful.

Experiences and Inside Tips

Deutsch and Willis utilize a planning outline of over a dozen important aspects for addressing the needs of an effectively planned software quality process.[8] The intent of the outline is to provide quality program planners with a summary of key implementation questions and considerations. Because the outline transcends the entire software PLC, it is also an excellent vehicle for presenting a list of SQA Program implementation successes. Summarized below are personal experiences and inside tips which should be considered when planning an SQA Program. These experiences will help expedite the subject task and/or help make an applicable quality requirement more effective.

1) Quality Requirements

- define a solid set of project requirements which is the cornerstone of the SQA Program
- establish SQA Program requirements via objectives and goals

2) Effective Plans

- create standardized software plans for development, quality, and configuration management; tailor plans to the needs of each project
- plan to "build quality into the product"
- plan the SQA Program as if you really mean it

3) Organization

- promote intra-organization communication: setup planning/coordination meetings with other organization well in advance of tasks to be completed/coordinated
- hire personnel based upon projects needs
- avoid being the organizational dump of problem employees
- ensure that the quality and test personnel are as capable as the software development personnel
- utilize low cost personnel such as clerks and technicians to free up senior personnel when possible

4) *Training*

- establish internal formal training programs based upon the project needs (i.e., languages, computer platforms, databases, networks, quality processes, testing, etc.)
- expose personnel to software industry advances via seminars, periodicals, texts, professional organizations, etc.
- cross-pollinate groups within departments via staff presentations

5) *Standards*

- develop software standards based upon the customer environment. Are IEEE, FDA, etc. standards required?
- utilize published guidelines, e.g., standards developed by the IEEE, DOD, NASA, etc., to tailor a process to your needs/product when standards are not "required"
- distribute standards and staff actions to affected groups

6) *Reviews*

- include requirements, design, code, test, documentation and process reviews
- establish written procedures; designate a review chairman [key guidelines: advanced notice and data, concentrate on design not designer, do not solve every problem in the review — take action items]

7) *Testing*

- test development should coincide with software development
- test personnel should be involved in all requirements, design and code reviews
- plans, specifications, cases, reports are a must
- automate where possible

8) *People*

- estimate staff size based upon experience; utilize cost/sizing models; collect, retain, analyze historical costs based upon each project task
- avoid percentage staffing — test or quality staff as a percentage of the development staff

9) *Procedures*

- develop procedures based upon required standards and product environment
- disseminate procedures, follow-up on concurrence and implementation

10) *Tools*

- investigate aids to expedite the software process or to measure quality
- ensure that internally developed quality tools are subject to a defined quality assurance process (practice what you preach)

11) *Facilities*

- plan for resources well in advance of need
- provide support personnel with the same equipment capability as the personnel developing the software

12) *Subcontractor Controls*

- do not allow your subcontractor to do any less than what is required of your own personnel; implement your SQA Program on their project
- establish points of contacts; conduct frequent status meetings
- establish contractual, measurable software milestones

13) *Measurements and Feedback*

- remember, you cannot improve what you cannot measure
- utilize data to locate both the problem and the source; perform appropriate corrective action

14) *Configuration Controls*

- establish: libraries, error reporting systems, review boards, version control methodologies, documented procedures, etc.
- consider that even if the other 13 points are exceeded in their implementation, if there is no configuration control, there is no identifiable product

16.8 IMPLEMENTING AN SQA PROGRAM: PROBLEMS, PAYOFFS AND LESSONS LEARNED (A CASE STUDY)

Objective

The previous section outlined the activities and implementation techniques which lead to a successful SQA program. The next section examines the experiences associated with the *actual start-up and enhancement* of an SQA program within the commercial sector. The following case study involves a fictitious company (MPA) that produces a fictitious product—an Auto Parts Management (APM) software package which includes parts tracking, location identification, accounts receivable ledgers, accounts payable ledgers and over the counter sales processing. However, the experiences, solutions and results are real. Only the names have been changed to protect the innocent!

The Setup—Defining the Product Environment

The MPA product environment included PC-based users of the APM software. The average software program was approximately 300,000 lines of code and was executed in various operational environments:

- various PCs (IBM "XT" to IBM "PS/2") including clones
- multiple versions of disk operating systems—DOS and OS/2

- multiple types of peripherals
- single user and LAN modes
- multiple and unique organizational configuration

Key organizations participating in the MPA SQA Program and their designated roles included:

- Marketing: participated in requirements reviews and project status meetings. Defined market/customer requirements.
- Software Product Development: analyzed requirements, created software design, generated code, performed unit testing, performed integration testing; conducted all requirements and design reviews.
- Quality Assurance/Test Group: assessed all software activities during the PLC (attend reviews/walkthroughs, review documentation), performed Functional, System, Performance and Acceptance Testing, oversaw Configuration/Disaster Controls, maintained/analyzed project metrics and trends.
- Software Support: assisted customers after product roll-out; provided inputs to the software product via PLC reviews based upon customer experiences.

The Approach—Setting the Stage for Improvement

MPA management immediately realized that up-front planning and a skillfully laid quality program framework were the keys to installing an effective software quality process. Consequently, MPA personnel focused their attention on two key tasks during the early phases of planning the SQA Program:

- defining the SQA Program Mission based upon the software/user product environment
- establishing the SQA Program objectives

The MPA SQA Program was viewed as a service mechanism attending to the needs of MPA software development personnel and MPA customers. The following MPA SQA Program Charter was established to help define the SQA Program's direction and future growth:

- represent MPA and its customers' interests to assure product quality via conformance to customer requirements and prevention of software defects
- provide outstanding customer service via increased software reliability and maintainability
- increase customer service and software personnel productivity via aggressive automation
- implement techniques and methodologies which measure software successes and failures to improve the overall quality process
- operate in evaluation/test environments which reflect the changing needs and preferences of MPA customers
- promote customer retention through product satisfaction

Then the following SQA Program objectives were established to meet MPA's Charter:

- emphasize defect prevention as well as defect removal
- prevent defect by embedding quality procedures into all phases of the PLC
  - controlled development process
  - conformance to standards
  - implementation of V&V techniques
- detect and remove errors early in the product life cycle
- implement an effective metrics program
  - you can't improve what you can't measure
  - collect data for product release decisions
- plan structured and documented organizational procedures consistent with successful software industry standard techniques

The ultimate goal was to develop and maintain an SQA Program that utilized state-of-the-industry, in-process, software PLC activities to evaluate software product quality. An example of the general activities of such a program is outlined in Table 16-1. An overview of the QA in-process activities of an ideal Quality Program consistent with the previously stated SQA Program Charter is summarized in Table 16-2.

The Need—Why Improve the Software Quality Process?

Why did MPA management choose to improve the software quality process?

Although MPA's software products consistently provided users with the desired results, e.g., part locations, over the counter prices, inventory status, they believed that the software development, test and maintenance processes could be improved to further increase software product quality and reliability. A review of the MPA

TABLE 16-1   A Comprehensive Software Quality Assurance Program

- Introduce and utilize QA tools, techniques and methods
- Define and monitor divisional software configuration control
- Develop, implement and monitor quality metrics
- Perform software verification and validation via
  - Passive QA techniques
    - Requirements reviews
    - Design reviews/walkthroughs
    - Code reviews/walkthroughs
    - Static tests
  - Dynamic/active QA techniques
    - Functional tests
    - Integration tests
    - System/acceptance tests
    - Special tests (LAN, stress, performance, regression)

TABLE 16-2   The "Ideal" SQA Program (In-Process Activities)

A. Quality Program Characteristics

- Effective Defect Prevention and Defect Removal Techniques
- Embedded Verification and Validation Techniques in Each Phase of the Software Product Life Cycle
- Extensive Metrics Program
- Planned, Automated, Structured and Documented

B. Quality Program Details

- Introduce QA Tools, Techniques and Methodologies
  - test case generators
  - test analyzers
  - commercially available tools
  - quality and test standards
  - CASE tools
- Oversee Divisional Configuration Control
  - Software duplication/production control
  - Off-site software storage
  - Error collection systems
  - Software baseline development and control (Librarian)
  - Code management systems
  - Departmental software library (golden masters)
- Develop, Implement and Monitor Quality Metrics
  - Error tracking and trends
  - Error review boards
  - Halstead volume
  - McCabe cyclomatic complexity
  - Tagging and seeding
  - Baseline stability/improvement
  - Reliability modeling
- Perform Software Verification and Validation via
  - Passive QA techniques
    Requirements review
    Design reviews/walkthroughs
    Code reviews/walkthroughs
    Static tests (reviews/formal analysis, symbolic execution)
  - Dynamic/Active QA techniques
    Unit test (white box) (path tests, breakpoints/diagnostic traces, assertion testing)
    Integration test (glass/gray Box)
    System/functional/scenario tests (black box)
    Special tests (LAN, random, stress, capacity, timing, baseline, etc.)
- Develop and Maintain Quality and Test Documentation
  - Quality program plans/procedures
  - Test plans, specifications, cases and reports

---

software development, test and deployment process revealed that the following improvement objectives could provide significant dividends:

- eliminate the presence of latent defects
- prevent ambiguous and changing requirements
- provide structure and definition to current non-rigorous testing approaches, i.e., what and how much has been tested

- improve the release decision making process (i.e., metrics usage)
- remove configuration ambiguity, e.g., what version has been tested, various authorized versions, disaster controls, etc.

MPA management believed that improvements in the above areas would increase the satisfaction levels of their customer base. However, in order to improve the above processes, MPA management needed to understand what caused the subject areas to be judged inadequate. Several of the contributing negative factors uncovered by MPA management were:

- Staff makeup: quality process review personnel and test personnel were heavily weighted with analytical skills; minimal programming knowledge; minimal formal training in quality or test techniques.
- Software Methodologies: ad-hoc, limited/informal procedures; elementary product life cycle; software quality effort back-loaded; limited configuration/disaster controls.
  Also: quality personnel used to find errors vs. V&V; minimal quality involvement (processes or personnel) in the up-front development process; minimal data gathering to support product deployment decisions.
- Test Approach and Environment: minimal automated test equipment in use; testing performed under ideal conditions.

Consequently, MPA management concentrated on the previously stated five improvement objectives by focusing attention on correcting the above three areas. The following section discusses how the negative elements in the three subject areas were corrected and how the resulting change significantly improved the software development and quality process.

Problems, Payoffs and Lessons Learned

Quality Staff Makeup
The roles of the Quality Assurance and Test Group were previously outlined as follows:

- assess all software activities during the PLC by attending reviews and walkthroughs, and reviewing specifications and documentation
- perform Functional, System, Performance and Acceptance Testing
- oversee Configuration/Disaster Controls
- maintain/analyze project metrics and trends

MPA management felt that of all the difficult changes that they had made, reorganizing and adjusting the staff makeup was perhaps the most arduous task. Staff adjustments were necessary in order to complement the strengths or to fill the voids of the QA/Test Organization. The successful planning and implementation of the QA/Test Group essentially consisted of the following activities:

- utilizing software consultants
- utilizing temporary and college personnel
- adding permanent staff with complementary backgrounds and knowledge
- centralizing key support services within the QA/Test Organization

Outlined below, in no particular order of importance are some lessons learned from the QA/Test staffing experiences:

Personnel Knowledge & Background.   It was evident in the early phases of the improvement efforts that if a QA/Test staff consists of x personnel, you do not need x QA personnel who are only product experts. Personnel with specific knowledge of testing, quality assurance, LANs, specification writing and programming were needed. The QA Group needed a proper mix of Analysts, Testers, Programmers and Clerks.

However, the importance of knowing the product under test should not be diminished. While it is impossible to require every QA/Test candidate who walks off the street to know MPA inventory or accounts receivable concepts, it was important to find ways to educate QA personnel with regard to MPA products. Training methodologies included: off-site seminars, on-site courses, tutorials given by in-house experts and the videotaping of key "chalkboard sessions."

Permanent Staff and Consultants.   Consultants were brought in for several reasons:

- to complement the existing staff's product knowledge with programming and test tool knowledge
- to alleviate the intensive labor requirements associated with the start-up of an automated test process

The use of consultants reinforced the above points regarding knowledge background. MPA needed to employ a QA/Test staff which was familiar with the many facets of the programming/MPA product world. Many of the cost saving tools, described later, that were built during the enhancement period were implemented by consultants based upon QA/Test Analyst's needs/requirements. Thus, several benefits were realized from employing consultants:

- the extra labor force expedited the test automation progress
- the utilization of programming skills found an important and necessary niche within the QA/Test group, including implementing code walkthroughs
- tools developed for QA and evaluation purposes were used by development and field support personnel

Many of the consultants who contributed extremely cost-effective QA/Test solutions were later hired and made a part of the full-time QA staff. Additionally, the increase in programming knowledge that occurred within the QA/Test Group also increased the Software Product Development Group's confidence in and respect for the QA/Test Organization.

Temporary/College Assistance.   As tests were planned and documented, low cost clerk and college level intern personnel supported the QA/Test efforts. Clerks and students were used to:

- collect/retain metric data utilizing simple database and spreadsheet programs which they developed
- document existing tests

- automate documented tests
- execute automated tests repeatedly
- perform simple edits of automated tests
- generate quality reports for management

Miscellaneous Support/Overhead.   During the enhancement period, the increase in QA/Test services and associated responsibilities also brought an increase in the need for additional administrative help. Activities such as regression testing, configuration management, error reporting/tracking, LAN Administration and documentation/software version control, all required dedicated clerk-type assistance. Some of the above services were replicated in numerous software product development groups. MPA was able to transfer some of the under-utilized clerks from the development groups to the QA/Test Group and centralize many of the duplicated services.

Organizational Structure.   After realigning the makeup of the QA/Test Organization, MPA implemented an organizational structure which took advantage of the improvements and diversity in the QA/Test staff. An example of MPA's current QA/Test Organization, including QA/Test Analysts, QA/Test Programmers, clerks, a Librarian and a College Co-Op Program is outlined in Figure 16-2. The responsibilities of each of the groups in the MPA QA/Test Organization are outlined below.

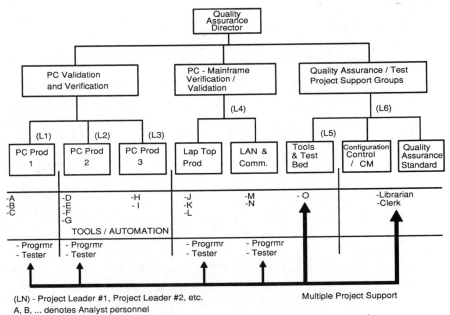

FIGURE 16-2. MPA quality assurance/test organization.

PC Verification & Validation Group

- Perform software Verification and Validation for PC products:
  - Requirements reviews, design reviews/walkthroughs, code reviews/walkthroughs, static tests, system/functional/scenario tests, special tests
  - Test plans, specifications and cases
  - Test execution, analysis and reporting

PC to Mainframe Verification & Validation Group

- Mainframe Interface issues: PC software product to Mainframe compatibility, PC to Mainframe test interface, testing of all Mainframe software which impacts PC software

Quality Assurance/Test Project Support Groups

- Measurements and Configuration Management
  - Develop, implement and monitor quality metrics
  - Oversee divisional configuration control:
    - Software duplication/production control
    - Off-site software storage
    - Error collection systems
    - Software baseline development and control
    - Code management systems
    - Departmental software library
- QA Standards: develop, introduce and enforce quality and test standards, methodologies and documentation (Quality Program Plans, Test Plans/Specifications, etc.)
- Provide LAN support services for the QA group: maintenance of software product release, QA test files, QA application software, QA LAN hardware configuration
- Introduce software tools to assist QA Analysts: test case generators, data reduction programs, test coverage applications, test analyzers, metric analyzers, commercially available tools, etc.
- Create and maintain a QA test bed: typical/atypical PCs, modems, printers, multiple software products, multiple LAN configurations, etc.
- Administer the QA/Test College Co-Op program.

Organization & Staffing Payoffs.   Summarized below are the resulting benefits as a result of the changes which were made in the QA/Test Organization:

Problem: not all QA personnel needed to be Analysts
Action: employed a mix of programmers, technical assistants and clerks
- created separate, but equal, career paths for Analysts and Programmers
- established the right jobs for the right personnel
- ensured cost effectiveness: clerks for repetitive jobs

> - utilized Co-Op students to infuse new technologies and assist with programming and test tasks

Problem: lack of formal QA or test training

Action: in-house and off-site seminars were offered

> - utilized available training or arranged for education in the areas of:
>   - tool usage
>   - networks
>   - company products
>   - quality and test techniques
>   - database products

Problem: programming not utilized as an effective QA tool

Action: hired consultants and "temps" with programming knowledge to meet short term milestones

> - alleviated intensive and nonrecurring automation start-up labor burden
> - designed and developed key software based tools to validate application software
> - complemented the existing staff's product knowledge

Problem: lack of support staff synergism: many configuration and metric activities resided within several development groups

Action: implemented standard processes for metric activities; reduced resources via centralized shift to QA/test

> - implemented activities included: error tracking, version control, software baseline builds for quality testing.

Software Methodologies

One of the key requirements of an SQA Program is a software PLC. MPA management realized the need for a PLC and therefore drafted and implemented a PLC. The PLC implementation included organizational reviews of draft approaches, company wide approval of the final PLC, dissemination of the PLC methodologies to all the affected personnel and conducting PLC training courses. The PLC documentation described several life cycle phases:

- Analysis and Requirements Definition
- Design
- Coding and Development Testing
- Functional Testing
- Integrated Systems Testing
- Quality Acceptance Testing
- Customer Installation Testing
- Field Pilot
- Field Rollout
- Final Analysis/Lessons Learned

The Life Cycle methodologies also included the:

- goals for each phase
- requirements necessary to complete a phase

- project team participants/responsibilities
- mechanisms for promoting project team communications (peer reviews, standardized documents, etc.).

Changes were also made to various software development and quality processes. Summarized below are the methodologies which required enhancement and the resulting benefit:

Problem: limited procedures, plans and specifications
Action: developed standardized QA Plans and Configuration Management Plans; created standardized test plan, specification and procedure data item templates
  - documented various levels of testing
  - implemented as part of the Project Life Cycle
  - utilized published standards from the IEEE and DOD as guidelines

Problem: limited concern for configuration/disaster controls
Action: implemented a full complement of configuration/disaster controls
  - master libraries
  - post production process (duplication) checkout
  - automated version control
  - off-site storage

Problem: testing was performed under ideal conditions
Action: creation of a dynamic test environment
  - procured clone and multiple brand PCs, modems, printers
  - began testing on multiple operating systems and LAN configurations

Problem: testing was a manual, time consuming process
Action: utilized automated test tools
  - spanned the entire test environment of white, gray and black box testing
  - freed up QA Analysts
  - reduced product release time
  - allowed for measurable testing coverage

Problem: no quality involvement in the up-front development process
Action: participated in specification reviews and code walkthroughs throughout the PLC

Problem: no techniques in place to gather the data needed to convince management that a product was not ready for shipment
Action: implemented a simple metrics program which included error trending, test progress, etc.; issued reports to management

Problem: need programming expertise and tools to test software
Action: developed a QA Tools Group
  - analyzed/procured tools
  - developed internal tools
  - tested products below the user interface level (i.e., utilized database and code knowledge)
  - developed tools which were also used by the Support staff

Test Approach and Environment

The Challenge.   The MPA process turnaround which paid the largest dividends was in the area of software testing. The challenge to enhance the test automation and test measurement programs was formidable because of the complexity of multiple PC hardware configurations and the corresponding inventory and accounting software applications. MPA's typical inventory and accounting PC applications are characterized by large numbers of data elements, relationships and processes. MPA knew that the challenge would continue to grow as many applications previously confined to their mainframe and minicomputers were ported to PCs.

MPA management addressed the challenges described above by outlining the following objectives:

- improve test coverage by exercising a greater percentage of code
- improve the accuracy of testing by having precisely defined and reproducible test cases
- improve the utilization of current resources by allowing QA Analysts to concentrate on the creation of tests instead of implementing them.

Testing Tools, Automation and Metrics.   MPA's verification of the implementation of a design involved many combinations of data and permutations of logical flow. Script writing and manual testing were perceived to provide an unsatisfactory percentage of functional test coverage of typically less than 50%. Automatic software testing was intended to increase the test coverage for the same or lesser cost as manual testing. Automatic testing also increased the quality of testing by exactly defining each test and making each test reproducible. Additionally, tests were run 24 hours a day, needing no human intervention once constructed. Test automation systems checked the contents of a screen, file or other I/O subsystem to verify conformity.

Initially, the MPA Quality/Test Group's Test Tool Set was made up of test aids which promoted automated and regressive execution of product test suites. Consequently, MPA decided to enhance the quality of their software products and broaden the capabilities of the QA/Test Group through the acquisition and development of software metrics and code coverage analysis tools. The tools allowed the group to effectively measure the quality of software during the evaluation process of the software development and testing phases. These software development and test measurements provided a proactive approach to improving product quality, increasing development productivity and reducing software PLC maintenance costs.

MPA management was guided by software industry studies which demonstrated that employing techniques such as software metrics including improvement feedback and code analysis resulted in increased productivity and fewer errors. The use of predictive metrics and code analysis were also shown to be much more cost-effective than utilizing only conventional black box software testing techniques.

Previously, the MPA QA/Test Group had concentrated only on removing defects during the Qualification Phase of the software life cycle. A software metrics and code analysis program was developed as an effective approach to removing defects in earlier phases of the software life cycle.

MPA found that an additional benefit of software analysis tools was the ability to identify software errors earlier in the software life cycle. Early error identification reduced overall development costs and also led to a reduction in software maintenance activities. MPA's results were consistent with Barry Boehm's widely published studies which demonstrated that errors exposed earlier in the software life cycle can be repaired at a fraction of the cost associated with allowing the error to propagate into the post development phases of the cycle. MPA's experiences were also consistent with other studies which noted that greater than 50% of software life cycle costs are spent after a system is deployed. Thus, MPA achieved its goal to reduce software maintenance, i.e., corrective, adaptive and perfective activities, by reducing the number of defects present in each PC product deployed to the field.

MPA management believed that the software metrics and code coverage analysis approach yielded the following benefits:

- provided significant cost savings due to defect prevention and the resulting decrease in software maintenance costs
- reduced rework due to the elimination of ripple effect errors
- allowed more efficient testing
- provided faster response time on product rollouts
- yielded a higher quality software product

General Test Approach.   MPA's QA/Test department had members from differing backgrounds: engineers, programmers, product support specialists, data processing operations, etc. MPA's newly implemented test automation and analysis cycle utilized these diverse backgrounds and expertise. For example personnel were organized into specialist groups:

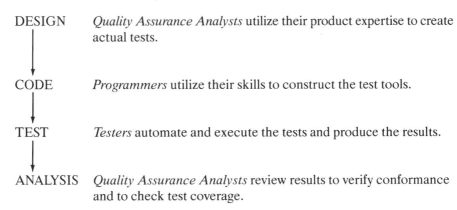

DESIGN   *Quality Assurance Analysts* utilize their product expertise to create actual tests.

CODE   *Programmers* utilize their skills to construct the test tools.

TEST   *Testers* automate and execute the tests and produce the results.

ANALYSIS   *Quality Assurance Analysts* review results to verify conformance and to check test coverage.

MPA management realized that the production and selection of the correct test tools were crucial. They also believed that self-sufficiency in tool technology allowed customization to exact needs.

Generally, MPA's test tools were intended for two purposes:

1. Testing/Analysis
2. Debugging

MPA's test tools also fell into three functional categories:

1. Black Box Testing—(e.g., record/playback tools)
2. White Box Testing—(e.g., database analysis tools)
3. Metrics—(e.g., code coverage analysis tools)

Outlined below are the classes of test tools which were either developed or procured by the MPA Quality/Test Group during the enhancement period.

Automatic Test Execution Tools.   Provides record and playback capabilities.

Features: Keystroke Replay, Screen Capture and Comparison with expected results. Dynamic flow and control of tests according to results found. Works on stand-alone Personal Computers.
Uses: Unit Testing, Functional Verification, System Testing, Capacity, Performance, Regression Testing.

Static (Quality Analysis) Systems.   Analyzes source code to improve code quality and maintenance activities.

Features: identifies source structure diagrams, measures structured programming attributes, determines module complexity.
Fundamentals of Operation: submit source to Analyzer.
Uses: analysis of source code and pseudo code during the requirements, design, code and unit test phases.

Dynamic (Test Coverage Analysis) Systems.   Executes tests on "instrumented code" to measure and improve test coverage.

Features: identifies modules, branch points, assignments.
Fundamentals of Operation: instrument source, generate audit trails, process trails to produce reports.
Uses: analysis of coverage by automated functional verification and system tests.

Dynamic Analysis/Data Base Analysis Tools.   Outputs the physical contents of a Database to an ASCII file before and after a Test. Comparison allows identification of changes to Database, both expected and unexpected.

The tools described above complemented each other during the QA/Test Group's repetitive test cycle. An example of MPA's typical automated test cycle is diagrammed below in Figure 16-3.

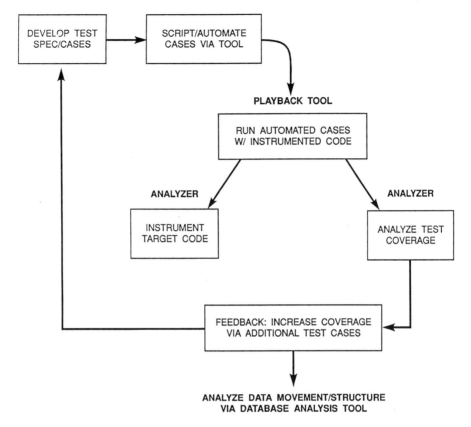

FIGURE 16-3. Example of MPA's automated test cycle.

Test Automation/Measurement Payoffs
Summarized below are the benefits and lessons learned from the changes made to MPA's test approach and environment:

- testing now performed at white, gray and black box levels
- metrics are defined for each test phase
- analysts analyze, programmers program and clerks run tests
- automated tools in use:
  - playback/regression
  - database analyzer
  - coverage measurement
  - complexity measurement
  - custom programs which utilize the design of software under test
  - CASE tools to generate test specifications
- test types: unit, functional verification, system, concurrent locks, performance, security, capacity

Benefits:

- test cases and data sets are accumulated assets
- code coverage increased with every release
- regression testing, once perfected, was very easy, low in cost and 100% accurate
- automatic tests ran 24 hours/day, 7 days/week
- test cases were held in an easily maintained Database and fed directly to the test tool
- exact test data and logic sequences causing a failure were known
- product differential over competitors was created by allowing the development and testing of far more complex software in a shorter time
- greater certainty and confidence levels were obtained regarding what had been tested

Possible disadvantages:

- caveat to regression testing (see above). Some of the playback and record tools would not allow an automated test to be constructed until the application software was error free.
- there were significant costs associated with the initial equipment setup and the addition of needed specialist staff/skills.

Future Directions:

- obtain good manual procedures before automating to prevent an automated mess.
- store all test data in a central database.
- plan test data sets and automatic software testing methodology with Database Administrators and integrate into CASE strategy/methodology.
- try to produce generic test tools and methodologies that can be applied across the whole product line.
- continued management support is paramount since automated software testing can be very expensive.
- insist that testing is performed by a group independent of the software development group.
- plan how to store, process, evaluate and report on the test data; test automation, once in place, generates mountains of data.
- plan on putting hooks into products to allow redirection of I/O for test analysis.

First Year Successes of the MPA SQA Program

Outlined below is a partial list of SQA Program accomplishments and enhancements achieved by the MPA Corporation:

QA/Test Process Definition and Documentation
- Defined and utilized quality metrics
- Created QA and test methodology standards
- Developed QA and test documentation standards

- Implemented duplication/release/storage controls
- Increased the emphasis on assuring critical product utilities
- Emphasized white box testing as well as black box testing

Test Automation
Planned, documented and utilized:

- Incoming Acceptance Tests
- Functional Tests
- System/Scenario Tests
- Capacity and Volume Tests
- Training Manual Tests

QA Support Tool Development
- Procured and built cost effective automation tools
- Developed in-house database analyzers
- Developed various test measurements (e.g., code coverage, application performance, product stability, etc.)

The enhancements to the SQA Program allowed MPA to make significant improvements in the overall software development, quality, test and management process. For example, some of the notable successes during the SQA Program implementation and enhancement period are outlined below:

- Built-up test coverage via automation & measurement
- Established simple metrics for release decisions
- Avoided major disasters via configuration control and in-process production testing
- Educated top management on the "science of testing"
- Attracted software developers to a more technical QA/Test Group
- Reduced the overall software test/release period
- Increased morale and job satisfaction

Future SQA Program Evolution and Goals

The ultimate goal of MPA management is to develop an SQA Program that utilizes state-of-the-industry, in-process, full product life cycle activities to evaluate software product quality. An overview of MPA's SQA Program's evolution which is currently in phase 3, and its future direction is outlined in Table 16-3.

16.9 COMMERCIAL vs. MISSION-CRITICAL SQA PROGRAMS—A FINAL COMPARISON

The following summary of the differences and similarities between military and commercial SQA Programs is based upon experiences in both types of programs. The experiences were the result of performing a wide range of roles regarding SQA Programs (e.g., manager, implementer, outside reviewer/auditor and consultant).

TABLE 16-3   MPA Software Quality Assurance Program Evolution

Phase/Emphasis	Description	Key Quality/Test Techniques
0 Initial State	Perform QA and support Investigate QA in other organizations/companies Describe formal QA program	AD HOC
1 Start-Up	Selling the QA function Staffing Investigating automation	Black box testing using product experts Random, manual testing
2 QA Implementation and Automation	Initial automation Training the QA staff: programming, testing, products Introducing programming and tools as aids to QA Analysts Basic metrics (error trends) QA and test standards Structured test methodology Configuration control Basic test bed Product roll-out control	Automated black box testing Some tools to perform limited white box testing Initial development of test specs and standards Control of software: internal, duplication and field Some error trending Test bed design
3 Advanced Implementation and Automation	Advanced metrics Enhancing the QA staff Interfacing with Mainframe quality and testing software which impact PC products Full test phase coverage Enhanced field/customer relations Advanced test bed Common test environment Increased design involvement	Full black, gray and white box testing Advanced measurement tools QA with programming knowledge Common test bed for all products Analyze customer use/experience Design and code reviews Documentation and Specification reviews
4 Refined QA	Automation, etc. Automated test documentation Test requirements traceability Reliability release modeling Integrated design, code, test	Statistical QA CASE tools Artificial Intelligence

Unique Characteristics

Commercial Sector
- Quality programs are generally not mandated by customers; must sell SQA Programs to management
- No consensus on the optimal software project reporting structure
- Emphasis on test role allows continuity/objectivity
- Total Quality Management (TQM), a recent DOD "buzz word" has been an industry trait.
- Similar to the DOD's Independent Validation and Verification (IV&V) role
  - Most Quality personnel actually *assure software* (see below)
- Quality personnel better equipped and trained due to their test roles

- Software procedures/methodologies may be in place, but not followed because there is no outside enforcement or compliance auditing
- Few paper requirements

Military Sector (Mission-critical)
- Quality programs are required
- Frameworks for software project reporting structures are provided
- Software procedures/methodologies are monitored by both internal and external agencies
- Many paper requirements
- Quality personnel are tasked with assuring the SQA Program
- Stresses documentation and requirements verification/traceability
- Emphasizes management of the Quality Program to assure effectiveness and monitor technical activities

Common Characteristics

- Use of design/test reviews
- Use of automated configuration controls
- Need for tools and automation
- Not enough emphasis on formal training

Many of the tools, techniques and methodologies required on military contracts can be used successfully in the commercial sector. Table 16-4 outlines actual examples of techniques used in commercial SQA programs which were borrowed from Mission-critical SQA programs.

TABLE 16-4   Mission-Critical SQA Program Methodologies Successfully Utilized on Commercial SQA Programs

Management	*Test*
• Peer Reviews/Guidelines	• Test Readiness Reviews
• Project Life Cycles	• Test Reports
• Documentation Standards	• Acceptance Tests
• Defect Prevention	• Incoming Tests
• Standardization	• Baseline Verification
• Cost Estimation Models	*Metrics*
Requirements/Design/Code	• Error Severity/Priority
• Requirements Traceability	• Trending/Cost of Quality
• Code Walkthroughs	• Complexity
• Engineering/QA Notebooks	• QA Sampling/Statistical Process Control
• Work Certification	

Configuration Management
- Change Control Boards
- FCA/PCA Concepts
- VDD Type Documentation
- Configuration Controls

While commercial and Mission-critical SQA Programs differ regarding organization role and project implementation requirements, there is one common point of agreement. Generally, after obtaining the necessary commitments in terms of management and customer support, financing, etc., both SQA Programs have the same objective: meeting the customer's requirements and needs.

16.10 SUMMARY

This chapter outlines the philosophy, framework, personnel roles, successes, benefits and lessons learned for an SQA Program in the commercial sector. Keys to the successful implementation of an effective SQA Program are:

- Obtaining commitment from management
- Meeting customer requirements/needs
- Providing/participating in full software life cycle coverage
- Providing accountability via measurements
- Acquiring customer/user confidence

References

1. Dunn, Robert H., *Software Quality Concepts and Plans* (Englewood Cliffs, New Jersey: Prentice Hall, 1990), p. 254.
2. Deutsch, Michael, and Willis, Ronald, *Software Quality Engineering* (Englewood Cliffs, New Jersey: Prentice Hall, 1988), p. 273.
3. Dunn, Robert H., *op cit,* pp. 11 and 255.
4. *Ibid,* p. 135.
5. *Ibid,* p. 135.
6. Dunn, Robert, and Ullman, Richard, *Quality Assurance for Computer Software* (New York: McGraw-Hill, 1982), p. 159.
7. Dunn, Robert H., *op cit,* pp. 159-173.
8. Deutsch, Michael, and Willis, Ronald, *op cit,* p. 272.

General References

Dunn, Robert, and Ullman, Richard, *Quality Assurance for Computer Software* (New York: McGraw-Hill, 1982).

Hetzel, William, *The Complete Guide to Software Testing,* (Wellesley, Massachusetts: QED Information Sciences, 1984).

Niech, Lawrence E., "Implementing and Effective Commercial Testing Program Utilizing DOD Software Experiences." Washington, D.C., *EDPMA Technical Conference Transactions* (1991).

Niech, Lawrence E., "The Pitfalls and Payoffs of Implementing a QA Program for Software." Washington, D.C., *NSIA Technical Conference Transactions* (1991).

Niech, Lawrence E., and Cheetham, Richard S., "Starting Up an Automated Test Group: Problems and Payoffs". San Francisco, California, *Quality Week Conference Transactions* (1991).

17

Statistical Methods Applied to Software Quality Control

C. K. Cho, Ph.D.

Computa, Inc.

17.1 GOAL—HIGH-QUALITY AND COST-EFFECTIVE SOFTWARE

According to *Webster's New World Dictionary of the American Language,* the term "quality" means the degree of excellence which a thing possesses and "productivity" means the state of being marked by abundant production. Quality and productivity are used as major weapons by enterprising organizations to gain control over product markets.

In the context of this article, software quality means primarily a piece of software being able to produce quality data for its user and software productivity means a group of people being able to develop quality software abundantly. Such other characteristics as software understandability, modifiability, portability, and so on, could be considered as primary quality attributes as well, depending on the user's priority. In general, the ability to produce quality data abundantly means user satisfaction. Else all of the other characteristics are meaningless. Software productivity requires an effective way to integrate different and unique routines, modules, and programs into a quality system.

The goal of software engineering and quality assurance study and practice is software quality excellence—that is, the development of high-quality and cost-effective software. This chapter presents a new methodology based on statistical quality control principles to help attain the goal.

17.2 TWENTY PROBLEMS IN SOFTWARE ENGINEERING PROJECT MANAGEMENT

Development of high-quality and cost-effective software has been always a challenge facing the computer and software industry. Although abundant literature on techniques and methodologies of software development exists, most of such methods deal with a very specific phase in the software development cycle and few treat a software process as a manufacturing process. Furthermore, good techniques for achieving specific software quality characteristics such as reliability, performance, and maintainability are still lacking. Although modern software development methodologies such as top-down design and structured programming are being practiced, their contributions to meeting the challenge have been meager. Many software projects have resulted in poor quality, cost overruns, late delivery, and dissatisfied users, as surveyed in Thayer.[1] In this interesting article discussing the challenge facing the software industry, the authors survey the current practices in software engineering project management (SEPM) and find that there are twenty problems urgently requiring solutions, as shown in Table 17-1. These problems are reflected in the so-called "software warranty" printed on software packages found in many computer stores:

TABLE 17-1   Twenty Problems in Software Engineering Project Management*

PLANNING

1. *Requirements:* Requirement specifications are frequently incomplete, ambiguous, inconsistent, and/or unmeasurable.
2. *Success:* Success criteria for a software development are frequently inappropriate, which result in "poor-quality" delivered software; i.e., not maintainable, unreliable, difficult to use, relatively undocumented, etc.
3. *Project:* Planning for software engineering projects is generally poor.
4. *Cost:* The ability to estimate accurately the resources required to accomplish a software development is poor.
5. *Schedule:* The ability to estimate accurately the delivery time on a software development is poor.
6. *Design:* Decision rules for use in selecting the correct software design techniques, equipment, and aids to be used in designing software in a software engineering project are not available.
7. *Test:* Decision rules for use in selecting the correct procedures, strategies, and tools to be used in testing software developed in a software engineering project are not available.
8. *Maintainability:* Procedures, techniques, and strategies for designing maintainable software are not available.
9. *Warranty:* Methods to guarantee or warranty that the delivered software will "work" for the user are not available.
10. *Control:* Procedures, methods, and techniques for designing a project control system that will enable project managers to successfully control their project are not readily available.

ORGANIZING

11. *Type:* Decision rules for selecting the proper organizational structure; e.g., project, matrix, function, are not available.

TABLE 17-1   (Cont.)

ORGANIZING

12. *Accountability:* The accountability structure in many software engineering projects is poor, leaving some question as to who is responsible for various project functions.

STAFFING

13. *Project manager:* Procedures and techniques for the selection of project managers are poor.

DIRECTING

14. *Techniques:* Decision rules for use in selecting the correct management techniques for software engineering project management are not available.

CONTROLLING

15. *Visibility:* Procedures, techniques, strategies, and aids that will provide visibility of progress (not just resources used) to the project manager are not available.
16. *Reliability:* Measurements or indexes of reliability that can be used as an element of software design are not available and there is no way to predict software failure; i.e., there is no practical way to show the delivered software meets a given reliability criteria.
17. *Maintainability:* Measurements or indexes of maintainability that can be used as an element of software design are not available; i.e., there is no practical way to show that a given program is more maintainable than another.
18. *Goodness:* Measurements or indexes of "goodness" of code that can be used as an element of software design are not available; i.e., there is no practical way to show that one program is better than another.
19. *Programmers:* Standards and techniques for measuring the quality of performance and the quantity of production expected from programmers and data processing analysts are not available.
20. *Tracing:* Techniques and aids that provide an acceptable means of tracing a software development from requirements to completed code are not generally available.

* Reproduced with permission from R. H. Thayer, A. Pyster, and R. C. Wood, "The Challenges of Software Engineering Project Management," IEEE *Computer*, Vol. 13, No. 8 (Aug., 1980), pp. 51–59. ©1980 IEEE.

This program is sold "as is" without warranty of any kind, either expressed or implied, including, but not limited to, the warranties of merchantability and fitness for your purpose. The entire risk as to the quality and performance of the program is with you. If the program is found to be defective, you (and not the developer or an authorized dealer) assume the entire cost of all necessary servicing, repair, or correction. . . . This warranty gives you specific legal rights and you may also have other rights which vary from state to state.

The developer does not warrant that the functions contained in the program will meet your requirements or that the operation of the software will be uninterrupted or error-free. The developer does warrant as the only warranty provided to you, that the diskette(s) or cassette(s) on which the program is furnished will be free from defects in materials and workmanship under normal use for ninety (90) days from the date of delivery to you as evidenced by your receipt.

Some of the problems in Table 17-1 are managerial while the remaining are technical. Problems 3, 4, 5, 10, 11, 12, 13, 14, 15, and 20 appear to be managerial and problems 1, 2, 6, 7, 8, 9, 16, 17, 18, and 19 are technical. Solutions to the managerial problems depend on solutions to the technical problems and on management support. The purpose of this chapter is to discuss the roots of and the solutions to some of the technical problems, and what top management must do to help solve the problems.

The proposed solutions are based on an essentially simple idea: the application of quality control to control software quality during software development. The term "quality control" as used here refers to the tool "quality control" developed during World War II to control the manufacturing and procurement of quality military hardware, described next.

Various aspects of the methodology discussed here have been applied to practical software development with success. References 2, 3, 4, 5, and 6 report some of the applications.

17.3 QUALITY CONTROL

As noted, the term "quality control" in the context of this article refers to a powerful and widely used tool to ensure product quality in modern manufacturing industries. It is a tool developed during World War II based on statistical methods including random sampling techniques, testing, measurements, inspection, defective cause findings, improvements, statistical inference, and acceptance sampling. During World War II, contracts for military procurement mandated that suppliers employ statistical quality control procedures in their processing and that random samples of finished goods be submitted for quality conformance inspection. Since then, the tool has been widely used in the United States and abroad and has become important to agencies of the federal government in enforcing production of quality products and to consumer groups. It also has become a competitive weapon enabling manufacturing organizations to survive in modern marketing.

Quality control activities in manufacturing industries may be summarized as follows from Cho:[7]*

A. *Set Quality Standard.* For each quality characteristic, a standard should be established as a product specification with which to compare the characteristic of the finished product. For example, the diameter and the acceptable tolerance variation of a steel ball to be used in a ball bearing should be specified, such as 0.25 ± 0.001 in. If the diameter of a finished ball falls within 0.0249 to 0.251 in., then the diameter of the ball is considered as acceptable. Otherwise it is considered defective.

---

*From C. K. Cho, *An Introduction to Software Quality Control.* Copyright © 1980 by John Wiley & Sons, Inc. Reprinted by permission of John Wiley & Sons, Inc.

B. *Plan to Attain the Quality Standard.* The achievement of the product quality requires careful planning and engineering of manufacturing process and equipment, acquisition of good quality materials, training operators, and so on.

C. *Determine Preventive Methods to Control Manufacturing Process.* The old saying "it is better to prevent than to cure" holds true in quality control. During the manufacturing process all possible factors affecting the quality characteristics of the product must be carefully controlled. For example, the purity of raw materials, temperature, and pressure control can affect the diameter of a steel ball.

D. *Determine Conformance of Quality.* The determination includes
   a. Interpretation of the product quality standard.
   b. Random sampling of product units for inspection.
   c. Inspection and measurements of the sampled product units.
   d. Comparisons of c with a for each sampled product unit.
   e. Judgment of conformance of quality of each product unit.
   f. Acceptance of rejection of the product lot by statistical methods.
   g. Documentation of the inspection data.

A factory in a manufacturing industry is a process that makes raw materials into useable products. It may be expressed mathematically as

$$U = F(R)$$

where R is a set of raw materials and U is a set of product units.

A factory possesses two major characteristics: (1) the raw materials are well-defined—types and quality characteristics such as properties and chemical components of each material type are specified—and (2) the product unit and product unit defectiveness, quality characteristics of each product unit are also well-defined. These characteristics enable the application of quality control to insure the quality of the products for the consumers.

The relationship between quality control and a manufacturing process, called the *quality cycle,* is depicted in Figure 17-1. The cycle starts with product concept formulation after human needs have been identified. The characteristics of the product are then determined. The product is designed for manufacturing; methods and engineering approaches are then devised to make the product; machinery and raw materials are procured; and equipment and instruments are installed. Finally, manufacturing begins. The products are then inspected to verify conformance of quality against the characteristics. Consumers buy and use the product with their experience being fed back to the cycle. The cycle then starts all over again.

Mass inspection of product units in determining quality conformance may not be feasible and economical due to the size of the product population. Therefore, statistical sampling inspection comes to play a major role here. Sampling inspection usually involves an estimate of the population defective rate θ. The rate is defined as $\theta = D/N$, where D is the number of defective units in the product population and N is the total number of product units in the population. The

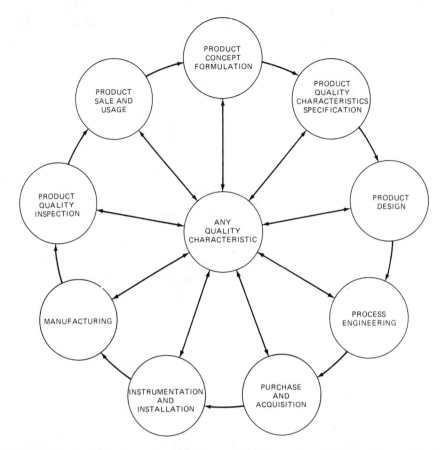

FIGURE 17-1. Manufacturing quality cycle. (From Cho, C. K., *An Introduction to Software Quality Control,* New York: John Wiley & Sons 1980. Copyright © 1980 by John Wiley & Sons, Inc. Reprinted by permission of John Wiley & Sons, Inc.)

estimate of θ can be easily done by using the binomial distribution, important in the study of probability, statistics, and quality control. The application of the distribution often arises when sampling from a finite population consisting of a finite number of units with replacement, or from an infinite population consisting of an infinite number of units with or without replacement.

The probability function of the bionomial distribution is given by:

$$b(x) = \binom{n}{x} \theta^x (1-\theta)^{n-x}$$

It gives the probability of getting x defectives in a sample of n units taken from a population having a defective rate of θ. The mean and variance of the distribution are given by:

$$\mu = n\theta$$
$$\sigma^2 = n\theta(1 - \theta)$$

Once the sample is taken and inspected, the defective rate θ° of the sample may be computed by $\theta^\circ = d/n$, where d is the number of defects in the sample.

The defective rate of the population can then be estimated from d. The estimate may be expressed in an interval called *100c% confidence interval*, where $0 \leq c \leq 1$. An approximate $100c\%$ confidence interval of the population defective rate may be computed by:

$$\left[\theta^\circ - t_{n-1,\,a/2} \frac{\sqrt{\theta^\circ\,(1-\theta^\circ)}}{n}, \quad \theta^\circ + t_{n-1,\,a/2} \frac{\sqrt{\theta^\circ\,(1-\theta^\circ)}}{n} \right] \tag{3.0}$$

where $t_{n-1,\,a/2}$ is called the *value of the Student t-distribution*[7] at $n-1$ degrees of freedom and $a = 1 - c$ is called a *risk factor*. (In statistics, a binomial distribution can be approximated by a normal distribution. In the normal distribution, there is a value represented by $z_{a/2}$, which is the number of standard normal deviate such that the area to its right under the normal curve is $a/2$. The value of $t_{n-1,a/2}$ is the same as $z_{a/2}$ if n is large, e.g., $n \geq 30$. A Student t-distribution table from which $t_{n-1,a/2}$ can be found when n is small, e.g., $n < 30$, is available in many statistics and quality control books, e.g., Cho.[7]

The accuracy of the estimates depends on the sample size. In general, the larger the size, the more accurate the estimate. The value of n may be computed by (see Cho[7]):

$$n = \frac{z^2(1 - \theta)}{a^2\theta} \tag{3.1}$$

where a is the desired accuracy factor such that $|\theta - \theta^\circ| = a\theta$, and z is the value of $z_{a/2}$. Since the population defective rate θ is unknown, the determination of n may take several iterations. The sample defective rate $\theta^\circ{}_i$, found at iteration i is used as θ in computing n at iteration $i + 1$. If n_{i+1} is less than n_i, the total number of units in the sample already taken, then the sample is completed. The final sample defective rate is then used to estimate μ and σ^2.

In any factory, it is hardly possible to produce a defect-free product lot: therefore, the conformance of product quality is usually measured by a defective rate less than an acceptable number, e.g., $\theta < 0.01$. With a statistical sampling method, a confidence level such as 95% sure can be imposed on the conclusion of the defective rate.

There is another measure in determining acceptability of a product population, called the *acceptance sampling*. In this method, a sample of K units is taken and inspected. If the sample contains less than an acceptable number of defective units c, then the population is acceptable, else unacceptable. In this sampling, there are two types of risks involved in reaching a conclusion: the *producer's risk* and the *user's risk*. The former is the risk assumed by the producer in having a good-quality product lot rejected by the sampling method. The latter is the risk assumed by the user in accepting a poor-quality product lot. The producer's risk is expressed by α_1 if his or her product population's defective rate is θ_1 while the user's risk is expressed by α_2 if the population's defective rate is θ_2, where $\theta_1 < \theta_2$ and α_1, θ_1, α_2, θ_2 are called the *acceptance criteria*. With these criteria, an acceptance sampling plan can be determined, i.e., the sample size K and the acceptable number of defective units c in the sample can be decided statistically to provide a fair protection to both of the parties.

The details of the sampling techniques may be found in Cho[7] and Juran.[8] For the purpose of this chapter, only the sampling inspection for estimating the population defective rate will be discussed with examples.

17.4 SOFTWARE QUALITY CONTROL

An analogy can be drawn between a manufacturing factory and a piece of software. Software input and output are the raw materials and finished goods of a factory.

If the software output is defined in terms of "product unit," then the output is a collection of product units called the *output population* of the software. For any nontrivial program, the population contains a very large number of units. The goal of software testing is to find certain characteristics of the population such as the ratio of the number of defective units in the population to the total number of units in the population. The ratio may be called the defective rate of the population and may be imposed on the software as the *software quality index*. Clearly a mass inspection of the population to find the rate is prohibitive. An efficient method is through statistical random sampling. With statistical quality control, one can build confidence in the quality of the population in numerical terms.

With this concept, the quality of the data must be built in from the beginning of manufacturing to the hand of the user. Similar to a manufacturing process, there is a close relationship called the *software quality cycle* between quality control and development of the software, as shown in Figure 17-2. An examination of Figures 17-1 and 17-2 reveals a close parallelism.

But if one investigates current software practices (Figure 17-3) in terms of the quality cycle in Figure 17-2, one would immediately notice three missing important ingredients: product concept formulation, product quality characteristics specification, and product design including definitions of product units and product unit defectiveness. Because of these missing ingredients as shown in Figure 17-3, the tool of quality control cannot be applied. This may be the root of the seven technical problems of requirements, success, design, test, warranty, reliability, and goodness of Table 17-1.

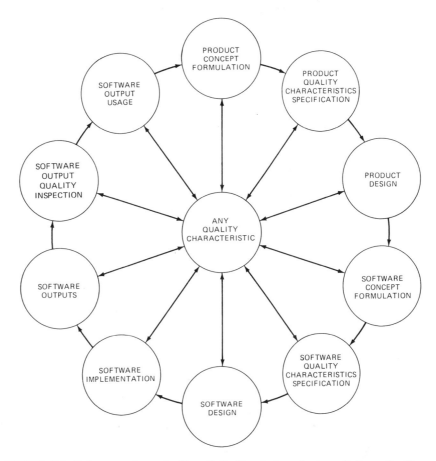

FIGURE 17-2. Software quality cycle. (From C. K. Cho, *An Introduction to Software Quality Control.* New York: John Wiley & Sons, 1980. Copyright © 1980 by John Wiley & Sons, Inc. Reprinted by permission of John Wiley & Sons, Inc.)

A methodology, called the quality programming, incorporating the tool of quality control along with the software quality cycle of Figure 17-2 will be discussed with an example. The solutions to the seven technical problems mentioned above will also be explained.

17.5 QUALITY PROGRAMMING

A software development process that implements the quality cycle of Figure 17-2 incorporating the tool of quality control is shown in Figure 17-4. Given a system to be developed, a model is developed to analyze and understand the "problem." The modeling activities may take several iterations (see backward arrow from model-

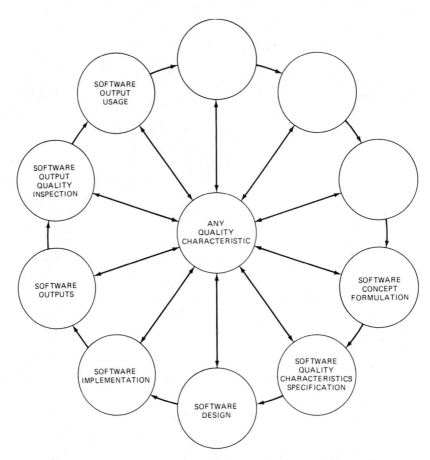

FIGURE 17-3. Incomplete software quality cycle, modified from Cho.[7]

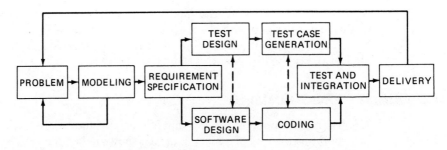

FIGURE 17-4. Quality programming life cycle.

ing to problem in Figure 17-4) to thoroughly understand the problem. Models including a description of the problem and the product to be generated by the software are built to form the basis of product design and the concept of the software being developed.

Requirements are then generated as a result of the modeling activity. Included in the requirements are software and test requirements. Software requirements define the functions the software is to perform and the quality characteristics such as response time, throughput, understandability, and portability. Test requirements define the product units and product unit defectiveness for statistical sampling, sampling methods for estimating the defective rate of the software population with which to judge software quality, statistical inference methods and confidence level of software output population quality, the acceptable software defective rate, and test input unit generation methods.

With well-defined requirements, software development can be divided into two channels which can proceed concurrently: software design and implementation, and software test design and implementation. Top-down design, structured programming, and critical-module-first implementation methods are used in the software channel. The formulation of sampling plans for estimating software defective rate and population acceptability, the design of input units, and the implementation of the sampling plans are used in the test channel. During the design and implementation phases, interfaces between the channels are incorporated to ensure that quality is built into the software at every stage of development. The two channels meet at the time of testing and integration. Testing and integration are performed again on a most-critical-module-first basis to ensure that the software is integrated on a quality-spare-part basis. If the software passes the test satisfying the test requirements, delivery to the user takes place. The user employs the quality control tool to determine the acceptability of the software output population, in turn the basis for accepting or rejecting the software. With the user's experience, modification, enhancement, and maintenance start from the beginning of the cycle again.

I. Modeling

Modeling is the activity of understanding the problems under consideration. The following are the major tasks that must be done well before software development begins:

A. Problem Description

This is the description of what the software being developed must do. An exact, unambiguous, and complete description is essential to smooth the development of the software, and is an integral part of a document to be produced at the modeling stage.

B. Types of Raw Materials

Definitions of the types of raw materials required are an integral part of a plan in building a factory. For any factory, the types and sources of raw materials, and the means of transporting the materials to the factory are well-defined before the factory is built. By analogy, the types of raw materials of a piece of software are the input variables. The variables can be numerical, nonnumerical, or both. The source(s) of the raw materials can be a data base, a terminal, or a real-time data acquisition system. An exact and complete definition of the raw materials constitutes an integral part of the modeling activity.

C. Characteristics of Raw Materials

Once the types and sources of all of the raw materials of a factory have been identified, the characteristics of each of the raw materials must also be analyzed: properties, chemical components, and so on. Are the characteristics of the materials suitable for the manufacturing? What side-effect does each characteristic have on the operations of the factory? Are there any constraints in using the materials? Is there any substitute for each of the materials? These are but some questions that should be answered before the use of these materials is finalized.

Similarly, the characteristics of the input variables of a piece of software to be developed should be analyzed. Is a variable assuming numerical values? What are the lower and upper bounds of the variable? If the variable assumes nonnumerical values, what kinds of data are to be assigned to the variable? What are the components of the variable? (E.g., if NAME is a variable containing people's names, the components would be FIRST NAME, MIDDLE NAME, and LAST NAME.) What are the characteristics of each of the components? (E.g., no numerical characters are to be in a FIRST NAME.)

D. Rules of Using Raw Materials

The order, and in many cases timing, in which raw materials are entered into a manufacturing process must be strictly followed. A variation of the rules may lead to poor-quality products, waste, or even disaster. Such rules must be defined before a factory is built.

Similarly, rules governing the use of data in a piece of software must be defined. For example, whether or not LAST NAME should precede FIRST NAME and MIDDLE NAME, or vice versa, in a data base management system should be decided well in advance.

E. Definition of Product Unit

The capacity of a factory can be measured in many ways. In the manufacturing of "discrete" products such as screws, nuts, and automobiles, capacity may be measured by the number of units produced per day. In the production of "continuous" products, such as gasoline and flour, measurement can be by volume or weight, such as gallons or tons, per day. The measurement unit (gallon or ton), may be considered as the *product unit.* With the definition of a product unit, product quality inspections using the quality control tool introduced in Section 14.3 can be conducted.

If a piece of software is viewed as a factory, the definition of product unit is necessary for software development. The quality of the software product population can be inspected using the same quality control tool. A piece of software is said to be of good quality only when it is able to produce a good-quality product population.

The lack of product unit definition in the software industry has been observed to be the root of many of the technical problems listed in Table 17-1. Product unit definition is crucial to solving these problems in developing high-quality and cost-effective software.

(The "product unit" produced by software shouldn't be confused with the development unit produced by people. The latter is an entity such as a routine, module, or program which, as a productivity measure, is usually measured in terms of lines of code generated by programmers per day. The use of "product unit" in this chapter specifically refers to the output produced by software, analogous to the output of a factory.)

F. DEFINITION OF PRODUCT UNIT DEFECTIVENESS

As the definition of product unit is the basis on which to apply the quality control tool, the definition of product unit defectiveness forms the basis on which to judge quality conformance of a product unit. The latter definition is generally difficult for a particular product. For example, an automobile is a product unit. The defectiveness of the unit may not be easily defined: it involves the identification of the quality characteristics of a car, such as weight, physical properties, chemical components of each spare part, gas mileage, tire life, the length of normal battery life, and so forth. It also involves the definition of defectiveness in terms of each of the characteristics. For example, gas mileage must be 30 miles per gallon on the highway; the mean time to failure of a battery is three years. The definitions become the quality standards which govern the manufacture of a product.

Similar observations can be made in viewing a piece of software as a factory. Without quality standards, it is difficult to attain the goal of developing high-quality and cost-effective software.

G. METHODS OF MANUFACTURING

Usually a product consists of many parts and more than one method can be used to produce a part. Therefore, many methods need to be investigated before determining which method to use to manufacture which part of the product. In addition, methods of assembling the parts into the product need to be studied to ensure smooth production.

Similarly, many methods can be used to solve a problem in software development. For example, there are many methods of finding the roots of equations of one variable, such as the bisection method, Newton's algorithm, secant method, fixed-point iteration, the modified regular falsi, Steffensen iteration method, and so on. As many methods as possible should be studied and documented at this point of development for later use.

H. Characteristics of Factory

The characteristics can be the production capacity, speed, size of the factory, types of buildings, materials used to build the factory, storage capacity for incoming raw materials, means of transportation within a factory, ways of handling materials in the factory, and so on. These characteristics should be well-planned before the factory is designed and built.

Similarly, the characteristics of a piece of software can be the output data generation capacity, speed, memory size, data storage capacity, data flows, and the like. They must be studied at this stage of software development.

I. Manufacturing Process

Since a product usually consists of many parts and the manufacturing of the parts requires many raw materials and some intermediate products fabricated within a factory, the flow of these materials and intermediate products constitutes a complex network. The smooth movement of the objects is essential to efficient manufacturing of the product. When and how to inspect the quality of the raw materials and intermediate products to insure that the finished goods are to be of good quality need to be studied at the beginning of this stage of development.

Similarly, the way the input data is flowing into a piece of software, the temporary storage of intermediate data, the way the data is structured to be processed before output data is produced should be analyzed to facilitate later development of the software.

J. Method of Building a Factory

While there are many ways of building a factory, the selection of one has a significant impact on how the building should be designed. Should the factory be built and installed on its site? Should it be fabricated somewhere else and transported to the site and then assembled? Should a model be built first? What effects will each building method have? Questions of this kind should be fully investigated.

The same questions can be asked of software development. Should the software be developed from scratch? Are there any existing software packages available? Should a software model be developed first? And so on. Answers to these questions will greatly facilitate the later software design stage.

II. Requirements Specification

The requirements for software development can be specified in two classes: software and test. The first includes the input domain, functions, and characteristics of the software being considered. The second consists of a test plan with which the software is to be tested and accepted. The document produced in the modeling stage is essential to this important software development task.

(1) Software Requirements

Software requirements include input, processing, and output descriptions of the software. The input requirements consist of the types, and characteristics of raw materials and the rules governing the use of the raw materials. The process requirements contain exhaustive listings of the functions the software must have. The output requirements include man-machine interface and other characteristics of the products to be generated by the software. The following are the detailed descriptions of the requirements.

A. INPUT DOMAIN

The input domain of a piece of software is the representation of all possible input data and the rules governing the construction of input to be processed by the software. With a well-defined input domain, random input units can be constructed to test the software. The input data used in daily production is in fact a subset of all of the possible input that can be generated from the domain. The input domain of a piece of software can be represented by a symbolic input attribute decomposition (SIAD) tree (a detailed description of the tree is given in Cho[7]). The following example is a demonstration of a SIAD tree representing mailing list software that maintains the accuracy of mailing addresses.

Example.   An address can be decomposed into name, street, city, state, and zip code. A name can be decomposed into first name, middle name, and last name. A first name can be either a full first name or a first initial. It is seen the decomposition of the components can be done into a number of levels. The results can be arranged in a tree, as shown in Figure 17-5.

The tree may be represented in a SIAD tree, as in Table 17-2. The tree has four columns: index, tree symbol, tree element, and rule index. The indices are for sampling use. The tree symbols preserve the tree structure of the tree elements in Figure (17-5). A tree element is a node in Figure 17-5 with some explanation of the node. A rule index points to a rule that governs the use of the tree element in constructing an input unit.

The rules governing the use of tree elements in a SIAD tree can be listed as shown in Table 17-3. A rule index is used to identify a rule to be used. The rule description is the rule of interest. The sub-rule index points to a sub-rule to supplement the use of the rule, as shown in Table 17-4.

Examples of constructing input units using the SIAD tree are given in Section 17.5, paragraph D, Sampling Methods.

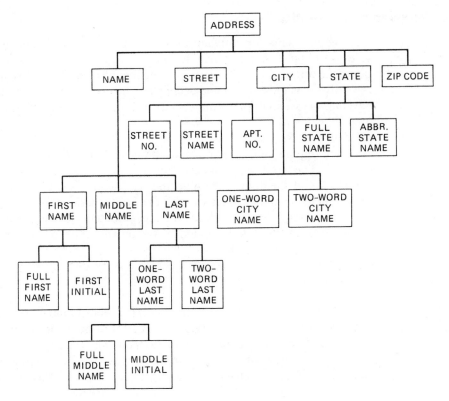

FIGURE 17-5. A tree structure of an address.

The foregoing discussion involves the representation of a nonnumerical input domain by a SIAD tree. Similarly, a numerical input domain can also be represented by a SIAD tree. An example is given in Tables 17-8 and 17-9.

B. Process

In building a manufacturing factory, this stage includes the description of all of the processes required to produce the goods that must be developed into real processes. Similarly, in developing software, the complete description of what all of the functions must perform must be created and developed in real executable code. The information given in Section 17.5, paragraph I is to be incorporated into the process section of the requirements document.

C. Output

Software output requirements include man-machine interface, the characteristics of the products to be generated by the software, response time, data input-output format and contents, and interpretation of data produced by the software.

TABLE 17-2   Example Nonnumerical SIAD Tree

INDEX	TREE SYMBOL	TREE ELEMENT	RULE INDEX
1	X1	ADDRESS, N1 alphanumeric characters	1 13
2	X1, 1	NAME, N2 alphabetic characters	2 12 13 14 16
3	X1, 1, 1	FIRST NAME, N3 alphabetic characters	3 13 14 15 16
4	X1, 1, 1, 1	FULL FIRST NAME, N3 alphabetic characters	3 13 14 15 16
5	X1, 1, 1, 2	FIRST INITIAL, N3 alphabetic characters	3 13 14 15 17
6	X1, 1, 2	MIDDLE NAME, N4 alphabetic characters	4 13 14 15 16
7	X1, 1, 2, 1	FULL MIDDLE NAME, N4 alphabetic characters	4 13 14 15 16
8	X1, 1, 2, 2	MIDDLE INITIAL, N4 alphabetic characters	4 13 14 15 17
9	X1, 1, 3	LAST NAME, N5 alphabetic characters	5 13 14 16
10	X1, 1, 3, 1	ONE-WORD LAST NAME, N5 alphabetic characters	5 13 14 17 19
11	X1, 1, 3, 2	MULTI-WORD LAST NAME, N5 alphabetic characters	5 13 14 15 18
12	X1, 2	STREET, N6 alphanumeric characters	6 13 15 16
13	X1, 2, 1	STREET NO., N7 alphanumeric characters	7 13 16
14	X1, 2, 2	STREET NAME N8 alphanumeric characters	8 13 15
15	X1, 2, 3	APARTMENT NO., N9 alphanumeric characters	9 13 15 17 19 20
16	X1, 3	CITY NAME, N10 alphabetic characters	10 13 14 15 17 19
17	X1, 3, 1	ONE-WORD CITY NAME, N10 alphabetic characters	10 13 14 17 19
18	X1, 3, 2	TWO-WORD CITY NAME, N10 alphabetic characters	10 13 14 15 19
19	X1, 4	STATE, N11 alphabetic characters	11 13 14 15 17 19
20	X1, 4, 1	FULL STATE NAME, N11 alphabetic characters	11 13 14 17 19
21	X1, 4, 2	ABBREVIATED STATE NAME, N11 alphabetic characters	11 13 14 15 17 19
22	X1, 5	ZIP CODE, N12 numeric characters	12 13 15 17 19

TABLE 17-3 Input Domain Rules for the SIAD Tree in Table 17-2

RULE INDEX	RULE DESCRIPTION	SUBRULE INDEX
1	N1 = N3 + N4 + N5 + N7 + N8 + N9 + N10 + N11 + N12	1 2 3 4 5 6 7 8 9
2	N2 = N3 + N4 + N5	1 2 3
3	N3	1
4	N4	2
5	N5	3
6	N6 = N7 + N8 + N9	4 5 6
7	N7	4
8	N8	5
9	N9	6
10	N10	7
11	N11	8
12	N12	9
13	Excluding characters + * / ' " $ & # @ /= ; :) (! ? =] [% ¢	
14	Excluding characters 0 1 2 3 4 5 6 7 8 9	
15	Including one character . or space	
16	Including character -	
17	Excluding character -	
18	Including character ,	
19	Excluding character ,	
20	Including space	

TABLE 17-4 Example Subrules of the Input Domain Rules in Table 17-3

SUBRULE INDEX	SUBRULE DESCRIPTION	REMARK
1	$1 \leq N3 \leq 24$	Length of FIRST NAME
2	$1 \leq N4 \leq 24$	Length of MIDDLE NAME
3	$2 \leq N5 \leq 40$	Length of LAST NAME
4	$1 \leq N7 \leq 10$	Length of STREET NO.
5	$1 \leq N8 \leq 20$	Length of STREET NAME
6	$1 \leq N9 \leq 10$	Length of APARTMENT NO.
7	$2 \leq N10 \leq 20$	Length of CITY NAME
8	$2 \leq N11 \leq 20$	Length of STATE NAME
9	$5 \leq N12 \leq 9$	Length of ZIP CODE

(2) Test Requirements

Test requirements are specified as the criteria for software testing and acceptance upon completion. They consist of definition of product units, definition of product unit defectiveness, software acceptance criteria, sampling methods, and software reliability confidence level.

A. DEFINITION OF PRODUCT UNIT

Once the modeling activities in Section 17.5 have been completed, the definition of product unit is transferred here into the requirement specification document. The information collected in Section 17.5, see items C, D, E and F under I. Modeling, is reviewed and refined to ensure that the definition is correct.

B. DEFINITION OF PRODUCT UNIT DEFECTIVENESS

The information obtained in Section 17.5, see items E and F under I. Modeling, is entered into the requirement specification document.

C. SOFTWARE ACCEPTANCE CRITERIA

With the definitions of product unit and product unit defectiveness, the acceptance of a piece of software is equivalent to that of the product population the software generates. Criteria are needed to determine the acceptability of the population. Such criteria can be divided into two classes: population defective rate estimate and population acceptance.

a. *Population Defective Rate Estimate Criteria*

The criteria are the values of a and z in equation (3.1). For example, $a = 0.1$ and $z = 1.96$ (the z value is for confidence level). A sampling plan for estimating the defective rate of a population can be formulated, as explained with equation (3.1).

One other criterion is required to decide the acceptability of the population— the acceptable defective rate. Intuitively, the output population defective rate must be 0 to be acceptable. But because of the size of the population, a mass inspection of it is infeasible. Equation (3.1) also indicates that the sample size n approaches infinity when the defective rate θ is 0. Therefore, after the defective rate has been estimated, the acceptability of the population is judged by $\theta < c$, where c is the acceptable defective rate.

b. *Population Acceptance Criteria*

The criteria are the values of a_1, θ_1, a_2, θ_2, where $\theta_1 < \theta_2$, for formulating an acceptance plan, as described in Section 17.3. The details of the formulation of a plan may be found in Cho[7].

D. Sampling Methods

The purpose of defining a software product unit is twofold: testing and usage. When a piece of software is viewed as a factory, daily processing of input units into product units becomes conceptually equivalent to taking random product units from the software's population. If the product units in the population are all of good quality, then the units taken will be of good quality.

Since the software product population is extremely large, and may be considered infinite, generation of the entire population and then taking a random sample from the population for estimating the defective rate is impossible. An easy way is through random construction of input units from the SIAD tree of the software. The random sampling may be done in four ways:

a. *Basic Sampling.* Let $w_1, w_2, \ldots, w_t$ be the weights to be placed on the input variables $v_1, v_2, \ldots, v_t$ (or on the SIAD tree elements $e_1, e_2, \ldots, e_t$) of the software. If $w_1 = w_2 = \ldots = w_t$, then the sampling is called basic sampling. In other words, each tree element in the SIAD tree has an equal chance of being taken from the tree for the construction of an input unit.

b. *Weighted Sampling.* The sampling method is the same as basic sampling, except some of the weights $w_1, w_2, \ldots, w_t$ are not equal, e.g., $w_1 \neq w_5$.

c. *Boundary Sampling.* This method is the same as basic sampling, except that each numerical variable of a piece of software assumes either its lower or upper bound value. If there are s such variables, $u_1, u_2, \ldots, u_s$, then there are 2^s input units of 2^s product units in the population. For example, there will be 2^{31} or 2,147,483,648 units that can be generated if the number of numerical variables is 31. Clearly, inspecting 2,147,483,648 units exhaustively is uneconomical if not infeasible. It is seen that random sampling of product units from the population is an easy and economical way of inspecting the quality of the population.

d. *Invalid Sampling.* This method is the same as basic sampling, except that some of the variables, $v_1, v_2, \ldots, v_t$ assumes some invalid data, e.g., assigning the value outside of the defined lower and upper bound of a numerical variable or embedding some invalid characters into the datum of a nonnumerical variable.

It is seen that a product population can be generated under each of the sampling methods. The software acceptance criteria given in the previous subsection can be imposed on each of the populations in the requirement specification document.

E. Software Quality Confidence Level

Equation (3.1) is for determining the sample size n required to estimate the defective rate θ of a software output population with a certain confidence level z and an accuracy factor a. For example, if $z = 1.96$ and $a = 0.1$, then one can be 95% (found from a normal distribution table with $z = 1.96$) confident that the population defective rate θ is not different from the sample defective $\theta°$ by $0.1\ \theta$. As the value of θ remains unchanged during testing of n input units, the larger the value of n, the more accurate the estimate of θ between θ and $\theta°$ (i.e., the smaller the value of a) and the higher the confidence level z, based on the equation. However, the larger the value of n, the more the cost in testing. Therefore, the user needs to define the values of z and a for equation (3.1) to fit his or her budgetary situation and, at the same time, can impose the quality requirement on the object software, e.g., the population defective rate to be less than 0.001 with a confidence level of 95% and an accuracy factory of 0.01 for sampling purposes.

III. Concurrent Software Design and Test Design

Software design and test design are two major tasks in the design stage of software development. With a well-prepared model and requirements specification documents, the tasks can proceed concurrently.

There are many software design methods in practice, such as structured design,[9] structured analysis and design technique,[10] and object-oriented design.[11] They may be classified into two groups: *function-oriented* and *object-oriented* methods. The first deals with general development of software using most programming languages, while the second is similar to the first but more suitable for developing software in the new Ada® programming language. Since the second method requires the Ada language, only the function-oriented design method is discussed here. The object-oriented design with Quality Programming may be found in Cho[15].

(1) Software Design

The major design tasks of the quality programming method include:

    A. Derivation of software functions from a software model.
    B. Organizing the functions into a tree structure (each of the functions becomes a software module).
    C. Generating input domain of each module in performing the function of the module.
    D. Design of user interface.
    E. Design of module interface.
    F. Design of module.

The design tasks should be performed in that order and should be refined with test design upon completion.

A. DERIVATION OF SOFTWARE FUNCTIONS FROM A MODEL

In any manufacturing, the building of a factory requires many blueprints. Each blueprint represents a portion of the factory which performs a specific function. In

------

order to generate the blueprints, the functions of the factory must first be identified. The identification of such functions are the results of studying the model of the factory, as described in Section 17.5.

B. ORGANIZING THE FUNCTIONS INTO A TREE STRUCTURE

After all of the functions have been identified, their interrelationships are defined. The functions are then organized into a tree structure to illustrate the relationships. Such a structure allows understanding of a complicated problem on a tree level-by-level basis. A function at a level in the tree is an abstraction of the subfunction(s) at a lower level and hides some detailed information from the subfunction(s). The resultant tree structure becomes the structure of the software being developed.

C. GENERATING INPUT DOMAIN OF EACH MODULE IN PERFORMING THE FUNCTION

Similar to a software system, the function of a module is to produce an output from an input. The input domain of a module must also be designed for module interfaces and can also be represented in a SIAD tree as described in Section 17.5, paragraph II. Requirements Specification. A module SIAD tree is required because:

  a. It insures testability of a module, since inputs to the module can be constructed from the tree to facilitate test design.
  b. It forms a convenient basis for module interfaces.
  c. It enables concurrent development of module design and module test design.

D. DESIGN OF USER INTERFACE

User interface consists of input preparation and output interpretation. Human factors must be considered in designing such an interface, e.g., easy to use and difficult to misuse.

E. DESIGN OF MODULE INTERFACES

The design is based on the SIAD tree of a module. The following factors should be considered in designing module interfaces:

  a. *To avoid bad common coupling,* two modules should not be "glued" together by the interface. A module, once developed, should be reuseable. For example, a variable in an interface should be given a significant name *within* the module, instead of being tied to the name of the function or calling module.

b. *To avoid control coupling,* the logic of a module should not depend on the logic of a calling module and vice versa. For example, in the segments of FORTRAN code:

```
        .
        .
        .
I = 1
CALL SUBA(I,A,B)
        .
        .
        .
I = 2
CALL SUBA(I,A,B)
        .
        .
        .
END
SUBROUTINE SUBA(I,A,B)
IF (I .EQ. 1) THEN A = B * 2 END IF
IF (I .EQ. 2) THEN A = B ** 2 END IF
        .
        .
    3 .
END
```

the logic of SUBA is controlled by the value of I and should be avoided.

F. Design of Module

A module consists of two parts: data structure and algorithm. There are many data structures and algorithms that can be developed to perform the intended function of a module. Design alternatives and simplicity should be considered in designing a module.

Module design can be expressed in a program design language (PDL). The PDL contains six major parts:

a. Module name: this is for module identification.
b. Level number: this is the level of detailed description of the module. (This level number should not be confused with the level of a tree structure.)
c. Description: this is the description of the function or subfunction(s) of the module, the constraints on the module, and other information related to the module.

d. Input: this is the description of the input domain of the module in terms of input variables with which data is to be passed to the module. The description includes the types and the structures of the variable and rules of constructing input data, and so forth.

e. Output: this is the description of the output of the module and is similar to that of the input variables.

f. Process: this is the body of module design. It uses a program design language (PDL) which is simple English to describe the constructs of module logic. The constructs include SEQUENCE, IF-THEN-ELSE, DO-WHILE, DO-UNTIL, and CASE, as described in Cho[7].

The input and output part of the design is the interface of the module with the "outside world."

If a module is complicated, then the design can be developed by refining the PDL level by level, e.g., level-1, level-2, and level-3 PDL of a module. The level-1 PDL is an abstraction of the level-2 PDL, hiding some detailed information from the level-2 PDL. Similarly, the level-2 PDL is an abstraction of the level-3 PDL, hiding some detailed information from the level-3 PDL; and so on. The lowest-level PDL is very close to the programming language to be used. The criteria in developing these levels of abstraction are shown in Table 17-5.

Figure 17-6 is an example of a 3-level PDL for a matrix multiplication module. The advantages of using the 3-level approach are:

a. After each level of PDL has been completed, a design review or walkthrough can be conducted to insure that nothing is missing from the PDL before the design of the next-level PDL.

b. After the review, the design is refined and the result is a design document for that level.

TABLE 17-5   Three Levels of PDL

PDL	LEVEL		
	1	2	3
Input Variable	Basic description and how it is used,	Adding the structure of the variable.	Adding data type, lower and upper bounds, rules of using the variable.
Output Variable	Basic description and how it is to be used by other modules.	Adding the structure of the variable.	Adding data type, lower and upper bounds, rules of using the variable.
Process	Basic functions and the logical order in which the functions are to be performed.	Decomposing each basic function into subfunctions, with description of necessary initialization and constraints.	Decomposing each subfunction into smaller pieces, with detailed description of initialization and constraints.

MODULE NAME: MODULA

LEVEL: 1

DESCRIPTION: This module performs multiplication of two matrices.

INPUT: A = This is a multiplicant matrix.

               B = This is a multiplier matrix.

OUTPUT: C = This is a matrix storing the result of the multiplication.

PROCESS:

   DO   ;

      Multiply matrix A by matrix B and store the result in matrix C   ;

   END   ;

END   ;

MODULE NAME: MODULA

LEVEL: 2

DESCRIPTION: This module performs multiplication of two matrices.

INPUT: A = This is a 2-dimensional multiplicant matrix.

               B = This is a 2-dimensional multiplier matrix.

OUTPUT: C = This is a 2-dimensional matrix storing the result of the multiplica-
               tion.
PROCESS:

   DO   ;

      Multiply each row of matrix A by each column of matrix B   ;

      Store the result in matrix C   ;

   END   ;

END   ;

MODULE NAME: MODULA

LEVEL: 3

DESCRIPTION: This module performs multiplication of two matrices.

INPUT: A = This is a 2-dimensional, double precision, of size 3 x 3,
               multiplicant matrix.

               B = This is a 2-dimensional, double precision, of size 3 x 3,
               multiplier matrix.

FIGURE 17-6. Matrix multiplication module (3-level PDL).

```
OUTPUT:   C = This is a 2-dimensional, double precision, of size 3 x 3, matrix
                storing the result of the multiplication.

PROCESS:

    DO  ;

        DO I FROM 1 TO 3  ;

            DO K FROM 1 TO 3  ;

                C(I,K) = 0  ;

                DO J FROM 1 TO 3  ;

                    C(I,K) = C(I,K) + A(I,J) * B(J,K)  ;

                END  ;

            END  ;

        END  ;

    END  ;

END  ;
```

FIGURE 17-6. (Cont.)

c. The level of abstraction in the PDL provides a "top-down" understandability of the design, enhancing tremendously the readability of the software being developed.

(2) Test Design

The tasks of estimating the software defective rate using statistical quality control include:

A. Review of product unit definition for sampling.
B. Review of product unit defectiveness definition.
C. Design of a sampling plan.
D. Construction of random input units by a random procedure using a SIAD tree.
E. Analysis of test results.
F. Statistical inference on product population defective rate.

Tasks A, B, C, and D are design tasks which can proceed simultaneously with software design. Tasks E and F are implementation tasks to be performed after software coding and debugging has been completed.

A. REVIEW OF PRODUCT UNIT DEFINITION FOR SAMPLING

In any manufacturing industry, the definition of product unit is the basis on which to apply statistical quality control. As a piece of software can be viewed as a factory producing discrete outputs, so each of the outputs can be defined as a product unit. With this concept in mind, we can view accepting a piece of software as equivalent to accepting all of the product units the software generates.

B. Review of Product Unit Defectiveness Definition

This definition is essential to classify a product unit being defective or nondefective. Depending on the degree of seriousness, a defective unit may fall into one of four categories:

i. Severely defective: it contain wrong and unuseable results. The use of the results can cause severe damage to its user.
ii. Seriously defective: it contains unuseable results. The use of the results can cause serious difficulty to its user.
iii. Minor-defective: it contains errors but will not affect its user.
iv. Irregularly defective: It contains odd results. The use of the results will not affect its user.

A defective unit in categories iii and iv may be regarded as nondefective for economical reasons.

C. Design of a Sampling Plan

The design of a plan for estimating the defective rate of a software population includes the determination of sample size n, the number of product units to be taken randomly from the population. As seen in equation (3.1), the value of n depends on two criteria: (1) the closeness of the accuracy between the population defective rate θ and the sample defective rate θ°, and (2) the desired level of confidence for determining the value of z in equation (3.1). The criteria should be given in the requirement specification document.

D. Construction of Random Input Units by a Random Procedure Using a SIAD Tree

The construction of a random input unit for testing begins with sampling from the tree elements of a software SIAD tree defined in a requirement specification document. Since there are three types of tree elements that can be specified in the tree—numerical, nonnumerical, and data value—the construction of a unit can be different.

i. *Numerical Elements:* If *LA* and *UA* are two tree elements representing the lower and upper bounds of a variable *A* in a SIAD tree, then the value of *A* may be generated randomly by

$$A = LA + (UA - LA)r$$

where r is a random number, $0 < r < 1$. For example, if $LA = -0.5$, $UA = 10$, and $r = 0.2314$, then $A = -0.5 + (10 + 0.5)0.2314 = 1.9297$.

ii. *Nonnumerical Elements:* If a tree element randomly sampled from a SIAD tree represents a nonnumerical datum, the actual data is to be chosen by the designer. For example, a piece of software maintains the accuracy of a mailing address data base and the product unit is defined to be the result of processing an input unit constructed from a tree element in Table 17-2. Suppose a random number 9 is generated to sample a tree element. Then the 9th element, LAST NAME, is to be used to construct an input unit to test if the software changes the content of a last name in the data base correctly. The construction of such a unit must follow rules 5, 13, 14, and 16, as shown in the RULE INDEX column of Table 17-2. Rules 5, 13, 14, and 16 are given in Table 17-3. Rule 5 indicates that the length of a last name in number of characters, N5, must follow subrule 3, as shown in the SUBRULE INDEX column in Table 17-4, which is $2 \le N5 \le 40$. Accordingly, the length of a last name can be randomly generated by

$$N5 = 2 + [(40 - 2 + 1)r],$$

where $[(40 - 2 + 1)r]$ is the whole number (or integer) part of the contents, and $0 < r < 1$, e.g.:

$$N5 = 2 + [(40 - 2 + 1)0.0252] = 2 + 0 = 2$$

Rule 13 in Table 17-3 states "Excluding characters $+ * / ' " \$ \& \# @ \ne ; :)$ $(! ? =] [\% ¢$." In other words, no valid last name can contain any of these characters. Rule 14 states "Excluding characters 0 1 2 3 4 5 6 7 8 9," meaning that no numerical characters can be in a last name. Rule 16 is "Including character -" which means that the character - can be embedded in a last name. Table 17-6 contains some examples of last names to be used as input by the software program prior to processing and updating the LAST NAME fields of some addresses.

It is seen in this example that the SIAD tree in Table 17-2 with the rules and subrules in Tables 17-3 and 17-4 represents the input domain of the example software. Within the domain, a sample of n input units can be constructed, each unit being a set of the elements in SIAD tree in Table 17-2.

TABLE 17-6   Last Names for Updating

INPUT UNIT	N5	LAST NAME	VALIDITY
1	2	XY	Valid
2	11	WAYSMITENIA	Valid
3	6	NENDOL	Valid
4	7	SM1THEN	Invalid
5	15	AMDJWXER-OQRSTK	Valid
6	3	N+A	Invalid

TABLE 17-7   Sample SIAD Tree

INDEX	TREE SYMBOL	TREE ELEMENT
1	Y1	X
2	Y2	MM
3	Y3	PPP
4	Y4	AAAA
5	Y5	FFFFF
6	Y6	HHHHHH

If an input unit is defined to consist of k elements of the SIAD tree, $1 < k$, then k random numbers, each being between 1 and 22, are generated. The tree elements that correspond to the k numbers are taken for construction of an input unit, following the process described above for each of the sampled elements.

iii. *Data Value Elements:* If a piece of data is specified directly in the SIAD tree, then it is entered into an input unit directly if sampled. For example, if a SIAD tree is specified to be that shown in Table 17-7, then AAAAXMM is an input unit if elements 4, 1, and 2 are randomly sampled in that order.

The discussion given above is basic sampling. The other three sampling methods—weighted, boundary, and invalid, as discussed in paragraph II. Requirements Specification, Item D, may be used to construct the input units for testing purposes.

The test design technique discussed in this section is applicable to both module and software development.

IV. Software Implementation

As shown in Figure 17-4, software implementation consists of two major tasks: coding and test case generation with expected results of processing the input units. The tasks are simply the implementation of software design and test design respectively. Proper program constructs including SEQUENCE, IF-THEN-ELSE, DO WHILE or DO UNTIL, and MODULE should be used for algorithm coding for better understandability. In addition, proper data structures including VARI-ABLE, ARRAY, LIST, STACK, QUEUE, TREE and NETWORK (or PLEX) should be used for efficiency of a particular algorithm. In the test case generation, n units should be generated using the design in the test design stage discussed in this section, where n is the sample size determined by equation (3.1).

Although there are many methods of software implementation, such as top-down and bottom-up, it has been this author's experience that a good method is top-down design with critical-module and bottom-up implementation. This method is based on the concept of building a thing on a "secured spare-part and assembly" basis. If bottom-up implementation cannot be done, then it means the software design is incomplete. Implementation of a software system with an incomplete design is asking for trouble!

A detailed description of software implementation methods is given in Cho[7].

V. Testing and Integration

After software design and test design have been implemented, the individual modules are to be tested before it is integrated into the software. Testing and integration should be done from the modules at the bottom level to the modules at the top level in the software tree. This is like building a factory based on a "quality-part" basis to avoid integrating a poor-quality part into the factory. After each module has been tested and its output population defective rate satisfies a design criterion $\theta_i < c_i$ where i identifies a module and c_i is a given small number, the module is then integrated into the software. The module output population defective rate θ_i can also be estimated by equation (3.0).

After all of the modules have been tested and integrated, the software is then tested using the test input units implemented from the software's input domain and rules SIAD tree. Finally, the software product population defective rate θ under each of the four sampling methods (regular, weighted, boundary, and invalid) discussed in the Test Requirements subsection of Section 17.5, is computed by equation (3.0). If the estimated rates do not satisfy the requirement $\theta < c$ under at least one sampling method, then the software should not be delivered. The developer should improve the quality by correcting the errors found during the test.

VI. Software Acceptance

If the developed software satisfies the quality requirement $\theta < c$, it is delivered to the user. The user can accept the software trusting that the requirement $\theta < c$ has been met, or the user can verify the rate θ by conducting a test following the same techniques discussed. The quality control tool is seen to be a powerful weapon to protect the user from being a poor-quality software victim.

17.6 QUALITY PROGRAMMING PRACTICAL EXPERIENCES

The Quality Programming technology has been applied to a number of projects in the U.S. and other countries in many different applications since the publication of Reference 15, which describes the invention and development of the technology. The technology has been applied to development and testing of new systems and to testing already-developed systems. The applications include:

- Air defense system
- Air traffic control system
- Large-scale defense systems
- Operating system
- Space decision support system
- Color graphics firmware system
- Printed circuit design system

- Multisensor tracking system
- Scientific systems

These systems were developed in the Ada, Assembly, COBOL, FORTRAN, and PL/M languages.

Following the technology in developing a new system, software quality is automatically built into the system. The test of such a system is fairly easy, as all of the ingredients necessary to the design and implementation of test have been built in the system along with the development process.[15] The major ingredients include the SIAD tree (input domain), definitions of product unit and product unit definitions, confidence in the test result, etc.[15]

Applying the Quality Programming technology to testing an existing system, developed using other software technologies, presents many difficulties. The ingredients necessary to apply the technology to the design and implementation of test are missing. Therefore, those ingredients must be made available after the fact for testing and software use purposes. This is one reason why many software systems are of poor quality—unusable!

Table 17.8 shows a number of existing systems tested for 25 projects using the Quality Programming technology. Each of the entries was obtained by applying Equations (3.1) in Section 17.4 of this book and/or (5.3a) in Chapter 5 of Reference 15, where the % chance of getting wrong results is the sample defective rate in the equations. For example, the user would get wrong results 77 times out of 100 from using the Project 9 software during the operation of the system under the defined conditions (the conditions are not shown).

It is important to note that the entries in the column of % chance of getting wrong results should be interpreted strictly under the conditions of SIAD tree (input domain), product unit, product unit defectiveness and quality confidence level defined for the software. (None of these conditions are shown.) The chances of getting wrong results must not be generalized. In other words, each chance is valid only when the software is used under its defined conditions. Each system must be retested under a different set of conditions. For example, the chance of getting wrong results for Project 2 system is 0, meaning that it is 0 only under the conditions defined for the software to operate. The chance may not be 0 if the user is to use the system under another set of conditions. Similarly, the chance is 100 percent for Project 8. This does not mean that the system is not usable under another set of conditions. The chance must be obtained by retesting the system.

The software reliability measure using the Quality Programming technology is simply the value of $1 - d$, where d is the % chance of getting wrong results in using a system. For example, the reliability of Project 1 is $1 - 0.225 = 0.775$ in Table 17.8. The reliability value so obtained is independent of software test and operation clock time. Conventionally, the software reliability is measured by the "mean time to failure" which is dependent on the software operation clock time. However, the value of $1 - d$ is the "mean 'time' to failure," where 'time' is the number of times a user uses the system under his defined conditions.

TABLE 17.8   The State of Health of, or Risks in using, the Software in 25 Projects.

Project	System	Number of Units Tested	Number of Defective Units Found	User's Risks (% Chance of Getting Wrong Results)
1	OS/MAINFRAME	50	11	22.50
2		60	0	0.00
3		60	31	52.00
4		53	1	1.80
5		60	4	6.70
	TOTALS	283	47	16.60
6	DBMS/PC	30	0	0.00
7		38	2	5.30
8		12	12	100.00
9		122	94	77.10
10		30	29	96.70
	TOTALS	232	137	59.10
11	DBMS/HOL/MINI	380	8	2.10
12		380	8	2.10
13		2080	12	0.60
	TOTALS	2840	28	1.00
14	DBMS/HOL/MINI	77	43	56.00
15		36	(5 errors)	*
16		88	(33 errors)	*
17	SCIENTIFIC	36	4	11.11
18		55	6	10.91
19		55	9	16.36
20		112	14	12.50
21		30	8	26.67
22		30	29	96.70
23		30	16	53.33
24		30	8	26.67
25		30	30	100.00
	TOTALS	408	124	30.39

Note: The conditions under which each project was tested are proprietary in nature and are not given.

*Only the number of errors were found in the test.

17.7 PROPOSED SOLUTIONS TO SOME TECHNICAL PROBLEMS IN SOFTWARE ENGINEERING PROJECT MANAGEMENT

An effective software development methodology based on statistical quality control has been proposed to help develop good quality and cost effective software.

The method answers the two basic questions in software development; when to stop testing and how good the software is after testing. The first question may be answered with equation (3.1). The second is answered with the software product population defective rate θ estimated from the sample defective rate θ° after n product units, determined by equation (3.1), have been tested and inspected. The basis of the method is the definitions of product unit and of product unit defectiveness.

It is seen that the method may also provide solutions to the software engineering project management technical problems 1, 2, 9, 16, 18, and 19 in Table 17-1 as follows.

Problem 1: Requirement

In general, what is missing in requirements specification for software development includes the input domain and rules of constructing input units from the domain (see sub-sections marked "A. Input Domain") and the test requirements. This may explain why the requirement problem exists. The input domain and rules expressed in the SIAD tree is consistent for both numerical and nonnumerical domains. The completeness of the tree is measurable and has no ambiguity. The test requirements are based on statistical quality control principles.

Problem 2: Success

The software product population defective rate θ discussed in this chapter and in Cho[7] may be used as a success criterion for software development. For example, the criterion previously given (see sub-section "C. Software Acceptance Criteria") is $\theta < c$, where c is a small acceptable number. Another criterion is the document generated at each of the six stages in Figure 17-4 and discussed in Section 17.5.

Problem 9: Warranty

The software population defective rate θ may be used to guarantee or warrant that the software delivered will work. For example, if the defective criterion ϵ is 0.1, 0.01, 0.001, 0.0001, or 0.00001, then the ROOTS procedure in Figure 17-13 can be guaranteed to work 100% according to the input domain and rules in Tables 17-8, and 17-9. However, if ϵ is 0.000001, then such a warranty is not valid, and the producer will risk about 10% in giving the 100% warranty.

Problem 16: Reliability

Although discussions of and models for measuring software reliability abound in the literature, most such discussions and models are not based on sound theoretical foundations.[12] As pointed out in reference 12, the only model whose theoretical foundations are sound is the Nelson model.[13] Based on this model, test cases are selected randomly according to some operational distribution. The reliability over the next run $R(1)$ is computed by

$$\hat{R}(1) = 1 - \frac{n_f}{n}$$

where n is the total number of test cases and n_f is the number of failures out of these tests. The following are the drawbacks of the model:[12]

1) In order to have a high confidence in the reliability estimate, a large number of test cases must be used.
2) It does not take into account "continuity" in the input domain. For example, if the program is correct for a test case, then it is likely that it is correct for all test cases excuting the same sequence of statements.
3) It assumes random sampling of the input domain. Thus, it cannot take advantage of testing strategies which have a higher probability of detecting errors, e.g., boundary value testing, etc. Further, for most real-time control systems the successive inputs are "correlated" if the inputs are sensor readings of physical quantities, like temperature, which cannot change rapidly. In these cases we cannot perform random testing.
4) It does not consider any complexity measure of the program, e.g., number of paths, statements, etc. Generally, a complex program should be tested more than a simple program for the same confidence in the reliability estimate.

Our method is based on the concrete theoretical foundations of statistical quality control principles. It removes the drawbacks of the Nelson model as follows:

1. According to Equation (3.1), the sample size n depends on the confidence level from the value of z and the estimate accuracy factor of a. The equation can be used to compute the value of z given a and n. The result of testing can answer when to stop testing and how good the software is after testing. The Nelson model seems not to address this aspect.
2. Continuity is implied in the test. The number of paths in a large and complex program is also large. Once a path is tested, the same path may not be tested more than once. This may not be considered as a drawback.
3. Our method does take advantage of testing strategies which have a higher probability of detecting errors. The sampling methods on p. 306 provide four different ways: basic, weighted, boundary, and invalid sampling for this purpose. The defective rate of each of the four populations can be given. Further, the random sampling in this chapter is based on the definition of product unit derived from the input domain and rules of a piece of software. The random sampling is different from the Nelson model which is based on number of runs.[12] In the case of real-time control systems where successive inputs are correlated if the inputs are sensor readings of physical quantities,

like temperature, which cannot change rapidly, the product unit is also defined with input rules.

For example, the product unit of temperature readings can be defined as follows: Let M be a desired number and $T_1, T_2, \ldots, T_k$ be the successive inputs, where only T_1 is a random input while $T_2, \ldots, T_k$ are computed from $T_i = T_i - 1 \pm rt$ for $i = 2, 3, \ldots, k$, and t is the maximum possible temperature variation between two successive inputs, r is a random number, $0 < r < 1$, and k is a random number between 1 and M inclusive. Therefore, n random product units $T_{j1}, T_{j2}, \ldots, T_{jk}$ for $j = 1, 2, \ldots, n$ are to be used to test, instead of just n temperatures.

4. Although the complexity measure of a program is not considered explicitly, it is considered implicitly in module testing, as discussed in sub-section "V. Testing and Integration."

It is seen that the software product population defective rate θ is a good software reliability measure, e.g., $R = 1 - \theta$.

Problem 18: Goodness

The software product population defective rate θ can also be used to measure the goodness of a program or to show that one program is better than another. Once a sample of n product units has been constructed, it can be used to test as many programs $F_1, F_2, \ldots F_p$ as are performing the same functions. The defective rates $\theta_{F_1}, \theta_{F_2}, \ldots, \theta_{F_p}$ can be used to compare the goodness of the programs.

Problem 19: Programmer

Conventionally, the quality of a programmer cannot be measured in a meaningful numerical term. But the defective rate θ can be used for this purpose. If the program developed satisfies the requirement $\theta < c$, then the performance of the programmer is good. However, since the software developed is the result of the modeling, requirements specification, concurrent software design and test design, and implementation activities, all of the people involved in these activities should be considered in measuring the programming personnel.

17.8 WHAT TOP MANAGEMENT MUST DO

In his world-famous seminar on Japanese methods for productivity and quality, Dr. W. Edwards Deming, the father of modern Japanese quality control, points out 14 obligations that the top management of any manufacturing organization must carry out for the improvement of quality, productivity, and competitive position.[14] Since a piece of software is indeed a factory and the tool of quality control is applicable to ensure product quality of the software, the obligations Dr. Deming stresses are applicable to the software industry as well. The following are 12 of the

14 obligations that the top management of a computer or software company must do to be responsible to software users:

1. To create a rigid goal toward improvement of software quality and productivity with a plan to become competitive and to stay in business. Top management is responsible to stockholders and to the general public as well.
2. To adopt a new philosophy. We are living in a new information age. We can no longer live with commonly accepted levels of delays, poor quality, and costly software.
3. To cease dependence on conventional software methods. Adapt, instead, statistical evidence to assure that quality is built into the software. Software managers have a new job and must learn it.
4. To end the practice of awarding software business on the lowest-bid basis. Instead, meaningful measures of quality along with price must be demanded. Software developers who cannot qualify with statistical evidence of quality must be removed.
5. To find problems. Everyone in a software organization must be provided with appropriate statistical methods by which to learn which software quality problems can be corrected "locally" and which belong to the system and require the attention of management. It is the management's job to work continually on the system (from requirement specification, design, implementation, testing, delivery, maintenance, improvement, to training supervision, and retraining).
6. To institute modern methods of training on the job, e.g., training software personnel with the method that uses the quality control tool.
7. To institute modern methods of supervision, e.g., award people with quality and quantity, rather than quantity alone. In the software industry, productivity is often measured by the number of lines of code produced per day. To require, instead, productivity as reducing the defective rate.
8. To drive out fear so that everyone within a software organization may work effectively.
9. To break down barriers between departments. People in software design and implementation must work as a team with people in software quality assurance to foresee problems of software quality that may be encountered in the development process.
10. To provide methods to measure software quality in meaningful numerical terms. (Cho[7] provides detailed discussions and may be used as a starting point.)
11. To institute a rigorous program of education and retraining.
12. To create a top management structure that will encourage and stimulate an everyday push on the above eleven action items.

References

1. Thayer, R. H.; Pyster, A.; and Wood R. C., "The Challenge of Software Engineering Project Management," IEEE *Computer,* Vol. 13, No. 8, (Aug. 1980), pp. 51-59.
2. Cho, C. K., *AERA Package 1 Test Bed Software Quality Assurance Tests of the*

Aircraft Data Manager, Working Paper No. WP-81W00285, The MITRE Corp., June 1981.

3. Eagles, S. L., *SIAD Tree Experiments,* Control Data Corporation, November 1983.

4. Miller, C. R., *SIAD Tree Report,* Control Data Corporation, November 1983.

5. Jump, L. B., *Software Quality Control: A Case Study,* Applied Data Systems, December, 1983.

6. Fultyn, R. V., *Computer-Assisted Software Testing,* Digital Equipment Corporation, 1982.

7. Cho, C. K., *An Introduction to Software Quality Control,* (New York: John Wiley & Sons, 1980).

8. Juran, J. M.; Seder, L. A.; and Gryna, F. M., Eds., *Quality Control Handbook,* 2nd Ed. (New York: McGraw-Hill, 1962).

9. Yourdon, E., and Constantine, L. L., *Structured Design: Fundamentals of a Discipline of Computer Program and System Design* (Englewood Cliffs, NJ: Prentice-Hall, 1979).

10. Ross, D. T.; Goodenough, J. B.; and Irvine, C. A., "Software Engineering: Process, Principles, and Goals," IEEE *Computer,* Vol. 8, No. 5 (May 1975), pp. 17-27.

11. Booch, G., *Software Engineering with Ada* (Menlo Park: Benjamin/Cummins, 1983).

12. Ramamoorthy, C. V., and Bastani F. B., "Software Reliability and Perspectives," IEEE *Transactions on Software Engineering,* Vol. SE-8, No. 4 (July 1982), pp. 354-371.

13. Nelson E., "Estimating Software Reliability from Test Data," *Microelectronics and Reliability,* Vol. 17 (New York: Pergamon, 1978), pp. 67-74.

14. Deming, W. Edwards, *Quality, Productivity and Competitive Position* (Cambridge, MA: Center for Advanced Engineering Study, Massachusetts Institute of Technology, 1982).

15. C. K. Cho, *Quality Programming: Developing and Testing Software with Statistical Quality Control,* (New York: John Wiley & Sons, Inc., 1987).

16. C. K. Cho, "Software Engineering with Statistical Quality Control," *Proceedings, (METS),* CIE/ROC and CIE/USA, Taiwan, Republic of China, 1986.

17. C. K. Cho, "Statistical Measurement and Software Warranty," *Proceedings, Software Cost & Quality Management,* The National Institute for Software Quality and Productivity, Inc., October 29-30, 1986, pp. C1-C34.

18. C. K. Cho, "Statistical Quality Control and the Software Warranty," *Proceedings, Software Cost and Quality Control,* The National Institute for Software Quality and Productivity, Inc., September 21-22, 1987, pp. C1-C17.

19. C. K. Cho, "Software Warranty," Computa, Inc. (to appear in 1991).

General References

Arden, B. W., Ed., *What Can Be Automated* (Cambridge, MA: The MIT Press, 1980).

Cho, C. K., *High Quality Software—An Introduction* (in Japanese), translated and published by Kinkai Kagaku Sha (Tokyo), 1982.

Cho, C. K., *Software Engineering and Quality Assurance,* Continuing Engineering Education Course No. 705 Handout, The George Washington University, December 1985.

Dahl, O. J.; Dijkstra, E. W.; and Hoare, C. A. R., *Structured Programming,* (New York: Academic Press, 1972).

Handler, S. L., and King, J. C., "An Introduction to Proving the Correctness of Programs," *Computing Surveys,* ACM, Vol. 8, No. 3 (September 1976), pp. 331-353.

King, J. C., "Symbolic Execution and Program Testing," *Communications of the ACM,* Vol. 9, No. 7 (July 1976), pp. 385-394.

Meyers, G. J., "A Controlled Experiment in Program Testing and Code Walkthroughs/ Inspection," *Communications of the ACM,* Vol. 21, No. 9, (September 1978), pp. 760-768.

Myers, G. J., *Software Reliability—Principles and Practices,* (New York: John Wiley & Sons, 1976).

Shooman, M. L., *Software Engineering,* (New York: McGraw-Hill, 1983).

Wegner, P., Ed., *Research Directions in Software Technology,* (Cambridge, MA: The MIT Press, 1979).

Weyuker, E. J., and Ostrand, T. J., "Theories of Program Testing," IEEE *Transactions on Software Engineering,* Vol. SE-6, No. 3 (May 1980).

Yeh, R. T., *Current Trends in Programming Methodology,* Vols. 1 and 2 (Englewood Cliffs, NJ: Prentice-Hall, 1977).

18

The Quest for Software Reliability

Robert H. Dunn

Systems for Quality Software

18.1 INTRODUCTION

The bottom line for software quality assurance is the reliability of the product. Admittedly, much has been made of the contributions of software quality assurance to programmer productivity, but the primary business of quality remains quality, and the most conspicuous attribute of quality is *reliability*. This chapter explores the connection between software quality assurance and software reliability. Underlying that connection is an issue that has in recent years attracted the attention of both software engineers and quality engineers: defining just what is meant by "software reliability." Perhaps it would be more accurate to say that the issue has to do with defining software reliability such that it can be attended by mathematical exactness comparable to that which attaches to reliability theory developed for hardware. Toward the end of this chapter, we shall have the opportunity to look at the intriguing steps taken in this direction, but for the present we must settle for less.

The literature of reliability engineering developed for hardware falls short of our purpose for the simple reason that it assumes that failure results from physical changes in state. If we exclude from our concern degradation of the medium holding the software of interest, an exclusion required if the real issue is not to be trivialized, we have no interest in the statistical behavior of randomly migrating molecules or similar phenomena that hardware reliability theory tacitly accounts for. Software reliability—more precisely, unreliability—results not from degradation of the condition of programs or data, but from the condition of the software *ab*

465

initio, or at least from the time of the last release. This is scarcely new knowledge, but it reminds us that we must make plain our use of the locution "software reliability" before we can try to improve the thing itself.

Apart from attempts to quantify it, what we mean by software reliability is the extent to which software can be depended on to correctly perform the functions assigned to it. An isolated failure to correctly perform is labeled just that: a failure. Ignoring (for the moment) misuse of a program, each failure results from one or more defects in the program or in the data supporting it. Thus, the context of software reliability is that of software defects: software entirely free of defects is entirely reliable. Even the most dogmatic reliability theorist would be willing to quantify that kind of reliability. If software quality assurance can favorably affect the reliability of a software product (including both stand-alone software systems and systems in which software is embedded), it will have to do something about the potential defect population of that product. How it does so is the substance of this chapter.

None of this is to suggest that reliability cannot also be enhanced by system architecture, and much has been done in the design of fault-tolerant systems. An outstanding example is ITT's System 12 telecommunications switch, which uses a totally distributed architecture employing hundreds or thousands of microprocessors, each controlling a maximum of 60 lines (e.g., connected telephones). To prevent an observable loss of service upon failure of any microprocessor, it was necessary for the software to be designed such that each control element autonomously performs recovery procedures in the event of a malfunction. Such opportunities to improve reliability through system design considerations are, however, rare. For the most part—certainly that part in which software quality assurance enjoys some prominence—it remains that the two topics of software reliability and software defects are inextricably intertwined.

For our immediate purpose, reliability has now been equated with dependability, an intuitive expedient that will serve until we get to Section 18.6 (Measuring Reliability). Also, reduction of the number of defects embedded in the fabric of software is seen as the obvious avenue for improving reliability. Achieving this reduction will be our focus. Any reduction in the defect population has to be a good thing, but an effective software quality assurance program can use a bit more knowledge about the primary enemies, the *defects* themselves.

18.2 DEFECTS COME IN ALL SHAPES AND SIZES

Let us return briefly to the earlier passing reference to the misuse of software. A payroll system designed only for operation in some Camelot in which withholding tax is unknown will surely fail to perform to the satisfaction of any business in the United States. Yet, without fail it may crank out penny-perfect paychecks in Camelot week after week. Shall we say that it contains defects when, after installation in New York City, it sends home a thousand happily bewildered workers of a Friday afternoon with swollen purses? Unfortunately, not all cases of misuse are as blatant as this example. Much more subtle instances adorn the archives of programs that performed unreliably. Many of these resulted from misunderstanding of information supplied by users (incorrect user information, however, *is* a true defect), but the more controversial cases have risen from an inadequately defined description of the operational conditions for which the software is intended.

In short, whether or not we are dealing with defects may be a matter of circumstances beyond the cognizance of the people developing the subject software. It is not, however, outside the purview of software quality assurance engineers. That is, software quality assurance engineers are concerned with every aspect of software products, starting with the conception of a project and continuing into its indefinitely long period of maintenance. Any time that the potential for human error can compromise the successful and dependable performance of software, an opportunity exists for the contributions of software quality assurance.

Still, most defects are more easily defined than those associated with an inadequate understanding of a program's mission, and looking at these in some detail provides insights that can lead to the formulation of profitable software quality assurance programs.

Defects Created During the Definition of Requirements

Although any defect can lead to failure, defects traceable to the requirements phase of development are the most vexing since they often propagate to many pages of code. Development management is particularly sensitive to these because of their adverse effect on programmer productivity. Those defects most likely to cause unpredictable operational behavior generally fall into one of the following classes.

Incorrect Reflection of Operational Environment

A close cousin to the misapplication of the Camelot payroll system to the United States is the failure to define software requirements that accurately reflect higher level specifications, such as those that define the desired characteristics of a large system incorporating software. In the allocation of elements of the solution to individual hardware and software constituents, something can get lost in translation. A typical defect found in programs embedded in instrumentation or communication systems is the stipulation of input rates or message rates less than those that will actually be encountered; generally a consequence of inadequate understanding of random components of the environment. In the data rate example, a brief flurry of input may cause some data to be ignored or may cause some to be processed incorrectly. Either response may be viewed as unreliable operation.

Incomplete Requirements

Similar to defects of the previous class are those associated with the correct but incomplete specification of functions and performance. Returning to message handling, we may have correct specifications for message rates but nothing said about the necessary response time for each message, not always the same as the minimum interval between any two messages. Worse, requirements documents have been written with entire functions omitted.

Infeasible Requirements
Here we have the response time specified, but inconsistently with the speed of the computer hardware and other necessary processing functions.

Conflicting Requirements
Functions that compete for processing time may be viewed also as conflicting requirements. A less subtle example of conflict is the specification of any two requirements that are pairwise incompatible. Consider pattern recognition. The probability of correctly identifying an image increases with redundancy. For real-time pattern recognition, one may need to process a great deal of data to meet accuracy specifications, but the amount of processing may be inimical with a quick-response-time specification. Faced with making a choice of speed vs. correctness, the software designers may select speed with the consequence of occasional erratic (read "unreliable") identification of images.

Software Requirements Specification Inconsistent with Other Specifications
The hardware environment in which the software is to operate may be overstated. More than one programmer has been brought up short when the N unrestricted registers he thought were available turned out to be half that number. As another example, we have the requirement, doomed to be unfulfilled by even the most diligent programmer, that two successive signals input from an 8-bit register be distinguished by any amplitude difference greater than 1 part in 1000.

Improper Description of the Initial State of the System
All aspects of systems are not zero-valued at start-up. But this is what programmers assume unless told otherwise. Failure to correctly initialize for a given initial system state may escape all testing, only to manifest itself months into the operational phase.

Incorrect Allocation of Error
In translating system specifications to software specifications, it is not unusual simply to equate allowable software errors with allowable system errors. We see this mostly with regard to instrumentation systems, for which the writers of the software requirements specifications have ignored measurement errors intrinsic to data-gathering subsystems.

Defects Created During the Design Phase

The people who define the requirements of software have no monopoly on the diversity of defects that can be implanted. Designers who implement the requirements also have a number of ways in which the potential for unreliable behavior can be introduced. Here are a few:

Range Limitations
The design may place inadvertent constraints on the range of input data. Boundary value testing is normally successful in finding such defects within the domain of physical data input. Range, however, can take on many forms, including the completeness of a character set capable of being processed by a lexical analyzer and other such easily overlooked set definitions.

Infinite Loops
Nothing can be less reliable than a program that is diverted from useful processing to the interminable repetition of a sequence of steps. The time that an aircraft pilot needs to know whether to turn left or right to intercept the final approach course is not the time for the flight computer to get caught in an endless loop caused by a design error.

Unauthorized or Incorrect Use of System Resources
A typical defect of this class is the indiscriminate misuse of architectural features of the hardware processor, such as reserved registers. Software resources may be misused also, often as the result of an incomplete understanding of the characteristics of library routines or operating systems.

Computational Error Improperly Analyzed
Designers generally recognize possibilities for individual truncation and roundoff errors, but they sometimes fail to properly account for the effect of these errors in concert. Also, the use of ill-suited techniques of numerical computation may result in odd results from time to time. (Descriptions of mathematical libraries sometimes read like advertising copy, setting traps for the unwary programmer.)

Conflicting Data Representations
If one module processes inches and another meters, we can expect to find the problem in testing. But more subtle conflicts associated with scaling and the like may await operation to be heard from.

Software Interface Anomalies
There are several possibilities here. Parameters may be passed to modules that are not designed to catch them. Module A may call Module B, which calls Module A, ad infinitum. Modules may be referenced but undefined.

Defenseless Design
From the point of view of software reliability, perhaps the archtypical design defect is the lack of adequate error traps. Input, encompassing data received from instrumentation hardware to characters generated from a keyboard, must be checked for validity. Sequences of input have also to be checked. Internal to the software system, passed parameters also must be validated to ensure that they

cannot cause catastrophic results. Moreover, good design calls for recovery action from the module trapping the error, not an all-inclusive "recovery module."

Inadequate Exception Handling

Defects of this class are related to the previous one. In focusing on the main body of the problem, designers occasionally forget to properly handle unique conditions. These are not always obvious, particularly when the exception is a possible, if unlikely, combination of discrete events—unlikely, but almost inevitable in the operational environment.

Non-Conformance to Specified Requirements

This omnibus category can include many of the above, depending on the scope of the specifications, but it also includes any design that is nonresponsive to stipulated functional, architectural, or performance features, whether by oversight or misinterpretation. We may observe that misinterpretation frequently results from ambiguity in the requirements documentation, in which case we are dealing as much with a requirements defect as a design defect.

Defects Created During the Coding Phase

Since these are the classic programming bugs, no description is really needed. However, it is worthwhile to enumerate the ones most likely to have a bearing on reliability:

- Misuse of variables (an exponent here, a flag there).
- Mismatched parameter lists.
- Improper nesting of loops and branches.
- Undefined variables and initialization defects.
- Infinite loops.
- Missing code.
- Unreachable code (assuming it is not "dead" code, left over from the last revision).
- Inverted predicates (A < B where it should have been B < A).
- Incomplete predicates (A AND B where it should have been A AND B AND C).
- Failure to save or restore registers.
- Missing validity tests (designed, but not coded).
- Incorrect access of array components.

In addition to these, we must more generally include any failure to implement the design as documented. (There is, of course, the opportunity to err in coding such that a design defect is exactly compensated for, but this may safely be ignored.)

Documentation and Installation Defects

The above lists of defects comprise those that ultimately are embedded in operating programs. However, failures can result from other sources. Incorrect or unclear information in user manuals can lead to operator errors and resulting failure. For example, no one has remembered to tell the new data entry operator that the CNTRL P operation on page 16 of the manual does not restore the screen as stated; rather, it wipes out all entries made since the last screen selection. As a result, the daily summaries are not posted in time for the 4:30 P.M. partners' meeting, a failure in their eyes whatever the cause.

Installation defects take diverse forms. Perhaps no one bothered to set the operating system parameter that automatically logs out all users on detection of a parity error. Each time this happens, every few weeks or so, many hours of work are lost, save for those captured in journals before the hardware starts to malfunction.

The word "installation" can be broadened sufficiently to include data base defects. The customer application information for a computer-controlled telephone exchange may have an incorrect datum that causes occasional irregularities in service for some of the telephone subscribers. Software quality engineers intent on improving reliability often have to look beyond the bounds of operational code to find potential sources of mischief.

18.3 SOFTWARE QUALITY ASSURANCE AND DEFECTS

It should be evident by now that the connection between software quality assurance and reliability resolves to the connection between software quality assurance and defects. In fact, there are two connections to defects: one of prevention and one of removal. As one reads through the defects listed in the previous section, it becomes plain that many are preventable. For example, the practice of writing requirements documentation in a clear, unambiguous fashion will markedly reduce the likelihood of misinterpretations by designers. With regard to defect removal, that same documentation can be examined to make certain that it encompasses all relevant functions of a higher-level specification.

Defects—their prevention and their removal—occupy the greatest part of a software quality engineer's workweek. Not all of this constitutes a direct attack on defects. Much of software quality assurance has to do with preventing projects from going out of control. The project that gathers enough undisciplined momentum to override management control not only will end up too costly and too late, but also it will likely have been inaccurately documented, insufficiently tested, and of doubtful configuration integrity. Thus the software quality engineer is concerned with assuring proper compliance to phase exit criteria, or with providing independent reports of status based on completion of tasks according to established standards. Moreover, as we shall see, software quality assurance is concerned with the merit of the standards themselves, and through measurement and analysis seeks always to upgrade them.

So there we have it: software quality assurance promotes software reliability by attacking the cause of unreliability—defects in the operational product. The next two sections of this chapter are given to the two prongs of that attack, prevention and removal.

18.4 DEFECT PREVENTION

Simplistic as it may sound, defect prevention really means only two things: (1) good programming, and (2) management support for good programmers, the support primarily in the form of adequate funds for programming tools.† Given a large development team, one comprising system analysts or engineers, designers, coders, testers, librarians, and whatever other job titles are in local use, there is no more definitive way to foster good programming practices than by defining them as the standard way to do things. The tangible forms of the definitions of good practice are, in fact, called *programming standards*. Software quality assurance works toward:

- The continual upgrading of the content of programming standards.
- The publication of programming standards.
- Compliance to programming standards.

For defect prevention, we look first, then, to standards.

Standards and Audits

Standards that help prevent defects address the employment of tools, the forms of documentation, the handover of interim products from one development group to another, configuration management, and the very methods used for problem definition and program design. Standards that define methodology are directed to an attribute of computer programs closely linked with defect incidence: complexity.

Decomposition

The organized attack on complexity begins with the process of decomposition. Specific methods for decomposition such as, transaction analysis, the Jackson approach, Parnas information hiding, and many others, underlie many of the locally defined stipulated approaches toward solving complexity. Common to all thoughtful decomposition methods is the goal of a sensible, structured, array of relatively small modules. Reference 1 describes several of the more popular decomposition methods. Other methods may be closely tied to the use of documentation techniques: Higher Order Software,[2] the Warnier-Orr approach,[3] SADT*,[4] and so on. Whether a published method or a home-grown one is selected, it should be common throughout the project—ideally, common to all projects undertaken by a programming department—and documented as a standard so that the method is applied by all designers. A documented standard also permits software quality engineers to audit compliance with the approved method.

---

†As used in this chapter, "programming" refers to all software design, code generation, and test activities performed by the development staff.

*SADT is a trademark of SofTech Inc.

Rapid Prototyping

Decomposition applies to both the requirements definition and the design activities required for software development. The frequently encountered difficulty of defining just what one wants software to do has been an historically infamous source of inadequate requirements specifications. To circumvent this, software departments increasingly are turning to the technique of *rapid prototyping*. A scantily defined set of requirements, possibly even a verbal set, is converted into executable (if inefficient) code written in one of several very-high-level languages. The potential user (customer, system engineer, and so forth) examines the results of the execution of this code and states the several deficiencies he or she finds. The process is iterated until the prototype system is found acceptable, at which time it becomes, if not a de facto requirements specification, at least a model of what the completed system should do. With the advent of prototyping, however, we find that old lessons must be relearned. Even prototyping must be performed in a controlled environment. Accordingly, standards must be established defining the prototyping process.

Software Functional Requirements

In the early 1990s, we find that the relatively new technique of prototyping has yet to displace the traditional attempt to fully define, prior to the initiation of design work, the functional requirements of software systems. Certainly, for software embedded in instrumentation or communications systems, satisfactory models of the on-line hardware are difficult to come by. In any case, in most programming environments it remains that requirements definition is a phase apart from and preceding the programming tasks. Formalized methodologies for arriving at a complete and correct requirements set are fewer in number than design methodologies. Many of the formalized systems in current use derive from techniques of structured analysis, especially DeMarco's.[5]

Documentation Standards

Perhaps the most conspicuous standards are those that address documentation. A standard way of writing requirements or design specifications permits a standard way of reading them. That is, the people who have to implement the specifications should know what to expect of them and know where to find things. Standards provide the writers of documentation an off-the-shelf format that encourages the more timorous writers to put down all the relevant information, while restraining the more adventurous ones from ill-focused flights of fancy. Finally, for the benefit of reviewers, the exposure of missing or contradictory information is abetted by documentation that follows carefully thought-out techniques.

VERIFIABLE LANGUAGES

No documentation techniques have the potential to abet defect prevention more than those that employ verifiable languages (e.g., ALPHARD,[6] SIMULA,[7] and

AFFIRM[8]), which lend themselves to formal analyses of correctness such as proofs in first-order mathematics. These are not used casually, however, as is natural language. Rather, much acquired skill is required of both the writer and the reader, which accounts for the limited use currently seen of such languages.

As a half-way measure, structured requirements and design languages have gained considerable popularity. Examples of these are Problem Statement Language (PSL),[9] Requirements Statement Language,[10] and any of a number of program design languages of which the best-known is the proprietary PDL,[11] of Caine, Farber & Gordon, Inc. Although these languages lack the mathematical qualities of verifiable languages, they are machine-readable and of formality sufficient for computer-generated reports (including lists of internal inconsistencies) invaluable for defect prevention.

FLOW-CHARTING

Even the most meagerly supported program design language provides a major increment of defect-prevention capability over the most widely used design documentation technique, flow-charting. Since design languages require the exposition of program flow to be structured,* programmers have to work hard at producing unstructured code when implementing the design. Also, since design languages are machine-readable, designs may more easily be updated, unlike flow charts, which are executed on paper. The belief that a picture is worth a thousand words has given the practice of flow-charting immortality, however. For those who insist on graphic representations of control flow, but would avoid the unstructured quality (call it the spaghetti-and-meatballs syndrome) of most flow charts, the Nassi-Schneiderman technique[12] may be used to generate flow charts that embody the precepts of structured programming.

FORMAT DOCUMENTATION STANDARDS

Software quality engineers are much concerned with the documentation techniques in local use, whether the foregoing or any of many others. Their concern with any technique, of course, is whether the method favors the implantation or the prevention of defects. Whatever practice is locally favored, software quality engineers insist on the formalization of that practice, that is, publication of a standard specifying the way documentation shall be accomplished. This stipulation applies not only to requirements and design documentation, but to user manuals, test plans, test specifications, and so on. Here, as elsewhere, standards promote stability, and stability promotes quality.

---

*At the risk of oversimplification, structured programming may be defined as a restriction permitting only one entry to and only one exit from each primitive processing segment. This provides a restraint on complexity at the module level.

Configuration Management

Of all standards, the ones most closely associated with stability are the standards that establish configuration management policies. War stories are legion of programs tested and delivered with pages of code of uncertain origin or even unknown purpose. Somehow the systems are made to work, but divine intervention should get as much credit for this as is given development effort. Reliability, in any case, frequently is poor, especially after an attempt is made to modify the program. The good fight against such mongrel programs is waged by configuration management standards, which define the means of releasing documentation and code, controlling these through the stages of design refinement and testing, and managing changes. Baselines, from which further work departs, are established at discrete points, and control boards are set up to evaluate any changes to these. Strict adherence to configuration management standards can be audited by software quality engineers.

Software Quality Audits

Software quality engineers—or at least their managers—lobby development personnel for the establishment of standards conducive to defect prevention. However, they spend far more of their time auditing the development process to ensure adherence to whatever standards are in place. Software development, particularly the development of large systems, can, for a variety of reasons, become frenetic. During the lengthy time—perhaps one or two years—that development proceeds, further front-end thinking often results in changes or additions to the specified software functions or to an understanding of the environment in which the software is to perform. It is learned that tools will not be available when planned. An influenza epidemic wipes out 50 labor weeks. Worse, the Personnel Department delivers only half of the candidates for additional staff that programming management had demanded. No matter how carefully planned the project is, events somehow conspire to cause scheduled progress milestones to be jeopardized.

As a scheduled interim completion date nears, meeting one's commitments becomes the predominant concern. Short cuts are sought, and none may appear as vulnerable as some of the practices dictated by management. The design language description of a module becomes:

Enter with a lot of data.
Perform the function Carrie wants.
Exit with the answer.

Well, maybe not quite that bad. But short cuts will be taken, in design descriptions, in test documentation, and with configuration control. One knows that in the long run they should be counter-productive, but one can always hope that this time luck will gain the day. Luck is not one of the fundamental precepts of software quality assurance, but auditing for adherence to standards is.

Here, let us merely note that through the mechanism of in-process audits, the software quality engineer acts as the cop on the beat, preventing not vandalism but defects.

Phase Exit Criteria

The handover of interim products from one group of people to another offers a powerful use of quality assurance audits towards the end of ensuring that planned development practices are followed. In handover procedures, the receiver's quality assurance group audits the records maintained by the deliverer to make certain that all open problem items have been resolved, that configuration control records are up to date and indicate that all controlled materials are mutually consistent, and so on. Alternatively, as when coded modules are handed over to an integration team within the same programming department, a quality assurance function common to both the integration team and the module producers performs the auditing function.

SQA Expectations

In addition to performing audits of records, software quality engineers want also to establish, whether by their own examination or in concert with deliverer and receiver representatives, that the product handed over conforms to the expectations for it. For example, at the time that a top-level design is handed over to those who will complete the design phase by filling in details, software quality engineers want confirmation that the design fulfills the requirements laid on it by higher-level design or requirements specifications. They also check to see that the design is documented in compliance with standards; moreover, for those elements of the design that have been documented in a programming design language, that the design language statements have been machine-processed with no error diagnostics. Most commonly, such confirmation takes place through the medium of a review, discussed in Section 18.5 as a defect-removal technique. However confirmation is achieved, the collateral function of establishing the successful completion of a phase is also achieved.

Determining that each development phase has been completed in conformance with its technical specifications and prevailing standards is an integral part of software quality assurance even when the completed phase does not result in material handed over to other people. Phase-completion milestones are conspicuous to several levels of management. Software quality assurance signatures on the reviews, tests, and audits associated with phase completions collectively represent tacit certification that the milestone has been, indeed, reached. A software quality assurance function report that all of the relevant material is as it should be—save for a few clearly identified items requiring correction or completion—provides management the information needed to start the next phase of work. The successful conclusion, then, of reviews, tests, and audits, as defined in the software quality standards, serves as the phase exit criteria that must be met before successor tasks are started, and assures against prematurely entering the next phase.

Let us summarize the defect prevention program thus far discussed: standards define favored ways of doing things; audits ensure that standards are followed; and the combination of standards and audits provide phase exit criteria that offer management visibility into true status. We have yet to address the *improvement* of one's standards. Enter measurement.

Measurement

To improve standards for the development of reliable software, we require knowledge of the effect of current standards. To acquire knowledge, we must measure. We must measure — that is, record and analyze — the source of defects. We must also measure the success of defect-removal techniques. Now, any function associated with software development can undertake a measurement program. However, we find that little measurement has been done by programming people. For whatever reason, programmers and their managers seem not to want to record information concerning software defects.* On the other hand, measurements have historically been an integral part of quality programs. Indeed, much of in-process quality control involves the trend of out-of-roundness measurements, defect rates of randomly selected part's lots, and so forth.

Tabulating Defects

So too with software quality assurance. By examining the records of requirements, design and code reviews, software quality assurance can determine whether the technology or tooling (or lack thereof) of any one activity is contributing an untoward number of defects. Later, with cooperation from program test personnel, more valuable data can be collected during the testing phases of development. In formal test activities, when a problem report is prepared for each anomaly detected, test data is fairly easily captured. Informal testing is more of a problem. Nevertheless, "bean-counting" forms, completed at the time of failure diagnosis, can be used to tabulate the number of defects attributed to earlier phases. This, of course, requires of those making the diagnoses a little extra effort and a willingness to use judgment. An example of such forms and their use can be found in reference 14.

Analysis of Defects Source

Given a tabulation, by origin, of the defect data pertaining to a given software system, one can go about determining the most likely activities that require shoring. Suppose, for example, we find that top-level design contributes twice the number of defects as does detailed design. If we know, also, that detailed design requires twice as many hours of labor as does top-level design, we are led to

---

*Two possible reasons that come to mind are lack of time and a disinclination to ponder the less attractive aspects of one's calling. For more detailed explanations see reference 13.

wonder why the top-level designers err at four times the rate of their (usually more junior) colleagues.* We have other information, however. For example, a program design language is used for detailed design, but none is used in the preceding phase. The requirements specification was changed eight times during top-level design, while the top-level design was changed only twice during the period of detailed design. Whatever the suspect causes, measurement provides the basis for knowing what to analyze, and the analysis may very well indicate where the existing standards need to be changed.

Future Payoff

Defect data measurement is essentially altruistic. The measurements made of a given project are made too late to be of substantial use to that project. The measurements are made mainly to the profit of succeeding projects. Although at small cost, measurement activity takes away from the present for the primary benefit of the future. All the more the pity that at present we have so little recorded history to help us.

Effectiveness Measure

But let us go on. Apart from knowing where defects arise, we are concerned also with how we find them. Anticipating the next section of this chapter, a number of defect removal activities attend the development of software systems. Typical ones are:

- Reviews of requirements specifications.
- Reviews of design specifications.
- Code reviews.
- Unit testing.
- Integration testing.
- Sub-system and system testing.
- Qualification testing.

For each, we may define an effectiveness measure, E.

$$E = \frac{N}{N + S} \text{ where}$$

N = the number of defects found by the defect removal activity
S = the number of those defects, found during all succeeding defect removal activities and operation that had existed at the time of the subject defect removal activity.

---

*Admittedly, this is somewhat simplistic. A one-to-one correspondence between errors and defects may not necessarily exist. Moreover, one has to take care not to count twice a defect generated in top-level design and propagated to detailed design. Also, the argument ignores the severity of defects.

As an example, if a code review turns up 20 defects, and if an additional 80 defects attributable to the requirements, design, or coding phases are found during testing and the first year of operation, then for that code review

$$E = \frac{20}{20 + 80} = 0.2$$

Alternatively, at the cost of more precise recordkeeping, one may prefer to include in S only those defects susceptible to the defect removal procedure. In the above case, for example, we should not expect the code review capable of finding defects in the requirements specifications, so we would subtract from 80 the number of requirements defects found during test and operation.

Use of Effectiveness Measure

Let us assume that E (unit testing) is half of E (integration testing). Now, if most of the defects detected during integration testing turn out to have been software interface defects, we should not be dismayed at the relatively poor harvest of defects found by unit testing. Suppose, however, that a disproportionate share of the defects found during integration turn out to be totally within the domain of the individual modules previously unit-tested. This may represent something less than prima facie evidence of inadequate unit testing standards and tools, but it is more than adequate to instigate an intensive analysis of their effectiveness.

Keep Standards Current

Measurement, then, is integral to the improvement of reliability through software quality assurance. Measurement guides the evolution of methodology and technology in productive directions—productive not only in terms of programmer productivity (often management's only interest in change) but of product reliability as well. Nor should we forget that there is nothing inevitable about the evolution of standards. If Homer thought, "The minds of the everlasting gods are not changed suddenly," his ghost ought to read the dates of issue on some of the standards in current use in programming shops. The standards of Section 18.4 need not only to be established, but to be continually revisited. Moreover, when standards are reappraised, there is no substitute for hard facts (read "numbers").

18.5 DEFECT REMOVAL

Computer programming, in all its parts, is fertile ground for error. Not even the most optimistic software engineer believes that it is possible to construct a perfect defect-prevention program. With the continuous invention of new techniques and tools, software development is, in theory, becoming less hazardous (less hazardous to the product, that is; the programmer was never in danger), but only in theory. The complexity and size of the current generation of programs continues to outpace the improvements in developmental method. Indeed, one is led to suspect that new technology directed to reliability is driven not so much by the goal of quality as by the necessity to maintain whatever levels existed in simpler times. One thing is, in any case, clear; software development is attended by a host of defects, and, along with the development people, software quality engineers must mount a vigorous attempt to root them out.

When we speak of defect removal, we are really speaking of defect *detection* followed by a *repair* operation. Most of the action attaches to defect detection, although software quality assurance assiduously tracks the taking of corrective action. Configuration control and (for defects found by testing) frequently elaborate retesting strategies also enter into repair procedures. For the most part, we shall focus on defect detection during the phases of development.

It is still within the memory of living programmers that defect removal meant testing a program before it was given over to its users. The short list of today's defect-removal opportunities, comprising reviews and several discrete testing stages, suggests the distance we have come. In the remaining pages of this chapter, we shall be able to do no more than touch upon the most prominent facets of a subject that, properly, requires a book to itself.*

Passive Defect Removal

The word "passive" is not intended to suggest a lack of aggressive defect removal activity on the part of programmers and software quality engineers. Rather, the term is used here to refer to procedures other than those in which code is actually exercised. Indeed, passive defect removal starts before there is any code available for execution.

Reviews

Software engineers and software quality engineers recognized early on that there were opportunities to remove defects well before code could be tested. The reason was obvious: defects are created in the requirements and design phases of development, not just during coding. Accordingly, the practice slowly developed of reviewing the products (documentation of various forms) of these two pre-code phases. The success of such reviews has led to their being extended to include code, as well.

Reviews can take a number of forms. They can be restricted to fellow workers, especially in the class of formats known as "peer walkthroughs," or can be expanded to include staff from other functions (e.g., system designers). The format of the review meeting can be formally structured, as in Fagan's design and code inspections,[15] or can be marked by the informality associated with Weinberg's "egoless programming."[16] Owing to the value of viewing higher-level designs from the perspectives of the several design functions associated with a single project, informal peer formats are less suited to the reviews of requirements specifications and top-level designs than are interdisciplinary reviews. Chapter 9

---

*Indeed, several such books have been written. Taking an example at random, we have Robert Dunn, *Software Defect Removal,* McGraw-Hill Book Co., 1984.

provides an exposition on the conduct and value of the more formal types of reviews. We shall here look only at the salient points having to do with reliability.

SUBJECTS OF REVIEWS

The subjects of reviews are these: requirements specifications, top-level design specifications, interface specifications, intermediate design specifications, detailed design specifications, code, and test specifications. Planning documents (e.g., program development plans) are also subject to review, but are not directly germane to the subject of defect removal. The objects of the reviews in which we are interested, save for those of test specifications, are several:

- Confirmation that the work reviewed is traceable to the requirements implicitly or explicitly set forth for it by predecessor tasks.
- Confirmation that the work reviewed is complete; that is, that all the information required to initiate the next work phase is present.
- Confirmation that the work has been completed to standards, thus giving reviews a further role in defect prevention, much like that of audits.
- Ascertaining that the work reviewed is not overly complex. (This really does not apply to interface specifications except in the sense of reviewing the complexity of a system design.)
- Ascertaining that the work reviewed is correct.

The last of these sounds like a copout, a clause used to cover any objectives that had been forgotten. It is that, but it is more, too. It means that inner workings of the interim product being examined are analyzed for consistency, for compatibility, for accuracy, and whatever. Notice also, that the last two of the objectives are not couched in terms of confirmation, but in the exploratory sense of "ascertaining." This is not a literary device to avoid further repetition of "confirmation." The change highlights the essence of defect removal.

Confirmation implies that we are looking for correct results. In establishing traceability to earlier work, or stages, we generally know what we are looking for, and we consider the absence of any expected item to be a defect. If the requirements specification states that the software will process three kinds of malfunction messages, one expects to find design referents to all three.

MAXIMIZING REVIEW FINDINGS

However, to gain maximum profit from reviews, one ought not look only for what is correct; the opportunity must be provided for incorrect work to evince itself. For example, in a code review the author (or someone else, depending on format) "walks through" the code with test cases. The test cases are, most likely, based on interpretations of the code's functional specifications. However, at any point—generally, at many points—the narrator is interrupted by "what-if" questions. "What if the interrupt comes before the register has been saved?" "What if the reassignment module doesn't respond with a validated address?" And on and on.

In defect removal, the object is *not* to prove the product correct; it is to prove that the product harbors defects.

EFFECTIVENESS OF REVIEWS

This philosophy is most evident in the formulation of test strategies, and we shall return to it there. That the foregoing tenet is often forgotten is one of the possible reasons for the wide range of effectiveness ratios (as defined earlier) for reviews. Requirements reviews range from 20 to 50 percent effective, design reviews from 30 to 70 percent, and code reviews from 35 to 85 percent. Even at the low end of the effectiveness percentage windows, reviews are probably worth the cost, since the cost of removing defects once they have propagated to controlled code is much greater than if removed directly on completion of the work in which they were created. At the high end of the percentage ranges, the cost-effectiveness is obvious.

REVIEW FOLLOW-UP

Of course, we must not forget that reviews only *find* defects. The defects must also be *removed*. Review minutes are usually lists of the defects found. (For whatever reason, defects noted in review minutes are generally called "correction items," a locution applied with equal fuzziness to discrepancies uncovered by audits.) The better of these lists include the name of the person assigned to the fix and the date by which it must be completed. Software quality engineers undertake the task of maintaining records of these completions, reminding—with increasing frequency—anyone whose due date has passed. Various mechanized tracking systems to reduce the bookkeeping effort have been devised by software quality engineers. These range from office automation calendars to various homegrown computerized tickler files.

REVIEWS AIDED BY MECHANIZATION

Before leaving the topic of reviews, let us note the extent to which mechanization is possible for the substance of the reviews themselves. Specifications prepared in requirements and design languages, especially the latter, can be processed to provide various reports (e.g., where defined data is used, or the calling structure implied by module interface specifications and procedure references) that reduce the effort required to comprehend the specifications, thereby increasing the likelihood of making certain defects more visible. Beyond acting as simple aids to reviews, the more ambitious processors (the term "pseudolanguage processor" is frequently used) directly find defects of several types, for example, conflicting data representations, use of undefined global data, and software interface anomalies.

Static Analysis

The analysis capabilities of pseudolanguage processors pale in comparison with the analysis tools for real code. Static analyzers, as they are called, operate on source code files as their input, producing reports analogous to those of the pseudolanguage processors that abet requirements and design reviews. Reports that simplify manual code reviews include data cross-references, module hierarchies implied by the code (as before), program graphs (distillations of the internal control structure), and so on. Again analogously to pseudolanguage processors, but more powerfully, static analyzers directly expose defects. Among those that yield to static analyzers are improper nesting, missing and unreachable code, and undefined variables. It must be understood, of course, that no two static analysis systems offer identical capabilities. Moreover, let us note that many compilers offer some static analysis features, particularly compilers for well-structured languages such as Pascal and Ada. This last note reflects the principal problem of static analyzers; each is inherently specific to a given language. The programming department working in five different source languages has five times the investment in static analysis that the department working in only one language has.

STATIC VERSUS DYNAMIC DEFECT REMOVAL

Used singly or in concert, code reviews and static analysis, as techniques for the passive removal of defects from code, offer an interesting contrast to the oldest (and still necessary) technique of defect removal: active defect removal, or, if you will, testing. In testing, one does not directly expose defects. Rather, a failure occurs, followed by an investigation (debugging) to find the cause of the failure (the defect). The labor time to find the defect may be as little as a few minutes, but it may be hours or days as well. Indeed, weeks have been spent attempting to find the source of a single problem. Worse, it has happened that after constructing all manner of diagnostic tests and painstakingly analyzing the results, the decision has been reached to abandon the search for the bug despite its obvious effect on reliability.

In contrast, the passive defect removal methods directly find defects. They may or may not find as many, but the ones they do find are quickly corrected. We may note, also, that they are roughly as effective as active testing. Experiments conducted by this writer and others have found that a code review even when conducted *after* unit test (in contradistinction to the recommended order) invariably uncovers at least one bug. The significance of this should not be lost on those who have argued—at least with regard to code reviews—that passive defect removal methods are overly labor-intensive.

Testing

Testing is sometimes viewed as the essence of software quality assurance. An extreme example of this is found in older military standards for software requirements and design specifications. These standards contained a section, entitled "Quality Assurance," that stipulated little more than that the contractor had to document the manner in which he planned to test the software. We now know that software quality assurance is of much broader scope. Nevertheless, software quality engineers still spend a large part of their time making certain that testing is properly planned and is performed in accordance with plans.

There are actually two objectives to testing: defect removal and demonstration of performance. The former, of course, is the one that bears directly on reliability. Nevertheless, for reasons too patent to need further comment, the second has also to be completed. The curious, and certainly disquieting, thing is that it is the demonstration of performance that has attracted most of the attention. Too often, test plans are constructed for the sole purpose of showing that a module, a subsystem, or a complete system performs a specific function or set of functions. When a function fails to be demonstrated, testing is halted, and the mode of operation switches to debugging. That is, defects are detected and removed, but only as an incidental byproduct of another activity. Software quality engineers need to make certain that the emphasis of testing is placed on the productivity of the process, with the understanding that defect removal is the product of testing. Thus, the following discussions on testing focus on the means by which productive testing can be assured.

Test Strategies

The first thing software quality engineers want to do is cooperate with the programming people in identifying discrete test stages, each directed to a specific objective or set of objectives. This provides a basis for visibility of progress, while at the same time lending assistance to the planning and scheduling tasks. Most important, though, a well-considered incremental test strategy permits a variety of types of testing diverse enough to provide confidence in the total efficacy of the testing process. A collateral advantage of the more successful incremental strategies is efficient diagnoses of failures.

There is no shortage of effective schemes that divide testing into discrete stages, some more appropriate to one kind of software system than another, and some more appropriate to one kind of development methodology than another. Still, it does not serve to talk only in abstractions. We need an example. A typical set of stages used for large software systems includes, in chronological order:

Unit, or module, testing
Integration testing
Subsystem integration testing
System testing
Qualification testing

In *unit testing,* each module is individually tested, affording the maximum capability of exercising each of its segments and each aspect of its function. In *integration testing,* the modules of each of the several subsystems constituting the overall software system are welded together, providing an opportunity to find defects in the structure of each subsystem and in the interfaces of its modules.* This stage can be combined with the integration of subsystems, but, assuming that each subsystem performs a unique set of functions directly related to divisible portions of the system specification, it is productive to exercise separately each of these sets of functions.

The test cases designed for subsystem integration are directed to the exercise of the interfaces between the subsystems and the overall control structure.

After all the parts of the system are in place, we come to *system testing,* the stage in which the development people, continuing in charge of the testing process, demonstrate that the product is sufficiently robust and defect-free to warrant the start of qualification testing.

Qualification testing represents a major departure from the preceding tests. Through system testing, the role of the software quality assurance function has been to make certain that test cases have been executed as planned, that corrective action has been taken after the failure of test cases, that defect data has been tabulated for later analysis, and that configuration control procedures have been followed. With qualification testing, we see a role reversal. Now, the software quality engineers take the responsibility of performing—or at least controlling—the tests, while the development people stand aside for a support role. The tests themselves are designed to demonstrate that the system is ready for operational use. Defect exposure here is secondary to the demonstration of performance. System testing has demonstrated that the software is sound; now we want to know that it can be released.

STRUCTURAL AND FUNCTIONAL TESTS

For each of the test stages (other than qualification), it is necessary to design test cases that will exploit the defect exposure potential. There are two fundamentally different kinds of tests that can be performed: *structural tests,* which probe the structure of the software, and *functional tests,* which span the set of functions that the software is required to perform. Structural tests are directed toward the execution of specified percentages of program statements, branches, or paths. Functional tests emphasize traceability to the original performance specifications.

The two kinds of tests are sometimes referred to as "glass box" (or "white box") and "black box," respectively. To design structural tests, or alternatively, to interpret the results of execution coverage-reporting mechanisms, we need to have the software structure visible. To design functional tests, we need only know the purpose of the software black boxes. Both kinds of tests are appropriate for each of the discrete test stages through systems test, although structural testing lends itself more easily to the earlier stages, gradually giving way to functional testing.

---

*Let this be the one piece written on software testing that does not rehash the top-down/bottom-up debate.

Functional Test Limitations

It might appear that either test type can suffice. If one truly wants to produce reliable software, however, both types are needed. Functional testing can exercise only a statistically insignificant portion of the total number of processing paths latent in a program. Functional testing is weak at finding undefined variables and initialization faults. Also, functional testing is weak at testing alternative outcomes of computations. This last shortcoming is so pervasive it rates an example.

The formula for finding the roots of the quadratic equation $y = ax^2 + bx + c$ involves the radical $SQRT(b^2 - 4ac)$. Included in a program, the evaluations of this radical will invoke different processing rules for real and imaginary roots. Yet, particularly if the subject code is toward the end of the set of possible program paths, a set of functional test cases directed to the functional specifications may totally ignore one of the two possibilities. This is not just a matter of leaving some section of the code unexercised; the computation, itself, may not be properly evaluated.

Structural Test Limitations

If functional testing has limitations, so has structural testing. In structural testing we may be satisfied with the correct answer even though it has been incorrectly computed. For example, if ($a = 2 * b$) is computed only for $b = 2$, we shall never know that the statement is not ($a = b * b$) as it should be. Structural testing does not reveal incomplete predicates. Nor, since it is directed solely to code that is present, can it demonstrate that code is missing (e.g., a missing error trap).

Value of Structural and Functional Tests

The bad news is that a regimen of only structural tests or only functional tests may detect as few as 20% of the defects present in a system. On the bright side, either functional or structural testing can find up to $\frac{2}{3}$* of the defects in the code itself. Therefore it is essential that these tests are well-planned. Since $\frac{2}{3}$ is still a long way from all of the defects present, the inescapable conclusion is that no matter how well we test functionally or structurally, we cannot be confident that software is reliable unless we use *both* kinds and use them well.

Functional Testing

One way to help make functional tests effective is to select the correct set of specifications for each test stage. Appropriate ones for the test stages identified earlier are the following:

- Unit testing—module functional specifications.
- Integration testing—top-level design specifications and subsystem functional specifications (or portions of the system requirements specification).

---

*Neither of these two fractions—$\frac{2}{3}$ and $\frac{1}{5}$—has a theoretical basis. Both are empirical averages based on the experience of the author and others.

- Subsystem integration testing—mostly the system requirements specification, but also any overall architectural design specifications.
- Qualification testing—system requirements specification unless there is a requirements specification senior to it.

TRACEABILITY

It helps, also, to be able to relate the lower-level specifications to the highest-level requirements specification. That is, it serves as a further check on the design of the system if the test cases selected can be couched in terms of the expected operational use of the program. To take the extreme, unit tests are directed to the module functional specifications. These tests are at a level considerably below that of operational requirements testing. Nevertheless, to make certain a measurement has not been missed, one wants—if possible—to select at least some test cases traceable to the highest-level specification.

Keeping track of the apportionment of that specification to elements of the design is a task that software quality engineers often undertake. Schemes to do this are frequently referred to as traceability matrices, although there may be nothing about them to suggest matrices. Indeed, one highly regarded method, system verification diagrams,[17] invented by Computer Sciences Corporation, is a graphic method.

ELEMENTS OF FUNCTIONAL TEST DESIGN

Apart from traceability, the more productive functional test cases derive from systematic test design. Given the presumption that one cannot (except for unit testing of certain small modules) test each function at every possible input value, nor multiple functions at more than a relatively few points of intersection, systematic test case design focuses on selecting a set of test cases having minimum redundancy.

In one manner or another, the input domain of the program or partial program is partitioned into functional classes. The object is to select at least one test case for each class, but no more than one except for extreme points (boundary testing). Thus, any time that two test cases are found to be members of the same functional class, one is rejected as redundant. A rigid definition of test case equivalency would require that the same variables be relevant to each, that the same transformations (in kind) result, and that the same output variables be affected. Test-case designers rarely have the time to be that scientific, but an intuitive sense of functional partitioning enters into the work of the more experienced ones.

The reference to *boundary testing* is to its most obvious aspect. In addition to boundaries of input and output domains, another kind of boundary selected for functional testing is the amount of data used for a test. For example, a telephone switch would be tested with a data base representative of the maximum number of lines the switch can handle; a compiler with the maximum number of symbols it can store. A software quality assurance imperative is to make certain such volume tests, as the data-processing community calls them, are performed.

Similar to boundary tests, but with time rather than the values or amount of data as the critical parameter, are *stress tests*. For example, testing a programmable signal processor at maximum input-data rates.

Software Quality Test Perspective

Software quality engineers often think of test cases in terms of three major components: test setup or conditions, input data, and expected output results. Although each functional class should have at least one test case complete with specific input and expected output, it often is appropriate to leave the input and output more loosely defined. For example, one may want to look for regions in which small changes of input values result in wide swings of output. These regions can then be tested further to determine if accuracy holds over the sensitive range.

A more common example is the use of *random input*. Here, there is no presumptive way to determine expected results, except as statistical expectations applied to the aggregate. It may be noted that random input is no substitute for analytically derived test cases. However, functional classes frequently can be defined only over domains so large they preclude exact design of a representative set of test cases. Within such classes, randomly selected data will at least have the virtue of not being influenced by human bias. An example of this is the testing of a program developed to efficiently sequence the operations of an automatic drilling machine. With no further definition, this is a one-class program. Random patterns of holes would be appropriate here, with the hole-to-hole traversals resulting from each pattern measured and analyzed to see if the objective of minimum total distance has been achieved.

Where the input domain can be decomposed into a hierarchy of subdomains, the SIAD technique of Chapter 17 can be applied to distribute random input such that it will have calculable meaning.

Adequacy of Testing

Given the most thoughtfully designed functional test cases, software quality engineers are still given to doubting that enough of the functional space of a program had been exercised. Especially with random input, one suspects that too many individual test points are really functionally equivalent. One would like to test not only the program but the tests as well. A method to do this is to emulate the technique of determining the number of fish in a pond. Catch some fish, tag them, throw them back, and see how many tagged fish are included in the next round of catches. The ratio of tagged to untagged fish provides an estimate of the total fish population.

The programming equivalent of tagging fish has two programming teams independently testing a program. One team finds A defects: the other finds B; and of the two sets, C defects (the retrieved tagged fish) are in common. The estimated number of defects that had been present before the start of testing is given by:

$$\hat{N} = \frac{A \times B}{C}$$

If the use of two test teams seems inefficient, one can deliberately sow the program with defects. In this case, *A* is the number of planted seeds, and *B* is the total number of defects found, of which *C* are seeds.

Assuming that the total number of detected bugs exceeds the number of seeds, the effectiveness of the tests can be gauged by the ratio

$$\frac{B - A}{\hat{N} - A}$$

which approaches 1 as the ratio of detected to seeded bugs approaches 1 but is sensitive also to the number of real bugs that were discovered.

INTRACTABLE DEFECTS

The interpretation of the results of seeding tacitly states that it may be acceptable to stop testing even though there is reason to believe that defects remain. Quality engineers may find this an anathema. However, what we are dealing with is less a blatant assault on the precepts of truth and beauty than an acceptance of reality. A large software system is capable of so great a number of discrete states that no feasible amount of "laboratory" testing can guarantee the exposure of all defects. But this is not the worst of it: software engineers may even have to accept that all exposed defects are not removed.

Two fundamental facts of software life account for this. First, the system may be so complex that an attempt to remove one defect may create several more. Through the process of requirements, design and code reviews, one attempts to reduce the complexity of the solution, but given even the most meticulous quality assurance regimen, the complexity of the problem that has been programmed may result in a system having some intractable defects. Software quality engineers may have no practical alternative to agreeing that the attempt to diagnose or permanently fix a problem be abandoned. Second, perhaps even more difficult for quality engineers to accept is the decision not to remove a defect because of the amount of retesting (regression) required. This is the case even during *qualification testing*—indeed, especially during qualification testing. Qualification testing may be a lengthy process, one of as much as two or three months. It is unthinkable to release a software product without a significant amount of retesting after a major surgical repair. For minor defects, it may be advantageous to leave the bug in the system rather than to fix it and retest. (This explains some of the euphemistically worded warnings found in user manuals.)

QUALIFICATION TESTING CONCERNS

All of which brings us to the subject of qualification testing and the ticklish problem of qualifying a product *known* to have defects. First, let us note that although the software quality engineers assigned to a project will have participated in the reviews of test case specifications for earlier test stages and will have been monitoring actual test activity, when it comes to qualification they are in charge. The software quality assurance function, in qualifying the product, implicitly accepts this responsibility on behalf of the end user.

Given the gravity, if it comes to it, of deciding whether a system with known defects should be released (unleashed?) to the user community, what aid can be offered the software quality manager? Not much, except for suggesting that he or she establish presumptive criteria for qualification, criteria agreed upon by all concerned parties (software management, marketing, customers, and so forth) well in advance of the start of qualification testing. Several possibilities for such criteria, taken singly or in combination, are:

- The number of defects exposed but left in the system, as a percentage of the number of lines of code.
- The number of undiagnosed test case failures, as a percentage of the number of lines of code.
- The ratio of test case failures to test case successes.
- The length of time the system may be run with random, or even arbitrary, input without incident.
- The result of reliability modeling or trend analysis (topics discussed in Section 15.6, Reliability).

FAILURE SEVERITY

With regard to failure counts (this applies also to reliability modeling), it may be necessary to define precisely what one means by failure. Many systems are designed with a certain level of fault tolerance. For example, automatic restart after a system crash may be tolerable if little downtime has elapsed and no data has been lost. The real reliability criterion is whether the users would perceive the crash as a disruption of service.

More generally, any qualification criteria entailing allowable levels of test failure should be sensitive to failure severity. We should not be so rigid that we include infrequent, brief brightening of screen menus in the same bag as unrecoverable system crashes. Three or four severity levels may be used. For example:

1. System did not complete an operation.
2. System did not complete an operation within the specified tolerance.
3. An operational anomaly occurred that would be inconvenient to users.

These severity levels, as well as the preceding acceptance criteria, must be translated into the operational characteristics applicable to the subject system. In a telephone switch, the third severity level would comprise such incidents as an interrupted ringing signal, the second level would be characterized by excessive waits for dial tones, and the first level might be represented by wrong numbers. All of this means that no amount of handbook codification of qualification practices can relieve the software quality engineer of having to exercise judgment in determining whether a product is sufficiently reliable to be released.

Of course, the number of hard decisions will be reduced by the thoroughness with which earlier functional testing has been achieved. It will also be reduced by the amount of structural testing.

Structural Testing

It was stated under Functional Testing that designers of functional test cases have as their objective maximum function coverage for a given number of tests (alternatively, providing a given function coverage for a minimum number of tests). This has an analogy in structural testing: maximize the number of statements, branches or paths covered for a given number of tests (and the obvious alternative). However, unmechanized selection of test cases directed to specific substructures of programs is a laborious process, more suitable to filling in coverage not attained by other means.

MANUAL TESTING

Manual test selection is mostly a matter of studying the code, selecting a path or decision point either because it is of some interest or because it has yet to be executed, noting the decision points leading to the selected code, and fashioning input data that will satisfy the predicates of these points plus any decisions internal to the selected path. If this does not sound tedious enough, consider the common situation wherein more than one relevant predicate references the same set of input variables, requiring the test designer to find input data satisfactory to both decision points, or all three, or all. . . .

There are several approaches, manual and mechanized, to improving matters a bit, but save for the observation that static analysis—last seen as a passive defect-removal technique—is the most promising, describing these is of less importance than discussing the mechanization that reduces manual test case selection to an auxiliary topic of structural testing.

MECHANIZATION OF STRUCTURAL TESTING

Mechanization starts with test coverage instrumentation, with which one can measure the coverage incidentally attained during functional testing or supplemented by additional tests. *Probes* (e.g., flags or counters) placed at strategic points within the program, can, during test postprocessing, report the execution of statements, decision-to-decision paths, or more complete paths. If this is not supported by the test environment software, it is still possible, at the expense of further changing the state of the program, to place one's own data collection arrays and routines directly in the program for this purpose.

Knowing where best to place the probes is, unfortunately, not very obvious. However, automatic probe insertion or semi-automatic interactive probe insertion is possible through static analysis. Moreover, mechanization of the next path to select and the data required to execute it is also possible if one has the requisite tools. Sadly, most program testers do not have such tools. *Dynamic analysis tools* (to give them the name that is frequently used) are relatively new and are known to a minority of software managers. Examples of such systems are the RXVP80™ system[18] for Fortran programs and JAVS[19] for programs coded in Jovial.

While on the subject of dynamic analysis, we should not forget the use of *executable assertions.* These are statements inserted at key points to confirm the expected relations among program variables. Test cases may result in correct output even though there are internal anomalies. For example, an incorrectly computed array subscript may from an adjacent (memory image) array pick up a value that coincidentally has no erroneous effect on the computation results. An assertion statement in the form of a Boolean predicate can be placed in the program to define the expected relation of the computed subscript to input or computed variables. If the predicate evaluates to TRUE, the testers never hear of it. But if it evaluates to FALSE during any traversal through the statement, the testers will be alerted to the presence of a defect. Perhaps the best-known of the systems that provide help in using assertions is PET.[20]

MUTATION TESTING

Recall, the use of defect-seeding to evaluate the overall effectiveness of a set of test cases. A more structural way of determining the effectiveness of one's test cases is to see how many continue to yield expected results if the program is slightly altered. If none of the tests responds to the mutated code, the effectiveness of the set of tests comes into question. Since a program may have many thousands of statements and a series of tests many input values, the process is quite impossible without mechanization. *Mutation testing,* as it is called by its inventors[21] has only recently emerged from university research, and it is almost unknown to industry. One available test system that incorporates mutation testing is the LDRA test bed offered by Liverpool Data Research Associates Ltd. in the U.K.

Whatever structural testing standards and tools are in place, it is an important part of a software quality assurance program to see that they are used and not ignored in feverish attempts to meet schedule commitments. Software quality engineers should understand the capabilities and limitations of the tools and should make certain that they are properly used and—opposite, again, to the undesirable haste flagged in the preceding sentence—that claims for their effectiveness are not overstated to the end of skimping on functional testing, either.

Debugging

Testing reveals the *presence* of defects. Debugging is the process by which the defects responsible for test failures are found and *removed.* Debugging may call for further, impromptu tests, and nearly always involves the study of source code listings. Debugging can be expensive; 10 minutes of test time can result in 10 hours of debugging time. The reasons are several.

One particularly nettlesome problem is that bugs tend to hide (mask) one another. In his search for a defect, the programmer, whether working from listings or the results of diagnostic tests or both, is frequently led astray by the presence of a second defect not directly associated with the failure that instigated the debugging session. Another vexing, if less common problem, is similar to one remarked in the discussion of dynamic analysis: diagnostic messages inserted in the program, much like instrumentation probes, can change the state of the program such that the effects of address-sensitive defects disappear when the failed test is rerun. There are other problems, as well, peculiar to debugging, but these are of less relevance to a quality assurance program than to the reinforcement of the tenet that passive defect removal techniques are, intrinsically, more economical than testing-debugging. Nor that we can do without testing; simply, we need to emphasize review and static analysis.

Symbolic Debugging

Increasingly, software managers are providing their programmers with the capability of *source-level* or *symbolic debugging*. Programmers who have the opportunity to set up diagnostic tests with reference to the meaningful names given to data and critical statements are better able to think a problem through using source code reasoning, thus placing their cognitive processes a bit closer than allowed by traditional debugging aids to the problem that the code is supposed to solve. Symbolic debuggers also provide a variety of powerful ancillary features that reduce debugging time. Curiously, in sharp distinction to the situation that prevailed in the early days of microprocessors, microprocessor development systems—whether stand-alone workstations or tool chains hosted on more powerful computers—provide some of the most powerful source-level debugging assistance that can be found.

Software quality engineers rarely participate in debugging. They do, however, often participate in the planning that leads to the development or acquisition of debugging tools. They nearly always participate in the planning of regression test strategies.

Regression Testing

One of the less cheerful facts of software life is that the removal of a defect found during testing often creates unexpected side-effects. The programmer, believing that he or she has found the cause of test failure, revises the code and is rewarded with a successful rerun of the previously failed test case. Unfortunately, the changed code creates a new problem, one that may not show up in the execution of the remaining test cases. With luck, however, one of the previously run test cases will be sensitive to the new bug; thus regression testing.

Now, one would not want to rerun all tests, starting with the first, every time a bug is removed. This can be absurdly time-consuming. Alternatively, if no tests are rerun until the end of the test series, the testers may—after some analysis—be greeted with the discovery that they have gravely destroyed the structure of the software through a series of ill-conceived repairs.

What is required is a strategy that entails criteria for determining when to retest (e.g., every time the global data structure or a module interface is altered) and, possibly, which test cases to rerun. Software quality engineers often recommend a regression test set consisting of small packets of test cases for use at various points in the testing process. The efficiency of retesting can be greatly enhanced by tools that permit the retention of test input and output on disk, perhaps as a byproduct of an interactive test control system that gives testers the ability to specify input conditions in problem-oriented language. Going one step further, a fully automatic regression test system compares the results of retest with the stored results of previously successful runs.

Another concern of software quality engineers is that a putative defect-removal operation may fall short of its promise because the code subsequently used to resume the testing process is either the original code that failed or code modified to provide diagnostic information; in any case, not the code that demonstrated that the problem had been resolved. This situation is most likely to occur in the early stages of testing, when software quality engineers are on the scene only infrequently and have less opportunity to personally observe configuration control procedures. Audits, of course, help. Audits of library control records serve also as reminders that there is a right way of doing things.

Summarizing debugging, we see that this most conspicuous of the defect-removal processes can be a defect-producing process as well. The procedures and tools used in debugging should, properly, be given ample attention by the software quality assurance program even though the work is performed at an entirely technical level.

Failure-Prone Modules

The remarks on the topic of debugging might lead one to believe that it is possible for debugging to make matters worse. Less pessimistically, it is more likely that debugging will not make a certain few modules much better. For various reasons, large software systems often have a few parts that seem to develop a new bug for each that is removed. Whether these modules are designed badly in the first place, lose their structure in the process of having new features added, or are ravaged by inept debugging, one wants to be able to identify and replace them. They will always be a source of unreliability.

The programmers testing the system may very well know of modules that qualify for the term *failure-prone*. It is, after all, difficult to test for several weeks without noticing those parts that again and again prove to be the source of test failures. For one reason or another, perhaps as little reason as the belief that no one is really interested, this knowledge often goes no further than the programmers. Defect measurement, however, will reveal the presence of failure-prone modules.

PARETO ANALYSIS

Given that defect measurement includes identification of the modules in which defects have been found, one can tabulate the number of defects found in each module. At some point late in the testing activity—say, at the end of integration

TABLE 18-1   Defective Modules

NUMBER OF MODULES WITH N DEFECTS	N
120	Less than 5
60	6 to 10
16	11 to 15
4	Over 15

testing—a Pareto analysis can be performed to see if there are any modules contributing an untoward number of defects. (For more on Pareto analysis, see Chapter 11.)

Consider a system of 200 modules as shown in Table 18-1. The four miscreants with $N > 15$ are examined further. Are any much larger than average? Have any been performing well in recent tests even if early performance was poor? Are any inherently much more complex (i.e., solving more complex problems) than the average? If answers to these and similar probing questions are negative for any of the four modules in the last category, serious thought should be given to returning them to the software drawing board. The schedule will suffer, but reliability will profit.

18.6 MEASURING RELIABILITY

During testing, once all the pieces of the system are in place, the time comes to question how much longer one has to test. Part of the answer (the lesser part) is arrived at by multiplying the average time to run a test case by the number of remaining test cases. This is quick, but grossly inaccurate. The greater part of test time will be spent debugging. Assuming that the average time to debug a failed test is known, a more accurate answer can be found by subtracting the number of bugs fixed from the number of bugs or estimated number (see equations $f(t)$ *and* $Z(t)$ later in this section) that existed at the start of testing; multiplying the difference by the average debug time; and adding this result to the result of the computation for the lesser part stated above.

Unfortunately, we do not know the actual number of bugs that existed at the start of testing. We may have some notion based on experience with similar projects or based on complexity modeling, but inklings do not score high on the scale of precise estimation. Seeding provides a better estimator (recall, from Section 18.5, the calculation of N), but it does not take into account the variable rate at which bugs are found. The defect rate may not directly affect the estimate of the remaining test time, but a rate that diminishes with time would affect the length of one's wait for the testing process to become more orderly and predictable, that is, for the software to become more reliable.

Decreasing the Defect-Detection Rate

Indeed, the defect-detection rate should diminish with time because tests early in the testing cycle exercise more code for the first time than do later tests. Despite the connection between functional test cases and specific programmed functions and despite the connection between deliberately selected test cases and code structure, code incidental to the functionality to which a test is directed is also exposed.

Any code, when exercised, may cause a failure. Accordingly, the earlier in the series of tests a given test case is run, the greater its opportunity to expose a defect. Once removed (assuming it is properly removed), the defect can cause no further trouble.

Exactly at what rate the defect-detection incidence (only, henceforth, let us call it *failure* incidence) decreases is a matter that has occupied a number of software and reliability engineers for some time. Whether the word "exactly," as used above, applies at all is questioned by an equal number of software and reliability engineers. As we get into the topic, the reasons will become apparent. However, even if one tends to take either side of the argument, the contemplation of the issues of software reliability modeling leads to new insights into defect population and reliability itself.

Classical Models

Software reliability models extrapolate from the history of failure to forecast the future of failure. With their statistical roots in the reliability theory originally developed for hardware, the many published models all share the definition of reliability in the time domain,

$$R(t) = \text{probability of no failure in the interval 0 to } t$$

The companion definition is the *failure function:*

$$F(t) = 1 - R(t)$$

Statistically, $F(t)$ is the cumulative distribution function, or cdf, of failure. If there is a cdf, there must also be a probability density function, or pdf, the familiar $f(t)$ of statistics:

$$f(t) = \frac{dF(t)}{dt}$$

Borrowed also from classical reliability theory is the hazard function or failure rate, written variously as $Z(t)$ or $\lambda(t)$. $Z(t)$ is the pdf of the time to failure, given no failure prior to t.

$$Z(t) = \frac{f(t)}{R(t)} = -\frac{dR(t)}{dt}$$

For the most part, it is the specification of $Z(t)$ that distinguishes one model from another. Several surveys of software reliability models have been published, three of which are included in references 14, 22, and 23. Rather than repeating material already available, we shall restrict the topic to the broader issues.

Most of the models produce an exponentially decreasing pdf, although S-shaped curves, a hypergeometric distribution, and Rayleigh distributions have also been modeled. The earliest models, in one form or another, specified that the hazard function between successive defect-removal operations is proportional to the remaining number of bugs. Implicit in such hazard functions is the assumption of a random distribution of defects with respect to test cases. For practical purposes, this amounts to the assumption that the defects are random with respect to the structure of the software. This is doubtful, although there certainly is no presumptive distribution more acceptable. Whether or not the model may hold in the early stages of testing, the presumption of randomness weakens in the late stages when (we should like to think) there are few bugs remaining in the system.

Accordingly (and shifting our focus a bit), an attempt to extrapolate within the bounds of statistical precision from the testing environment to that of operational use appears ill-advised. On the other hand, if the failure distribution appears to have been well-behaved and has sustained a level asymptotic to a zero failure expectation, it is reasonable to expect the condition to continue through the transition to operation, assuming no significant differences between the testing and operational environments.

This assumption is, in fact, one that several models have questioned and attempted to account for. There are other assumptions, as well, that shape the hazard functions of software reliability models. A partial list of assumptions influencing models includes:

- Debugging time vs. testing time.
- Availability of testing and debugging personnel.
- Effectiveness of debugging procedures.
- Uniformity of testing time with calendar time.
- Probability of correctly fixing a problem.
- Probability of introducing a new defect.
- Homogeneity of defect tractability.
- Test stress vs. operational stress.
- Timewise uniformity of hazard rates between failures.

Bayesian Models

The difficulty of specifying the effects of these influences, individually or severally at a time, underscores the problem of fixing reliability to environmental causality.

Enter the Bayesian modelers. Their underlying thesis is that whatever hazard distribution one assumes, if its tuning parameters are well-chosen, the model will improve rapidly with failure experience. As failure data accumulates, all of the models are expected to improve, of course; the issue is whether the Bayesian models, with their scant assumptions of causality, can improve more rapidly than their "frequentist" counterparts (to use the word given to classical models by Bayesian adherents).

Littlewood's stochastic Bayesian model[24] takes account of the question of the random distribution of defects. Like most of the Bayesian models, it assumes a gamma distributed failure rate; but it also assumes that each bug may have its own. This, at least, does away with the tenuous assumption that bugs are evenly distributed with respect to test history.

Frequentist or Bayesian, most of the models imply that the probability of failure increases as the time since the last failure. This may be mathematically consistent, but intuitively it is unsatisfactory. With fairly new products, our perception of reliability increases to the point of complacency as the product continues to uninterruptedly perform without incident. Littlewood's model, as did a predecessor to it, has the reliability increase as the time from the last failure. This seems more tidy, its acceptability tarnished only by the observation that on encountering a failure the model does not, by sharply increasing the failure rate, disabuse its user of the system's trustworthiness.

If each model depends on a body of statistical data, we have a paucity of data on independent validation of models. Many of the models have been validated by people other than the authors of the models, but the total number of programming projects that have been used as validation references, especially for comparison purposes, is much less than one might expect. Part of the reason is the difficulty of acquiring time-domain failure data from large systems, not to mention defect-by-defect time data, execution time data, and other statistics required by one model or another. In any event, the independent validation data that does exist is inconsistent, and there is not enough of it to match the goodness of fit with the accuracy—when it can be ascertained—of the assumptions. In at least one case, excellent fits were obtained with three different models, each model working well for a period of testing, then (all but the last) abruptly becoming inaccurate for no evident reason. Despite the inconsistencies that exist in model validation, it should be emphasized that some programming installations have had success with the use of models.

Testing Time

This section started with the topic of estimating test progress. Before continuing with the larger issue of reliability, let us digress long enough to conclude the business of timewise test progress measurements. If we view the time domain reliability models as sophisticated trend analyzers, we should remain aware that there are other useful, if simpler, indicators of how well things are going during the testing process. One easily constructed indicator applies to testing conducted under a regimen (as might be found in system or qualification testing) wherein new test cases continue to be run while failures are analyzed by programmers who are independent of the testers. One can plot, against calendar time, the cumulative number of problems that have occurred and the cumulative number of problems that have been fixed. If, after an appropriate time, the number of problems opened exceeds the number closed by an ever-increasing amount, trouble is plainly indicated. If the difference between opened and closed problems remains fairly constant or decreases, one can predict with reasonable success the time at which testing will be complete. Of course, even this implies restrictive assumptions, such as a constant debugging labor force.

An even simpler trend analysis derives from the graph of the ratio of failed tests to attempted tests plotted against time. The interpretation is similar to the preceding trend technique. The failed-attempted graph may be simpler to use, but unlike the other it lacks the virtue of being able to account for trends in the subtlety of disclosed defects. Many projects have experienced the phenomenon of encountering increasingly problematic failure diagnosis as testing wears on.

Chapter 19 addresses the IEEE standardization process for the measurement for software reliability with copious examples in its appendix.

So much for digression. Let us turn back to the topic of reliability.

18.7 SOME CONCLUDING OBSERVATIONS

In focusing anew on reliability, we shall do so not mathematically as in the preceding section, but in a manner reflecting the opening pages of the chapter, and in the course of things perhaps find the crux of software quality assurance.

The IEEE *Software Glossary* provides two definitions of reliability. The first is given in the Glossary of Chapter 1, incorporating probability. The second reads: "The ability of a program to perform a required function under stated conditions for a stated period of time." Ignoring the implicit allusion to statistics, the reference to required functions and stated conditions gets to the real nub of reliability: expectations. The perception of a reliable program is one that relates its performance to our expectations of usable computer output: that which is correct and available when needed. Now, let's look at what we mean by "correct" and "when needed."

Correctness

Correctness has to do with the accuracy of output, at least the extent to which the accuracy is adequate for the purpose. A telephone switching system that generally connects to the wrong terminal is not accurate enough; it is unreliable. A payroll system that is frequently off by small amounts of money is unreliable in terms of correctness. On the other hand, a spacecraft guidance system that intermittently produces inaccurate steering commands may be reliable.*

---

*If the steering output occurs at intervals too short for the differential thrust apparatus to respond to abrupt commands, little is lost. Spacecraft guidance systems work in closed loops with respect to position sensors, enabling the system to self-correct in short order.

Availability

Availability may have several meanings, even as correctness may refer to analog or discrete errors, to accuracy or precision. The availability of a batch system has to do with system crashes. The availability of the spacecraft navigation system has not only to do with system crashes, but also with the program's capability of keeping up with the *rate* at which input arrives. For the same navigation system for which we can tolerate intermittent inaccuracy, we probably cannot tolerate much in the way of slowness, as this might produce cumulative errors that do not self-correct. We certainly cannot tolerate system crashes. On the other hand, for the batch payroll system that we perceive as unreliable if it outputs checks that are off by few cents, we can tolerate occasional system crashes. For the telephone switch that should seldom connect one to the wrong party, we can tolerate periods of slowness every now and again; but we cannot tolerate system crashes.

Back to Expectations

In short, our perceptions have to do with what we expect in the way of *usable* output. This is what reliability is all about. If one is to design for reliable performance, one must take into account the operational environment and understand the uses to which the program will be put. Then one can take whatever pains seem appropriate to design the program such that it will not exhibit performance judged intolerable by its users. Although reliable performance is generally equivalent to good performance, a distinction should be made between a program designed for reliable performance and a program of good design.

By "good design" we mean modularity, structure, and all the other shibboleths of modern programming. If we are to focus on reliability, however, we must not only use good design techniques, but we must also emphasize the goodness of the design as it applies to what the user expects, what can and cannot be tolerated. Moreover, we must take pains to focus on the detection and removal of defects specific to those performance characteristics that enter into satisfying the user's expectations. This is the reference that frames the role of software quality assurance.

To take but two examples, first, for the batch payroll system, where accuracy of calculation is preeminent, software quality engineers would be startled by the choice of floating-point arithmetic. That would scarcely be designing for reliability. Moreover, they would not accept functional test cases designed to demonstrate that the average value of the paychecks printed equalled the average of those that were supposed to be printed. They would insist that each be checked individually. For the spacecraft guidance system, on the other hand, floating-point arithmetic would be quite appropriate; and with regard to testing, the trend (short-term average) of guidance corrections is possibly more useful an indicator of performance than individual steering outputs.

Once one understands what the goals must be to conform to what the user perceives as reliability, any design output, code, or test technique that does not support the identified goals is a defect. Keeping defects out of operational software is the contribution made by software quality assurance to software reliability.

References

1. Bergland, Glenn, and Gordon, Ronald, *Tutorial: Software Design Strategies,* IEEE EH0149-5, 1979.

2. Hamilton, M., and Zeldin, S., "Higher Order Software — A Methodology for Defining Software," *IEEE Transactions on Software Engineering,* Vol. SE-2, March 1976, pp. 9-32.

3. Orr, Kenneth, "Introducing Structured Systems Design", *Tutorial: Software Design Strategies,* IEEE EH0149-5, 1979, pp. 79-82.

4. Ross, D. T., and Schoman, K. E., Jr., "Structured Analysis for Requirements Definition," *IEEE Transactions on Software Engineering,* Vol. SE-3, January 1977, pp. 6-15.

5. DeMarco, Tom, *Structured Analysis and System Specifications,* (New York: Yourdon, 1978).

6. Shaw, M., et al., "Abstraction and Verification in ALPHARD: Defining and Specification of Iteration and Generators," *CACM,* Vol. 20, August 1977, pp. 553-563.

7. Dahl, O., "Simula — an ALGOL-Based Simulation Language," *CACM,* Vol. 9, September 1966, pp. 671-678.

8. Musser, David, "Abstract Data Type Specification in the AFFIRM System," *IEEE Transactions on Software Engineering,* Vol. SE-6, January 1980, pp. 24-32.

9. Teichroew, D., and Hershey, E. A., III, "PSL/PSA: A Computer Aided Technique for Structured Documentation and Analysis of Information Processing Systems," *IEEE Transactions on Software Engineering,* Vol. SE-3, January 1977, pp. 41-48.

10. Davis, C., and Vick, C., "The Software Development System," *IEEE Transactions on Software Engineering,* Vol. SE-3, January 1977, pp. 69-84.

11. Caine, Stephen, and Gordon, E. Kent, "PDL — A Tool for Software Design," *Proceedings of the 1975 National Computer Conference,* Vol. 44 (Montvale, NJ: AFIPS Press, 1975), pp. 271-276.

12. Nassi, I., and Shneiderman, B., "Flow Chart Techniques for Structured Programming," *SIGPLAN NOTICES,* Vol, 8, ACM, August 1973, pp. 12-26.

13. DeMarco, Tom, *Controlling Software Projects* (New York: Yourdon Press, 1982), pp. 195-232.

14. Dunn, Robert, and Ullman, Richard, *Quality Assurance for Computer Software* (New York: McGraw-Hill, 1982), pp. 244-247.

15. Fagan, Michael E., "Design and Code Inspection to Reduce Errors in Program Development," *IBM System Journal,* Vol. 15, No. 3 (July 1976), pp. 182-211.

16. Weinberg, Gerald, *The Psychology of Computer Programming,* (New York: Van Nostrand Reinhold, 1971).

17. Fischer, Kurt, and Walker, Michael, "Improved Software Reliability through Requirements Verification", *IEEE Transactions on Reliability,* Vol. R-28, August 1979, pp. 233-240.

18. Dehaan, W., *RXVP80™ A Software Documentation, Analysis, and Test System,* (Santa Barbara, CA: General Research Corporation)

19. Miller, E. R., *Methodology for Comprehensive Software Testing,* General Research Corporation, released by Rome Air Development Center, Rome, NY, as RADC-TR-75-161.

20. Stucki, Leon, and Foshee, Gary, "New Assertion Concepts for Self-Metric Software Validation," *Proceedings 1975 International Conference on Reliable Software,* IEEE 75CHO940-7CSR, pp. 59-71.

21. Budd, T. A.; Demillo, R. A.; Lipton, R. J.; and Sayward, F. G., "Theoretical and Empirical Studies on Using Program Mutation to Test the Functional Correctness of Programs," *Seventh Annual ACM Symposium on Principles of Programming Languages,* January 1980, pp. 220-223.

22. Dale, C. J., *Software Reliability Evaluation Methods,* ST26750, British Aerospace Dynamics Group, Stevenage, September 1982. v
23. Swearingen, D., and Donahoo, J., "Quantitative Software Reliability Models—Data Parameters: A Tutorial," *Workshop on Quantitative Software Models,* IEEE TH0067-9, 1979, pp. 143-153.
24. Littlewood, Bev, "Stochastic Reliability Growth: A Model for Fault Removal in Computer Programs and Hardware Designs," *IEEE Transactions on Reliability,* Vol. R-30, October 1981, pp. 313-320.

19

Software Reliability Management

James H. Dobbins, CQA
Defense Systems Management College

19.1 THE MANAGEMENT OF SOFTWARE RELIABILITY

The science of measurement and the practice of software quality assurance (SQA) have not always been bedfellows. They are still often considered diverse activities rather than companion disciplines. It is time that the practice of SQA and the discipline of measurement of software quality, in all aspects, merge and speak with a common voice. Quality cannot be assured if it cannot be measured. It is not enough to implement a technique or process. The result must be evaluated, and evaluation implies some form of measurement technique.

Attempts at the measurement of software quality have suffered from a lack of positive direction and this has led to a plethora of measurements of questionable utility. If it is understood that quality is an umbrella characteristic which covers many other selective aspects, such as reliability, then it is possible to begin to provide focus and direction on the measurement process and the intelligent selection and evaluation of the measurement applied. It is the purpose of this chapter to provide the framework for evaluation of one aspect of software quality, that of reliability, and do so in such a manner that reliability can be continually assessed and managed throughout the entire development life cycle. This assessment will allow the optimization of reliability, and this optimization will be seen to be the maximization of reliability within project constraints such as cost, schedule, resources, and the like.

19.2 PERSPECTIVE

To ascertain the place at which this discipline has arrived, it is important to examine its brief and recent history.

The science of hardware reliability measurement has long been understood and practiced through the application of statistical models, usually either Bayesian or Poisson, by which the user can calculate how long a piece of hardware will operate in a given physical environment before it likely will fail. The mean time between failure (MTBF) is an important characteristic to the user in determining the spare parts requirements, and certainly is a significant input to any consideration of system availability. These techniques have been proven over time and have been shown to be quite valuable.

Software reliability is a much more recent science which began with the assumption that the measurement of software reliability should be accomplished using the same techniques as are used for hardware reliability. During the 1970s, several models came into being; the majority fall into one of two fundamental categories: deterministic or seeding.

The deterministic models, which measure mean time between failures (MTBF) or mean time to next failure (MTTF), have certain inherent assumptions and each has its own set of considerations making it more or less applicable to a given environment. Deterministic models usually assume random testing and the recording of exact test-time periods, and random testing is generally not accomplished in a laboratory environment. The more usual case is the execution of predetermined test procedures at a specific time and for a specific period to test a given functional performance. Depending on the data collection needs of each particular model,[1] the model may or may not consider whether an error is serious or minor, within specification or out of specification or any of a number of other factors which are important to management or the user community.

Seeding models (see Chapters 11 and 18) have certain fundamental assumptions which are difficult or impossible to verify. These are usually those related to the types of errors seeded. It is assumed that seeded errors are the same types and in the same proportion as indigenous errors. On the basis of how many of the seeded errors are found during test, the models calculate the number of remaining indigenous errors left to be removed and, in some cases, approximately how much longer it will take to find them. If all of the seeded errors are found, one can allegedly infer that all the indigenous errors have been found and testing can cease.

A subtlety that is often overlooked in discussions of the accuracy or validity of software reliability models is the effect of the tests themselves. Any model depends heavily on the test data as input for the model. It necessarily depends on the robustness of the test and the accuracy of recording the ancillary parameters, such as the time period for which the test was conducted. The models also tend to presume that all of the software is being exercised continuously during the test period, and that is a largely invalid assumption. We have all seen numerous cases, especially for real-time systems, in which the total system is operating, but various functional subsystems may or may not be actively processing data, depending on whether the operator, or test conductor, has chosen to activate that function of the system. When considering these elements, we must ask ourselves whether we are measuring the reliability of the software or the test. A test conductor can run two separate tests on the same software, one test being very robust and the other much less so. The results of the two tests may likely yield significantly different results in terms of errors detected. If the test data from the two tests are fed into any of the models, the result will be significantly different in terms of measured reliability, even though the software being measured by the two tests is identical. We tend to treat the results from the models as an inherent characteristic of the software being tested, and not think of it as indicative of the tests themselves. We also know that during tests of real-time systems, the operator has considerable control over which functions are being exercised at any time. If the Mean-Time-Between-Failure (MTBF) is the desired reliability measure, and assuming perfectly robust tests and perfectly designed models, we would still have to keep completely accurate records of the time each functional subsystem is processing data, assuming that is even possible, in order to provide accurate and relevant data to the model. And, finally, we also know that software is data environment responsive, not physical environment responsive. Hardware is physical, and tends to break or wear out after being subjected to certain kinds of physical stress (friction, heat, etc.) for periods of time. But software is not physical, and it responds to data environments. The tests to date for a given suite of software may indicate that the software has a certain MTBF, but if the operator finds an environmental condition (data sequence, data type, data rate, etc.) that the system cannot respond to, then the operator can cause the system to fail on command, as often as he or she wants to create the condition. Conversely, once the condition is discovered, the operator can purposely avoid that condition. Either of these conditions will have a dramatic impact on the reliability measurement, but in either case the reliability measurement will not be indicative of the true operational reliability.

Without going into lengthy discussion on the many different models and their subtle differences, which can already be found in the literature,[2,3] suffice it to say that the models, whatever their individual strengths or restrictions, generally require that the system be well into test before the necessary data can be collected and the model applied. Also, no one model has been identified by the professional community as that which should be used.

With these restrictions on the application of models, and the absence of a generally accepted model, there would seem to be no tool or set of measurements available for the software community to use any earlier than the test period itself. By this time, the software is developed, the design and implementation costs have been expended, and there is most likely to be an already established reliability for the software programs that will be altered very little (short of a redesign) by any activity during the later test phases. What is needed is a means to manage the reliability of the software from the conceptual phase all the way through to the operational phase.

19.3 THE FUNDAMENTAL NEED

Hardware models give us reasonably accurate data on the time it will take hardware to break. However, software does not break; but it does respond to environmental stimuli. There is little sense to speak of a MTBF for software which does not break. Spare parts do not help since the spares will have the same defect. Whatever defect(s) the software has, it has had since the software has been in existence and the defect will remain thus until environmental conditions cause it to manifest itself. For example, an incorrect result is obtained or the software ceases to perform altogether. Then the opportunity is available to fix the problem, and once fixed, it should be fixed forever. When the software finally does fail, it does so because test conditions or user environmental conditions finally occur which force the software to execute in a manner it was not specified to handle or could not handle, either because of a hardware failure or inherent design inadequacy.

During development, it is not so much the actual software failures which determine the results of any given software reliability model, but rather the effectiveness of the test plans and procedures in presenting a sufficiently thorough environment to allow software faults to manifest themselves as failures. If the test procedures are inadequate, the reliability measurement will look great because so few errors are being detected. If the test procedures are sufficiently comprehensive, the reliability measurement result may be quite poor because many errors are being found. In either case, the software is the same, and must therefore have the same inherent reliability.

Therefore, the true fundamental need is not a statistical model, but a means for managing the reliability of the software from concept to delivery. No single model or measurement will accomplish this. Reliability, if it is to be managed, must be maximized under conditions which account for cost, schedule, available resources, and the like. If reliability is so optimized, then there must be a *series* of measures which can be applied throughout the development process, which can provide an orthogonal view of the software at each development phase, and which will allow the development manager continuously to perform self-assessment and correction as the software progresses. At each phase, one must examine multiple aspects of the software to avoid being led astray by only one point of view of the product at any given time.

Equally important is the need to convert the data obtained from the measures into information which can be readily understood and utilized by management. In doing so, the measures and the information should be developed in light of three important characteristics: Primitives, Flexibility, and Graphics.

Primitives

Primitives are those things which are directly countable or observable. Some primitives may be measures. Other measures are derived by mathematical manipulation of one or more primitives. When establishing a database, the database should be constructed or primitives. If only the computational results producing measures are included in the database, the fundamental data upon which the measures are based is lost. The fundamental data from which to compute other additional measures is also lost. This also means that the ability to, at some time in the future, develop new measures based on some combination of these primitives cannot be accomplished with any historical perspective upon which a trend analysis might be performed.

Flexibility

Flexibility is the ability to respond to changing needs and conditions. The set of measures chosen at one point in time for the project may not be the same measures needed at a later time. The change in the measures may be due to the change in life cycle, or may be the result of a change in the condition of the project necessitating a different set of measures to evaluate the changed condition. This means that the database must be flexible enough to respond to these management needs, while retaining all of the requirements of rigorous database design. This can be done if the database is constructed from primitives data.

In IEEE Standard 982.1[4] and IEEE Guide 982.2,[5] the primitives are identified at the beginning as one set which satisfies the needs of all the measures described in the documents. Once the data as described by the primitives are collected, any measure in the standard can be computed.

Graphics

In converting any set of data into management information, it is highly recommended that the output be produced in the form of graphics. The graphics can convey a large amount of information very quickly, and if the detail background data is required for support it can always be obtained directly from the database. Few managers have the time to spend pouring over reams of digital data in trying to glean those bits of information needed to make the best decisions required for the life-cycle management of software reliability.

19.4 ADVANTAGES

The advantages of such an approach to the task of measurement for reliable software are numerous. Such a measurement approach allows the development manager to apply a variety of measurements to the product rather than only one. The confidence level achieved when the variety of measures gives a consistent or at least understandable picture of the software at any point in time is necessary for the decision-making process. The visibility into the product status provided by the measurements is a necessary ingredient to these decisions. It is only through such measurements that effective self-assessment and correction, can take place. The aspect of reliability being measured can be assessed, and the result will help determine whether the product proceeds to the next phase or remains in the present phase until the measurement is what is desired.

Without the measurement's availability, the decisions are made in a vacuum, largely as a result of gut-feeling or intuition based on some level of experience. The critical advantage of this measurement type of reliability management is the ability to perform the self-assessment and correction in real time. It is no longer necessary for reliability measurement, and reliability management, to be an after-the-fact process. Reliability management can now be based on a series of intelligently selected exit criteria which determine if and when the software will pass from one development phase to the next. Without the measurement availability, the exit criteria selection and evaluation are largely a process of whistling in the wind.

This is a conceptual leap which many will have difficulty adjusting to, partly because of the historical concepts and practices related to hardware reliability measurement which have been confined to an after-the-fact application of a statistical model.

But, it is no longer sufficient to learn what the reliability is; the manager must now also know what it *will* be, how to control it, and how to exercise that control through knowledge obtained from indicators of reliability measured at any point in time. Through the application of reliability management, the level of reliability will be determined and planned. If it is insufficient at any given phase, if the exit criteria are not being met, there will be a means for assessment to determine why, with the resultant opportunity to make the necessary corrections and reassess the product. In today's competitive environment, with the lives and safety of fellow citizens being ever more dependent on the reliability of the software products which so subtley affect them, the only approach which makes sense is to design and manage the reliability of the systems we produce. *How* to measure, and *what* measures to employ are really the only questions which should remain.

19.5 STANDARDIZATION

The literature is replete with measures of all types, each with its own data collection requirements and each more or less useful to the task facing the developer. Before any measurement selection process takes place, there should be some frame of reference through which discussion of candidate measures can be accomplished and which will afford some medium of evaluation.

The Institute of Electrical and Electronic Engineers (IEEE), through the Computer Society, recognized this need, and in 1982 initiated Project 982. This project was given the task of providing the community with a set of measures which could be used for the management of software reliability. This required that the members of the working group sort through the maze of measures discussed in the literature and select a candidate set to meet the project needs. This working group, made up of over 300 men and women, from industry, government and academia, and from many countries around the world, accomplished this task and submitted their candidate standard to the governing board in 1985. There was considerable discussion as to whether such a set of measures should be standardized. It was decided that standardization was necessary to an orderly development of this field. The work continued and the project was balloted, approved, and published by IEEE in 1988 in the form of IEEE Standard 982.1 and IEEE Guide 982.2.

There is no standardization imposed by the document regarding what measures the manager *must* utilize. This is clearly a matter of personal choice made by the developer. The standardization aspect comes into play once the selection has taken place. The document provides a set of 39 measures which may be used during development. The manager of a project is clearly free to choose any measure desired. However, if one of the measures contained in the IEEE document is selected, then the standardization governs how the measure is computed, when data is collected, and how the result is interpreted.

If application of the measures contained in the standard is consistent and uniform, then there is a basis for common discussion about the measures between professionals. However, if measures were applied in different ways and with different data collection requirements, there would be virtually no basis for common discussion.

Therefore, the standardization process is not applied to force the use of any one measure. In fact, the document is structured so that the set of measures may be modified as measurement science progresses. The set of measures is applied to increase communication and provide a firm basis for a common understanding of the application of measures if the selection is made from the measures discussed in the document.

In order to accomplish this goal, each measurement section of the IEEE Guide 982.2 contains a common structure. This means that for each measure contained, the following should be known:

a. A description of what the measure does and what it might be used for.
b. An identification and definition of each of the primitives needed. (A primitive is a parameter which is a fundamental input to the selected measure. It may be the result of another measure or it may be a parameter which is directly measured rather than derived through the application of a formula or other technique. For example, temperature is a directly measurable parameter.)
c. How the measure is to be implemented.
d. How the results are to be integrated.
e. Any special considerations related to that particular measure.
f. Any special training or experience required of one who applies the measure.
g. A specific example of the application of the measure.
h. A summary of the more important benefits of the measure.
i. The experience history in using the measure.
j. One or more published references on that measure.

By doing this, the developer is not left with only a formula to apply. The entire framework for the measure is provided and the avenue for meaningful discussion is thereby created.

The appendix to this chapter contains some of the measure tables from the final pre-publication draft, which are virtually intact in the published version, of the

IEEE Standard 982.1 and IEEE Guide 982.2. They are included here as examples of the type of information provided and the degree to which a measure has been discussed in the available literature. Some of the measures have had considerable evaluation reported in the literature and others, felt worthy of inclusion, may have had little publicly discussed evaluation but significant unpublished evaluation within one or more companies. It is hoped that their inclusion in IEEE Std 982.1 and IEEE Guide 982.2 will result in significant public discussion of the results of application of each of the measures selected.

The factors which have contributed to the inclusion of the measures in the IEEE 982 documents are:

1. The ease with which the primitive data may be collected.
2. The relationship between the measurement results and eventual operational reliability.
3. The ease with which the results may be interpreted.
4. Usefulness of the results in the management of the aspect being measured.
5. The need for measurements of multiple aspects at each life-cycle phase.
6. The ease of implementation.
7. The cost of implementation.

With these factors in mind, it should be clear that a considerable amount of evaluation has gone into the selection of the measures. This by no means implies that there are no other good or useful measures available. It simply means that the measures included in the document were found to serve the purposes and objectives for which the IEEE 982 documents were written. Attention to the foregoing list helps to shorten the selection process when measures are being evaluated. Since the document was written for general application and not directed to any one segment of industry, such as defense or nuclear power generation, it should be intuitively clear that no project should attempt to apply *all* of the measures in the document; each has its own requirements. Some measures require that a certain process be implemented, such as the inspection process.[6] If that requirement is not in place, then the measure cannot be applied.

In order to assist the manager, who may not be immediately familiar with the measurements which are available, a matrix is provided in the IEEE Guide 982.2 which gives a cross-reference between the general categories of the measures, the measures themselves, and the life-cycle phases in which the measures may be applied. These matrices, when used in conjunction with the measure descriptions, should offer considerable assistance to the one responsible for selecting the measures to be applied on a given project.

19.6 GOVERNMENT POSTURE

The Joint Logistics Command (JLC) has actively participated in the standardization process and continues to provide industry with the challenge to increase the quality, and therefore reliability, of the products delivered under government contracts. The history and brief summary of the software standard DOD-STD-2167A and the software quality standard DOD-STD-2168 and provided in Chapter 6. The

DOD-STD-2168 is markedly different from MIL-S-52779(A) in that it does not offer superficial guidance on the evaluation of a quality assurance program by a government representative. It will require that the contractor offer a specific software quality evaluation program and therefore a measurement program throughout the entire software development cycle. These two standards are written and designed to operate as a pair on any contract, DOD-STD-2168 specifically referring throughout to DOD-STD-2167A. Each also provides for specific tailoring, recommended by the contractor but subject to approval by the government.

In short, these standards force the contractor to scrutinize the project under development and select a set of measures which will allow the evaluation of quality, and therefore reliability, on a continuing basis and provide the customer with visibility into that process. They are driving the art of software quality assurance away from the arm-waving process of monitoring and inspecting which has been traditional and into the twenty-first century of effective measurement and analysis of the quality aspects of delivered products. The numbers selected for these two standards come from the feeling that they will take us into the twenty-first century and the fact that they are the 67th and 68th iterations of the documents, respectively.

And so, we have a choice. We either evaluate and therefore measure ourselves in some intelligent fashion, or the customer will not approve our development programs, with the resultant loss of business that will entail.

19.7 APPLICATION

Application of the measures advocated in the IEEE Project 982 standard requires an intelligent selection process. IEEE Standard 982.1 and IEEE Guide 982.2 contain 39 measures and is not intended to apply as a whole to any one project. The only way to select intelligently the measures which should be applied is to choose those which meet a given project's specific goals and which can also be implemented within the project constraints of time, cost, schedule, manpower, experience, and the like. Clearly, if it would be necessary to delay a project in order to apply a particular measure, selection of that measure when the schedule is very ambitious is not in the best interest of the project.

19.8 SELECTION

Selection of a measurement base should always be the result of intelligent evaluation. The selection process is first dependent on experience. If experience in measurement is limited, one or a small number of measures should be selected and applied. As experience is gained, additional measures may be added to the base. The IEEE STD 982.1 and IEEE Guide 982.2 provide the software professional or project manager, or both, a basis for discussion with other professionals. Judicious use of the IEEE 982 documents will significantly shorten the learning curve in measurement technology. Certainly, familiarity with the P982 document and Guide will enable the software quality assurance person with expertise in software measurement to aid management significantly in the measurement selection process.

Selection is likewise dependent on the type of project under development. Each project type will require a different level of reliability when delivered and this will drive the set of measures selected to meet those goals. If the varied user base is examined, the differences may be readily seen. Such diverse projects as a nuclear power plant, a manned space flight series, commercial software for off-the-shelf use by multiple nonprofessional users, military weapons systems, financial industry applications, software games and satellite communications systems applications will each have its own set of reliability requirements. Within each of these varied applications will be found a unique set of project goals and constraints.

19.9 OPTIMIZING RELIABILITY

Examination of the project goals and constraints is a necessary prerequisite to the intelligent selection of the measures to be applied on a project. Many program managers become enthusiastic in their establishment of project goals, but the manager selecting the reliability measures must be cognizant of both the goals and the constraints. A few of these possible goals and constraints are:

  a. Develop the system for no more than x dollars.
  b. Develop using only entry-grade programmers.
  c. Develop within x months or years.
  d. Develop using no more than x programmers.
  e. Develop assuming the customer will do most of the software testing.
  f. Develop a system for use in millions of homes.
  g. Develop a critical life-dependent system.
  h. Develop for analysis of medical data.
  i. Develop a state-of-the-art weapons system.
  j. Develop for nonmilitary governmental use, such as IRS or National Weather Service.
  k. Develop with a fixed specification.
  l. Develop with no available specification.
  m. Develop with a rapidly changing specification.
  n. Develop one or more subcontractors.
  o. Modify already produced product where original may have been developed in-house or by another company.

These, and many others, make up the possible set of goals and constraints facing every development manager. A realistic evaluation of the full set of parameters aids in the proper selection of the measures to be applied, since the measures are only chosen to aid in the realization of those goals within those constraints. Measures inconsistent with these project parameters will be of little use to the program manager.

Assuming consistency with goals and constraints, measures should be selected for their ability to provide meaningful feedback to the developers. This feedback is in the form of an evaluation of the parameter under investigation, the intelligibility of the data derived, the correlation between the measure and a process required for its application, the ability to use the data to make a management decision to correct the product or process or to proceed with development, and the amount of additional information provided in light of information already being gathered. If complexity is already being measured, it may not be best to choose another complexity measure but rather a measure of some other aspect of the software so as to gain the maximum insight into the condition of the product. Through intelligent selection, based on identified exist criteria for each stage of development, the reliability of the product can be optimized.

19.10 MANAGEMENT

Reliability management will be achieved through continuous optimization during development. This requires that there be a clear commitment to the measurement process by the management team. To accomplish this, the management team must be willing both to apply the measures and to learn from the results of the measurements. Through educated use of the measurement results, the management team can gain sufficient visibility into the product to achieve the optimal software reliability.

A corollary is that managers must not use the measures as a club to hold over the heads of the individual programmers during performance evaluations. This does nothing to maximize reliability and will be detrimental to the collection of accurate data on the project. Any competent manager does not have to depend on the results of a few measurements to find out if a programmer or software test individual is performing properly. The objective of the measurements task is to optimize software reliability, a considerable task in itself.

Reliability management also requires periodic examination of the selected measures in light of results already achieved and possibly a change in goals or constraints or both. The required measures are also determined by whatever change may come about in the exit criteria previously identified for a given life-cycle phase. A change in exit criteria may result from increased education in the selection and use of the measures, or it may come about from changes in the project itself.

19.11 MATRIX CONTROL

Inherent in the idea of reliability measurement selection and management is the idea of measurement control. Implementing this need requires that a set of measures be applied, and the results tracked throughout the application process. To accomplish this, a project application cross-reference matrix should be developed showing the measures selected, the phase or phases during which each can be applied, the goal or constraint affecting or affected by each, whether each has been actually applied, and the degree of satisfaction with the measurement result. This last point should *not* be confused with satisfaction with the condition of the software.

The IEEE Guide 982.2 has various tables (two are provided in Tables 19-1 and 19-2) set up in matrix format which provide significant information regarding the measures. Some show all of the measures, and reflect the general categories of

TABLE 19-1   Error/Faults/Failures Counting

MEASURES	LIFE-CYCLE PHASE							
	CONCEPTS	REQUIRE-MENTS	DESIGN	IMPLEMEN-TATION	TEST	INSTAL-LATION AND CHECKOUT	OPERA-TION AND MAINTE-NANCE	RETIRE-MENT
1. Fault Density	△	△	△	△	△	△	△	△
2. Defect Density		△	△	△	△	△	△	△
3. Cumulative Failure Profile	△	△	△	△	△	△	△	△
4. Fault-Days Number	△	△	△	△	△	△	△	△
7. Requirements Traceability		△	△					
8. Defect Indexes		△	△	△	△	△	△	△
12. Number of Conflicting Requirements		△						
23. Requirements Compliance		△						

TABLE 19-2 Overall Risk/Benefit/Cost Explanation

MEASURES	LIFE-CYCLE PHASE							
	CONCEPTS	REQUIRE-MENTS	DESIGN	IMPLEMEN-TATION	TEST	INSTAL-LATION AND CHECKOUT	OPERA-TION AND MAINTE-NANCE	RETIRE-MENT
5. Functional Test Coverage					◁	◁		
11. Man-Hours per Major Defect Detected			◁	◁	◁	◁	◁	◁
20. Mean Time to Remove Next K faults					◁	◁	◁	
33. Rely	◁	◁	◁	◁	◁	◁	◁	
34. Software Release Readiness					◁	◁	◁	◁

measure, process measure or product measure, to which each belongs. Other matrices are broken down by specific type of measure (ex: Error, Faults, Failures (Table 19-1); Complexity; MTBF) and show in which life cycle phases each can be used. These matrices were included to assist the manager in selecting the measures which should be used on a given project, recognizing that many managers will not be familiar with most of the measures described. These matrices can be of considerable help on defense contracts now that the IEEE STD 982.1 has been included as a reference standard in several Request for Proposals (RFPs), and even more so since February 1991 when the new DOD Instruction 5000.2 was signed. The new DODI 5000.2 mandates the use of metrics on software projects.

When the reliability measurement program starts with a select few measures, and accurate records on the results achieved are kept, the selection and evaluation process is made much easier than it would be otherwise. If, for example, a selected measure turns out to be less utilitarian than anticipated, and if that is because the data the measure provides is really not important to the achievement of a particular result, then this information would suggest that it and similar measures be dropped from the set of selected measures. Such a tracking system will be a substantial aid in communications among those applying similar measures, particularly in deciding whether the measures should be retained, altered, or dropped.

19.12 SUMMARY

Software reliability measurement is in its infancy, but is rapidly approaching puberty. As it progresses through puberty into maturity, the degree to which meaningful communication is achieved among those who practice this discipline will in large measure determine the direction it takes and the credibility it achieves in the reliability community. A great deal has to be accomplished in a short time to meet the rapidly developing needs of the market and of end users.

References

1. Duvall, L., Martens, J., Swearingen, D., and Donahoo, J., "Data Needs for Software Reliability Modeling," *Proceedings Annual Reliability and Maintainability Symposium,* 1980, pp. 200-208.
2. Farr, W. H., *A Survey of Software Reliability Modeling and Estimation.* Technical Report NSWC TR 82-171, Dahlgren, VA: Naval Surface Weapons Center, September 1983.
3. Schnick, G. J., and Wolverton, R. W., "An Analysis of Competing Software Reliability Models," *IEEE Transactions on Software Engineering,* Volume SE-4, No. 2 (March 1978), pp. 104-120.
4. IEEE Standard 982.1—1988, June 12, 1989.
5. IEEE Guide 982.2—1988, June 12, 1989.
6. Fagan, M. E., "Design and Code Inspections to Reduce Errors in Program Development," *IBM Systems Journal,* Vol. 15, No. 3 (July, 1976).

Appendix (Chapter 19)

Sample Measures for Reliable Software (From IEEE Guide 982.2)*

4.1 FAULT DENSITY

4.1.1 Application

This measure calculates the total faults per 1000 source lines of code (KSLOC). It can be used to:

—Predict remaining faults by comparison with expected fault density.
—Determine if sufficient testing has been completed, based on predetermined goals for severity class.
—Establish standard fault densities for code type and programming organization to use for comparison and prediction.

4.1.2 Primitives

i = failure sequence number.
d_i = failure date.
S_i = severity of failure.
Cl_i = class of failure.
C_i = type of fault.
$KSLOC$ = source lines (e.g. executable) of code, in thousands.

4.1.3 Implementation

The implementation steps are:

—Establish a classification scheme for severity and class of failure.
—Observe and log each failure.
—Determine the severity and class of failure.
—Determine the program fault(s) that caused the failure. Additional faults may be found resulting in total faults being greater than the number of failures observed. Or one fault may manifest itself by several failures. Thus, fault and failure density may both be measured.
—Determine total lines of source code.
—Calculate the fault density (n_f):

$$N_T = \sum_i n_i = \text{the total faults found, where}$$

n_i = the number of faults found per failure i.

$n_f = N_T/KSLOC.$

---

*Published June 12, 1989.

4.2 DEFECT DENSITY

4.2.1 Application

The defect density measure can be used after design and code inspections. If the defect density is outside the norm after several inspections, it is an indication that the inspection process requires further scrutiny. This measure is a variation of the fault density measure [*see* 4.1]. It is considered a separate measure because it focuses on the inspection process rather than the software product.

4.2.2 Primitives

i = inspection sequence number.
D_i = total number of defects detected during the ith design or code inspection process.
n = total number of inspections.
$KSLOC$ = source lines (e.g. executable) of code, in thousands, which have been inspected to date.

4.2.3 Implementation

At each inspection meeting, record the total lines inspected and the total defects. After several inspections have been completed on about 8-10 KSLOC, the total product volume and the total defects are summarized. The computation should be performed often (weekly) during design and code phases. If the design is not written in a structured design language, then this measure can be applied only during the code phase.

The measure is computed as follows:

$$\text{Defect Density } (DD) = \frac{\sum_{i=1}^{n} D_i}{KSLOC}$$

4.3 CUMULATIVE FAILURE PROFILE

4.3.1 Application

This is a graphical method used to:

—Predict reliability through the use of failure profiles.
—Estimate additional testing time to reach an acceptably reliable system.
—Identify modules, subsystems, etc. which require additional testing.

4.3.2 Primitives

i = failure sequence number.
d_i = failure date.
t_t = failure time.
S_i = severity of failure.
Cl_i= class of failure.
C_i = type of fault.

4.3.3 Implementation

Establish severity, and class of failure, and fault types. Failure classes might include I/O, user, incorrect output, etc. Fault types might include design, coding, documentation, initialization errors, etc. Observe and log failures (severity and class) and the time of failure. Determine fault(s) causing each failure. Plot cumulative failures versus a suitable time base. Calculate the failure rate and plot versus time.

4.6 CAUSE AND EFFECT GRAPHING

4.6.1 Application

Cause and Effect graphing aids in identifying requirements which are incomplete and ambiguous. This measure explores the inputs and expected outputs of a program and identifies the ambiguities. Once these ambiguities are eliminated, the specifications are considered complete and consistent.

Cause and Effect graphing can also be applied to generate test cases in any type of computing application where the specification is clearly stated (i.e. no ambiguities) and combinations of input conditions can be identified. It is used in developing and designing test cases which have a high probability of detecting errors that exist in programs. It is not concerned with the internal structure or behavior of the program.

4.6.2 Primitives

List of causes: a distinct input condition.
List of effects: an output condition or system transformation (an effect of an input on the
state of the system).
A = number of ambiguities in a program.

4.6.3 Implementation

A Cause and Effect graph is a formal translation of a natural language specification into its input conditions and expected outputs. The graph depicts a combinatorial logic network.

To begin, identify all requirements of the system and divide them into separate identifiable entities. Carefully analyze the requirements to identify all the causes and effects in the specification. After the analysis is completed, assign each cause and effect a unique number.

To create the Cause and Effect graph:

—Represent each cause and effect by a node identified by its unique number.
—Interconnect the cause and effect nodes by analyzing the semantic content of the specification and transforming it into a Boolean graph. Each cause and effect can be in one of two states: true or false. Using Boolean logic, set the possible states of the causes and determine under what condition each effect will be present.
—Annotate the graph with constraints describing combinations of causes and/or effects that are impossible because of syntactical or environmental constraints.
—Identify as an *ambiguity* any cause which does not result in a corresponding effect, any effect which does not originate with a cause as a source, and any combination of causes and effects which are inconsistent with the requirement specification or impossible to achieve.

The measure is computed as follows:

$$CE = 100\% \left(1 - \frac{A_{\text{existing}}}{A_{\text{total}}}\right)$$

where A_{existing} = number of ambiguities remaining to be eliminated.

A_{total} = total number of ambiguities identified.

To derive test cases for the program, convert the graph into a limited entry decision table with "effects" as columns and "causes" as rows. For each effect, trace back through the graph to find all combinations of causes that will set the effect to be TRUE. Each combination is represented as a column in the decision table. The state of all other effects should also be determined for each such combination. Each column in the table represents a test case.

4.7 REQUIREMENTS TRACEABILITY

4.7.1 Application

This measure aids in identifying requirements which are either missing from, or in addition to, the original requirements.

4.7.2 Primitives

$R1$ = number of requirements met by the architecture.
$R2$ = number of original requirements.

4.7.3 Implementation

A set of mappings from the requirements in the software architecture to the original requirements is created. Count each requirement met by the architecture ($R1$) and count each of the original requirements ($R2$). Compute the traceability measure:

$$\frac{R1}{R2} \times 100\%$$

4.8 DEFECT INDEXES

4.8.1 Application

This measure provides a continuing, relative index of how correct the software is as it proceeds through the development cycle. Application is a straight-forward phase dependent, weighted, calculation which requires no knowledge of advanced mathematics or statistics. This measure may be applied as early in the life cycle as the user has products which can be evaluated.

4.8.2 Primitives

For each phase in the life cycle:

i = phase indicator.
N_i = total number of defects found.
S_i = number of serious defects found.
M_i = number of medium defects found.
T_i = number of trivial defects found.
$KSLOC$ = source lines (e.g. executable) of code, in thousands.
W_1 = weighting factor for serious defects (default 10).
W_2 = weighting factor for medium defects (default 3).
W_3 = weighting factor for trivial defects (default 1).

4.8.3 Implementation

The measure is generated as a sum of calculations taken throughout development. It is a continuing measure applied to the software as it proceeds from design through final tests.

At each phase of development, calculate the following expression, P_i, associated with the number and severity of defects found.

$$P_i = W_1 \frac{S_i}{N_i} + W_2 \frac{M_i}{N_i} + W_3 \frac{T_i}{N_i}$$

The Defect Index (DI) is calculated at each phase by cumulatively adding the calculation for P_i as the software proceeds through development:

$$DI = \sum_{i=1}^{n} i * P_i / KSLOC$$
$$= (P_1 + 2P_2 + 3P_3 + \ldots)/KSLOC$$

where each phase is weighted such that the further into development the software has progressed, such as phase 2 or 3, the larger the weight (i.e., 2 or 3, respectively) assigned, and the sum of calculations is normalized according to program size, $KSLOC$.

The data collected in prior projects can be used as a baseline figure for comparison.

4.9 ERROR DISTRIBUTION(s)

4.9.1 Application

The search for the causes of software errors involves the error analysis of the data collected during each phase of the software development. The results of this analysis can be best depicted by plotting error information to provide the distribution of errors according to different criteria.

4.9.2 Primitives

— Error description.
— Pointer(s) to fault(s) originated by the error.
— Cause of the error.
— Error classification of the phase (date) when the error was introduced.
— Error weight: assignment due to severity/delay in error revelation.
— Steps to prevent the error.
— Reasons for earlier nondetection of faults.

4.9.3 Implementation

The information for each error is recorded and the errors are counted according to the criteria adopted for each classification. The number of errors are then plotted for each class. Examples of such distribution plots are shown in Figure [19A-1]. In the three examples of Figure [19A-1], the errors are classified and counted by phase, by the cause and by the cause for deferred fault detection. Other similar classification could be used such as the type of steps suggested to prevent the reoccurrence of similar errors or the type of steps suggested for the early detection of the corresponding faults.

4.10 SOFTWARE MATURITY INDEX

4.10.1 Application

This measure is used to quantify a software maturity index for a software delivery, based on the functions (modules) that include changes and additions from the previous delivery. The primitives counted may either be functions or modules.

4.10.2 Primitives

M_T = number of software functions (modules) in the current software delivery.
F_c = number of software functions (modules) in the current delivery that include internal changes from a previous delivery.
F_a = number of software functions (modules) in the current delivery that are additions to the previous delivery.
F_{del} = number of software functions (modules) in the previous delivery that are deleted in the current delivery.

4.10.3 Implementation

The software maturity index (*SMI*) may be calculated in two different ways depending on the available data (primitives).

4.10.3.1 IMPLEMENTATION #1

— For the present (just delivered or modified) software release, count the number of functions (modules) that have been changed (F_c).

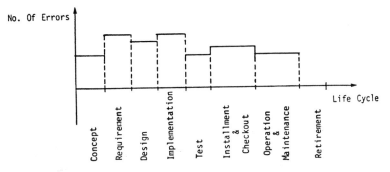

(a) Error Distribution By Phase

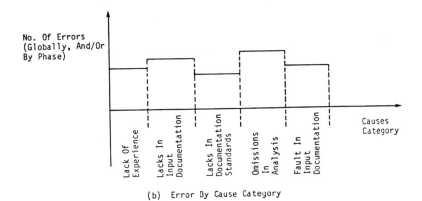

(b) Error By Cause Category

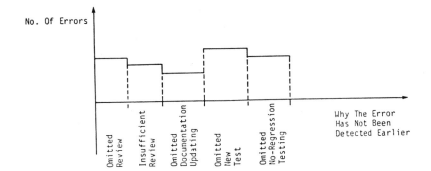

(c) Suggested Causes For Error Detection Deferral

FIGURE [19A-1]. Error analysis.

— For the *present* software release, count the number of functions (modules) that have been added (F_a) or deleted (F_{del}).

— For the *present* software release, count the number of functions (modules) that make-up that release (M_T).

Calculate the maturity index:

$$\text{Maturity Index} =$$

$$\frac{\begin{array}{l}\text{Number of}\\\text{Current}\\\text{Functions}\\\text{(Modules)}\end{array} - \left(\begin{array}{l}\text{Number of Current}\\\text{Release Functions}\\\text{(Modules) That}\\\text{Have Been Added}\end{array} + \begin{array}{l}\text{Number of}\\\text{Functions}\\\text{(Modules)}\\\text{Changed}\end{array} + \begin{array}{l}\text{Number of Current}\\\text{Release Functions}\\\text{(Modules) That}\\\text{Have Been}\\\text{Deleted}\end{array}\right)}{\text{Number of Current Release Function (Modules)}}$$

i.e., $SMI = \dfrac{M_T - (F_a + F_c + F_{del})}{M_T}$

Notice that the total number of current release functions (modules) equals the number of previous release functions (modules) plus the number of current release functions (modules) that were added to the previous release minus the number of functions (modules) that were deleted from the previous release. In the maturity index calculation, the deletion of a function (module) is treated the same as an addition of a function (module).

4.10.3.2 IMPLEMENTATION #2

The Software Maturity Index may also be calculated as the ratio of the number of functions (modules) that remain unchanged from the previous release to the total number of functions (modules) delivered in the present release, but this method of calculation is more appropriate.

$$SMI = \frac{M_T - F_c}{M_T}$$

The change and addition of functions (modules) is tracked and the maturity index is calculated for each release. Problem reports that would result in a software update subsequent to the tracking period are included in the maturity analysis by estimating the configuration of the subsequent releases.

20

Effective Methods of EDP Quality Assurance

William E. Perry, CPA, CIA, CISA, CQA

Quality Assurance Institute

20.1 WHAT IS QUALITY ASSURANCE?

Quality assurance is a rapidly growing part of data processing. Organizations establish quality assurance to improve their applications, process, and image. It is one of the cornerstones of an effective EDP function.

Quality assurance begins with the definition of quality standards, methodology, and procedures; in other words, bringing order and control to the environment. Some systems analysts feel that a quality assurance group is an impediment by management to hinder them from doing their job on time. This may be true if the function is established and operated incorrectly. If the quality assurance process itself is burdensome, it may not work.

Quality must be a routine habit in the department—it can't be imposed upon people at particular points in time, but the quality assurance group must build a quality environment. Looking at a single application will not improve data processing productivity. Looking at several applications, the symptoms of problems in the environment can be identified and analyzed, after which recommendations can be made to improve the whole quality of the data processing function. Table 20-1 summarizes the embodiment of QA.

The Quality Assurance Institute surveyed its membership in mid 1989; the results of the survey were tabulated by the DATAFAX Company (a market research company) in Winter Park, Florida. The highlights of the survey follow.

TABLE 20-1   Embodiment of QA

- Need an unambiguous, rigorous definition of QA standards, rules, and methodologies.
- Ties various methodologies into unified, cohesive program.
- Defines responsibilities, interdepartmental interfaces.
- If it is too burdensome, it won't work.
- More than life cycle, or project control system.
- In summary, concepts must be reduced to ROUTINE HABIT.

1989 EDP QUALITY ASSURANCE SURVEY*

The significant findings of this 1989 EDP quality assurance survey are:

1. The primary focus in the QA groups represented by the respondents is now on standards and procedures development and improvement.
2. The inability to obtain management's commitment and involvement is viewed as the major impediment facing QA groups.
3. Many organizations have been able to prove the value of quality and quality's positive relationship to productivity. These organizations report that this is what they receive most recognition for within their companies.
4. Measurement continues to be one of the most important new activities QA groups are focusing on.
5. QA's view of its own mission is shifting from a passive role and/or one focused on corrective action to a leadership role and/or one focused on process management.

The survey conclusions are:

1. The members of the QA function will need to develop strong 'soft skills' in the area of communications and marketing if they want to overcome the problems of management commitment that they continue to face.
2. Measurement data will also be needed to prove the value of quality and gain management's long term commitment to quality.
3. The mission of the QA function must move towards one of leadership and one which will lead the Information Services organization into a culture of continuous process improvement.

Using the survey findings and conclusions Quality Assurance Institute recommends the following two actions for QA managers

1. Position QA as a leadership function. Leadership requires establishing a vision, then developing programs to accomplish that vision. QA managers

---

should begin this process by establishing small short term visions that can be accomplished with your current staff. Success builds credibility.

2. Demonstrate that quality works. Select one or two results desired by MIS managers (e.g., fewer production ABENDS); results that the quality programs can help achieve. Develop a measurement program, then benchmark the current status for those results. Present a plan to move the results in the desired direction. Work hard and make the quality program work.

Age, Size and Growth of Quality Assurance

The age of the quality assurance function within the organizations surveyed continues to increase to an average of 3 years. This is composed as follows: 26% at < 1 year, 24% at 1-2 years, 20% at 2-3 years, 16% at 3-5 years, and 14% at > 5 years.

The size of the quality assurance staff in relation to total systems development and programming professional staff follows: 50% of the companies at 2% or less, 32% of the companies between 2% to 5%, and 18% of the companies at > 5%.

According to the survey quality assurance will grow by 25% in 18% of the companies and by 50% or more in 20% of the companies.

Quality Assurance Activities and Information Received

While the quality assurance activities vary from industry to industry, the overall ranking of quality assurance responsibilities in order of importance are:

1. Attendance at outside conference/seminars
2. Acquisition of software tools/methodologies
3. Conducting in-house training sessions
4. Reviews/walkthroughs of application systems
5. Special studies
6. Testing computer software
7. Survey of end users
8. Involvement with auditors
9. Software inspections
10. Cost-justification of the QA function
11. Quality circles

Other major activities reported were: standards and procedure and Software Development Methodology development and improvement, process improvements, change management/control, and measurement.

The activities and/or products that QA has evaluated in order of frequency are:

1. New system development
2. Program change control
3. Enhancements to existing software

4. Repair maintenance
5. Computer operations
6. Development center
7. Microcomputers

Other activities and products mentioned as being evaluated by QA are test plans and testing, project management process, and standards.

The information that the QA organization regularly receives in order of frequency is:

1. Problem reports
2. Project status reports
3. Program change requests
4. Data processing schedules
5. Data processing budgets

Other information mentioned as being regularly received by the QA organization is software deliverables, process suggestions and improvements, audits, and project documentation.

Quality Assurance Accomplishments and Impediments

The most significant accomplishments reported by the QA organizations surveyed in order of importance are:

1. Implemented or improved standards
2. Installed tools and methods
3. Installed or revised the software development life cycle methodology
4. Improved processes
5. Started the QA function
6. Conducted quality training programs
7. Increased awareness or commitment

Other frequently mentioned accomplishments include: a) improved testing, b) implemented change control/management, c) expanded QA function and coverage, d) implemented walkthroughs, reviews, and inspections, e) implemented problem reporting, f) implemented a measurement program, and g) improved project management.

The major impediments to the QA function in order of importance are:

1. Obtaining management commitment and involvement
2. Lack of resources (time, money, people)
3. Attitude/culture

4. Current organizational structure
5. Focus on short term; meeting schedules

Other frequently mentioned impediments include: a) lack of awareness of quality impact, b) lack of adequate education/training, c) cannot get quick results; cannot prove benefits, d) no standards (obsolete or unenforced), e) QA is misused, f) communication of concepts, and g) lack of corporate direction or planning.

Quality Assurance Measurements and Tools

Of the QA organizations surveyed 45% perform mathematical measures that quantify quality or productivity. The areas being measured are:

1. Defects in system development
2. Production defects
3. Defects in software maintenance
4. Computer time availability

Other measurement areas frequently mentioned are: productivity, customer satisfaction, performance, and program structure.

The most important tools used by QA are:

1. Communications/networks/contacts
2. Personal computers for graphics, statistics, etc.
3. Word processing
4. Standards
5. Methodologies

Other tools frequently mentioned are program management and change management, software reviews and inspections, metrics, training, code analyzers, status reporting, test tools, project management systems, restructuring tools, and quality councils.

Specific automated tools mentioned are:

—VERIFY	—INSPECTOR
—HARVARD PM	—CAPEX
—SAS	—COMPAREX
—SMF	—WORDPERFECT
—GRAMMATIKS	—INFOMAN
—FOCMAN	—CMS (Code Mgmt. System)
—PATHVU	—DTM (DEC Test Manager)
—LOTUS	—CICS Playback
—TRAPS	

Recognition for the Quality Assurance Function

The QA actions taken during the year prior to the survey that received the most recognition:

1. Demonstrated value of quality programs through on time delivery of projects
2. Selling quality and gaining management commitment
3. Implemented tools and methodologies
4. Established or improved the QA organization
5. Established or improved the standards programs
6a. Conducted training in quality concepts
6b. Testing
7. Established and administered quality teams
8a. Implemented or improved change control
8b. Implemented walkthroughs, reviews and inspections
8c. Conducted audits
9a. Improved customer satisfaction
9b. Conducted customer interviews and surveys

The Quality Assurance Mission

These 190 quality assurance professionals assessed where they thought the QA mission was and where they thought that mission should be. The results of that assessment are:

	Now	Should be
Independent test	26%	23%
Quality catalyst	63%	40%
Quality leader	38%	58%
Mgmt. of processes	36%	49%

The areas where the QA professionals thought that assistance is needed in fulfilling the QA mission are:

1. Measurement tools
2. Quality education and training
3. Testing process, methods, tools
4. Selling QA and quality
5. Software inspection and review processes

Other areas mentioned were CASE technology (see chapter 12), standards, project management training, change management tools, life cycle training and publications, quality control processes, and communications skills.

The best summary of the QA attitude found in the survey and the conference where the survey was conducted came from an Information Services manager: "I came to this conference to learn more about QA, what my QA manager was trying to accomplish, and what I could do to help. I have seen a lot of frustration with QA people [at the conference]. At times I felt like crawling out of some sessions. I wonder if QA people remember that management of their companies created QA. Maybe this was done for the 'wrong' reasons (consultant recommendation, audit) or the 'right' reason (concern for quality being delivered). No matter what the reason—*they exist.* Now the challenge is to make it work . . . I strongly believe most management would like to get involved—they just need to be shown the way."

20.2 QUALITY ASSURANCE AS A MEASUREMENT SCIENCE

The key to a successful quality assurance group is to define and measure quality. This requires some reeducation of DP management and staff. What is needed by a QA group is a methodology for defining and measuring quality. The following methodology for defining and measuring quality is based on research performed by Rome Air Development Center, Air Force Systems Command.

There has been an increased awareness in recent years of the critical problems that have been encountered in the development of large scale software systems. These problems not only include the cost and schedule overruns typical of development efforts, and the poor performance of the systems once they are delivered, but also include the high cost of maintaining the systems, the lack of portability, and the high sensitivity to changes in requirements.

Software metrics measure various attributes of software and relate to different aspects of software quality. The potential of the software metric concepts can be realized by their inclusion in software quality programs. They provide a more disciplined, engineering approach to quality assurance and a mechanism allowing a life-cycle viewpoint of software quality. The benefits derived from their application are realized in life-cycle cost reduction.

During the past decade, the evolution of modern programming practices, structured and disciplined development techniques and methodologies, and requirements for more structured, effective documentation has increased the feasibility of the effective measurement of software quality.

However, before the potential of measurement techniques could be realized, a framework or model of software quality had to be constructed. An established model, which at one level provides a user or management-oriented view of quality, is described in the perspective of how it can be used to establish software quality requirements for a specific application.

The actual measurement of software quality is accomplished by applying software metrics (or measurements) to the documentation and source code produced during software development. These measurements are part of the established model of software quality and through that model can be related to various user-oriented aspects of software quality. (See Chapter 10 for an application of software metrics to the Pareto Principle in a practical case.)

Metrics can be classified according to three categories:

- Anomaly-detecting
- Predictive
- Acceptance

Anomaly-detecting metrics identify deficiencies in documentation or source code. These deficiencies usually are corrected to improve the quality of the software product. Standards enforcement is a form of anomaly-detecting metrics.

Predictive metrics are measurements of the logic of the design and implementation. These measurements are concerned with form, structure, density, and complexity. They provide an indication of the quality that will be achieved in the end product, based on the nature of the application, and design and implementation strategies.

Acceptance metrics are measurements that are applied to the end product to assess its final compliance with requirements. Tests are a form of acceptance-type measurements.

The measurements described and used in this manual are either anomaly-detecting or predictive metrics. They are applied during the development phases to assist in identification of quality problems early on so that corrective actions can be taken early when they are more effective and economical.

The measurement concepts complement current quality assurance and testing practices. They are not a replacement for any current techniques utilized in normal quality assurance programs. For example, a major objective of quality assurance is to assure conformance with user/customer requirements. The software quality metric concepts described in this manual provide a methodology for the user/customer to specify life-cycle-oriented quality requirements, usually not considered, and a mechanism for measuring how well those requirements have been attained. A function usually performed by software quality assurance personnel is a review/audit of software product produced during a software development. Software metrics add formality and quantification to document and code reviews. Metric concepts also provide a vehicle for early involvement in development since there are metrics which apply to the documents produced early in the development.

Testing is usually oriented toward correctness, reliability, and performance (efficiency). Metrics assist in the evaluation of other qualities like maintainability, portability, and flexibility.

Procedures for Identifying Software Quality Requirements

The primary purpose of applying software quality metrics in a quality assurance program is to improve the quality of the software product. In other words, rather than simply measuring, metrics exert a positive influence on the product in that they improve its development.

FRAMEWORK

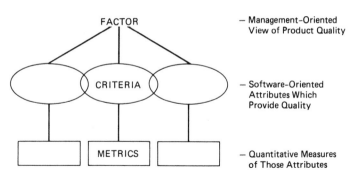

FIGURE 20-1. Hierarchical model of software quality.

The vehicle for establishing performance requirements is the hierarchical model of software quality. This model, shown in Figure 20-1, has at its highest level a set of software quality factors which are expressed as user/management-oriented terms and represent the characteristics which comprise software quality. At the next level for each quality factor is a set of criteria which provide the characteristics represented by the quality factors. These criteria are software-related terms. At the lowest level of the model are the metrics which are quantitative measures of the software attributes defined by the criteria.

The procedures for establishing the quality requirements for a particular software system utilize this model and will be described as a three-level approach, the levels corresponding to the hierarchical levels of the software quality model. The first level establishes the quality factors that are important; the second level identifies the critical software attributes; and the third level identifies the metrics which will be applied and establishes quantitative ratings for the quality factors.

Once the quality requirements have been determined according to the procedures described in the subsequent paragraphs, they must be transmitted to the development team. If the development is being done internally, the quality requirements should be documented in the same form as the other system requirements and provided to the development team. Additionally, a briefing emphasizing the intent of the inclusion of the quality requirements is recommended.

Procedures for Identifying
Important Quality Factors

The basic tool to be utilized in identifying the important quality factors will be the software quality requirements survey form shown in Table 20-2. The formal definitions of each of the quality factors are provided on that form.

A preliminary briefing should be given to the decision makers who will use the following tables and figures, prior to soliciting their responses to the survey. This should be done so that only meaningful quality factors will be measured for a

TABLE 20-2   Software Requirements Survey Form

1. The 11 quality factors listed below have been isolated from the current literature. They are not meant to be exhaustive, but to reflect what is currently thought to be important. Please indicate whether you consider each factor to be Very Important (VI), Important (I), Somewhat Important (SI), or Not Important (NI) as design goals in the system you are currently working on.

Response	Factors	Definition
_____	Correctness	Extent to which a program satisfies its specifications and fulfills the user's mission objectives.
_____	Reliability	Extent to which a program can be expected to perform its intended function with required precision.
_____	Efficiency	The amount of computing resources and code required by a program to perform a function.
_____	Integrity	Extent to which access to software or data by unauthorized persons can be controlled.
_____	Usability	Effort required to learn, operate, prepare input, and interpret output of a program.
_____	Maintainability	Effort required to locate and fix an error in an operational program.
_____	Testability	Effort required to test a program to insure it performs its intended function.
_____	Flexibility	Effort required to modify an operational program.
_____	Portability	Effort required to transfer a program from one hardware configuration and/or software system environment to another.
_____	Reusability	Extent to which a program can be used in other applications—related to the packaging and scope of the functions that programs perform.
_____	Interoperability	Effort required to couple one system with another.

2. What type(s) of application are you currently involved in?

_____

3. Are you currently in:
   _____ 1. Development phase
   _____ 2. Operations/Maintenance phase

4. Please indicate the title which most closely describes your position:
   _____ 1. Program Manager
   _____ 2. Technical consultant
   _____ 3. Systems Analyst
   _____ 4. Other (please specify) _____

project, i.e., with the avoidance of unnecessary measurements for less meaningful quality factors. The decision makers may include the acquisition manager, the user/customer, the development manager, and the QA manager. To complete the survey, the following procedures should be followed.

Consider Basic Characteristics of the Application
The software quality requirements for each system are unique and are influenced by system or application-dependent characteristics. There are basic characteris-

TABLE 20-3   System Characteristics and Related Quality Factors

CHARACTERISTIC	QUALITY FACTOR
• If human lives are affected	Reliability
	Correctness
	Testability
• Long life cycle	Maintainability
	Flexibility
	Portability
• Real time application	Efficiency
	Reliability
	Correctness
• On-board computer application	Efficiency
	Reliability
	Correctness
• Processes classified information	Integrity
• Interrelated systems	Interoperability

tics which affect the quality requirements; therefore each software system must be evaluated for its basic characteristics Table 20-3 provides a list of some of these basic characteristics.

For example, if the system is being developed in an environment in which there is a high rate of technical breakthroughs in hardware design, *portability* should take on an added significance. If the expected life cycle of the system is long, *maintainability* becomes a cost-critical consideration. If the application is an experimental system where the software specifications will have a high rate of change, *flexibility* in the software product is highly desirable. If the functions of the system are expected to be required for a long time, while the system itself may change considerably, *reusability* is of prime importance in those modules which implement the major functions of the system With the advent of more computer networks and communication capabilities, systems are increasingly being required to interface with other systems and the concept of *interoperability* is extremely important. These and other system characteristics should be considered when identifying the important quality factors.

Consider Life-Cycle Implications

The 11 quality factors identified on the survey can be grouped according to three life-cycle activities associated with a delivered software product. These three activities are product operation, product revision, and product transition. The relationship of the quality factors to these activities is shown in Table 20-4. This table also shows where quality indications can be achieved through measurement and where the impact is felt if poor quality is realized. This size of this positive impact determines the cost savings that can be expected if a higher-quality system is achieved through the application of the metrics. This cost savings is somewhat offset by the cost of applying the metrics and the cost of developing the higher quality software product as illustrated in Figure 20-2.

TABLE 20-4   The Impact of Not Specifying or Measuring Software Quality Factors

LIFE-CYCLE PHASES FACTORS	DEVELOPMENT			EVALUATION	POST-DEVELOPMENT			EXPECTED COST SAVED VS. COST TO PROVIDE
	REQMIS ANALYSIS	DESIGN	CODE & DEBUG	SYSTEM TEST	OPERATION	REVISION	TRANSITION	
Correctness	△	△	△	X	X	X		High
Reliability	△	△	△	X	X	X		High
Efficiency	△	△	△		X			Low
Integrity	△	△	△		X			Low
Usability	△	△	△	X				Medium
Maintainability		△	△			X	X	High
Testability		△	△	X		X	X	High
Flexibility		△	△			X	X	Medium
Portability		△	△				X	Medium
Reusability		△	△				X	Medium
Interoperability	△	△		X			X	Low

Legend: △—where quality factors should be measured.   X—where impact of poor quality is realized.

FIGURE 20-2. Cost vs. benefit trade-off.

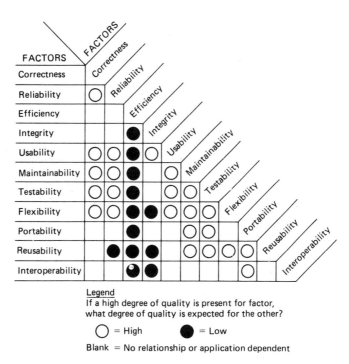

Legend
If a high degree of quality is present for factor,
what degree of quality is expected for the other?

◯ = High   ● = Low

Blank = No relationship or application dependent

FIGURE 20-3. Relationships between software quality factors.

This cost to implement versus life-cycle cost reduction relationship exists for each quality factor. The benefit versus cost-to-provide ratio for each factor is rated as high, medium, or low in the right-hand column of Table 20-4. This relationship and the life-cycle implications of the quality factors should be considered when selecting the important factors for a specific system.

Perform Trade-Offs Among the Tentative
List of Quality Factors

As a result of the first two steps, a tentative list of quality factors should be produced. The next step is to consider the interrelationships among the factors selected. Figure 20-3 and Table 20-5 can be used as a guide for determining the

TABLE 20-5   Typical Factor Trade-offs

Integrity vs. Efficiency	The additional code and processing required to control the access of the software or data usually lengthen run time and require additional storage.
Usability vs. Efficiency	The additional code and processing required to ease an operator's tasks or provide more usable output usually lengthen run time and require additional storage.
Maintainability vs. Efficiency	Optimized code, incorporating intricate coding techniques and direct code, always provides problems to the maintainer. Using modularity, instrumentation, and well-commented high-level code to increase the maintainability of a system usually increases the overhead, resulting in less efficient operation.
Testability vs. Efficiency	The above discussion applies to testing.
Portability vs. Efficiency	The use of direct code or optimized system software or utilities decreases the portability of the system.
Flexibility vs. Efficiency	The generality required for a flexible system increases overhead and decreases the efficiency of the system.
Reusability vs. Efficiency	The above discussion applies to reusability.
Interoperability vs. Efficiency	Again, the added overhead for conversion from standard data representations and the use of interface routines decrease the operating efficiency of the system.
Flexibility vs. Integrity	Flexibility requires very general and flexible data structures. This increases the data security problem.
Reusability vs. Integrity	As in the above discussion, the generality required by reusable software provides severe protection problems.
Interoperability vs. Integrity	Coupled systems allow for more avenues of access and for different users who can access the system. The potential for accidental access of sensitive data increases as the opportunities for deliberate access increase. Often, coupled systems share data or software, which further compounds the security problems.
Reusability vs. Reliability	The generality required by reusable software makes providing error tolerance and accuracy for all cases more difficult.

relationships between the quality factors. Some factors are synergistic while others conflict. The impact of conflicting factors is that the cost to implement will increase, which will lower the benefit-to-cost ratio described in the preceding paragraph.

Provide Definitions

The definitions in Table 20-6 should also be provided as part of the specification. The relationship of these criteria to the quality factors is discussed next.

TABLE 20-6   Criteria Definitions for Software Quality

CRITERION	DEFINITION
Traceability	Those attributes of the software that provide a thread from the requirements to the implementation with respect to the specific development and operational environment.
Completeness	Those attributes of the software that provide full implementation of the functions required.
Consistency	Those attributes of the software that provide uniform design and implementation techniques and notation.
Accuracy	Those attributes of the software that provide the required precision in calculations and outputs.
Error Tolerance	Those attributes of the software that provide continuity of operation under nonnominal conditions.
Simplicity	Those attributes of the software that provide implementation of functions in the most understandable manner (usually avoidance of practices which increase complexity).
Modularity	Those attributes of the software that provide a structure of highly independent modules.
Generality	Those attributes of the software that provide breadth to the functions performed.
Expandability	Those attributes of the software that provide for expansion of data storage requirements or computational functions.
Instrumentation	Those attributes of the software that provide for the measurement of usage or identification of errors.
Self-Descriptiveness	Those attributes of the software that provide explanation of the implementation of a function.
Execution Efficiency	Those attributes of the software that provide for minimum processing time.
Storage Efficiency	Those attributes of the software that provide for minimum storage requirements during operation.
Access Control	Those attributes of the software that provide for control of the access of software and data.
Access Audit	Those attributes of the software that provide for an audit of the access of software and data.

(Cont.)

TABLE 20-6   Criteria Definitions for Software Quality Factors (cont.)

CRITERION	DEFINITION
Operability	Those attributes of the software that determine operation and procedures concerned with the operation of the software.
Training	Those attributes of the software that provide transition from current operation or initial familiarization.
Communicativeness	Those attributes of the software that provide useful inputs and outputs which can be assimilated.
Software System Independence	Those attributes of the software that determine its dependency on the software environment (operating systems, utilities, input/output routines, etc.).
Machine Independence	Those attributes of the software that determine its dependency on the hardware system.
Communications Commonality	Those attributes of the software that provide the use of standard protocols and interface routines.
Data Commonality	Those attributes of the software that provide the use of standard data representations.
Conciseness	Those attributes of the software that provide for implementation of a function with a minimum amount of code.

TABLE 20-7   Software Criteria and Related Quality Factors

FACTOR	SOFTWARE CRITERIA	FACTOR	SOFTWARE CRITERIA
Correctness	Traceability Consistency Completeness	Flexibility	Modularity Generality Expandability
Reliability	Error Tolerance Consistency Accuracy Simplicity	Testability	Simplicity Modularity Instrumentation Self-Descriptiveness
Efficiency	Storage Efficiency Execution Efficiency	Portability	Modularity Self-Descriptiveness

Integrity	Access control
	Access audit
			Machine
			  Independence
			Software System
			  Independence

Usability	Operability Training Communicativeness	Reusability	Generality Modularity Software System Independence
Maintainability	Consistency	Interoperability	Modularity Communication Commonality Data Commonality

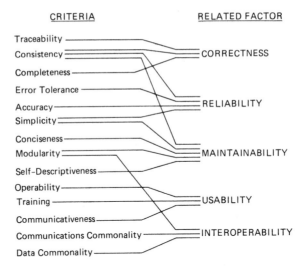

FIGURE 20-4. Criteria for related factors.

Procedures for Identifying Critical Software Attributes

Identifying the next level of quality requirements involves proceeding from the user-oriented quality factors to the software-oriented criteria. Sets of criteria, which are attributes of the software, are related to the various factors by definition. Their identification is automatic and represents a more detailed specification of the quality requirements.

Table 20-7 should be used to identify the software attributes associated with the chosen critical quality factors. For example, using the relationships provided in Table 20-7, the criteria listed in Figure 20-4 would be identified as shown.

20.3 MOVING QA FROM A CONCEPT TO A REALITY

Quality assurance works if the concept of quality is implemented. It has taken many corporations years to develop a formula that makes quality assurance really effective (see Table 20-8). Although most corporations agree with quality assurance at the conceptual level, when faced with compliance with standards and increased productivity, they encounter many problems. A quality assurance analyst may feel that a system is not complying to standards, and the systems analysts often feel that in order to comply with standards the implemented system will be late and run over budget. Usually the decision is made to get it in on time and worry about quality later. The price corporations pay for this compromise is huge.

Defining and Enforcing QA as a Priority Activity

Excitement and enthusiasm over quality is a goal itself. Quality assurance personnel are marketing people—they have to sell their staffs on the fact that quality is

TABLE 20-8   What Makes QA Actually Work?

• Must go from a CONCEPT to actual IMPLEMENTATION.

• Everybody agrees at the conceptual level.

• Needed:

—An embodiment (organized set of QA procedures used as part of everyday routine).

—Centralized function (someone who is responsible).

TABLE 20-9   Typical Problems in Implementing QA

PROBLEM	QA APPROACH OR SOLUTION
• Resistance to change	Education, successful pilot project, some will never be converted.
• Big brother	Education, QA works with PM, matters resolved at lowest level.
• Not responsive	Skilled competent QA staff, QA must assist team.
• No teeth	Approval authority, management followup.
• Too burdensome	Less paper-driven, practical procedures, flexible.
• Too conceptual	A prescribed routine, habit.

important. Japanese automobile factory managements post on their walls the names of their workers and the number of defects reported from the field based on the parts made by the responsible workers. This policy could be adopted in data processing departments. If the names of erring programmers were put on a chart with checkmarks by their names for each problem inflicted on users, some different concerns about quality would evolve. One organization has bestowed the name "Captain Quality" on its quality assurance manager, who becomes excited over various concepts and gets the staff equally enthused.

The quality assurance examination can be compared to a medical examination. Certain tests must be done to determine if the "patient" is well or sick. There can be no guesswork on what quality is: quality must be predetermined and then checks made to assure it exists as specified. Resistance to change is a problem managers have in getting quality accepted. (See Table 20-9 for the typical QA implementation problems.) When people have done something a certain way and they are asked to change, they will fight the concept. Still, through its acceptance of all concerned the image of quality assurance simply as a policeman must be overcome.

In order for a quality assurance group to function effectively, it must be backed by management. Management must make the staff aware of what it will and won't support. The systems analyst must be made to believe he or she is being judged on user satisfaction, and getting projects done on time and within budget. Failure to receive a salary increase when expected because of a system being poor in quality will unequivocably show the systems analyst the importance the company attaches to quality.

It is very difficult for many systems analysts to be enthusiastic about quality because a lot of other pressures take priority on their time. To implement quality concepts in their organizations, companies have devised several seemingly drastic means to assure quality is controlled. One company has given the production library and source library to quality assurance. If a systems analyst wants to place a compiled program into production, it first must be approved by quality assurance. Before programs can be placed into the source library, the data processing analyst must first write design specifications and submit them to quality assurance. Another company requires the systems analysts to sit in the computer room every time a program is run on which adequate operations documentation is not completed; the company schedules the run from midnight to 2:00 A.M. to get the point across. Still another company fails to promote or transfer people until their systems are certified by quality assurance.

Positioning the QA Manager

The QAI study revealed that the higher in the organization the centralization of the function reports, the more successful it is (see Table 20-10). If it is too low, it is ignored, and being too high can also cause problems; the person managing this activity—the QA manager—needs to be placed on a par with the other managers in the department. The study showed that pay grades for quality assurance managers range from three below a senior systems analyst to three above, which is a wide range in the organizational structure. The quality assurance manager must strive to get cooperation from other department and middle managers, to get involved in the operation and application of the program or user's system, and to get involved in the development of standards because quality problems occur throughout the organization.

Opening Communications from Vendor to User

Some time ago, through the mail I ordered an animal trap from the—Company. When it finally arrived, I eagerly ripped open the package only to find a lot of unassembled parts. I looked in vain for instructions to assemble the parts into an animal trap, but since the instructions were missing I worked with the parts until

TABLE 20-10   Centralized QA Function

- QA must be placed at high level in organization.
- If too low, it will be ignored.
- If too high, it may lose detailed, operational effectiveness.
- QA and project manager must strive for concurrence.

completely frustrated. The next morning I called up the company to request that they forward me the instructions for assembling the animal trap, only to be informed by a young lady on the other end that they were only in the business of making parts—they didn't make instructions. My next question to her was as to what kind of animal I could catch in the event I was lucky enough to get the trap put together. She quickly responded that I could catch anything I wanted with it—they didn't make decisions.

Many software products obtained from vendors come without instructions, like those parts in the box. There are things called *controls* and *features,* but nobody tells you how to put these together or how to optimize the software for your organization. This lack of communication between seller and buyer or developer and user forces many organizations to rely on the decisions of software programmers who are usually not familiar with the buyers' or users' business and may have no more than minimal loyalty to their own organizations. These software programmers have made major quality decisions which each organization's quality assurance department is forced to understand and work with.

Growth and Maturity of QA

The National Bureau of Standards defines quality as a three-phase approach: (1) the development of the standards, procedures, and guidelines; (2) automating segments of the EDP process; and (3) automating and integrating individual segments (see Table 20-11). Phase 1 includes the acquisition and use of a systems development life cycle. This phase has brought order out of some of the chaos that existed during the 1960s. Phase 2 involves improving quality by automating the individual pieces, such as data dictionaries and libraries. In Phase 3, the individual pieces are automated and integrated. For example, the data dictionary is integrated into the data base management system; and high-level programming languages will unify the programs under one roof, i.e., make them relatively computer-independent, as well as speed their development. This integrated systems environment is very important in increasing productivity in a quality environment.

Quality assurance is a new, rapidly growing discipline which is implemented in

TABLE 20-11   Phases of Quality

Phase 1
STANDARDS, PROCEDURES, GUIDELINES
Phase 2
AUTOMATING SEGMENTS OF EDP PROCESS
Phase 3
AUTOMATING AND INTEGRATING INDIVIDUAL SEGMENTS

hundreds of companies. While in many companies it is still a fairly small function, it is maturing and in some companies involves 50 or more people within data processing departments of 500–600. When it gets larger, quality assurance encompasses the disciplines of data base administrations, education, production control, software programs, development of standards, compliance with standards, project review, project scheduling, tracking of projects, error analysis, and S.W.A.T.-team concepts to make data processing work. Two especially promising techniques to define and measure quality, supplementing the foregoing, are metrics and risk analysis.

A successful quality assurance function can be recognized as the group that does many of the nonproduction functions. These people, who are not building, maintaining, or operating systems, belong under the quality banner because the discipline of assurance in all functions is necessary. Stand-alone standards require real-world interaction with projects. Enforcing and tailoring standards give a different view from writing standards. Good standards are essential because systems analysts/programmers will not follow them if they are bad.

The effective quality assurance group increases productivity rather dramatically. As experience in the quality assurance group grows, the corporation experiences fewer problems, fewer user complaints, fewer requests for changes, quicker maintenance, and fewer hang-ups in the computer area. The quality assurance group that is able to focus on the concept of quality and productivity pays for itself over and over again.

With management support and good objectives, quality assurance is the solution to productivity in the 1980s and beyond. The quality assurance function in a data processing department makes its members visible within their corporation as a function that has done something positive to improve quality and productivity.

Reference

1. Perry, William E., *Hatching the EDP Quality Assurance Function,* Quality Assurance Institute, 9222 Bay Point Drive, Orlando, Florida 32811, 1981.

General References

Burrill, Claude W. and Ellsworth, Leon W. *Modern Project Management: Foundations for Quality and Productivity* (Tenafly, NJ: Burrill-Ellsworth, 1980).
———, *Quality Data Processing—The Profit Potential for the 80s* (Tenafly, NJ: Burrill-Ellsworth, 1982).
Crosby, Philip B., *Quality is Free: The Art of Making Quality Certain* (New York: New American Library, 1980).
GUIDE International, Inc., *A Guide to Implementing Systems Quality Assurance,* GUIDE International, Inc., 1979.
McCall, James A., and Matsumoto, Mike T., *Software Quality Metrics Enhancements* (2 vols.), Rome Air Development Center Air Force Systems Command, Griffiss Air Force Base, N.Y., 1980.

Perry, William E., *Effective Methods of EDP Quality Assurance,* (Wellesley, MA: Q.E.D. Information Sciences, 1981).

————, *Management Guide to EDP Quality Assurance,* (U.S. Professional Development Institute, 1983).

————, *Quality Assurance System Development Reviews,* (Orlando, FL: Quality Assurance Institute, 1981).

————, *Report Writing for Quality Assurance Analysts* (Orlando, FL: Quality Assurance Institute, 1981).

Appendix A

GLOSSARY OF ACRONYMS

4GL. Fourth generation language
10X. ten times
ABENDS. Abnormal endings
AC. Aircraft
AD/Cycle. Application Development/Cycle
ADP. Automated Data Processing
AFSCP. Air Force Systems Command Pamphlet
ANSI. American National Standards Institute
APM. assistant project manager
APM. Auto parts management
AQAP. Allied Quality Assurance Publication
AQL. acceptable quality level
ASQC. American Society for Quality Control
ATIS. A Tools Integration Standard
BET. Break Even Time
BIT. Built in test
CASE. computer aided software engineering
CCB. Configuration Control Board
CCD/Plus. Common Data Dictionary/Plus
cdf. cumulative distribution function
CDR. Critical Design Review
CEO. Chief Executive Officer
CIDS. Critical Item Development Specification

CM. Configuration Management
CMM. capability maturity model
CND. can not duplicate
COCOMO. constructive cost model
CODSIA. Council of Defense and Space Industry Associations
COQ. Cost of Quality
COT. commercial off the shelf
CPIN. computer program identification number
CPM. Critical Path Method
CPU. Central Processing Unit
CRISD. Computer Resources Integrated Support Document
CRM. Computer Resources Management
CSC. Computer Software Component
CSCI. Computer Software Configuration Item
CSDM. Computer System Diagnostic Manual
CSM. Computer Software Management
CSOM. Computer System Operator's Manual
CSU. Computer Software Unit
DBDD. Data Base Design Document
D.C. Developmental Configuration
DD. data dictionary
DEC. Digital Equipment Corporation
Dem-Val. Demonstration and validation
DFD. data flow diagram
DI. Data Item
DID. Data Item Description
DLA. Defense Logistics Agency
Doc. documentation
DOD. Department of Defense
DODI. Department of Defense Instruction
DOS. Disk Operating System
DPRO. Defense Program Review Office
DT. development test
ECP. Engineering Change Proposal
EDP. Electronic Data Processing
EPA. Environmental Protection Agency
ESD. Electronics System Division (Air Force)
ETTF. Estimated Time to Fix
FAA. Federal Aviation Administration
FCA. Functional Configuration Audit
FM. Figure of Merit
FQR. Formal Qualification Review
FQT. Formal Qualification Test
FSD. Full scale development
FSM. Firmware Support Manual
Funct. Functional
FURPS. functionality, usability, reliability, performance and supportability
F/W. Firmware
HDBK. Handbook

HOL. High Order Language
H-P. Hewlett Packard
H/W. Hardware
IO. High Level inspection
I1. Low level inspection
I-1. Requirements documents inspection
I2. Code Inspection
ICBM. Intercontinental ballistic missile
ID. identification
IDD. Interface Design Document
IEEE. Institute of Electrical and Electronics Engineers, Inc.
IPO. input, processing, output
IPSE. Integrated Project Support Environment
IQUE. In-plant Quality Assurance
IR. Incident Report
IRS. Internal Revenue Service
IRS. Interface Requirements Specification
ITT. International Telephone and Telegraph
IV&V. Independent Verification and Validation
I^2V&V. Internal, Independent Verification and Validation
JCG. Joint Coordinating Group
JLC. Joint Logistics Command
JPCG. Joint Policy Coordinating Group
KLOC. Thousand Lines of Code
KLOSC. Thousand Lines of Source Code
LAN. Local Area Network
LL. lower level
LLCSC. Lower level computer software component
LRU. Line Replaceable Unit
MCCR. Mission Critical Computer Resource
Mgmt. management
MIL-S. Military Specification
MIPS. millions of instructions per second
MIS. Management Information System
MPA. Fictitious company name
MPT. Mid-point of Test
MTBE. Mean Time Between Error
MTBF. Mean Time Between Failures
MTR. Modular Tree Representation
NAS. Network Application Support
NASA. National Aeronautics and Space Administration
NATO. North Atlantic Treaty Organization
NBS. National Bureau of Standards
NCOQ. Non Cost of Quality
NEC. Nippon Electric Company
NOAA. National Oceanographic Atmospheric Administration
NOE. Number of Errors
NOEL. Number of Errors Left
N_p. number of program paths

OCD. Operational Concept Document
OOD. object oriented design
OS/2. Operating System 2
OT. operational test
PA. Product Assurance
PC. Personal Computer
PCA. Physical Configuration Audit
P-D-C-A. Plan-Do-Check-Analyze
pdf. probability density function
PDL. Program Design Language
PDR. Preliminary Design Review
PERT. Program Evaluation and Review Technique
PIDS. Prime Item Development Specification
PLC. Product life cycle
PM. Program/Project Manager
PP & C. program planning and control
Prelim. preliminary
PSA. Program Statement Analyzer
PSL. Program Statement Language
PSQM. project software quality manager
Q. quality
QA. Quality Assurance
QAI. Quality Assurance Institute
QC. Quality Circle
QC. Quality Control
QIT. Quality Improvement Team
QP. quality program
QROI. quality return on investment
Qual. qualification
RADC. Rome Air Development Center
RAM. Random access memory
Rdb. Relational data base
RFP. Request for Proposal
Rqmts. requirements
ROM. Read only memory
SAA. Systems Application Architecture
SCCB. Software Configuration Control Board
SCM. Software Configuration Management
SCMP. Software Configuration Management Plan
SCO. Software Change Order
SDD. Software Design Document
SDDD. Software Detailed Design Document
SDF. Software Development File
SDL. Software Development Library
SDLC. System Development Life Cycle
SDN. Software Development Notebook
SDP. Software Development Plan
SDR. Software Design Review
SDS. Software Development Standard

SEE. Software Engineering Environment
SeCS. self check system
SEI. Software Engineering Institute
SEPG. Software Engineering Process Group
SERN. Software Engineering Release Notice
SIAD. Symbolic Input Attribute Decomposition
SIVVP. Software Independent Verification and Validation Plan
SLBM. Sea launched ballistic missile
SLC. Software Life Cycle
SLCSE. software life cycle support environment
SLOC. Source lines of code
SMLC. Software Maintenance Life Cycle
SN. signal to noise
SOW. Statement of Work
SPC. Statistical process Control
Spec. specification
SPM. Software Programmer's Manual
SPR. Software Problem Report
SPS. Software Product Specification
SQA. Software Quality Assurance
SQAIR. Software Quality Assurance Inspection Report
SQAM. Software Quality Assessment and Measurement
SQAMP. Software Quality Assessment and Measurement Plan
SQAP. Software Quality Assurance Plan
SQC. Software Quality Control
SQC. Statistical Quality Control
SQCS. statistical quality control system
SQE. software quality evaluation
SQEP. Software Quality Evaluation Plan
SQMAT. software quality measurement and assurance technology
SQP. Software Quality Plan
SQP. software quality program
SQPP. Software Quality Program Plan
SQS. Software Quality Standard
SRR. Software Requirements Review
SRS. Software Requirements Specification
SSDD. System/Segment Design Document
SSF. Space Station Freedom
SSPM. Software Standards and Procedures Manual
SSR. Software Specification Review
SSS. System/Segment Specification
STD. Software Test Description
STD. Standard
STLDD. Software Top Level Design Document
STP. Software Test Plan
STPR. Software Test Procedure
STR. Software Test Report
STR. Software Trouble Report
SuCS. successive check system

SUM. Software User's Manual
SVVP. Software Verification and Validation Plan
S/W. Software
SYSGEN. system generation
T & E. Test and Evaluation
T & I. Test and Integration
TL. top level
TLCSC. Top level computer software component
TQM. Total Quality Management
TRR. Test Readiness Review
USDF. Unit Software Development File
UT. Unit Testing
VDD. Version Description Document
VHSIC. Very High Speed Integration Circuits
VLSI. Very Large Scale Integration Circuits
V & V. Verification and Validation
WRA. Weapon Replaceable Assembly
WWMCCS. World Wide Military Command and Control System

Subject Index

Author Index